The
Beginnings
of
Christianity

The Beginnings of Christianity

AN INTRODUCTION TO THE NEW TESTAMENT

Howard Clark Kee

t&t clark

NEW YORK • LONDON

T & T Clark International
Madison Square Park, 15 East 26th Street, New York, NY 10010

T & T Clark International
The Tower Building, 11 York Road, London SE1 7NX

T & T Clark International is a Continuum imprint.

Cover design: Brenda Klinger

Library of Congress Cataloging-in-Publication Data

Kee, Howard Clark.
    The beginnings of Christianity : an introduction to the New Testament / Howard Clark Kee.
        p.   cm.
    Includes bibliographical references and index.
    ISBN 0-567-02731-7 (hardcover) — ISBN 0-567-02741-4 (pbk.)
    1. Church history—Primitive and early church, ca. 30–600.   2. Bible. N.T.—Introductions.   I. Title.
BS2410.K43   2005
270.1—dc22

                                                                2005015641

Printed in the United States of America

05 06 07 08 09 10   10 9 8 7 6 5 4 3 2 1

Contents

Methods and Resources for the History of Christian Origins

Agenda and Method for the History of Christian Origins

To understand the historical beginnings of Christianity requires one not only to examine the documents that the movement produced, but also to scrutinize other evidence—historical, literary, and archaeological—that can illumine the sociocultural context in which Christianity began and how it responded to the influences that derived from that setting. This involves not only analysis of the readily accessible content of the relevant literary evidence, but also attention to the worldviews and assumptions about reality that are inherent in these documents and in other phenomena that have survived from this period. Important for historical analysis is attention to the roles of leadership and the modes of formation of social identity in Judaism and the continuing influence of these developments as Christianity began to take shape.[1]

In methodological terms, the historical study of Christian origins in all its diversity must involve three different modes of analysis: (1) epistemological, (2) sociological, and (3) eschatological. The first concerns the way knowledge and communication of it were perceived. The second seeks to discern the way the community or tradition preserving and conveying this information defined its group identity and its shared values and aims. The third focuses on the way the group understood and affirmed its ultimate destiny and that of its members in the purpose of God. These factors are interrelated, and features of one mode of perception strongly influence details of

1

the others, but it is useful to consider each of them separately to discern with greater precision the specific historical features that appear in the surviving evidence concerning the origins of Christianity.

Ancient Antecedents and Models for Historical Reconstruction of Christian Origins

Interest in the historical beginnings of Christianity is not an intellectual phenomenon that first took shape in the age of Constantine through the apologetic medium of Eusebius's *Ecclesiastical History* and then emerged in an intellectually critical mode in the post-Enlightenment era. Indeed, historical interests and truth claims are already evident in the New Testament itself. Thus, the Gospel of Luke begins with the declaration by the author to the patron or official to whom his two-volume work was addressed[2] that he was engaging in a historical enterprise for which there were abundant precedents:

> Since *many* have undertaken to set down an orderly account of the events that have been fulfilled among us, just as they were handed on to us by those who from the beginning were eyewitnesses and servants of the word, I too decided, after investigating everything carefully from the very first, to write an orderly account for you, most excellent Theophilus, so that you may know the truth concerning the things about which you have been instructed. (Luke 1:1–4)

Obviously taking a position in the historical tradition, the author of this gospel is keenly interested in historical evidence, the reliability of the witnesses to whom he has turned for evidence, the preparation of a systematic record of the events and testimony, and convincing his readers of the veracity of his report. Thus, concern for historicity is not a modern innovation, but is as old as the New Testament writings themselves.

The only known surviving precedents and sources for Luke's gospel are (1) the Gospel of Mark and (2) the hypothetical Sayings Source (Q), upon which the author of Luke draws.[3] Yet he does claim to have examined the relevant evidence "carefully" and comprehensively: "everything"!

A similar claim is implicit in the preface to Luke's second volume, the Acts of the Apostles, where he refers to having "dealt with *all* that Jesus began to do and teach" (Acts 1:1). Luke asserts unequivocally that there were "many" others who were compiling accounts concerning Jesus. Yet Luke's story in Acts of the movement of the gospel from Jerusalem to Rome and the emergence of the new covenant community as a consequence of the proclamation about Jesus is unique within the New Testament canon. This history of the origins and development of this religious movement, written in the early years of the second century CE, seeks to correlate those Christian features that were represented by the gospel traditions and those embodied in the Pauline letters (the authentic and the pseudonymous), and to place those events in the wider context of the Roman world.[4] But Luke 1:1 claims that there were multiple precedents for his historical undertakings concerning the origins of Christianity.

As for the history of Judaism in the centuries before the common era, precedent for historical analysis and reconstruction of the origins of Jewish religious tradition—from preexilic times down into the Hellenistic and Roman periods—is abundant from both canonical and noncanonical sources. In the Hebrew scriptures, there are two distinctive traditions concerned with the history of Israel: the Deuteronomist[5] and the Chroniclers.[6] In the view of the Deuteronomist historical account, "God is at work in the historical process . . . and the obedience or self-will of kings leads to blessing or punishment." According to this material, for the prophetic groups led by Elijah and Elisha, "the word of God became action against a religion and politics that glorified power and rode roughshod over the weak." Following the return of Israel from exile, the conviction that Israel and Judah were the people of God is evident in the books of Kings, which in their final form articulated hope for the future, combined with warnings about the past.[7] The somewhat different aims of the Chroniclers have been effectively summarized as follows: "In Chronicles, the past history of Israel is perceived and presented from the viewpoint of a worshiping, temple-based community. This sense of the sovereignty of God is such that there is a scaling down of human achievement and an exaltation of what God can do with even the most unpromising material."[8]

In the deuterocanonical Jewish literature included in the Septuagint, there is an analogous appeal to history to serve as instruction and guide for the religious community. Chief among these is 1 Maccabees. Dating from the first century BCE, this book describes the effective resistance of the Jewish leadership against the efforts of the Seleucid rulers to impose Hellenistic religion and culture on the Jews of Palestine.[9] The Maccabees are depicted as the divinely chosen and empowered agents for the deliverance of God's people from the political and religious domination of the Hellenistic rulers, and for the restoration and guidance of the covenant people in obedience to the Law of Moses and faithful worship of God in the temple. Second Maccabees shifts from Jewish nationalistic goals to an emphasis on true piety and the sanctity of the Jerusalem temple—the only place where God is present among his people.[10] The emphasis on personal devotion is even stronger in 3 Maccabees, which resembles a Hellenistic romance.[11] Fourth Maccabees uses the historical experiences of the Maccabean period to illustrate a philosophical thesis on the supremacy of reason (4 Macc 1). Thus, in this body of literature, historical reporting is a major factor, although it is carried out in a variety of modes and with a range of intentions.

In the writings of Josephus we have not only comprehensive historical treatises—*Antiquities of the Jews* and *The Jewish War*—but also an extended essay on historical method, *Against Apion*, in which he seeks to confirm the antiquity of the Jewish people and the moral integrity of the law of Moses by which they live. He links the history of the Jews with historical evidence from Egyptian, Chaldean, and Phoenician sources.[12] In contrast to the Greek historians, whose work is more recent, more interested in style than accuracy, and lacking public records as documentation,[13] the Jewish sources are based on official records prepared by successive priestly leaders.[14] Reports concerning the Jews in antiquity are preserved by such Greek historians as Manetho[15] and the Chaldean historian Berossus,[16] as well as by other Greek authors.[17] Josephus also points to the anti-Semitic features of some of the Greek historians, especially Apion.[18] This contrasts with the special favors bestowed on the Jews by such Hellenistic leaders as Alexander and the Ptolemies.[19] Further, Josephus discredits the false charges that were subsequently brought against the Jews.[20] He asserts instead that Moses is the most ancient of all legislators,[21] and that as a result, the Jewish people have the finest law and the purest understanding of God, of morality, and of true worship.[22] Here, then, Josephus is engaged in analytical historiographic study combined with certain clear apologetic features—as well as historical reconstruction based on an impressive range of evidence from the ancient world.

Concurrent with such efforts in critical analysis and reconstruction based on historical sources, there emerged in the Hellenistic period another mode of reporting past events and depicting past leaders that was more concerned with evoking sympathetic response from the reader than in recounting facts. This form of communication, which flourished in the Hellenistic and Roman periods, is designated *the romance* by literary historians.[23] One of the most important examples of the Graeco-Roman romance is *The Life of Alexander of Macedon by Pseudo-Callisthenes*.[24] Elizabeth H. Haight, the translator, concurs that this is a primary example of the Hellenistic romance, some of which were written as early as the first century BCE. Most were produced in the first centuries of the common era.[25]

In *The Form of the Greek Romance*, B. F. Reardon describes the romance as "prose fiction" in which humans are depicted in both a social and a divine context, historical in setting and dramatic in method. For example, Apuleius's *Metamorphoses* is a sermon against excessive human ambition and sensuality and offers an invitation to submit to the divine will. The typical pattern of the romance is: (1) a problem is presented; (2) conflict arises; (3) the issues develop; (4) a solution appears. The moral or spiritual message is made more attractive to the reader by the historical mode in which it is conveyed.[26] The motifs in the romances include travel, adventure, warfare, love, miracle, and divine intervention; the modes of communication range from historical, didactic, comic, and tragic to marvelous, sentimental, moral, missionary, and pastoral. The aim of the romances is to enable the reader to deal with the loss of the old world and to experience the new in which a fresh and enriched meaning of the tradition may be gained.[27]

There are two types of romances: historical and romantic. Pervo suggests that the earlier Jewish romances—such as *Ahigar*[28] and Tobit—represent an even older Aramaic literary category, which he designates "sapiential novels."[29] These also portray historical developments, however. Also of this type is the apocryphal work Baruch, which consists of a mixture of narrative and wisdom and purports to come from the time of Nebuchadnezzar (ruler of Babylonia from 605 to 562 BCE), but is actually a call for obedience to Torah as essential for the Jews to be liberated from domination by the Seleucids.[30] Prime examples of Jewish novels that may be characterized as "romantic" are Judith and *Joseph and Asenath*.[31] These stories include emotional and human relations factors, as do the well-known Graeco-Roman romances: Chariton, *Chaereas and Callirhoe*; Xenophon of Ephesus, *Ephesiaca*; Longus, *Daphnis and Chloe*.

Thus, the methods of reporting past events in the early centuries of the common era included not only historiography in the formal sense—as represented by Josephus and subsequently by Eusebius—but the romantic mode as well. Influence of both these modes is evident in the subsequent early Christian narrative writings, canonical and apocryphal. To understand the beginnings of Christianity in the sociocultural context in which it arose as well as its subsequent development in the wider Roman world requires analysis of these kinds of evidence: both the worldviews that are implicit in the content of this literature and the literary modes in which the information and insights are conveyed.

The Enduring Impact of Aspects of Babylonian and Iranian Culture on Judaism in the Postexilic Period

Discernible in the later Jewish scriptures is the enduring impact on the perceptions and beliefs of the Jews from their extended exposure to Babylonian and Persian culture during their forced exile to Babylon, which began in the opening years of the sixth century BCE. Permission was given by the Persian ruler, Cyrus the Great (550–530 BCE), for the Jews to return to their land after the Persians took over Mesopotamia in 540 BCE. This is reported in 2 Chron 36:23 (and Ezra 1:1–4) as having been initiated by God's impact on the "spirit of King Cyrus." Persian control of the land of the Jews continued until the invasion and takeover of the Middle East by Alexander extended to the border of India in 325.

Chief among the conceptual features of Babylonian and Persian culture that significantly influenced Jewish thinking in this period but had no counterpart in older Jewish tradition were certain perceptions of (1) the origin of evil, and (2) human history as the outworking of a cosmic purpose.

The Akkadian documents from the third century BCE include eschatological features, such as prophetic oracles, that proclaim the continuity of divine purpose between recent events and those about to occur in the future.[32] Also significant in other Babylonian literature as indications of kinship with what developed as Jewish apocalypticism are the interpretation of dreams as predictions of the future, and mantic wisdom, which interprets the future through signs and depicts the establishment of a divinely determined order. The Persians had well-developed apocalyptic traditions, which included belief in the struggle between light and darkness, activities of angels and demons, and the division of history into successive periods.[33] In the basic Persian religion, Zoroastrianism, time was divided into three periods: (1) Creation; (2) Mixture (when the evil deity, Angra Mainyu, brought evil and death); and (3) Separation, when the true god, Ahura Mazda, triumphs over evil and the righteous reach paradise. Plutarch (46–120 CE), in his treatise *On Isis and Osiris*, attributes to Theopompus (a Hellenistic historian from Chios, born in 378 BCE) the report that the Persians believe in two rival gods—Ahura Mazda, the god of light; and Ahriman, the god of darkness. Each of these gods will dominate the world for three thousand years, at the end of which one smashes the domain of the other. In the end, the rule of evil will be fully overcome: happiness and rest will prevail.[34] Variants of this scheme of the final triumph of the god of light appear in reports of Persian beliefs found in other Hellenistic writers.[35]

Thus, this religious tradition of a future era in which the powers of evil would be overcome and those of good would triumph was dominant in the land of Israel's exile from the reign of Cyrus (560–530 BCE) onward, and it was he who gave the Jews permission to return to their land.

It is only in the later Jewish biblical traditions, however, that a superhuman adversary—*Satan*—is indicated. Elsewhere the word is used with reference to an earthly, human opponent. But in Job 1 and 2, *Satan* is the one who in the presence of God seeks to discredit the character of Job. Similarly, in Zech 3, Satan brings accusations against the high priest Joshua in the presence of "the angel of the Lord." The most explicit attribution to Satan of evil action appears in the account in 1 Chron 21:1, where he is the instigator of David's sin in invading a divine secret by taking a census of Israel. In the parallel narrative in an earlier historical writing, 2 Sam 24:1–2, it is Yahweh whose anger against Israel incites David to sin by numbering the people. Significantly, in the Jewish tradition, the serpent in Gen 3 that leads Adam to sin was not identified as Satan until the rabbinic period.[36]

In these writings, the following items are described:

1. There exists a cosmic opponent to God, as indicated above, whose defeat by divine action is necessary before God's rule of the earth and his people will be complete.

2. Divine intervention is expected in human history to establish a rule of justice for those who live by the divinely given norms.

3. The divine agent and the specifics of God's purpose are disclosed through mantic wisdom: a series of predictions that describe past and future events.

4. A sequence of time periods is depicted in which the cosmic conflict and the renewal of the creation in accomplishment of the divine purpose will take place. This feature, which was important in Iranian culture,[37] especially from the time of Cyrus, is directly reflected and linked with his name in Isa 45.

5. Perspective on these developments in history is provided through apocalyptic images, which are granted to and interpreted for the faithful remnant of the people of God. The prime Jewish example of such a document is the book of Daniel, which purports to have been written during the time of the Babylonian empire (605–539 BCE), but which took its present form in the mid-second century BCE, as hopes faded for nationalistic renewal of God's people under the Jewish Maccabean rulers.[38]

For many Jews, as a consequence of what came to be regarded as the self-serving tactics of the Maccabees, the focus shifted from the political to the cosmic realm—to the hoped-for divine intervention and renewing vindication of God's covenant people. In the Jewish apocryphal and pseudepigraphic writings produced in the centuries just before and after the turn of the eras, Satan—the divine adversary—is mentioned or identified by several different names, including [H]asmodeus, Mastema, and Beliar.[39] John Collins has offered a useful and insightful characterization of apocalyptic, which he sees as having developed from late Jewish prophetic tradition, powerfully influenced by Babylonian and Iranian thought and literature: "Apocalypse is a genre of revelatory literature with a narrative framework, in which a revelation is mediated by an otherworldly being to a human recipient, disclosing a transcendent reality which is both temporal, insofar as it envisages eschatological salvation, and spatial, insofar as it involves another supernatural world."[40]

It was during the period of Israel's exile in Babylon, and especially after the Persian dominance of the Mesopotamian region, that this mode of understanding human destiny and divine purpose penetrated the thinking of Israel and set a conceptual and literary pattern that was to have enduring influence on the emergence of Christianity from Judaism. These developments in understanding the destiny of God's people were expanded and refined in the era dominated by Hellenistic culture. In chapter 1, we consider in some detail the political, social, and cultural features of the Hellenistic world, and the consequent impact on Judaism and nascent Christianity.

Notes

1. Critical analysis of the changing modes and assumptions by which historians have undertaken the analysis and reconstruction of early Christianity in the post-Enlightenment period is the theme of my monograph *Knowing the Truth: A Sociological Approach to New Testament Interpretation* (Minneapolis: Augsburg-Fortress, 1989).

2. Insightful discussion of the identity of Theophilus is offered by Joseph Fitzmyer in his commentary on Luke: *The Gospel according to Luke I–IX* (Garden City, NY: Doubleday, 1981), 299–300.

3. On the content of the Q document and its use by Luke, see my *Jesus in History* (3rd ed.; Fort Worth: Harcourt Brace, 1996), 74–115.

4. An analysis of Acts that highlights the feature of outreach of the early Christian movement to the wider Graeco-Roman community is offered in my commentary on Acts, *To Every Nation under Heaven* (New Testament in Context; Harrisburg, PA: Trinity Press International, 1997).

5. Building on the mode and approach of the book of Deuteronomy, a historian developed the books of Joshua and Judges, 1 and 2 Samuel, 1 and 2 Kings.

6. 1 and 2 Chronicles, Ezra, Nehemiah.

7. Eric M. Meyers and John Rogerson, *The Cambridge Companion to the Bible* (Cambridge: Cambridge University Press, 1997), 146.

8. Ibid., 160.

9. My introduction to and notes on the books of Maccabees appear in the *Cambridge Annotated Study Apocrypha* (Cambridge: Cambridge University Press, 1994), xxiv–xxvii, xxx, xxxii.

10. Ibid., xxvii.

11. See discussion below of the Hellenistic romance, 37–39. Perceptive analysis of the text and contents of 3 and 4 Maccabees is provided by Hugh Anderson in *The Old Testament Pseudepigrapha* (ed. J. H. Charlesworth; Garden City, NY: Doubleday, 1985), 2:509–64.

12. *Contra Apionem*, 1.8.

13. Ibid., 1.19–27.

14. Ibid., 1.28–31.

15. Ibid., 1.69–105.

16. Berossus (330–250 BCE), I.128–53.

17. *Contra Apionem*, 1.161.

18. Ibid., 1.223–2.42.

19. Ibid., 2.43–65.

20. Ibid., 2.65–144.

21. Ibid., 2.154–74.

22. Ibid., 2.175–235, 291.

23. More recent studies of the novel or romance include: B. F. Reardon, *The Form of the Greek Romance* (Princeton: Princeton University Press, 1991); Shadi Bartsch, *Decoding the Ancient Novel* (Princeton: Princeton University Press, 1989).

24. The critical edition of the Greek text, *Historia Alexandri Magni (Pseudo-Callisthenes)* was edited by W. Kroll (Berlin: Weidmann, 1958); a translation with notes was prepared by Elizabeth H. Haight, *The Life of Alexander of Macedon* (New York: Longmans, Green, 1945).

25. Earlier, Haight also wrote a series of studies of this genre: *More Essays on Greek Romances* (New York: Longmans, Green, 1945).

26. Reardon, *Form of Greek Romance*, 8, 94, 103–6.

27. Richard I. Pervo, *Profit with Delight: Literary Genre of the Acts of the Apostles* (Philadelphia: Fortress Pres, 1987), 105n12.

28. Introduction and translation by J. M. Lindenberger, *Old Testament Pseudepigrapha*, ed. Charlesworth, 479–508.

29. Pervo, *Profit*, 120. The probable date of Tobit is around 200 BCE, as suggested by Carey A. Moore in his article on Tobit in *The Anchor Bible Dictionary* (ed. D. N. Freedman; Garden City, NY: Doubleday, 1992), 6:591.

30. G. W. E Nickelsburg, *Jewish Literature between the Bible and the Mishnah* (Philadelphia: Fortress, 1981), 109–44.

31. "Joseph and Asenath," translation and introduction by C. Burchard, in *Old Testament Pseudepigrapha*, ed. Charlesworth, 2:177–247.

32. A. Kirk Grayson, "Akkadian Apocalyptic Literature," *ABD*, 1:282.

33. John J. Collins, "Foreign Influences on Apocalyptic," in "Apocalypses and Apocalypticism," *ABD*, 1:284–85.

34. *Plutarch's De Iside et Osiride* (trans. J. Gwyn Griffiths; Cardiff: University of Wales Press, 1970), 480–81, sec. 46–47.

35. Ibid., 180–481.

36. *Sanhedrin* 29a.

37. Mary Boyce, *Zoroastrianism: Their Religious Beliefs and Practices* (London: Routledge and Kegan Paul, 1979), 25–28.

38. A sketch of the origins and structure of Daniel is included in my notes for the *Cambridge Annotated Study Bible* (Cambridge: Cambridge University Press, 1993), 63–65. A masterful analysis of Daniel is offered by John J. Collins in his commentary on Daniel for the Hermeneia series (Minneapolis, MN: Fortress Press, 1993).

39. Tobit 3:8; Jubilees 10:11; Belial, frequently in the Dead Sea Scrolls.

40. Collins, "Apocalypses and Apocalypticism," *ABD*, 1:279.

CHAPTER ONE

The Impact of Graeco-Roman Politics and Culture on Judaism

The Changing Political Status of the Jews under the Persians, the Successors of Alexander, and the Romans: The Social and Religious Consequences

The social, literary, and conceptual changes that took place within Judaism from the time of the Jews' return from exile to the period of domination by the Romans are central features in that history and contributed directly to the origins of Christianity.

The Antecedents: The Jews under Persian Rule

Effective control over the Middle East and the eastern Mediterranean region was established by the Persians under Cyrus II (ruled 550–530 BCE) and Cambyses (530–522 BCE). This dynasty, known as the Achaemenids, conquered the ancient kingdoms of Media, Lydia, Babylonia, Syria, and Egypt, and lasted until the coming of Alexander in 330. Cambyses respected and protected the regional sanctuaries and their deities in lands taken over by the Persians, and was designated by the Egyptians as pharaoh. The goal of the Achaemenids was to reconcile central power with a degree of autonomy for local subjects, whose lives were, however, ultimately subject to Persian control through the imperial army. The construction of extensive royal roads facilitated Persian dominance of the empire. Cyrus's son, Cambyses, was the

11

one who by 525 had extended the empire as far west as Egypt and as east as Lydia in western Asia Minor.

The winner of the dynastic struggle after Cambyses's death was Darius (ruled 520–486). He launched the takeover of Greek cities in Asia Minor and Greece, but was ultimately defeated at Marathon by a coalition from Athens and other Greek cities. The resulting agreement worked out with the Athenians brought about a diminution of Achaemenid power in terms of its geographical extent, but from the fifth century onward, its cultural influence on the subject peoples—including the Jews—was great.[1]

Each region had considerable autonomy, including the right of regional residents to continue worship of traditional deities. In keeping with this policy, Cyrus II (the Great), who reigned from 550–530, authorized the rebuilding of the temple in Jerusalem by the Jews, whom he permitted to return to their land from their exile in Babylon when he took over that city in 539. Consequently, he was hailed by the Israelite prophet now referred to as Deutero-Isaiah as "the anointed (*meshiach*) of the Lord."[2]

The Jews under the Hellenistic Rulers: Their Political Status and Religious Development

The defeat of the Persian ruler, Darius, by Alexander the Great—heir to the throne of Macedon—at Issus on the border of Syria in 333 BCE, had opened the way for the Macedonian domination of the Middle East from the Nile to the Indus River, not only militarily but culturally. After the death of Alexander in 323, the lands were taken over and ruled by his generals: Ptolemy in Egypt, and Seleucus in Mesopotamian and Persian territory. Palestine, however, was initially ruled by the Ptolemies from their newly created capital in the Nile Delta, Alexandria. From that city, both political and cultural dominance of the eastern Mediterranean world was fostered with remarkable effectiveness. Subsequently, in 200 BCE, the Seleucids took over all of southern Syria and Palestine, continuing to rule the latter until the harsh policies of Antiochus IV toward the Jews led to their successful revolt and the establishment of an independent Jewish state under Judas Maccabeus, who regained control of the Temple Mount in Jerusalem in 164 BCE, as described below.

Until the first half of the second century BCE, the Seleucid rulers allowed the Jews—as well as people in the other lands they dominated—to worship their ancestral deity. An aggressive shift in policy came when Antiochus IV Epiphanes[3] took the Seleucid throne in 175 BCE. A Jew named Jason, who was the brother of the incumbent high priest Onias III, was appointed high priest by the Seleucid king in response to his promise to provide the king a share in the abundant revenues collected through the temple. Hellenistic culture was promoted by constructing sports and educational facilities. In Jerusalem, the upper classes constituted a council through which they ruled the city and its surrounding territory.[4] The ruling classes were encouraged to adopt features of the Hellenistic culture and, under Antiochus Epiphanes, to honor the Seleucid king as a manifestation of the divine, as his title implied.[5] When Antiochus IV first took over the city of Jerusalem and the land of the Jews in 167, he destroyed all copies of the Torah, and forbade possession of any copies of it. In 168, obedience to its laws was prohibited, including the observance of Sabbath and circumcision. On the altar of burnt offerings in the temple, Antiochus erected some stone pillars that were intended to foster the worship of another deity—probably Baal, the ancient Middle Eastern fertility god of the Canaanites. This profanation of the temple altar is referred to in Daniel as "the abomination of desolation."[6] Resistance to the promotion of this deity and what was seen by pious Jews as the corruption of the temple of Yahweh led to martyrdom for the courageous critics of this pagan worship.

Those who remained faithful to the God of Israel and the law of Moses in spite of the pressure from the Hellenizing rulers were referred to as the Hasideans—the pious ones. They formed protest groups that sought to maintain traditional Jewish standards for belief and practice, in spite of the enormous power of the Seleucid rulers. But a new crisis came for the Jews when the Romans took over the eastern Mediterranean world.

The Social and Cultural Impact of the Graeco-Roman World on Judaism

Changing Social Structures in the Hellenistic and Roman Periods: The Effect on Jewish Life

Urban centers, such as Alexandria in Egypt and Antioch in Syria, were built to serve as dramatic symbols and concrete embodiments of the values and features of human life in accord with the ideals of Hellenistic society and culture. They also functioned as hubs for commercial activity. The abundance of Greek coins and pottery of this period found at archaeological sites in Syria and Palestine shows the great extent of the commercial and cultural interchange that the Hellenistic policies effected. Encouragement for fostering both cultural and commercial ends was a major factor behind the federation of groups of cities in Asia Minor and Syria.[7] A prime example of this civic acculturation enterprise developed in the Palestinian region: the Decapolis (meaning [a confederation of] "ten cities"), which included Gerasa,

Damascus, Philadelphia, Scythopolis (Beth Shan), and Pella. Thus, the language and culture of the Hellenistic world penetrated the entire region, with powerful effects on the values, language, and literature produced in the Graeco-Roman period. This is dramatically evident in the modes of wisdom that developed in Judaism, as discussed below.

The basic instrument of administration was the city, the local governments of which carried the major responsibilities for controlling the life of both the city itself and its region, through construction and operation of public buildings and the supervision of commercial and public life. The Romans did not impose a unitary system of legal institutions upon the diverse peoples over whom they gained control; instead, the legal relationships within the communities were basically as they had been before.[8] The provincial governors were able to exercise "untrammeled discretionary power," including the right to intervene in administrative affairs of the subject cities, "most strikingly in [the] power of life and death over [their] provincial subjects."[9] In the Greek and Hellenistic periods, the key institution was the council (*boule*)—also known as the *synedrion*—whose members were respected local leading citizens, often designated as elders (*presbuteroi*). They approved measures advanced by the wider group of residents, the assembly. The specific roles and functions of the provincial government and leadership under the Romans among the Jews were characteristic of the imperial rule as a whole.

The empire was divided for administrative purposes into provinces, the governors of which were appointed by the senate or by the emperor. All governors selected by the emperor were of senatorial rank and were designated procurators. In many provinces they were aided by nonprofessional staff, although some had junior senators as aides. The procurators were chosen from the equestrian rank to supervise the imperial states and property. Each province had a board of executives and a permanent deliberative council, which was composed of the local ruling class, civic magistrates, and councilors. Taxation was a major responsibility and was carried out by the provincial governor or by officials of senatorial or equestrian rank. Taxes were collected on the land and income of individuals, on inheritances, and on goods in transit through the province. The money was necessary to maintain roads and transport, and was gathered by local tax collectors who, in addition to aiding the provincial administration, could assign taxes for their own advantage. Thus, tax collectors were regarded as collaborators with the Romans, and hence as exploiters of the advantage they gained from their position.

The major role of the provincial system was to maintain the social order and to preserve peace. Only the governor had the right to impose capital punishment and to free the province from the impact of criminals. Yet the local system was expected to apprehend and detain criminals—for example, brigands and robbers. When full-scale hearings were necessary, they were conducted with a regional advisory council, comprised of friends of the governor and local elites. Final decisions were made by the governor, but those with Roman citizenship could appeal to the emperor. Yet local authorities had jurisdiction in civil cases involving their own people and maintained control over internal administrative affairs. But the governor had "untrammeled discretionary power to intervene in the administrative affairs of the subject cities of his province."[10] Yet overall, "Roman rule was predicated on, recognized and enhanced the social and political hierarchy of the provinces."[11]

The Jews under Roman Rule

An important feature of Roman politics and society was the designation of certain individuals throughout the empire as citizens. For example, an edict of Octavian to the council and people of Rhosus on the coast of Syria announced the grant of citizenship and tax exemption to "Seleucus son of Theodotus, citizen of Rhosus," who had fought under Octavian, unflinching in spite of great risk, and evidencing complete loyalty to him. This grant was not only to this faithful soldier, but to his parents, his wife and children, and included "the fullest legal rights and privileges."[12] The issue of citizen rights emerges also in Acts 16:35–39, when Paul has been beaten by the Roman soldiers in Philippi and later in Jerusalem (22:22–29), and appeals to his own status as a Roman citizen as precluding his being scourged before he has been given a proper trial.[13] Clearly, the status of Jews under Roman domination was ambiguous and diverse, ranging from legal protection for collaborators with the Romans—as well as agents operating officially in behalf of the Romans—to helpless victims denounced and punished for plans or acts seen as threats to Roman control.

Later under the Romans, there were two types of official supervisors in the provinces: those appointed by the senate—the prefects—and those appointed by the emperor—the praetors or procurators, who were his agents and kept him informed about problems and prospects for development. In the eastern provinces, the cities remained relatively independent and responsible for local social conditions, having their own magistrates and council. The latter continued to be known as *boule* or *synedrion*—a system of regional government in continuity with the Hellenistic civic structures. The tasks undertaken by the regional councils included providing food for the populace, building roads and harbors to facilitate transport, and maintaining law and order. Taxes were collected by those who bid for or were assigned to the task. The income served to furnish support for the military and governmental processes.[14] The strategy of the Hellenistic monarchs—which was followed by the Romans—was to assign responsibility to these councils comprised of the local elite for the cities of the realm, while maintaining ultimate control in the hands of the monarch. This mode of shared political responsibility was likewise operative in the decision reached in the Roman era by the procurator, Pontius Pilate, in consultation with the council in Jerusalem, to have Jesus executed.

In addition to the official leaders of the Jewish people as a whole, it is essential to recognize the roles of certain functionaries within Jewish society at the regional or local level during the Graeco-Roman period. For example, an important but somewhat puzzling feature of social structure among the Jews and other people of the Middle East in the Graeco-Roman period is the role of the scribe.[15] The Greek term, *grammateus*, translates the Hebrew word *sofer*, which means "writer," and is used with reference to a wide range of roles in writing, education, and administration. It is also linked with record keeping and school activity in Egypt and Mesopotamia, as well as in Israel. Ezra 7:1–10 describes Ezra the priest as "a scribe skilled in the law of Moses" who intended to study and "teach the statutes and ordinances in Israel." Artaxerxes responded favorably to Ezra's request for permission to return to Jerusalem and resume the worship of God there, and commissioned him to "appoint magistrates and judges" to see that the law is obeyed (7:21–26). On their return to Jerusalem, however, it is Nehemiah who is identified as the governor, while Ezra is the religious leader who leads the people in prayer and sacrifice.

In some early Jewish texts, on the other hand, the scribes have a teaching role, transmitting and interpreting the biblical tradition.[16] Josephus mentions "the scribes of the temple" in the reign of Antiochus III (223–187 BCE), and though their function is not clear, it may have involved financial and organizational matters.[17] By the first century CE, there appear to have been three levels of scribes: (1) the lowest level was the village scribe who kept official records and wrote letters, or was an elementary teacher; (2) the middle level was an agent of the central government in a bureaucratic post, subordinate to leading families and priests or to the Roman-appointed ruler; (3) at the highest level were those who came from or joined the governing class, keeping records and handling official communications as well as supervising instruction in law, history, and tradition. There is no evidence that the scribes were a hereditary group, like the priests, or that the term was sharply defined. Each occurrence of "scribe" must be analyzed in its own context.

Modes of Adaptation to Graeco-Roman Culture

Although the Jewish groups and their leaders sought earnestly to maintain the special identity of the people of Israel as members of God's covenant people, there were at the same time ways in which many of them made adjustments that enabled them to survive and even to flourish in a culture dominated by features so different from the historic traditions of Israel. These modes of adaptation were linguistic, conceptual, literary, and political.

Linguistic Adaptation

An important development under the Hellenistic rulers was that Greek became the essential language for international economic, political, and cultural interchange—and this readily penetrated the Jewish communities. The most dramatic evidence for this appeared in the decision to translate the Hebrew scriptures into Greek. An account of that decision and the process by which it was reportedly accomplished is offered in the *Letter of Aristeas*, which is probably a mixture of history and legend. This translation undertaking is said to have been initiated by one of the Egyptian kings named Ptolemy,[18] who was eager to have a Greek version of the Jewish Bible among the hundreds of thousands of books that were being assembled for the royal library in Alexandria. The librarian is reported to have recommended and the king to have authorized that there be a translation of "the lawbooks of the Jews," prepared by seventy-two translators assigned to the project by Eleazar, the high priest in Jerusalem—six from each of the twelve tribes of Israel. As a reward, the king sent a generous gift of gold and silver to the temple, "as a thank offering to the Most High God."[19]

The men chosen for the assignment are said to have been of the highest merit and of excellent education, including not only Jewish but also Greek literature.[20] It is highly significant culturally that the translators' moral qualities are described in basic Stoic terms: justice, moderation in all things, piety, and self-control.[21] They are said to have agreed on the results of their translating activities and produced the definitive copy—all in seventy-two days![22] And no revisions were to be permitted.

This translation of the original Hebrew was supplemented over the next centuries by works originally written in Greek, such as the Wisdom of Solomon. Found among the Dead Sea Scrolls were fragments of Greek versions of Exodus, Leviticus, and Numbers, as well as of Tobit and Sirach. Thus, there is no mistaking that in the Graeco-Roman period, communication in Greek was an important feature of Jewish life and practice—not only in the Diaspora, but also in the land of Israel.

Other Jewish authors of Greek writings during this period are known only by name or by fragments that have survived. Of the Greek writings that have been preserved, the best known are the historical works of Josephus[23] and the treatises by Philo of Alexandria. The latter offer analyses of biblical themes and allegorical expositions of scripture based on his synthesis of Platonic and Stoic philosophies.[24] A significant number of the Greek writings by Jewish authors in this period are modeled on the Hellenistic romances, which are discussed below and also in the introduction.

Conceptual Influences on Judaism from the Graeco-Roman World

PHILOSOPHY

The wisdom literature of Judaism in the Graeco-Roman period shows the powerful influence on Jewish thinking from Greek philosophy—that is, from Platonism but especially from Stoicism. Plato's concept of the world was that it was formed by ideas, which are eternal and unchanging and exist in a super-celestial sphere, where the soul in its preexistence has perceived them. The earthly, sensually perceptible things are mere shadows of the world of ideas, which is conceived to be an immutable, eternal order of universal types and laws and values. The eternal forms are not perceived by the senses, but by the intellect, which is capable of discerning the underlying pattern and plan of reality that transcends the realms of time and space. These ideas represent true being, and constitute the meaning and the moving forces that shape the world as it is. Contemplation of these eternal forms enables one to move beyond the diversity and ever-changing quality of the sensory world to the perception of a unified vision of unchanging reality. Such a concept of reality was adopted and employed in the understanding of the scriptural traditions offered by Philo of Alexandria, and was influential among early Christians, as is evident in the Letter to the Hebrews. In that document, the repeated, ephemeral sacrificial system of Judaism, based on the law of Moses, is contrasted with the unique and eternal—once-for-all—sacrifice and renewal of God's people accomplished through Jesus.[25]

The impact of Stoicism on early Christian thinking is evident in the New Testament letters, especially those of Paul and James. In the Stoic philosophical tradition—founded by Zeno (344–262 BCE) and developed more systematically by his successors Cleanthes and Chrysippus—philosophers saw themselves as providing support for moral life by encouraging humans to live by natural law. They rejected the metaphysical dualism of Plato and Aristotle, encouraging instead knowledge of the unity of the natural world and conformity to the aims and values of divine providence. God was perceived by Stoics of the Roman period as the soul of the world, and humans were called to obey the moral principles inherent in the universe. The universal capacity by which humans might recognize and heed the natural law was called "conscience," which meant common knowledge, shared by all humanity. Life based on these views and resources would result in a sense of unity with the divine, and in a way of life characterized by justice and by a sense of kinship between God and the human race. We shall see that Paul's ethical appeals, while linked with specifics to the law of Moses, the prophets, and the teachings of Jesus, are articulated by his use of the technical ethical terminology of the Stoic tradition.

Another feature of Stoic philosophy of major importance in Judaism of the Second Temple period and in early Christianity was the perspective for

Stoics—as well as for adherents of other philosophical schools, especially Cynicism and Platonism—on the future, and the hope for moral and cosmic renewal. This view of the world and of human destiny shared many aims and values with Jewish and early Christian apocalypticism. The details of these Graeco-Roman philosophical perspectives on the future are discussed later in this book in "Excursus 5: Facing the Future: Common Themes in Jewish Apocalyptic and Graeco-Roman Philosophy and Literature."[26]

MYSTICISM

In the Hellenistic period, there was considerable interest in gaining direct access to the divine so that in one's personal experience—as an individual, or as a member of a questing group—one might participate in the divine presence and power. The chief Jewish exponent of this mode of religion was Philo of Alexandria, whose account of these mystical participations is set forth in his symbolic and allegorical interpretations of scripture, as considered below.[27]

A significant element in postexilic Judaism was the belief that God enabled certain chosen individuals to enter the divine presence. The term that came to be used for this vision of God derives from the Hebrew word for chariot, *merkabah*, and the vision itself appears to have built on—or at least is consonant with—the story of Elijah's being transported to heaven in a chariot of fire (2 Kgs 2:11). Ezekiel uses the chariot imagery, but offers comparisons rather than direct descriptions, as when he describes "something like a throne . . . and seated above that likeness of a throne was something that seemed like a human form" (Ezek 1:26). Ithamar Gruenwald has suggested the following features as characteristic of theophanies in this tradition: God is sitting on a throne; has a human appearance (that of a white-haired old man); abides in a palace. An important element in the divine visions is the presence of angels who accompany, serve, and recite hymns honoring God.[28] The impact of such mystical experience is evident in the New Testament, as when Paul—with seeming reluctance and restraint—in 2 Cor 12:1–10 reports having been transported to heaven. An invitation to come up to the heavenly throne and some details concerning the presence of God are also described in Rev 4.

A Century of Jewish Political Independence: The Maccabees

In 167 BCE, a militant Jewish resistance movement against the Seleucid rulers was launched in Judea by a priestly family, the Hasmoneans, led by Judas, who was given the nickname "the Maccabee" (= hammerlike). He and his supporters effectively confronted the Syrian troops and killed those who collaborated with the Seleucids. By 164, Judas and his supporters had regained control of the temple courts, where he ordered purification from the effects of the pagan sacrifices and ceremonies that had been performed there. It is this rededication of the temple that is still celebrated by Jews as Hanukkah.[29] The traditional pattern of worship was resumed, along with the proper cycle of biblical and historical feasts and procedures for worship of the God of Israel.

After the death of Antiochus IV, two Syrian generals struggled to take control of the regency of his son, Antiochus V. This provided Judas the opportunity to conduct successful campaigns in Galilee and across the Jordan in order to extend the territory under Jewish control. Jews from these territories were encouraged to return to Judea in order to strengthen Judas's power there. A violent Syrian response against this enterprise resulted in the death of Judas, but the Syrians made a peaceful settlement with his brother Jonathan.[30] Jerusalem continued to be officially under the rule of the Seleucids, but the Jewish community there was divided in the effort to exercise actual control. Jonathan and his brother Simon connived to take over the high priesthood and other offices. In 152, Jonathan was appointed high priest by the Seleucid ruler, Alexander Balas. In the ongoing dynastic struggle among the Seleucids, Simon was able to take over several important cities and to expel the Syrian garrison from the Akra, the military fortification overlooking the Jerusalem temple. He was approved as high priest by the Jewish council of priests and leaders and by the people.[31] As a consequence, the Hasmonean dynasty was in power for about one hundred years.

During the power struggle after the death of Antiochus, Jewish forces had launched successful attacks in support of Jewish communities in Galilee and Transjordan. But a contest developed among members of the Hasmonean family seeking to attain power over the Jews. Jonathan, who was high priest for ten years (152–142), was succeeded in 140 by his brother Simon, with the approval of the priests and the people, and was able to expand the territory under Jewish authority. Further expansion was accomplished by John Hyrcanus (134–104), who conquered the coastal area and converted the Idumeans[32] to Judaism. Alexander Jannaeus took over land east of the Jordan and south of the Dead Sea, and broke the power of the independent Hellenistic cities in the area.[33] During his reign from 104 to 76 BCE, he crucified his opponents, their wives, and children. When he was serving as high priest at the Festival of Booths, people threw citrons at him. After his death, his sons fought among themselves for control. The resultant civil strife ended when the Romans invaded the land in 63—at the request of certain Jewish leaders!

The Impact of Roman Imperial Power and Policy on the Jews

Roman Rule in the Middle East

The pattern of military dominance and administration of the Middle East employed by the Romans had earlier been established by them in Macedonia, Greece, and portions of Asia Minor in the second century BCE. For a time, however, it was threatened by three neighboring groups: the Persians, the Armenians, and Mithridates of Pontus, on the southern coast of the Black Sea. When Mithridates and the ruler of Armenia tried to take over all of Asia Minor and Syria, Roman armies defeated them (in 74–66 BCE). Pompey—who with Julius Caesar and Crassus formed the triumvirate that in 60 had taken control in Rome—brought troops into the eastern Mediterranean, defeating Mithridates and driving out those seeking to retain Seleucid power in Syria. In Palestine, the contest for rule between the two sons of Alexander Jannaeus on the death of their mother led to an invitation to Pompey (who was then in Syria) to take action. He was able to end the siege of Jerusalem, which had developed in the struggle between the brothers.

Pompey horrified the Jews, however, by entering the holy of holies in the temple, although he did not harm or plunder the temple. He confirmed Hyrcanus of the Hasmonean family as high priest and removed the coastal regions and Samaria from Jewish control. He vested political power over the Jewish region in a non-Jew, Antipater, the governor of Idumea, whose son, Herod, would become the ruler in Galilee, southern Syria, Samaria, and finally in Judea and the land east of the Jordan.

The most notable accomplishment of Herod's rule (which lasted from 37 to 4 BCE) was his launching a splendid rebuilding of the temple in Jerusalem, which was not completed until after his death. But even that great contribution did not win him respect from many of the Jews. When he died, a Jewish delegation was sent to the emperor Octavian (Augustus), asking him not to execute Herod's will, in which his sons were to be appointed his successors. Riots broke out in Judea, which the Roman governor of Syria, Varus, sought to quell. The emperor, ignoring the request of the Jews, confirmed the division of the region among Herod's three sons: Archelaus become ethnarch of Judea from 4 BCE to 6 CE; Herod Antipas was tetrarch of Galilee and Perea (east of the Jordan) from 4 BCE to 39 CE; Philip was tetrarch of an area east and northeast of the Sea of Galilee, predominantly Gentile in population.[34]

In 6 CE, Archelaus was deposed for incompetence and ruthlessness toward his opponents, and Jerusalem and Judea were placed under direct Roman administration by a series of procurators from that year until 66 CE.[35] During this period there were fourteen procurators[36]—most of whom were incompetent in administration and ruthless in dealing with Jews who opposed their policies and actions. As noted above, the formal link between the Roman authorities and the residents of the various regions under their control was the *boule*, more often designated the *synedrion*, comprised of the wealthy and powerful among the Jewish residents.

Modern historical perception of the role of the *synedrion* in the life of Jews resident in Palestine in the first century CE has been shaped largely by the Mishnah tractate *Sanhedrin* and the Tosefta, which interpret and supplement the Mishnah in the rabbinic tradition. There it is depicted as the long-standing supreme Jewish religious body, whose task was to interpret the law of Moses and enforce it in the ongoing life of the Jewish people. But, as indicated, the *synedrion* was the regional legislative and judicial body, presided over by the political head of state—king or governor. In Greek literature the term is used for a variety of types of conferences and consultations; for example, an informal gathering of philosophical scholars,[37] a council of war,[38] a place of meeting,[39] and the Roman and regional senates, as evident in a second/third century CE inscription from Hierapolis, in which appears *synedrion tes gerousias*[40] (council of the elders). In 1 Macc 12:6, however, the Jerusalem council is referred to as *he gerousia kai to koinon ton hieron* (the body of the elders and the council of the priests), so it is clear that *synedrion* was not a formal term for the Jewish body that was defining and enforcing the law of Moses. The council (*synedrion*) in Jerusalem was consulted by the procurator, but ultimate decisions rested with him. The troops stationed in the area were there to enforce or coerce the populace to conform to the procurator's will and purpose.

The Romans continued the policies of the Hellenistic rulers in centralizing regional rule and in encouraging the development of city-states through the local bourgeoisie and aristocrats who comprised the city councils. Indeed, the empire has been appropriately characterized as a commonwealth of city-states.[41] In a wide range of cultures across the empire, colleges of regional priests were also recognized and encouraged to exercise authority in fostering the indigenous religion.[42] The residents of rural areas were relatively unaffected by the Greek and Roman culture, and retained their traditional customs and way of life, as well as their indigenous languages. The aristocracy controlled the villages and owned the farms, which were operated by tenants. Apart from Damascus and Antioch, there was no significant urbanization in greater Syria, so that Galilee and Samaria, as well as most of Judea, consisted mostly of villages, which were inhabited chiefly by peasants and craftsmen.[43]

The widespread presence of Roman military forces was an essential factor in the exercise of imperial power. Augustus (as Octavian came to be known), who ruled as Caesar from 27 BCE to 14 CE, had set the pattern for this imperial dominance of the army by shifting to himself the control over it. Some of the provinces suffered from civil wars, but many settlers moved to new colonies, initially in Asia Minor. Troops were stationed on the frontiers of the empire, including both regular Roman legions and those of the praetorian guard under senators and knights. A major factor attracting recruits for the army was the promise of citizenship at the end of one's effective term of service. The army was professional in its training and steady in its composition and role. Auxiliaries were recruited from Romanized provinces, however, especially in the East. Augustus was so effective in organizing military power and using it to establish and maintain peace throughout the empire that he was celebrated as a divine agent, and acclaimed as such by poets and by the development of a cult honoring him as god and savior.[44]

The resistance of Jews to obeying orders from the central government to participate in offering honors to a human ruler who claimed to be divine was firm in both the Hellenistic and Roman periods, and led to revolts against the pagan powers—to which we now turn.

The Jewish Revolts against the Romans[45]

Clearly, in postbiblical Judaism both the political and priestly roles were important in messianic hopes. Both features likewise were carried over into the imagery and perspectives on the future that took shape in early Christianity. The crises for the political and priestly future of Judaism arose dramatically in the first and second centuries of the common era. Beginning in the middle of the first century CE, a succession of four Roman procurators—Felix (52–60), Festus (60–61), Albinus (62–64), and Florus (64–66)—were all actively hostile toward the Jews. A group of Jewish revolutionaries known as the Sicarii—the dagger men—promoted a rebellion against the Romans, killing Romans as well as Jews who opposed the revolt. Albinus took bribes from both the Sicarii and the chief priests, whose positions of power were assigned by the Romans and who sided with the latter in opposition to the revolutionaries. Ananus, who was high priest between the terms of Festus and Albinus as procurator, executed many Jews whom he regarded as forming the opposition, including James, the brother of Jesus.

In the spring of 66, Florus the procurator took from the temple treasury seventeen talents[46] of gold. A riot ensued, in which the people attacked the troops sent by Florus to suppress them and succeeded in taking control of the Temple Mount, including destroying the bridge that connected the temple area to the adjacent Roman fortress, the Tower of Antonia. The grandson of Herod the Great, Agrippa II, brought in troops to enable the chief priests to take control of the city, but his effort failed; nor was he able to gain the support of the people as a whole. Instead, Jewish rebels took over the city, destroying the palaces of Agrippa and of the high priest, Ananias, whom they murdered. The Roman governor of Syria, Cestius Gallus—whose province included Palestine—intervened, but was unable to crush the revolt. In 67, leading priests and Jewish aristocrats began to prepare for a war against the Romans by fortifying cities and towns, but not all the people favored the revolution.

In that year, the Roman army, led by Vespasian, came to the land of Israel, and leading cities of Galilee submitted to him and his troops. He prepared for an attack on Jerusalem, but in 69, he was declared emperor by the armies of the east, and was soon accepted as such by the empire as a whole. All Judea submitted to Vespasian and his troops, except for the Herodian fortresses, still occupied by the revolutionaries, and the city of Jerusalem. In 70, Vespasian's son, Titus, began the siege of Jerusalem—a city severely weakened by the lack of an adequate food supply and by Jewish factions warring against each other, claiming as their own various parts of the city. The Romans brought battering rams and succeeded in breaching the city walls. They took control of the Temple Mount, destroyed the temple, and killed its defenders. The Roman soldiers plundered the city, and many of the inhabitants were sold into slavery or killed. In a single day, nearly twenty thousand Jews were put to death there. All the Jewish and Christian religious groups were driven away, leaving no social structures or central leadership for the Jewish people. In the smaller cities and villages, Jewish practice and identity continued, however, fostered by the wealthy land-owning families. The seat of Roman rule was transferred to Caesarea on the Mediterranean coast, which was designated the provincial capital.

In 115, in the eastern Mediterranean area, Jews once more began a revolt against the Romans—who at this time were ruled by the emperor Trajan. The result was that many Jews in Palestine were slaughtered, but the revolt continued. In 132–135, after decades of heavy taxation and repression by the Romans, two acts of the emperor Hadrian led to a second and more extensive Jewish revolt: (1) his prohibition of circumcision,[47] and (2) his program for rebuilding Jerusalem as Aelia Capitolina, with a temple of Zeus as its central feature.

The Jewish revolutionaries were now led by Simon bar Kosiba, whose followers called him Bar Kochba (son of the star) on the basis of their perceiving him to be the messiah, in fulfillment of the prediction in Num 24:17 of the coming of a ruler who would free Israel from domination by its enemies. Later Jewish writers named him Bar Koziba, "son of the lie," however, when his claim to inaugurate a new era for Israel proved to be untrue. For a time he did restructure the leadership of the land and issued coins heralding the arrival of the new age for the Jews. Recently found letters from him to his military leaders—written in Hebrew, Aramaic, and Greek—provide evidence concerning the course of the war against the Romans. It is clear that the major goal of the revolutionaries was to regain control of Jerusalem, to rebuild the temple there, and to resume the annual cycle of feasts—especially the Feast of Tabernacles. The letters indicate that B. Kosiba had taken over various cities that served as capitals of their respective districts, such as Herodium and En Gedi—thus indicating that his administration was still operating there.[48]

Thwarting this expectation, the Romans sent in several legions, which gradually captured scores of Jewish forts and took over hundreds of villages, killing thousands of Jews and finally defeating Bar Kochba at his stronghold southwest of Jerusalem.[49] Hadrian thereupon rebuilt the city, but Jews were forbidden to go there to mourn for the now-destroyed temple. The name of the entire region was changed to Syria Palestina, and two Roman legions were stationed there permanently. In various parts of the land, temples were built honoring Roman deities, and laws were passed prohibiting Sabbath observance, circumcision, and the study of Torah. The Christians fled from the Jerusalem area, and the leaders of the emergent rabbinic movement moved their operations to Galilee.

Clearly, with the failure of these two Jewish revolts, neither the political nor the priestly messianic agents of God were perceived to be in power. If the prophetic promises were to be fulfilled, it had to be by a mode or agent radically different from those advanced by the insurrectionist movements of the late first and early second century CE.

Jewish Religious Leadership and Movements in Response to Roman Rule: Priests, Sadducees, Pharisees, Essenes

Roman dominance of the Jews was most clearly evident in the fact that from the outset, Roman authority determined who might serve as high priest. Consequently, the priestly hierarchy was obliged to coordinate its activities with Roman policy. The priests were thus part of the official religious system and were obliged to support and conform to the pattern of Jewish submission to the Roman powers. Because of contributions to the temple made by the pious visitors and the fees charged by the priests for providing them with appropriate sacrifices, the temple was the largest financial enterprise in that part of the Roman Empire. It was both religiously and economically essential that it be preserved and operative effectively.

Yet in the Hellenistic and Roman periods, several significant groups within Judaism arose that shaped Jewish life and thought in a variety of directions, not only then but also in the ensuing centuries. The major issues that differentiated these Jewish groups from each other concerned the specifics of the ways in which identity as members of the covenant community was defined and maintained. This identity could no longer be based on political independence, or even on participation in worship at the temple in Jerusalem—which was destroyed in 68–70 CE—but on compliance with the purpose of God for his people as set forth in Torah, and more specifically as defined and interpreted in diverse ways by the leaders of the various Jewish groups.

For a time, one group, the Sadducees, who considered themselves to be the true heirs of the priestly role and alone qualified to guide the operation of the temple,[50] enjoyed a dominant role in the Jewish council. They recognized only the law of Moses as the scriptures, and rejected the prophetic and apocalyptic traditions as not authoritative.

The Pharisees, however, regarded as scripture not only Torah but also the prophets and other holy writings concerned with wisdom and worship (e.g., Job, Psalms, Proverbs). They also developed oral tradition for interpretation of the Law, which later provided the method and pattern for what would result in the rabbinic formation of the Mishnah (beginning between 180 and 200 CE) following the destruction of the temple and the disappearance of the priesthood.[51] In the Mishnah is a mixture of (1) second-century CE interpretation and application of Torah as it evolved under the rabbis, and (2) earlier legal tradition. This ongoing application and interpretation of the Law fostered and was based on the notion that there had always existed an oral law paralleling and making the ancient Torah relevant in the present.

A third distinctive Jewish group was the Essenes, known from the writings of Josephus and Philo of Alexandria[52] and now believed to have been the originators of the community that in the latter part of the second century BCE moved from the settled area of Israel and took up residence on a bluff overlooking the Dead Sea, where the Dead Sea Scrolls that they produced were found in the mid-twentieth century. They were critical of the Hasmonean leaders who engaged in what the Essenes regarded as secularization and illegitimate claims to the priesthood. They believed that God had disclosed to their leader, the Teacher of Righteousness (or The One Who Teaches What Is Right), how the true, faithful community should live. They saw themselves as serving in the final age of the world in a role analogous to that of ancient Israel receiving the Torah at Sinai: they were the true covenant community, to whom God had given the essential rules[53] and the proper interpretation of scripture,[54] as well as a description of what the true worship of God would be like in the ultimate temple.[55] The community and its center were destroyed, probably by the Romans during the siege of Jerusalem in 68 CE, but their precautions in hiding their documents in caves in the vicinity of their center enabled these scrolls to survive until their modern discovery, beginning in 1947. There is no way to determine the size or significance of the Essene movement during the Maccabean period, when it presumably was launched, but it represents an important example of dissent from those who sought to establish the covenant community—either by political and military force—by finding ways to maintain covenantal identity while making accommodations to pagan rule under the Romans.

The Evolution of the Synagogue

A major development within Judaism that probably began during the period of Jewish exile in Babylon—when there was no longer the possibility of worshiping God in the Jerusalem temple—was the emergence of groups of pious Jews who gathered to engage in reading and application of the Jewish scriptures to their common life in the new circumstances. After the return of most Jews from the exile, which began with the Persian initiative of Cyrus the Great in the sixth century BCE, the Jerusalem temple was rebuilt, but it appears that the practice of the pious to meet for study and worship continued to be a significant feature of postexilic Judaism. These gatherings—in Greek, *synagogai*—seem to have taken place in homes or in whatever public space was available for groups to assemble. Analysis of the use of *synagoge* in literature from the Graeco-Roman period, as well as from inscriptions recovered from excavations of sites from that era, shows that there was no distinctive architectural model as a setting for these gatherings until the late second century CE and subsequently.[56]

The development of synagogues as distinctive buildings was a constructive response to the destruction of the Jerusalem temple by the Romans in 66–70 CE. In the earlier period, the term that was used for the place of community gathering for worship, prayer, and study was the *proseuche*, meaning "place of prayer."[57] As W. Schrage has noted,[58] terms used to designate these Jewish places of assembly include (in addition to *proseuche*): *proseuterion*, *eucheion, sabbateion, agios topos, hieron, ho oikos, didaskaleion.* The archaeological evidence—much of it recovered in recent years—shows that the earliest structures that clearly were designed and used as places for devout Jews to gather for prayer and worship date from the late second century CE.[59] Characteristic features of these synagogue buildings include a *bema* or podium from which the scriptures were read, and a Torah shrine in which the scriptures were kept. In the Diaspora, where synagogues date mostly from the third and fourth centuries CE, there are often additional features: ornamented mosaic floors and paintings of biblical scenes, of which the most notable examples are from Dura Europos.[60] But none of these items is found in the multipurpose assembly places of the earlier period, when the *synagogue* was the designation of a gathered group of the pious.

Jewish Hopes and Agents for Liberation and/or for Renewal of the Covenant

The diversity and the vigor of these Jewish movements in the early Roman period indicate the climate and potential for growth—as well as for differences and conflict—within yet another group that evolved from Judaism at this time and became what is now known as Christianity. Before turning to an analysis of the early Christian documents and other evidence for the origins of Christianity, however, it is essential to survey (1) the various models adopted by groups within Judaism to define the role of the agent(s) they believed God would provide to bring them freedom and covenant renewal; and (2) the range of literary instruments employed by Jewish writers in this period to express their hopes for divine intervention that would result in that renewal. It was these models of divine agency, as well as the kinds of literature produced in Judaism in this period, which depict the process by which the divine purpose was to be achieved. These perceptions had a continuing effect on the thinking and self-understanding of the Christians in their claim to be the people of the new covenant. In what follows, we survey first the ways in which the role of the liberator is defined, and then analyze representative examples of the literature in which these hopes are expressed.

Central in Jewish hopes for freedom and renewal was the definition of the role of the agent through whom that liberation would be achieved. The prophetic promise that God would renew his covenant with his people had its most emphatic articulation in the familiar words of Jer 31:31:

> The days are surely coming, says the Lord, when I will make a new covenant with the house of Israel and the house of Judah. It will not be like the covenant which I made with their ancestors . . . a covenant which they broke. . . . But this is the covenant that I will make with the house of Israel . . . I will put my law within them, and I will write it upon their hearts; and I will be their God, and they will be my people.

Since the perceptions within Judaism subsequently in the Graeco-Roman period were so diverse as to how the divine purpose for the future of the covenant people was to be achieved—repressed as the Jews were by pagan powers—the hopes and the agendas formed among them in the first century of the common era varied widely as well. Those hopes ranged from formation of political and military power in order to gain independence from the Romans to types of expectation of divine intervention that would achieve the defeat of the human and cosmic powers of evil and vindicate the true, faithful community of God's people. For those more concerned about personal piety than political freedom or about correct perception of the law of God, there were hopes of divine disclosure that would convey true wisdom or correct perception of the law of God, and thereby establishment of the right relationship between God and his people.

The range of models of new communities and their liberators or founders in the Graeco-Roman period is indicated dramatically in the title—and the contents—of an important collection of essays, *Judaisms and Their Messiahs at the Turn of the Christian Era*, edited by Jacob Neusner, William S. Green, and Ernest Frerichs.[61] In the volume's introductory article, "Messiah in Judaism: Rethinking the Question," Green asserts,

> It is no longer possible to justify the standard, homogeneous reading of the varied Jewish writings or to assume that different Jewish groups, even within Palestine, shared a single outlook, social experience or religious expectations simply because they were Jews. The evidence in this [collection of essays] shows that preoccupation with the messiah was not a uniform or definitive trait, nor a common reference point of early Jewish writings or of the Jews who produced them.

Further, Green rejects the statement of Gershom Scholem that the messianic hope compelled a life "lived in deferment"[62]—that is, lived in expectation of the coming of the messiah.

The essays in the volume on the multiple Judaisms and their messiahs show, by the examination of a range of Jewish writings—including some that became designated as canonical and others that did not—a great diversity in the titles or designation of the divine agents who were to effect renewal of God's people and that these differences were a direct reflection of the way in which the community by and for whom the writing was produced perceived itself as the true community.[63]

It is these alternative movements within Judaism at the turn of the eras that must be examined in order to discern the diversity of hopes and fears, of aspirations and visions alive within Judaism at that time, which helped to shape the hopes and agenda evident in the beginnings of Christianity.

Hope for Recovery of Political Independence: Messiah, Son of David

The account in 2 Sam 7 of "the word of the Lord" conveyed to David through Nathan declares that God will "appoint a place for my people Israel and will plant them, so that they may live in their own place . . . and I will give [them] rest from their enemies." Through the offspring of David, the house of the Lord will be built and "the throne of the kingdom will be established forever" (7:13–16). This prophecy probably received its present form in the seventh or sixth century BCE, as the Deuteronomic history was taking shape.[64] Such an expectation is also affirmed by the Prophets and in Psalms.

Earlier, in Isa 7–9, Ahaz, king of Judah (c. 735–715 BCE), was addressed as "house of David" and told that following the impending Assyrian invasion (Isa 8:1–15), God would intervene on behalf of his people, and that a "son" would be given to them who would establish "endless peace." This "child" would be named "Wonderful Counselor, Mighty God, Everlasting Father, Prince of Peace," and would uphold "the throne of David and his kingdom. . . . with justice and righteousness from this time onward and forevermore" (9:6–7). A similar prophecy about the peaceable kingdom to be ruled by the offspring of David is recorded in Isa 11:1–9. A portrait of the king anointed as God's son and ruling from Zion to "the ends of the earth" is offered in Ps 2. In Ps 89, the offspring of David is promised supremacy among the kings of the earth and is to be the one who will achieve confirmation of God's covenant with his people (89:20, 28, 34).

The Chronicler's account of the Persians' grant of permission for the people of Judah to return to their land from exile in Babylon (520–515 BCE), however, places a different emphasis on the role of David as leader of the covenant people. As in the word of Yahweh to the people through Moses at Mount Sinai (Exod 19:6), they are told, "You shall be for me a kingdom of priests and a holy nation." Accordingly, the emphasis in the books of Chronicles, Ezra, and Nehemiah, as well as in the contemporary prophets, Zechariah and Haggai, is on David's role in having established the central shrine for the worship of Yahweh on the mount in Jerusalem. The major motivation for the return of the people to Jerusalem was "to rebuild the house of Yahweh there" (Ezra 1:5). Zerubbabel made it possible for worship to resume there, as the restoration began under him (Ezra 3), was interrupted, and then resumed (Ezra 4–5). Accordingly, he was acclaimed by the prophets as the Davidic messiah (Zech 4:6–10; Haggai 2:20–23). Subsequently, in Judaism the expectation developed that God would establish two messiahs: a royal, Davidic messiah, and a priestly messiah. These appear in the Dead Sea Scrolls,[65] as well as in such Old Testament Pseudepigrapha documents as the *Testaments of the Twelve Patriarchs*.[66]

It is important to note further that in Israel's royal tradition the king was at times designated not only as the "anointed" of the Lord, but also as his "son."[67] In the prophetic tradition, the "son," who is also called "mighty God, Everlasting Father, Prince of Peace," is to sit on "the throne of David" and will establish God's rule "from this time onward and forevermore."[68]

The Bearer of Divine Wisdom: The Biblical Tradition and the Impact of Hellenistic Philosophy

The Jewish biblical tradition shared with the wider literature of the ancient Near East a conviction concerning the importance of wisdom in guiding leaders as well as the lives of the people. This is attested in documents preserved among ancient Egyptian and Babylonian sources.[69] The two major types of wisdom material in this ancient literature are (1) instructions for young men, especially those entering leadership roles in society or the government; and (2) description of the cosmic order in the created world, which is to be the basis for truth and justice in human society. The latter theme is especially important in the ancient Egyptian sources. Humans are to live in accord with this divinely established order in the universe. In the Hellenistic period, however, the theme of cosmic order in the Wisdom literature took on more abstract features, adopting concepts of order and justice from the major Greek philosophical schools—Stoic,[70] Platonic, and Aristotelian—as we shall discuss below.

In the Hebrew Bible, the perspectives on the establishment and maintenance of divine order are set forth in different ways in Proverbs, Job, and Ecclesiastes. The author of Proverbs assumes that God grants wisdom and assures justice for those in the world, while contrasting the transience of human life with the unchanging purpose and the order divinely established and maintained. This understanding is expressed clearly in Prov 8:22–31, where it is asserted that wisdom was created at the beginning of the world, that the resulting moral structure is to be recognized by humans, and that their lives are to be conformed to it. The injunctions and insights of the Proverbs are intended to foster this ordering of human life in a way that is consonant with the divine purpose. Ecclesiastes, on the other hand, portrays the transience of human life, with death as the great leveler of all human existence. Injustice is condemned, but the ultimate message is the inevitability of death. The book of Job combines the vivid narrative of the trials through which Job passes with a discussion of the problem of human suffering: Is righteousness rewarded, and is wickedness punished? The ambiguity of life in this world is vividly depicted, and although the basic questions are not answered unequivocally, the point is made that great and undeserved suffering can bring a new awareness of the presence of God in the life of earnest seekers.

Ben Sira

In later Jewish writings, Wisdom is linked with the Law, as is made explicit in Baruch,[71] where Wisdom is depicted as the female companion given to Israel: she has come to earth to "live with humankind" and is "the whole way to knowledge" (3:36–37). She is thereupon identified as "the book of the commandments of God, the law that endures forever." The promise and warning are given that "All who hold her fast will live, and those who forsake her will die" (4:1). The faithful are to endure and remain obedient during the time of tribulation that they are going to experience because of their failure to obey the law fully (4:21–29).

Wisdom is also explicitly linked with the law in Ben Sira (or Sirach, also known as Ecclesiasticus). After a vivid description of the role of Wisdom in the creation of the world and its coming to dwell in the sanctuary of Israel on the Temple Mount, where it is compared with the life-giving qualities of a river, it is identified with the Law: "the book of the covenant of the Most High God" (24:1–34). In Ben Sira, the role of Wisdom in the creation and sustaining of the universe is celebrated in 42:15–43:33. The correlation of the disclosure of wisdom with the history of the ongoing life of the Jewish people, which is alluded to in Baruch, becomes an important theme in the Wisdom of Ben Sira and is a major factor in the Wisdom of Solomon.

Sirach 44:1–50:21 "sings the praises of famous men," including figures in the history of Israel—beginning with Enoch (44:16; Gen 5:24) and extending through the period of the kings and prophets down to Simon II, who was high priest from 220–195 BCE and is here praised for the restoration of the temple and its precincts. A central figure in Sirach as a whole, however, is the one who studies the Law and the prophets as well as other ancient wisdom (38:34–39:2), is a teacher (39:8), and is an advisor to rulers (39:4). Such a set of roles is linked with the diversity of functions associated in other Jewish traditions with the scribe. Sirach's views of the world and of human moral responsibility are set forth in language that shows the impact of Stoicism on the author.[72] The substantial influence of such philosophy on Jewish historiography in the Graeco-Roman period is even more directly evident in 4 Maccabees, which is discussed below.

The Wisdom of Solomon

Although the book does not mention the name of Solomon, the author identifies himself as the king of Israel whose major goal was to obtain and convey wisdom, as is reported in Solomon's prayer in 1 Kgs 3:9 and much later in an extended form in Wis 7–9. Wisdom is there depicted as a female figure—perhaps from the influence of the Egyptian mystical cult of Isis—who is "easily discerned by those who love her" and "makes herself known to those who desire her" (6:12–13). The facets of the knowledge that Wisdom provides cover a wide range of the metaphysics and physical sciences in the Greek intellectual tradition (7:15–22a), and the depiction of her in 7:22b–8:1 uses metaphors and abstract terms—such as emanation, reflection, mirror—which were basic for the tradition of Platonic philosophy, as well as being important in the writings of Philo of Alexandria. The eternal power and wisdom of God are transcendent, but copies or reflections of these ultimate realities are disclosed to the human mind through the divine light. Hence, Wisdom is "a reflection of eternal light, a spotless mirror of the working of God, and an image of his goodness" (7:26). The temple in Jerusalem (9:8) is a symbol of the way in which—through Wisdom—the faithful can have access to divine knowledge and ultimate truth (9:8–18).

Aristobolus

It is evident from the Wisdom of Solomon that the pattern had been set for the use of insights and perspectives from Graeco-Roman philosophy to illuminate, clarify, and specify the Jewish understanding of God's self-disclosure to his people through the leaders chosen by God to communicate divine wisdom, and that this wisdom is not incompatible with other modes of human wisdom. Indeed, it is clear from the passages attributed by Eusebius in his *Ecclesiastical History* to a second-century BCE Egyptian writer named Aristobolus[73] that the compatibility in certain respects between biblical texts and those of Greek philosophers was perceived to have been the result of the philosophers' having read and been influenced by the biblical writers! Adela Y. Collins's analysis of this material[74] leads to the conclusion that the work was written in the latter part of the reign of Ptolemy VI Philometor (155–145 BCE), probably in Alexandria, by a Jewish scholar seeking to reconcile Jewish biblical tradition and Hellenistic philosophy. In that case, he would be the first known Jewish philosopher. Fragment 5 implies that Jews were using symbolic numbers in the style of Pythagoras. Allegorical method is employed in the account of the descent of Yahweh on Mount Sinai, and God's speaking is interpreted in terms of the *logos*, by which the cosmos was established and which conveys to humans the knowledge of divine matters. Aristobolus's conclusion is that the similarities between the Torah and Greek philosophy are to be accounted for by assuming that Socrates, Plato, and other Greek philosophers knew the Jewish Law. Aristobolus also notes similarities between the Law and passages from Orpheus and Aratus (mentioned in Fragment 4)—who, of course, is quoted by Paul in the Acts account of his address to the Athenians (Acts 17:28). Whether the claim of Aristobolus about philosophers' familiarity with the Torah is true or not, it shows that Jewish scholars in the Hellenistic period were eager to discern—or to establish!—links between their biblical tradition and the dominant philosophical modes of their day.

4 Maccabees

The impact of Stoic and Platonic philosophy on Judaism is likewise evident in 4 Maccabees.[75] The importance of philosophy is explicit in the opening word of the text: "philosophical" in the superlative. Features from Plato's *Gorgias* are pervasive: the appeal to live and die practicing justice and virtue; death is to be seen as preferable to wrongdoing; the certainty of true future judgment; the assurance of life after death for the just; and the use of athletic imagery to depict the disciplined life. Wisdom is defined in characteristically Stoic terms: rational judgment, justice, courage, and self-control, with rational judgment as supreme.[76] The bravery and perseverance of the seven brothers martyred by the pagan king leads to the conclusion: "Devout reason is sovereign over the emotions."[77] Reverence for God, who is referred to as "divine and all-wise Providence,"[78] was the victor in this struggle, and "gave the crown to its own athletes."[79] The prize for this endurance was "immortality in endless life."[80] Thus, Greek philosophical perspectives and terminology provided those in the Jewish tradition with a framework for perceiving the nature and fostering the values of the true moral life.

The Agent of Cosmic Renewal: The Son of Man

In the older biblical tradition, down to the major prophets, the Semitic phrase translated literally as "son of man"[81] emphasizes the humanity, and hence the limits, of humans. The term occurs in Ezek 2:1, when Yahweh appears to the prophet and commissions him, and then is repeated ninety-two times in that book, emphasizing human limits as contrasted with divine transcendence. In Ps 8, however, "the son of man" is said to have been uniquely honored by having been "crowned with glory and honor" and granted "dominion" over all creatures. This celebrates the role assigned by God to humans at creation to "subdue the earth and have dominion over . . . every living thing that moves upon the earth" (Gen 1:28).

In Dan 7, however, the "son of man" is linked with the eschatological triumph of God over the forces of evil. The term itself appears in Daniel as a comparison, "one like a son of man"—apparently contrasting the human agent through whom God's will is to triumph with the evil powers represented as fearsome beasts. The vision of the four beasts depicts the succession of vicious kingdoms that controlled the Middle East: the Babylonians, the Medes, the Persians, and the Hellenistic rulers, culminating in the "little horn" (7:8), who is Antiochus IV Epiphanes (ruled 175–164 BCE). His having made "war with the saints and prevailed over them" (7:21) is the final event before the coming of "*one like a son of man*" into the presence of God ("the Ancient of Days," 7:13): it is he who will receive the universal and everlasting kingdom (7:14).[82] The explanation is then offered in Daniel that the recipient of the kingdom is not an individual, but "the saints of the Most High" (7:18)—the faithful, obedient community of the people of God.

In the Parables of Enoch,[83] on the other hand, the Son of Man is an individual who combines features of the Davidic royal messiah and the Servant of the Lord pictured in Second Isaiah.[84] He is also called the Elect One,[85] the First Word,[86] and the Antecedent of Time.[87] His name is disclosed to the faithful. He will overcome the wicked on the earth, and will remove evil from it.[88] His "righteousness [or, setting things right] will continue forever."[89]

Second Esdras[90] and 2 Baruch, which probably date from the end of the first century CE or the first part of the second century,[91] develop the image from Dan 7 of the "fourth kingdom," which is clearly the Roman Empire. The agent for establishing God's rule, however, is not the "son of man," but "the man" who is called God's "son"[92] or "my anointed one."[93] A role like that of the Son of Man in Daniel continues in the subsequent Jewish visions of divine renewal,[94] but the title itself was ultimately abandoned—probably to the Christians!

The Literary Instruments for Portraying Divine Renewal

In the Graeco-Roman period there developed within Judaism a wide variety of literary modes for portraying the ways in which God was at work, seeking to accomplish the renewal of the covenant people. These included (1) historical writings different in content and method from the biblical modes discussed earlier; (2) legendary and romantic expansions of the historical tradition; (3) treatises on the role of Wisdom on behalf of renewal of the people, as well as (4) apocalypses, (5) testaments attributed to the patriarchs of ancient Israel, (6) new prayers and psalms. The common theme in these diverse documents is that God is at work to achieve renewal of the faithful community. The differences in them lie in (1) the modes by which the divine purpose is seen as being accomplished, and (2) the variety of ways in which the renewed community is defined.

Jewish Historical Writings in the Graeco-Roman Period: Expanding the Scriptural Records and Modifying the Historical Method

We noted above the historical accounts in Ezra and Nehemiah of the resumption of worship in the Jerusalem temple following the return of Jews from exile in Babylonia, and how this led to the rewriting of the history of Israel in the books of Chronicles. First Esdras, a writing known in the Septuagint as *Esdras A'*,[95] consists of the rearrangement of material from 2 Chron 35–36, canonical Ezra, and Neh 7–8. The fluidity of the historical traditions is clearly evident.

By the turn of the eras, the history of God's people and its leaders was perceived in a variety of ways and depicted in a diversity of modes, as is evident in four works that are similar in title but focus quite differently in recounting the history of the Jews in the period beyond Israel's return from exile: 1, 2, 3, and 4 Maccabees.

First Maccabees praises Judas and his brothers for their establishment of their dynasty, and indicates that God has been at work through them to free his people from oppression and to establish the Jewish Law as the rule of the people. It was the military effectiveness of the Maccabees—and especially of

Judas[96]—that overcame the oppression of the Jews by Antiochus Epiphanes and his attempt to force them to give him divine honors. The esteem for the Romans and the alliance with them reported in 1 Macc 8 indicates that the book was written before the Roman takeover of Palestine in 63 BCE. The author perceives that it was God at work through the Maccabees that achieved the deliverance of Israel from her enemies.

Second Maccabees claims to be the condensation of a five-volume work by Jason of Cyrene (2:19–23) describing the antecedents and causes of the Maccabean revolt. The plight of the Jews was the result of their being punished by God for their impiety, not that they were the victims of pagan aggression. Their ability to withstand the hostile nation was the result of (1) the inherent power of the temple, and (2) the fidelity of the people to God and his law. God acted directly when the purity of the temple was violated. The book discloses inner conflict among the Jewish people, and indicates that a significant factor in their ability to be courageous in the face of martyrdom was their belief in the resurrection of the just.

Third Maccabees describes the conflict of Jews with Ptolemy and the Egyptians, and was probably written in Alexandria. Ptolemy IV Philapator (221–205 BCE) defeated the Seleucid king Antiochus II at Raphia and then went north to Jerusalem, where he entered the temple. Only intervention by an angel prevented him from entering the holy of holies. The book attests God's care of those who defied Ptolemy's decree requiring the subjects to accord him divine honors, and documents the founding of a new Jewish festival: Purim. Although the details of the story portray Ptolemy as confused when the elephants he had drugged to trample the Jews turned on his own troops, the dominant theme in the book is the importance of the Jews' maintaining right relationships with the incumbent civil authority.

Fourth Maccabees reports historical events in order to celebrate the sovereignty of reason: devout reason is the ground of human behavior. Extolled as virtues are reason, justice, courage, and self-control—concepts derived from Platonism and Stoicism. Yet the specifics of moral value are defined through the law of Moses. For example, the dietary laws are not to be dismissed as irrational, but are to be obeyed as evidence for one's having achieved self-control.

Clearly, this group of four historical writings shows that in the Graeco-Roman period there were no normative Jewish patterns for recounting the history of God's people. Yet, in spite of their differences in assumptions as to how God works and how such perceptions were to be communicated, these and other writings contemporary with them were to become the canonical historical accounts of the development of Israel in the postexilic period and thereafter.[97]

Other Modes of Historical Narrative:
Tales and Romances

A significant feature of the postexilic literary depictions of the life of the covenant people—and especially of the impact of crucial, dramatic figures in that unfolding story—is the recounting of tales and romances that highlight crucial events in the lives of these individuals and the implications of their personal experiences for the covenant people as a whole, or for a distinct social group within Judaism. In the canonical texts there are antecedents for this literary phenomenon, which became prominent in the Jewish literature of the Graeco-Roman period.

The prose prologue and epilogue of the book of Job[98] frame the poetic speeches attributed to Job, addressed to his so-called comforters and to God (3:1–42:6). Job is portrayed as a rich man of profound piety who became the innocent victim of a contest between God and Satan. In the speeches, Job is critical of God and of the suffering God has brought upon him, an innocent man. In the narrative portion of the book, however, Job is a model of piety and submission, and rejects his wife's suggestion that he curse God and die (2:9). Instead, he is penitent and submissive while his friends are humiliated (42:7–9), and his fortunes are restored doubly (42:10–17). It seems clear that the introduction and conclusion are much later than the poetic core, and probably date from the early Hellenistic period, when a popular medium for propagating religious beliefs and insights took the form of a tale about the encounters of a human with the gods.

Another example of the sacred tale as an instrument to communicate a religious insight is Jonah. A prophet by that name was active in the reign of Jeroboam II (782–747 BCE) and is mentioned in 2 Kgs 14:25, where he is said to have predicted that Israel would fully regain its lost territory. The book of Jonah describes Jonah's punishment for embarking on a ship to Tarshish instead of obeying God's instruction to him to go by land to Nineveh in order to call the people there to repentance. Jonah's punishment for his disobedience is pictured as the arrival of a fierce storm, which leads him to confess his misdeed and to declare that he should be cast into the sea. He is swallowed by a great fish, in the belly of which he utters a psalm, and then is spewed out on dry land (1:17–2:10). He proceeds to Nineveh, calls the people to repent, but is deeply disappointed when no doom falls on the city and is rebuked by God for his lack of concern for the people of that Gentile city.[99] Clearly, the book was written at a time when the Jews were being encouraged to reach out to Gentiles and bring them into positive relationship with the God of Israel—an enterprise that seems to have flourished in the Hellenistic period and is enhanced by this dramatic tale.

Esther is a story set in the time of the Persian king Ahasuerus (or Xerxes, 485–465 BCE). Esther became the queen and informed the king of a plot to assassinate him, and later of a plan by the plotter, Haman, to kill all the Jews throughout the Persian realm. The Jews were also forewarned and attacked their enemies, killing thousands of them. It is this deliverance from enemies that is celebrated in the Jewish Feast of Purim.

Ruth is the story of a Moabite woman, Ruth, who was married to a Bethlehemite, Boaz, and whose son by him would become the grandfather of David. The result was that a non-Israelite displays the wisdom and courage to enter into a marital relationship that made possible the ancestry of David, the archetypal king of God's people.

In these romances, a vivid, compelling tale is recounted with the aim of describing the religious experience of the leading figure in the story.[100] Indicating the flourishing of this literary mode in the literature of Egypt in the Graeco-Roman period, Martin Braun observed that those writings contained "neither pure history nor pure fiction, but a strange mixture of both."[101] This fascination with the supernatural element in depicting the history of God's people is evident in the stories, which might be characterized as edifying novels, and which are included in what is known as the Old Testament Apocrypha.

Two of these writings in the Apocrypha are Tobit and Judith. Although Tobit describes events taking place during the Jewish exile in Mesopotamia in the sixth–fifth centuries BCE, it is full of serious errors and anachronisms, and was likely written about 200 BCE. Tobit was a native of the northern tribes of Israel, but had continued to worship God in the temple in Jerusalem. Taken into captivity in Nineveh, he defied the royal decrees by burying the exposed bodies of Israelite victims (1–2). Though he was blinded by sparrow droppings, his sight was later restored by an angel, Raphael, who guided his son, Tobias, on a journey to Media, where he met and married Sarah. They returned to Tobit, who thanked God for the future restoration of Jerusalem and the return of the people to their land.

Judith was probably written about 100 BCE in the mid-Maccabean period, and the author—like Tobit—mixes names, places, and epochs.[102] The aim is to show that God is at work in history in ways that transcend human expectations and customs. The extended siege of the Israelites in Bethulia (an unknown city!) by the Assyrians resulted in a deadly water shortage, which made the leaders yield to the besiegers. A pious widow, Judith (whose name means, "a Jewish woman"!), protested the plan, and then successfully carried out a scheme that took her into the presence of Holofernes, the leader of the invading troops. She enticed him into coming to her alone, whereupon she beheaded him, and returned with his head to her people. The Assyrians fled, and the Israelites celebrated the victory through Judith. The most remarkable feature of this story is its celebration of a *woman* as the instrument of deliverance of the covenant people. As in the other stories sketched above,[103] Judith's story is not told to convey historical information about the past of the Jewish people, but to stimulate interest and faith by describing the remarkable ways in which God is at work through chosen agents to enrich the lives of his people.

Perhaps the outstanding example of Jewish literary adaptation of the Hellenistic romance is *Joseph and Asenath*, as Christoph Burchard has shown.[104] He perceives a kinship with such erotic romances as Chariton's *Chareas and Callirhoe*, Xenophon of Ephesus' *Ephesiaca*, and Apuleius's *The Golden Ass*. Burchard comments, "Much like these stories, *Joseph and Asenath* relates a love which is achieved with difficulty, only to find oneself exposed to dangerous adventures to which a happy end is brought by the hand of a benign Fate . . . In particular, as an utterly conceited heroine who is swept off her feet by a handsome male and then thrown into the blackest despair, from which she disentangles herself by self-abasement and supernatural assistance." A central feature of the romances—religious conversion—is the main theme of *Joseph and Asenath*, as depicted in the prayers by which Aseneth turns to the God of the Hebrews (11:17–18) and commits herself to Joseph and his God (12–13). She is washed and purified, permitted to eat "the bread of life," to drink "the cup of immortality," and is then anointed with the "ointment of incorruptibility" (16:16). As the bride of Joseph, she is transformed into a heavenly beauty (18:6–11) and is identified by Joseph as the symbol of "the City of Refuge," where the sons of God will live forever under God's eternal rule (19:8–9). Her conversion is confirmed by the declaration of the heavenly man, by her marriage to Joseph, and by her transformation into the "City of Refuge," where the nations and peoples of the world may come to know the true God (14–15) and become members of God's people (19).

Joseph and Asenath was very likely written in Egypt for the Jewish community between the first century BCE and the early second century CE.[105] Clearly, there is no evading the evidence that a powerful factor shaping Jewish writings in the Graeco-Roman period was the Hellenistic romance.

Testaments of the Patriarchs

Using Gen 49 as a model, with its report of Jacob, just before his death, predicting judgment and blessings for his twelve sons, there appeared in Judaism from the second century BCE and on into the third century CE a series of writings purporting to be the last will and "testament" of a range of Old Testament figures, from Adam through the sons of Jacob down to Moses and Job. These documents vary in style and literary method, but they often make use of apocalyptic features and offer ethical appeals. As in Gen 49, these patriarchal figures, facing death, utter predictions, promises, and warnings concerning the future.

The *Testaments of the Twelve Patriarchs* extends the pattern of Gen 49 by offering the testaments of each of the sons of Jacob. Written in Greek, probably in Syria, this work includes the expectation of two messiahs: one royal and the other priestly. A radical dualism is perceived in the world, which is divided between the spirits of truth and the spirits of error. Humanity is grouped in two categories: those guided by the angels of the Lord, and those guided by the angels of Beliar (= Satan), who will ultimately be defeated by God's agents of salvation. Virtues are described in terms derived from Stoicism, rather than from specific legal items found in Torah. The moral resources for humans are the Spirit of God and the conscience. Wisdom and law are virtual synonyms, and are embodied in the universal law of nature—which is a basic Stoic principle.[106] Similarly, in the *Testament of Abraham*, which probably originated in Egypt about 100 CE, good works are defined in terms of the commonplace Graeco-Roman virtues, such as hospitality and charity, rather than derived from the law of Moses.

The *Testament of Job* was written in Greek around the turn of the eras, probably in Egypt—perhaps by a member of the Jewish sect, the Therapeutae, described by Philo of Alexandria in his *On the Contemplative Life*. It shows the influence of a belief in magic and of the Jewish *merkabah* mystical tradition, which focused on the chariot (*merkabah*) of God as the vehicle of divine disclosure. The author assumes cosmological dualism, and foresees the passing away of the present age and its kingdoms, to be followed by the triumph of the heavenly world.[107] The *Testament of Moses*—also written in Greek—dates from the first century CE. It asserts that God will vindicate his people, whose innocent suffering is symbolized by the trials experienced by one Taxo, whose death will result in divine vengeance on the wicked.[108]

Clearly, these testaments represent a movement within Judaism in the Graeco-Roman period that affirms the importance of the covenant people's obedience to the Law, but which perceives that law in terms compatible with Hellenistic, especially Stoic, philosophy. Also operative in these testaments is the belief in the impending divine action that will overcome the powers of evil and vindicate the faithful. This latter perspective—which had its counterpart in Stoic philosophy[109]—found expression in Judaism in this period primarily in the literary and conceptual mode known as apocalyptic (meaning that which is divinely revealed), to which we now turn.

Apocalypses

An apocalypse is a report of a divine disclosure of the purpose and plan of God for his people, and through them, for the renewal of the world. The only complete apocalypse in the Hebrew scriptures is Daniel,[110] although passages akin to the apocalyptic mode are also found in the Prophets, such as Isa 24–27 and Zech 9–14. This section of Isaiah envisages the punishment of the earth and the host of heaven, which have brought evil and oppression upon humanity but will be overcome when "the Lord of Hosts will reign" (24:23). Similarly, Zech 9–14 foretells the defeat of the Greeks[111] (9:13) and the victory in Jerusalem following an attack on it by "all the nations of the earth" (12:3)— events that seem to point to the period of domination of the land of Israel by Graeco-Roman forces. Jews dispersed throughout the world are seen as returning to worship "the king, the Lord of Hosts" (14:16). The multinational involvement seems to envision a cosmic event rather than simply the renewal of the people of Israel, which is the hope regularly expressed in the Prophets. As noted above, the single completely apocalyptic document in the Jewish scriptures is the book of Daniel, which is analyzed below.

This kind of literature offers a panoramic view of history, depicting the ongoing conflict between good and evil and culminating in a vision of the age to come when God's purpose for his people and for the creation triumphs. The visions are filled with mythological imagery of the battle for control of the universe between God and his adversary—at times depicted in superhuman terms and in other apocalypses in terms of historical figures. This worldview and its literary expression developed within Judaism in the postexilic period, probably influenced by Babylonian speculation about the future and by the importance in that culture of mantic wisdom. Similar perceptions of the periods of history and the ultimate triumph of divine justice are evident in the Persian tradition and in writings of Greek historians and philosophers into the Hellenistic and Roman periods, however. The visions concern the future of a group—often in crisis.[112] The linked themes of prophecy and consummation of the divine purpose are significant features in that Graeco-Roman literature, but this phenomenon is often overlooked in scholarly studies of Hellenistic and Roman literature.[113]

Jewish and early Christian apocalyptic writings offer a panoramic view of history, but reach their climax in a vision of the age to come. The information and insights about past and future realms are conveyed in the form of mythological imagery, portraying the battle of good and evil. The dualism is both ethical and ontic, representing the struggle to control history and the world. In Jewish apocalyptic, the basic conviction is that, if the religious community remains obedient to God during the present and impending conflicts with the powers of evil, God will act to vindicate the faithful when he establishes his rule over the world in the age to come. The trials through which the righteous community is now passing are essential to prepare for the new order of peace and justice that is to follow.

It is important to examine some documents that display features of the development of apocalyptic in Judaism. All the Jewish apocalypses that have been preserved are pseudonymous. This was a widespread literary feature in the Graeco-Roman world, and was not regarded as a means of deceiving the reader as to the origins of the writing, but as a sign of respect for a worthy figure in history. Further, this literary device served to highlight the belief that God had been and was still at work in human history to accomplish his purpose for his people and for the whole of creation.

As noted above, Daniel is the only complete apocalypse in the Hebrew canon,[114] although apocalyptic features are found in the writings of the prophets—perhaps as additions during the Hellenistic period. Daniel is written partly in Hebrew (1:1–2:4a; 8:1–12:13) and the rest is in Aramaic (2:4b–7:28). The tales in chapters 2 to 6 have been designated by modern scholars as novels or "court tales," which is a typical literary feature of the Hellenistic period,[115] in which Daniel furnishes models for how pious Jews are to live in and relate to the life of an alien nation and culture.

It may be useful to repeat John J. Collins's excellent definition of the term "apocalypse": [It is] "a genre of revelatory literature with a narrative framework, in which a revelation is mediated by an otherworldly being to a human recipient, disclosing a transcendent reality which is both temporal, insofar as it envisions eschatological salvation, and spatial insofar as it involves another, supernatural world."[116] Further, he states that this genre normally serves "to interpret the present, earthly circumstances in light of the supernatural world and of the future, and to influence both the understanding of the world and the behavior of the audience by means of divine authority."[117] The aim of Daniel is to show how the faithful community is to live in the midst of an alien nation. There is no call for a revolution against the prevailing pagan power such as the author's Jewish contemporaries, the Maccabees, became engaged in. Instead, they are to remain faithful to the law of God in defiance of the royal decrees calling for divine honors to the Gentile ruler, since they are to be confident in their ultimate vindication by God. Then the faithful, who died as martyrs for their commitment to the divine purpose for God's people, will be raised from the dead (12:3). They are the *maskilim*: the "wise ones" to whom God has granted insight and understanding of his ultimate purpose for the world.[118]

Sibylline Oracles

From the fifth century BCE onward, the Graeco-Roman world produced writings that purported to have been the ecstatic utterances of an aged woman prophetess known as Sibyl. The themes dealt with in these oracles include an expectation of some major cosmic disaster, followed by the transformation of the world. The third book of Egyptian *Sibylline Oracles* comes from the middle of the second century BCE. References in it to Macedonia and to Egypt suggest that it originated in Ptolemaic Egypt.[119] Wisdom is related to Isis and to Cleopatra, whose involvement with Rome brought Egypt more directly into the Roman military and political complex.[120] John Collins thinks that these oracles were written by Jews deeply influenced by Hellenistic culture, who saw continuity between their revelation and what was reported in the Gentile oracles, though they expected the destruction of the Gentile political power.[121] These Hellenistic writings became a model for certain Jewish claims of oracular disclosure of the consummation of the divine purpose for the chosen people.

Similar views of divine action that would establish in the world the ultimate rule of peace and justice were advanced by such leading Roman figures as Seneca and Virgil. In *On Providence*, Seneca (4 BCE–65 CE) declares that human suffering is a feature of divine discipline and is a sign of love for those the gods approve. In *To Marcia on the Death of her Son*, he indicates that the world and the whole of creation continue to be renewed by cycles of conflagration and restoration (21:1–3). In his *Fourth Eclogue*, Virgil affirms the Stoic view articulated by Posidonius of Apamea concerning the future purging by fire (*ekpyrosis*) and the subsequent rebirth (*palingenesia*) of the universe.[122] Thus features characteristic of Jewish apocalypses are also evident in the literature of imperial Rome.

4 Ezra

Evidence that the Jewish apocalyptic perception of God's outworking of the divine purpose for his people continued to have proponents down into the Roman period is provided by *4 Ezra*.[123] The work claims to have been written by Ezra in the reign of the Persian king, Artaxerxes (465–424 BCE), but its imagery builds on the vision of the four successive kingdoms found in Daniel. Further, like *2 Baruch* 36–40, the fourth of these kingdoms is identified as the Roman Empire, and the image of the eagle with three heads probably symbolizes the trio of Flavian Roman emperors: Vespasian (69–79 CE), Titus (79–81 CE), and Domitian (81–96 CE).

The original core of the book is most likely chapters 3–14, where the messiah is seen to be descended from David but identified as the Son of Man—building on the Daniel tradition. Chapters 1 and 2, which are probably a late preface, declare that God is going to replace historic Israel with a new, truly obedient covenant community. In the preface (2:33–48), Ezra is commissioned by God on Mount Horeb to convey his message to the people. Horeb is another name—instead of Sinai—for the mountain where Moses met God and received from him the law for Israel (Exod 3:1).

Depicted in a series of visions is the coming end of the age (5:1–12:39), the defeat of the pagan powers, and the appearance of the Man from the Sea, who is God's agent for renewal of the world and of his people. There are warnings of severe judgments that will fall on the pagan powers, as well as painful trials to be experienced by God's people as they await ultimate divine vindication.[124] The features of the prototypical apocalypse—Daniel—are clearly evident here in *4 Ezra*: (1) the need for God's people to preserve their integrity and obedience; (2) the certainty of persecution that they will suffer at the hands of the pagan powers; (3) the intervention of a divine agent of deliverance that they should await; (4) the ultimate consummation of the divine purpose in the renewal of the world.

Expanding and Expounding the Scriptures

A major feature of the new forms of covenant community that were being defined in the Graeco-Roman period by various Jewish leaders and by the diverse groups that were then taking shape was their fresh interpretation and appropriation of the scripture traditions of Israel in ways that would inform and strengthen their constituency. This move employed two different modes: (1) to expand the scriptural accounts, and (2) to expound the scriptures by means of commentaries.

Expansion of the Scriptures and the Move Toward a Canon of Scripture

A prime example of the expansion approach to scripture is the book of *Jubilees*,[125] which is alluded to in the Dead Sea Scrolls and probably dates from about 100 BCE.[126] The major concern of the book is to confirm the authority and relevance of the law of Moses, and it purports to contain revelation for all Israel, not merely for a special group, such as the Dead Sea community. The title shows that of prime importance is the temporal outworking of the plan of God for his people through the divinely determined pattern of weeks of years (= 49 years), which is perceived to have been operative throughout the history of Israel and is seen as now in the course of consummation for the faithful community. In depicting this chronological process, the stories about Adam, Noah, Abraham (including an account of his death), Jacob, and Moses are retold—with the most extensive treatment being of Jacob and his family.[127]

Three different kinds of exegetical literature found among the Dead Sea Scrolls expound scripture to show its relevance for the present claimants of participation in the covenant community: (1) paraphrases of scripture, (2) interpretations of scripture, and (3) expansions of scripture. The first type is represented by Targums on Leviticus (4Q156) and Job (4Q157), but especially by what is sometimes referred to as 4Q *Reworked Pentateuch* (4Q158).

These interpretive documents include some that offer verse-by-verse commentaries, and others that represent studies of themes in the scriptures. *Pesharim*, "interpretations," is the self-designation for the many commentaries that have been found among the Dead Sea Scrolls: they expound the books of Isaiah, Hosea, Micah, Nahum, Habakkuk, Zephaniah, Malachi, and the Psalms. One important find was the *Genesis Apocryphon*, which interprets the account in Genesis that runs from Lamech (Noah's father), the birth of Noah, the flood and its consequences, to the coming of Abraham, including his stay in Egypt. The scriptural narratives are seen as not merely providing a record of the past of Israel, but also as expressing the implications of these stories for the present community of those who perceive themselves to be God's people. There is the explicit claim that the interpretation "concerns the last days" (4Q162), and that what is referred to in the scriptures concerns the leadership and membership of the Dead Sea community. For example, in 1Q Micah Pesher, there is a direct identification of the community's founder, the Teacher of Righteousness, and of his council. In 1Q Habakkuk Pesher there is a claim that God has sent the Teacher to foretell the fulfillment of the divine promises for the faithful community (II), and that the Wicked Priest will defile the Sanctuary of God (XII).

The expansion of the corpus of sacred scriptures at Qumran is represented by the *Temple Scroll*, which builds on the book of Deuteronomy, offering detailed instructions for worship in the ultimate temple. It is written in the first-person singular, conveying the claim that "I, YHWH, reside among the children of Israel." This is a clear implication that the eschatological renewal of God's people and of the temple and the sacred city is expected to take place soon in fulfillment of these divinely granted predictions of God's presence with the faithful community.

In his article on "Canon,"[128] James A. Sanders offers an analysis of the process by which limits were imposed on the growing body of Jewish writings as to which were to be regarded as authoritative. He concludes that the definition of normative scriptures was not fixed in scope or sequence until at least the end of the first century CE. The differences operative up until that time are apparent from the Septuagint and from the Dead Sea Scrolls. The tradition that a council at Jabneh (Jamnia) in the late first century BCE established the definite list and order of the Jewish scriptures is not historically reliable. It was probably around 100 CE, through Pharisees and those who were to launch the rabbinic movement, that the reduction of the list of Jewish writings to be considered as scripture began. These writings had been produced over a period of fifteen hundred years, from the Bronze Age to the Graeco-Roman period. With the temple destroyed and the priesthood irrelevant, it was essential to provide norms and background for establishing and maintaining the identity of those who claimed to be the people of God.

Expounding the Scriptures

A significantly different mode of scriptural interpretation and application from those sketched above—one that was to have an important impact on nascent Christianity—is that which was developed by Philo of Alexandria in the first century CE.[129] As a member of a prominent Jewish family among the hundreds of thousands of Jews resident in Alexandria, Philo was so highly regarded by them that he was chosen to lead an embassy to the Roman emperor Gaius Caligula (37–41 CE) to protest abuses of the Jews there.[130] His many writings consist largely of expositions that he offers of both the narratives and the laws in the Hebrew scriptures—which he interprets in their Greek translation. His method in his extended treatises on the biblical texts is to disclose to the reader the *spiritual* meaning in them, which for Philo meant the underlying perceptions and insights that lie beneath the surface of the texts, compatible with what he regarded as lofty insights from the Greek philosophical tradition.[131] For example, he sought to bring out the spiritual meaning that underlies the narratives concerning the patriarchs. Specifically, in his study *On the Migration of Abraham*, he makes the point that the intent of the narrative is not simply to describe the wanderings of some ancient nomads but to depict the spiritual journey of one who moves from the realm of sense perception (symbolized by Ur of the Chaldees) to the place where one may gain a true vision of God. The names, numbers, and details of the biblical stories are interpreted symbolically to disclose the divine purpose and the world of ultimate reality, which Philo perceives in terms of the Platonic distinction between the ideal realm of eternal models and the transitory world of ephemeral copies. This spiritual transition is the point in his recounting the story of Abraham's "migration."

In the treatise *On the Embassy to Gaius* (4–7), Philo makes the point that the insight into the nature and purpose of God for his people that the unaided human intellect (*logos*) fails to attain, the Jew with his special perception can gain through mystical experience.[132] Israel, which Philo understands to mean "one who sees God," is the true humankind. The Greek concept of universalistic *philanthropia* was affirmed by Philo, but he understood that it had been disclosed by God primarily to the Jews, who through their laws and worship were the center of humankind, and who were to be the instruments through whom this concept would be spread to all humanity.[133] The cosmic order of the world promised by God will be gained by bringing the law of Moses and its virtues to all the nations and to the world of nature, since this is the cosmic law that presents the conditions for fulfillment of human hopes.[134] The ethical values enjoined in the Torah are correlated by Philo with the Stoic concepts of justice and order. Both the interpretive method of

Philo and the philosophical presuppositions that he derived from the Graeco-Roman intellectual tradition were to have profound influence on early Christian writers and leaders.

Fostering True Worship

From the sixth century BCE exile of the Jews in Babylon onward, the historic experiences of the Jews, by which they were deprived of access to the temple in Jerusalem where God was believed to be present and accessible to the priesthood in the holy of holies, required them to develop other modes of worship. This led subsequently to the evolution of the synagogue, as noted above, and to the elevation of rabbis to a status equivalent to the priestly leadership in worship. Even while the temple was still in operation, however, there were those who were persuaded that the incumbent priesthood was impure and unworthy, as is evident from the Dead Sea Scrolls. It is to these developments in worship within Judaism that we now turn.

Worship in the Dead Sea Community: The *Temple Scroll*

The *Temple Scroll* (11Q19)[135] heightens the purity requirements for the true covenant community in the awaited time of fulfillment (xlix–l), and attaches special importance to the tribe of Judah (xxiii). For example, no blind person is to be permitted to enter the holy city or the temple (xlv). All the law is to be obeyed (liv), and the people are called to be perfect (lx). The priests are to be obeyed (liv), and the wicked are to be killed, including worshipers of other gods (lxi), a defiant son (lxiv), and one who is a "glutton and a drunkard" (lxiv).[136] Rules are set down for kings, judges, and magistrates (li), and for observance of such holy days as Pentecost (frag. 6) and the Day of Atonement (xxv). The emphasis is not so much on guidance for worship by devout individuals as for purity of the city, the temple, and the true and renewed people of God.

New Resources for Worship: Prayers and Psalms

The canonical collection of 150 psalms was apparently not finalized until the end of the first century CE, and prior to that time other psalms were regarded as authoritative for the guidance of certain Jewish communities.[137] Four such psalms (Ps 151A, 151B, 154, and 155) have been found among the Dead Sea Scrolls.[138] But another Qumran scroll, 1Q Hodayoth,[139] contains hymns that include quotations from 120 of the canonical psalms, as well as eight not found in the Masoretic text, and four known from the Septuagint or the Syriac Psalter. The hymns offer the following recurrent themes: the central concern for fostering the community of the covenant;[140] the mysteries divinely disclosed;[141] the identification of Beliar as the source of untruth and evil.[142] This perception of the demonic enemies is repeated in the *Songs of the Sage* (4Q510) and in the *Psalms of Exorcism* (11QPsAp). The necessity for overcoming the demonic powers, which is such an important feature of the gospel tradition,[143] is clearly pervasive in the liturgical material preserved among the Dead Sea Scrolls.

The Antecedents of Rabbinic Judaism

A mode of interpretation and appropriation of the biblical tradition very different from those sketched above developed in the postexilic period as a central feature in what was to become the locus of Jewish worship: the synagogue. This phenomenon seems to have begun evolving during the exile of the Jews in Mesopotamia as they assembled to share the traditions of Torah in an alien land. Such gatherings apparently developed programs of study and worship to confirm the commitment of the community to the covenantal tradition. This practice spread among Jews in their dispersion across the Mediterranean world, and was continued and more formally developed by Jews after they returned from exile to their land. Only after the destruction of the temple and the failure of the two revolts against the Romans did the synagogue develop its institutional forms and its distinctive architectural features.[144] From the outset, this process resulted in the highlighting of the public reading and interpretation of scripture as a central feature for the ongoing life of Jews, and especially for those who could not reach the temple in Jerusalem. Those who took leadership in this process of study and scriptural interpretation were the progenitors of those who became the rabbis of Judaism in the second and subsequent centuries CE.

The interpretive methods these leaders developed and the results of their analyses and debates began the evolution of what became the Mishnah and the Talmud—the process that has been so ably traced and documented by Jacob Neusner in his extensive writings.[145] He dates the beginnings of the Mishnah to around 200 CE, with its sixty-three tractates covering six kinds of activity: (1) economy, including the provisions of rations for priests—who by that time no longer had any official function, since the temple was gone; (2) observance of holy days, with special attention to what happened in the temple; (3) the status of women; (4) civil, commercial and criminal laws, with a government based on the temple and the king; (5) cultic rules for the temple and rules for its upkeep; (6) rules for dealing with the unclean. Clearly, these rules and interpretations projected an ideal situation in which the monarchy, temple, and priesthood would be restored, but they dealt with day-to-day issues as well. The process of development of post-temple Judaism is implicit in the term "formative," which Neusner has used effectively, as in the title of one of his books, *Formative Judaism: Religious, Historical and Literary Studies*,[146] and in the title of the collection of essays strongly influenced by his insights: *Judaisms and Their Messiahs at the Turn of the Christian Era.*[147]

The implications of these developments in Judaism for Christian origins are set forth by Neusner in his preface to *Judaism in the Matrix of Christianity*:[148]

> The Judaisms under discussion here do not wholly conform to a single pattern, and the evidence at hand also proves diverse . . . In ancient times, as in every age of the history of the Jewish people, diverse groups of Jews have defined for themselves distinctive ways of life and world views . . . A Judaism therefore constitutes a worldview and the way of life that characterize the distinctive system by which a social group of Jews works out its affairs.

He notes that the different groups all appeal to scripture, though each group bases its identity on a different set of scriptures, and each of them builds a different system of group identity and divine purpose. The same diversity is evident in the material produced by the various early Christian groups, so that the historian is faced with "Christianities and Judaisms."[149]

An important and insightful comparative study of Judaism and Christian origins by a major Jewish scholar is Alan Segal's *Rebecca's Children: Judaism and Christianity in the Roman World.*[150] At this time, when biblical scholars and theologians are rightly concerned with the historic connections between Judaism in the period of the Second Temple and the origins of Christianity, Alan Segal's book offers a fresh, perceptive, profoundly insightful statement of the issues and the historical developments. Unlike others who in recent decades have written in this field, the author neither papers over basic differences nor champions a later orthodoxy, Jewish or Christian. Instead, Segal has undertaken a sensitive, evenhanded description that takes into account not only conceptual factors, but also social and cultural dimensions. The result is a major contribution to historical inquiry as well as to interreligious understanding.

The title of the book points to an extended metaphor, according to which the twin heirs of the covenant first vie with each other for dominance, and then go separate ways. In Segal's scenarios, Jacob (= Judaism) rivals Esau (= Christianity). Yet the metaphor is not overextended, since he makes clear that there were wide differences among Jews in the Hellenistic and Roman periods as to the nature of covenantal identity and responsibility. The Jesus movement and then Pauline Christianity emerge as significantly different options within the broad field of covenantal definition. From the outset, covenant between Israel and God was not merely a theological concept, but a model of social practice that shaped personal behavior and public policy. The shared story of the origins of Israel and God's activity among his people is mingled with the specifics of individual and group obligation: hence, the centrality of Torah and the necessity for renewing and rethinking the covenant.

The shift from monarchy to hierocracy in the Persian period had heightened the importance of Torah for Israel. And the aggressiveness of the Hellenizers meant that the ancestral convictions could no longer be taken for granted, but must be promoted and defended. Complicating these basic adjustments were the socioeconomic factors of the split between Hellenized Jewish urban aristocrats and entrepreneurs on the one hand and the exploited Jewish rural people living mostly as tenant farmers in an Aramaic-oriented rural culture on the other. To preserve covenantal identity required more than the continuing of the official cultus located in the temple, led by the priests, and supported by groups like the Sadducees.

The synagogue—which, as explained above, means "gathering"—emerged as an informal meeting in homes for the purpose of study of Torah and the reinforcement of religious identity in the new social conditions, fostered by the emergent Pharisaic movement. The formal features of special buildings for this purpose and a rabbinate for synagogal leadership do not appear until after the second Jewish revolt in the second century CE. As noted above, the Sanhedrin was originally only a local council, set up by the Hellenistic and Roman rulers, but in the second century the name was taken by the emerging corps of rabbinic leaders as a designation for their central leadership group. The Essenes at Qumran based themselves on the model of Moses and his people, poised in the desert until God would act to reestablish them in the promised land and place them in charge of the renewed central shrine. The root metaphor for all these groups was covenant, even though the locus and focus for covenantal identity of each group were so very different. The term messiah was not a title or an office or an idealized future king, but a designation of someone chosen of God to perform a function on behalf of the covenant people (65).

In sharp contrast to these Jewish groups, all of which made ritual purity central for covenantal identity, Jesus was opposed to ritual purity as a requisite for participation in the covenant. Similarly, "Jesus, the Jewish revolutionary," as Segal calls him, was also critical of the temple (82, 84). His championing of the poor and his denunciation of the rich by appeal to the prophetic traditions were perceived as politically revolutionary—if not in intent, at least in their implications (81). The Jewish scriptures were appealed to by Jesus—and more extensively by those who passed on the Jesus traditions—for justification of his challenge to the religious and political leadership, of his promise of a new covenantal order, and of his own death and ultimate vindication by God (88–95).

On the basis of the apocalyptic orientation (which Paul took over from the Jesus tradition) and his own mystical encounter with Christ in his conversion experience, Paul defined the covenant community as those who are "in Christ" (108), a relationship entered into by baptism, which transcends ethnic differences and is experienced in the predominantly Gentile house churches (109). As a Jew, Paul continued to respect the law. Though he no longer saw it as the instrument for human salvation, its significance for both Gentile and Jewish Christians was a problem with which he continued to struggle (114–15).

The Pharisees and their rabbinic heirs wanted to make the Torah relevant to contemporary life in an altered situation where they lacked political autonomy and a central shrine. By transferring the focus of Torah from the temple to their fellowship groups, and by employing imaginative principles of exegesis that were then set forth as the original meaning of the texts, the rabbis were able to give to the ancient legal traditions a sense of both venerable antiquity and contemporary relevance (122). Given the socially and culturally threatening circumstances and the loss of geographical or political territory of their own, Jews sought to maintain identity by major emphasis on purity through the establishing of ritual boundaries that demarcated them as the covenant people from all other peoples (123–27).

On the Christian side, as the numbers of Jewish Christians dwindled and the permeation of the church by those reared in Graeco-Roman culture increased, the Christian notions of covenant became not only different from, but also hostile toward the emergent rabbinic definition. This is apparent in the gospels, especially in Matthew (146–47).[151] The Jewish reaction to these developments was to draw a clear line between the true members of the covenant people and the *minim* (the outsiders), so that by the third century, the rupture was complete (160–61). The major center of contention was the Christian claim about Jesus' unique relationship to God, which the rabbis saw as compromising the unity and uniqueness of God (151–57). Yet, since both of "Rebecca's children"—Jewish and Christian—claimed to be the true heirs of the covenantal tradition, and therefore the true Israel, the differences between them are historically comprehensible, but ultimately incompatible (179).

One may have quarrels with Segal over details, such as whether Paul did indeed insist that Jewish Christians continue to obey Torah, or what the connotations of the title "messiah" were in this period. But his work, along with that of Jacob Neusner (whose literary and historical judgments about the evolution of the rabbinic traditions Segal in general accepts) makes clear to both Jewish and Christian scholars that it is grossly anachronistic to read the viewpoints of Mishnah and Talmud back into the first-century documents. Instead, both rabbinic Judaism and Christianity must be seen as in process of concurrent evolution—and controversy—in the early centuries of the common era.

Accordingly, this study of the origins of Christianity must seek to identify and describe the major diverse ways in which this movement originated within its Jewish context and then grew and spread into the wider Gentile world.

Conclusion

This survey has sought to show that, as a result of the politically and culturally aggressive actions of the Hellenistic and Roman rulers who dominated the Jews during the period of the Second Temple, there is abundant evidence from the surviving Jewish sources of the development there of not only literary and liturgical features, but also of many essential concepts that were to have a basic impact on the origins of Christianity. Many of these concepts—hopes, anxieties, perceptions of evil, ethical norms, social and political models, expectations of divine intervention in human history—which were being articulated in Judaism in response to the Roman world in the time before and after Jesus appeared on the scene, had a significant and substantive impact on Christianity, the movement which began to develop in the name of Jesus, based on the belief in his messianic role as "the Christ." It is to the import of these conceptual and cultural developments for nascent Christianity that we now turn.

Notes

1. The successors of Darius included Xerxes (486–465), Artaxerxes I (646–424), Darius II (425–405), Artaxerxes II (404–358). Probably the mission of the Jewish leader Nehemiah to the Persian ruler (Neh 1–2) was to Artaxerxes I in 427, and that of Ezra (Ezra 4) was to Artaxerxes II (404–359) in 398.

2. Isa 45:1–3.

3. This assumed title, Epiphanes, implied that Antiochus was the manifestation of a divinity. *Epiphanes* derives from the Greek word *epiphaion*, "manifest, disclose," and was used as a title that implied manifestation of the divine.

4. These regional councils were variously designated as *boule* and *synedrion*. For the subsequent development of these political entities, see below.

5. A compact, insightful historical analysis of Antiochus IV's accession to power and its consequences for the Jewish people is offered by A. J. Saldarini in sec. 2 of his study of Jewish responses to Greco-Roman culture in *The Cambridge Companion to the Bible* (ed. H. C. Kee; Cambridge: Cambridge University Press, 1997), 306–54.

6. Dan 9:27; 11:31. The "four great beasts that came up out of the sea" (Dan 7:3) represent the successive empires that dominated the Middle East: Babylonian, Median, Persian, and Greek/Hellenistic. This is specified in 8:19–21.

7. M. Rostovtzeff, *The Social and Economic History of the Hellenistic World* (Oxford: Clarendon, 1964), 1:153–55.

8. J. A. Crook, *Law and Life of Rome* (London: Thames & Hudson, 1967), 10–11.

9. Graham Burton, "Government and the Provinces," in *The Roman World* (ed. J. Wacher; London and New York: Routledge & Kegan Paul, 1987), 434. The description offered here is based on Burton's analysis of Roman administrative policy (423–39).

10. Ibid., 434.

11. Ibid., 439.

12. From "Letters and Edicts of Octavian to the Rhodians between 41 and 30 B.C.E," in *Documents Illustrating the Reigns of Augustus and Tiberias* (2nd ed.; ed. V. Ehrenburg and A. H. M. Jones; Oxford: Clarendon Press, 1976), no. 301, 133–35.

13. Discussed in the excursus on Roman citizenship in my commentary on Acts, *To Every Nation under Heaven* (Harrisburg, PA: Trinity Press International, 1997), 200–201; the issue is also raised when Paul is on trial in Jerusalem (257–63). The specifics of Roman citizenship are described by Peter Garnsey and Richard Saller in *The Roman Empire: Economy, Society and Culture*, particularly in chap. 6, "On the Social Hierarchy" (Berkeley, CA: University of California Press, 1987), 107–25.

14. M. Rostovtzeff, *The Social and Economic History of the Roman Empire* (Oxford: Clarendon Press), 1:46–49, 384–88.

15. A perceptive and comprehensive analysis of the evidence concerning the role of the scribe in the Jewish tradition is offered by A. J. Saldarini in *Pharisees, Scribes and Sadducees in Palestinian Society: A Sociological Approach* (Wilmington, DE: M. Glazier, 1988), 241–76.

16. Ibid., 248.

17. Josephus, *Jewish Antiquities* 12.3.3.

18. Which king by the name of Ptolemy the letter refers to is uncertain: the dynasty of Ptolemies ruled Egypt from 323 to 30 BCE. A likely possibility is Ptolemy Philometor, who reigned from 181 to 145, part of the time sharing the throne with his younger brother, Ptolemy VII Euergetes II, and with their sister Cleopatra as queen and wife of Philometor. Surviving records show him to have been a friend and promoter of Greek culture. It was he, perhaps, who arranged for the translation of the Jewish scriptures into Greek. In his introduction to the letter, R. J. H. Shutt thinks a date around 170 BCE date is most likely. *The Old Testament Pseudepigrapha* (ed. J. H. Charlesworth; Garden City, NY: Doubleday, 1985), 2:9.

19. *Letter of Aristeas* 20–33.

20. Ibid., 121–22.

21. Ibid., 131–33, 209, 237, 255, 279.

22. Ibid., 302.

23. Josephus's major works include *Jewish Antiquities, Jewish War, The Life* (his autobiography), and *Against Apion*.

24. The titles of Philo's work include: *On the Creation, Allegorical Interpretation, On the Cherubim, On the Sacrifices of Abel and Cain, The Worse Attacks the Better, On the Unchangeableness of God, On Noah's Work as a Planter; On the Confusion of Tongues; On the Migration of Abraham; On Flight and Finding, On the Change of Names, On Dreams, On Abraham, On Joseph, Life of Moses, On the Decalogue, On the Special Laws, On the Virtues, On Rewards and Punishments, Every Good Man is Free, On the Contemplative Life, On the Eternity of the World, On Providence, Questions and Answers on Genesis.* Examples of his mode of exegesis are offered below.

25. The crucial term, *ephapax*, with reference to the once-for-all sacrifice of Christ, occurs in Rom 6:10, and in Heb 7:27; 9:12; 10:10. An analysis of Heb 8–10, pointing out its appropriation of the Platonic view of reality and contrasting ephemeral recurring factors with the eternal model of reality, is offered in my discussion of the Letter to the Hebrews in *Cambridge Companion to the Bible*, 511–14, and is summarized below in the analysis of Hebrews in chap. 3.

26. Pp. 463–80.

27. A prime example of this feature of Philo's interpretation of scripture is in his tractate, *On the Migration of Abraham*, analyses of which are discussed below.

28. Extra-biblical theophanies mentioned by Gruenwald include those in *1 Enoch* 14 and 71, *2 Enoch*, *Apocalypse of Abraham*, *Ascension of Isaiah*, *Testament of Levi* (in *Testament of the Twelve Patriarchs*), and *3 Baruch*. The subsequent development of this mystical mode in postbiblical Judaism is traced by P. Alexander in his analysis of *3 Enoch* (Charlesworth, ed., *Old Testament Pseudepigrapha*, 1:223–54), and in his notes on his translation of the text.

29. Cf. 1 Macc 4:36–61; 2 Macc 10:1–8.

30. 1 Macc 6:28ff; 9:1–22.

31. 1 Macc 14:25–49.

32. Idumeans were descendants of the biblical Edomites, whose territory was around the lower end of the Dead Sea.

33. As noted above, one group of these cities came to be known as the Decapolis (ten cities), which included Scythopolis, Gadara, Gerasa, Pella, and Philadelphia (Amman).

34. His tetrarchy included Iturea, Trachonitis, Batanea, Auranitis, Gaulanitis, and Panias.

35. There was a brief period (41–44 CE) when the whole of Herod's former realm was assigned to his grandson, Herod Agrippa I.

36. The Roman governors of Palestine in the first century CE were:

Coponius	6–9
Ambibulus	9–12
Rufus	12–15
Valerius Gratus	15–26
Pontius Pilate	26–36
Marcellus	36
Marullus	36–41
Cuspius Fadus	41–46
Tiberius Julius Alexander	46–48
Ventidius Cumanus	48–52
Felix	52–60?
Porcius Festus	60–62
Albiunus	62–64
Gessius Florus	64–66

37. Plato, *Protagoras* 317d.

38. Xenophon, *Historia Graeca* 1.1.31ff.

39. Herodotus 8.79.

40. In *Supplementum Epigraphicum Graecum* (ed. H. W. Plaket and R. S. Stroud; Amsterdam: J. C. Gieber, 1984), SEG XXXIII, no. 1138.

41. So M. Rostovtseff, *Social and Economic History of the Roman Empire* (rev. ed.; Oxford: Oxford University Press, 1957), 1:49.

42. Ibid., 1:103.

43. Ibid., 193–270nn22, 35.

44. Virgil and Horace proclaimed Augustus to be god and savior. Similar divine honors for him were declared through public art.

45. The following account of the Jewish revolts against the Romans is a digest of the fine survey of these events—based on the primary ancient source, *Jewish War* by Josephus—offered by A. J. Saldarini under the title "The Wars Against Rome" in his presentation of "Jewish Responses to Greco Roman Culture" in *Cambridge Companion to the Bible*, 408–19.

46. A talent weighed about 42.5 kilograms, or 93 pounds.

47. The law was actually a prohibition of castration, but it seems to have been understood by those enforcing it as forbidding circumcision, as well.

48. A description of their discovery in caves near the Dead Sea and an analysis of their contents is in Michael O. Wise's article, "Bar Kochba Letters," in the *Anchor Bible Dictionary* (ed. D. N. Freeman; Garden City, NY: Doubleday, 1992), 1:601–6.

49. A perceptive, cautious analysis of the literary and archaeological material relating to Bar Kochba is offered by Benjamin Isaac and A. Oppenheim in an article on him in the *Anchor Bible Dictionary*, 1:598–601. The letters between him and and his military aides, written in Hebrew, Aramaic, and Greek, provide evidence of the course of the Jewish war against the Romans. The major goal of the revolutionaries was to regain control of Jerusalem, to rebuild the temple there, and to resume the annual cycle of feasts, especially the Feast of Tabernacles. The letters indicate that Bar Kosiba had taken over various cities in the region, which served as capitals of their districts, such as Herodium and En Gedi. It is clear that in these areas his administrative control was for a time operating.

50. Their self-designation probably derived from the name Zadok, who was declared to be the legitimate heir of the priestly role of Aaron (1 Kgs 1:28–28) with the accession of Solomon to the throne of Israel.

51. The evolution of the interpretive traditions of the Pharisees and its central role in the formation of the Mishna and Talmud has been effectively traced by Jacob Neusner in a series of studies, going back to *From Politics to Piety: The Emergence of Pharisaic Judaism* (Englewood Cliffs, NJ: Prentice-Hall, 1973) and *Pharisees: Rabbinic Perspectives* (Hoboken, NJ: KTAV, 1985). The tensions between the Pharisees and nascent Christianity are discussed below in the analysis of the gospel tradition.

52. References to the Essenes in the works of Josephus include *Jewish War* 2.120–161; *Jewish Antiquities* 13.171, 298; 15.371; 18.18–22. Philo describes the Essenes in *That Every Good Person Is Free* 75; *On the Contemplative Life* 1; *Hypothetica* 2.1–18.

53. *The Manual of Discipline* or *Rule of the Community*. English translations of this and the other documents found at Qumran, adjacent to the ruins of the community center, are in F. G. Martinez, *The Dead Sea Scrolls Translated* (2nd ed.; Leiden: Brill; Grand Rapids: Eerdmans, 1996).

54. For example, the Habbakuk commentary found among the Dead Sea Scrolls.

55. *The Temple Scroll*. A compact description of the Dead Sea community, its beliefs, and its mode of life is offered in H. C. Kee, *Understanding the New Testament* (5th ed.; Englewood Cliffs, NJ: Prentice-Hall, 1993), 62–70.

56. I have assembled the linguistic, literary, and archeological evidence in my article, "Defining the First-Century Synagogue," *NTS* 41 (1995): 481–500. Careful reading of the Greek literature, including the Septuagint, shows that *synagoge* was a general

term for a collection of people, animals, etc., and did not designate a special building where the gathering took place. Details of this development are offered in my article, which now is included in a volume of essays I have edited: *The Evolution of the Synagogue* (Harrisburg, PA: Trinity Press International, 1999). The authors include the presenters of papers on this theme at the Philadelphia Seminar on Christian Origins and others who have made distinctive contributions to understanding the development of the synagogue.

57. Details are offered by Martin Hengel in his festschrift article for K. G. Kuhn, "Proseuche und Synagoge: Juedische Gemeinde, Gotteshaus und Gottesdienst" (ed. J. Jeremias; Gottingen: Vandenhoeck & Ruprecht, 1971); repr. in *The Synagogue: Studies in Origins, Archaeology, and Architecture* (ed. J. Gutmann; New York: KTAV, 1975), 27–54.

58. In the article on *synagoge* in the *Theological Dictionary of the New Testament* (trans. G. W. Bromiley; Grand Rapids: Eerdmans, 1964–76), vol. 7, W. Schrage accepts as reliable the claim by A. Deissmann that the construction of the synagogue mentioned in the Theodotus inscription found in Jerusalem early in the present century took place before 70 CE (in *Light from the Ancient East* [trans. L. R .M. Strachan; New York: G. R. Doran, 1927], 439–41).

59. In addition to my survey of the archaeological evidence, similar conclusions are drawn by A. J. Saldarini in his article "Synaogue," in *Harper Collins Bible Dictionary* (ed. Paul Achtemeier; San Francisco: Harper San Francisco, 1996), 1079–81; and by Eric M. Meyers in his article on "Synagogue" in the *ABD*, 6:252–62. Meyers traces a similar account of the development of the synagogue building in the second and subsequent centuries CE from a basilica type (probably with a portable Torah shrine), through a broadhouse type, to an apsidal type in the fifth through the eighth centuries, with the apse containing the Torah and pointing in the direction of Jerusalem.

60. Rachel Hachlili, "Diaspora Synagogues," *ABD*, 1:260.

61. Cambridge: Cambridge University Press, 1987. Green quote is on page 22.

62. In *The Messianic Idea in Judaism* (New York: Schocken, 1971), 35.

63. Both the choice of titles of these essays and the substance of them disclose the range of ways in which "messiah" was perceived in the Graeco-Roman period of Judaism. Burton L. Mack surveys the Wisdom literature to show that the concepts of wisdom in this literature represent social notions for the ordering of society, based on models drawn from Torah (chap. 2, 15–48). George W. E. Nickelsburg shows how in much of the Enoch literature there is "salvation without a Messiah," brought by the force of nature and the lives of the righteous. Where there is an agent, he may be a transcendent, heavenly figure, as in the Parables of Enoch. And the roles of kings in bringing renewal differ widely (chap. 3, 49–68). Jonathan A. Goldstein, in discussing "How the Authors of 1 and 2 Maccabees treated the 'Messianic Promises'" (chap. 4, 69–96) observes that the expectation of the Davidic messiah-king is not in Daniel or in the writings of important Jewish groups in the second and first centuries BCE. J. J. Collins also discusses "Messianism in the Maccabean Period" (chap. 5, 97–109), noting that there are only traces of messianism in this period, and no single notion of messiah. Instead, the occurrences of the term reflect political attitudes and circumstances, although there is strong interest in messiah in the writings from Qumran and in the testaments of Levi and Judah (*Testament of the Twelve Patriarchs*). Richard D. Hecht, in "Philo and Messiah" (chap. 7, 139–68), concludes that for Philo, the "first line of meaning for Messiah and the Messianic Era" was inner experience, by which the soul was transformed. George MacRae, in "Messiah and Gospel" (chap. 8, 169–85), observes that the gospels' designation of Jesus as Son of Man and Son of

God employ categories that are not central for Judaism of that period. H. C. Kee's "Christology in Mark's Gospel" observes that there was in Judaism of this period no neat set of definitions of messiah, and that Mark's portrayal of Jesus' mission is contrary to much of the spectrum of Jewish definitions and is shaped by Mark's radical redefinition of the covenant community (chap. 9, 187–208). J. H. Charlesworth, in "From Messianology to Christology" (chap. 11, 225–64), correctly concludes, "Jewish messianology does not flow majestically into Christian christology" (255). In the concluding chap. 12 ("Mishnah and Messiah," 265–82), Jacob Neusner deduces from the evidence that "the Messiah became precisely what the sages of the Mishnah and their continuators in the Talmud most needed: a rabbi-Messiah, who will save an Israel sanctified through Torah" (283).

64. Possibly this passage was formed during the reign of Josiah (640–609 BCE); the issue is discussed by E. Meyer and J. Rogerson in *Cambridge Companion to the Bible*, 76, 129–32.

65. As in the *Rule of the Community* 9.7, 11, where the priestly messiah is "of Aaron" and the royal messiah is "of Israel."

66. *Testament of Judah* 24–25; *Testament of Levi* 18. *Testaments of the Twelve Patriarchs* probably were written in the second half of the second century BCE. Cf. discussion of the date and origins of this work in H. C. Kee, "Testaments of the Twelve Patriarchs," in Charlesworth, ed., *Old Testament Pseudepigrapha*, 1:777–78.

67. Ps 2:2–7.

68. Isa 9:6–7.

69. Much of this wisdom material is available in translation in J. B. Pritchard, *Ancient Near Eastern Texts Relating to the Old Testament* (3rd ed.; Princeton: Princeton University Press, 1969), 405–619.

70. On the influence of Stoicism on Judaism and early Christianity, see Excursus 4, "The Multiple Impact of Stoicism on the Origins of Christianity," pp. 451–62.

71. Although Baruch purports to come from the time of Belshazzar, son of Nebuchadnezzar (605–562 BCE), it probably was written in the second century BCE—perhaps in the reign of Antiochus V Eupator (164–162), who is reported in 2 Macc 11:22–26 as having decreed religious freedom for the Jews. Further discussion of the date and origins of Baruch is offered in my notes on this book in *Cambridge Annotated Study Apocrypha* (ed. H. C. Kee; Cambridge: Cambridge University Press, 1994), xxii.

72. Cf. Martin Hengel, *Judaism and Hellenism* (Philadelphia: Fortress, 1974), 1:146–50.

73. Aristobolus is also cited by Clement of Alexandria, in *Stromata* 1, 5, and 6, which are included by A.-M. Denis in *Pseudepigrapha Veteris Testamenti Graece* (Leiden: Brill, 1970), 3:217–28.

74. In Charlesworth, ed., *Old Testament Pseudepigrapha*, 1:831–36.

75. The philosophical features of 4 Maccabees are detailed in my introduction and notes on this work in *Cambridge Annotated Study Apocrypha*, xxxii, 234–47.

76. 4 Macc 1:18–19.

77. 4 Macc 13:1.

78. 4 Macc 13:19.

79. 4 Macc 17:15.

80. 4 Macc 17:12.

81. In Hebrew, *ben-adam*; in Aramaic, *bar-nasha*. The NRSV translation of the phrase figuratively as "human being" is a commendable effort to avoid the implicit

sexual preference for males in the phrase "son of man," but it obscures the importance of the term itself in its variety of connotations in the biblical texts.

82. In Daniel, the "son of man" means "one like a human being," and hence is a description of a person, not a title, as it is in the Similitudes of Enoch. In the latter document, the Son of Man existed since before the creation of the world (*1 Enoch* 48:3), as Wisdom does according to Prov 8, and is explicitly identified as the Messiah (48:10; 52:4). See J. J. Collins, *Daniel: A Commentary on the Book of Daniel* (Hermeneia, ed. F. M. Cross; Minneapolis: Fortress, 1993), 79–84. Early on, the Son of Man came to be understood as a being of heavenly origin and exalted status (82).

83. *1 Enoch* 37–71. A fine translation of Enoch is that of E. Isaac in Charlesworth, ed., *Old Testament Pseudepigrapha*, 1:5–89.

84. This perception of the Son of Man in the Parables of Enoch is developed by G. Nickelsburg in the article on Son of Man in the *ABD*, 6:138–40.

85. *1 Enoch* 45:3.

86. *1 Enoch* 61.

87. *1 Enoch* 71.

88. *1 Enoch* 69.

89. *1 Enoch* 71.

90. Known in the Latin Vulgate as 4 Esdras. It claims to have been written in the time of Artaxerxes (king of the Persians from 465 to 424 BCE), but its use of the imagery of Dan 7 (from the second century BCE) and of the eagle with the three heads (which is very likely adapted from a Roman symbol of the three Flavian emperors: Vespasian [69–79 CE], Titus [89–81], and Domitian [81–96]) suggests a date in the second century CE for this portion of the apocalypse.

91. That is, in the period that included the First and Second Jewish Revolts, when suffering was experienced and the takeover of land, temple, and people by a pagan power was being experienced.

92. *4 Ezra* 13:32, 37, 52.

93. *2 Baruch* 29–30.

94. The "son of man" is discussed below in its various literary appearances in the New Testament.

95. In the Greek and Latin versions of the Jewish scriptures, the name Esdras [= Ezra in Hebrew] designates several books. In the Latin versions, 1 Esdras is canonical Ezra; 2 Esdras is canonical Nehemiah; 3 Esdras is a translation of the Greek *Esdras A'*. My analysis of these writings appears in *Cambridge Annotated Study Apocrypha*, xxviii, 178–92.

96. 1 Macc 3:3–5.

97. A more complete analysis of the changing historiographical modes used in Jewish historical literature is offered in Excursus 1.

98. Job 1:1–2:13; 42:7–17.

99. Jonah 4:9–11.

100. In his important study, *Three Greek Romances* (Indianapolis: Bobbs-Merrill, 1953), Moses Hadas makes the point that romances developed as "apologetics for a cult, or more probably for the cultural minority who were its devotees" (ix). The stories include hairbreadth escapes, separation, resounding triumphs against overwhelming threats, miraculous reunions, sensational recognitions, scenes in courts of law or of exotic potentates, and endings depicting the vindication of the hero or heroine (x). Reinhold Merkelbach (in *Roman und Mysterium in der Antike* [Munich and Berlin: C.H. Beck, 1962]) noted that often the stories are variations of popular myths such as

Psyche and Eros, which is based on the Isis-Osiris myth, and depicts the journey of the soul, a sacred marriage, a ceremonial death, and a divine renewal of life (1–55). Bryan P. Reardon, in *The Form of Greek Romance* (Princeton: Princeton University Press, 1991), notes how the divinities operate in the lives of the central figures in the romances, as in Chariton's *Chareas and Callirhoe* and in Apuleius's *Metamorphoses*, which ends with a moralizing address warning against human ambition and sexual excess, followed by an invitation to submit to the divine will (94).

101. M. Braun, *History and Romance in Graeco-Roman Literature* (Oxford: Oxford University Press, 1938), 28.

102. The anachronisms and geographical inaccuracies are indicated in my notes for Judith in the *Cambridge Annotated Study Apocrypha*, 14–15.

103. Other novelistic stories from this period include the Additions to Esther and the *Testament of Solomon*, translation and notes by D. C. Duling, in Charlesworth, ed., *Old Testament Pseudepigrapha*, 1:935–87. The latter work emphasizes divine authority over the demons, and includes features from astrology, angelology, demonology, magic, and medicine from the period of the Second Jewish Commonwealth.

104. Burchard's introduction to and translation of this text appear in Charlesworth, ed., *Old Testament Pseudepigrapha*, 2:177–247.

105. Ibid., 187–88.

106. Translation and introduction by H. C. Kee in Charlesworth, ed., *Old Testament Pseudepigrapha*, 1:775–828.

107. Translation and introduction by R. P. Spittler to *Testament of Job* in Charlesworth, ed., *Old Testament Pseudepigrapha*, 1:829–68.

108. Translation and introduction by John Priest in Charlesworth, ed., *Old Testament Pseudepigrapha*, 1:919–34.

109. See Excursus 4, "The Multiple Impact of Stoicism on the Origins of Christianity."

110. Distinctively apocalyptic features of Daniel have been noted above; see also my further analysis of apocalypse in the Jesus tradition in chap. 2 of this book, where the influence of Daniel on the New Testament apocalyptic traditions is considered.

111. The term here means specifically the Hellenistic monarchs who ruled the eastern Mediterranean region from the late fourth to the mid-first century BCE.

112. So David Hellholm, "The Problem of Apocalyptic Genre and the Apocalypse of John," *SBL Seminar Papers 1982* (Chico, CA: Scholars Press, 1982), 168. Also, George Nickelsburg in *Apocalypticism in the Mediterranean World and the Near East* (ed. David Hellholm; Tuebingen: Mohr, 1983), 649. The links between Pauline eschatology and that of the Stoics are discussed in my article, "Pauline Eschatology: Relationships with Apocalyptic and Stoic Thought," in the W. G. Kümmel festschrift, *Glaube und Eschatologie* (ed. E. Graesser and Otto Merk; Tuebingen: Mohr Siebeck, 1985), 135–58. The kinship of early Christian eschatology with Stoicism is also discussed below in Excursus 4.

113. See my discussion of this factor below, and in my book, *Who Are the People of God?* (New Haven: Yale University Press, 1995), 40–44.

114. Other apocalypses from the centuries just before and after the turn of the eras include *4 Ezra*, *Jubilees*, *Assumption of Moses*, *Testament of Abraham*, and *2 Baruch*. Introductions and translations of all the extant noncanonical Jewish apocalyptic writings are in Charlesworth, ed., *Old Testament Pseudepigrapha*, vol. 1.

115. So W. Lee Humphreys in an article, "Lifestyle for the Diaspora," *JBL* 92 (1973): 211–23.

116. Cf. Collins, *Daniel*, 61–70.

117. Collins, in *Semeia* 14 (1979): 9; and in his commentary on *Daniel*, 54.

118. Collins, *Daniel*, 61–70.

119. J. J. Collins, *The Sibylline Oracles of Egyptian Judaism* (SBLDS 13; Missoula, MT: SBL, 1974), 33.

120. Ibid., 71.

121. Ibid., 114–15.

122. Virgil, *Fourth Eclogue* 4.4–17; 46; 60–61. See also Jonathan Z. Smith, "Wisdom and Apocalyptic," in *Map Is Not Territory* (Leiden: Brill, 1978).

123. Known as *2* or *3 Esdras* in some Eastern versions of the Bible, this work does not appear in the Septuagint.

124. Chaps. 15 and 16 are probably a later appendix, dating from the second or third century CE.

125. A fine introduction to and translation of *Jubilees* is that of O. S. Wintermute in Charlesworth, ed., *Old Testament Pseudepigrapha*, 1:35–142.

126. There is mention in the Dead Sea Scroll document the *Covenanters of Damascus* (CD 16:24) of the book of the division of time according to their jubilees and weeks—which surely means the writing that is known as *Jubilees*.

127. Out of a total of fifty chapters, forty-one concern Jacob and his sons.

128. *ABD* 1:837–52.

129. A highly perceptive analysis of the method employed by Philo in interpreting the scriptures and demonstrating their relevance for him and his Jewish contemporaries is Peder Borgen's *Philo of Alexandria: An Exegete for His Time* (NovTSup 86; Leiden and New York: Brill, 1997).

130. This process and the issues at stake are documented by Philo in his *On the Embassy to Gaius*.

131. Borgen warns against the efforts of some scholars to link Philo with Gnosticism or with Middle Platonism, which he thinks is not adequately definable (*Philo*, 5–9).

132. E. M. Smallwood, *Philonis Alexandrini Legation ad Gaium* (2nd ed; Leiden: Brill, 1970), 155.

133. Here is summarized the detailed account that Borgen sets forth in chap. 14 of *Philo*, 243–60.

134. Borgen, *Philo*, 276–84.

135. Most of the *Temple Scroll* material is found on the scroll to which the number assigned is 11Q, although some of the material exists only in fragments.

136. The phrase is from Deut 21:20, and it is quoted by Jesus' critics in Luke 7:34. The guilty individual is to be executed by stoning.

137. Noted by J. H. Charlesworth in his introduction to "Prayers, Psalms and Odes," in the second of the volumes he edited, *Old Testament Pseudepigrapha*, 2:607.

138. In the *Psalm Scroll* (11QPsa), J. A. Sanders, ed., *The Psalms Scroll of Qumran Cave 11* (DJD 4; Oxford: Oxford University Press, 1965).

139. Also called 1Q Hymns; translation in *The Dead Sea Scrolls Translated: The Qumran Texts in English* (2nd ed.; ed. Florentino Garcia Martinez; trans. W. G. E. Watson; Leiden: Brill; Grand Rapids: Eerdmans, 1994), 317–62.

140. 1QH7.19; 8.23; 11:21; 12:24.

141 1QH15.27; 19.10.

142. 1QH13.26–28. Cf. the mention of Beliar above.

143. See the analysis of the gospel tradition below.

144. This process is mentioned above but is traced and documented in my article, "The First Century Synagogue: Problems and Progress," *NTS* 41, no. 4 (1995): 481–500, and more fully in Kee, ed., *Evolution of the Synagogue.*

145. Neusner's replacement of the long-standing anachronistic perception of rabbinic Judaism as a formally and institutionally established feature in the Maccabean period (as set forth in G. F. Moore, *Judaism in the First Centuries of the Christian Era* [Cambridge, MA: Harvard University Press, 1932]) began with his studies in the rise of Pharisaism, *The Pharisees: Rabbinic Perspectives* (Leiden: Brill, 1971; repr., Hoboken, NJ: KTAV, 1985), and has been developed in scores of scholarly volumes down to the present.

146. Chico, CA: Scholars Press, 1983. A comprehensive analysis of formative Judaism is offered by Neusner in *The Foundations of Judaism: Method, Teleology, Doctrine* (Philadelphia: Fortress, 1983–1985): vol. 1, *Midrash in Context: Exegesis in Formative Judaism*; vol. 2, *Messiah in Context: Israel's History and Destiny in Formative Judaism*; vol. 3, *Torah: From Scroll to Symbol in Formative Judaism.*

147. Cambridge: Cambridge University Press, 1987.

148. Philadelphia: Fortress, 1984.

149 Jacob Neusner, *Judaisms and Their Messiahs* (Cambridge: Cambridge University Press, 1988), ix–xiv. The same features of diversity within Judaism are noted in the Mishnah in Neusner's preface to the second printing of *Judaism in the Matrix of Christianity* (South Florida Studies in the History of Judaism 8; Atlanta, GA: Scholars Press, 1991). He differentiates between the Judaism of the Mishnah and that of the Talmud: in the former (which began development before Christianity was a significant, organized system), there is no explicit theory of scriptural authority, no "teleology focused on the coming of Messiah as the end and purpose of the system as a whole" (liv), and no stress on the Torah as a symbol. Instead, the emphasis is on the stability and continuing sanctity of the land and the people, to be sustained by study of Torah. In the Talmud, however, Neusner sees no theory of Messiah, or of the end of the age, and no reliance on historical arguments. Instead, the aim is to construct order and rules for classification of everything in earth and heaven and for the ordering of life. The aim is to fashion "an essentially ahistorical system of timeless sanctification, worked out through the construction of an eternal rhythm which centered on the movement of the moon and the stars . . ." (lxvii). The messiah is perceived as a sage, whose aim is to bring "Israel's total submission" to God (lxix).

150. Cambridge, MA: Harvard University Press, 1986. The analysis given here is based on my review of this book in *JBL* 107 (1988): 317–19.

151. See the analysis of Matthew, 121–76.

CHAPTER TWO

The Jesus Tradition and the Formation of the New Covenant Community

Of great significance for understanding the emerging Jesus tradition are the reports of his moral teachings and his instructions to the new covenant community comprised of his followers and those persuaded by them to join the movement, as well as his challenges to the established religious and political institutions and the leaders of Judaism. These challenged features included (1) the priesthood and the temple, (2) the major interpreters of the Jewish religious tradition, and (3) those Jewish leaders—the rich and the powerful—who collaborated with the imperial authority as members of the regional council (*synedrion*) established by the Romans. Jesus' challenges to the Jewish tradition include what he taught his followers and all who listened to him, as well as his defiant actions and critical declarations in relation to the civil and religious authorities. Thus, his teaching is not merely instructive, but radically critical of those in control of the established political and religious powers and institutions of his time.

Added to these accounts of confrontation with the authorities but central for faith in Jesus as the Anointed of God crucified by the Romans are the diverse reports that God had raised him from the dead and exalted him to heaven. These narratives of his career, of his teachings, of his confrontation with the Jewish leadership, of his execution by the Romans, and of his reported resurrection, constitute the type of literature that now begins the New Testament: the gospels. In them, the emphasis is on Jesus' career and activities as they convey and demonstrate his message concerning God's present and future actions in establishing the divine rule in the world. And they also indicate how the faithful community perceives how it will share in this new order. Jesus' major term for the ultimate outcome of the divine undertaking through him is—in his oft-repeated phrase—the kingdom of God. This is the central theme of his teaching and the focus of his acts of healing and human renewal by which the powers of evil are being overcome.

What Jesus' reported message calls for is understanding of this divine purpose for human renewal, which will lead to trust in this promise and consequently to transformed ethical behavior by members of the new community. This new covenant people is defined—implicitly and explicitly in the Jesus tradition—in terms of (1) how one may become a member; (2) how one is thereby to live in relation to God, to the other members, and to the wider world; (3) how one is to celebrate membership; and (4) what one is to expect as God fulfills his purpose for and through this new people. Reports of these teachings, activities, and expectations, as well as indications of the formation of the nuclear new covenant community, constitute the four gospels that now stand at the beginning of the New Testament. The wider expansion of the new community across the Roman world is described in the Acts of the Apostles, which significantly ends with an account of an unresolved confrontation of the leaders of the new movement with the imperial powers in Rome.

The letters included in the New Testament are chiefly concerned with the meaning and significance for the community of Jesus' life, death, and resurrection—how this affects the lives of the members, their relations within the group, and their dealings with the outside social and political world. These themes are also developed along various lines in treatises included in the New Testament—though often designated as letters—such as Ephesians and Hebrews. The latter two documents are not addressed to the needs and questions of a specific Christian community, but in general terms and in some detail they treat the theological significance of Jesus and the consequent formation of the new people of God, as well as the responsibility of members toward one another and the wider world. The expectations as to the ultimate import and impact of Jesus for the future of the community—and for the world as a whole—are considered in the other New Testament books, but these are the primary themes set forth in the apocalypse known as the Revelation of John—which fittingly brings the New Testament to a close on a note of expectation and hope for the triumph of the purpose of God through Jesus.

This process of describing the career of Jesus and clarifying the ongoing significance of his life, death, and resurrection continued into the second century CE and beyond, thus producing an abundant and diverse literature within the early Christian movement. Collections of some of these writings are known as the Apostolic Fathers[1] and the *Didache*, or the Teaching of the Twelve Apostles.[2] Five themes appear in all these writings: (1) the prospect of possible martyrdom for those committed to Jesus and the new community; (2) the need for obedience to the leaders of the church; (3) how Christianity is to be differentiated from its origins in Judaism; (4) how Christians are to behave within their own community and in the wider world; (5) what is true Christian doctrine, and what Christians are to expect in the future. These writings contain no neatly uniform set of answers to these questions, and other writings were produced that diverge significantly in content and aim from the mainstream Christian writings and from each other. The divergent documents include what scholars have identified as the New Testament Apocrypha: analyses of these are offered in chapter 4.

In addition to this range of Christian literature concerned with Jesus, his teachings, and their import for the Christian community, there are references to him in non-Christian sources—both Roman and Jewish. Brief analyses of these materials are offered below.

Jesus' major role as it is portrayed in the gospels is to convey by his word and actions the ground and intent of God's program through him for the renewal of God's people and of the creation. Hence, the dominant feature of the portrayals of Jesus represented by the four gospels in the New Testament is his role as teacher—and, consequently, the gospels offer the content of his teachings.

This evidence about Jesus' role as teacher has often been eclipsed by the major concentration of theologians on the significance of his death, burial, and resurrection—which Paul identifies as "the gospel" in 1 Cor 15:1–8. In the gospel tradition, however, although there are predictions of and descriptions of the crucifixion and resurrection of Jesus, the emphasis is primarily on his role as conveyer of the purpose of God for his covenant people. We shall highlight that role below, following analyses of the extra-biblical and New Testament evidence concerning his life, teachings, death, and resurrection.

Two of the central claims of the early Christians that differentiated them from Jews of the first and subsequent centuries were (1) that Jesus was the Christ/Messiah awaited in the Jewish tradition, and (2) that his followers constituted the renewed covenant people promised in the Jewish prophetic tradition.[3] To understand the origins of these Christian convictions, one must examine (1) the diverse historical evidence concerning Jesus from Roman, Jewish, and Christian sources, and (2) the claims that were made by him and by his followers on his behalf. To discern the distinctive features of these claims, one must also consider the range of messianic hopes and the models of covenant community that were operative in Judaism at that time, as reflected in the literature we have examined in chapter 1. We begin with an analysis of the evidence concerning Jesus that has survived from non-Christian sources, and then turn to the ancient Jewish sources relevant to historical knowledge concerning Jesus.

Perceiving the Jesus of History:
Ancient Non-Christian Sources Concerning Jesus

The Roman Sources: Pliny, Suetonius, and Tacitus

The oldest reference to Jesus in writings of Roman authorship occurs in the *Letters* of Pliny the Younger (62–113 CE). About the year 110, when he was governor of the Roman province of Bithynia in Asia Minor on the Black Sea coast, he wrote to the emperor Trajan (98–117 CE) requesting guidance in the matter of dealing with Christians.[4] Their numbers had increased dramatically, with the result that those taking part in the ceremonies in the area temples devoted to the officially recognized Graeco-Roman gods and goddesses had decreased alarmingly. Pliny reports that Jesus was worshiped "as a god," and he refers to the group practices of the Christians by which they celebrated their special relationship to God and the divine presence that they declared was among them. These included the love feast of the community and participation in the Eucharist. Written about eighty years after the crucifixion, this letter shows that the movement begun in the name of Jesus was a significant factor across the Mediterranean world during the decades following the Romans' crucifixion of Jesus.

The Roman historian Suetonius, a contemporary of Pliny, reported in his *Lives of the Twelve Caesars* that there was a serious disturbance among the Jews in Rome during the reign of Claudius (41–54 CE) that became so intense they were forced to leave the city. He wrote that the culprit who instigated this struggle was a man named Chrestos, and Claudius forced them all to leave.[5] Suetonius stated, "Since the Jews constantly made disturbances at the instigation of Chrestos, he [Claudius] expelled them from Rome." Chrestus is the Latinized form of the Greek word *chrestos*, which has a range of meanings: "useful, advantageous, honest, merciful, generous." It was used as a name or an epithet, and would be a common term in Greek, unlike *Christos*, which means "anointed." and which likely did not become widely used until later in the first century. The disturbance within the Jewish community was almost certainly not the result of the arrival in Rome of someone named Chrestos, but of the coming to that city of Christian preachers with the claim that Jesus was the Messiah—Christos. This may have begun even earlier, during the reign of Tiberius (14–37 CE). But the tensions within the Jewish community caused by the proclamation of Jesus as the *Christos* there seem to have become severe and publicly visible during the reign of Claudius (41–54 CE). This development also probably lies behind the report in Acts 18:1–4 of Paul's collaboration at Corinth with a Christian couple, Priscilla and Aquila, who had migrated there from Rome, following the decree of Claudius expelling the Jews from the capital city.[6] All that the passage in Suetonius shows us concerning Jesus, however, is that as early as 49–50 CE, a visible and active group in Rome claimed that the Messiah (*Christos*) awaited by Jews had indeed come, and thus a community of Christians was a visible feature there.

The most detailed account of Christianity in the Roman historical writings is that of Tacitus (c. 55–120) in his *Annals*.[7] He was a senator and held a number of official positions in the Roman government, beginning in the reign of Vespasian (69–79) and continuing under Nerva (96–98). He may have outlived Trajan (98–117). His *Histories* cover the period from Galba (69) to the close of Domitian's reign (81–96). In the fifth book of the *Histories*, he offered a highly inaccurate account of the Jewish people, including their religion. The *Annals* cover the period from Tiberius (14–37) to Nero (54–68), but extensive sections (including the last three years of Nero's reign) are missing. In *Annals* 15.44, Tacitus describes the Christians, who, in order to divert suspicion from themselves, were accused by Nero of having set fire to the city of Rome:

> Neither human help, nor imperial munificence, nor all the modes of placating heaven, could stifle the belief that the fire had taken place by order, i.e., of Nero. Therefore, to scotch the rumor, Nero substituted as culprits and punished with utmost refinements of cruelty, a class of men, loathed for their vices, whom the crowd called Christians. Christus, the found of the name, had undergone the death penalty in the reign of Tiberius, by sentence of the procurator Pontius Pilate, and the pernicious superstition was checked for a moment, only to break out once more, not merely in Judea, the home of the disease, but in the capital itself, where all things horrible or shameful in the world collect and find a vogue. First, then, the confessed members of the sect were arrested; next, on their disclosures, vast numbers were convicted, not so much on the count of arson as for the hatred of the human race. And derision accompanied their end: they were covered with wild beasts' skins and torn to death by dogs; or they were fastened on crosses, and when daylight failed were burned to serve as lamps by night. Nero had offered his gardens for the spectacle, and gave an exhibition in his Circus, mixing with the crowd in the habit of a charioteer, or mounted on his car.

Even though Tacitus, in his description of the religious sects in Rome—which he scorned—may have exaggerated the size of the Christian community in Rome, it was clearly large and visible enough to invite hatred from the masses as well as from their political and intellectual leaders. His account of the time, the circumstances, the official agent, and the mode of execution of Jesus match well the reports in the Christian sources. The movement launched by Jesus and his continuing significance for his followers after his death are attested in these Roman sources, although there is no evidence from them that goes beyond—or contradicts!—reports of these features in the Christian literature.

Jewish Sources

Josephus

Flavius Josephus, the Jewish historian (37–100? CE) who became a collaborator with the Romans when they invaded and took over direct control of Palestine in response to the Jewish revolt (67–70 CE), twice refers to Jesus in his *Jewish Antiquities*.[8] The first of these (18.63) reads in the widely used Greek text of this work as a witness by the author to Jesus as Messiah:

> About this time[9] there lived Jesus, a wise man, if indeed one ought to call him a man. For he was one who wrought surprising feats and was a teacher of such people as accept the truth gladly. He won over many Jews and many of the Greeks. He was the Messiah. When Pilate, upon hearing him, accused by men of the highest standing among us, had condemned him to be crucified, those who had in the first place come to love him did not give up their affection for him. On the third day he appeared to them restored to life, for the prophets of God had prophesied these and countless other marvellous things about him. And the tribe of the Christians, so called after him, has still to this day not disappeared.

L. H. Feldman, the translator of Josephus in the Loeb Classical Library, has also produced a huge volume, *Josephus and Modern Scholarship (1937–1980)*,[10] in which he provides summaries and critical observations on more than thirty-five hundred books and articles dealing with Josephus and his writings.[11] Section 23 of the work is devoted to the bearing of Josephus's writings on the history of Christianity, of which a major portion deals directly with the "Testimonium Flavianum," as it came to be designated by scholars. The overwhelming consensus is that this passage has been interpolated by Christians. Feldman observes that early Christian writers such as Origen and Eusebius—who knew the work of Josephus, do not appeal to it as Jewish support for Christian claims about the messiahship of Jesus.[12] Indeed, as early as the third century CE, Origen of Alexandria (185–253) raised doubts about the authenticity of this attribution to Josephus of an affirmation of Jesus' messiahship.

Josephus's second reference to Jesus appears in *Jewish Antiquities* 20.200, where he is dealing with the struggles for power that characterized life in Judea prior to the revolt of 66 CE. James, the brother of Jesus, had succeeded to the leadership of the Christians in Jerusalem,[13] and seems to have been highly regarded by many of the Jews there as well. He is further identified here by associating him with another well-known figure: Jesus. No information about the activity of Jesus is provided here, but his identity and association with the movement that was launched in his name can be simply assumed.

The Import of the Dead Sea Scrolls for Christian Origins

Josephus also described the various voluntary groups within Judaism at the turn of the eras, including not only the Pharisees and Sadducees—who are mentioned in the New Testament—but also a group called the Essenes. The latter believed that God was directly active in human life, that the divine purpose for his people had been disclosed through their leaders and was to be detailed through their own interpretations of the scriptures. As noted above, they were convinced that the incumbent priests were corrupt, that the temple was not where God dwelt among his people, and that their group must call their contemporaries to proper worship of God and prepare them for the coming new age in which the purified covenant people and the true temple would be established.

These Dead Sea documents foster an apocalyptic view of this new Jewish community, which claimed to be the true covenant people and perceived the collaboration of the Jewish leadership with the Hellenistic rulers (and later, with the Romans) as evidence of corruption and actions contrary to God's purpose for his true people. Hence the members of the true People of God were to withdraw to "the wilderness" in order to "prepare the way" for the fulfillment of God's purpose for them.[14] There they were to live in complete obedience to the Law and the Prophets.

The claimed disclosure of the divine purpose to this chosen community is perceived to have come through one who is identified as "the Teacher of Righteousness," to whom God had revealed correct understanding of the message of the prophets, which was seen as foretelling what was going to happen to God's people.[15] They were "to walk perfectly in all the ways commanded by God . . . straying neither to the right nor to the left and transgressing none of his words."[16] On entering the community they were to take an oath to obey every commandment of Moses "in accord with all that has been revealed to the Sons of Zadok, the Keepers of the Covenant and the Seekers of his Will": the leaders of the Dead Sea community.[17] They were to live "in the wilderness" by these precepts until there would come to them the Prophet, the Messiah of Aaron, and the Messiah of Israel—the royal and priestly messiahs.[18]

In the *Messianic Rule* (1Qsa) found among the scrolls, those to be excluded from the "assembly of God" are the paralyzed, the lame, the blind, and the deaf. The *War Rule* (1QM) describes the eschatological conflict with the powers of evil—Light against Darkness—which will lead to the defeat of these evil forces and the vindication of the People of God. The agent through whom this triumph will come is "a star out of Jacob" (Num 24:17–19).[19] The leaders of the group are seen in the *Temple Scroll* (11QTs) to include priests, whose task is to interpret the Law (LVI), so that even the king is to be subject to their legal formulations (LVII). The rebellious individual is to be labeled "a glutton and a drunkard" (LXIV)—the epithet from Deut 21:18–21 that was applied to Jesus by his critics according to the Q tradition (Luke 7:33–35) as a result of his having befriended "tax-collectors and sinners."[20] The appropriate way to deal with such a violator of what were considered to be the boundaries of the covenant people was for the community to stone him or her to death.

The *Midrash on the Last Days* (4Q174) announced the coming of two Messiahs: the Branch of David, and the Interpreter of the Law. In the Qumran document 11Q, Melchizdek (building on Gen 14:17–20) is portrayed as the head of the "sons of heaven," who serves as God's agent of justice—a role that will continue until the final eschatological judgment and the defeat of Satan, the Prince of Darkness.[21] It is expected that this leader will denounce those who rebel against God and that he will announce the coming of peace and of the "anointed prince" and comfort those who mourn.[22]

Clearly the aims of this Jewish movement as reflected in the Dead Sea Scrolls—to redefine the covenant community and to identify the messianic agents through whom the definition and the actualization will occur—were shared by the early Christians. But the scrolls are seen as articulating the divine promises that are now perceived as in process of fulfillment. The resolution of these issues by the early Christians, however, was radically different from that of the Qumran community.

References to Jesus in Rabbinic Sources

The references to Jesus in rabbinic sources have been thoroughly examined by both Jewish and Christian scholars. The major documents employed in these analyses are the records of the oral interpretation and exposition of the Torah attributed to the rabbis of the first two centuries of the common era who came to be designated as the Tannaim. But these materials have clearly been modified by later editors when they were brought together and codified as the Mishnah in the third century CE. In the fourth century, this tradition was further modified and supplemented in the collection known as the Jerusalem Talmud, as it was again in the fifth century in the Babylonian Talmud. However, this rabbinic material, which is attributed by scholars primarily to rabbis of the third to the fifth centuries, may include earlier material stemming from the Tannaim of the first two centuries. The latter would be more relevant to Christian origins, but there is clearly a tactic on the part of the editors of the rabbinic traditions to lend weight to certain traditions—especially some of a polemical type—by attributing them to the Tannaitic interpreters of Torah. Jacob Neusner has discussed this tactic in detail in over more than three decades of scholarly publications on rabbinic Judaism. He has pointed out the shift in Judaism of the early centuries of the common era from politics (seeking national independence for Jews) to personal and communal piety, which was fostered in the synagogues by the rabbis, who were their instructors.[23] The specifics of this development of Judaism are perceived by Neusner to be significantly different from those involved in the origins of Christianity—a theme likewise implicit in the title of one of his more recent works: *Jews and Christians: The Myth of a Common Tradition.*[24]

These important and basic insights contrast sharply with the scholarly assumptions of those in the early twentieth century who were attempting analysis of the historical origins of Christianity in the setting of first-century Judaism. Yet little attention was paid to Jesus in this level of the rabbinic tradition. In the early rabbinic material, Jesus is called "Ben Stada" or "Ben Pandira" (or Panthera), and the explanations of the name indicate that Jesus was seen as an illegitimate child and a fool. The intent of this material is clear: to show that (1) Jesus was engaged in magical practices, and (2) his birth was illegitimate.

Useful summaries of this rabbinic material are offered by Joseph Klausner for the Tannaitic period, and by R. Travers Herford for the later talmudic sources. The former summary follows:

> There are reliable statements to the effect that his name was Yeshu'a of Nazareth; that he practiced sorcery (i.e., performed miracles, as was usual in those days) and beguiled and led Israel astray; that he mocked at the words of the wise [the officially sanctioned interpreters of Torah]; that he expounded scriptures in the same manner as the Pharisees [emphasizing its relevance for moral responsibility in the present]; that he had five disciples; that he was not come to take aught away from the Law or to add to it; that he was hanged (crucified) as a false teacher and beguiler on the eve of the Passover which happened on a sabbath; and that his disciples healed the sick in his name.[25]

Herford's summary of the later rabbinic material reads:[26]

> Jesus, called a Notzri [the Nazarene], Ben Stada, or Ben Pandera, was born out of wedlock. His mother was Miriam, and was a dresser of women's hair. Her husband was Pappos ben Jehudah. Her paramour was Pandira. She is also said to have been descended from princes and rulers, and to have played the role of a harlot with a carpenter.
>
> He was a magician, and led astray and deceived Israel. He sinned and caused the multitude to sin. He mocked at the words of the wise and was excommunicated. He was tainted with heresy. He called himself God, also "the son of man," and said that he would go up to heaven. He made himself to live by the name of God . . . He was tried in Lud[27] as a deceiver and as a teacher of apostasy . . . on the eve of Pesah [the Passover], which was also the eve of the Sabbath. He was stoned and hung, or crucified . . . Under the name of Balaam, he was put to death by Pinhas the robber [Pontius Pilate] and at the time of his death was thirty-three years old. He was punished in Gehinnom [the Valley of Hinnom; the dump area southwest of Jerusalem] by means of boiling filth. . . . Under the name of Balaam[28] he is excluded from the age to come.

Clearly, a pattern had developed of modifying the traditions about Jesus in order to discredit him and to depict him as subversive of proper understanding of God's purpose for his people and of covenantal identity. Yet there is no denial of his existence, of his extensive public activity of teaching and healing, and of his confronting the religious and political authorities, resulting in his public execution by the Romans. The assertion that Jesus was "near to the kingdom" is probably to be understood as recognizing the centrality in his teachings and actions of the direct link that he claimed with the coming of the new age of God's rule, as well as the threat to the established religious and political order that was implicit in his words and acts.

The Christian Sources

The Scholarly Search for the Central Features of the Early Jesus Tradition: From Jesus to Paul, or from Paul to Jesus?

Before examining the ancient sources that report the activity and teachings of Jesus, it is important to observe the range of ways in which these diverse materials were analyzed by scholars over the past two centuries with the aim of identifying the central features of the Jesus tradition. The major focus in this investigation was on what was perceived to be the historical relationship between the features of Jesus as they appear in the gospels and in the letters of the New Testament—especially those of Paul. As we shall note, some considered the Pauline material to be the primary source, while the accounts of Jesus in the gospels were later and historically secondary.

In the middle of the nineteenth century, F. C. Baur proposed a quite specific solution to the problem of the relationship between the message preached by Jesus and known to us through the Synoptics and the message preached about him by Paul. In Baur's view, the message of Jesus historically was fundamentally one of "absolute moral command,"[29] according to which "the inner is opposed to the outer, the disposition to the act, the spirit to the letter."[30] Jesus' moral ideal was expressed through Jewish concepts, as we would expect of a historical person living under the intellectual and cultural conditions of first-century Judaism. One group of his followers restricted themselves to "the cramping and narrowing influence of the Jewish national Messianic idea" and therefore were never able "to surmount the particularism of Judaism at all."[31]

The wing of the church that launched the Gentile mission, on the other hand, of which Paul was the chief representative, built on the "moral universal in [Jesus], the unconfined humanity, the divine exaltation, which gave his person its absolute significance," and thereby "introduced Christianity to its true destination as a religion for the world, and enunciated, with a full sense of its vast significance, the principle of Christian universalism."[32] Baur found Jesus' moral and spiritual ideal set forth in all the gospels, and with particular clarity in Matthew's Sermon on the Mount.[33] In Luke, however, he saw an additional development: Luke emphasized the universal element in

Jesus' message, modifying the tradition so as to bring out the universal dimension stressed in Paul's message.[34] Baur assumed that Luke was indeed a companion and disciple of Paul, but saw the culmination of New Testament universalism in the Gospel of John, in which "Christianity is established as a universal principle of salvation; all those antitheses which threatened to detain it within the narrow limits of Jewish particularism are merged in the universalism of Christianity."[35] For Baur there was no essential discontinuity in the conceptual movement from Jesus to Paul and on to the Catholic Church of the late first and early second centuries. Paul's polemics against the Judaizers were necessary in order to help the church shed its excess baggage of Jewish images and perspectives. Only through such a conflict could the church emerge to the stage of conceptual reconciliation at which the pure, spiritual intention of Jesus was comprehended and expressed in terms freed of the connotations of Jewish particularism.

With his value judgment that Paul's universalism was good and the Jewish particularism of the Synoptic Gospels was bad, Baur discouraged serious attention to the interpretations of Jesus embodied in the Synoptics. Accordingly, Mark's view of Jesus in history finds no significant place in Baur's critical reconstruction of primitive Christianity, except as it provides evidence of the Jewish particularism that had to be outgrown.

One hundred years after Baur, Rudolf Bultmann was at work on his own formulation of the relationship of the message of Jesus to that of Paul and the later New Testament writers. According to Bultmann, the essential message of the New Testament cannot be found in the message of Jesus in the Synoptics; rather, it is to be seen in Paul and in the Gospel of John. The preaching of Jesus as we have it in the synoptic tradition is only the presupposition of New Testament theology and is not to be considered *kerygma*, or the proclamation of the Christian message.[36] As a historical person, Jesus should be thought of within the sphere of late Judaism[37] and not as the inaugurator of Christian faith. Christian faith began with Easter; that is, with the belief that God made the crucified one Lord, the church asserted that Jesus was present in the kerygma, in the "proclaiming, accosting, demanding and promising word of preaching."[38]

Although for Bultmann the message of Jesus is by no means to be considered kerygma,[39] the Synoptics may serve a kerygmatic function: repetition of Jesus' preaching under the impact of kerygma make "the past present in such a way that it puts the hearers (or readers) before the decision for (or against) a possibility of self-understanding disclosed in the preaching of the historical Jesus."[40] But for Bultmann, it is the Jesus present in the kerygma who is the saving event, not the historical Jesus of the Synoptic Gospels. Only to the extent that the post-Jesus kerygma influenced and shaped the present form of the Synoptic Gospels can the Synoptics be called kerygmatic.

Bultmann made a brilliant contribution to the study of the gospels, however, through his *History of the Synoptic Tradition*, in which he developed and utilized form criticism to differentiate older from later strata of the tradition incorporated in the Synoptic Gospels; but he did not close the gap between the message of Jesus and the message about him. For example, he made no attempt to show the continuity between Jesus' proclamation of the kingdom of God and Paul's proclamation of Jesus as eschatological event.

That he failed to close this gap is evident too in his brief but highly suggestive analysis of the distinctive features of Mark's editing of the tradition.[41] In discussing Mark's purpose, Bultmann states only that Mark combined the tradition of the story about Jesus with Hellenistic, or Pauline, kerygma.[42] Thus, according to Bultmann, even in Mark the Pauline message is basic, and the Jesus tradition is little more than an embellishment. He remarks that Mark was "not sufficiently master of his material to venture on a systematic construction himself."[43] As we shall see in this chapter, Bultmann seems not to have recognized that Mark did in fact present a theological construction of his own—one that has some elements in common with the Pauline kerygma, though it does not adopt Paul's cross-resurrection theology as its basis.

In the so-called new quest of the historical Jesus, New Testament scholars have reversed their direction in their search for an answer to the problem of the relationship between Jesus and Paul. Instead of moving from Jesus to Paul, they move from Paul back toward Jesus. Of course, this sequence is required by the fact that in terms of literary chronology alone, the documentation of the cross-resurrection kerygma antedates by thirty-five years the earliest gospel writing. If Paul's claim is accurate that there was no difference between his kerygma and that of the original group of apostle-disciples—Peter and the Twelve—is it possible that they too had no more interest than Paul in the kind of material that someone later incorporated into the gospels? This theory would suggest that the real Christian message was to be found only in the gospel preached by Paul, a message that he shared with the apostles. But then we should be completely at a loss to know why the gospels were ever written, or why they were included in the same collection—the New Testament—that contained the letters of Paul. Certainly, Paul has only a few allusions to sayings of Jesus (for example, 1 Cor 7:10); Acts attributes to Paul a quotation from the teaching of Jesus that is not otherwise known (Acts 20:35). But Baur long ago recognized the foolishness of those who try to demonstrate Paul's reliance on the Jesus tradition.[44]

Most attempts to trace the links between Paul and the gospels have proved to be evasions of the problem or blind alleys. Baur's suggestion that Luke was a Paulinized gospel,[45] as well as more recent theories about Mark that depict this gospel as filled with Paulinisms, do not bear up under critical scrutiny, however.[46] Both the theological concepts and the distinctive vocabulary of Paul are missing from all the gospels. The extended treatment of the public ministry of Jesus, which is central to the synoptic tradition, has no place in Paul's letters, and seems clearly to have no role in his understanding of the central Christian beliefs about Jesus. Even when Paul appeals to a saying of Jesus for parenetic purposes, as in 1 Cor 7:10 ("I give the charge, not I but the Lord"), he quotes himself with equal authority in the next breath ("I say, not the Lord," 1 Cor 7:11).

Given the fact that leading historical critics have not differentiated between the Markan message and the message of Paul, it is not surprising that theologians have perpetuated this confusion. For example, Martin Kähler took a position that has exercised wide influence on the issue of the relationship between the understanding of Jesus recoverable from critical assessment of the gospels and the understanding of him set forth in the church's kerygma. Having taken as his theological foundation "the kerygma"—which means for Kähler the message of Paul—he declares it invalid even to investigate the differences between Paul and the gospels or to look behind the traditions to their possible historical origins:

> From these fragmentary traditions, these half-understood recollections, these portrayals colored by the writers' individual personalities, these heartfelt confessions, these sermons proclaiming him as Savior, there gazes upon us a vivid and coherent image of a Man, an image we never fail to recognize. Hence, we may conclude that in his unique and powerful personality and by his incomparable deeds and life (including his resurrection appearances) this man has engraved his image on the mind and memory of his followers with such sharp and deeply etched features that it could be neither obliterated nor distorted.[47]

But Kähler's subsequent remarks show that however "deeply etched" the features may be, for him it is not legitimate for faith to inquire into any of the details by which the gospel portraits have been traced: "It is erroneous to make [faith] depend on uncertain statements about an allegedly reliable picture of Jesus that has been tortuously extracted by the modern methods of historical research."[48] It is obvious that Kähler is interested in the gospel accounts only as they transmit to the hearts of believers "the mind of Christ."[49] Indeed, the more uncertain the historical reconstruction, the more discernible is the inspiration of the gospel writers. As Kähler puts it, "The more obscure the course of events remains which have preceded the literary activity, all the more certainly can we sense the invisible hand of Providence over the primitive community's carefreeness in the transmission of the tradition."[50]

The systematic theologian Paul Tillich had a more positive attitude than Kähler about historical research, but his conclusions concerning the results of gospel criticism and the differences between the gospels and Paul are paradoxical, if not downright contradictory. On the one hand, he praises Protestantism for its courage in subjecting its holy writings to critical analysis[51] and for "the immense historical material which has been discovered and often empirically verified by a universally used method of research."[52] He also asserts that it is not enough to reconstruct a *gestalt* (simple basic model) of Jesus after all questionable details have been eliminated; an essential picture "remains dependent on details."[53] But when he speaks of the transforming power of the biblical picture of Jesus as the Christ, through which the New Being is transmitted, he declares: "No special trait of this picture can be verified with certainty. But it can be definitely asserted that through this picture the New Being has power to transform those who are transformed by it."[54] With how little seriousness Tillich took the work of historical criticism—in spite of his commendatory generalities—is evident in this statement: "Harnack was wrong . . . about Jesus. There is no substantial difference between the message given by the Synoptic Jesus and the message about Jesus given in Paul's Epistles."[55]

Perceptions of the Different Understandings of Jesus in the Gospels and Paul

By such approaches as these, the problem of the relationship between the portraits of Jesus in Paul and Mark remains not only unanswered but unaddressed. The question is not merely one of historical continuity from Jesus to Paul or from Paul back to Jesus. Some theologians have made the easy assumption that there is no fundamental difference between Paul's kerygma and the kerygmatic significance of Jesus in Mark, and this assumption has prevented them from seeing clearly Mark's perspective. To make the distinction between Mark's perspective and Paul's, it may be useful to take up Bultmann's contention that the kerygma announces that a historical event has become an eschatological event.

Bultmann uses the words "historical" and "eschatological" in a special way, however, that derives from existentialist philosophy. For Bultmann, "historical" concerns not the past, but what he calls the historicity of self, which is constituted by an event or a word through which a human finds the meaning of his or her own existence. Similarly, Bultmann does not perceive "eschatological" as a term for dealing with the end of the world at some future date, but rather as describing any moment in the present when the individual is called to make a fundamental decision that requires freeing oneself from reliance on the institutions and powers of the past and to open oneself to the future. In making the decision, one experiences an event that transforms one's outlook on oneself and the world, on which one has relied for standards and stability. By making this radical decision, one "dies." But God gives one a new life, so that, in the language of the New Testament, one enters "the life of the Age to Come." For Bultmann, Jesus' summons to individuals to follow him, in light of his own decision to accept death rather than conform his life to the political and even the religious institutions of his time, constitutes a historical event that for faith becomes an eschatological event.

Bultmann considered the Gospel of John (in an expurgated form) to be the purest version of the kerygma. He asserted that John's basic message—"the Word became flesh"—is the simple declaration *that* God addresses humans in a historical individual: Jesus of Nazareth.[56] Paul is assumed by Bultmann to have come close to the purity of this insight by leaving out of consideration the ethical and eschatological teaching of Jesus, locating Jesus' obedience in a decision to do God's will made by him as the heavenly Christ before he took the form of the earthly Jesus (Phil 2:5–8) and limiting his kerygma to the "'that' of the life of Jesus and the fact of his crucifixion."[57] Through the cross, God announces the end of the old age and the coming of the new; therefore, to accept God's Word through the cross is to enter now the life of the age to come. Having died to the old world, one is raised by faith to the new life.

Bultmann's representation of Jesus as historical event become eschatological event is appropriate and illuminating for understanding some of the major aspects of Paul's and John's thought, although it does not provide a satisfactory perspective for dealing with their beliefs about the eschatological future. But for Mark, the axiom is wholly inadequate. That notion would be useful in interpreting Mark only if both "historical" and "eschatological" were assigned meanings quite different from those Bultmann intends, but which are inherent in Mark.

Although Paul does not repudiate the apocalyptic element in the gospel he preaches, he does not give it a central place. Or, more accurately, even when he includes the apocalyptic elements of the Christian message, he does so without reference to the past ministry or message of Jesus. The only roles Jesus plays in Paul's eschatological scheme are those of the crucified-exalted Lord and the agent who will bring the cosmos into subjection to the will of God. There is no appeal to precedent or guideline for Christian behavior in the activity or message of the earthly Jesus.

For the gospel tradition, as for late Judaism and particularly for Jewish apocalypticism, the coming of the New Age was a far more complicated matter than a shift of self-understanding. Whatever one may think of Albert Schweitzer's reconstruction of the life and message of Jesus, Schweitzer has shown beyond doubt the thoroughly eschatological and, indeed, apocalyptic outlook of Jesus, in terms of which his message of the coming kingdom of God was formulated.[58]

In our analysis of the synoptic tradition, we shall see that the central concerns in the gospels are precisely what is missing in Paul: Jesus is seen as the eschatological salvation-bringer in the context of his *historical* public ministry and without reference to his heavenly existence prior to his appearance as man or to his *Parousia*, his future coming in glory. No one before Mark had undertaken to bring together the tradition in a sequential way. What pre-Markan documents there were seem to have been structured by topical or mnemonic arrangement. Thus, in any study of the gospels, Mark poses this problem: How, in a church that (to judge from most of the New Testament) was dominated by Paul and his kerygma and whose major concern was to proclaim the crucified and risen Lord, did there arise a literary creation like the Gospel of Mark, with the theological understanding of Jesus it embodies? Why did the author write such a work, which has come to be called "a gospel"?

Before offering an analysis of the contents of Mark, the oldest of the gospels, however, it is essential to recognize and examine the evidence for a body of tradition about Jesus and his teaching that antedated any of the gospels, and was used by two of the gospel writers as a basic source for their reports of the teaching and aims of Jesus. This material has been designated by scholars as the Q source—a term probably derived from the German word for source, *Quelle*.

What Is a Gospel? The Meaning of *Euangelion*

The problem of what "gospel" means becomes apparent immediately when we recognize that *euangelion*, or gospel—the word Mark (or the early church for which he was a spokesman) chose as the heading for his little book—was Paul's favorite term for his kerygma. For Paul the word meant the announcement of the eschatological events leading to the formation of the new people of God and the triumph of God's purpose in the world. This was effected by God through the crucifixion and resurrection of Jesus. Therefore, the one who preaches the gospel could be perceived as the Deutero-Isaianic messenger of Yahweh, who "proclaims the victory of Yahweh over the whole world."[59] He not only announces it, but his word of good tidings brings about salvation for those who respond in faith. "By the fact that he declares the restoration of Israel, the new creation of the world, the inauguration of the eschatological age, he brings them to pass."[60]

The noun *euangelion* as used by Mark (1:1) may carry some of the connotation of the verb in Second Isaiah, but its meaning and use lie closer to the term as it was employed in the imperial Roman cult, where it meant an announcement of the benefits the empire enjoyed through the gracious authority of Caesar, viewed as the divinely appointed ruler of Rome. Although the fuller documentation for this meaning of *euangelion* comes in part from post-New Testament writers, such as Plutarch (46?–120? CE) in *De Fortuna Romanorum*,[61] there is inscriptional evidence going back to the time of Augustus for the use of *euangelion* in connection with the imperial cult: "The birthday of the god was for the world the beginning of tidings of joy [*euangelion*] on his account."[62] Gerhard Friedrich has summarized what the term implied when associated with the saving power and person of the emperor: "The ruler is divine by nature. His power extends to men, to animals, to the earth and to the sea. Nature belongs to him; the wind and the waves are subject to him. He works miracles and heals men. He is the savior of the world who also redeems individuals from their difficulties."[63]

The emperor's divinity was believed to have been attested by signs in the heavens at both his birth and his death, which showed that he belonged among the gods. Although some leading scholars have denied the link between the meaning of *euangelion* as applied to the first four books of the New Testament and the connotation it carries in the imperial cult,[64] the connection has rightly been reaffirmed in an important study of gospel origins by Wilhelm Schneemelcher.[65]

It would be wrong to assume, however, that the primary meaning of *euangelion* was taken over from the Hellenistic conceptual world and that the Old Testament belief in the significance of Yahweh's saving acts as set forth in Second Isaiah was added later. The likelihood is rather the reverse. For Mark, the Hellenistic term was a useful propaganda tool for setting forth his understanding of Jesus' divine kingship, a form of rulership that rested on conceptions of power and divine purpose in the world entirely different from those in non-Christian circles. This radical divergence is explicitly declared in Mark 10:42–45: "You know that those who are supposed to rule over the Gentiles lord it over them, and their great men exercise authority over them. But it shall be not so among you; but whoever would be great among you must be your servant, and whoever would be first among you must be slave of all. For the Son of man came not to be served but to serve, and to give his life as a ransom for many."

Without assuming that Mark 10:45 is a direct allusion to the Suffering Servant theme of Isa 53 (this cannot be demonstrated on philological grounds),[66] we can see that casting Jesus in the role of a servant on the eve of his entry into Jerusalem as a kingly figure (Mark 11:1–10) is clearly intentional. Mark wants to use the terminology of Gentile kingship—including *euangelion*—but to redefine in a radical way what kingship involves. This redefinition, reflecting his understanding of Yahweh's sovereignty, is drawn not from imperial Rome but from the eschatological kingship of Second Isaiah and the later prophets and apocalyptists.

Although Paul refers to Jesus' turning over "the kingdom" to God after the defeat of the evil powers is complete (1 Cor 15:24–28), this phrase is not central in Paul's thought. Indeed, he uses it at times in a way that sounds more like early-twentieth-century Protestant liberals than like Mark: "the kingdom of God does not mean food and drink but righteousness and peace and joy in the Holy Spirit" (Rom 14:17). Apart from the 1 Cor 15 passage, in which Paul sets forth a kind of eschatological calendar of events, the king-dom plays no significant role in Paul's thought as we know it from his letters. It may be that the eschatological wisdom was kept for the inner core of the theologically mature believers in the Pauline churches,[67] which could account for the brief attention it receives in his public letters. But even if this were the case—and the hypothesis has great plausibility—the central concern for Paul was the cross-resurrection kerygma.[68]

What we are confronted with, therefore, is not merely a difference between "gospel" as message in Paul and as a narrative account in Mark, but a different understanding of the meaning of Jesus for faith. The problem is not only the relationship of Jesus' message to that of Paul, but also the understandings of Jesus that underlie the synoptic tradition on the one hand and Paul on the other. It is not enough to say that the gospel form developed by a process of enriching the basic message about the cross and resurrection.[69] Kähler's oft-quoted dictum that the gospels are passion stories with extended introduc-tions[70] is likewise inadequate. Although the story of Jesus' suffering and death are an essential element in Mark's scheme, it is not the main event for which the events of Jesus' ministry are no more than inconsequential preliminaries. Nor is Kähler any closer to the truth of Mark's intention when he says that the gospels are interested not in *what* happened but in *who* acted and *how*.[71]

Mark's Unique Literary Contribution

What led Mark to arrange the Jesus tradition in the literary form we know as a gospel? Answers to this question were already being offered by the early second century, although there is a certain speciousness about them. Papias of Hierapolis, famed for the low estimate of his intellect advanced by Eusebius[72] and for the tantalizing bits of information about gospel origins attributed to him,[73] reports that Mark,

> ". . . [h]aving become the interpreter of Peter, wrote down accurately—but not in order—all that he remembered of the things either said or done by the Lord. For he had neither heard the Lord nor followed him. But later he followed Peter, who used to make available the teachings as needed, not in order to pro-duce an orderly account of the Lord's sayings. Thus Mark did no wrong in pro-ducing some written accounts as he remembered them, for he set as his goal not to omit anything he had heard, or to report falsely of any of these things."[74]

Justin Martyr (100?–165? CE), relying on the testimony of Papias, refers to the Gospel of Mark as the "memoir" of Peter.[75] By the very choice of this des-ignation, Justin elevates the gospel as a literary form into the realm of known types of Hellenistic literature. The implication seems to be that before the apostolic generation passed away, Peter and other apostles (or apostolic asso-ciates, such as Luke) authorized or allowed their followers to produce memoirs of their associations with Jesus. These memoirs would guarantee an immediacy of witness to what Jesus had said and done and would serve as the last possible eyewitness accounts. As much as a twentieth-century scholar interested in the origins of Christianity might wish to have access to such documents, it must be acknowledged that the gospels do not match the description that Justin Martyr offered for them in the middle of the second century CE. The Gospel of Mark is not a "memoir" of Peter, either in the sense that it recounts in a special way the associations of Peter with Jesus or in the sense that Mark reports someone's firsthand recollections about Jesus. The material on which Mark drew passed through a long process of retelling and modification and interpretation, and it reflects less special interest in Peter than does Matthew's gospel. Thus, for example, in Matt 16:13–20—especially verses 17–19—Peter is singled out for a special place of authority, but these details have no parallel in the other gospel accounts of the incident.

Does the Gospel of Mark fit the model of the memoir? As a literary type, the memoir, *apomnemoneuma*, is best exemplified by the *Memorabilia of Socrates*, written by Xenophon (434?–355? BCE). The analogy between this life of Socrates and the gospels, first developed by Justin Martyr in his apologetic writings, has been widely discussed for the past century and a half by biblical scholars.[76] Although the theory of apostolic memoirs has been appealed to as a way of ensuring the reliability of the gospel accounts, it does not in fact provide any such guarantee. Indeed, the analogy is not even an appropriate one, since Xenophon's *Memorabilia* represents a conscious literary effort, rather than the popular kind of writing that makes no pretension of being "literature." The distinction is accurately brought out in the contrast between the two German words, *Hochliteratur* and *Kleinliteratur*, which might be rendered respectively as "pretentious" or "unpretentious literature," with the gospel fitting the second category. To make such a distinction is in no way to dismiss the Gospel of Mark as beneath academic notice; it is rather to recognize it for what it is: a propaganda writing produced by and for a community that made no cultural claims for itself but offered its writings as a direct appeal for adherents rather than as a way of attracting the attention of intellectuals or literati of the day.

Recently an attempt has been made to place the gospels, especially Luke (the use of contemporary literary conventions shows that the writer of Luke wished to be considered an author and a historian[77]) within a genre of literature produced in the late Hellenistic-early Roman period (150 BCE–150 CE): the aretalogy.[78] Though the term is not used in Greek, it appears in a Latinized form, *aretalogus*, to designate "one who (professionally) speaks the wondrous deeds of a deity or a divinely gifted human."[79] The aretalogy, then, is a narrative in which a heroic figure is portrayed. Plato's portrayal of Socrates is considered by some scholars—most notably Moses Hadas and

Morton Smith—to be "the source for all subsequent aretalogies, pagan and Christian."[80] As artist and teacher, Socrates was portrayed by Plato in *Phaedo* and the *Apology* in such a way as to establish a kind of archetype, in terms of which subsequent ages represented "certain saintly figures, who like Socrates, had selflessly devoted themselves to the spiritual improvement of the community and had accepted the suffering, sometimes the martyrdom [that Socrates had]."[81]

When the detailed evidence is adduced to support this thesis, however, it turns out not to be persuasive. There is no pattern discernible that can be called a common literary element in the "aretalogies" summarized by Morton Smith, nor do three of them—Porphyry's *Life of Pythagoras*, Philo Judaeus's *Life of Moses*, and Philostratus's *Life of Apollonius of Tyana*—depict their respective heroes as dying a martyr's death. This is something of a letdown after the moving description of the martyred Socrates, who has been proposed as the archetypal subject of the aretalogy. The two elements that seem to be shared with the gospels by these biographies are that miracles were attributed to all the heroes and that each had his own kind of divine wisdom to offer his faithful followers. The form and content of these four lives, however, do not demonstrate sufficient similarities as a literary genre to consider the aretalogy—if indeed it is a specific literary form—identifiable as the model for the Gospel of Mark or the other gospels.

The conclusion reached by K. L. Schmidt in his study of this subject a half century ago is the only one warranted by the evidence: that the writer of the first gospel, Mark, had no model or precedent to follow. In writing his gospel, he created a new genre of literature for which, as a whole, there was no precedent.[82] He followed neither the patterns of the literary memoirs or the popular biographies of his time,[83] although analogies to the narrative style can be found in collections of anecdotes in Jewish and pagan folk literature.[84] A major feature of the gospel writers (with the exception of Luke) and the authors of anecdotes and miracle stories is their lack of consciousness of being an author or of creating a literature.[85] Stated another way, for the preliterary stages of the origin of the gospel tradition, parallels can be shown in Jewish and pagan sources; but for the gospel as a literary whole, there is no real precedent.[86] The impact of the pagan miracle stories is most evident at the written stage of the development of the synoptic tradition, so it is possible to distinguish in Mark between what was probably the original intent of the tradition that he incorporated and what it had come to mean to him. But even where this pagan influence can perhaps be observed, as in the heightening of the miraculous element, it is apparent in details of stories and sayings, not in the structure of the gospel as a whole or in Mark's goals in writing it.

Chief among Mark's aims was the determination to show that the meaning of Jesus for faith was manifest in the arena of world history. His view of history was derived from that of Jewish apocalypticism, especially from the book of Daniel. He was not content with the notion that God's purpose for creation was disclosed through the words or teachings of Jesus: he wanted to demonstrate that the revelation came through a public person performing public acts in interaction with the civil and religious authorities of his time. For Mark, faith offered not an escape from the world, but the divinely granted key to the meaning of the past, the present, and the future of the world. It is in that cosmic context that his report of Jesus is placed. And it was in the interests of that goal that he appropriated and edited the Jesus tradition.

There is no way to determine who wrote the gospel attributed to Mark. The special attention to Peter in this gospel (he is mentioned seventeen times) and the references elsewhere in the New Testament to a close relationship between Peter and Mark[87] led very early to the assumption that this gospel was written by a companion of Peter named Mark. The fact that it expects the siege of Jerusalem and the destruction of the temple but does not describe these events in detail such as one finds in Luke probably indicates that it was written before those catastrophes took place. And the prediction in Mark 13:30 that some followers of Jesus who were young adults were told in Mark that they should to expect to live to the end of the age suggests that he was writing while they were still alive. The probable date for the Gospel of Mark, therefore, is about 65 CE. Prior to that, however, there was a source that preserved mostly sayings of Jesus, but which included reports on some of his activities as well. It is this source that has become known among scholars as Q.

The Earliest Gospel Tradition: The Q Source

In the early nineteenth century, Johann Gottfried Eichhorn, in his *Introduction to the New Testament*,[88] proposed that the gospel material shared by Matthew and Luke but not found in Mark derived from a specific sayings source. The first scholar to refer to this source by the term Q appears to have been J. Weiss, late in the nineteenth century.[89] In his detailed analysis of the development of the Q source, W. G. Kümmel comes to the conclusion that Q was mostly sayings tradition with a few narrative features, that it was probably arranged with sayings grouped on the basis of content, and that the material concerning John the Baptist was the first, while that dealing with Parousia and judgment was at the end.[90] The same basic conclusion about the use of a common sayings source by Matthew and Luke is offered by Raymond E. Brown in his monumental and magisterial *Introduction to the New Testament*.[91] He asserts that, while no solution to the Synoptic Problem solves all the difficulties, the most plausible is the priority of Mark and the common use of a source (Q) by Matthew and Luke, in addition to their own special sources. He rejects the hypothesis of some that the original Q portrayed Jesus as a wisdom teacher in the

Cynic-Stoic tradition, with no apocalyptic message.[92] Instead, he perceives the Q source as having a strong eschatological thrust, including warnings, woes, and parables depicting the future, and offers a likely reconstruction of Q.[93]

These sound perceptions are in sharp contrast to a hypothesis advanced and defended in recent years, which claims that the original Q should be designated "The Sayings of a Wise Man," on the assumption that the historical Jesus was to be seen primarily as carrying out the traditions of Jewish wisdom, conveying timeless truths. Only subsequently, according to this theory, was this material altered by the introduction of references to the age to come and to miracles performed by Jesus.[94] This perception of the Q source was adopted and has been refined by John Kloppenborg in *The Formation of Q*,[95] where he purports to trace the development of Q from its original collection of wisdom sayings to the present mix of apocalyptic and miracle features. This process has also been affirmed by Helmut Koester,[96] among others.

In a highly perceptive recent work, *Q and the History of Early Christianity: Studies on Q*,[97] Christopher M. Tuckett has shown that Q does not fit the model of the Sayings of a Wise Man. There are certain common features that match or reflect Jewish wisdom, as in the reference in Luke 11:49 to "the Wisdom of God" and the declaration of Jesus in Luke 7:35 that the justification for his controversial message and the activity carried out by him—and earlier by John the Baptist—will be provided by "wisdom." Indeed, it is precisely these warnings of persecution and rejection that have no parallel in the Wisdom literature, but are instead crucial features in the apocalyptic tradition, represented by Daniel, Enoch, and *Jubilees*.

As noted by R. A. Piper[98] and Ben Witherington,[99] the sayings of Jesus in the Q tradition are not witty, timeless truths, but radical calls to obedience in light of impending conflict and the hope of divine deliverance. Membership in the new people of God is not based on conformity to Torah, as in the Jewish wisdom tradition's equating of wisdom and the Law of God,[100] or in the *Rule of the Community* from Qumran, where the opening lines declare that members must live in full obedience to do "what is good and right [as God] commanded by the hand of Moses and all his servants the prophets." The scholarly misperception of Q—as well as of Jewish Wisdom literature—is the consequence of the hypothesis that differentiates sharply between apocalyptic (with its orientation toward conflict and future cosmic renewal) and what are assumed to be the perspectives of the popular philosophies of the Graeco-Roman period: Cynicism and Stoicism. But in fact, both these philosophical modes stressed the importance of divine rule in the future and present moral accountability in preparation for that new order. These themes in such philosophical traditions are spelled out in Excursus 3, below.

The reconstruction of the Q source, based on identifying it as the non-Markan material common to Matthew and Luke, is not only conceptually plausible, but is indeed visually evident in editions of gospel parallels, where the twofold parallels between Matthew and Luke contrast sharply with the threefold parallels with Mark.[101] The material to be included as deriving from Q may be classified as to formal structure in the following categories:

1. Narratives, which recount the activities of Jesus.

2. Parables, which consist of instructions offered by Jesus by means of analogies between features of human experience and the outworking of the divine purpose.

3. Oracles, which are warnings of conflict and doom for the wicked.

4. Beatitudes, pronouncements of God's special favor for the faithful.

5. Prophetic Pronouncements, which predict what God is going to do for his people and to judge the forces of evil.

6. Wisdom Words, which are more nearly proverbial in form, but which emphasize the fulfillment of divine promises.

7. Exhortations, which concern the shared life within the new community that is being called into being.

These formal modes of Q material are oriented toward the future: the fulfillment of God's purpose for and through his people. The symbols used below for these categories are Narratives (Na), Parables (Pa), Oracles (Or), Beatitudes (Be), Prophetic Pronouncements (PP), Wisdom Words (WW), Exhortations (Ex). The conceptual themes in the Q tradition are likewise eschatological in substance: (1) Discipleship: Its Privileges and Trials; (2) The Prophet as God's Messenger; (3) Call to Repentance; Warning of Judgment; (4) Jesus as Revealer and Agent for Establishing God's Rule.

On the basis of these formal modes, the components of the Q source may be identified as follows:

PP	3:7–9, 16b–17	John's Eschatological Preaching
Na	4:2b–12	Jesus' Struggle with Satan
Be	6:20–23	Beatitudes: The Poor, the Hungry, the Hated
WW	6:27–36	Promised Reward for Love and Forgiveness
WW	6:37–42	Rewards of Discipleship
Pa	6:43–46	Parables of Moral Productivity
Pa	6:47–49	Discipleship Must Survive Testing: A Parable of the House with and without a Foundation
Na	7:2–3, 6–10	Healing of the Centurion's Slave
PP	7:18–23	Response to the Question from John the Baptist

PP	7:24–35	John's Place in God's Plan
PP	9:57–58 (–62?)	Leave Behind Home and Family
PP	10:2–12	Disciples Commissioned to Extend Jesus' New Community Work
Or	10:13–15	Doom on Unrepentant Cities
PP	10:16	Disciples Share in Jesus' Rejection
PP	10:21–22	God's Gift of Wisdom to His Own
Be	10:23–24	Beatitude: Those to Whom Wisdom Is Granted
Ex	11:2–4	Prayer for the Coming of God's Kingdom
WW	11:9–13	God Answers the Prayers of His Own
PP	11:14–23	Jesus' Defeat of Demons as a Sign of the Kingdom
Or	11:24–26	The Return of the Unclean Spirit
PP	11:29b–32	The Sign of Jonah and the One Greater than He: Jesus as Prophet and Wise Man
Pa	11:33–36	Parabolic Words of Light and Darkness
Or	11:39–40, 42–43	Woes to the Pharisees
Or	11:46–48, 52	Woes to the Lawyers
PP	11:49–51	Wisdom Predicts the Martyrdom of Prophets and Apostles
PP	12:2–3	What Is Hidden Will Be Revealed
Or	12:4–5	Do Not Fear Martyrdom
Pa	12:6–7	Parable of God's Care for His Own
PP	12:8–10	Confirmation of the Confession/Denial of the Son of Man
PP	12:11–12	God's Support of the Persecuted
Pa	12:22–31	Freedom from Anxiety about Earthly Needs
Pa	12:33–34	Freedom from Possessions
Pa	12:35–40	Parable of Preparedness: The Returning Householder
Pa	12:42–46	Parable of the Faithful Steward
PP	12:51–53	Jesus as the Agent of Crises
Pa	12:54–56	Signs of the Impending End of the Age
Pa	12:57–59	Parable of Preparedness for Judgment
Pa	13:20–21	Parable of the Leaven
WW	13:24	Difficulty in Entering the Kingdom

Pa	13:25–29	Parable of Exclusion from the Kingdom
PP	13:34–35	The Rejection of the Prophets and the Vindication of God's Agent
Pa	14:16–23	Parable of the Eschatological Banquet
PP	14:26–27	Jesus Shatters Domestic Ties, and Summons Disciples to Bear the Cross
Pa	15:4–7	The Joyous Shepherd
WW	16:13	Inevitable Choice Between Masters
PP	16:16	The End of the Old Era and the New Age Proclaimed
WW	16:17	Confidence in God's Promise
Ex	16:18	Prohibition of Divorce and Remarriage
Ex	17:3–4	Forgiveness within the Community
Ex	17:5–6	Faith within the Community
Or	17:23–37	Sudden Judgment to Fall
Pa	19:12–13, 15–26	Parable of the Returning Nobleman and Rewards for Fidelity
PP	22:28–30	The Promise to the Faithful of Sharing in the Kingdom of God

The conceptual themes of the Q material are identified in the following analysis of the components of this source, some of which appear in even the sparse narrative features, of which the clearest example is the story of Jesus Healing the Centurion's Servant [Na] (7:2–3, 6–10).[102] Law-observant Jews would consider the centurion off limits because he was not only a Gentile, but also an agent of the oppressive power of the Roman Empire. Clearly, a central concern of this pericope is Jesus' intent to include non-Israelites in the new community that he is calling into being by his teachings and his actions. In Matthew's version of this tradition, the centurion himself told Jesus about the illness of his servant (Matt 8:5), while Luke reports that the Roman military officer sent Jewish elders to inform Jesus about the illness of his slave and to request that he come to heal him (Luke 7:3). Capernaum was a Roman garrison town and a fishing center on the northwest shore of the Sea of Galilee, and was used by Jesus as the headquarters for his activity of preaching and healing in preparation for the coming of the kingdom of God.[103]

The only other narrative pericope in Q is the detailed account of the temptation of Jesus ([Na] 4:2b–12), which expands well beyond the succinct Markan report of his forty days in the wilderness (Mark 1:12–13). The latter describes the Spirit *driving* Jesus there, his encounter with the wild beasts, and the assistance provided him by the angels, in addition to his being "tempted by Satan." But the Q account provides the details of the tempta-tion. His forty days were a time of fasting, and the "devil"—which means "accuser"—tried to entice Jesus into using his extraordinary powers by over-coming his hunger through converting stones into bread, by displaying pub-licly and dramatically his alleged divine support by leaping down from a pinnacle of the temple, and by gaining sovereign authority over the king-doms of the world through engaging in the worship of Satan/the devil. Jesus' response to these temptations is in each case focused on a quotation from scripture.[104] What is at issue in this pericope is not the nature of divine wis-dom, but Jesus as faithful agent of God's sovereignty over the universe.

The dominant themes in Q, as noted above, are set forth in the texts that comprise this body of tradition. They concern the resources and the respon-sibilities of God's new people, the role of Jesus as God's messenger, the cen-tral importance of major changes in attitude and behavior, and the ultimate consequences (repentance or judgment). Importantly, they also describe the role that Jesus fulfills in preparing for the renewal of God's covenant people. As indicated above, these themes may be summarized as follows:

1. Discipleship: Its Privileges and Trials
2. The Prophet as God's Messenger
3. Repentance or Judgment
4. Jesus as Revealer and Agent of God's Rule

Discipleship

The beatitudes in Luke's version (6:20–23) offer promise of divine support and compensation for the poverty, hunger, hatred, and exclusion that the faithful can expect to suffer. The "great" divine reward for fidelity in spite of such deprivation and antagonism is already prepared in heaven, and is cer-tain to be provided. The overcoming of ordinary human conflict by works of love is enjoined on the new community: loving one's enemies; seeking bless-ing for those who bring curses, abuse, bodily harm, and robbery. Generosity is to be shown to beggars and even thieves. Love of enemies is to be manifest not merely in attitude but in action, including works of mercy. The promise of divine reward is declared for those who avoid judgment and condemna-tion of others, and who instead give generously to those who are in need (6:27–39). There is to be no striving for a superior role or moral status, or criticism of others rather than forthright self-examination (6:40–42). Crucial are the moral state and performance of the individual in response to the eth-ical message of Jesus—doing "what I tell you" (6:43–46). Only such moral performance—hearing and doing Jesus' words—will enable one to survive the eschatological judgment, here pictured as a stream that brings down the flimsy house in which the self-reliant one foolishly lives, in contrast to the solidly built house of those who hear and do the words of Jesus (6:47–49).

The factor of discipleship appears in two different modes in the Q source. The first of these describes the impact on ordinary human relationships that comes from accepting the role of disciple. The second concerns the process and results of God's disclosure to his people of his new purpose through Jesus. To accept the call to discipleship will result in a radical break with one's earthly family, and even the possible loss of one's domicile. The unconditional commitment to follow Jesus means that one must be ready to abandon not only the security of a family home ("the Son of Man has nowhere to lay his head") but also the traditional obligations to one's parents (9:57–62) if one is to fulfill the task of announcing the coming of the kingdom of God and to qualify for sharing in it. Jesus did not come to promote peace within families; instead, heeding his call to announce and prepare for the coming of God's kingdom will result in conflict among family members. One must recognize the portents of coming struggle and divine judgment, just as one can be aware of the coming of earthly storms (12:49–56). Animosity with family members will develop for those who accept the call to discipleship. One cannot become a disciple of Jesus unless one is prepared to suffer and even to be put to death: "to bear one's cross" (14:26–27). Ordinary patterns of family relationships and traditional expectations of peace and order must be set aside by those who heed Jesus' call to be his disciple.

The insights and resources provided by God for his new people are also set forth in the Q tradition. That the basis of participation in the covenant people is about to undergo radical change from the simple claim of Abrahamic ancestry is made explicit in the Q material, which reports the message of John the Baptist. He declares, "God is able from these stones to raise up children to Abraham" (3:8). He also predicts that the agent that God is about to send forth will gather his true people and purge "the chaff" (3:17–18). When Jesus has begun his mission, he declares that, important as the work of John has been, it represents a crucial transition in the outworking of God's purpose—from the preparatory era of the law and the prophets to the consummation that will come with the establishment of the kingdom of God (16:16). It is for the establishment of God's kingdom that Jesus instructs his disciples to pray to the Father, meanwhile asking God to supply their daily needs for food, forgiveness, and deliverance from temptation (11:2–4, 9–13). Participation in the kingdom of God is vividly depicted in the parable of the Great Supper (14:16–23), in which the pious and proper are so preoccupied with their ordinary routines that they fail to respond to the ultimate invitation to share in the kingdom of God. Instead, it is the poor, the ailing, and the outsiders who accept the call and are thereby brought in to share in the fellowship of God's new people.

There is also a solemn warning that the followers of Jesus can expect to undergo hostility and even martyrdom, analogous to Jesus' own rejection and execution by the authorities (11:49–51). Indeed, that is said to have been the fate of God's messengers and agents throughout the whole biblical period, from the death of Abel in the first book of the Hebrew canon (Gen 4:8) to the death of Zechariah in the last book (2 Chron 24:20–21). Ironically, those in the past who have sought and heeded the message of God for his people include those who are outsiders by standards of Jewish covenantal identity. The two examples cited in Q are "the Queen of the South"—the ruler from a kingdom in the southwest Arabian peninsula in what is now Yemen—who came to hear the wisdom of Solomon (1 Kgs 10:1–10); and "the men of Nineveh" in Assyria who "repented at the preaching of Jonah" (Jonah 3:5). Both of these references are to non-Israelites who sought and heeded God's word for human beings.

Those who have received God's revelation through Jesus and accordingly are being persecuted can be certain that their public acknowledgment of Jesus as the agent of God will result in their vindication in the presence of God and his angels (12:2–10). Therefore, they are to be confident when brought before the earthly authorities, and they will be given guidance by the Holy Spirit (12:11–12). Until the Son of Man comes to establish God's rule, however, they must remain faithful to the laws of love, kindness, and sobriety (12:30–46). The prime model for this life of compassion and concern is that of Jesus, who expresses his loving concern for the city of Jerusalem as the symbol of the religious leadership and their followers who have consistently rejected God's message and messengers (13:34–35).

How are the members of the new community to live in the present, aware as they are of the execution of Jesus and the likelihood of their own suffering and martyrdom? They are to go forth into the towns and cities around them, proclaiming Jesus' message of the coming of God's kingdom. They are not to take money or other resources, but instead are to accept food and housing that will be provided for them by the hearers who respond in faith. Unbelief and rejection in certain Galilean towns is contrasted with the potential openness of Gentile cities (Tyre and Sidon), and will result in divine judgment, since the response to these messengers is matched by their negative response to Jesus, who is the center of their message (10:1–16).

The Prophet as God's Messenger

It is through the prophets that God has disclosed—and continues to disclose—his purpose for the renewal of the covenant people and for the establishment of the divine rule over the whole created order. We have noted (1) John the Baptist's prediction of the new "children" that God will raise up for Abraham (3:8) and of the "coming one" who will purge and burn "the chaff" = those who falsely claim to be God's people (3:17); and (2) Jesus' announcement that the era of "the law and the prophets" ends with John (16:16).[105] Now the whole of God's purpose is to be revealed, and is to be proclaimed by the messengers whom Jesus has sent (12:2–3). Those who identify themselves with the Son of Man in the presence of others will be acclaimed by Jesus in the presence of God ("before the angels of God") and those who reject him will be rejected before God (12:8–10). They can expect to be challenged by religious and political authorities, but through the Holy Spirit they will receive instruction how to respond (12:11–12). Because of the rejection and martyrdom of the prophets by the religious leadership in Jerusalem and the refusal of many to obey the divine summons to come together as the children of God, judgment is to fall on the city. Ultimate renewal will come only when Jesus is acknowledged there as the one who "comes in the name of the Lord" (13:34–35; Ps 118:26).

Yet in the Q source there is a report of a direct question by John addressed to Jesus concerning his role in the purpose of God: "Are you the one who is to come, or should we look for another?" (7:19). Jesus' response is to direct attention to the works of healing he has performed and his proclamation of the good news to "the poor"—the deprived and the outsiders (7:22–23). The healings that Jesus is reported as doing on behalf of the blind, the lame, lepers, the deaf, and the dead are all identified as acts of eschatological renewal, in fulfillment of prophetic promises reported in passages from the Isaiah Apocalypse and Second Isaiah.[106] Jesus' description of John's role in the purpose of God, on the other hand, identifies him as "my [= God's] messenger," as predicted in Mal 4:5, and as unexcelled "among those born of women" but also as one destined to await but not to share in the kingdom of God (7:28). Jesus then is reported as contrasting the abstemiousness of John with his own open association with those who did not observe ritual or ethnic purity. As a consequence, Jesus was denounced by religious leaders as "a glutton and a drunkard," in that he befriended "tax-collectors and sinners"—those who by collaboration with the Romans or by personal lifestyle violated the strict boundaries of Jewish piety and covenantal identity (7:34). The epithets by which Jesus says he has been labeled are taken from a passage in Deut 21:18–21, where the rule is laid down that a rebellious son who violates the rules of his family is to be considered a threat to the integrity of the larger community, and is to be denounced as a "glutton and a drunkard" and killed by stoning on the initiative of the town elders.[107] Clearly, Q represents Jesus as foreseeing his own rejection by the community leadership,[108] and accordingly warns his followers to expect similar hostile reactions. Ironically, it is as Son of Man that he expects to experience this denunciation by the religious authorities.

In Q's expanded version of the Markan pericope that describes Jesus as being accused of performing exorcisms by being an agent of Beelzebul, "the prince of demons,"[109] Jesus' response to this accusation raises two issues: (1) If all exorcisms are carried out through the "prince of demons," then that would apply to all Jewish exorcists (Q 11:18). (2) But Jesus makes the explicit claim that his ability to expel demons is the consequence of his being a divine instrument—"the finger of God" (11:20), which is a term used by the Egyptian magicians in Exod 8:18–19.[110] The significance of Jesus' expulsion of a demon is said to be the inbreaking of the kingdom of God into the present experience of Jesus and his contemporaries—including that of his critics and detractors in this pericope.

Repentance or Judgment

How is one to respond to these claims and actions of Jesus? The results of responses will lead to divine reward or punishment. As noted above, unlike the pagan queen and the Ninevites who responded positively to God's messengers, Solomon and Jonah, this generation has not repented in response to God's message through the Son of Man: Jesus (Q 11:29–32). The Pharisees are denounced for their strict attention to ritual purity requirements, while their way of life is characterized by "extortion and wickedness" instead of by "justice and the love of God" (11:37–43). Like their predecessors, they go through the public display of honoring the tombs of the prophets, but inwardly they share in the hostile response to the prophets that culminated in their contemporaries persecuting and executing them (Q 11:47–49). This is made explicit in the warning to Jerusalem that its continuation of the violence accorded the prophets—which has thwarted God's program to call together the faithful community ("your children")—will result in destruction of the city and severance of the special relationship with God until they acclaim as "Blessed . . . he who comes in the name of the Lord."[111]

God has given light to humans by disclosing to them his purpose for them and for the world, but a major issue is: How will they respond to the light? Will they conceal it or ignore it, by putting it "in a cellar or under a bushel"? Or will they allow it to pervade their "whole body" and to be transmitted through them to others? (Q 11:33–36). They can be sure of being held accountable when the vindicated, triumphant Son of Man comes (11:40), just as the absent householder expects his servants to be fulfilling their tasks faithfully whenever he may return (Q 12:36–46). Yet they must be prepared to accept deeply divisive results within human families for those who receive Jesus as God's agent of human renewal. His followers must be prepared for severe cosmic difficulties and testings—"fire," "division," "scorching heat" (12:49–56)—in the unpredictably extended interim before Jesus returns in triumph as Son of Man to establish God's rule.

His hearers are warned to be ready to accept responsibility for their way of life, like an accused individual taken before a magistrate (Q 12:57–59).

They must avoid the complacent, self-gratifying way of life that ignores the warnings of impending divine judgment that will come with the return of the Son of Man, just as most of Noah's and Lot's contemporaries ignored the predictions of doom and accordingly were destroyed when it fell on the world (Q 17:22–30). They must choose between serving "God and mammon," which symbolizes the human craving for possessions (Q 16:13). And they are reminded of the comprehensive and enduring claim of Torah upon them as God's people: Not "one stroke of the letter of the law is to be dropped" (Q 16:17). The parable of the Returning Nobleman serves as a warning against misuse or waste of the capabilities and responsibilities that have been entrusted to the members of the new community, for which they will be held accountable when the Lord returns (Q 19:12–13, 15–26).[112]

Jesus as Revealer and Agent of God's Rule

In the extended Q account of Jesus' having been tempted by the devil (Q 4:3–13),[113] the issues raised by the devil deal with major themes concerning the identity of Jesus, his relationship to God, and his role in the coming of the kingdom of God. The issue is not: Does Jesus have extraordinary powers? Instead, it is: By what authority and for what purpose will he exercise these capabilities? The tempter's first test of Jesus is the proposal that he transform stone into bread; that is, use his power in order to satisfy personal needs. His response here, as in reaction to all the successive temptations, is to quote scripture: to appeal to God's word for the faithful community. Here the quote is from Deut 8:3, where Moses is reported as reminding the people of Israel of God's gift to them of bread from heaven after they have left Egypt and are on their way to Sinai (Exod 16). The source of true life for God's people is not daily food, but "every word that comes from the mouth of the Lord." Here Jesus' central concern is not to perform spectacular miracles, but to be the instrument through whom God's word reaches his people.[114]

The second temptation in the Q account (4:5–8) is based on the assumption that Jesus is to have a role in the rule over "all the kingdoms of the world," by which there will be manifest the "authority" and "glory" of such sovereignty. The tempter promises to deliver this role immediately, if only Jesus will acknowledge the sovereignty of the devil. The issue is: Who will rule the world? Will it be the kingdom of the devil or the kingdom of God? Jesus' answer is to quote Deut 6:16, with its prohibition of acknowledging any other god but the Lord (Yahweh). The quote is from the section of Deuteronomy that follows the account of the second giving of the law through Moses—the first having been described as taking place when the Israelites first reached Sinai (Exod 19–20). Here, following the giving of the Ten Commandments (Deut 5), is the summary declaration of what has come to be known as the Great Commandment (6:1–6) and the series of warnings about the consequences of violation of the commandments. Then comes the instruction referred to by Jesus in this section of the temptation narrative: that the Lord alone is to be feared, served, and invoked in oaths (6:13).

The third phase of the temptation story in Q is the devil's proposal to Jesus that he publicly show off his claimed special relationship with God by leaping down from a pinnacle of the temple. The devil is described here as paralleling the strategy of Jesus by quoting scripture to make his case that the angels will support him and protect him from the consequences of the fall.[115] Jesus' reaction is to quote the injunction in Deut 6:16 against putting "the Lord your God to a test."

Thus, the Q account of the temptation of Jesus is more than a test of personal piety, though it does portray Jesus as appealing to scripture in demonstration of his total devotion to the will of God. But the story also shows that what is at stake includes the claim that Jesus is the Son of God (4:3; 4:9) and that he is perceived to have a central role in the establishment of God's rule over the world: the coming of the kingdom of God. That facet of the Q tradition is likewise indicated in the Q version of the Beelzebul controversy, where the issue is not whether Jesus has power to expel demons, but rather: What is the source of his power?

The basic story appears in Mark 3:22–27, where the scribes are reported as charging Jesus with performing exorcisms as an agent of Beelzebul,[116] a name given to the chief of the God-opposing powers at work in the world, usually designated as "Satan" (adversary) or "the devil" (accuser, or calumniator). In Mark's version of this tradition, Jesus responds to the charge by pointing out that Satan would not be an agent in combating his own aides: the demons (Mark 3:22–26). But in the Q version, there is an additional significant feature: Jesus asks how his opponents' "sons" perform exorcisms if all who expel demons do so through the agency of the "prince of demons." Then, as indicated above, he goes on to propose that he expels demons "by the finger of God" (11:19–20). That phrase derives from the tradition in Exod 8–9, where God sends seven plagues on the Egyptians to convince them to allow the people of Israel to leave for their new land. Aaron's ability to convert the dust of the earth into gnats is perceived by the Egyptian magicians to be the work of "the finger of God" (Exod 8:16–19). Thus, it is appropriate for Jesus to carry forward that term in relation to his own controversy with the official leadership over his ability to overcome the powers of evil. The inference is obvious: it is God's power at work through him that enables him to perform the exorcisms. What is new is the claim that these manifestations of the defeat of Satan and his powers provides evidence that God's kingdom is no longer merely a future hope, but is already present and operative in the experience of his hearers (Q 11:20).

As discussed previously, the Q tradition asserts that John the Baptist is the crucial transitional figure. It is he who sends his disciples to Jesus to ask him: "Are you the one who is to come, or are we to wait for another?" (Q 7:19). When the question is reported to Jesus, he tells the messengers to report to John what they have seen and heard concerning the healings and exorcisms that he has performed. Jesus' recital of his activities (Q 7:22) is a composite of phrases from Isaiah: restoration of sight to the blind and hearing to the deaf (Isa 29:18–19; 42:18), the lame are able to walk (35:5–6); the dead are raised (26:19).[117] These accomplishments of Jesus in fulfillment of prophetic hopes[118] are to be reported to John.

John's role as the one through whom the era of the law and the prophets has come to an end and the violence linked with the coming of the kingdom of God has begun is asserted in Q 16:16. That perception of John as the crucial transitional figure is expanded in Q 7:24–35. Here Jesus is reported as explaining to his disciples that he had not gone out "into the wilderness"— that is, the barren area adjacent to the place where the Jordan River flows into the Dead Sea, which was the traditional location of John's baptismal activity—to see someone of wealth and splendid garb, "gorgeously apparel ed" (7:25). That would have been possible in the area, since graphic evidence of the splendid winter palaces of the first century CE was provided when the palace of Herod—as well as those of earlier Hasmonean aristocrats—were discovered and excavated not far north of Jericho.[119] Jesus says that he went out into this region to see "a prophet . . . and more than a prophet" (7:26). He then explains that John's unique role is that of "messenger" whom "I am sending ahead of you" (7:27). This is a paraphrase of the promise to Israel at Sinai that God would send an "angel in front of you, to guard you on the way and to bring you to the place that I have prepared" (i.e., Canaan; Exod 23:20). Although John is a human being—"among those born of women no one is greater than John"—yet his role in the purpose of God is purely preparatory for the coming of the kingdom of God. Hence, even "the least in the kingdom of God is greater than he" (7:28). The contemporaries of Jesus and John have rejected both of them and their messages: John's abstemious way of life ("eating no bread, drinking no wine"), and Jesus' open, accessible and friendly way, which reaches across moral, ritual, and occupational boundaries ("a friend of tax-collectors and sinners," Q 7:33–34). Hence, Jesus is being denounced as one who violates the boundaries of the covenant people: "a glutton and a drunkard." His rejection and martyrdom are clearly anticipated in this Q tradition.

In the Q tradition Jesus also articulates his special relationship with God, and then his joy that God's purpose through him has been communicated to his followers (Q 10:21–22, 23–24). What God intends for his people in the establishment of his kingdom is hidden from those who claim to possess wisdom, but it has been disclosed to "babes"—the simple people who make no claim to having achieved wisdom or special status. They are the ones to whom God has chosen to reveal his plan. Jesus is the crucial intermediary agent in this process, since everything has been delivered to him by the Father. God alone fully knows who Jesus is, and he alone fully knows the Father. But he has chosen to reveal this knowledge to certain ones: his disciples. Hence, he tells them of the special blessing they have received in the form of these insights—which neither prophets nor rulers in the past have been able to attain. In a supreme irony, the people of Jerusalem are denounced for their persistent rejection of the prophetic messengers and the martyrdom of the agents of God who have been sent to them. It has been the aim of Jesus to gather there the "brood" of the new community, but they have refused and judgment is to fall upon the leadership of the people until they make a major shift and acknowledge him as the agent of God for human renewal, saying, "Blessed is he who comes in the name of the Lord" (13:34–35; Ps 118:26).

Nevertheless, Jesus is pictured in Q as seeking out the lost and the needy—a role evident in the parable of the Lost Sheep (15:4–7), in which God is pictured as rejoicing at the recovery of the alien and estranged who now are part of the flock of God's people. The ultimate outcome of the mission of Jesus as depicted in Q is indicated in 22:28–30. Those who have remained faithful to Jesus during the difficulties and sufferings that he is to experience as he prepares to carry out his role in the establishment of God's kingdom are told that they will share the new life intimately with him when God's rule is attained in the world. They will take part in the work of Jesus as God's agent for accomplishing the kingdom, and they will share in meting out justice to those who have not accepted Jesus as God's agent for renewal of his people and of the creation.

Conclusion Concerning the Aims of the Q Source

It is a serious misreading of the Q source to perceive it as a medium of timeless wisdom, or to suppose that it represents Jesus as the conveyor of some sort of universal conceptual truths. Instead, Jesus' actions and his depiction of his relationship to God and of his role in the divine purpose are represented as involving a unique agenda and capacity that aim to defeat the powers of evil at work in the world and to summon into a new community those who—regardless of their ethnic origins, their cultic or social practices—perceive Jesus as the agent (1) to establish God's rule in the world, and (2) to make possible the emergence of a new community that understands and affirms this role and the goal as announced by Jesus.

Meanwhile, God's work in preparing for the establishment of his rule in the world goes on, unnoticed by most of humanity, like leaven hidden in measures of flour (Q 13:20–21). God's purpose through Jesus and the followers whom he calls is compared with a shepherd whose concern for a single lost sheep leads him to abandon temporarily the flock as a whole, going into the wilderness to find the lost one, and returning filled with joy at its recovery (Q 15:4–7). Reconciliation of the lost and estranged has a higher priority in the Q portrayal of Jesus than does maintenance of the religious status quo within the traditional covenant people. Jesus has a special commendation and a promise for those who have remained faithful to him during his time of trial and hostile treatment by the religious and political authorities. He describes them in Q 22:28–30 as "those who have stood by me in my trials," and then promises them a share in the common life ("eat and drink") in the new era when God's rule will be established and participation in the judgment that will come for the traditional "twelve tribes of Israel." His disciples thus are seen as having a significant role in the evaluation and redefinition of the people of God that will take place when God's kingdom is established.

This is the culmination of the designation of and agenda for the people of God as set forth in the Q tradition. It does not give a comprehensive view of the career of Jesus or of his origins, as the canonical gospels do, but it presents a clear and vivid picture of God's purpose for renewal of his covenant people and the crucial role that Jesus is fulfilling in accomplishing that end. Thus, there is continuity in aim, but difference in strategy and content between Q and the literary mode that came to be known as a "gospel."

The Pauline Tradition about Jesus

In the Pauline letters, the primary interest in Jesus is his role as God's Messiah. There is statistical evidence for this in the fact that, while there are 147 references to Jesus by name, there are 187 places in which he is designated as *kurios* and 270 where he is called "the Christ," fifteen in which he is identified as "son" or "Son of God." Passages in Paul do refer to his human birth and the circumstances into which he was born. In Gal 4:4–6 we read that when God's chronological scheme reached the appropriate point ("when the fullness of time had come"), Jesus was born of a human mother ("God sent forth his Son, born of a woman"). The time of his coming was when the Jewish law was a dominant factor: "born under the law." The communication of God's message to his people has come "through the Spirit of His Son," so that those whose relationship to God was based on the obedience to the law of Moses may be transformed from that of slave to the law to children whose intimate link with God is conveyed in the affectionate term, "Abba."

In the Christ hymn of Phil 2:5–9, Jesus is said to have willingly stepped aside from the rank of "equality with God" and taken the role of a "servant," which entailed birth in human likeness and a life of obedience that led to his death in humiliation "on a cross." This was rewarded by God's exaltation of him and his future role in which everyone in earth and heaven will bow "at the name of Jesus." In 1 Thess 4:13–18, there is a similar reference to the fact that "Jesus died and rose again," and that at his return in triumph, both the faithful who have died and those who are alive at his coming will be taken up "to meet the Lord in the air, and so we shall always be with the Lord." The role of Jesus as the agent and prototype of the resurrection of the faithful is set forth in more elaborate form in 1 Cor 15:21–28, where it is the man Jesus who has experienced both death and resurrection, unlike Adam and all his descendants who face only death. Christ is the exemplar of the new humanity—"the first fruits"—who, having completed his role as agent to establish God's rule ("kingdom") in the world and defeating all the agents of evil, hands it over to God. Thus is fulfilled the promise of total sovereignty of the universe to God, as promised in Psalm 8.

The one passage in Paul's letters that deals directly with an issue raised in the teachings of Jesus according to the gospel traditions is 1 Cor 7:10–12. There the issue is whether divorce and remarriage are proper for members of the new covenant community. Divorce is viewed negatively: the wife is instructed to remain single if she is divorced, or if possible to be reconciled to her husband. The husband is not to take the initiative in divorcing his wife. The basis for this set of rules is what "the Lord" taught in Mark 10:10–12, where divorce and remarriage are forbidden for husband and wife.[120] For Paul, divorce is unacceptable, even when there is an unbelieving spouse, since there can be a conveyance of holiness to the unconverted through the Christian spouse. Paul is wrestling with a difficult issue in the new community, addressing it by appeal to and interpretation of the tradition derived from Jesus.

The redemptive role of Jesus is spelled out in greater detail in the deuteropauline letter to the Ephesians (2:11–22). There Gentiles, who by birth are "alienated from the commonwealth of Israel and strangers to the covenant of promise," are said to have been "brought near by the blood of Christ." He has made one new people of God by "abolishing the law with its commandments and ordinances, so that he might create in himself one new humanity. . . ." It was for this end that "he came and proclaimed peace to you who were afar off and to you who were near," with the result that Gentiles "are no longer strangers and aliens, but saint and members of the household of God, built upon the foundation of the apostles and prophets." Although there are no quotes from Jesus' teaching and no references to his associations with Gentiles as reported in the gospel traditions, it is clear that in the letters of Paul and the Pauline tradition that built on them, Jesus' message is of paramount importance, even though the ultimate agent for reconciling humans to God is his death on the cross: "You who once were afar off have been brought near by the blood of Christ."

The Roles of Jesus and the Images of the New Community in the Canonical Gospels

It is essential to note that the four gospels in the New Testament differ not only in what they report about Jesus' life and teachings, but also in the way they represent the community of his followers, including the criteria for participation and their ultimate destiny. Clearly, by the time the gospels were written, there was not a single model for the perceptions of Jesus as Messiah or for defining the new people of God whom Jesus was believed to have called together. This range of perceptions of the role of Jesus and the consequences of what he said and did for the formation of the new covenant people are set forth in the canonical gospels.

The Apocalyptic Community: Mark

As indicated above, the theory that Mark is the oldest gospel, as well as the oldest extant gospel, seems to be the most plausible explanation for the literary relationships among the Synoptics.[121] But the question immediately arises: What sources and what literary models within the Christian tradition did Mark have on which to build? The author may have had collections of stories about Jesus or sayings of Jesus, but there is no evidence that, prior to Mark, they were woven into a continuous narrative as we now have them. The parables may have constituted one such group of sayings, just as the cluster of shorter miracle stories in Mark 2 and 3 and of longer stories in Mark 4 and 5 may have constituted collections of narratives on which Mark drew. A similar case could be made for individual sayings or collections of them that offered criticism of the Jewish tradition (Mark 7 and 10), presenting accounts of controversies with Jews (Mark 12) and containing eschatological themes (Mark 13). On the other hand, the present topical grouping could well come from Mark. Theories proposed for written sources of Mark are dubious, with the possible exception of collections of miracle stories.[122] Even in the case of the passion narrative—the only extended narrative sequence in the gospels—there is no sure evidence (as form critics have assumed)[123] that Mark had access to an existing document for Mark 11–16, or for any part of it. The same characteristics are evident there as are found in other parts of Mark. Mark 11–16 stresses that the events at the end of Jesus' life were divinely initiated, hence bringing about the fulfillment of scripture, so that the critical reader cannot tell whether the events have been conformed to scripture or (as seems likely in several cases) that scripture has been modified to fit the event. Almost everywhere in Mark the connective tissue by which Mark has joined together the sayings and narrative units is secondary; that is, it is the work of Mark himself. Almost certainly he had no sequential or chronological framework available to him, other than the obvious fact that the baptism of Jesus came at the outset of Jesus' ministry and the crucifixion came at the end. C. H. Dodd's attempt to prove otherwise is not persuasive.[124] There are a few points at which place names may have been preserved in the tradition on the basis of actual historical memory, as in the scene of the confession of Peter, which is located in the theologically and dogmatically insignificant vicinity of Caesarea Philippi (Mark 8:27).[125]

The freedom felt by the gospel writers to rearrange the order of events in the gospel tradition for programmatic or literary purposes is shown by Luke's placing Jesus' rejection at Nazareth at the outset of his public ministry (Luke 4), whereas in Mark it comes in the middle of the story of Jesus' activity (Mark 6:1). The miracle stories of Mark (Mark 1 and 2) are moved by Matthew to a point following the Sermon on the Mount (Matt 5, 6, and 7) because that best suited Matthew's arrangement of material in alternating panels of activity and discourse.[126] The sense of movement and sequence that the reader receives in Mark's gospel comes from Mark's own arrangement of the tradition, as K. L. Schmidt showed in his pioneering form-critical study, *Der Rahmen der Geschichte Jesu* [The Framework of the History of Jesus]. As Schmidt points out, "in Mark's introductions to the pericopes, there can still be traced vestiges of an itinerary."[127] But only traces of an itinerary remain, and these are confused as a result of Mark's lack of detailed knowledge of Palestinian geography. The report that Jesus went from Tyre and Sidon through the cities of the Decapolis on his way back to the Sea of Galilee sounds as odd to one who knows Palestine as to say that a man stopped off in Boston on his way from New York to Philadelphia. Designations of temporal connections are rare, but where they do occur, as in Mark 9:1—"after six days," that is, one week later— they show us only that Mark may have preserved the few temporal links that he found in the tradition,[128] although these phrases could as well be Markan stylizations intended to impart dramatic movement to the story sequence.

The Gospel Tradition as Received by Mark

Mark seems to have received his material in a period of oral transmission, or perhaps when pre-gospel documents were available in addition to the oral transmission process, which continued even after the gospels had been written.[129] But what Mark received came to him in isolated pericopes of two main types: sayings tradition and narrative tradition, the various modes of which may be defined as follows:

SAYINGS TRADITION

The sayings tradition in the gospels may be grouped in the following categories:

1. Aphorisms. Brief, proverb-like statements of exhortations. Example: "He who has ears to hear, let him hear" (Mark 4:9). Mark positioned this type of saying where he thought it fit, a judgment that does not always correspond with the opinion of modern commentators and critics.

2. Parables. Comparisons are offered in a descriptive or narrative mode. Example: the parable of the Productive Seed (= the parable of the Sower, Mark 4:3–8). Mark interprets this parable as an allegory of the variety of hearers of the gospel in the church (Mark 4:14–20).

3. Sayings clusters. These are of two types:

   a. Topical groupings. Example: the salt words (Matt 5:13–16).

   b. Formal groupings. Example: the Beatitudes and Woes (Luke 6:20–26).

NARRATIVE TRADITION

These traditions may be grouped in the following categories:

1. Anecdotes. Example: the story of the demoniac in the synagogue at Capernaum (Mark 1:23–26). These are brief biographical narratives.

2. Aphoristic narratives. Example: the plucking of grain on the Sabbath (Mark 2:23–28). A blending of narrative and sayings material, these narratives culminate in pithy sayings.

3. Wonder stories. Example: Mark 5:1–20. In these stories, the main point is the wonder itself, the miraculous as such.

4. Legends. These are narratives in which the divine is directly or publicly manifest. They are of two types.

   a. Biographical legends. Example: the temptation story, especially in the Q form found in Matthew and Luke (Matt 4:1–11; Luke 4:1–12). The main interest in the legends is in the divine as disclosed in Jesus' life and activity.

   b. Cult legends. Example: the Feeding of the Five Thousand (Mark 6:30–44). The main interest is in authorization of or grounding for the church's cult, which is here the Eucharist.

5. Passion story. In its present form, this is the only extended sequential account preserved in the gospel tradition. The extent to which it (1) preserves pre-Markan reports of the course of events, or (2) to which it has been given this continuity by Mark in the interest of demonstrating Jesus' trial and death as the fulfillment of scripture is difficult to determine.

Working with these disconnected elements as components for writing his gospel, it would not have been possible for the author to infer a series of sure cause-and-effect links that would offer an explanation for the dynamics of

Jesus' ministry or the sequence in the events that led to his crucifixion. Nor is there the slightest possibility of reconstructing any detailed inward process by which Jesus came to understand his own role in God's plan or in what terms he came to view his own impending death. To the extent that such a developmental pattern of messianic role can be discerned in the Gospel of Mark, it is probably to be attributed to Mark himself and to the literary method by which he presents and expands his basic themes.

One must distinguish between Mark's themes and the gospel outline he uses to give what is mostly the appearance, but in part also the strategy, of a historical sequence of events. Mark placed the traditional material into the following structural framework:

1. Preparation for Ministry (1:1–20)
2. The Kingdom Announced in Word and Act (1:21–8:26)
3. What Messiahship and Discipleship Mean (8:27–10:45)
4. Preparation for the Events of the End (11:1–14:25)
5. The Passion and the Parousia (14:26–16:8)

The sense of urgency and tension in Mark's account is heightened not only in editorial ways, such as his twelve-times-repeated "immediately," but also in the recurrent juxtaposition of challenge and rejection, of confession and denial, which highlights both the feeling of eschatological imminence and the importance for the reader of a faith decision.

The Major Themes in Mark's Gospel

Intertwined in the Gospel of Mark (so that more than one theme may be present in a single pericope) are the following major themes:

1. Jesus as the Fulfillment of Scripture
2. The Messianic Roles and Titles of Jesus
3. Jesus as Salvation-Bringer in His Public Ministry
4. The Apocalyptic Necessity of Jesus' Death; His Return in Triumph
5. Ministry, Ethics, and Cultus in the New Community

Each of these themes, as we shall see, is fundamental to Mark's overall thesis that the eschatological event proclaimed in the kerygma had its beginning in the historical figure of Jesus of Nazareth.[130]

JESUS AS THE FULFILLMENT OF SCRIPTURE

It is tempting to suppose that the gospel writers appealed to scripture frequently in their portrayals of Jesus as an apologetic tactic, in order to lend authority to the claim of the early church to be the new people of God developed on the foundation of Jewish hopes and expectations. This somewhat condescending estimate is made the more appealing by the fact that, gauged by modern interpretive standards, the New Testament writers exercised an embarrassing degree of freedom in applying an Old Testament text to their situation. The fact that the rabbis were performing the same sort of exegetical sleight of hand (or even that similarly fanciful essays in Old Testament hermeneutics have been discovered at Qumran)[131] does not dispel the impression that the methods are artificial judged by modern scholarly standards. Historically trained Christian interpreters are made more than a little uncomfortable by what they find the New Testament claiming to have happened "according to the Scriptures."[132] But far more important than the documentation provided by scripture was the power of the belief, shared by the Qumran Essenes and the early church, that the scriptures were not so much chronicles of the past as blueprints for the future that God had in store for his creation in general, and for his people in particular. It was the belief in the actualization of the eschatological plan laid down in the scriptures, and now being rightly interpreted and carried out in and through contemporary events, which was the ground of the importance of scripture in the first century CE. Thus Mark launches into "the beginning of the gospel" (Mark 1:1) with the claim that through Jesus' baptism at the hand of John were fulfilled both the promise of an eschatological messenger (Mal 3:1) and the announcement of the act of the one who would prepare for the Lord's coming (Isa 40:3). The fact that the quotation as a whole is wrongly attributed to Isaiah and that Second Isaiah's expectation was of the coming of Yahweh, not explicitly of Jesus Christ as Lord, does not obscure the theological assertion that is being made: it is for God's Son, Jesus of Nazareth, that John the Baptist was sent to prepare the way. In a way that could not have been anticipated by the human author of these prophecies, the promise of God is seen as being fulfilled through Jesus.[133]

It is impossible to tell how much of the detail given in the tradition concerning John the Baptist is historical recollection about him that is being passed on from his contemporaries and how much is Christian interpretation of his role in the light of the Old Testament. If there are historically reliable features, then the Baptist may have modeled his attire after Elijah (2 Kgs 1:8), whose coming is announced in Mal 4:5 as an agent to bring about eschatological judgment, as was widely expected in late Judaism.[134] If the latter— that is, if Mark shaped his picture of John by recalling such Old Testament allusions to the Lord's forerunner as Mal 3:1–2—then we see that in this case also it was the belief that God's redemptive plan was nearing completion that motivated Mark's and the tradition's appeal to scripture as finding fulfillment in Jesus. Early Christian faith deemed it essential that there be discernible correspondence between what the scriptures announced and what was actually occurring, since the apocalyptic view of history required that the outworking of the divine purpose be seen in current events or in the recent past. Whether the modern reader finds the alleged correspondence convincing is not the point: what was essential at Qumran and for the author of Mark was the demonstration in the realm of observable history of the fulfillment of what God had announced beforehand through the prophets. Only in this way could one be certain that the eschatological schedule was leading to the redemptive climax for the covenant people.

The statistics for scriptural quotations and allusions in Mark are revealing.[135] There are hundreds of these in Mark as a whole, of which more than fifty-seven are in Mark 11–16. Only eight of these are from the Torah, and all but one of those appears in the controversies over the law in Mark 12. Two references are from the historical writings, twelve are from the Psalms, twelve from Daniel, and the remaining twenty-one are from the other prophetic writings. As for the 160 allusions to scripture in this part of Mark, half are from the prophets (excluding Daniel) and the rest are evenly divided from Daniel, Psalms, Torah, and noncanonical writings. The influence of Daniel on Mark is also evident in his blending of miracle stories, predictions of martyrdom, personal (Mark 9) and cosmic revelations (Mark 13). Thus, the influence of apocalyptic on Mark is evident in both the structure and the contents of the discourse material—especially, of course, in the synoptic apocalypse of Mark 13.

Unlike Jewish apocalyptic, however, with its emphasis on the special moral and cultic demands for the faithful and on the rewards they are to receive for participation in the people of God, Mark pictures Jesus as defining a community that is to be accessible to non-Jews and to Jews who do not conform to the dominant covenantal standards. Jesus is pictured in Mark as frequently having physical contact with those whose ailments would consign them to the ritually impure, and as rejecting the notion that sickness or disabilities are evidence of divine disfavor or punishment. Jesus touches Peter's paralytic mother-in-law and heals her (1:31), as he does a leper (1:40–45) and a paralytic, whose sins he declares to be forgiven (2:1–12). He violates the law as then widely understood by healing a man with a withered hand on the Sabbath, and defends his action by declaring that one should do good on the Sabbath (3:1–6). The controversial nature of these actions is dramatically evident in the report that, as a result of these ritually illegal actions, the Pharisees and the Herodians begin to conspire to destroy Jesus. These touchings and healings of the sick lead to his rejection in his hometown of Nazareth (6:1–6).

Further compounding his role and fostering opposition from the law-observant is Jesus' reaching out to those in need of healing from outside the people or the land of the Jews. In 3:7–12, the multitude that comes to be healed by him are from not only Jewish regions (Galilee, Judea, Jerusalem), but also from Idumea and beyond the Jordan, as well as from Tyre and Sidon. One of the most extended accounts of his performing exorcisms concerns a demoniac from Gerasa, one of the Hellenistic cities of the Decapolis; and it is in those cities that the cured man proclaims what Jesus has done for him. Conversely, Jesus was rejected at Nazareth, as Mark reports (6:1–6). His work continues in Hellenistic regions, as at Gennesaret and apparently adjacent villages and countryside, where the sick are brought to touch him—even the fringe of his garment (6:53–56). Healings continue in the vicinity of Tyre and Sidon, where the Syro-Phoenician woman appeals to him on behalf of her demon-possessed son (7:24–30), and in the region of the Decapolis (7:31–37). The import of these actions as a challenge to ethnic and cultic separation (which is evident in the Dead Sea Scrolls and the Pharisaic traditions) is intensified in Mark when Jesus is reported as rejecting the notion that defilement comes through outward, physical contact, and as insisting that the locus of defilement is the human heart (7:1–23).

The picture of Jesus as setting aside ethnic and ritual boundaries in calling men and women to share in the covenant community includes the parallel Mark offers between (1) the miraculous feeding of the five thousand (6:30–44) in an arid setting reminiscent of Moses' role as the agent through whom manna came to the people of Israel in the desert of Sinai, and (2) the feeding of the four thousand (8:1–10), which he reports as taking place in Gentile territory. The contrasting imagery is heightened by the symbolic figures of the food remnants in each story: in the first story, twelve baskets of fragments, matching the number of the tribes of Israel as well as the twelve apostles; in the second story, there are seven baskets, which is the number of leaders chosen for the Gentile-oriented Hellenists and approved by the apostles in the account in Acts 6:1–6. The numerical symbolism of these two accounts of what in the Gospel of John is pictured as God's provision through Jesus of bread from heaven[136] seems to be intended in the Markan tradition of these two feeding stories: the first for Jews who share in the new covenant people, and the second for Gentiles who become part of this new community.

The form of appeal to the Old Testament in Mark varies widely. In most instances, a passage is directly quoted or alluded to quite explicitly. At other times, the correspondence between the narrative of the gospel and a prophetic passage must be inferred, as in Mark 11:1–9, where the details of the lowly king's entry match the prophecy of Zech 9:9—a link that is made explicit in Matthew's expanded version of the incident (Matt 21:1–9). The apocalyptic discourse in Mark 13 is filled with direct and indirect allusions to Old Testament passages. Details of the passion story are reported as corresponding closely with the Old Testament; indeed, there are more Old Testament allusions here than elsewhere in Mark. In the details of the crucifixion alone

(Mark 15:24–34), there are at least three recollections of Psalm 22. Thus, the Old Testament may have helped to shape the narrative, although the incidents must have been in some way analogous to Old Testament stories or prophecies from the outset in order for the parallels ever to have been noticed. One gospel passage, however, Mark 9:12, refers to what is "written," as though alluding to scripture, but no known Jewish writing contains such a prophecy (that is, of the suffering of the Son of Man).

The three major subjects pointed to by the Old Testament quotations in Mark are: (1) the judgment on Israel, (2) the reinterpretation of the commandments of God, and (3) the fulfillment of messianic hopes. All these are eschatological functions, of course, since the repristination of the law of God was one of the divine actions expected in late Judaism to occur in the end time. At Qumran, it was the Teacher of Righteousness, the eschatological prophet, who was to fulfill this role. In Mark, Jesus performs this function in denouncing the blindness of the faithless (Mark 4:12 = Isa 6:9–10); in criticizing the practice of allowing human traditions to supersede the divine command (Mark 7:6 = Isa 29:13); and in defending the belief in the resurrection (Mark 12:18–27 = Exod 3:6), even though in this case the weight of the argument is lost on the modern reader. No matter whether the arguments are still perceived as persuasive or not, the fact remains that Mark presents Jesus as one whose ministry among men was characterized by the work of interpreting anew God's law, and doing so not in continuity with rabbinic methods of interpretation (1:22) but with his own unprecedented authority. Clearly, Mark wants his reader to see in Jesus of Nazareth the eschatological messenger who restores what is now seen to be the true understanding of God's will in the end time. Mark spells out this role in relation to specific issues: the precedence of human need over Sabbath observance (2:26 = 1 Sam 21:1–6) and the priority in the created order for marriage over divorce, which is a concession to human frailty (10:2–12 = Gen 1:27; Deut 24:1–4).

Most important of all, however, is the correspondence that Mark and his tradition see between the Old Testament messianic hopes (as set forth in Pss 110 and 118 in particular) and the meaning of Jesus. Both these psalms were interpreted eschatologically in Judaism;[137] by pointing out the fulfillment of them in Jesus' teachings (12:10) and actions (11:9), Mark wants to show his readers that Jesus, who is worshiped as Lord in the church, was already the eschatological king in the days of his historical ministry, as reported in the synoptic tradition. Something of the difficulties that the early church had in interpreting Jesus in relation to these messianic categories is to be observed in the inconclusive controversy story that Mark pushed back into the ministry of Jesus (12:35–37). Anachronistically, Jesus is there depicted struggling with christological questions about himself only a few days before the crucifixion. But what Mark wants to show is that this issue was already implicit in the authoritative earthly ministry of Jesus. The historical critic knows, however, that the struggle over titles almost certainly did not take shape until after Easter.

THE MESSIANIC ROLES AND TITLES OF JESUS IN MARK

The disciples regularly refer to Jesus as "Rabbi" or "Teacher" (*didaskalos*), even in such circumstances as the storm on the lake, when, presumably, their thoughts were not on instructional matters (Mark 4:38). Mark's use of these terms may show that he has preserved the actual titles conferred on Jesus by his followers, probably after their vision of him having been raised from the dead. Paul's favorite title for Jesus, Lord (*kurios*), is rare in Mark (5:19 and 11:3); the occurrences probably betray an unconscious shift to the terminology of the church's post-Easter kerygma: "Jesus is Lord" (Phil 2:11, 1 Cor 12:3), which even on Mark's terms is not appropriate until after the resurrection. Mark's clear preferences as titles for Jesus are Son of God and Son of Man.

Son of God. Because Mark is convinced that the kingdom of God began to break into the old age in the person and ministry of Jesus, it is wholly fitting for him to locate the eschatological titles, Son of God and Son of Man, in Jesus' earthly ministry. In addition to sounding forth the title of Jesus as "Son of God" in his opening words (Mark 1:1), Mark reports that at Jesus' baptism, by a private, divine disclosure he was declared to be Son of God (Mark 1:11). The words attributed to the voice of God form a blend of phrases from Psalm 2 and from Isa 42. The first was addressed to David (or his successors) as those who ruled in God's stead; the second was uttered to the Servant of Yahweh, who is commended for his humility and persistence and endowed with God's Spirit to enable him to establish justice in the earth among the nations (Isa 42:1–4). Mark 10:42–45 expresses the view that the one chosen by God to establish the kingdom of God on the earth accomplishes his mission not by the exercise of brute force but by humble, self-sacrificing service. No claim is offered in either Psalm 2 or Isa 42 that God's agent of redemption is a divine being, so "Son of God" in Mark 1:1 is not to be perceived as an explicitly metaphysical term, which it subsequently became. Indeed, Mark gives no hint of a supernatural birth for Jesus; if there is any belief in the virgin birth abroad, Mary gives no hint of it in Mark's narrative. Indeed, she and her other sons are so unprepared for his authoritative way of commissioning disciples, expelling demons, and accepting acclaim as God's Son (3:11, 14) that they conclude he is crazy (3:21) and try to remove him from the public scene (3:31).[138]

Although the term *Son of God* is not used (as in Matthew) in connection with the confession of Peter (Mark 8:29), the title used, Christ, refers to the anointed figure or figures who were to reestablish the true kingship and the true cultus in the end time. The Christian faith in Jesus as a single kingly figure, to whom priestly functions are assigned in a peripheral manner (except in Hebrews, which is itself near the periphery of the canon), cannot obscure the fact that in late Judaism there was widespread belief in two anointed figures: the kingly figure from Judah and the priestly figure from Levi.[139] First attested in Zech 4 and 6, the theme of two anointed eschatological figures is a dominant one in the *Testament of Levi* (fragments of which have been found at Qumran).[140] However, since no contrary evidence is present in Mark, we can assume that for him the terms *king*, *Son of God*, and *Christ* are interchangeable: all point to the man divinely appointed to establish God's rule over his people and, through them, over the whole creation. What is new in Mark is his linking this kingly hope with the eschatological servant of Second Isaiah. The importance for Mark of the servant role of Isa 42 is stressed by the fact that Mark sees in Jesus' baptism the fulfillment of the prediction in 42:1, which describes God's pouring out his Spirit upon the servant to enable him to carry out his redemptive role. At Jesus' baptism he is acclaimed Son of God by a heavenly utterance (Mark 1:10–11).

The other crucial text in which the term "Son of God" is used is Mark 15:39. At the cross, having observed the darkness that covered the earth, the cry of Jesus, the scorn of the crowd, and the ripping of the temple veil, the centurion said: "Truly this man was a son of God!" Although the definite article is not used (not "*the* Son of God"), the pagan soldier's testimony is central for Mark. Through the cross, even Gentiles will recognize in Jesus the redeemer of mankind. The term *Son of God* seems to have carried quite different connotations in Gentile thinking, and Mark's account is not uninfluenced by these. The practice of deifying a great leader or wise man of the past was common throughout the Hellenistic and Roman worlds, but it is almost surely too much to claim that there was a fixed type, the *theios anēr*,[141] to which Mark conformed the image of Jesus. This notion, which arose in the heyday of the history of religions school, has been repeated so often that it has come to be accepted as a fact.[142] But in truth, except for a widespread fondness for apotheosis of great men, there is no set type or model of *theios aner*. That is not to say, however, that the tendency toward apotheosizing Jesus is not at work in Mark, nor in the tradition on which he drew. What is clear is that this does not constitute a major, conscious aim of Mark. The basic function of Jesus as Son of God in Mark is as bringer of the eschatological salvation, in keeping with the expectations of Jewish apocalypticism around the turn of the eras.

Son of Man. The influence of apocalypticism is even more apparent in Mark's use of the title Son of Man. Scholarly opinions about the meaning of this term in the gospel tradition vary widely.[143] Some scholars think that only future Son of Man words are authentic;[144] some are convinced that only the present Son of Man sayings go back to Jesus;[145] others are persuaded that all or nearly all the sayings are genuine;[146] and a few think that none of the sayings can be attributed to Jesus.[147] The background of the term, whether used by Jesus of himself or by the synoptic tradition in its interpretation of him, is Jewish apocalypticism.[148]

The hypothesis with the greatest potential for explaining the development of the various categories of Son of Man words as we now find them in the gospel tradition is the one advanced by H. E. Tödt.[149] According to Tödt, Jesus gathered around himself an eschatological community to whom he announced the coming of the Son of Man, who would judge men and women based on their response to him and his ministry. His message of the coming kingdom of God and the signs of its inbreaking, evident in his healings and exorcisms, called men and women to decision: the Son of Man would confirm that decision in the eschatological judgment (Mark 8:38).

When Jesus' fellowship with his own followers was reconstituted in the post-resurrection appearances, they came to believe that Jesus was himself the Son of Man, whose coming as judge they still awaited. In the light of this conviction, the gospel tradition read back into his earthly ministry this insight into who Jesus was: the Son of Man. The pre-Markan tradition went on from that interpretive point to consider Jesus' suffering as a necessary part of his role as Son of Man (Mark 8:32; 9:31; 10:32–34). But before examining the eschatological framework in which Mark presents the passion of Jesus, we must look more closely at his description of Jesus' public ministry and message.

In Mark, Jesus receives confirmation of his unique role as God's agent for renewal of the covenant people and for establishing God's rule in the world in a variety of ways. Noted above is the voice at his baptism acclaiming him as Son of God (3:8–11). His ability to still the storm (4:35–41) leads the disciples to raise the question: "Who then is this, that even wind and sea obey him?"—the clear implication being that he embodies the power of God. The multiplication of loaves and fishes to feed the five thousand (6:30–44) and then the four thousand (8:1–10) recalls God's provision of food for Israel in the wilderness (Exod 16; Num 11) as they were being led by God's agent, Moses, from slavery in Egypt to establishment as God's people in their own land. Jesus' walking on the water (6:45–50) recalls God's control of the waters as described in Gen 1:6–7 and when the Israelites were enabled to cross the sea into the Sinai peninsula (Exod 14:21–30). This divine capability is extolled in Ps 89:8–9 and in the Song of Moses (Exod 15:1–18).

JESUS AS SALVATION-BRINGER IN HIS PUBLIC MINISTRY

Mark's understanding of the intention of Jesus' public ministry is expressed succinctly in Mark 1:15: "The time [*kairos*] is fulfilled, and the kingdom of God is at hand; repent, and believe in the gospel [good news]." What is involved in Jesus' gospel is made clear immediately in the story of the demoniac in the synagogue at Capernaum (Mark 1:23–26). A central element in the story is the question of the demon (or the demoniac as his spokesman): "Have you come to destroy us?" The tradition could scarcely make its point more forcefully. To destroy Satan and his hosts is precisely what Jesus has come to do. The interrogative style is replaced by a straight declarative mode in a related passage (Mark 3:22–27) in which a series of sayings point to Jesus' role as the agent through whom Satan's dynasty will be shattered and his possessions plundered. The Q version of this incident makes the point even more explicitly: "If it is by the finger of God that I cast out demons, then the kingdom of God has come upon you" (Luke 11:20). Mark, however, uses a technical term in the exorcism accounts, *epitimao*, which translates a Semitic word meaning "to utter a commanding word by which an enemy is subjugated."[150] This is the significance attached to Jesus' exorcisms, and perhaps to his healings, in the earliest tradition: by Jesus' powerful acts, Satan's control over the creation was being wrested from him as a necessary step toward the establishment of God's rule. Mark modified this intention of the miracle stories somewhat by shifting the focus at times (especially in Mark 5:1–20) to the thaumaturgic, or wonder-working, technique and to the person of the wonder-worker, as in pagan miracle tales. But Mark's changes do not obscure or conflict with his own overall aim of presenting Jesus as the bringer of the message and the signs of the new age.

Mark shares with Q the belief that Jesus is the eschatological bringer of salvation, but he lays great stress on Jesus' "mighty works" as manifestations of the inbreaking of the rule of God. Q, as we have observed, holds the same view of the meaning of Jesus' exorcisms, but in fact the Q material is almost wholly limited to sayings tradition. Mark differs from Q also in the sense of apocalyptic urgency that pervades his gospel. The message of the imminently coming kingdom is directly set out in the apocalyptic discourse (Mark 13) and metaphorically proclaimed in the parables of the kingdom (Mark 4). Although Mark reproduced the older—and almost certainly more nearly original—form and intent of these parables, with their encouragement to the messengers of the kingdom to carry out their work without calculating the results (which are, after all, in God's hands), he also added allegorical explanations that turn attention to the inner state of the eschatological community.[151] But the apocalyptic images of the harvest still predominate: by retaining the emphasis on the judgment, Mark kept the parables within their original eschatological atmosphere. The shorter parabolic sayings, such as those dealing with the bridegroom and the wineskins, are likewise built on apocalyptic imagery and remind the hearer or reader that the day of reckoning lies ahead (Mark 2:18–22). As a result, the churchly question about whether or not to fast is settled based on an eschatological pronouncement: "The days will come. . . ."

In the context of the announcement by Jesus of his suffering and death (8:27–31), Mark introduces the apocalyptic prediction of the coming in glory of the Son of Man (8:38) that is linked with the coming in power of the kingdom of God (9:1). Precisely because this section of Mark is composite in its present form, we can be sure that Mark placed these materials together with full intent: Jesus' acceptance of the cross and Peter's satanically originated remonstration (8:32–33) are linked with the prophetic words about the coming Son of Man and the coming with power of God's kingdom. Jesus' message and ministry, as well as his passion and death, are set by Mark within a sequence of apocalyptic events: a schedule of eschatological actions by which God will establish his rule over creation.

The direct pronouncement of the apocalyptic role of Jesus is given in Mark 13, which is likewise composite. How much of this apocalyptic discourse goes back to Jesus is variously assessed,[152] but Mark placed it in a strategic spot—just before the passion narrative and just after the prediction of the destruction of the temple—in order to show Jesus' crucial role in the apocalyptic scheme of things. After all these catastrophes have occurred on earth and in the cosmos, "the Son of man" will be seen "coming in clouds with great power and glory" (Mark 13:26). In keeping with the conventions of apocalyptists, Mark asserts that the end will be soon, within the lifetime of Jesus' hearers (13:30), but that the exact time is known only to God (13:32). Thus, it is in the interest of documenting his reading of the tradition concerning Jesus that Mark, or the source on which he drew, assigns to the earthly Jesus throughout his gospel the titles Son of God (king) and Son of Man (eschatological salvation-bringer). The implications of these features for the perception of Jesus' role and for the life of the new community are examined in the next sections.

THE APOCALYPTIC NECESSITY OF JESUS' DEATH; HIS RETURN IN TRIUMPH

Mark presents Jesus' passion as an essential element in a series of eschatological events rather than as the basis of a developed doctrine of the atonement. From the first prediction of the passion onward, Mark reports Jesus as describing his impending death in terms of apocalyptic necessity (*dei*),[153] or simply as certain to occur in the apocalyptic scheme of things ("how is it written of the Son of Man that he should suffer many things?"—Mark 9:12). Although we know of no such apocalyptic document in which the suffering of the Son of Man is predicted, Mark's appeal to what is "written" suggests that he either had such a document or assumed its existence. In any case, he makes no claim for having originated the idea of the Son of Man who must suffer. From this (perhaps hypothetical) document, Mark concluded that the passion of Jesus was a necessary event in the working out of the divinely determined apocalyptic scheme of "history," both past and future.

The apocalyptic necessity of Jesus' death is underscored in Mark not only in the explicit predictions of the passion[154] but also in metaphorical allusions to it: the bridegroom taken away (2:20), the cup of suffering, and the baptism to be endured (10:38). The nearest Mark comes to an interpretation of Jesus' death as an atonement is in 10:45, where the life of the Son of Man is said to be given "as a ransom for many." In spite of learned efforts to link this phrase with Paul or with Isa 53, the fact remains that the verse says only that in some unspecified way Jesus' giving up his life will effect release "for many." This notion of the redemptive benefits from the death of a righteous man could be understood in terms of the cult of the martyrs,[155] or simply as a part of the messianic woes that "must" occur before the new age dawns (Mark 13:7–8). The closest one can come to an interpretation of the death of Jesus in Mark is in the eucharistic word (Mark 14:24–25) and in the parable of the Vineyard Workers (12:1–11). In the first instance, the life given ("blood . . . poured out") is associated with the covenant,[156] a term that is given eschatological significance by Mark's placing beside it the saying about Jesus drinking the fruit of the vine on "that day . . . in the kingdom of God." Similar positive meaning is given to the death of Jesus in the parable of the Vineyard Workers, where his rejection is presented as a necessary step prior to his becoming the "head of the corner," in fulfillment of Ps 118:22–23. What is at stake, as is shown by (Jesus'? Mark's? the tradition's?) use of the allegorical representation of Israel as a vineyard, purged (Isa 5:1–7) and then reconstituted, is the founding of a new people: an eschatological community. In rejecting Jesus as the embodiment of God's final prophetic word, the leaders of the Jewish nation are unwittingly laying the foundation for the new community. This seems to be the fundamental meaning given by Mark, and/or the tradition on which he drew, to the death of Jesus.

Because the cross is not described in Mark as the basis for a doctrine of the atonement—other than the statement of Jesus to the disciples that "the Son of Man [is] to give his life as a ransom for many" (10:45)—there is no problem of moving from his death to the Parousia or of linking the Parousia with the resurrection. Following the Last Supper, as Jesus and the disciples move out to the Mount of Olives, he warns them that their impending desertion of him (the scattering of the sheep after the shepherd has been struck, Zech 13:7) will be followed by his preceding them to Galilee, a promise of which they are reminded by the young man at the tomb who tells them that Jesus has been raised from the dead (16:7). Both resurrection and parousia are terms Mark uses to represent a single, central apocalyptic event: the vindication of Jesus as triumphant Son of Man and founder of the eschatological community. The explicit predictions of the passion are also always announcements of the resurrection (8:31; 9:31: 10:32–33). Jesus' metaphorical warning, couched in apocalyptic language, that the shepherd is about to be struck (14:27),[157] leads directly to an announcement of his resurrection and the reassembling of the eschatological community under Peter (14:28). This is a promise recalled by the supernatural messenger in the post-resurrection scene (16:6–7) in which the cross is once more presented as a prelude to the reconstitution of the circle of followers: "Do not be amazed; you seek Jesus of Nazareth, who was crucified. He has risen, he is not here. . . . But go, tell his disciples and Peter that he is going before you to Galilee; there you will see him, as he told you."

MINISTRY, ETHICS, AND CULTUS IN THE NEW COMMUNITY

Because Mark regards history as the chain of events by which the divine purpose is worked out through struggle and seeming defeat, it is not surprising that he can discover authorization in the period of Jesus' earthly ministry for the practices that are the concern of the eschatological community as it awaits the final, victorious disclosure of God's redemptive agent, Jesus, the Son of Man. Accordingly, the ethical norms, the missionary practices and pitfalls, and the cultic life of the community are all read out of—or back into—the lifetime of Jesus.

In the course of setting forth his account of Jesus' ministry, Mark addresses the specific problems the early Christian church faced in relation to the conventions and circumstances of the day, especially those that prevailed in law-abiding Judaism of the first century CE. Since the new covenant community pictured in Mark was so deeply conscious of itself as heir to the promises made to Israel, it could not merely brush aside the distinctive features of Jewish piety. What should the attitude of the church be toward Sabbath observance, fasting, prayer, dietary laws, eating a meal with those who are ritually or religiously impure? Each of these issues is addressed by Jesus in the Markan gospel.

In addition, problems arose from the historical circumstances of life in first-century Palestine. What should be the relationship of the Christians to Roman authorities? Further, how was a Christian to understand God's seeming judgment on Judaism, as evidenced by the destruction of the temple? What right had the church to announce the forgiveness of sins? What lay behind the sacraments of baptism and the Eucharist? Why had not Jesus' claim to the fulfillment of scripture—which was so obvious to the Christians' way of thinking—been recognized by the Jews who knew and searched the scriptures? These and related issues remain largely implicit in Mark, but are the subject of direct address and proposed solutions in the other gospels, as is indicated in the analyses of them below.

The clue to the new community's understanding of God's purpose through Jesus, and the lack of such comprehension among outsiders, is made explicit in Mark's account of Jesus' private explanation of his parables to the twelve disciples: "To you has been given the secret [or mystery] of the kingdom of God, but for those outside everything comes in parables" (Mark 4:10–11). Here "parable" is perceived as not simply a rhetorical form of communication based on a comparison, but as a divinely intended enigma, the meaning of which is reserved for the faithful community. This perception closely resembles the claim set forth in the *Habakkuk Commentary* found among the Dead Sea Scrolls (1QpHab), which states that comprehension of visions is perceptible only to those who have been granted divine interpretation. A similar apocalyptic view that God grants meaning only to those inside the faithful community appears in Daniel.[158] In Mark, however, Jesus immediately offers an explanation of the parable of the Sower, which promises divine support for those who avoid preoccupation with worldly values, but warns of loss of privileged participation for those who are satanically deprived of the message from Jesus ("the word," 4:15), or who fail to endure when persecution comes (4:13–19). These are contrasted with those to whom the divine insights have been granted, and who persevere in faith and fruitfulness (4:20) as productive members of the community (4:22–25).

The parables in Mark point to both the mixed results of their efforts and the great productivity of God's work in preparing for the coming of his kingdom: the diverse yields of the sowing of seed (4:1–9; 13–20); the mustard seed, smallest of all, produces the greatest of shrubs (4:30–32). Though the understanding of the parables is intentionally secret (4:11–12), it is reserved for and disclosed to the disciples, for whom Jesus is said to have provided private explanations (4:33–34). It is they, of course, who have the crucial role in spreading the gospel and inviting a wide range of humanity to become part of the new covenant people who await the coming kingdom of God.

Mark's Perception of Jesus' Challenge to Jewish Institutions and Eschatological Hopes

Jesus as depicted in Mark is engaged in a broad and deep challenge to Jewish authorities and institutions as he announces the coming kingdom of God and demonstrates the transforming power by which this new age will arrive and the covenant community will be redefined.

Two of the most controversial issues are evident in Jesus' challenge to the ancient Jewish rules that require (1) fasting and (2) abstinence from work on the Sabbath. In 2:18–22, there is a report of the question raised by two devout and law-abiding Jewish groups—the Pharisees and the disciples of John the Baptist—as to why Jesus' disciples do not observe the pious practice of fasting. In the Jewish tradition, fasting, or abstaining from food, included both public and private observances. It was regarded as a sign of the community's confession of its sin and its call to repentance (Neh 9:1–3). Public fasts are reported to have been called for in 2 Chron 20:3 and in Ezra 8:21–23, where one is called to reinforce a prayer for divine protection of the people of Israel as they returned to their land. In Joel 1:8–2:17, the prophet calls for a fast by the people as a sign of penitence for sins that have resulted in the devastation of the land by locusts. Private fasts include those of Ahab, whose fasting after his rebuke by Elijah led to his avoiding divine destruction (1 Kgs 21:17–28).

The response of Jesus to the question why his disciples do not fast makes two points. First, Jesus' presence among them is an occasion for joy, like that of wedding guests when the bridegroom is with them; when he has been taken from them, there will be a time for penitence and sorrow represented by fasting. Second, a new reality has come into the world with the arrival of Jesus, and there is no more sense in applying old practices to the present than there would be to put a new patch on a worn-out garment or to put new wine in process of fermentation into old, stiff wineskins.

The second issue raised by the Pharisees concerns Jesus' and the disciples' violation of the prohibition of work on the Sabbath (Exod 20:8–11), which is perceived as a commemoration of God's rest on the seventh day of creation (Gen 2:1–3). Jesus' response is that there is scriptural precedent for his disciples' having helped themselves to grain in a field belonging to others; it is not a violation of the Torah, since it is permitted to do so to meet one's daily need (Deut 23:25), just as David ate the sacred Bread of the Presence in the sanctuary (1 Sam 21:1–7) when he was without food during his flight from Saul. Jesus' point is that the Sabbath was established to benefit humans, not as an institution to which they are obligated even in a time of deprivation. Jesus makes a similar point when he heals a man on the Sabbath (3:1–6): human need and the opportunity to help others transcends the obligation to observe the Sabbath. The seriousness of this violation of Torah is seen as having led the Pharisees to conspire with an unlikely group—the Herodians, the Jews who gained power by collaborating with the Romans.

A third factor in the conflict of Jesus with the Jewish religious leadership concerns his making physical contact with those who by physical condition or ethnic origin or chosen occupation would be considered unclean and untouchable by the norms of Jewish piety in that era. The kosher laws of Jewish separation are simply set aside by Jesus as he is seen in the Markan tradition. Thus, Jesus, on meeting Simon Peter's ailing mother-in-law, reached out his hand to touch her and heal her (1:29–31). The significance of physical contact with those who are sick—and hence ritually impure—is likewise evident in the story of the woman with the issue of blood who touches Jesus and is healed, and in the report of Jesus touching and healing the sick following his rejection in his hometown, Nazareth (6:1–6). The radical nature of this redefining of the basis for participation in the covenant people is perhaps most dramatically formulated in the Markan tradition when Jesus is notified that his family has come seeking him. To this he responds that his true brothers and sisters and parents are those who "do the will of God" (3:31–35)—which of course implies the will of God as he perceives and articulates it.

The inclusiveness of this new community is further evident in Mark's reports of the places of origin of those who come to Jesus seeking to be healed: not only from distinctively Jewish areas (such as Galilee, Judea, and Jerusalem) but also from Gentile regions: Idumea and beyond the Jordan, Tyre and Sidon (3:7–12). The most dramatic evidence of this inclusiveness of Jesus' healing activity comes in the story of his expelling the demons from the possessed man from the region of Gerasa—one of the cities of the Decapolis (Ten Towns), the confederation of cities built and operated in the Hellenistic style as to architecture,[159] facilities, and organization.

But Jesus' outreach to non-Jews is further indicated in the accounts of his landing at Gennesaret, a Hellenized region overlooking the Sea of Galilee from the northeast, from the villages and countryside of which were brought the ailing to be healed by touching Jesus (6:53–56). Other Graeco-Roman places Jesus visited to heal the sick include "the region of Tyre and Sidon" (7:24), "the region of the Decapolis" (7:31), and "the villages of Caesarea Philippi" (8:27)—a city located well north of the Sea of Galilee and the location of a shrine of Pan, the Greek and Roman nature god. It was rebuilt by Herod's son Philip, who renamed it in honor of the Roman emperor and himself. The nexus of the role of Jesus in establishing the new covenant community and the wide cultural context in which this was taking place could scarcely be more dramatically evident.

Jesus' Pronouncement of the End of the Temple and the Redefinition of the Davidic Messiah

The temple in Jerusalem, which was perceived to be the place where the God of Israel dwelt among his people and hence was known as "the House of Yahweh," had been a central feature of the religion of Israel from the time of its erection under Solomon in the tenth century BCE. The inner sanctuary, where God was believed to dwell (1 Kgs 6:13), was accessible only to the high priest, and only once a year on the Day of Atonement.[160] Destroyed by the Babylonians in 586 BCE (2 Kgs 25:8–17), the temple was rebuilt on a much smaller scale under the Jewish governor, Zerubbabel, appointed by the Persians and a descendant of David (Hag 2:3; Ezra 3:12). But Herod erected on the site a magnificent structure in Graeco-Roman style, with impressive gates and imposing colonnades—probably motivated by a mixture of pride and a desire to ingratiate himself with his Jewish subjects. It was destroyed by the Romans under Titus in response to the First Jewish Revolt, although the image of the temple as the place where God dwells among his people continued to appear in Jewish—and in early Christian—literature.

Jesus' major challenges to the temple were threefold. First, he drove out from its courts those engaged in operations essential for the functioning of the temple: those who sold sacrificial animals and those who changed money into the special temple currency to be presented as offerings (Mark 11:15–19). Further, in a pair of quotations from the prophets he reminded his hearers that the temple had been intended as "a house of prayer for all peoples" (Isa 56:7) and that it had been converted into "a den of robbers" (Jer 7:11). Then he announced that the temple was going to be totally destroyed (Mark 13:2). These pronouncements and predictions challenged the basic Jewish convictions about the special ethnic and ritual identity of the people of Israel and the unique locus of God's presence in their midst.

The redefining of the covenant people is furthered in both explicit and metaphorical fashion in the Markan tradition, and in a manner that makes direct claims to the establishing of the kingdom of God in the tradition of David. On entering Jerusalem on the colt of an ass (11:1–10), Jesus is publicly claiming to be the expected king of Israel (Isa 62:11; Zech 9:9; which is directly quoted in the Matthean parallel [Matt 21:5–6]) and permits his supporters to make this claim explicit in their acclaim of him in words taken from Ps 118:25–26: "Hosanna! Blessed is the one who comes in the name of the Lord! Blessed is the coming kingdom of our father, David!" The traditional Jewish expectations of the coming of the kingdom of God are further challenged by Jesus' raising the question as he was teaching in the temple as to how David—to whom is attributed the passage from Ps 110:1 that refers to the one who defeats the enemies of God and is granted the seat of honor and authority at God's right hand—could refer to this agent of God as both "his son" and "his Lord" (12:35–37a). No direct answer is provided in Mark, but the implication is clear: Jesus as Messiah is both descendant of David and his Lord.

The Plot to Kill Jesus

In Mark's account, the response to Jesus' challenge to his Jewish contemporaries reaches a climax in the secret plot of the Jewish leaders—priests and scribes—"to arrest him by stealth, and kill him" (14:2). Jesus is seen as anticipating his death (1) when a woman came to him in Bethany, just outside Jerusalem, and poured costly ointment on his head (14:3–9), and (2) when he tells the disciples as they have gathered in Jerusalem to celebrate the Passover (14:12–21) that one of them is going to betray him to the chief priests (14:12–21). He identifies the shared bread and wine as his body and blood, about to be offered to seal the new covenant (14:22–24), the ultimate consequence of which will be his sharing with them in the coming "kingdom of God." God's vindication of him will make this possible. Meanwhile, however, all the disciples will abandon him when he is seized and executed by the civil authorities—which he sees as anticipated by the prophet Zechariah

(14:27 = Zech 13:7). Nevertheless, he will join them again in Galilee (14:28). Peter's claim that he will remain faithful to Jesus is countered by the prediction of his threefold denial (14:29–31), described as taking place in the courtyard outside the building where the high priest is examining Jesus (14:66–72). The hearing takes place before the regional council, the *synedrion*, whose members were those of wealth and power in a region who were given a degree of local autonomy in exchange for retaining ultimate control in the hands of the imperial monarch. In the Jerusalem area, the chief local authorities were the high priest—who was appointed by the Roman senate—and his associates. The council could find no charge against Jesus that would warrant execution. False witnesses gave inconsistent testimony that he had predicted his destruction and rebuilding of the temple, to which Jesus repeatedly refused to offer any defense (14:57–60). In response to the high priest's direct question, however, he did claim to be the messiah, and further claimed his future exaltation at God's right hand and his glorious return to earth (14:61–62). The council was unanimous in considering his answer to be blasphemy and thus in condemning him to execution. Yet the case was turned over to the Roman authority, Pilate, whose accusation was political: that Jesus claimed to be "King of the Jews" (15:1–3). The offer to release Jesus or one of the other insurrectionist prisoners (15:6–15) underscores the report that it was as a political pretender that Jesus was to be executed—an inference confirmed by (1) the fact that the mode of execution was Roman, crucifixion; (2) by the mockery of Jesus by the soldiers (15:18) and formally by the charge affixed to the cross: "the King of the Jews" (15:26). Mockery of his role as king is reflected in the crown of thorns and the robe of royal purple (15:20), and by the chief priests saying that the one who claims to be the messiah, king of Israel, should come down from the cross (15:31–32). The divine sorrow for Jesus' suffering is to be seen in the three hours of darkness and in Jesus' own rhetorical question expressed in the words of Ps 22:1, "My God, My God! Why have you forsaken me?" This cry was wrongly understood by some bystanders as Jesus' calling to Elijah, who (as noted in Mal 3:1–2) was expected to return before "the great and terrible day of the LORD" (Mal 4:5), which would bring judgment on the evil world. A symbol of the new access to God that was to be provided through the crucifixion and resurrection of Jesus was tearing of the great curtain in the temple, which was perceived to be a divinely established barrier between the worshipers of God and the inner sanctuary where God was believed to dwell (15:37–39). Significantly, this event is described as taking place at the moment of Jesus' death, which is perceived to have made possible this new access to the presence of God. It is the Roman military officer, the centurion, who then acclaims Jesus as Son of God. A major group witnessing these events "from a distance" consists of a considerable number of women who had followed

Jesus to Jerusalem from Galilee—presaging the fact that, unlike most Jewish movements of this period, women were to play a crucial role in the new covenant community (15:40–41).

The burial of Jesus was carried out by Joseph of Arimathea, who was so brave—and so devoted to the coming of the kingdom of God as announced by Jesus—that he requested and received permission from Pilate to prepare for the speedy burial of Jesus in a tomb hewn from the rock so that its exposure would not defile the impending Sabbath (15:42–46). Once again, Mark reports that it was women—Mary Magdalene[161] and Mary the mother of James[162]—who saw where the tomb was in which the body of Jesus was laid (15:47). Hence, it is appropriate that the women came as soon as the Sabbath has passed and approach to the tomb was possible—"very early on the first day of the week when the sun had risen" (16:1–2). En route to the tomb they were discussing how they might find someone who could roll away the massive cylindrical stone that covered the entrance—only to find it already rolled back, and a young man sitting there in a white robe. He knew that they were seeking the body of the crucified Jesus, but announced to them that he had been raised from the dead—as they could infer from the empty tomb—and that he had left instructions for Peter and the other disciples that he was preceding them to Galilee, where they would see him. Overcome with fear and astonishment, the women are reported as having fled, too fearful to tell anyone what they had seen and heard at the tomb (16:3–8). That this was the original ending of Mark is clearly indicated by the fact that both Matthew and Luke follow Mark to this point, and then sharply digress from Mark in the next stages in their accounts of the risen Christ.

The manuscript tradition that includes the so-called shorter ending of Mark tells of their reporting to "Peter and those with him" what they had seen and heard, which led Peter to launch the mission of the gospel "from east to west." The longer ending of Mark (16:9–20) reports an appearance of the risen Jesus to Mary Magdalene, who told the mourning disciples that Jesus was alive, but they did not believe her. Subsequently he appeared to two of them, and then to the eleven faithful disciples, scolding them for their unbelief, but then commissioning them to carry out a mission of the gospel to the world, promising them signs of support in the form of the ability to expel demons and to "speak in new tongues"[163] to further the spread of the good news across the world and to confirm its divine origin by these extraordinary signs.

The Origins of the Gospel of Mark

As indicated above, there seems to have been no direct model for the author of what came to be known as the Gospel of Mark. The author—or perhaps initially the community for which he served as editor—brought together oral traditions and written sources about Jesus, the differences among which are evident in the mixture of styles in the gospel as we have it. Sometimes the material seems to have been copied, and at other times, rephrased. There is no firm evidence for such sources, although some scholars have proposed that a predecessor of Mark was the Gospel of Thomas, or that he drew upon collections of miracle stories. But the Gospel of Thomas, as we shall discuss below, shows the influence of Gnosticism in its demeaning of the material world, and although there may have been collections of miracle stories, they give no evidence of having included the overall canonical gospels' perspectives on the career of Jesus, his challenge to the Jewish establishment, or the central significance of the cross and resurrection as perceived in Mark.

In the New Testament references to Mark—or John Mark—he is associated with both Peter and Paul. Acts 12:1–17 is an account of the execution of James and the arrest and imprisonment of Peter by order of Herod Agrippa I (10 BCE–44 CE), grandson of Herod the Great, who was made king of Judea and Samaria by the emperor Claudius in 41.[164] Peter is reported in Acts 12:6–11 to have been miraculously delivered from prison by an angel, and to have sought refuge in "the house of Mary, the mother of John whose other name was Mark" (12:12). When Barnabas and Saul returned to Antioch from Jerusalem, after having delivered to the church there the relief contribution from the churches of Syria (11:29–30), they brought with them John/Mark (12:25). Following their return to Jerusalem for the council of the apostles and elders on the issue of the obligation of Gentile converts to Christianity to conform to aspects of the Jewish ritual code (15:1–19) and their subsequent report of this decision to the church in Antioch (15:30–40), Paul and Barnabas split over the issue whether Mark should accompany them on their next visit to the new churches. Mark went with Barnabas, and Paul chose Silas to accompany him (15:36–41). In Phlm 24, however, Paul mentions Mark among his coworkers, as is the case in Col 4:10, where he is identified as Barnabas's cousin.[165] In the pseudepigraphic letters of 1 Pet 5:13 and 2 Tim 4:11, Mark is identified respectively as Peter's "son" and as Paul's useful helper. It is possible that John Mark was known to Peter, associated with Paul, became alienated from him and then reconciled, ultimately going to Rome, where he assisted Paul and Peter prior to their martyrdom there.[166] That this John Mark wrote the first gospel is clearly an early—though mixed—tradition. But the one feature of this gospel that is clear is its unique contribution to the beginnings of Christianity as a new literary mode, and the first composite report of the sayings, career, and death of Jesus, as well as of the rise of the convictions (1) that God raised him from the dead and (2) that a movement emerged in his name claiming to embody the establishment of a new covenant community.

The Community of the New Torah: Matthew

In contrast to the eschatological orientation of the Gospel of Mark, where we have seen that a dominant theme is the importance of the covenant community's being prepared for the imminent return of Jesus as the triumphant messiah, the Gospel of Matthew displays the structuring and ordering of a people to whom has been disclosed the procedures that are to characterize an ongoing community. In Mark, Jesus challenges the Jewish rules with regard to fasting, abstinence from work on the Sabbath, and avoidance of contact with people who are ritually unclean or non-Israelites. But in Matthew, the redefining of the people of God over against dominant views in first-century Judaism is more extensive and more explicit, and includes new rules. The aim is not a rejection of the hopes and divine promises to Israel, but a fresh perception as to how they are being fulfilled through Jesus. Accordingly, strong emphasis is placed on the fulfillment and transformation through Jesus of the promises made by God to the covenant people, Israel. Jesus is portrayed as the successor to Moses, through whom God is now giving the new law to his redefined people. This transformation is evident in the structure of Matthew, in the portrayal of Jesus as the successor to Moses, and in the rules for the present and expectations for the future that are offered in this gospel.

The Structure of Matthew

Clearly indicative of these aims of Matthew is the literary structure in which he has placed the gospel tradition. The revealing clue to this structure is to be found in the phrase repeated five times, "when Jesus had finished," which appears at the end of each of five of the major discourses in the gospel:

The Sermon on the Mount (7:28)

The Messianic Mission (11:1)

The Parables of the Kingdom (13:53)

Rank and Responsibility in the Kingdom of God (19:1)

Revelation of the End of the Age (24:32–25:46)

The concluding address is Jesus' Commissioning of his Disciples (26:1–28:20)
As in the narrative antecedents to the giving of the law to Israel through Moses at Sinai and the consequences as Israel enters the promised land (Exod 1–Deut 34), so Matthew's gospel recounts the divine preparation for the birth of the Messiah, the calling of his followers and emissaries, and concludes with the account of his sacrificial death and divine exaltation and the assignment to his disciples to spread the message worldwide and to foster the new community. But above all, the Gospel of Matthew—like the Torah—is

concerned with the communication of the criteria for participation in the new covenant people: their life together in a hostile world, and their mission to "proclaim the good news of the kingdom throughout the world' (24:14) and thereby to "make disciples of all nations" (28:18). The survey of Matthew that follows, while offering analyses of the opening and closing sections—the coming of God's Messiah, and the commissioning of the disciples—focuses on (1) the five portraits of Jesus as the agent of the new covenant, and (2) the five descriptions of the resources and responsibilities of the members of the new community.

In setting out these portrayals of Christ and his people, there is a mixture of continuities and contrasts with the earlier leaders of the covenant people of Israel and with the principles by which they were called to live. The continuity of Jesus with the history of God's people is explicit, however, from the genealogy of Jesus with which the book begins (Matt 1:1–17), and culminates in the commissioning of the new covenant people on a mountain, recalling Moses and Israel at Sinai. The individuals and the events highlighted in 1:1 are (1) the progenitor of the covenant people, Abraham, in whom "all the families of the earth shall be blessed (Gen 12:3); (2) David, the archetypal king of Israel, whose offspring will rule all the nations (Ps 2:6–7); and (3) the deportation of Israel to Babylon as punishment for its disobedience (Jer 27:2; Kgs 25). In Matt 3:4, the food eaten by John the Baptist conforms to the rules in Torah (Lev 11:22), and his garb matches that of Elijah, who was God's messenger to his disobedient people, a critic of the royal establishment, and the prophet expected to come at the end of the age (2 Kgs 1:8; Mal 4:56). John's being identified with Elijah is explicit only in Matthew (17:13).[167] Only in Matthew's account of Jesus' baptism does John declare that he should be baptized by Jesus and does Jesus instruct him to perform the baptism in order "to fulfill all righteousness" (3:15). And the declaration of Jesus' divine sonship by the voice from heaven is not a private disclosure to Jesus, as in Mark 1:11 and Luke 3:22 ("you are my beloved Son"), but a public announcement in the words of the messianic Psalm 2:7 "This is my beloved Son" (Matt 3:17)

The forty days and forty nights of Jesus' being tested in the wilderness (Matt 4:1–11) match precisely the time and setting that (1) Moses is reported to have experienced on the mountain where God promised to give him the law on the tablets of stone and where God was revealed to him "like a devouring fire" (Exod 24:12–18), and (2) when Elijah was instructed by the Lord on a mountain how Israel was to be enabled to renew the covenant and to receive a king and a prophet (Elisha) to lead the people in obedience to God (1 Kgs 19:11–16). Though Matthew is building on the Q tradition as well as on the briefer Markan account,[168] this gospel adds the detail that it was "to a very high mountain" that the devil took Jesus. His resistance to the temptations is said in each case to have been supported by an appeal to scripture.[169] After Jesus' return to Galilee, Matthew alone reports his move from Nazareth to Capernaum, which is said to be "in the territory of Zebulun and Naphtali," and hence to be in fulfillment of the prophecy of Isaiah[170] that God will bring light in "Galilee of the Gentiles" to those who sit "in darkness . . . and the shadow of death."

As noted above, the role of the mountain in Matthew as analogous to its function in the biblical account of Moses continues. The initial major instruction for the new covenant people as to how they are to live in obedience to God is offered on a mountain (5:1). As in Mark, after the report of Jesus having fed the five thousand, he withdraws to a mountain to pray (14:23), and it is on a mountain that he is transfigured (17:1). But only in Matthew is Jesus' post-resurrection commissioning of the disciples reported as also taking place on a mountain to which he directed them (28:16–20). Thus, the imagery of the mountain as the locus for God's revelation and instruction to his people in the Moses/Sinai tradition of Torah is a dominant factor in Matthew's account of Jesus as the one through whom the new covenant has been established and its guidelines are communicated to the new people of God.

The law code for the people of the new covenant is the Sermon on the Mount (Matt 5–7). Just as Moses went up on a mountain to serve as God's agent for conveying to his people the divine purpose and moral expectations for them, so Jesus is seen in Matthew to ascend a mountain to inform his new people what obedience God expects of them. In contrast to the direct and explicit moral injunctions of the Q tradition—such as Luke 6:20, "Blessed are you poor—Matthew reports Jesus as pronouncing more general and spiritualized teachings: "Blessed are the poor in spirit" (5:3). The community is given a series of social and moral injunctions that are to be obeyed by the new community to characterize their life as God's people, people who await the coming of "the kingdom of heaven" but are to be prepared to wait.

In the analysis of Matthew that follows, we shall employ a variation of the outline of Matthew offered above and instead will examine in sequence (1) Matthew's depiction of the role of Jesus as the agent of God for establishing the new covenant, and (2) the range of insights, resources, and responsibilities assigned to that new covenant people.

Jesus' Coming as God's Agent of Covenant Renewal (Matt 1–2)

The effectiveness and historical comprehensiveness of the divine purpose to be achieved for God's people through Jesus is evident in the genealogy set forth in Matt 1:1–17. Highlighted in 1:1 are David, the prototypical king, and Abraham, the progenitor of the covenant people. The great catastrophe of the deportation of Israel to Babylon is mentioned, and serves as a kind of turning point for the genealogy as it moves toward the birth of Jesus. Each of these events is separated from those that succeed them by fourteen generations—apparently seen as twice the sacred number seven (1:17).

The Holy Spirit is responsible for Mary's conception of the child, whose name, Jesus (from Yehoshua, "May Yahweh save"), highlights his role in the purpose of God to renew his covenant people—as is specified in 1:21. This miraculous birth is seen to be the fulfillment of the promise of a child born of a virgin who will embody God's presence with his people: Emmanuel (1:23; Isa 7:14).[171] His birth in Bethlehem likewise fits with the prophetic promise in Mic 5:2-6 that—in the purpose of God—a child born in this small city in an area south of Jerusalem[172] is to rule Israel, caring for his people, honoring the name of the Lord, recognized "to the ends of the earth" for his greatness, and an instrument of peace.

The potentially universal recognition of Jesus as God's agent for renewal of his people and of the creation is indicated in Matthew's account of the coming of wise men (magi) from the East to Jerusalem seeking "the one who has been born king of the Jews" (2:1-2). Their arrival is dated here to the reign of Herod, which was from 40 to 4 BCE,[173] and the reason for their coming is that they had seen the star of the king, and had come to worship him. They are astrologers, and the account of their search for the new king implies the cosmic and cross-cultural significance of the birth of Jesus. Herod, troubled by the reason for their coming, assembles the priests and scribes—the authorities for the Jewish cultus and for the interpretation of their scriptures—to ask of them where the messiah is to be born, and is told that it is to take place in Bethlehem. The magi go to where the mother and child are, prostrate themselves before him and present their gifts (2:11), and then return secretly to their own country.

The story of the flight into Egypt by Joseph, with the child and the mother (2:13-18), and their subsequent return is reported in Matthew as analogous to the experience of the people of the ancient covenant, as is indicated directly by the quotation in 2:15 of the prophetic word comparing God's leading his people from exile in Egypt to the promised land to a father calling his son (Hos 11:1). Herod's cruel attempt to destroy the pretender to the throne of Judah (2:13-17) likewise recalls the prophetic lament in Jeremiah over the children being slaughtered (31:15-16) even as the people are promised the renewal of their covenant with God (31:31-37). After Herod died and the rule of Judea, Samaria, and Idumea was assigned to his son, Archelaus (Matt 2:22), Joseph returned from Egypt with the child and his mother, but chose to reside in Galilee rather than in Judea. He chose Nazareth, a small agricultural village not far from the Via Maris, which was a major trade route between Egypt and Syria. Yet it is never mentioned in the Jewish scriptures, Josephus, or the rabbinic sources. The alleged quote from the prophets, "He shall be called a Nazarene," seems to be based on references in Torah, the Prophets, and the historical writings to "nazirites," who were men and women who achieved a holy state of consecration.[174] The conditions of purity and conformity to the will of God for his people are radically redefined by Jesus, although in Matthew there is the constant claim that through him the scriptures are being fulfilled.

Jesus' Activity as Agent of the New Covenant (Matt 3–4)

Matthew's gospel on the whole follows his Mark and Q sources in these chapters, but adds some distinctive features and makes some significant alterations. Matthew 3:14–15 reports John the Baptist's objection that he should not baptize Jesus, implying that he considers himself to be inferior to him. Jesus' response is to let things stand as they are, since it is appropriate for him to demonstrate the need for purification—"to fulfill all righteousness"—by being publicly baptized. The fostering of righteousness is a pervasive and central theme in Matthew.

Matthew's account of Jesus' return to Galilee following the arrest of John the Baptist by the civil authorities (4:12) includes the detail that he moved his place of residence from the inland village of Nazareth to Capernaum by the Sea of Galilee. The specifics of its locale—"in the territory of Zebulun and Naphtali," near the sea (or lake), "across the Jordan"[175]—and the designation of the area as "Galilee of the Gentiles" (or "nations")—come from the scripture quoted: Isa 9:1. The prophetic promise is altered slightly to announce that those who have "sat in darkness have seen a great light," overcoming the "shadow of death." The message that brings this new and transforming light is the announcement of the nearness of the kingdom of God (Matt 4:17). Matthew's commitment to features of traditional Jewish piety are evident in his substitution of "kingdom of the heavens"—the eternal dwelling place of God—for the phrase found elsewhere in the Jesus tradition, "the kingdom of God."

The comprehensiveness of Jesus' preaching and healing are highlighted by Matthew in his expansion of the summary statement of Jesus' preaching and exorcisms in Galilee in 4:23–25. There he reports that he healed "every disease and every infirmity among the people"—a claim that is repeated in Matt 9:35. Further, his fame is said to have spread "throughout all Syria," so that "all the sick" were brought to him, and a list of the ailments is given: "various diseases and pains, demoniacs, epileptics and paralytics." Those who followed him consisted of "great crowds," not only from Galilee and Jerusalem and Judea, but from the Gentile cities of "the Decapolis" and "beyond the Jordan." The worldwide outreach of the gospel is already dramatically anticipated in Matthew's account of Jesus' ministry of word and act.

The Authority of Jesus' Ministry (8:1–9:35)

Matthew, while including many of the stories of Jesus' healings and exorcisms from the Markan gospel, frequently condenses them, while highlighting certain details that are important for his agenda. The healing of the leper (8:1–4) culminates in the instruction to the cured leper to show himself to the priest and make the offering prescribed by Moses. Jesus expects him to conform to the law.

The story from the Q source about Jesus' healing the paralyzed servant of the centurion who approached him in Capernaum appears in Matt 8:5–13 in a somewhat abbreviated version. But he not only reports Jesus' declaration that "not even in Israel have I found such faith," but he links with it another Q saying[176] that predicts the coming of many "from the east and west [to] sit at table with Abraham, Isaac and Jacob in the kingdom of God," while those who claim to have a place in God's people ("the sons of the kingdom") are "thrown into outer darkness; there men will weep and gnash their teeth"—an expression used repeatedly by Matthew as a sign of deep contrition.[177] Following the summary description of Jesus' healings and exorcisms (8:16–17), we read that Jesus "healed all who were sick," and the note is added that these acts of Jesus were fulfilling the words of the prophet Isaiah (53:4) that "he took our infirmities and bore our diseases." A similar claim to divine authorization for Jesus is added by Matthew to his version of the Markan story of the healing of a paralytic (Mark 2:1–12): "When the crowds saw it they were afraid, and they glorified God who had given such authority to humans (*anthropoi*) (Matt 9:8).

Matthew's report of the Markan call of Levi (2:13–17) differs most obviously in that the tax collector who in Mark is called Levi by Jesus is identified as "Matthew" (Matt 9:9). As in Mark, the call is followed by Jesus' sharing a meal with tax collectors—collaborators who took money from fellow Jews to support the pagan Romans—and other "sinners." To the report of the Pharisees' challenge to Jesus and his disciples for this flagrant violation of kosher laws, Matthew has added a quotation from the prophet Hosea (6:6 = Matt 9:13) that implies that God is concerned for acts of mercy rather than for the cultic sacrifices.

Matthew's abbreviated version of the linked stories of the healing of Jairus's daughter and of the woman with a hemorrhage differs from Mark's (5:21–43) in several details: the ruler (*archon*) is not linked with a synagogue; the daughter is already dead; at her house the flute players and a crowd have gathered for the funeral ceremony; instead of the prohibition of telling others what had occurred, "the report of this went throughout all that district" (Matt 9:26). Thus, the more public nature of Jesus' act of raising the dead becomes known throughout a wider region. Clearly, for Matthew the wide outreach of the good news had already begun during Jesus' lifetime.

This theme is highlighted in the transitional passage (9:35–36) leading to Jesus' commissioning of the twelve disciples.[178] Jesus' initial outreach as depicted in Matthew is comprehensive—"all the cities and villages"—but focused primarily on the Jews, since it is in "their synagogues" that his preaching and healing are carried out. His competence is likewise comprehensive, since he is able to heal "every disease and every infirmity."

Jesus' Role Defined (11:2–12:50)

Matthew addresses the question of the specifics of Jesus' role as God's agent of covenant renewal in his abbreviated version of the Q traditions' account of the question sent to Jesus by John the Baptist as to whether he is "the one who is to come" (Matt 11:3). As noted above in our analysis of Q, Jesus' response is to define his role as the agent of God by pointing to his works of healing and renewal of life and his outreach to the neglected or excluded ("the poor") with the good news of the inbreaking of the kingdom of God. His final note is an expression of hope that others will not be offended by his work of outreach and renewal, which violates strict rules of ritual purity: "Blessed is the one who takes no offense at me" (11:6). John is directly identified in Matt 11:14 as Elijah, the prophet whose coming is predicted in Mal 4:5–6, prior to "the great and terrible day" when God's judgment will be poured out on disobedient humanity. The repentance that he will evoke among parents and children will stave off the fall of divine judgment. Yet from the time of John the Baptist until the period of Jesus' proclamation of the kingdom of heaven by word and action, there has been violent opposition to it (11:12). What justifies the enterprise launched by Jesus in which the covenant community is now engaged are the results ("deeds") being produced in the transformation of lives and the overcoming of the powers of evil (11:19).

The Markan report of Jesus' response to the Pharisees' challenge of his disciples' plucking and eating grain on the Sabbath (Mark 2:23–28) is repeated by Matthew (12:1–4) with a significant addition: 12:5–7. The biblical precedents cited here for the priority of human hunger over strict ritual and Sabbath regulations include not only David and his associates having eaten the Bread of the Presence when they were hungry (1 Sam 21), which is mentioned in Mark (2:25–25), but also the special sacrifices to be prepared and presented on the Sabbath (Num 28:9–10), which presumably were eaten by the priests. But the argument goes on to assert that "something greater" than either the temple or its sacrificial system has come through "the son of Man [who] is Lord of the Sabbath" (12:6). For Matthew, the whole of the cultic system is perceived as outmoded and superseded.

In Matthew's version of the Beelzebul controversy story (12:25–36),[179] Jesus claims that he casts out demons "by the Spirit of God" rather than "by the finger of God." The warning against falsely attributing Jesus' powers to anything but the Spirit of God is "a sin and blasphemy," and will not be forgiven "either in this age or the age to come." To speak "a word against the Son of Man" will be forgiven, but not "the blasphemy against the Spirit" (12:31–32). Since this "brood of vipers" is evil, they cannot speak good (12:34). It is on the basis of the words that they speak that they will be "justified" or "condemned" on the day of judgment (12:36–37).

In response to the request from some "scribes and Pharisees" for a sign from Jesus to attest his status, as reported in Q 11:29–32, Matthew quotes Jesus as denouncing the present generation as not only evil but "adulterous" (12:39). The significance of the "sign of Jonah" mentioned in Q is here (Matt 12:40) said to be the "three days and three nights [Jonah] was in the belly of the whale" (Jonah 1:17). Unlike Q, the reference to the burial and resurrection of Jesus is now explicit: "three days and three nights in the heart of the earth." A similar denunciation of the present generation appears in Matt 12:43–45, where the picture of the empty house that comes to be occupied by seven evil spirits is specified as referring to "this present evil generation" (Matt 12:45).

Conversely, Jesus' true relatives are described as those having an intimate relationship to God, who is here designated by one of Matthew's favorite terms, "my Father in heaven."[180] The motif of the new family of God is implicit in Matt 13:53–58 in the questions that arise about the source of Jesus' "wisdom and mighty works," since his family members are known to his critics (Matt 13:532–58). This opens the next section of this gospel in which Jesus encounters direct opposition and challenges.

Jesus Confronts Opposition and Competition (13:53–16:12)

The section is introduced by the Matthean summary reference to Jesus' teaching in parables ("When Jesus had finished . . . ," 13:53), the report of which is now concluded. It is his own choice—"he did not do many mighty works there"—rather than his inability to do so, as implied in Mark 6:5, that curtailed his healing activity. Thus, Matthew assumes the sovereignty of Jesus and omits any surprise on the part of Jesus in reaction to the unbelief of those from "his own country." The accounts of (1) Herod Antipas's astonished assumption that Jesus is John the Baptist risen from the dead (Matt 14:1–2) and (2) the execution of John (14:3–12) are markedly condensed from their Markan sources (6:14–16, 17–29). Two details added by Matthew, however, are (1) that when Jesus first saw the throng, "he had compassion on them and healed their sick" (14:14); and (2) that in addition to the five thousand male recipients of the abundant food Jesus provided were "women and children." Once more, Matthew's theme of the inclusiveness of the new community is evident.

The Markan story of Jesus walking on the water (Mark 6:45–52) is expanded by Matthew (14:22–33) to include the account of Peter's requesting and receiving the call from Jesus to walk on the water. On doing so, Peter becomes anxious because of the wind and calls for help, whereupon by Jesus he is saved from drowning and is rebuked for his "little faith." Also distinctive in Matthew's version of this incident is the response to Jesus of those in the boat, worshiping him and acclaiming him as Son of God. This feature clearly anticipates the Matthean version of Peter's confession of Jesus as "Messiah, the Son of the Living God" (16:16).

Jesus' outreach to non-Jews and to those whose physical condition or occupation excluded them from acceptance into the ritually pure covenant people is depicted in Matt 15:21–39. He also is critical of the inability of the Pharisees and Sadducees to discern in his words and acts signs of divine support and empowerment: they can predict the weather by obvious indicators, but they are like the contemporaries of the prophet Jonah who could not recognize the signs of God's purpose for his people through his chosen agent (16:1–4).

Jesus' Redemptive Role: The Crucified and Risen Messiah (16:13–17:13)

Building on the Markan tradition of Peter's acclaim of Jesus as Messiah,[181] Jesus is reported in Matthew as adding another phrase to the confession: "the Son of the living God," and then describing the major role Peter will have in building the new community, the *ekklesia* (16:17–19). He is addressed by Jesus—not by his nickname, Peter (the rock), or as Cephas, its Semitic equivalent—but by his Semitic name, "Simon Bar-Jonah." Peter's insight as to the role of Jesus has not come from human sources ("flesh and blood") but from "my Father who is in heaven," which we have already noted is Jesus' preferred designation of God, according to Matthew. In a play on the meaning of his name—in Greek, *petros/petra*; in Aramaic, *kepha/kephas*—Peter is described by Jesus as the rock on which "I will build my church." In spite of opposition from "the powers of death [Hades],"[182] the church will remain. Access to the kingdom of heaven and control of life there will be given to him, and binding decisions or grants of freedom made by him will be confirmed in heaven—that is, by God.

Matthew's account of the transfiguration (17:1–8) follows that of Mark (9:2–8) on the whole, but adds the details of Jesus' face having "shone like the sun." It omits Mark's mention of the disciples being "exceedingly afraid" (9:6), however, and instead speaks of their falling down before him because they were "filled with awe," and therefore being advised by Jesus to "have no fear" (17:8). In the subsequent explanation by Jesus of the prophecy in Mal 4:5–6 of the coming of Elijah "to restore all things," the implication in Mark

9:9–13 that this has already occurred with the coming of John the Baptist is made explicit in Matt 17:12–13, as is the prediction that both he and Jesus will suffer at the hands of "the scribers," the Jewish interpreters of scripture.

Jesus Defines the Laws by Which the New Covenant People Are to Live and His Role as the Messiah (17:14–27; 19:1–22:46)

Matthew has adapted or supplemented the Markan material in such a way as to describe the qualities that are to characterize the new covenant people. But he has, as is often the case, abbreviated the story of the healing/exorcism of the epileptic boy (17:14–21; cf. 9:14–29). Jesus' response to the disciples' question why they had been unable to expel the demon is to charge them with having "little faith" (17:20). Even faith the size of a tiny mustard seed would be sufficient to move a mountain; indeed, for faith, nothing is impossible. The noun used here, *oligopistia*, as well the corresponding adjective, are found only in Christian writings, and in the New Testament—with a single exception (Luke 12:28)—only in Matthew (6:30; 8:26; 14:31; 16:8). The same point as to the power of faith is made in Matt 21:20–22, which is somewhat abbreviated in Mark 11:20–25.

Only in Matthew (17:24–27) is the story told of the divine provision of a shekel—in the mouth of a fish!—for payment of the temple tax collected from the Jewish population, as required by the law of Moses from everyone over the age of thirty (Exod 30:11–16). The payment of this tax and the collection of tithes to support the worship of God were economically essential features of Judaism, and the support of the priests in this way probably continued even after the temple was destroyed.[183] Jesus explains the justification for paying the tax even though he points out that "the sons of the kings of the earth" are free from doing so. This may imply that he is here claiming to be the Son of God, or that the new people he is calling together are the sons or people of God, or both. A discussion of the issue for members of the new community of obeying the Torah and the laws of secular society appears in Matt 22:17–21 and 23:1–28.

The journey of Jesus and his disciples from Galilee to Judea marks the transition in the synoptic accounts from the broad ministry of Jesus by words and works to the focus of his confrontation with the civil and religious authorities in Jerusalem, which leads to his seizure, trial, and death. In addition to the events that lead to his trial and crucifixion, Jesus is depicted as challenging the norms by which the traditional covenant community of Israel was defining itself, and as providing new insights and rules for the people of God.

New features of the new covenant community as depicted here include new perceptions of sexual behavior for the members, such as "those who have made themselves eunuchs for the sake of the kingdom of heaven" (19:10–12), and the depiction of children as those who belong to the community (19:13–15). To the Markan extended account of Jesus' conversation with the rich young man and his subsequent discussion of the issue with the disciples (Mark 10:17–31), Matthew (19:16–30) adds the promise that his twelve disciples will have an eschatological role, serving as judges "when the Son of Man shall sit on his glorious throne" to judge "the twelve tribes of Israel" (19:28). Thus, the leaders of the new community will have a major role in defining the ultimate destiny of the traditional covenant people.

The parable of the Laborers in the Vineyard, unique to Matthew (20:1–16), expands the theme of Jesus' role in the day of judgment. Those who came to work in the vineyard at various times throughout the day were astounded that, when evening came, they all received the same wages: a denarius, which was considered a full day's pay. Those who had worked during the heat of the day thought they should receive higher pay than those who came last. The crucial factor is the generosity of the owner, who reminds them (1) that the right to such decisions is his—"Am I not allowed to do what I choose with what belongs to me?"—and (2) that they should not begrudge him his generosity to everyone. The main point here is that the gifts of grace are extended to all humans regardless of their efforts or self-esteem.

A similar point is made in Matthew's version (20:20–38) of the request that the sons of Zebedee, James, and John be promised special places of honor when Jesus assumes his seat of power in the coming kingdom. Matthew attributes this to their mother rather than to them, as in Mark 10:35. Jesus points them instead to the primary role of servant within the people of God, and to his expectation that as Son of Man he will "give his life as a ransom for many."

Again, Jesus is seen in Matt 20:29–34 as challenging the notion that his role as Messiah is basically one of royal power. Instead, when the two blind men are rebuked by the crowd for calling out to Jesus for merciful assistance to regain their sight, Jesus in pity reaches out and heals their blindness. In Mark's narrative (10:46–52), a single blind beggar named Bartinmaeus calls to Jesus as "Son of David" and then as *rabbouni* when he is led to Jesus and cured. Matthew reports him as calling to Jesus repeatedly, "Lord have mercy on us, Son of David." Thus, the address of Jesus as "Lord" is clearly a higher Christology, as in the confessional hymn quoted by Paul in Phil 2:6–10: "Every tongue shall confess that Jesus Christ is Lord."

The royal role of the Messiah is made explicit in Matthew's account of Jesus' entry into Jerusalem (21:1–9). The symbolic implication of his riding into the city on a colt in Mark's version (11:1–10) is made specific to the evangelist's observation that "this took place to fulfill what was spoken by the prophet, saying [in a linking of Isa 62:11 and Zech 9:9], 'Tell the daughter of Zion, Behold your king is coming to you, humble, and mounted on a donkey, on a colt, the foal of a donkey.'" Similarly, the acclaim of Jesus is said to be by "the crowd," which is directed explicitly to Jesus as "the Son of David," who has "come in the name of the Lord."

Matthew's account of Jesus in the temple (21:10–17) combines and expands the two passages in Mark describing Jesus and the temple: (1) 11:11, which merely reports his entering and leaving; (2) 11:15–19, which tells of his disrupting the commercial activities in the temple and of his teaching there about the contrast between its intended purpose, "a house of prayer" (Isa 56:7), and its actual function, "a den of robbers" (Jer 7:11). Matthew alone depicts Jesus as fulfilling a multiple role: healing the blind and lame; receiving the acclaim of children as Son of David; and the indignant reaction to this on the part of the chief priests and scribes. To this, Jesus responds by an appeal to Ps 8:2, but to a version that differs radically from the Hebrew text,[184] and exults in the "praise" uttered by children.

Matthew's report of Jesus' ability to curse the fruitless fig tree (Matt 21:18–19) omits both the peculiar detail in Mark's version that "it was not the season for figs" (Mark 11:14) and the appeal to be forgiving as one prays (Mark 11:23). The emphasis falls, therefore, on the power of faith to produce results. The uniquely Matthean parable of the Two Sons (21:28–32) also involves working in a vineyard, but the point concerns whether or not one responds in faith to the invitation to "go and work in the vineyard," which here means to engage in God's work among his people. Those hearers who consider themselves to be righteous did not repent and accept the invitation to the "way of righteousness" as announced by John, while such violators of the law as "tax collectors and harlots" did, and entered the kingdom.

A parable from Mark (12:1–12) concerning a vineyard is modified substantially in Matthew (21:33–46) by the addition of some radical details. The parable builds on the Song of the Unfruitful Vineyard in Isa 5. There the vineyard is identified with the people of Israel and Judah (5:7), and the destruction of the vineyard is God's response to the failure of the people to achieve justice. The Matthean version of the parable is even more clearly an allegory in that the details are intended as references to specific individuals and groups: God is the householder; the tenants are those who claim to be God's people; the servants who were beaten and killed are the prophets and messengers God sent to them; his "son" is clearly Jesus, whom the tenants killed. These features are present in the Markan original, but the added details in Matthew heighten the antagonism between Christians and the Jews who do not become part of the new community by denouncing the tenants (the Jewish leaders) as "wretches" who will experience "a miserable death." The "other tenants" are those who respond to Jesus in faith, and accordingly produce "the fruits of their season." After repeating the quote from Ps 118:22–23 in Mark 12:19, which shifts the image to a new structure for which the rejected stone "has become the head of the corner," Matthew adds an explanatory note that presages the new "nation producing the fruits" of the vineyard (21:43).

Lest there be any failure to grasp the point, Matthew concludes with the statement that the chief priests and Pharisees—the cultic and scribal leaders of the people—perceived that Jesus "was speaking about them." Accordingly, they tried to arrest him, but were fearful of the support he was gaining from "the multitudes," who were convinced he was a "prophet." Thus, the distinctive role of Jesus as Matthew perceives it is to carry out the purpose of God by establishing an obedient people, with full and proper understanding of the law and the prophets. The religious leaders who reject him and his message are to fall under divine judgment, which was probably seen by the author of Matthew as having already occurred in the destruction of the temple and the fall of Jerusalem to the Romans.

Matthew's final parabolic image of the role of Jesus in the purpose of God appears in the appendix to the Q parable of the Banquet (Matt 22:11-4). But the parable itself has been altered significantly by Matthew as well (22:1-10). Instead of a banquet for an unspecified celebratory occasion, as in Luke 14:16-24, the parable has become a well-developed allegory. The picture of the coming kingdom "of the heavens" is now linked to a "marriage feast" celebrated by the "king to honor his son." The anger of the king at the failure to attend the festivities by those previously invited leads to a radically different reaction in Matthew's version: instead of the Q account of the householder's compassion in inviting marginal people—the poor, the maimed, the blind, the lame—to come to the banquet, Matthew describes the angry king as sending his troops "to destroy those murderers and burn their city." The details clearly reflect the Roman attack on Jerusalem and the ruin of the temple following the First Jewish Revolt in 66-70 CE.

But the assembled guests who responded to the invitation—which in Q was to share in the new covenant people—are now said to represent a mixed group, including both "bad and good." The Matthean addition to the parable (22:11-14) describes one who sought to enter the feast without the proper "wedding garment"—clearly a symbol for proper moral and ritual condition. The inappropriately attired guest is unable to explain his condition, and the king ordered him to be expelled to "outer darkness"—the Matthean image for Hades, the abode of the dead and the place of punishment of the unrighteous.[185] The invitation to share in the kingdom goes out to "many," but only a "few are chosen" and respond to it in faith and obedience, and so are able to enter the "kingdom of heaven."

The extended discourse materials in Matthew that deal with (1) the rules for the new community in contrast to those formulated by the Pharisees

(23:1-6) and (2) Matthew's expanded version of the final apocalyptic discourse of Jesus are examined below, in the sections titled "Defining the New Covenant Community and its Role," "False Criteria for the New Community" (Matt 23), and "The Consummation of God's Purpose for the New Community" (Matt 24-25). It is essential, however, to perceive how Matthew pictures the final events in the life of Jesus.

The Crucial Events to Establish the New Covenant (26:1-28:20)

While relying primarily on the Markan narrative, Matthew includes details in his account of Jesus' arrest, trial, crucifixion, burial, and resurrection that are unique. When Jesus tells the disciples about his impending seizure and execution (26:2), he refers to himself as "the Son of Man," just as in his question concerning his role as Messiah addressed to the disciples at Caesarea Philippi (16:14), "Who do men say that the Son of Man is?" The official plot to destroy him is attributed to "the chief priests and elders" (26:3), rather than to the priests and scribes (Mark 14:1).[186] This coalition of religious leaders formed to destroy Jesus and his movement is said to have convened "in the palace of the high priest"—a detail that heightens the message of official Jewish opposition to Jesus.

Matthew's interest in noting the correspondences between (1) what Jesus said and did and (2) what was foretold in the scriptures is evident in the detail that the bribe paid to Judas to betray Jesus to the authorities was "thirty pieces of silver." This is the amount paid to the prophet in connection with his role that was to bring divine judgment on the disobedient covenant people (Zech 11:12). That scripture-fulfillment feature is elaborated in Matthew's account of the suicide of Judas by hanging (27:3-10), where there are links with other scriptures through the reported purchase of the potter's field (cf. Jer 18:2-3; 32:6-15). In response to Judas's question to Jesus as to whether he is to serve as the traitor, Jesus does not answer categorically, but simply replies, "You have said so" (26:25). He responds similarly to the question of the high priest as to whether he claims to be "the Messiah, the Son of God" (27:64).

Jesus' special relationship to God is implicit in Matthew, however, in his repeated reference to God as "my Father" (26:42, 44) and his claim to a special role "in my Father's kingdom" (26:29). Yet that claim does not carry with it the assurance that he will be delivered from suffering or death. When one of his supporters, at the moment that he was being taken captive, reached out with a sword and cut off the ear of a slave of the high priest, Jesus rebuked him. Then he went on to say that he could appeal to God for angelic support and deliverance ("Twelve legions of angels"), but instead it was essential to the purpose of God that he die. Only in this way would "the scriptures be fulfilled" concerning his sacrificial death (26:52-55).

In his version of the description of the trial of Jesus before the Jewish council (*synedrion*), Matthew follows the Markan sequence, unlike Luke, who departs in a significant way. Matthew's special interest in Peter is evident in that he adds the detail concerning Peter's sorrow: after having three times denied that he even knew Jesus, he "went out and wept *bitterly*" (26:75). The breadth of responsibility among Jewish officials for the death of Jesus is accentuated by Matthew's report that those who took council to execute him included "*all* the chief priests and elders of the people" (27:1). Only here is there a report of the death of Judas: by suicidal hanging (27:3–10).

Jesus' refusal to offer a defense of himself in the hearing before Pilate is more emphatic in Matthew, who reports that "he gave no answer, not even to a single charge" (27:14). Only in this version of the trial are there a number of features that highlight that Jesus is innocent of violating Roman law. Thus, Pilate's wife reports to him her dream, which leads her to advise him to "have nothing to do with this righteous man" (27:19). Pilate not only declares Jesus' innocence verbally, but does so symbolically by washing "his hands before the crowd." The thrust of Matthew's aim in placing the blame for Jesus' death on the Jewish people is apparent in his report of the reaction attributed to "all the people," who cry out, "His blood be on us and on our children." Probably no verse in the New Testament has contributed more to anti-Semitism in the modern world than this Matthean detail of Jesus' trial.

The scornful onlookers at the crucifixion mockingly declare that, since Jesus claimed to be the Son of God, if God is really concerned with him, he will "deliver him" from this horrible death (27:43). Matthew alone reports that at the moment of Jesus' death, in addition to the tearing of the temple veil, there was an earthquake, rocks were split, tombs were opened, and saints were raised from the dead and appeared in the holy city. Clearly, the latter are the prototypes of the new people of God who are expected to share in the ultimate resurrection of the dead (1 Cor 15:22–28). The prototype of the resurrection is said to have been witnessed by the Roman centurion and his associates, as well as by the women mentioned in Mark's version (15:40–41).

Forewarned by the Jewish officials, Pilate arranges to have the guards there informed of the alleged plot of the disciples to steal Jesus' body from the tomb in order to support the claim that he would be raised from the dead, and thus Matthew tells of the sealing of the tomb and the establishment of a guard (27:62–66). The angel of the Lord who instructs the faithful women that Jesus has been raised from the dead in Mark's account (16:1–8) appear to the guards at the tomb as well, according to Matthew, with the message reinforced by an earthquake (28:2–4). Then Jesus' appearance to the women is described in Matt 28:9–10, with the instruction to be given by them to the disciples to go to Galilee, where they will see him. Only here is the story told of the bribing of the soldiers to give out the report that they had fallen asleep, during which time the disciples had come and stolen the body of Jesus (28:11–15). Apparently, the accusation by opponents of the Christian movement that the disappearance of the body of Jesus was the result of a clever act by his followers, rather than of his resurrection, is thus being discredited.

The final verses of Matthew (28:16–20) are of paramount importance for Matthew's portrait of Jesus and his role in founding the new covenant people. As noted above, he appears to them on a mountain, recalling God's appearance to Moses and the tribes of Israel on Sinai. They recognize his divine origin and role, as is evident in their having "worshipped him" there. Not all are persuaded, however: "Some doubted." Jesus' claim is of sovereign, universal authority. The disciples are to launch a worldwide mission, reaching out not merely to convert their hearers into believers, but to enlist "disciples" from "all nations." The rite of admission to the new covenant people is baptism, and the formula by which this is to be administered is explicitly Trinitarian. Above all, new members are bound to observe new laws—"all that I have commanded you." And they are given the promise of Christ's continual presence among them until the present age ends and the ultimate kingdom of God is established (28:16–20).

The Inclusive Community: Luke

The Distinctive Literary and Historiographical Features of Luke and Acts

Both the contents and the literary style of the Gospel of Luke—and its companion work, the Acts of the Apostles—were clearly intended to reach out to a wide readership in the Graeco-Roman world at the beginning of the second century CE. Ancient tradition, as gathered by Eusebius of Caesarea (260–331) in his *Ecclesiastical History*, attributed this gospel to Luke, who is mentioned in the New Testament as an associate of Paul. Irenaeus reported that, after the death of Paul, Luke "put down in a book the gospel which was preached by him."[187] Origen also noted that Luke wrote the Gospel of Luke and Acts "for those from the gentiles who [came to believe] the gospel that was preached by Paul."[188]

In the New Testament, Luke is included by Paul among his "fellow workers" in the greetings sent by him in his letter to Philemon (v. 24). He is also mentioned in Col 4:14 as "the beloved physician" apparently accompanying Paul, and in the deuteropauline 2 Tim 4:11 as Paul's sole companion at the time of writing. The extent to which these later letters in Paul's name are historically accurate with regard to Luke's continuing association with Paul is impossible to determine. The fact that parts of the narrative in Acts are reported in the first-person plural, as in Acts 16:10, has long been understood by some to indicate that the book was written by a companion of Paul: hence, Luke. But in fact, there is evidence in Hellenistic literature of narratives that shift back and forth between first-person plural and third-person style, so that any inference about identity of authorship on the basis of "we" passages is dubious. All that one can conclude from this evidence is that from the second century on, it was this coworker of Paul who was regarded as the author of both the Gospel of Luke and the Acts of the Apostles.

What is clear, however, is that the author of Luke and Acts knew and respected the literary and historical methods of his cultural contemporaries, and wanted to produce writings in comparable style. This is shown by the stylized introductions to the gospel, including a reference to his patron, Theophilus (Luke 1:1-4), and the mention of "the first book" in Acts 1:1, followed by a summary of the gospel and a compact account of Christ's ascension (Acts 1:1-11). The orientation of the author of this gospel to historical method of the first century is evident from his references to important events in Roman history, as when he points out that the reason for the journey of Joseph and Mary from their hometown of Nazareth in Galilee to the "city of David," Bethlehem, where Jesus was born in fulfillment of the prophetic prediction (Mic 5:20),[189] was the "decree from the Emperor Augustus that all the world should be registered." References to secular rulers, to governmental decrees and actions appear throughout both Luke and Acts.[190] The range and depth of involvement of the early Christians in confrontation with the empire is also a major theme in Luke-Acts, as noted below in some detail.

It is important to see how the author of Luke-Acts—whom, for convenience, we shall designate simply as "Luke"—was influenced by the historiography of his time in two different modes: (1) the historiographic and literary methods that were employed by Roman historians (and their Hellenistic predecessors) in the first century CE, including the more popular literary style known as the *romance*;[191] (2) the Jewish theological perspective on history that assumed that the past, present, and future of the covenant people are in the hands of God, whose purpose was announced and prepared for in the past, and was being shaped by present actions in history, which would come to its divinely intended consummation in the future.[192]

The romance, or ancient novel, is a type of literature widely produced in the first centuries of the common era. An accurate description of it has been provided by Thomas Hagg in his study, *The Novel in Antiquity*:

> Gods, oracles, cults of different kinds are organically integrated into the course of events in human experience. In Xenophon [*Ephesiaca*] . . . there is hardly any important stage in the action that is not accompanied by an invocation, a prayer, a sacrifice or a hint at some involvement with a god. And in Heliodorus the missionary tendency in favor of the Helios cult is unmistakable. . . . It is also quite possible that direct allusions to mystery rituals, to be understood only by the initiated, were hidden in the texts.[193]

Thus, these romances were not intended to be merely entertaining, but were written as propaganda for the cult of the deity involved. A similar aim seems to be clear in Luke-Acts, which seeks to engage the reader in the recognition and worship of Jesus as the Messiah, through whom God is calling into being a new covenant community that is ethnically and culturally inclusive. The author seems to have combined the features of Graeco-Roman historiography and the romances in order to make his case for Christianity.

With regard to the specifically historical strategy employed by Luke, an important model for his method is the one presented by Lucian of Samosata in his second-century CE work, *How to Write History*. He points to the work of the late-fifth-century BCE historian Thucydides, who, in his *History of the Peloponnesian War*, declared that the purpose of writing history is to convey to the reader what is true and useful, and thereby to enable people in the future to learn from the past. He wrote, "I have written not for immediate applause but for posterity, and I shall be content if the future student of these events . . . finds my narrative of them useful." The preface to the history aims to engage and instruct the reader; the speeches are written to convey the situation of the reader and his audience, although the author may subtly use the speeches to demonstrate his own eloquence as well. What is essential in analysis of ancient histories—as is the case with any literary document—is to seek to reconstruct the historical situation, the then-current modes of communication, the basic assumptions, and the models of reality (human and divine) that are taken for granted by the historian and that shape the written result.[194] It is these factors that must be kept in focus in the analysis of Luke-Acts, as well as the other early Christian writings.

Luke's Perception of History

A most revealing feature of the Gospel of Luke with respect to the assumptions of the author about the overall divine scheme of history, and one that reflects his engagement with Jewish perceptions of the divine plan operative in the history of God's people, appears in Luke 16:16: "The law and the prophets were in effect until John [the Baptist]; since then the good news of the kingdom of God is proclaimed, and everyone tries to enter it by force." What is implied is that there are three stages in history: (1) the era of the law and the prophets, which terminates with John the Baptist; (2) the proclamation by Jesus and his followers of the "good news" about the coming of the kingdom of God; (3) the establishment of God's rule. What is distinctive about Luke is his declaration that the kingdom of God is no longer an event to be expected in the future—as in the prayer taught by Jesus, "May your kingdom come" (11:2)—but that it is a reality already at work through Jesus in the present age in a way that guarantees and points to the ultimate triumph of God's purpose for his people and for the creation. This is also affirmed in the Q tradition—"If it is by the finger of God that I cast out demons, then the kingdom of God has come to you"—as well as in Luke's special material (17:20), "In fact, the kingdom of God is among you."[195]

As will be indicated in the subsequent analysis of the Gospel of Luke, a major feature of this work—and one that appears for the most part only in this gospel—is the development of the theme from the prophets of Israel that the good news of God's renewal of his people and of the creation is to go out to Gentiles, as well as to Jews. This is explicit in the account of Simeon's acclaim of Jesus on the occasion of his being circumcised in the temple, which appears only in Luke. As he took up the child "and blessed God," he declared,

> "My eyes have seen your salvation,
>   which you have prepared in the presence of all peoples,
> a light for revelation to the Gentiles
>   and for glory to your people Israel." (Luke 2:25–32)[196]

This theme appears repeatedly and uniquely in Luke's gospel. Its implications are spelled out in detail in the Acts of the Apostles and form the climax of Jesus' charge to the apostles just prior to his ascension: ". . . You will be my witnesses in Jerusalem, in Judea and Samaria, and to the ends of the earth" (Acts 1:8). Also in Acts, Peter's address to the people of Jerusalem, who have seen the outpouring of the Holy Spirit on him and the other apostles, begins with a quotation from the prophet Joel that affirms, "I will pour out my spirit *on all flesh*" (Acts 1:17; Joel 2:28).

Thus, in Luke and in Acts, participation in the covenant people is no longer perceived as limited to Jews and to those who conform to their ritual and legal qualifications. Now Luke's gospel describes detailed preparation for this inclusive community and its worldwide outreach, especially in Jesus' association with those who would have been regarded by pious Jews of the first century as untouchable—sinners, tax collectors, the sick—or as ineligible for full participation in the covenant people: women, the poor, "the lost." The import of this outreach as depicted in Acts is analyzed below.

As shown by Joseph A. Fitzmyer in his superb commentary on Luke,[197] this gospel describes what was accomplished through the person, ministry, death, and resurrection of Jesus for the salvation offered to all humanity. Jesus is depicted as the agent through whom the eschatological purpose of God for his people and for the creation is being achieved.[198] The enabling power of God that comes upon Jesus through the Holy Spirit—at baptism (3:23), in his temptation (4:1), but especially as he launches his ministry in Galilee (4:14, 18)—is the central agent in Acts for the instruction and empowerment of the apostles (Acts 1:2; 2:1–12) and is declared by Jesus (Luke 4:18 = Isa 61:1–2) and by Peter (Acts 2:17 = Joel 2:28–32) to be in fulfillment of the promise of God through the prophets. Thus, the works and words of

Jesus and the apostles are perceived as the eschatological outworking of the divine plan for the renewal of God's people. The invitation to share in this divine enterprise is to go out "to the ends of the earth" (Acts 13:47).

Outline of the Gospel of Luke

1. The Prologue (1:1–4)

2. The Birth and Boyhood of Jesus (1:5–2:52)

3. Jesus' Preparation for his Ministry (3:1–4:13)

4. The Ministry and Message of Jesus in Galilee (4:14–9:50)

5. Jesus' Journey to Jerusalem (9:51–19:27)

   a. 9:51–13:21

   b. 13:22–17:10

   c. 13:11–19:27

6. Jesus' Ministry in Jerusalem (19:28–21:38)

7. The Last Supper, Trial, Death, and Burial of Jesus (22:1–23:56)

8. Jesus' Appearances to His Followers in Jerusalem (24:1–53)

   a. At the Empty Tomb (24:1–12)

   b. On the Road to Emmaus (24:13–35)

   c. In Jerusalem: The Ascension (24:36–53)

Analysis of Luke

THE PROLOGUE (1:1–4)

The introductory words with which this gospel begins are addressed to the one who is presumably the patron of Luke, having authorized and supported his preparation of this writing and volume two, the Acts of the Apostles. His Greek name is symbolic: Theophilus, which means "friend of God." The events reported here have two notable features: (1) they were not random occurrences, but constituted the fulfillment of a divine purpose; and (2) the reports of them were transmitted, not only by "many" previous writers who sought to present what happened in an "orderly" manner, but have been based on reports by "eyewitnesses" who were involved "from the beginning" and who had become devoted to the spread of the message: "servants of the word." Theophilus is not merely a potentially interested observer, but he has been receiving instruction and is now being helped by this writing to "know the truth" concerning the matters about which he has been taught.

Clearly, there are multiple sources in use concerning Jesus and the impact of his life and ministry, and there are procedures operative through which instruction is being offered in these matters. Luke wants to set the record straight, having engaged in extended and careful investigation of the evidence "from the very first," or "for a long time." Since the author differentiates himself from those who were eyewitnesses "from the beginning," he clearly is not from the generation of Jesus' original followers, but is carefully examining and organizing the evidence that they produced and preserved. Accordingly, he considers what he has produced in these two volumes, Luke and Acts, to be "an orderly account." And the announced aim of the work is for the members of the recipient community to "know the truth concerning the things of which [they] have been informed." Thus, there is a claim to historical reliability and an assumption of the direct relevance of the contents for increased understanding of the matters concerning Jesus, his life and teaching, about which community members have received instruction.

As indicated above, what is evident throughout these two works is Luke's familiarity with the historical methods and literary style of the Graeco-Roman tradition and his ability to utilize them for conveying to a wide range of his contemporaries his perception of the life and message of Jesus and of Jesus' impact on the life and work of the apostles and the converts and communities that emerged in response to their work. His skill in utilizing these modes of communication from the wider culture is both symbolic and functionally significant for fostering the outreach of message and membership in the Roman world. Although there is no clear basis for dating this undertaking, it seems likely to have taken place in the last decades of the first century CE.

THE BIRTH AND BOYHOOD OF JESUS (1:5–2:52)

Implicit in Luke's account of the birth of John the Baptist and his role in preparing Jesus for the work that God was to do through him is Luke's aim to show that both the context and the specifics of the birth and career of Jesus were divinely planned and determined, building on and transforming the traditions of Israel. The dating of these events to the reign of "King Herod of Judea" is a bit problematic, since the reign of so-called Herod the Great was from 37 to 4 BCE. Either the subsequent calculation of the date of Jesus' birth was incorrect, or the reference may be to one of this Herod's successors: Herod Archelaus, who ruled Judah, Samaria, and Idumea from 4 BCE to 6 CE, or Herod Antipas, who ruled Galilee and Perea from 4 BCE to 39 CE. The vital link with pagan rule comes in Luke 2:1, where it is specified that it was under Caesar Augustus (ruled 30 BCE to 14 CE) that all the people in the inhabited world were to be enrolled in a kind of census, which involved the listing of the properties owned by all the subjects with a view to imposing imperial taxes. The date is further specified by mention that this occurred when Quirinius was governor of Syria. Josephus notes that such a census took place under him in 6 or 7 CE,[199] so that Luke's dating it during the reign of Herod is highly dubious. What is important is not the precision of the date but the intention of Luke to show that what happened in the life and career of Jesus was not a private matter but was directly involved with secular powers and public events. The need to register for the census in the family hometown required the journey to Bethlehem, which was associated with the kingship of Israel and was specified in the prophecy of Micah (5:2) as the place from which would come the ruler of God's people.[200] Thus, the decree of the pagan emperor is perceived by Luke to have resulted in the fulfillment of the prophecy concerning the birth in Bethlehem of the Son of David, through whom the rule of God was to be established in the world.

Before that occurs, however, Luke recounts the circumstances and events through which John, the divinely chosen agent, is brought forth, who by his message and by ritual act will prepare for the coming of God's Messiah. His aged father, Zechariah,[201] is a priest, married to Elizabeth but childless, and is described as "righteous before God, walking in all the commandments and ordinances of the Lord" (1:5–6). An angel informs them that they are to have a son, who will be an ascetic and filled with the Spirit even before he is born. He will call his people back to God, and will function like Elijah,[202] leading parents to care for their children and the disobedient to conform to divine wisdom, and he will thereby redefine the people of God (1:27). When Mary visits the pregnant Elizabeth, she pronounces her blessed and utters what has come to be known as the Magnificat (1:46–55). In this hymn, God's special care for lowly women is noted and praise is offered for God's mercy but also for his strength, which will be evident in his abasing the proud and caring for the poor—promises that have been made to God's people since the time of Abraham.

John is born (1:57–80), and his father celebrates his coming as a sign that God is remembering and renewing "his holy covenant" and will bring salvation and renewal to his people, guiding their feet "into the way of peace." After the child is born, he takes up residence "in the wilderness," which recalls the preparatory experience of ancient Israel prior to the move into the promised land. Before describing the change in role of John from a solitary figure in the desert to a preacher of repentance and the agent of baptism in the vicinity of the Jordan River (3:3–4), Luke extends the quotation from Isa 40 found in Mark's report (1:2–3) to include the prediction that the result of this call to "prepare the way of the Lord" is that "*all flesh*" shall see the salvation of God" (3:6).

Drawing on the Q tradition (3:7–9), Luke quotes John as predicting that, in contrast to the disobedient who claim Abraham as their father, "God is able from these stones to raise up children to Abraham." In other words, from the least likely source will come the new members of the covenant community. This is evident from the report in 3:10–14 that among the inquirers responding to his call are those from two most unlikely groups—both of which serve the pagan power, Rome: tax collectors and soldiers. John's response to the inquiry as to whether he is himself the messiah who will bring about this great change is to contrast his baptism in water with that of the one whose baptism will be "with the Holy Spirit and with fire" (3:15–18). He will gather his own people ("the wheat"), but he will also be the agent to bring down "unquenchable fire" of judgment on the wicked. Luke alone reports the seizure and imprisonment of John by Herod Antipas, who, as noted above, ruled Galilee and Perea from 4 BCE to 39 CE, and whom John is reported here to have reproved for marrying his niece, Herodias. Thus, Luke's account of Jesus and the origins of Christianity describes a movement that was in multiple ways involved with public life and political leadership.

In his report of Jesus' baptism by John, Luke adds two significant details to the Markan version: that it was the *Holy* Spirit that came upon Jesus, and that it came "in bodily form"—not merely as an invisible and intangible entity. Similarly, Jesus is described by Luke as returning from the Jordan "full of the Holy Spirit, and led "by the Spirit" into the wilderness for the time of testing, during which he ate nothing and "was hungry"—a sign that the Messiah is truly human (4:1–2). This is emphasized by the added detail that the devil's leaving him was only "until an opportune time" (4:12). With this narrative, Luke's account of Jesus' preparation for ministry ends.

JESUS' MINISTRY AND MESSAGE IN GALILEE (4:14–9:50)

Jesus' return to his own region, Galilee, is said by Luke to have been "in the power of the Spirit." The message he proclaims as he launches his public ministry (4:16–30) includes an important detail that is additional to the Markan version (Mark 6:1–6). The location for this address of Jesus in a synagogue is not simply "his own country" but is specified as "Nazareth, where he had been brought up" (Luke 4:16). His finding his place in the book of Isaiah for the text he is interpreting implies his ability to read and his familiarity with the scriptures. The passage read (4:18–19) is a combination of Isa 61:1–2 and 58:6—which he forthwith proclaims is being "fulfilled in [their] hearing" (Luke 4:21). His claims thus include (1) that his agenda are derived from the prophetic promises; (2) that it is the Spirit of God that is enabling him to carry out his task; (3) that he has been "anointed,"[203] a term akin to the designation *christos*; (4) that he is to bring good news to the "poor"—the neglected and excluded; (5) that he is to bring release for the captives; (6) that the blind will receive their sight; (7) that the oppressed will be liberated. All of these prophetic promises of renewal and liberation are now to be fulfilled through the work of Jesus. And finally, he is "to proclaim the acceptable year of the Lord"—the new era when God's purpose for the renewal of his people and of the creation will be achieved.

The response to this message and these claims is a mixture of wonder and perplexity. Is not he merely the son of Joseph? (4:22). Since Jesus has not performed the miracles in Nazareth that he is reported to have done in Capernaum, he anticipates a request by the people of his hometown to do so there, while acknowledging that prophets do not find acceptance in their own country (4:24). Prime examples of this are that those benefiting from the miraculous powers of Elijah and Elisha were, respectively, a widow in the land of Sidon and Naaman the Syrian.[204] The response to these claims and to Jesus' failure to perform miracles for them on demand leads those gathered in the synagogue to try to put Jesus to death by group action, as seems to have been a social feature of Jewish life in this period. But Jesus escaped from their plot to destroy him and returned to Capernaum (4:25–31). Thus, the pattern for Jesus' career is set in this Lukan passage: though he will meet with hostility from the Jewish leadership, his wider outreach to the people, and to Gentiles, will continue through his work of healing and his message of renewal based on the prophets. He announces that he has been sent out—implicitly, by God—to "preach the good news of the kingdom of God to the other cities" (4:43).[205]

The brief account in Mark 1:16–20 of Jesus' call to Simon Peter and his brother Andrew to follow him and thereby become "fishers of humans" is expanded in Luke 5:1–11 into the story of the miraculous catch of fish on the Lake of Galilee in response to Jesus' instruction to Simon Peter to "put out into the deep water and let down your nets for a catch." The results are astonishing as the nets begin to break and the overloaded boats begin to sink, which attracts the attention of James and John, the sons of Zebedee and partners of Peter. Jesus reassures them, and informs them that "from now on you will be catching people," whereupon they abandoned their boats, "left everything and followed him." The Markan narrative has become a vivid allegory in Luke.

The Markan accounts of the healing of a leper,[206] the healing of the para-lytic,[207] and the call of Levi the tax collector[208] are told with only slight modifi-cations. An example of a change is in Luke 5:17, however, where Jesus is reported to be under observation by "Pharisees and teachers of the law who had come from every village of Galilee and Judea and from Jerusalem," thereby highlighting the scrutiny of Jesus by religious authorities and the geographical scope of the interest that his activities evoked. The detail of his being watched by "scribes and Pharisees" (Luke 6:7) is also added to the Markan account of the healing of the man with the withered hand (Mark 3:1–6).

Luke's briefer combining of Jesus' teaching in a manner comparable to Matthew's Sermon on the Mount appears in Luke 6:20–49. This follows Luke's account of the call of the twelve disciples, who are here designated "apostles" (6:12–16). As in Matthew (5:1–2), the hearers of these teachings are the disciples (Luke 6:20), but here the Beatitudes are addressed directly to them and deal with literal needs: for example, "you poor" rather than "the poor in spirit" (Matt 5:3); "you that hunger now" rather than "those who hunger and thirst for righteousness (Matt 5:6). Added to these in Luke are woes pronounced on those who are now rich, well fed, happy, and enjoying a good reputation (6:24–26). It is in the coming day of divine judgment—"that day" (6:23)—that God will call humanity to account for their treatment of his messengers and faithful people. The remainder of the instruction to the disciples matches well the parallel passages in the Sermon on the Mount.[209]

The next section of Luke (7:1–50) consists mostly of material drawn from the Q source: the Healing of the Centurion's Servant, with the added feature of his generosity to the synagogue (Luke 7:1–10); the Healing of Peter's Mother-in-law (4:38–39), which is based on Mark 1:29–31; Jesus' Words about John the Baptist (7:24–35, which is discussed in some detail in the Q section, Matt 11:7–19). Luke 7:36–50, however, consists of a major revision and expansion of the Markan story of Jesus' being anointed by a woman on the eve of his crucifixion (Mark 14:3–9). The different features are as follows:

	According to Mark	According to Luke
Location:	the house of Simon the leper	the house of a Pharisee
The woman:	unidentified	woman of the city; sinner
The ointment:	very expensive	ointment of pure nard
Her action:	poured it on his head	stood behind him; wet his feet with her tears, wiped them with her hair; kissed and anointed his feet with the ointment
Response of onlookers:	Ointment could have been sold and the money given to the poor	Jesus should have recognized her as a sinner and refused to let her touch him
Jesus' response:	woman is commended for her preparing his body for burial; her story will be told wherever the gospel is preached	Jesus tells a parable of a "beautiful" act of a creditor who forgave two debtors, who owed him respectively 500 and 50 denarii

Jesus then asks, "Which of them will love him more?" When his critic says it was the one who received greater forgiveness, Jesus points to the analogy of the sinful woman whose loving care for him they have witnessed. This leads to his telling her she is forgiven, that her faith has saved her, and that she should now "Go in peace."

Thus, the story is a symbolic picture of the forgiveness of sinners that was to characterize the significance of Jesus for faith, and especially to the place for women—even sinners—in the new community. What is evident is that in Mark, the anointing of Jesus by the woman is a symbolic act that points to his coming death and burial. In Luke, however, the major issue is Jesus' ignoring the laws of ritual purity, and the point is that the mutual love that is to characterize the new community transcends moral, ritual, and economic boundaries.

The role of women in the Jesus movement is detailed in the unique Lukan passage, 8:1–3, where he is reported as being accompanied on his wide preaching mission not only by the Twelve but also by some women who had been healed or had demons expelled from them. They included women of wealth and social standing, such as Joanna (one of the first to find the tomb of Jesus empty; 24:10), and the wife of Chuza, who was steward of the estate of Herod Antipas.[210] Thus the supporters of the new community being called into existence by Jesus come from across sexual, moral, ritual, social, and economic boundaries.

In 8:4–18, Luke reproduces from Mark (4:1–25) the parable of the Sower and Jesus' explanation of parables, with only minor modifications. In his account of the interpretation of the parable of the Sower (8:11–15), Luke does add references to "the pleasures of life" that choke "the seed which is the word of God" and that hinder maturity. Conversely, the seed in good soil produces the standard Graeco-Roman Stoic virtues: "an honest and good heart, and brings forth fruit with patience." Analogously, the series of Markan miracle stories (Mark 4:35–5:43) are reported with changes only in a few details: the disciples awakened by the storm as they cross the lake appeal to Jesus not as "teacher" (*didaskalos*), but by the more exalted term, *epistata*, used by the Greeks for master teachers and supervisors, including those who gave instruction to the deities![211] Luke expands slightly Mark's report of the disciples' fear-filled question as to "Who then is this, that he commands even in wind and water, *and they obey him*?" (8:25).

The other miracle stories from Mark (5:1–43) of the Gerasene demoniac and the linked accounts of the raising of Jairus's daughter and the healing of the woman with the bloody flow are included by Luke with only slight changes (Luke 8:26–56). One possibly significant variation is the omission by Luke of the report in Mark that the ailing woman had "suffered much under the many physicians, and had spent all that she had" (Mark 5:26). Perhaps this was not included by Luke because of the traditional linking of the author of this gospel with "the beloved physician" (Col 4:14). The subsequent Markan account of Jesus' rejection in the synagogue at Nazareth (6:1–6) is also omitted by Luke.

Jesus' sending out of the Twelve in Luke's account has the added features that they are "to preach the kingdom of God and to heal" (9:2). The description of the death of John the Baptist (Mark 6:17–29) is omitted by Luke. And following the slightly abbreviated accounts of the return of the Twelve and Jesus' feeding the five thousand (Luke 9:10–17; Mark 6:30–44), one encounters Luke's major omission from Mark (6:45–8:26). The Markan narrative is rejoined at Luke 9:18 (= Mark 8:27), although there is no mention of these events taking place at Caesarea Philippi. Peter's confession of Jesus as Messiah adds "the Christ *of God*," but omitted from the narrative are Peter's rebuke of Jesus' prediction of his suffering, death, and resurrection, and Jesus' rebuke of Peter (Mark 8:32–33). As in Mark, the call to discipleship and the promise of divine vindication and sharing in the coming kingdom of God (Mark 8:34–9:1; Luke 9:23–27) are followed by the description of the transfiguration of Jesus (Luke 9:28–36). This supplements the Markan account (Mark 9:2–8) with a report of (1) Jesus' conversation with Moses and Elijah about his impending "departure"—*exodus*—that is to take place in Jerusalem; (2) the awakening of the slumbering disciples to see Jesus' glory and the historic visitors; and (3) the note that "in those days" the disciples kept silent about what they had seen, without having been so instructed by Jesus, as in Mark 9:9–10.

JESUS' JOURNEY TO JERUSALEM (9:51–19:27)

Following Luke's briefer version of Jesus' advice about allowing non-followers to expel demons in his name (9:49–50), the material from Mark 9:41–10:12 is either omitted by Luke or placed elsewhere in his sequence. Luke 9:51, which is unique to Luke, introduces a special section of that gospel (9:51–18:14) describing Jesus' preparation of his followers and of himself for the trial and execution that are to take place in Jerusalem. The section begins with an account of the rejection of his followers by the Samaritan villagers and Jesus' rebuke of James and John for offering "to call down fire from heaven and consume them" (9:54–55). To the Q tradition (9:57–59), Luke adds further words of Jesus calling for his followers to sever their obligations to their earthly families as they prepare for the coming of the kingdom of God (9:60–62).

Luke also places in a distinctive framework the Q traditions about Jesus sending out the disciples and how they are to react to hostility that they confront (10:1–16). In addition to the Twelve sent out earlier—whose number matches that of the tribes of Israel—he appoints "seventy others" to go before him in pairs to the towns where he is to come. Seventy was the traditional Jewish number for the nations of the world, as reflected in the designation of the Greek translation of the Hebrew Bible as the Septuagint: "the seventy."[212] They are to announce the divine "harvest" that is impending: when God calls all humanity to account, gathers the faithful, and punishes the wicked who reject the good news. They are to take no supplies with them, but to depend on the hospitality of the townspeople wherever they go, while warning of the dire punishment that will befall those in the towns that spurn the message and its messengers. Such cities as Tyre and Sidon will fare better in the day of judgment than the Galilean towns that scorn the works and words of Jesus and his emissaries. Only Luke (10:17–20) includes the report at their return of their ability to control the demons and the powers of evil, to which Jesus responds that he is the source of their having this capacity. It should lead not to pride, but to joy at their identity as God's people, whose "names are written in heaven." This is followed in Luke (10:21–22) by a prayer of rejoicing "in the Holy Spirit" that God has disclosed his purpose to his simple followers—"the babes"—rather than to those who pride themselves in their wisdom. Jesus as Son of the Father is the one through whom this truth has been revealed, and his followers can rejoice in these insights unknown by "many prophets and kings" (Luke 10:23–24).

Following Luke's version of the Markan tradition (12:28–31) about which is the primary commandment of God—which Luke adapts as an answer to the question of how one may gain eternal life (10:25–28)—this gospel presents more unique material: the parable of the Good Samaritan (10:29–37), Jesus' evaluation of Mary and Martha (10:38–42), and the parable-like story of the Friend at Midnight (11:5–8). The Samaritan is the one who, unlike the religious leaders (priest and Levite), demonstrates true love of one's neighbor by providing immediate and long-term aid to the victim of the robbers on the road from Jerusalem to Jericho. The one who pays proper attention to the teaching of Jesus is Mary, "who sat at the Lord's feet and listened"—not Martha, who was preoccupied with housekeeping. The Lord's Prayer is reported in a more personal and less liturgical mode—and probably, in a more nearly original form—than by Matthew (Luke 11:1–4l; Matt 6:9–13). The story of the one who at midnight asks a friend for basic needs and receives what he asked for is a model of the importance of persistence in prayer. Luke's version of the Q tradition of seeking answers to prayer ends with the rhetorical question about the generosity ("good gifts") that will be provided by "the heavenly Father epitomized in the gift of the Holy Spirit" (Luke 11:9–13). Only here in Luke (11:27–28) does Jesus respond to the pronouncement of the blessedness of his mother for having born and suckled him by declaring the blessed state of those who "hear the word of God and keep it." The importance of the scriptures is a dominant motif throughout Luke and Acts.

The themes set forth here by Luke, based mostly on the Q tradition, are (1) the superiority of Jesus to the role of Jonah with his warning to the people of Nineveh of impending disaster and the role of Solomon as the conveyor of divine wisdom to Israel (11:29–32); (2) the essential importance of divinely provided light to illumine the whole human body and its functions (11:33–36); (3) warning against the Pharisees, whose preoccupation with such external items as ritual purity, tithing, and preferential seating in the synagogue results in their neglect of "love and justice" (11:37–43). The Wisdom of God quoted here is an unknown source and is not referred to in Matthew's version of this material (23:34), which is included in his diatribe against the Pharisees and scribes and predicts the coming of "prophets, wise men, and scribes." Appropriate for Luke's interest in divine wisdom, however, is the version that promises "wise men and *apostles*" (Luke 11:49). To the Q tradition, which places on "this generation" the blame for the death of the prophets as those who speak for God throughout the scriptures—from Abel in Gen 4 to Zechariah in 2 Chron 24—Luke adds the provocative and threatening reaction of the scribes and Pharisees (Luke 12:53). This leads into Luke's report that, as thousands gather to hear Jesus' message, he offers a private warning to his disciples concerning the false teaching—"leaven"—of the Pharisees, which he denounces as "hypocrisy" (12:1).

Luke then turns to the connected themes of punishment and vindication (12:2–12), drawing on the Q source. No human actions are truly secret: the acts and their motivations will be disclosed, so for evil deeds one should expect punishment at the hands of God, who has the "power to cast into hell" the offenders, as well as to care for and to vindicate the faithful—and especially, those who publicly acknowledge Jesus as Son of Man, and hence will be acknowledged before God as members of the covenant people (12:8). Even those who speak against Jesus as Son of Man will receive forgiveness, but not those who denounce God's work through "the Holy Spirit" (12:10). The Spirit will instruct the faithful who are brought for interrogation before the Jewish and the Roman authorities as to what they are to say by way of testimony (12:11–12).

Luke then includes the parable of the Rich Fool (12:13–21), in which Jesus, with a warning against greed, tells the story of a prosperous man whose crops were outstandingly fruitful. But he foolishly assumes that if he stores all of these, he will guarantee a safe, prosperous, and wholly pleasurable future. God warns him, however, that his life might be taken that very night, and none of these treasures will benefit or belong to him. He has not understood how one can be "rich toward God." This leads to material from Q (12:23–34) that reminds the listener how God cares for the needs of birds and flowers and grass in ways that exceed human efforts to achieve splendor, and therefore how he will care for his people, enabling them to meet their basic needs. Instead of being preoccupied with such ephemeral needs, his people—here called "little flock"—are to look to God to grant them a place in his "kingdom," and in preparation for this eschatological event, are to sell what they own and give generously—thereby storing up eternal benefits in heaven. They are to live in readiness for the return of their master—Jesus—whenever he may come, occupied with God's work. For this, they will receive a reward, while those who exploit or pervert the role assigned to them will be punished at his coming (12:35–46). The Q source is supplemented by Luke (12:47–48) with a further word of warning about the punishment that will come for those who do not live and act in readiness for the master's return.

Luke expands the Q tradition (12:49–56) to detail the "fire" of conflict and threatening conditions that will precede the coming of the Son of Man. For the present, his agenda consists of "fire," the "baptism" of suffering, divisions within families across generations, and marital links. Unlike predictions of the weather based on present winds and clouds, his hearers are unable to interpret the present situation and to discern its implications for the future. They are to come to terms with their present condition (12:57–59), making whatever adjustments will serve them well for the future. Above all (in a unique Lukan passage, 13:1–9), Jesus is reported as using the examples of maltreatment of certain Galileans by the imperial authorities and the disaster that occurred in Jerusalem when a tower fell on eighteen people and killed them to make the point that these were not especially wicked people who received divine punishment. Rather, all humans should be aware that all will be held accountable for their behavior and outlook on life, and hence all are called to "repent"—that is, to change their view of life, and thereby to come to terms with themselves and the uncertainties of human existence.

Two unique stories of healings are in Luke 13:10–17 and 14:1–6. Both the woman with a spirit that crippled her and a man with dropsy are healed on the Sabbath—in the first case, in a synagogue, and in the second, while Jesus was eating a meal at the home of a leader of the Pharisees.[213] Jesus' question to the "lawyers and the Pharisees" as to the legality—in terms of Torah—of healing on the Sabbath evoked no verbal response. After healing the man, Jesus' question suggests an analogy between his act and what a parent or the owner of an ox would do on the Sabbath to rescue an endangered son or beast, but they also had no reply. Hence, Jesus' justification for an act of healing on the Sabbath remains a challenging question, rather than a dictum.

The crucial geographical and sociocultural shift in the subsequent section of Luke that portrays Jesus' journey to Jerusalem (9:51–19:27) is clearly anticipated at this point with the juxtaposed announcement of Jesus' plan to go there (13:31–33) and the lament over Jerusalem that follows (13:34–35). Declaration of the necessity of Jesus' going to Jerusalem follows the warning he receives from some Pharisees about the intention of Herod Antipas to put him to death. As a messenger of God to his people—hence, a "prophet"—he knows that he must pursue his course to the city where those who fulfill such a role must die. This is linked with (1) the denunciation of the city as the killer of those sent by God, (2) an indication of Jesus' effort to call together the people of God that has been thwarted by the religious rulers, and (3) a prediction of the destruction of the "house" that they saw themselves as constituting.

A unique feature of Luke is the way he builds on the Q tradition of Jesus' having affirmed God's outreach through him to invite "the poor"—that is, those excluded by legal standards—to share in the life of the age to come (Luke 6:20): "Blessed are you poor, for yours is the kingdom of God." This theme is set forth in two parables of feasts: Luke 14:7–14 and 14:15–24. In the first of these, he advises those invited to a wedding feast not to choose for themselves the seats of honor but to take the lowest places, from which the host will then call them to "come up higher." Then he gives a proverbial word of advice—which appears in several contexts in the synoptic tradition (Matt 18:4 and 23:12; Luke 18:14)—not to exalt oneself and then be humbled, but to humble oneself and then to be exalted. The further advice to the host of the feast is to invite those whom Luke pictures as of special concern of Jesus: "the poor, the maimed, the lame, and the blind."

This theme is repeated in Luke's version of the Q parable of the Great Dinner (14:15–24), which depicts participation in the kingdom of God. The procedure was to notify the prospective guests that there was to be a dinner; subsequently, when the arrangements were complete, to inform them that the time for it had arrived. Those initially invited are so occupied with ordinary matters—buying land, acquiring cattle, getting married—that they do not attend the banquet. The host then sends the servants out to invite the deprived, and they come. Luke adds a third stage in extending the invitation to complete outsiders—those in "the highways and the hedges" (14:23)—in order that "my house may be filled." None of those initially invited will share in this great symbolic feast.

This parable serves a useful function, not only in describing the successive stages of the invitation to share in the kingdom of God, but also in accounting for the failure to respond to Jesus' message on the part of his respectable, established contemporaries. As noted above in the analysis of the Q tradition, Matthew has converted the parable into an allegory of a royal wedding, with subsequent conflict pictured as the messengers are maltreated and killed and troops are sent to destroy the city. These details obviously reflect the Christians' understanding of the consequences of the Jewish Revolt of 66–70 CE: (1) the persecution experienced by the messengers of the gospel at the hands of religious and political leaders, and (2) the siege and destruction of Jerusalem by the Romans.

Luke continues to draw on and expand the Q tradition in his reports of those who respond to the message of Jesus. In 14:25–35, there are warnings about being prepared for what following Jesus as a disciple will cost. These include *hating* the whole range of one's family relationships: parents, siblings, and offspring. One must be willing to accept the possibility of execution by the authorities—"to bear one's own cross"—as the consequence of having become a follower of Jesus. Preparation for the future is also compared with the necessity of a builder of a tower having the resources to complete his intended program, and of a monarch lacking an adequate number of troops to confront his adversary and having to work out a compromise peace agreement. True discipleship must involve complete renunciation of reliance on one's own resources. The final proverbial words about "salt" (14:34–35), building on material from Mark (9:50) and Q (cf. Matt 5:13), point to the importance of a disciple fulfilling his or her intended function, and hence seen as "good," in contrast with failure to do so, which results in being thrown away.

The continuing series of parables in Luke 15 and 16 include Q and uniquely Lukan material. The Q parable of the Lost Sheep and the Lost Coin (15:1–10) incorporates Q material[214] but here is placed in a context of the contention of the Pharisees and scribes with Jesus for his having drawn to him large numbers of "tax collectors and sinners" and sharing meals with them, in violation of ritual rules (Luke 15:1–2). Luke then expands the Q parable to depict the shepherd whose concern for the single lost sheep leads him to leave his flock for a time in order to find and restore the lost one. He then invites friends and neighbors to join him in rejoicing for the recovery of the lost one—a response he compares with the "joy in heaven" at the recovery of even a single penitent sinner. Similarly, a housewife who has lost a drachma (a silver coin that was a day's wage for a worker) searches diligently until she finds it, and invites her friend in to share in the joy of its recovery. These parables in Luke point to the joy in the presence of God over the repentance of even one sinner. What is implicit but highly significant here is that participation in the covenant people is not dependent on conformity to ritual or even to moral requirements, but is the consequence of and a grateful response to the manifestation of divine love and forgiveness.

That point is made vividly in the first of two unique Lukan parables: the Prodigal Son (15:11–32) and the Dishonest Manager (16:1–9). In the first of these, the younger son, who asked for and received his share of the property and then squandered it in "dissolute living," found himself as an ill-fed servant feeding swine. Returning to his father with true penitence, he was received with compassion and rejoicing at his restoration as a lost son who has now been found. The older son was enraged by this most cordial reconciliation of the father and the erring son, and reminds the father of his own consistent obedience. He is commended for that, but invited to join in the joyous celebration of the return of the repentant brother who is not dead, but alive; not lost, but found. The dishonest manager is a model of someone who, however scheming and unscrupulous, is shrewd in coming to terms with those indebted to his master. Hence, "the sons of light" can learn even from such scheming characters that one must confront reality and come to terms with it in such a way as to meet one's obligations, and thereby be prepared for the future day of reckoning.

At the same time (16:10–13), the people of God are called to be faithful in discharging whatever their responsibilities are, even in caring for what belongs to others. Only one master can be served: God, not worldly possessions. This teaching evokes scorn from the Pharisees, who are here depicted as "lovers of money" and as taking pride in their way of life, but their real values are "an abomination in the sight of God."

Returning to the Q tradition (Luke 16:16–17), Jesus makes a pronouncement of major significance concerning the radical change in the outworking of God's purpose for the history of his people. John the Baptist is said to be the crucial turning point, in that he brings to a conclusion the preparatory era of "the law and the prophets." After John—with the launching of Jesus' message and ministry—"the kingdom of God is proclaimed." Those who respond positively, however, must be prepared for encountering force and violence. Nevertheless, the promises and obligations that are set forth in the law continue to be in force: not one of its tiniest literary features—"one stroke"—will be dropped. An example of the binding character of the law is given in this version of the rules concerning divorce and remarriage (16:18; cf. Deut 24:1), which here prohibits such a practice, denouncing it as "adultery."[215]

A radically negative view of wealth is set forth in the Lukan story of the Rich Man and Lazarus (16:19–31). The fine clothing and sumptuous food of the former are contrasted with the impoverished one, who is eating what falls from the rich man's table and is covered with sores that dogs licked. The poor man died and was taken by angels to the presence of Abraham, among God's true people, while the rich man died and was being tormented in Hades. In response to his request to have Lazarus go and warn his brothers of their destiny in hell, he is told by Abraham that they should read Moses and the Prophets. But aware that they do not heed these sources, he asks that someone go to them from the dead, and then is told that such heedless individuals will not be persuaded even by someone rising from the dead. The aim of the passage is to explain why many complacent individuals who are exposed to the scriptures will not be "convinced," even when Jesus rises from the dead.

Luke 17:3–4 contains a simpler version than Matthew (18:15, 21–22) of the Q sayings about forgiving one's brother repeatedly. A variant of the power of faith that is comparable to a mustard seed in Mark 4:30–32 appears in Luke 13:18–19 as an image of the kingdom of God. Luke 17:7–21 and 18:1–14 are found only in Luke; 17:7–10 is a parable of the necessity for those who consider themselves to be servants of God to fulfill their responsibilities toward others beyond merely specified obligations. As Jesus travels along the boundary between Galilee and Samaria, he heals ten lepers and instructs them to show themselves to the priests in order to gain formal recognition of their having been cured. The only one of the ten who returns to thank Jesus is not a Jew, but a Samaritan—"not one of us!"

Three distinctive Lukan passages deal with the issue of when and how God's kingdom is to be established on the earth. The first, spoken in response to an inquiry from the Pharisees as to the time of its coming, states that there are no real clues or signs as to when or where the kingdom is to come (17:20–21). Instead, Jesus declares that it is already "among you." Its presence is to be seen in the actions of Jesus, which demonstrate the defeat of the powers of evil, and in the transformation of lives that is taking place within the new community. Expanding on a Q tradition about the coming of the Son of Man (17:22–37), Jesus declares that there will be no advance indicators as to the time of his coming. Rather, it will take place instantly, like lightning crossing the sky. Luke apparently adds the prediction of the suffering and rejection of the Son of Man (17:25), which has no match in the Matthean parallel (24:26–27). Instead, the present generation is compared with the self-satisfied routine of life of the wicked in the time of Noah (Gen 6–7) and of Lot (Gen 18–19), which leads to divine punishment. Those who are self-serving must be prepared to leave behind their worldly goods, not looking back longingly, as Lot's wife did (Gen 19:26). Luke's special interest in women[216] as participants in the new community is evident in his final note here (17:35, 37) about the two working women who are warned that vultures will be gathered around the corpses of those whose main concern is merely to continue their present mode of existence.

Two more parables that appear only in Luke are the Unjust Judge (18:1–8), and the Pharisee and the Tax Collector (18:9–14). In the former, an importunate widow continues to plead with an irreligious and inhumane judge to support her against her opponent. Her persistence overcomes his earlier indifference and he vows to bring justice to her—a process that is then compared with God's concerned response to obtain justice for the members of the elect community who appeal repeatedly for help. The other parable contrasts two who enter the temple to pray: (1) the Pharisee, whose prayer is filled with pride because of his moral and ritual piety as well as his fidelity in paying his tithes; (2) the tax collector, who prays, bows his head, and beats his breast as he asks for God's mercy toward him, since he serves as an agent taxing and exploiting his people for the benefit of the Romans. The latter went home in right relationship with God ("justified"), while the proudly pious one can expect to be "humbled."

At 18:15, Luke resumes following the Markan sequence (Mark 10:13) with the account of Jesus blessing the little children, to whom "belongs the kingdom of God" (18:17). This is followed by Luke's basic reproduction of Markan material through the third prediction of the passion (Luke 18:31–34; Mark 10:32–34), to which is added the note that the Twelve did not perceive the significance of this: "what he said was hidden from them, and they did not grasp what was said (18:34). To the story of the healing of the blind man near Jericho (Mark 10:46–52) is added that, when he was cured and followed Jesus, he "glorified God," as did "all the people" (18:43). Only Luke tells the story of Jesus' encounter in Jericho with Zacchaeus, the "rich" tax collector who had climbed a tree to see Jesus as he passed (19:1–10). Jesus invites himself to stay at his house, which would have been a violation of both the ritual and political standards of pious Jews, as is evident in the charge that Jesus "has gone to be the guest of a man who is a sinner." Zacchaeus tries to promote what he regards as his own piety: generosity to the poor and repayment of any wrongful financial transactions. Jesus declares that this man is experiencing renewal ("salvation") as a member of the covenant people of Abraham, and that such acts of deliverance and acceptance are essential features of his own role as "Son of Man."

The Q parable of the Pounds (19:11–27) depicts a nobleman destined to be designated and empowered as king in a far country where he goes to receive his kingdom and then to return. Ten of his servants were given money with which to trade until his return.[217] The returning king rewards those entrusted with the money in proportion to the effectiveness of their use of the funds: the one who increased the investment to ten additional pounds is given authority over ten cities; the second made five pounds and is rewarded with five cities; the third merely kept the pound safe, out of fear of the severity of the donor. His lack of productivity results in his money being given to the most productive of the three, while the unfruitful one is deprived of what he has (19:20–24). Those in the realm who were hostile toward the newly appointed king are brought before him and executed, but to the fruitful "will more be given." The parable points to the divine reward for those who faithfully and effectively spread the good news and expand its power over an ever-wider portion of the people. This brings to a close Luke's section concerning the journey to Jerusalem of Jesus and his disciples.

JESUS' MINISTRY IN JERUSALEM (19:28–21:38)

The account in Luke of Jesus' preparation for and entry into the city of Jerusalem (19:28–38) closely follows the Markan narrative, but at 19:37, there is an added detail. As Jesus was descending from the Mount of Olives, there was a "whole multitude of disciples" who began to praise God for all the great deeds that they had seen him perform. He is hailed in words from Ps 118:25–26, which have been expanded to greet him as "*the King* who comes in the name of the Lord," to call for "peace in heaven" and "glory in the highest." This is reported by Luke in another distinctive passage, which leads to Jesus' prediction of the destruction of Jerusalem (19:39–44) and to his defense of their acclaim of him by quoting from Habbakuk (2:11) the prediction that "the stones will cry out" against the actions of the wicked (Luke 19:39). Other prophetic features of this coming disaster are detailed in language reminiscent of Isa 29:3 (the siegeworks that will surround the city); Ps 137:9; Nahum 3:10 (the smashing of children on the ground). Luke omits the Markan account of Jesus simply entering the temple (11:11) and gives a shorter version than Mark (11:15–19) of Jesus' driving the merchants and moneychangers from the temple as well as of his teaching there. The desire of a coalition of religious leaders—the chief priests and the scribes and the principal men of the people—to find a way to destroy him is not yet fulfilled, while "all the people hung upon his words" (Mark 11:15–19; Luke 19:45–48).

Luke reproduces Mark's parable of the Vineyard and the Tenants (Mark 12:1–12) with only minor changes (Luke 20:9–19), which include the omission of building a tower and a wine vat (Mark 12:1; Isa 5:2) and the reversal of the order for maltreating the son: first casting him out of the vineyard and then killing him. The import of this is that Jesus is shown here by Luke as having been rejected from participation in the traditional covenant people and then being put to death (20:14–15). Jesus' hearers in Luke respond to this prediction by uttering the petition "May it not be so!" to which he replies, as in Mark, by quoting Ps 118:22 that the stone rejected by the builder has become the chief cornerstone.[218] But Luke adds the further prediction (20:18) of the judgmental role of "that stone," which will break in pieces those who fall on it, and crush anyone on whom it falls"—imagery of eschatological judgment that echoes the prophecies in Isa 8:13–15 and Dan 2:34, 44. Those who perceive that this parable is a severe criticism of them are identified in Luke (20:19) as "the scribes and the chief priests."

The plot by these religious leaders to rid themselves of Jesus includes, according to Luke (20:20–26), the use of spies who pose as being sympathetic with Jesus, but whose role is to provide the governor with the evidence of his subversive teachings. Building on the Markan material (12:13–17), they are described as first flattering Jesus as one who "truly teaches the way of God" and then asking questions for which they hope to get an anti-Roman answer. His response is the familiar Markan "Render to Caesar the things that are Caesar's, and to God the things that are God's"—which leaves the spies with no basis for a charge of political subversion, but astonished by his answer.

Luke 20:27–50 matches the basic aim and content of Mark 12:18–40, which consists of a series of controversies between Jesus and the various Jewish religious groups: Sadducees, scribes, and Pharisees. The issues debated concern (1) the resurrection (20:27–40); (2) The question about the messiah as David's Son (20:41–44); and (3) the woes against the Pharisees (20:45–47), which has already been dealt with by Luke, drawing on the Q tradition in 11:39–42, 44, 47–51. A shortened version of the Markan story of the poor widow's contribution to the treasury (12:41–44) makes the same point: that, in contrast to the rich who give out of their abundant wealth, she gave all that she had.

As in Mark 13, Luke's report of Jesus' prediction of the destruction of the temple (21:5–7) leads into his version of the Synoptic apocalypse (Mark 13:5–37; Luke 21:8–26). Significant Lukan variations from the Markan source begin with the promise in 21:15 that the faithful will be given divine wisdom, which none of their "adversaries will be able to withstand or contradict." This matches the importance attached to wisdom and eloquence that runs throughout Luke and Acts.

The importance for Luke of political powers and the worldwide dimensions of the apocalyptic battle that is being depicted are evident in his mention that, as the pollution of the temple draws near, "Jerusalem [will be] surrounded by armies" (21:20) and "will be trodden down by the Gentiles until the times of the Gentiles are fulfilled" (21:24). The people there will experience "great distress" and divine "wrath," dying by "the sword" and being "led captive among all the nations." The outcome of this cosmic struggle will be a new epoch in human history, dominated by Gentile rule and hence known as "the times of the Gentiles." The signs of this radical change will appear in the sun, moon, stars, and in the disturbances of the waters of the earth, and humans will be overcome with "fear and foreboding" at these signs of cosmic change (21:25–26). The divine resolution of these struggles will begin with the coming of the Son of Man (21:27), but even as these universal struggles are launched, the faithful should look up in expectation of the divine liberation and renewal that is "drawing near" (21:28). The signs give assurance to the community that "the kingdom of God is near" (21:31). And, as in Mark 13:30, there is the promise that all these events will take place before "this generation" has passed away (21:32).

Thus, Luke's epochal view of history perceives the consummation of the divine purpose in history as taking place within the lifetime of his readers. His version of the apocalyptic discourse ends with a solemn warning to avoid dissipation and worldly cares, since they will divert attention from the cosmic transformation that is to come. All humans will confront this event, and members of the community are urged to avoid involvement in earthly matters so that they may be able to escape the effects of the disasters and take their places in the presence of "the Son of Man" (21:34–36).

In anticipation of his seizure, trial, and execution by the civil authorities, Jesus is described in Luke 21:37–38 as teaching large groups of people daily in the temple, while residing nightly on the Mount of Olives.

THE LAST SUPPER, TRIAL, DEATH, AND BURIAL
OF JESUS (22:1–23:56)

Luke follows closely the brief Markan account of the conspiracy of the "chief priests and the scribes" as to how to put Jesus to death (22:1–4; Mark 14:1–2),[219] but there are some differences in details. For example, Satan is blamed for impelling Judas to betray Jesus to the authorities with whom he conferred, who are identified by Luke as "the chief priests and officers."[220] Judas is then said to have "sought an opportunity to betray him to them in the absence of the multitude (22:3–6). Preparation for Jesus to celebrate the Passover with his disciples (Mark 14:12–16) is assigned by Luke to "Peter and John" (Luke 22:8), but the narrative of their preparation follows the Markan account. Jesus' prediction of his betrayal is moved by Luke to after the meal (22:21–23), and is followed by an account of the dispute among the disciples concerning rank (22:24–30), which appears earlier in a briefer form in Mark (10:42–45) and is supplemented here by material from Q (Luke 22:27–30). This calls for a reversal of roles: the greatest is to become as the youngest, and the leader as one who serves. By human standards, the greater one is the one served, not the servant, which is the role Jesus is fulfilling among them: "as one who serves."

His disciples have remained faithful to him as he has passed through his "trials"—that is, his times of testing and maltreatment at the hands of the religious and civil authorities. Accordingly, he is designating a role in his kingdom for them in which they will share the common life of the leadership—eating and drinking at his table—as well as in the role of judges of the new "twelve tribes of Israel" that constitute the covenant people in the age to come. In a unique Lukan addition (22:35–38), the disciples are reminded how their life was sustained in the past when they were sent out without the customary equipment—"purse, bag, sandals." Now, however, they are to be prepared for meeting their basic needs, as well as for fierce opposition, represented chiefly by Jesus' own arrest and execution as a "transgressor" of Jewish and Roman law. They reply that they have the basic instruments for self-protection: "two swords."

In Luke's version of Jesus' being taken captive by the agents of the priestly leadership (Luke 22:32–47), Jesus observes that they did not seize him when he was "day after day in the temple," but that his situation has changed radically. He says to those who are seizing him, "This is your hour and the power of darkness" (22:53), a somewhat briefer comment than its basic Markan source (Mark 14:32–52). Omitted are Jesus' acknowledgment that his soul is sorrowful and his prayer that he might escape from this situation (Mark 14:34–35), as well as his thrice-repeated observing of the sleeping disciples (14:37–41) and his announcement of his betrayal "into the hands of sinners" (14:41–42). Instead, on finding them asleep (Luke 22:45–46) he merely advises the disciples to pray for escape from temptation. At this point, a crowd arrives, led by Judas and including "the chief priests and officers of the temple, who had come out against him." The sequence of events concerning Jesus' hearing before the council is also changed in Luke (22:54–71) from the Markan original (14:53–72), with the result that Peter's denial of Jesus is recounted prior to Jesus' confronting the council. In Luke's account, when "the Lord turned and looked at Peter" (Luke 22:61), he was filled with regret and sorrow for his denial that he knew Jesus, that he was one of his followers, and that he was a Galilean (22:56–61). Only in Luke's account of the hearing before the council is Jesus asked, "Are you the Son of God?" (22:70), and then the whole of the council unambiguously takes on the role of bringing Jesus before Pilate (23:1). The political features of the charges brought against Jesus by the religious authorities are explicit in Luke 23:2: "And they began to accuse him, saying, 'We found this man perverting our nation, and forbidding us to give tribute to Caesar, and saying that he himself is the Messiah, a king.'"

The further, unspecified accusations reported by Mark (15:3) are not mentioned by Luke, nor is Jesus' refusal to respond to the charges (15:4–5). Instead, in Luke's account Pilate simply notifies the chief priests and the crowds that he can "find no basis for an accusation against this man" (23:4). They respond by claiming that, by his teaching in Galilee and Judea, "he stirs up the people" (23:5). The political implications of this charge are clear, though no evidence to support it is offered.

Only Luke reports that Pilate, on learning of Jesus' Galilean residence and activity, sent him to Herod Antipas, whose tetrarchy included Galilee and Perea from 4 BCE to 39 CE. Luke notes Herod's personal interest in seeing and hearing Jesus, about whom he had heard so much and by whom he might see a sign performed (23:6–8). He interrogated Jesus, but received no answer. The chief priests and scribes are said to have made violent accusations against him, and so Herod and his soldiers, responding to what was apparently a charge that Jesus was an agent of revolution and a claimant to the throne, are said to have joined in "treating him with contempt and mocking him, arraying him in gorgeous apparel." Then Jesus was sent back to Pilate, which resulted in the transformation of their formerly hostile relationship into friendship (23:9–12). Thereupon Pilate is described as convening the priests and Jewish leaders—and the people—to tell them that neither he nor Herod was able to find any basis for their charges of political subversion or any other capital crime. He proposes, instead, to "have him flogged and release him" (23:13–16). Luke is extending his case, as he was subsequently to do in the book of Acts, that the movement launched by Jesus was not politically subversive.

Luke condenses the report of the call of the leaders and the people to set a culprit free: not Jesus but Barabbas, who had been convicted of insurrection and murder in the city (23:25). Their call to have Jesus crucified evokes Pilate's third declaration that he has found Jesus guilty "of no crime deserving death," and he offers once more to have him flogged and then released. Finally, Pilate accedes to the prevailing voices of the crowd, releases the man convicted of insurrection and murder (23:24), and turns Jesus over to the will of the crowd. As in Matthew, the evidence is presented in such a way as to place the blame for Jesus' death primarily on the Jewish leaders. Luke omits features reported in Mark: the mocking of Jesus by the soldiers, their dressing him and hailing him as a king, and then leading him out to be crucified (Mark 16:16–20).

Instead, Luke mentions the compelling story of Simon of Cyrene carrying the cross behind Jesus (23:26; cf. Mark 15:21), but then provides his own depiction of the multitude that follows him—not urging his impending execution but bewailing it (Luke 23:27–32). The imagery and the description of the mourning echo the language of the prophets. The special mention of women in the throng of mourners reflects the response in Zech 12:10–13:1 of the inhabitants of Jerusalem—and especially of the women—who mourn the death of God's agent, "whom [the authorities] have pierced."[221] In Jer 9:17–21, women are summoned to lament the consequences of Israel's having "forsaken the law that [God] set before them." Now they are to lament the rejection of God's Messiah by the Jewish leadership. The appeal to the women as "daughters of Jerusalem" recalls the use of that term in both the poetic and prophetic traditions: Song of Songs 2:7; 5:16; 8:4; Isa 37:22; Zeph 3:14, but especially Zech 9:9, where the "daughter of Zion"—i.e., the people of Jerusalem—are called to rejoice at the coming of God's ruler for his people. Now, however, they are to mourn as they and the people await divine judgment. The call for the hills and mountains to fall on them echoes the cry of the leaders and the people of Israel who have turned to idolatry and are to undergo divine punishment in exile (Hos 10:7–8). The imagery of green wood and dry wood (23:31) mirrors the prophecy in Isa 10:16–17, which foresees the fire of divine judgment consuming the faithless people.

Only Luke's version of the crucifixion (23:33–43) includes Jesus' prayer of intercession for his oppressors (v. 34) and identifies those executed with him as "criminals" or "evildoers"[222] rather than as "robbers,"[223] which is the term used by Josephus with reference to revolutionaries and insurrectionists.[224] Luke, however, avoids this political implication in his account of Jesus' crucifixion. He also reports Jesus' having interceded with God on behalf of these criminals, asking that they be forgiven for their unknowing misdeeds. He is scoffed at for his messianic claims by unidentified "rulers" (23:35), who are presumably the same Jewish leaders that participated in the denunciation of him at the hearing before Pilate (23:10). Luke juxtaposes with this detail the initiative of the Roman soldiers in offering him vinegar, which contrasts with one of the criminal's urging Jesus in mocking fashion, "If you are the Messiah, save yourself!" The other criminal, however, rebukes him, acknowledges the guilt of the two of them, but affirms the complete innocence of Jesus. His appeal to Jesus, "Remember me when you come into your kingdom," evokes Jesus' response, "Truly I tell you, today you will be with me in paradise" (23:43).[225]

In his description of the death of Jesus (23:44–49), Luke adds to the report of "darkness over the whole land" the detail that "the sun's light failed," but omits Jesus' cry of divine dereliction and his being offered vinegar (Mark 15:34–36). Instead, he describes Jesus as calling out—in full confidence, rather than in despair, as in the Markan tradition—"Father, into your hands I commend my spirit" (23:46). The centurion, instead of affirming Jesus' divine sonship, as in Mark 15:39, declares his innocence publicly (23:47). The multitudes that had gathered and seen what had happened to Jesus returned to their homes "beating their breasts" as a sign of contrition and regret at what he had suffered. Luke then joins Mark in describing his women followers from Galilee watching these events "at a distance" (23:49).

The Jewishness of Joseph of Arimathea is underscored by Luke, who describes his hometown as "Jewish" and depicts him as "a good and righteous man" but as having "not agreed to [the council's] plan and action" (23:50–51). He asked for and was granted the body of Jesus, which he planned to bury in a tomb that was ritually pure, since in it (Luke alone reports) "no one had ever been laid."

JESUS' APPEARANCES TO HIS FOLLOWERS
IN JERUSALEM (24:1–53)

Customary preparation of the body with "spices and ointments" could not be carried out then by the women followers from Galilee since it was time to prepare for the Sabbath, which was about to begin—a detail not included by Mark or Matthew.[226] In compliance with the Sabbath laws, the women rested instead of applying the materials to Jesus' body (23:56), waiting instead for the first available time: early Sunday morning, after the Sabbath was over. Luke's distinctive version of the story of the empty tomb varies considerably from the Markan account (16:1–8). On their arrival at the tomb and finding the stone door rolled back and the body of Jesus gone, "suddenly two men in dazzling clothes stood beside them" (24:4) and asked the women, who had prostrated themselves, "Why do you look for the living among the dead?" Then the men at the tomb recall for the women Jesus' prediction that "the Son of Man must be handed over to sinners, and be crucified, and on the third day rise again" (24:7). Recalling these words, the women go back from the tomb to report to the eleven disciples—who are also designated "the apostles" (24:10)—and the other members of Jesus' followers what they had seen and heard (24:8).

The initial response of the apostles to this report is incredulity (24:11): "These words seemed to them an idle tale, and they did not believe them." But Luke then has an additional, unique tradition that he provides to his readers: the story of Jesus' appearance to two unnamed disciples (24:13–35) and subsequently to all of them (24:36–48). In the first of these stories, the two are walking to Emmaus and discussing what has happened. Unrecognized by them, Jesus joins them and they tell him that Jesus, who was a "prophet mighty in deed and word" in the perception of "God and all the people," and whom they expected to set Israel free, had been crucified three days earlier by a plot of the "chief priests and leaders." But some women had reported finding his tomb empty and being told by angels that he was alive. Subsequently, Peter also visited the tomb and confirmed that the body was gone.

On the road to Emmaus, Jesus—whom his followers failed to recognize—met and rebuked two of his followers[227] for their failure to realize what the prophets had "declared" about his suffering and glorification. Then he began to show them from "Moses and all the prophets" the truth about him as Messiah. Responding to their invitation to him to join them at a meal, it is when he—conforming to the eucharistic model—"took bread, blessed and broke it" that they recognized him, and he vanished. They attested to each other that their hearts were burning within them as he talked with them and opened the scriptures to them (24:24–32). Returning to Jerusalem and the eleven, they learned that Simon Peter had also seen the risen Christ, and then reported how he had become "known to them in the breaking of bread" (24:33–34).

Then Jesus appeared among the gathered disciples, who were frightened and thought he was a ghost. He assured them of the tangibility of his body—demonstrating his bodily existence by eating some broiled fish before them. Luke is eager to show that the resurrection of Jesus was not merely a spiritual vision, but the demonstration of a transformed human body. Jesus is then portrayed as showing from the scriptures that his suffering, death, and resurrection were all discernible there, and then going on to commission them to preach "forgiveness of sins . . . in his name to all nations, beginning from Jerusalem." They have witnessed the events on which this message is based, and there in Jerusalem they are to become empowered by God to bear witness to these truths.

Luke then describes Jesus blessing them, and his being taken up to God, while his disciples remain "in the temple blessing God" (24:53). The fulfillment of that promise of divine empowerment is, of course, the first major event in the second volume of Luke's work, The Acts of the Apostles.[228] Thus, the historical basis for the church's message about Jesus, the foundation of the promise of forgiveness, the significance of his death on the cross, and the basic charge to his disciples about how to live as the new covenant people and what to do to spread the message across the world—are all set forth in this gospel.

The Community of Mystical Participation: John

Although there are certain features the Gospel of John shares with the Synoptic Gospels—an account of Jesus' public ministry, including his activities and his teaching and culminating in his conflict with the civil and religious authorities, his arrest, crucifixion, burial, and resurrection—the style and the details of his career, the content and mode of his teaching, the depiction of his relationship to God, and his post-resurrection appearances are communicated in a significantly different way in what has become known as the Fourth Gospel. Not surprisingly, therefore, and linked with the differences noted above, is the fact that the way in which the new community is pictured as being formed in this gospel is radically different from the other three as well. Yet paradoxically, in spite of the culturally and conceptually brilliant way in which Jesus' relationship to God and the nature of the covenant community he calls into being are communicated in this gospel, the author's perception of Jesus is conveyed in deceptively simple language and literary modes. One might say that the profundity of thought in the Gospel of John is expressed in the language of a primer.

To link the Gospel of John with the community of mystical participation in a conceptually and historically responsible way requires some investigation of the characteristics of mysticism in the Graeco-Roman world as well as in the Jewish mystical traditions that existed prior to or concurrent with the emergence of Christianity. At the same time, one must avoid imposing on the mystical feature of John's gospel the radically individualistic approach to religion—and especially to Christianity—that characterized much of theology and biblical studies in the late nineteenth and early twentieth centuries. This approach might be said to have culminated in the existentialist analysis and interpretation of the Gospel of John produced by Rudolf Bultmann in his commentary on this gospel.[229] In his perception, John's gospel is radically individualistic in its representation of Jesus and his message, and hence Bultmann has no place for understanding the mode of community definition implicit in the text.[230] Careful study of the mystical tradition in the Graeco-Roman period, however, in pagan as well as in Jewish and Christian sources, shows that sharing in what was regarded as a divine mystery was not a private experience but involved participation in the life of a seeking, committed community.[231]

Mystical Traditions in Judaism and the Graeco-Roman World

The Greek term *mysterion* derives from the verb *myein*, which means to shut the mouth or close the eyes of all except those to whom the insights have been granted: the *mystai*. In the Greek tradition, this granting of insight was thought to take place under the guidance of a *hierophants*, a revealer of sacred things. The initiate went through four stages: (1) preliminary purification; (2) communication of the mystical knowledge; (3) the experience of revelation of holy things (*epopteia*); (4) the crowning of the mystic. The central revelation was an act or sacred drama symbolizing the access to the holy wisdom, not merely conveying information. Secrecy was essential because one was dealing with deities who wanted to safeguard these insights from the impure or those not properly prepared. The dramas depicted the actions of the deities in gaining and maintaining divine order for the benefit of human life. Initiation into the mysteries provided comfort and assurance of divine purpose and control, rather than merely information.

One of the best-attested examples of the adaptation of myths to provide insight and hope concerning divinely granted access to truth is that of Isis in the early Roman imperial period. Isis was originally a deity praised and honored for her role in the continuing fertility of the world, but through adaptation of features from Greek philosophical tradition, she came to be perceived as the agent through whom humans could gain insight and participate in divine life. Already in the first century BCE, Diodorus Siculus describes Isis as the one who brings immortality to her devotees. By the turn of the second century CE—which is the probable date of the Gospel of John, as well—Plutarch, in his allegorical interpretation of the Isis myth, refers to her role in restoring her murdered husband Osiris to life, and correlates this experience with Greek philosophy and, most notably, with the philosophy of Plato. Of special relevance for our purposes is the central importance of the *logos*. God, who is the Good and the One, requires intermediaries in order to communicate with the world: the primary intermediary agent is the Logos. In developing this thesis, Plutarch draws on the *Symposium* and the *Phaedrus* of Plato, though he goes beyond Plato in his *Dialogue on Love* when he perceives Eros (love) as the divine agency that enables one to ascend from the tangible world to the realm of ideas and finally to the vision of Beauty. In his *On Isis and Osiris*, Plutarch portrays the ideas as what John Dillon described as "the content of the immanent logos. And in Plutarch's *On the Divine Vengeance*, God is seen as the totality of the Ideas, and as the model for the physical world, and especially for human beings, who are made in God's likeness."[232] The role of the *logos* in the Gospel of John is clearly akin to these Platonic concepts of the creation and ordering of the world as expressed in a work contemporary with the writing of the Fourth Gospel. The major emphasis in Plutarch's use of the Isis myth to describe how humans can attain divine knowledge is on the participation of the seeker in kinship with others in the community of those who strive to understand the divine purpose and to share in its benefits.

Thus, of major importance in investigation of the mystical traditions—among both Jews and Gentiles in the Graeco-Roman period—is the recognition that the divine mystery was not perceived in exclusively experiential terms that could not be articulated. In the Jewish traditions, disclosure of divine purpose and of the means for personal renewal was an important feature of the wisdom tradition. The books of Job and Ecclesiastes, for example, while differing in literary strategy and conceptual orientation, are both "intensely personal versions of . . . seeking for meaning behind the seeming chaos of human existence." Like other wisdom writings, they "include a questing, personal struggle to understand and affirm God's workings in human life, and in some cases to discern basic principles of divine action and human response." As an activity of a seeking community, this search can be characterized as not private and purely intellectual, but as mystical and group oriented. Similarly, some of the psalms are addressed to God by individuals, speaking in the first person singular (e.g., 23, 51, 54, 59, 69, 71, 102, 116, 130), but they are also intended to be heard and heeded by the whole of Israel. This is explicit in Ps 130, which begins with the profoundly personal appeal, "Out of the depths I cry to you, O Lord. Lord, hear my voice!" but which ends with:

> O Israel, hope in the LORD!
> For with the LORD there is steadfast love,
> and with him is great power to redeem.
> It is he who will redeem Israel
> from all its iniquities. (130:7–8)

An important and well-documented mystical mode in Judaism in the first century CE and subsequently was what came to be called *merkabah* mysticism—the designation deriving from the notion that God ruled the universe from a chariot-throne.[233] The prophet's vision of God in Ezekiel (1:4–28) included his seeing a chariot, the heavenly dome, the throne of God, and the radiant cloud of glory that was perceived as the presence of God. This perception of the divine throne is found in liturgical songs recovered among the Dead Sea Scrolls, which have been published as "Songs of the Sabbath Sacrifice."[234] The despair and disillusionment that set in among Jews after the Maccabean rulers fell and control passed into the hands of the Romans led to the writing of hymns and texts that promised mystical ascent into the presence of God and provided hope and perceptions about the renewal of the life of the community of faith in the present. It was believed that contemplation of the divine chariot-throne would make possible this renewal for members of the seeking community. The basic hope of access to God for those to whom God had disclosed his purpose parallels that which one encounters in the Gospel of John, but the image of the chariot throne is not found in this gospel.

Thus, Jewish mystical participation in divine renewal is deeply emotional and personal, but it is not private. Instead, it is to be part of the experience of God shared by the covenant community as a whole. These features of mystical encounter with God have a counterpart in the Gospel of John, where the images of participation in the new life that God has granted to his people are depicted through a range of vivid narrative and discourse models, as well as a series of metaphors portraying the new community and Jesus, its revelatory founder. These mystical features are evident in the corporate images found throughout this gospel.

Outline of the Gospel of John

Prologue (1:1–18)

1. Jesus' Signs, Summons, and Claims (1:19–13:38).
2. God's Glory Revealed by Jesus to the Community of Faith (14:1–17:26).
3. Jesus' Death and Vindication: His Disclosure of Himself to his Followers (18:1–20:31).

Epilogue (21:1–31)

Analysis of the Gospel of John

PROLOGUE (1:1–18)

The themes of the opening lines of this prologue are widely recognized as reflecting motifs and language used in the beginning of the Septuagintal version of the book of Genesis. Creation begins when God speaks, and light appears, dividing day from night and launching what is to be the "first day" of history, and on the successive days God shapes the heavens and the earth, living creatures, and finally humanity "in his image" (Gen 1:1–27). Each stage of creation takes place in response to God's word. John opens with the assertion that the *logos*—one meaning of which is "word"—was there from the beginning (1:1). This is not simply chronological beginning, but the conceptual and purposive base for all that came into being (1:2). The *logos* is the agent through which everything in creation came into being (1:3), and it is also the source of life and the instrument through which humanity gains illumination and information about reality (1:4). There is a force, however, which seeks to thwart or extinguish this divinely provided light: "darkness," but it has not been able to overcome the divine power and purpose.

Testimony to "the true light" was borne by John the Baptist, whom God sent so that potentially "all" might come to trust in the light, which was to provide illumination for all humanity (1:6–8). Indeed, the world was made through this Word, yet it did not recognize or acknowledge him as its creator. When the Word appeared in human form, he came into a situation and circumstances in the sphere of Judaism that was properly his own, but that people as a whole—and as is made clear in the subsequent account, especially their leaders—did not accept him as the instrument of God for their enlightenment and renewal. Others who perceived him to be God's messenger and agent took that opportunity, however. Since they trusted in his divine authority and empowerment to carry out this role—"believed in his name"—they were granted the right to become God's children: the new covenant community. Their right to this relationship was not based on ancestry or on human effort or will, but came wholly and solely from God (1:9–13).

The agent of God to convey and accomplish the divine purpose to create this new community came in fully human form: "the Word became flesh." Living among other humans, he nevertheless displayed in a unique way the gracious purpose of God, the ultimate truth about God's intention for his people, and even the divine glory, recalling the radiant presence of God that was believed to exist in the inmost sanctuary of the temple, the holy of holies. He is indeed the unique "Son from the Father"—the human agent and manifestation of divine purpose for those created in the divine image. John the Baptist acknowledged that the Jesus whose appearance was subsequent to his own actually preceded him in existence and rank: "He was before me" (1:16). In contrast to Moses, through whom the law was given by God to his people, Israel, "grace and truth" have come through Jesus Christ (1:17). And it is he alone, now in the intimate presence of God, who has enabled human beings to know God as he truly is (1:18).

It is important to mention that here John affirms the goodness of creation rather than making a distinction between the material world as inherently evil and the spiritual world as good, such as emerged later in Gnosticism. Nor is there the notion that in principal only an elect minority has access to the truth about God: rather, it is "every human" (*panta anthropon*) who can accept and be illumined by the light God provides concerning the origin and purpose of the world and of humanity (1:9). There are no prior ethnic or cultural limits on those who may come to know God. The decisive question is whether or not one trusts in Jesus' "name" (1:12)—that is, puts one's confidence in his identity and role as "the true light."

JESUS' SIGNS, SUMMONS, AND CLAIMS (1:19–12:20)

This major section of John contains a combination of reports of (1) the testimony of John the Baptist as to the identity and significance of Jesus, (2) Jesus' call of his disciples, (3) the miraculous acts of Jesus—called here "signs,"[235] (4) the claims of Jesus concerning his role in the purpose of God for his people, (5) the transformation that will take place in the lives of those who participate in the new community, and (6) predictions of the official opposition that he will confront. As in the other gospels, it is John the Baptist who recognizes Jesus as God's agent of renewal of his people (1:15) and who articulates what Jesus' role is to be as "Son of God."

The Voice in the Wilderness: John the Baptist (1:19–34)

The narrative of the Gospel of John begins with an account of an interchange between John the Baptist and interrogators from the Jewish leadership in Jerusalem. Their question was, "Who are you?" by which they clearly meant, "What role in the purpose of God do you see yourself as fulfilling?" His response was to renounce a claim to messiahship (1:20), and then to disclaim that he was either Elijah, whose coming was predicted in Mal 4:5 as occurring in preparation for the final time of divine judgment, or a prophet like Moses, whose coming is foretold in Deut 18:15. Instead, he is the one to "prepare the way of the Lord" and, in the barren terrain on the eastern side of the lower Jordan Valley, to "make straight the way of the Lord" (Isa 40:3). Only here in the gospel tradition does John identify Jesus as "the Lamb of God who takes away the sin of the world" (1:29), but he does match the synoptic tradition in linking the baptism of Jesus with the descent of the Holy Spirit with the prediction that Jesus would baptize with the Spirit (1:32–33; Mark 1:8; Q 3:16) and with the identification of Jesus as "Son of God" (1:34; Mark 1:11). The hopes and promises expressed in the Prologue of John are already perceived to be in process of fulfillment with the coming of Jesus.

Jesus' Call of his Disciples (1:35–51)

Omitting any reference to the temptation of Jesus or to his launching his preaching/teaching in Galilee (Mark 1:12–15), John describes Jesus' call of his first disciples (1:35–51). They are two disciples of John the Baptist, who heard him declare Jesus to be the "Lamb of God" and who thereupon left their former leader to follow Jesus. One was the brother of Simon Peter, who told him, "We have found the Messiah" (1:41). On coming to Jesus, Simon is given the nickname Cephas/Peter/Rock by him (1:42). In Galilee, Jesus called Philip to follow him, and he in turn invited Nathanael to "come and see" Jesus, whom he claimed to be the fulfillment of the law and the prophets (1:43–46). Jesus' ability to have seen Nathanael before Philip called him leads him to acclaim Jesus as not only a teacher ("rabbi"), but as "Son of God" and "king of Israel." He is promised by Jesus that he will see "greater things," including divine attestation of the role of Jesus as "Son of Man" (1:47–51). John is introducing his account of Jesus' message and role by linking him with messianic titles. Thus far, the significance of Jesus is conveyed by John in primarily verbal terms, but at this point, the gospel shifts to the symbolic, revelatory acts of Jesus, referred to in this gospel as signs.

The First Sign: Wine at the Wedding (2:1–11)

The first of these is the account of Jesus—invited as a guest to a wedding feast with his mother and his disciples—coming to the aid of the host when the wine supply gave out (2:1–11). At the word of Jesus, more than one hundred gallons of water become premium wine. The symbolism is multiple:

1. The event takes place at a wedding, which in both the prophetic and the wisdom traditions of Israel was a figure for the special, loving, ideal relationship of God to his people. Hosea 1:10–2:23 describes God's intention to restore unfaithful Israel by overcoming the idolatry of the people and their devotion to pagan deities and establishing their loving relationship with Yahweh. The Song of Solomon, which may have been originally based on an erotic poem in a pagan cult, serves in the Jewish scriptures as a celebration of the special relationship of God to his people.

2. Wine, while in excess potentially harmful (Prov 20:1), is also a symbol of joy at the triumph of God's purpose for his people, as in the promise of defeat of Israel's enemies and divine deliverance in Isa 25:6. The eschatological significance of this event is indicated in the note that, contrary to custom, the good wine has been kept "until now" (John 2:10), with the coming of Jesus and the work of renewal that he is pictured here as accomplishing. It is through this sign that Jesus first "manifested his glory," evoking faith from his disciples (2:11).

The New Temple where God Dwells (2:12–25)

Directly following this in John's narrative—though described as occurring near the end of Jesus' earthly career in the other gospels[236]—is the story of Jesus' cleansing of the temple (2:13–22). It combines features that appear in other contexts in the synoptic tradition: the link with the Passover (2:13; Mark 14:12–16); Jesus' denunciation of the commerce carried on in the temple (2:14; Mark 11:15–17); the prediction of the destruction of the temple (2:19; Mark 14:58). In this way, John confronts his readers early in his gospel with Jesus uttering prophetic criticism and predictions that are evident only later in the other gospels. But John further alters the account by reporting Jesus' prediction that, though the temple is destroyed, it will be raised up in three days—which he then treats as an explicit prophecy of the resurrection (2:18–22). The reference to scripture in v. 22 may be to Ps 16:9–11, where one's destiny is not in the grave or Sheol (the gloomy abode of the dead), but in the presence of God.

The section ends with a note that, although many had now come to trust in Jesus based on the signs he performed, he did not entrust himself to any of them, because he knew what frailty characterized humans. The narrative now shifts to an account of Jesus' power to renew and transform human life.

The New Birth from Above (3:1–21)

One of those impressed by the signs Jesus performed was Nicodemus, who in spite of his Greek name—meaning "conqueror of the people"—is described as having fine Jewish credentials: a Pharisee, and a "leader [*archon*] of the Jews," which may mean that he was a member of the council [*synedrion*] that exercised a degree of local autonomy in cooperation with the Roman authorities. He addresses Jesus as "Rabbi" and indicates that the basis of his interest in and respect for Jesus is that his teaching is receiving divine confirmation in the form of the signs that Jesus is doing (3:2). Jesus then tells Nicodemus that he must experience a new birth if he is to take part in the coming kingdom of God, describing this birth as *anothen*, which can mean "again" or "from above" (3:3). Nicodemus responds in basic human terms, assuming that rebirth would involve reentering the womb, but Jesus declares that it is brought about by two factors: "water and the Spirit." These terms refer to the two modes by which individuals become members of the people of God: the external mode is baptism ("water"), by which the public commitment to the new community is expressed; the internal mode is the work of the Spirit of God within, renewing and transforming life.

Although no one can determine the source or goal of the wind, one can identify the work of the Spirit by the results it produces in changed lives (3:4–9). The heavenly origin of the Spirit and its work are then described against the background of the one who has come down from heaven: Jesus, the Son of Man. Yet his role in the purpose of God involves another mode of being "lifted up": like the bronze serpent raised on a pole by Moses as a cure for the plague that befell the dissident people of Israel in the wilderness (Num 21:1–9), so Jesus will be "lifted up" on the cross as a provision for dealing with human sin and enabling the faithful to share in eternal life (3:14–15). John then explains the significance of Jesus' death as combining a mode of bringing judgment on human sin with the supreme sacrifice by which one may come to the light and be delivered from the power of sin (3:16–21). The potential for inclusion in this new community of the "saved" who experience this deliverance and renewal involves an invitation extended to "the world," which is the object of God's love, as evident in the outreach at work in Jesus' launching of this program for human renewal.

John the Baptist Speaks about the Son, the Spirit, and the New Life (3:22–36)

The important transitional role of John the Baptist is indicated in this section of the gospel, in which Jesus and John seem to be in competition for candidates to baptize. When John is informed that many are now going to Jesus for baptism, John makes a sharp distinction between them: he is not the Messiah but the one "sent before him"; he is the friend of the bridegroom who rejoices that the new community of faith—"the bride"—is now coming to the true bridegroom: Jesus. John's joy is now full, but his role must diminish. He is of earthly origin and speaks of earthly matters, but Jesus is "from above and utters the words of God" and is the one through whom the Spirit is given. Those who trust in the Son already share in "eternal life," but those who do not already are subject to divine judgment (3:36). The true community is constituted of those who have heard and trusted God's word through Jesus.

New Access to the People of God (4:1–42)

Although the prophets of Israel foresaw that a wide range of humanity would participate in the life of God's people, the historic break between the northern and southern tribes of Israel resulted in a radical break between them, including different versions of the scripture and different sanctuaries where God was said to dwell among them. The northern tribes regarded the temple on Mount Gerizim in the area known as Samaria as the place where God dwelt among them and the appropriate worship was to be carried out, while of course the tribes of Judah considered the temple in Jerusalem to be the holy place of Yahweh.

En route to Galilee, Jesus passed through Samaria and stopped at a well near Sychar—which almost certainly is Shechem[237]—to get a drink from a woman there. This act violated the wall of separation that Jews sought to maintain between themselves and Samaritans, and thus astounded the woman and shocked his disciples (4:16–30). But Jesus declares that the time is coming when true worship will occur in neither of these temples, but will take place "in spirit and in truth" (4:20–24)—that is, in response to the power, purpose, and insight that John depicts Jesus as conveying to those who respond in faith to him and his message. The woman is so impressed that, in spite of Jesus' having noticed her sexual promiscuity (4:16–19), she perceives him first as a prophet (4:19) and then responds affirmatively to his claim to be the Messiah, inviting other Samaritans to hear him (4:25–30). Many of them do so and conclude that he "is indeed the Savior of the world"—not merely of a select, ethnically or ritually exclusive community (4:39–42).

Meanwhile, Jesus is shown instructing his disciples that the "food" that sustains his life is doing the will of the God who sent him (4:31–34). Changing the imagery, he then compares the work to which they are called with sowing and harvesting, the benefits of which they are already enjoying (4:35–38). It is not their ethical origin or their missionary achievements that have brought them to share in the life of the new community but their joy in accepting what God has provided.

New Life and New Authority (4:43–5:47)

Journeying farther north from Samaria to Galilee, his family's residence,[238] Jesus is cordially received there, especially by Galileans who had seen his works in Jerusalem during the feast. John 4:44 ironically includes the synoptic tradition (Mark 6:4; Matt 13:57; Luke 4:24), which describes the negative response Jesus received in Galilee, even though 4:45 affirms that he was welcomed there because of his notable deeds.[239]

Reports of Jesus' deeds had reached one of the royal officials in Galilee, where Herod Antipas was designated by the Romans as tetrarch but often referred to as king, in the tradition of his father, Herod the Great, whose realm extended from Idumea (at the lower end of the Dead Sea) northward through Judea, Samaria, Galilee, and from there north and east of the Jordan, almost to Damascus. The official urged Jesus to come to Capernaum and heal his ailing son, who was near death. Jesus told him that his son was healed, and the man believed him. On returning home, he found the son well, having begun to recover at the hour when Jesus had promised his healing. Thereupon, he and his entire household trusted in Jesus.[240] Participation in the community of faith and sharing in the new life Jesus provides now extend socially and culturally even to those in the service of the pagan power of Rome.

Back in Jerusalem for "a feast,"[241] Jesus stopped at a pool at which many "invalids, blind, lame, paralyzed" were gathered (5:1–8). They are said to have been awaiting some disturbance or bubbling of the water, which may have been caused by intermittent springs but was thought to be an indication that the pool had healing powers. Although major Greek manuscripts here identify the pool as "Bethzatha" or "Bethsaida," the reference is probably to Bethesda. This is the name of a pool on the eastern slope of the hill of Jerusalem that is mentioned in the Dead Sea Scrolls; the excavation of it some forty years ago[242] fits this location in John. The lame man who had been waiting there for thirty-eight years to be healed but had not been able to get into the water at the crucial time was told by Jesus to get up, take up the mat on which he lay, and walk. He did so, and was healed. But it was on the Sabbath that Jesus instructed him to pick up and carry his mat, which violated the law against labor on that holy day of rest (Exod 20:8–11). In the fifth century BCE, as the Jewish people were being restored to their land from exile, this law was reaffirmed and intensified (Neh 13:15–22), as it had been by the prophet Jeremiah (17:19–27). Now Jesus not only encouraged breaking the Sabbath law in order to serve basic human need, but by declaring that his actions were based on his special filial relationship with God, he was "making himself equal with God" (5:18).

The import of this claim is spelled out in what follows (5:19–46). The intimate relation of Son and Father includes not only the love they share, but the roles assigned to the Son: to give life; to effect judgment; to share in the divine honor; to raise the dead. That new life is to come to fulfillment in the future, when the dead are raised and face judgment, but it may already be experienced now by those who hear and heed "the voice of the Son of God." Jesus' testimony is not based on something that he possesses as an independent individual, but derives wholly from God. John the Baptist was granted the insight and ability to testify concerning Jesus' coming role, but superior witness has been provided by God through the works that Jesus has been enabled to perform and through right understanding of the scriptures, which on his behalf "testify that the Father has sent me" (5:36).

His opponents search the scriptures on the assumption that thereby they will gain life, but their refusal to accept Jesus as God's agent for human renewal and their seeking "glory from one another" will result in their condemnation on the basis of the law of Moses. They wrongly assume that their hope lies in conformity to the law, but—rightly understood—Moses' testimony would lead them to trust in Jesus (5:46). Thus, the law of Moses is not rejected or displaced, but its true meaning is perceived as being disclosed only through Jesus as God's word to his people.

New Bread from Heaven (6:1–71)

The linking here of the stories of Jesus' feeding the five thousand (6:1–15) and of his walking on the water (6:16–21) obviously correspond not only to the experience of Israel on the pilgrimage from Egypt to the promised land, but also to the accounts in the synoptic tradition.[243] But there are a number of significant modifications. Mark notes that Jesus called the disciples to go with him "to a deserted place" (6:31–32)—which recalls the Sinai desert—but John says only that a "multitude followed him" and that he then "went up on a mountain" (6:3), which also matches the setting for Israel's receiving the covenant at Sinai. John alone notes that "the Passover . . . was at hand" (6:4) and that Jesus asks the disciples how bread is to be bought to feed this multitude "in order to test them" (6:6). The availability of five loaves and a few fish and the number of those to be fed (5,000) are the same in both versions, although Mark specifies that they were "male" (*andres*, 6:44), while John does not initially designate their sex (*anthropous*, 6:10), but then specifies that of the people who sat down, the number fed was five thousand males. In the synoptic versions, Jesus is described as looking up to heaven, uttering a blessing, and breaking up the food for distribution (Mark 6:47),[244] but in John he "gave thanks" = *eucharistesas*—which of course matches the language of the Lord's Supper[245] as well as the Markan account of Jesus' feeding the four thousand (8:6; also in Matt 15:36).

John describes two reactions of the people to this sign performed by Jesus—which is soon to be interpreted by him as "bread from heaven" (6:22–40)—(1) the acclaim of Jesus as "the prophet who is to come into the world" (6:14), and (2) the scheme of the people to force him to become their "king." In Deut 18:15–22, the people of Israel gathered in the wilderness beyond the Jordan are promised that God will raise up for them a prophet like Moses who will speak God's word to them. At the end of Malachi (4:1–5) is a warning of doom on the disobedient but a promise of (1) light for the faithful from "the sun of righteousness," and (2) of the coming of the prophet Elijah, who will call the hearts of God's people to obedience and responsibility. It is these prophetic expectations that are perceived as being fulfilled through Jesus. The movement to make him king, however, is represented as a misconception of Jesus' role: that he has come to foster political power and material prosperity. Accordingly, he is seen as withdrawing to the mountain, where he is in communion with God.

The account of Jesus' walking on the water recalls two important features of the Jewish scriptural tradition: (1) Israel's escape from slavery in Egypt by crossing the Red Sea and the subsequent launching of the people's existence as the covenant people in their own land (Exod 14–15); and (2) God's control of the waters as a major step in the creation and ordering of the world (Gen 1:1–23). It is wholly appropriate, therefore, that when his disciples are filled with terror as they see him walking on the water, he identifies himself (literally) as "I am" (*ego eimi*). This is, of course, the Greek translation of the ineffable name of God, Yahweh, which was disclosed to Moses on the holy mountain of God (Exod 3:3–15). Now Jesus is depicted by John as sharing in that divine name (John 6:20)—a theme that runs through the discourses of Jesus in this gospel. In addition to the implicit claims of Jesus' oneness with God that pervades the gospel, there is the explicit declaration in 10:30, "I and the Father are one." That oneness is depicted throughout John in terms of love, overcoming the powers of evil, and, through grace, achieving unity in spite of diversity of backgrounds.

The specific effects of Jesus' multiple roles as God's word become human are spelled out in distinctive material throughout this gospel in the form of "I am" pronouncements of Jesus. The first of these is spoken to the people who had shared the bread he provided, but who mistakenly wanted more of this food to sustain their ordinary existence instead of seeking for the divine support for humans "which endures to eternal life" (6:27). There is nothing they can do to earn this kind of divine sustenance; instead, they are called by Jesus to put their trust in him as the one whom God "has sent" (6:29). He recalls how God sustained his people in the wilderness by sending down on them "bread from heaven" that sustained them day by day (Exod 16). But now, God's people are promised "the true bread from heaven," which has the potential to give "life to the world" (6:33). The function of this bread is to sustain life in its fullest sense, so that those who share this "bread" will never hunger or thirst. All of their deepest and continuing needs will be met through this living bread. Sharing in this bread will be those given by God to Jesus, who become participating members of this new community and to whom is promised eternal life, including being raised from the dead "at the last day." Although the emphasis falls here on the present sharing in the new life through the bread from heaven, the promise is still held out of transformation and renewal that will take place when the present age comes to an end "at the last day" and God's purpose for his people is fully accomplished.

Jesus' critics insist that they know his earthly, family origins, including his parents, and that there is no basis for his claim to have come down from heaven (6:41–42). But he responds that only those drawn by the Father will come to him in faith, and it is they who will be raised "at the last day" (6:44). Only Jesus has seen the Father, and those who trust in him already *have* eternal life, unlike those who ate the manna in the wilderness and died. He is the living bread, and those who share in this will live forever, since he is to give his very body ("flesh") in order for the world to share in the eternal life he brings (6:48–51). This "bread" is Jesus' flesh and body: eating of it involves not only participation in the Eucharist, which represents his sacrificial death, but also abiding in him (6:56), which involves sharing in the transformed life of the new community that he makes possible and that endures eternally (6:55–58).

In defending and explaining his claims to his puzzled disciples, he points to two factors that—rightly understood—will confirm his assertions: (1) his ascension to be with the Father, and (2) the coming of the Spirit, which will work to transform and empower their lives. They should not expect that everyone will be convinced by his claims: those who participate are those to whom "it is granted by the Father" (6:60–65). Many of his followers are offended by these claims, especially Judas, his betrayer, who is here called by Jesus "a devil" (6:70–71). Peter, on the other hand, affirms his confidence in Jesus' words that bring eternal life and declares that he is indeed "the Holy One of God."

Jesus' New Claims to Be the Messiah (7:1–52)

Among those who are shown in John as failing to be convinced by Jesus' claims of messiahship and of his unique relationship with God are members of his own family (7:5). Yet they urge him to go to Jerusalem for the Feast of Tabernacles,[246] ostensibly because they want his followers—as well as the wider world—to see his amazing works (7:3). But secretly, they are hoping that the authorities there will confront him and kill him (7:1). This Festival of Booths was a celebration of the autumnal harvest and included giving thanks for what was produced from the threshing floor and the winepress. Jesus' response urges his brothers to go to the feast, while noting that—unlike him—they are not hated by the world. And his time to suffer because of the world's hatred of him "has not yet fully come" (7:9).

Nevertheless, he does go to Jerusalem, but "in secret" rather than publicly (7:10). People were looking for him at the festival, and a private debate arose as to whether he was a good man or a deceiver of the people (7:10–13). Jesus then appears in the temple courts and begins to teach. His learning makes his hearers wonder at the source of his knowledge, since he has had no formal training (7:14–15). His response is to call his hearers to realize that he does not seek to gain their esteem but to bring glory to the one who sent him (7:16–18). The opposition to Jesus has been built on his alleged failure to understand the purpose of the law: his critics are more concerned about detailed legal observance than about human welfare and renewal (7:23).

Jesus' critical hearers in Jerusalem claim to know his origins, while no one will know the origins of the Messiah. But he responds that they do not know where he comes from: the One who sent him is "true," and his critics do not know this one (= God, 7:28), in spite of their claims to possess knowledge of God and the law. Many of the onlookers believed Jesus, asking how one could imagine that when the messiah appears, he could perform more signs than Jesus has done (7:31). The indication of growing popular support for Jesus leads the priestly and Pharisaic authorities to arrest him, but he informs them that he will go away and they will be unable to find him. Ironically, they raise the question as to whether he will go out into the wider Graeco-Roman world, where in fact many Jews had gone, thus constituting "the Dispersion" (7:35). The reader who acknowledges that Jesus is God's Messiah will know, of course, that Jesus is here predicting his return to be with the Father—where there will be no place for those who reject him as God's agent for renewal of his covenant people.

Before continuing the theme of the division that will result from acceptance or rejection of Jesus (7:40–52), John discusses the difficulty posed by Jesus' identification as being "from Galilee," while the prophet (Mic 5:2) had foretold the birth in Bethlehem, the village of David, of the one who was to be "ruler in Israel" (7:40–42). That tradition of Jesus' birth there is not mentioned in John's gospel, and the implication of Jesus' failing to meet this messianic qualification is seen here as a source of conflict and opposition to him (7:42–43).[247]

Jesus, the Light of the World (8:12–9:41)

Jesus' role as "the light of the world" is set forth by John in his report of Jesus' declarations concerning his role (8:12–59) and in the symbolic action he performs and explains in restoring sight to a man born blind (9:1–41). Jesus is shown from the Prologue of John onward as the one who brings to the world the light of the knowledge of God and his purpose for the world—and especially for his people. John 1:4–5 describes the life of Jesus as the light that goes out to humans and continues to shine forth in spite of opposition ("darkness"). This role was attested by John the Baptist (1:6–8), and it continues to provide the possibility for enlightenment to every individual who comes into the world. This light was a central factor in the creation of the world (Gen 1:1–5), yet the world as a whole has failed to recognize that light. Even when the light came in human form, the people to and among whom he came did not accept the light that he embodied (John 1:9–11).

Those who see in him the light of the world "walk in the day"; those who reject this light walk in the night and stumble (John 11:9–10). Later in this gospel Jesus calls his hearers to become "sons of light," since he has "come as light into the world" (12:35–36, 46).[248] As in the story of Jesus walking on the water, the theme of the transforming power of light recalls the creation—in which the Word had a central role (John 1:3), including that of bringing light to humans (1:4)—and points to the new creation, which is to be experienced by the new covenant people.

The religious leaders, however, dispute Jesus' claims to be the light from God (8:13), to which he replies that his testimony to himself is true and is being confirmed by the One who sent him, and hence fulfills the requirement of the law for two witnesses (8:14–18).[249] Yet his opponents recognize neither who he is nor who is his Father (8:19, 27), and hence they are part of this world order—which Jesus is not (8:23). He declares rather that they will die in their sins unless they believe that he is one with God: "that I am (*ego eimi*).[250] He reaffirms that his origin and the message that he declares to the world are from God, who is "true"—right and trustworthy. But his critics still do not perceive that the "father" who sent him is God. That relationship will be manifest when the Son of Man is "lifted up": they will turn him over to the Romans who will "lift him up" on the cross; but God will "lift him up from the dead" (8:28). Indeed, he claims that his Father has always been with him, enabling him to speak with divine authority and to act in accord with the divine will (8:28–29).

The divided response to Jesus by his Jewish contemporaries is described in 8:31–59. To those who trust him, he promises truth and freedom (8:32). Those who are enslaved to sin, however, fail to recognize that he is the unique Son of the one whom they claim as Father. Their rejection of the truth that he has disclosed to them shows that their father is not God but the devil, whose fostering of murder they will soon emulate in the scheme to have him executed, and whose promoting of lies they follow by refusing to believe the truth that Jesus has told them. If they were truly children of God, they would hear God's word that he is declaring to them (8:44–47).

His critics denounce him as a deviant from the true covenant—a Samaritan—and as having a demon, to which he replies that he seeks only to honor God, and that those who heed his message "will never see death" (8:48–51). Unlike Abraham and the prophets, who died, he claims to be glorified by the Father, and asserts that Abraham looked forward with joy to seeing the new age in which God's agent for renewal of his people would be living and active. He thereupon declares, "Before Abraham came into being, I am" (*ego eimi*, 8:58). The reaction to this claim of oneness with God moves the throng to gather stones in order to execute him by corporate action.[251] But Jesus was able to escape their intended attack on him in the temple (8:59).

Preceding Jesus' affirmation of his sharing existence with God is the phrase "amen, amen," which means truly, truly (8:58)—an expression that appears in its duplicated form twenty-three times in the Gospel of John, and nowhere else in the New Testament. It is, of course, a transliteration of a Hebrew word that means certainty, reliability, and fidelity. In each case, it implies certainty as to the claim that Jesus is making or to the event being foretold. In John, the phrase is linked with Jesus' predictions about the future, declarations as to his identity, and promises and warnings to the new community.[252]

The symbolic version of Jesus as the bringer of light to the people of God is presented in John's story of Jesus healing the man who was born blind (9:1–41). The man's ailment is not to be considered a punishment resulting from his or his parents' misdeeds, but as providing the occasion to display "the works of God." An era of judgment is coming when darkness will prevail and good works cannot be done, but Jesus' role now is to serve as what he is: "I am the light of the world." This role is dramatically demonstrated as Jesus makes clay of spittle, anoints the man's eyes, and sends him to wash in the pool of Siloam—from which he returns "seeing" (9:7). Again, this act of Jesus is reported as taking place on the Sabbath and hence as in violation of the law against labor on the Sabbath—raising the question for strict law observers as to how Jesus could possibly be from God. The blind man affirms that he is a prophet, which is consonant with the predictions of Isa 35:5, and especially 43:6–7, where the servant of the Lord is foreseen as the one who will bring "light to the nations" and "to open the eyes that are blind." The healed man's parents confirm for skeptics that he had indeed been born blind, but refuse to give credit for this to Jesus, since John reports that those who affirm that Jesus is the Messiah will be ostracized from the synagogue (9:21–23). Instead, the investigators are to ask the son himself. In the bitter interchange that follows between him and the religious leaders, they accuse him of being a disciple of Jesus, but he responds that only someone sent and empowered by God could open the eyes of the blind, as Jesus has done. Thereupon, the interrogators denounce and expel him. Jesus then sought out the man and introduced himself to him as "the Son of Man," describing his role as twofold: showing the blindness of those, such as the Pharisees, who claim to see, but do not perceive who Jesus is; and bringing light and vision to those seeking insight and renewal (9:35–40).

Thus, the portrayal of Jesus here, as throughout the Gospel of John, resembles the role of the divine agents in the mythology of the mystery religions of the Graeco-Roman period in that the divinely endowed figure—such as Isis or Asklepios—as bringing perception of the divine purpose and making possible participation in the life of the community of those who trust in the deity.

The Good Shepherd and the True Flock (10:1–42)

Here are juxtaposed two parables portraying the new community and its relationship to Jesus and his roles on behalf of its members. The first parable concerns leading the flock out of the sheepfold (10:1–6), and the second depicts the role of the shepherd caring for the flock (10:7–18). They are followed by a controversy with the Jewish leadership over Jesus' claim to a unique Father/Son relationship with God (10:19–42). The point of the first parable is not how to gain access to the flock of God's people, but how Jesus brings "his own sheep" out of the larger conglomerate of those who claim to be the covenant community and then leads them (10:3–4). They recognize the voice of a false claimant to the role of shepherd and flee from his effort to dominate them (10:5–6). The gatekeeper here is God, who enables Jesus to call and assemble his true flock in this way (10:3). The point of this extended metaphor is lost on the hearers, however, so Jesus is then reported as telling the parable that highlights his role in terms of two images: as the door of the sheepfold and as the shepherd (10:9, 11).

Both these symbols are linked by John with Jesus' claim to be one with God: "*I am* the door of the sheep"; "*I am* the good shepherd." The sheepfold is an image of the new community, to which he alone provides access. The members do not live their lives in total separation from the wider world, however, but "go in and out" to find sustenance for their lives. Those who come to harass or kill them are here characterized as thieves and wolves—in contrast to Jesus' role, who gives his life for them. His knowledge of them and theirs of him match the mutual knowledge of Jesus and "the Father" (10:14–15). Those who will share in the life of this new flock include those not in the Jewish tradition ("other sheep, that are not of this fold," 10:16). All who heed the voice of the good shepherd—regardless of ethnic origin or ritual status—will constitute the "one flock" of God's people, and it is for them that he will lay down his life and then "take it again," as God has commissioned him (10:17–18).

These claims evoke a mixed response from the Jewish people: some assume that he is demon-possessed or mad, while others cannot attribute to a demon his ability to restore sight to the blind (10:19–21). The leadership, however, wants to force Jesus to make explicit his claim to be the messiah (10:22–24). The setting for this confrontation is symbolic: it takes place in the splendid portico of Solomon, a great colonnaded public area in the temple. Jesus' response is to recall the claims he has already made, and the confirmation provided by the works he has performed—all of which they have rejected (10:25). He explains their failure to accept him as messiah as the consequence of their not being members of "my sheep"—who hear his voice, are known by him, and follow him, and to whom he has already given eternal life. They are safely in his hand and in the hand of the Father, who gave them to Jesus (10:28–30).

The violently hostile reaction of the Jewish leaders is defended by them as an appropriate response to the blasphemy he has uttered by claiming to be one with God (10:31–33). In 10:34, Jesus is quoted as referring to Ps 82:6, where, in terms of origin and divine intention, the people of God are designated as "gods, children of the Most High, all of you." This recalls Gen 1:26, where God is said to have created humankind "in our image."[253] It was to such creatures that God has spoken his word, so that it is not blasphemy for Jesus to refer to himself as "Son of God." The works he has been performing are to be seen as God's work in the world and should lead to the conclusion that there is a profound mutual relationship between Jesus and God: "That you may know and understand that the Father is in me and I am in the Father" (10:38). There no speculation about metaphysical features of the relationship, as developed in later credal controversies; instead, what is pointed to are the tangible results of Jesus' works displaying divine power and purpose. The attempt of the authorities to arrest Jesus failed (10:39).

Jesus, the Resurrection and the Life (11:1–44)

The most dramatic of Jesus' signs and of the claims that he makes for his role in the purpose of God appear in the course of John's account of the death and restoration to life of Lazarus (11:1–44). Mary, his sister—whose subsequent anointing Jesus with ointment and wiping his feet with her hair (12:3) recalls an incident described in the synoptic tradition[254]—joins her sister Martha in sending Jesus notice of the illness of Lazarus, who is described as being loved by Jesus (11:2). After remarking that this illness would not end in death but would bring glory to God, for two days Jesus delays going to Bethany in Judea where they lived. His response to warnings that there were those in Judea who sought his death is followed by an assertion contrasting his walking "in the day," because his way is illuminated by "the light of the world," with those who "stumble . . . in the night" (11:9–10). Then he tells the disciples, "Lazarus has fallen asleep" (11:11), using the term for the death of believers found in the letters of Paul (1 Cor 15:51; 1 Thess 4:13–16). The disciples take this literally, as well as Jesus' assertion that he will waken Lazarus from his sleep, so Jesus explains that he is dead and declares that what is to happen will lead them to "believe" (11:15). Thomas, however, expects that they all will die with him.

On their arrival in Bethany, the friends of the sisters have gathered to join them in mourning, and Martha declares that Jesus could have kept Lazarus from dying. When Jesus asserts that her brother "will rise again," she assumes he is referring to the future resurrection of the just, which was a basic feature of Pharisaic belief and attested in Dan 12:2 as an event at the end of the present age. Jesus, however, declares that he is the embodiment of both "the resurrection and the life," and that those who trust in him but die will live, and those who continue to live and trust in him "shall never die" (11:25). Once more, this utterance is prefixed by "I am"—the crucial phrase by which Jesus' words and deeds and being are linked with Yahweh.

Jesus is described as "deeply moved" by the mourning of Mary and the Jews who had joined her, and he also "wept" (11:35). Some onlookers ask if Jesus, who can heal the sick, could not have "kept this man from dying." At his urging, the stone is removed from the tomb of Lazarus, and Jesus—expecting a manifestation of "the glory of God" and thanking God that, as always, he is hearing his prayer—summons Lazarus from the tomb (11:40–43), and he emerges, still bound in the wrappings for the dead, from which Jesus orders that he be freed (11:44). Jesus perceives this event as evoking faith from the onlookers that God has sent him (11:42).

The Hostile Response of the Jewish Leaders (11:45–54)

Although many of those present trust in Jesus, others report this occurrence to the religious and civil leaders who comprise the council [*synedrion*]. The latter are apprehensive that the popular following that Jesus is evoking will result in action by the Romans, destroying the Jewish temple and nation (11:48). In an ironic pronouncement, the current high priest declares that it would be better for this one man to die than for the whole Jewish nation to perish, unwittingly predicting the atoning death of Jesus that would result in the emergence of a new "nation," which would include not only the regional people of God but also those who are "scattered abroad" across the civilized world (11:51–52). Yet, focusing on their perceived need to be rid of this troublemaker, the leaders begin to plan how to have Jesus put to death (11:53). He withdraws to Ephraim, which was probably in the hills northeast of Jerusalem, overlooking the Judean desert and the Jordan Valley.

Jesus Faces Tragedy and Triumph (11:55–12:50)

As the time for the Passover approaches, and the crowds of the pious begin to gather in Jerusalem, the priestly and scribal leaders begin to scheme how they might arrest Jesus, whom they expect to come as well (11:55–57). He does come to the Jerusalem area before the Passover and is welcomed as a guest in nearby Bethany by Lazarus and his sisters. It is then that Mary anoints Jesus' feet, an act which he regards as pointing to his own death and burial, but which Judas Iscariot declares to have been a waste of much money—which he actually coveted (12:1–8). Because Lazarus has been raised from the dead, he becomes a major focus for pious sightseers, many of whom become followers of Jesus, so the priestly leaders decide to have Jesus put to death. A great crowd welcomes Jesus as he prepares to enter the city riding on a young donkey and he is acclaimed as the one through whom the prophecies of the coming of God's future king are being fulfilled

(Ps 118:36; Zech 9:9). The crowd's interest in and esteem for Jesus are heightened by the report of those who had witnessed Lazarus's being raised from the dead, and the religious leaders are in despair that "the world has gone after him" (12:12–19).

Some Greeks who had come for the feast ask two of the disciples with Greek names—Philip and Andrew—to see Jesus. When this is reported to him, he announces that "the hour has come for the Son of Man to be glorified," and proceeds to warn the disciples that he—and they—must be prepared to give up their lives in the service of God in order to gain "eternal life" (12:20–26). He then explains to the disciples that preceding the exaltation that God will give him in the future and that will result in the glorification of the name of God, he must be "lifted up." As noted above,[255] Jesus' being lifted up involves not only his being put up on the cross to die, but also his being raised from the dead and exalted to the presence of God. His call to God to glorify the divine name is answered by an audible heavenly assurance that the name of God—symbolizing not only his identity but his purpose and power to achieve that purpose—has been glorified and will be in the future.

What is then announced is that the judgment of this world is not to be viewed as an event in the distant future, but as something that is already happening in the moment of people's response to Jesus. Through him—his words and his works—the satanic "ruler of this world is already being overcome. Conversely, those who now walk in the light Jesus provides and who rely upon it may even now become sons and daughters of light (12:36). Yet many of those who hear and observe Jesus' signs are unconvinced, as the prophet Isaiah is said to have warned, even as he foresaw the coming disclosure of God's glory (12:37–41; Isa 53:1; 6:10). Even some of the Jewish authorities who believe in Jesus are reluctant to confess it publicly, lest they be excluded from the synagogue (12:42–43). The basic issue, however, is not simply having faith in what Jesus as an individual says and does, but in how one responds to the God who sent him as light for the world, and for whom he speaks (12:44–50).

Washing the Feet: A Sign of Loving One Another (13:1–35)

Knowing that the time of his departure from life in the present world was at hand and moved with unwavering love for his followers, Jesus began to act in a way that was intended to demonstrate to them that love was more than a kind of feeling. Rather, it involved direct, public action that demonstrated concern for the other and willingness to accept a menial role in order to show publicly one's desire for the other to be renewed and to reestablish the purity of right relationship. The symbolic act to demonstrate this was to assume the servant's role and wash the feet of one's friend or associate. It also pointed to the conviction that, while his disciples, like other humans, are besmirched by contact with the ordinary life of the world, they do not need to be totally cleansed, but simply to have the traces removed of their routine, impure experiences. To Peter's objection that Jesus do this for him, Jesus replies that their basic relationship remains inviolate, even though there will be passing acts that will stain it. Peter, again mistakenly, asks for a more complete cleansing, but is told by Jesus that what needs attention are only the daily, minor misdeeds. He then urges the apostles to help one another by this symbolic act of forgiveness and renewal of relationship. That possibility does not exist for Judas, however, since he has already acted to violate that relationship by betraying Jesus to the officials who want to destroy him. And this is seen to be in fulfillment of Ps 41:9, where the psalmist describes the trusted friend as lifting his heel against him. In response to Peter's inquiry, Jesus—as in the synoptic accounts[256]—identifies Judas as the one who will betray him to the authorities, but John adds that Satan entered him, that Jesus told him to carry out his plot "quickly," and that when he went out it was—symbolically— "night." What is performed as a betrayal of Jesus to destroy him will result in his glorification and his departure for a place where the disciples cannot come. Yet, as he had done when he washed their feet and in spite of this pending betrayal, he urges them to "love one another" (13:31–35). At the meal, rather than on the way to Gethsemane (as in the synoptic account),[257] Jesus predicts that Peter will deny him three times (13:26–38).

John points out repeatedly that these events took place before the Passover rather than following it, as reported in the other gospels, where Jesus eats the Passover meal with the disciples and makes explicit for them the symbolic significance of the broken bread and poured out wine (Mark 14:12–16, 22–25).[258] Thus, the day of Preparation for Passover in John coincides with the day of Jesus' death (19:31).

GOD'S GLORY REVEALED BY JESUS TO THE COMMUNITY OF FAITH (14:1–17:26)

Jesus Prepares the Way to the Father (14:1–31)

The mystical dimension of the new community is dramatically evident in Jesus' explanation that the outcome of his impending suffering and death will be his going into the presence of God, that there he will prepare dwelling places for each of his followers, and that there he will be with them as the Messiah, God's agent for human renewal. This mystical dwelling will take place if his hearers trust him as the one who knows and provides access to this way to God. Thomas articulates ignorance about Jesus' destination or the way to get there (14:5), to which Jesus responds by asserting he *is* the Way to God, the truth concerning God and his purpose for his people, and the only one through whom his followers may achieve this transformed life, which he both embodies and provides to the faithful (14:6). Only through him can one gain knowledge of God (14:7), since Jesus and the Father share being and action (14:8–11). Accordingly, those who trust in Jesus will be enabled to perform works like his, and even greater works when he returns to the Father. Their petitions are to be addressed to God in the name of Jesus, and he will perform according to their petitions, with the result that through these divinely enabled works, "the Father may be glorified in the Son" (14:12–14).

The disciples' love of Jesus is to be demonstrated by their obeying his commandments, and they will have access to divine advice and truth through the Spirit that Jesus will send to dwell within them (14:15–16). Although the world will no longer see Jesus, the disciples will be able to, and they will perceive that the mystical unity that binds together the Father, the Son, and the new community has been achieved. The loving relationship experienced by the people of God will evoke obedience on their part and divine disclosure to them on the part of Jesus and God. A lack of love on the part of some of them will be evident in their failure to obey the words of Jesus, which stem ultimately from the Father (14:18–24). The promise of the Spirit as counselor and teacher is repeated, as is the advice that the disciples should not be troubled by his impending departure, since he is going to the Father, whom he has loved and obeyed (14:25–30). The mystical participation of the members of the community has direct results in their obedience to God, and manifests to the world the love of God (14:31).

The True Vine and the Fruit of Love It Produces (15:1–17)

The identification of Jesus as the True Vine builds on the imagery of the Psalms and the Prophets concerning God's purpose for calling into being the covenant people of Israel and urging them to a shared life of fidelity to the divine purpose, a life of moral purity and productivity. Psalm 80:7–19 is a call for God to restore his disobedient people, which recalls how, like a vine, God brought Israel out of Egypt and planted this people in their own land, whereupon they flourished. Now, however, their disobedience has resulted in their being ravaged, and so there is a call for God to look down from heaven and restore the moral fertility of his people. Isaiah 5:1–7 contains a vivid picture of Israel and Judah as a vineyard planted by God to produce grapes and wine, which has instead yielded wild grapes. Now it is to be abandoned, its walls broken down, its space overgrown with briars, and it will cease to be supplied with rain. Jeremiah 2:15–21 compares Israel's having turned to the worship of pagan deities with his having planted them as "a choice vine from the purest stock" and their having become "a wild vine," engaging in idolatry and rebellion.

Jesus depicts himself as the True Vine (15:1), using the term *ego eimi* (I am) and thus affirming his unique relationship with God. The branches are the members of the new community (15:5). The Father is the one who controls which branches will remain attached to the vine and which will be removed. The former are those who maintain the intimate relationship with him; those who do not are to be discarded and "burned"—thus implying that eschatological judgment will befall those who do not "bear fruit." Bearing fruit is the image for those who obey Jesus' commandments, as he has obeyed those of the Father. But the vine is subjected to pruning when its branches are unfruitful. Those who live as conscious participants in the life of this vine are morally clean and fruitful in that they share in the vitality that Jesus produces in his people and transmit it to others, who are thereby drawn to this new corporate mode of life.

This process brings glory to God and enables the participants to share in God's love, which Jesus conveys to those who are obedient, and it brings joy in abundance to those who share in this life. The primary commandment— here as elsewhere in the Gospel of John—is to love one another, for which Jesus set the model when he gave his life for the rescue and renewal of his friends. Thus, the relationship between Jesus and his people will not be that of master and slave, but of friends[259] whom he chose, to whom he has revealed all that God has told him, and whom he now calls to share in the life of this true vine and to produce enduring results for their efforts to renew the lives of others (15:14–17).

The World's Hatred of God's People (15:18–16:4)

Three reasons are offered for the world's hatred of the new community: (1) its members are no longer part of this world order, because Jesus chose them and called them out of the world so that they might become a distinct people (15:19); (2) the world does not know the God who sent Jesus (15:21); (3) Jesus' message and works made the people of this world aware of their sin and now their sense of guilt manifests itself in their hatred toward God, toward Jesus, and toward his new people (15:22–24). All of this is seen to be in fulfillment of scripture (Ps 35:19; 69:4) and pseudepigraphic tradition (*Psalms of Solomon* 7:1), where we read that those who have sought to obey God have become the objects of hatred in the wider world. But for the new community, reassurance will be given them through the Paraclete or Counselor who is coming, and who is here called "the Spirit of Truth" (15:26), who is coming from the Father and bears testimony to Jesus. Because those addressed here have been with Jesus "from the beginning," they are qualified to serve as witnesses to him—to his role in the purpose of God and to his teachings (15:17). The work to which they are called is to be carried out by them in spite of the fierce hostility they will encounter, just as Jesus' words and works evoked violent reaction among the civil and religious leadership, culminating in his death.

A supreme irony lies in the way in which this gospel depicts the "world" (*kosmos*) as, on the one hand, the focus of God's love in sending his Son, whose role was to save the world rather than to condemn it (3:16–17), and, on the other hand, as the source of hatred toward both Jesus and his new people. A major factor in the opposition and attempted repression that the new community will encounter is here seen to be the Jewish leadership, which will expel from the synagogues the followers of Jesus and will view their execution as a service to God. The reason for their antagonism is their lack of true knowledge of either God the Father or Jesus the Son. This knowledge has been granted and received, however, by the mystical community that is here being called to fidelity to Jesus as the agent and conveyor of God's truth.

The Work of the Spirit in the New Community (16:5–33)

Here the followers of Jesus are told not to lament his impending departure from them, but to recognize it as an essential next step in God's provision for their perception of "all the truth"—i.e., both the difficulties and the ultimate cosmic renewal that lie ahead for them, as well as their understanding of the Father and of Jesus (16:13–15). They must realize that, although he will soon be taken from them—in death and return to the Father—and this will cause them to be sorrowful, the ultimate outcome will be joyous. Just as a mother's birth pangs result in a newborn child, so their time of distress over the death of Jesus and his departure will lead to a new era of joy when he "will see [them] again" (16:22). Then they will be filled with unceasing joy and will have the assurance that if they ask anything of God in Jesus' name, it will be given to them (16:23–24).

In more explicit language than the imagery that pervades this address to the community ("no longer . . . in figures," 16:25), Jesus states that (1) they will have access to God in his name because they believe that he came from the Father; (2) that he is leaving them in order to go to the Father; (3) that, in spite of their present claim to believe him, their reaction to his impending seizure and execution by the authorities will be to abandon him and flee (16:31); (4) that God will remain with him; and (5) that as his followers endure tribulation resulting from the world's hostility to him and them, they may be confident that he has "overcome the world" (16:25–33). Thus, both the conceptual insights and the spiritual provisions they are receiving will enable them to continue as faithful members of the community.

Jesus' Prayer for His People (17:1–26)

Jesus' final preparation for his impending arrest, trial, and execution is portrayed in John as an extended prayer. Aware that the crucial moment has arrived for the events in the divine scheme that will launch the renewal of the covenant people, Jesus is here depicted as calling on God to "glorify the Son"—a process that will begin, ironically, with his arrest, trial, and crucifixion, but will then culminate in his resurrection and the consequent outpouring of God's Spirit on his people. The impact of these events will be God's power manifested, transcending all human limitations ("all flesh") and giving eternal life to those who will share in the new community. The sign of God's approval of and support for this undertaking will be for Jesus to return to the presence of God, regaining the glory that was his before the world was made through him (17:1–5; cf. 1:2–3). Jesus' work of human renewal is already achieving its intended results. God's name and purpose for his people have been disclosed through Jesus to those who through him have heard and heeded God's word, so that now they know that God has sent him to establish the covenant community. It is for them Jesus is praying—not for the hostile world—and he asks that God will keep them through the power of the divine name that he shares with God and experience unity analogous to the unity of the Father and the Son (17:6–11). Those in the community of which his disciples are the prototype have remained faithful—except for Judas, who betrayed him, here designated "the son of perdition." There is in scripture no explicit reference to this traitorous act (17:12), but that designation does appear in the LXX version of Prov 24:22, and in the plural in Isa 57:4.[260]

The disclosure of God's purpose for his new people is seen to be taking place in the world so that they might share in his joy at the transformation of the new community he has launched (17:13). Yet, like him, they will experience hatred in the world, because, like him, they are "not of the world" (17:14, 16) in that they do not share its aims and values. The prayer is not that his followers might escape from this world, but to preserve them from the actions of "the evil one," and that they might be made holy through their having heard and grasped God's truth (17:17). They are commissioned by Jesus to extend his message and mission in the wider world, and he prays again that they might become in truth the holy people of God (17:19).

He also prays for those who will come to trust in him as God's agent of renewal through the word that the new community proclaims and for their unity—that it may match the unity of Jesus and the Father. If this is perceived by those who hear them, it will help to persuade the world that Jesus was sent by God and enable those who share in God's love for him to come to be with him and thus to share in perceiving the glory that God bestowed on him before the creation of the world (17:20–24). It is they who, unlike the world as a whole but like Jesus, will know that he was sent by God, and thus will honor and proclaim God's name. In this way, the love of God that has gone out to Jesus will unite him and the new community. Thus, in this section of the Gospel of John, participation in the life of the divine—a basic aim of Graeco-Roman mysticism—is dramatically depicted here in Jesus' prayer.

Jesus' Death and Vindication: His Disclosure of Himself
to His Followers (18:1–20:8)

John does not include details found in the synoptic tradition that point to the coming death of Jesus: his anointing by a woman in Bethany in preparation for his death (Mark 14:3–9; Matt 26:6–13); the preparation for the Passover (Mark 14:12–16; Matt 26:17–19; Luke 22:7–13); the institution of the Lord's Supper (Mark 14:22–25; Matt 26:26–29; Luke 22:15–20); Jesus going with the disciples to Gethsemane (Mark 14:26–31; Matt 26:30–35; Luke 22:39–46).

But from the Prologue onward, the Gospel of John describes the ways in which the redemptive death of Jesus and his resurrection have been foretold. In 1:29 and 36, John the Baptist acclaims Jesus as the "Lamb of God who takes away the sin of the world." Jesus' prediction of the raising up of the soon-to-be-destroyed temple in three days points to his resurrection from the dead (2:20–22). The lifting up of the Son of Man as the instrument by which the faithful will gain eternal life is described in 3:14–18, and later more fully explained as the crucifixion of Jesus (12:27–36). The resurrection of the faithful is promised in 5:25–29, as it is in 6:51–58. In the parable of the Good Shepherd (10:7–18), Jesus depicts himself as laying down his life for the sheep, his new people. At the death of Lazarus (11:23–26), Jesus identifies himself as "the resurrection and the life" and promises eternal life to those who trust in him. When the Jewish high priest makes his ironic pronouncement before the council that "one man should die for the people," this is described in John as a prophecy concerning the mode by which the scattered children of God will be gathered into one (11:50–52). Martha's anointing of Jesus' feet is seen as a sign pointing to his death and burial (12:3–8). But his glorification is also foreseen (12:12–16) when the hour comes for the Son of Man to die and be glorified (12:23–2), which is again here described as his being "lifted up" (12:27–36). His resurrection and return to the Father are likewise repeatedly announced (13:1; 14:1), as is the betrayal that will lead to his death (13:21). Thus, the absence from John of the explicit predictions of the passion and resurrection of Jesus that appear in the other gospels does not obscure the frequent and largely symbolic way in which John offers predictions of these salvific events.

JESUS' DEATH AND VINDICATION: HIS DISCLOSURE OF HIMSELF
TO HIS FOLLOWERS (18:1–20:31)

Jesus' Betrayal and Interrogation (18:1–38a)

In this gospel, however, the accounts of Judas's arrangements with the civil and religious authorities to arrest Jesus[261] are radically condensed, and he is pictured as taking the initiative to obtain a band of soldiers and temple officers with the assistance of "the chief priests and Pharisees" to seize Jesus. John's portrayal of Jesus as divine is heightened here (1) by the statement that he knew in advance all that was going to occur; (2) by his taking the initiative in identifying himself, rather than in Judas doing so by kissing him;[262] (3) his identification of himself as "I am" (*ego eimi*) and the consequent falling to the ground of those who have come to seize him; (4) his repeated affirmation of himself as "I am" (18:4–8). His request that his followers be released is said to fulfill his earlier prediction that not one of them would be lost (18:9; cf. 6:39). The brief account of Peter's cutting the ear of the high priest's slave matches the tradition in Mark 14:47; Matt 26:51; Luke 22:50, but does not include the detail in Luke that Jesus healed him (22:51).

Jesus' Crucifixion and Burial (18:38b–19:33)

The account of the treatment of Jesus in preparation for his crucifixion follows the Markan tradition (Mark 15:15–20) in describing the scourging of Jesus, the soldiers plaiting a crown of thorns, and their mocking him as king of the Jews. Here Pilate repeats that he has found Jesus to be guilty of no crime (18:38b; 19:4). The Jewish leaders claim he is to be executed because he has violated the Jewish law forbidding anyone to claim to be the Son of God (19:7). Jesus refuses to defend himself or to seek release by Pilate, while informing him that the real source of his power is God ("from above," 19:11). The Jewish leaders, on the other hand, press the political charge that Jesus wants to usurp the royal rule from Caesar, and so they deny that Jesus is king and declare that they "have no king but Caesar." As in the synoptic accounts, the charge that leads to Jesus' execution is his claim to be "king of the Jews" (19:17–22)—a claim that the chief priests formally reject. John alone reports the soldiers' taking Jesus' garments, which is perceived to be in fulfillment of the scriptures (19:23–24), quoting Psalm 22, which was widely perceived by the early Christians as foretelling the death of the Messiah (Ps 22:10). As in Mark (15:40), it is women who remain at the cross, but also "the disciple whom Jesus loved," who is told by Jesus that Mary is to be his mother and who thereafter takes her to his home (19:25–27).

Another psalm (69:22) that describes the pain and trials of one who is undergoing persecution mentions that the victim is given vinegar to drink—which is here seen as being fulfilled when Jesus announces his thirst (19:28–30). Jesus' final utterance, "It is finished," implies that the plan of God is now complete for the one whose death would "take away the sin of the world" (1:29) and bring eternal life to the faithful (3:14–16). In order to assure that Jesus was indeed dead before the Sabbath (also Passover in John's chronology) began at sundown, his side is pierced but his legs are not broken—fulfilling the rules concerning the death of the Passover lamb (Num 9:12; Exod 12:26), as well as the prophetic predictions of the deep contrition to be felt by the people of God when they realize that they have destroyed God's messenger to them (Zech 12:10).

According to John (19:38–42), the burial of Jesus is carried out not only by Joseph of Arimathea (as in the Markan account, 15:42–47) but with the assistance of Nicodemus, the Pharisee and Jewish leader to whom, according to John (3:1–14), Jesus explained the necessity of being born again/from above. The Jewish burial customs were followed and were carried out quickly in order not to violate the impending Sabbath/Passover.

The Encounter of the Disciples with the Risen Christ (20:1–29)

As in Mark (16:1–9), it is Mary Magdalene who goes to the tomb on the first day of the week to prepare the body of Jesus for burial, since it had been placed in the tomb with great haste (20:1–10). On finding the stone rolled back from the entrance to the tomb and the body of Jesus gone, she reports to the first disciple she finds—Peter—which fits with the instruction given to the women by an unidentified "young man" in Mark 16:7, but here Mary does make such a report (20:2), while in Mark, the women say nothing to anyone out of fear (Mark 16:8). According to John, Peter and "the other disciple, whom Jesus loved"[263] hurry to the tomb, where they find the cloth wrappings, but not the body of Jesus. The "other disciple" arrived first, and having seen the empty tomb, "believed" (20:8)—thus anticipating the faith that would be engendered when the women and the other disciples encountered the risen Christ.

The first one to be met by the risen Jesus, according to John (20:11–18), was the same one who first saw the empty tomb: Mary Magdalene. According to Mark 16:1–8, the women are the first to see the empty tomb,[264] as is the case in Luke's version (24:1–11) and in Matthew (28:1–10). But Matthew adds that when the risen Christ appeared to the women, he told them to instruct the disciples to go to Galilee (28:1–10). In John, however, this story is in an expanded version, according to which the women see two angels and then Jesus, whom they mistake for the gardener until Jesus calls Mary by name and she recognizes him as Teacher/Rabboni. He tells her not to cling to him, but to tell his disciples that he is ascending to God the Father. Mary then reports to them, "I have seen the Lord," and tells them what he said (20:18).

Following this is John's account (20:19–23) of his appearance to the disciples in a closed place to which they have retreated because of "fear of the Jews." In Matt 28:16–20, Jesus appears to the eleven disciples in Galilee and commissions them to "make disciples of all nations" and to baptize them in the name of the Trinity. In Luke 24:13–35, however. the women's report of seeing the risen Christ initially meets with unbelief from the disciples, but he does appear to two of them not far from Jerusalem, instructs them concerning the necessity of the suffering he endured as foreseen in scripture, and then is recognized by them in the breaking of bread. Luke also describes a second appearance to the disciples in Jerusalem (24:36–49) in which Jesus confirms his bodily state as the risen Christ, instructs them in the understanding of scripture, calls them to bear testimony to his death and resurrection, and then is taken up to heaven (24:50–51).

Jesus' encounter with doubting Thomas is recounted in John 20:24–29. Thomas, who was not with the disciples when Jesus appeared to them, is skeptical that what they claim to have seen was indeed the risen Christ. He insists that he must see and touch distinctive marks in Jesus' body (the pierced hands and side) before he will believe that Jesus has been raised from the dead. Eight days later, Jesus appears to his disciples in a closed room and invites Thomas to see the wounds in his hands and side. Thomas, who in John's account represents the skeptics who thought that the claims of an encounter with the risen Christ were based on pious imagination, is persuaded, and addresses Jesus in the words of Christian confession: "My Lord and my God." Jesus replies that there will be those who have not seen the risen Jesus in bodily form and yet believe that God has raised him from the dead and hence will be blessed.

EPILOGUE (20:30–21:25)

Verses 20:30–31 are almost certainly the original ending of this gospel. There the reader is told that the acts of Jesus—"signs"—reported in this book took place in the presence of the disciples, but have now been written down in order to foster belief on the part of the readers in Jesus as Messiah, Son of God, and thus to enable them to share in the new life that he has made possible.

John 21:1–14 is the first of three additional accounts of encounters of the disciples with the risen Christ. The stories are filled with multilevel symbolism, pointing to the disciples' roles as missionaries, Jesus' presence with them in the Eucharist, and the possibility that present members of the new community would live until his coming again in triumph. The seven disciples to whom Jesus appears here have returned to their former occupation of fishing, but are catching nothing. When they follow Jesus' explicit instructions as to where to cast the net, the results are overwhelming. The number of fish—one hundred and fifty-three—may be symbolic in some way, or may simply indicate the dramatic results of following Jesus' instructions.[265] His invitation to them to "Come have breakfast" may symbolize that he will provide for their needs as they begin what might be called a new day, as his messengers extend their mission to the wider world. The provision of bread and fish (21:13) fits this interpretation as indicating divine support, as does the message that this took place at one of the repeated ("third time") appearances to them of the risen Christ.

Jesus' questions and advice to Peter here (21:15–19) highlight (1) the loving relationship of the disciples to the risen Lord; (2) their need to care for and sustain the recent ("lambs") and the more mature members ("sheep") of the new community; and (3) the warning of persecution and martyrdom faced by those devoted to the service of Jesus is epitomized in his appeal to them, "Follow me." Peter is told (21:20–23) that the beloved disciple, who at the Last Supper had asked Jesus about the identity of the one who would betray him (13:23–25), may remain alive until Jesus returns in triumph, if Jesus so wills. Thus this disciple is—at least implicitly (21:24)—identified as the author who is reporting these traditions in this gospel. The record is not complete, it is acknowledged, since the books necessary for such a comprehensive account of Jesus' words and works would more than fill the world.

The work as a whole is consistent, however, in that its aim is to communicate to the world how the message and actions of Jesus are—literally!—the incarnation of the purpose of God for his people and the account of how this will be achieved. The mode of communication involves both words in the form of discourses and actions of Jesus—what he does for others and what is done to him by the authorities—which are conveyed in direct speech and narrative, but also through symbolic and multilevel speech. Those who grasp this message are thereby enabled to share in the new life that God is giving to his covenant people through Jesus, as summarized in 1:12—"To all who received him, who believed in his name, he gave power to become children of God."

Jesus and the New Community in the Apocryphal Gospels

A learned and comprehensive translation, survey, and analysis of early Christian writings not included in the New Testament—including gospels as well as writings related to the apostles and apocalypses—was edited by Wilhelm Schneemelcher and subsequently translated into English under the title *New Testament Apocrypha*.[266] In volume 1, there are translations of texts and analyses of the contents of materials akin to the canonical gospels, including the gnostic gospels found at Nag Hammadi in Egypt a half century ago. There is also an examination of the issue implicit—and at times explicit—in early Christians writings as to which documents produced in the variety of early Christian contexts were to be considered normative for the church. The prevailing scholarly conclusion is that it was in the latter part of the second century that a consensus began to emerge as to which of these writings were to be considered as authoritative, not only for what came to be called the New Testament, but for the writings that comprised the Old Testament as well.

Notable evidence of this movement toward establishing a New Testament canon is offered in the writings of Irenaeus, and especially in his affirmation of the fourfold gospel as normative[267]—a position also affirmed by Clement of Alexandria[268] and in the Muratorian Canon, which probably dates from around 200 CE. The canon was officially closed in the fourth century, decisions for which were probably linked with the emergence of a Rule of Faith, so that anything incompatible with the Rule was excluded from "true" and "genuine" tradition in the New Testament. This point of view concerning the twenty-seven books of the New Testament is attested in the 39th Festal Letter of Athanasius of Alexandria in the year 367.[269] A history of the research and scholarly analysis of this apocryphal material—which tells us much about the creativity and diversity of the early Christians, but which was excluded from the emergent New Testament canon—has been gathered and edited in what is now known as the New Testament Apocrypha.[270] In addition to the apocryphal gospels examined below, there are apocryphal accounts of the roles and teachings of the apostles, to which were given the title of *Acts* of Andrew, of Peter, of Paul, etc.

The nonbiblical material about Jesus is classified by Schneemelcher as follows: (1) that which has only an uncertain connection with canonical tradition—the so-called Agrapha, consisting mostly of scattered sayings attributed to Jesus; (2) tradition shaped in order to make a particular theological point—as in the gnostic reworking of the Jesus tradition that resulted in the *Gospel of Thomas*; (3) documents called "gospels" that differ widely from the canonical gospels, though retaining Jesus' message as their decisive theme: e.g., the *Gospel of Philip*; (4) writings that consist solely of conversations and debates, as in the Dialogues of the Redeemer; (5) writings that substantively supplement or alter the accounts in the canonical gospels, such as the *Protevangelium of James*, and the *Gospel of Nicodemus*.

Even the basic meaning of "gospel," *euangelion*, was shifted from "message of good news" to being perceived as primarily a literary mode.[271] The aim of the canonical gospel writers was to foster the faith and common life of the community and to strengthen and propagate that faith. These noncanonical gospels, however, do not represent a further development of the synoptic type of gospel, nor do they offer a definable alternative model. Instead, they vary in style and strategy as well as in content, though they do seek to supplement or adapt to a significantly different orientation the traditions of the words and works of Jesus. They employ the tactics of legendary additions, of remodeling canonical sayings in order to shift the basic meaning, and of polemics in order to fight for the position of the author's community.[272]

These observations about the apocryphal gospels may be illustrated by examination of representative elements in the following types of gospel. In terms of the range of contexts in which these documents were produced, the following classification is useful:[273]

1. Fragments of Unknown Gospels
2. Gnostic Gospels
3. Jewish-Christian Gospels
4. Infancy Gospels
5. Other Gospels

Here we shall examine briefly a representative example of each of these categories.

Fragments of Unknown Gospels

An example of such a gospel is the Papyrus Egerton 2,[274] which probably dates from the mid-second century and gives evidence of knowledge of all four of the canonical gospels, although the author's fluidity in use of this material may have resulted from knowing it through oral rather than strictly written transmission. Although the canonical gospels seem to be the major source, writings like this suggest that the oral tradition was continuing to develop and to modify the earlier written sources.

Gnostic Gospels

A prime instance of this category is the *Gospel of Thomas*. Written in Sahidic—probably in Syria in the mid-second century—its quotations from the earlier gospel tradition indicate the ultimate source to have been Greek. It consists of 114 logia of Jesus, but begins with the claim: "These are the secret words which the living Jesus spoke . . ." The emphasis is on esoteric knowledge available only to the closed community, as indicated by the opening lines: "These are the secret words which the living Jesus spoke, and which Didymus Judas Thomas wrote down. And he said: He who shall find the interpretation of these words shall not taste death." The internalization of knowledge and hence of human renewal is indicated in Saying 3: "The kingdom is within you, and it is outside of you. When you know yourselves, then you will be known, and you will know that you are the sons of the living Father. But if you do not know yourselves, then you are in poverty, and you are poverty."

There is also in this gospel a radical transformation of the expectation of a new age of cosmic, eschatological transformation, as shown by Saying 18: "The disciples said to Jesus: Tell us how our end will be. Jesus said: Since you have discovered the beginning, why do you seek the end? For where the beginning is, there will the end be. Blessed is he who shall stand at the beginning, and he shall know the end, and shall not taste death." Further, Jesus is represented here as an immanent force pervading the universe, including the material world, as in Saying 77: "Jesus said, I am the light that is above them all. I am the all; the all came forth from me, and the all attained to me. Cleave a piece of wood and I am there; Raise up a stone, and you will find me there."

Jewish-Christian Gospels

A typical example of this category is the *Gospel of the Ebionites*—a name that derives from a Jewish-Christian sect that developed in the mid-second century. Calling themselves "the poor" (*Ebionim*), they observed Jewish legal requirements, including Sabbath and circumcision, and eagerly awaited the messianic age to come and to be centered in Jerusalem. The *Gospel of the Ebionites*, which has survived only in quotations from the church fathers, was said by Epiphanius to have been their perverted version of the Gospel of Matthew. In it, they declared that Christ was not begotten of God, but was "created as one of the archangels . . . that he rules all the creatures of the Almighty," and that he asserted: "I am come to do away with sacrifices, and if ye cease not from sacrificing, the wrath of God will not cease from you." Likewise, Jesus is said to have rejected the proposal that "at this Passover I eat flesh with you."[275] Clearly, this critique wants to make a radical break with the Jewish context of Christian origins.

Infancy Gospels

These gospels expand the supernatural features of the canonical gospel accounts of the birth of Jesus, and seek at the same time to reconcile and blend the somewhat diverse accounts in Luke and Matthew. A specific aim was to combat the Jewish claim that, since Jesus was born of a virgin, he could not be considered a descendant of David, and therefore was not qualified for the role of messianic king, as claimed by the Christians. In the *Protevangelium of James*, which dates from after 150, the story is developed of the birth and growth of Mary, and there is a protracted struggle with the priests and the interpreters of the law of Moses over the issue of the divine origin of Jesus.

Other Gospels

In his analysis of three related documents—the *Gospel of Nicodemus*, the *Acts of Pilate*, and *Christ's Descent into Hell*, Felix Scheidweiler[276] describes the complex process by which the early Christians sought to combat the charge that Jesus was born of fornication and to resolve the question of the credibility of the claim that Jesus had been raised from the dead. In the *Acts of Pilate* (XVII)

Joseph of Arimathea is depicted as describing to the rulers of the synagogue and the priests and Levites (1) how Jesus had descended into hell and raised up others as he was raised from the dead; and (2) how Jesus taught those who were there that God's eternal purpose was being worked out through him for overcoming Satan and the powers of evil. This writing probably was given its present form in the fourth century.

Thus, these apocryphal writings served multiple purposes: (1) to expand and detail the accounts in the canonical gospels; (2) to combat charges that were being made against the character and credibility of Jesus as well as the false claims that were being made in his behalf; and (3) to provide documentation for credal claims concerning the career and cosmic role of Jesus.

Imposing Unity on the Gospel Tradition: The Diatessaron of Tatian

Tatian, who was born in Mesopotamia of Syrian parents, was educated in Greek culture and tradition and was initiated into one of the Greek mystery religions. Subsequently, he was converted to Christianity and went to Rome to study that tradition. There he became a pupil of the apologist Justin Martyr (100–167 CE), but subsequently he promoted the gnostic doctrine of the Encratites, according to which the material world was evil, marriage was forbidden, and strict asceticism was fostered, including abstinence from wine or meat. Hence, Tatian is reported to have partaken of only the bread in the celebration of the Eucharist.

Of his several writings, only two have survived: his *Address to the Greeks* (written in his more orthodox period) and the *Diatessaron* (= "through the four"), in which he wove the texts of the four canonical gospels into a single consecutive document. This scheme of harmonization set the pattern for the continuing efforts of the Christians to bring the diverse four gospels of the New Testament into a literarily and conceptually unified form—a point of view that continues to have its advocates down to the present day.

Notes

1. The Greek texts and a translation were edited by Kirsopp Lake (LCL; London: Heinemann; Cambridge, MA: Harvard University Press, 1952).
2. This document was found in 1875 at the Patriarchal Library in Istanbul; a fine edition by Robert A. Kraft is *Barnabas and Didache* (vol. 3 of *The Apostolic Fathers: A New Translation and Commentary*; ed. R. M. Grant; New York: T. Nelson, 1965).

3. Most notably, in Jer 31:31–34.

4. Pliny, *Letter* 10.94. The complete text in English, with a commentary, is in A. N. Sherwin-White's *Fifty Letters of Pliny* (New York: Oxford University Press, 1967).

5. Suetonius, *Lives of the Twelve Caesars* (trans. Joseph Gavorse; New York: Modern Library, 1931; repr. 1959), 25.4.

6. The presence and activity of Priscilla and Aquila in Corinth are mentioned by Paul in his letters to Corinth (1 Cor 16:19) and to Rome, to which they had apparently returned (Rom 16:3). An analysis of the evidence concerning this couple and Paul's continuing association with them is offered in my commentary on Acts, *To Every Nation under Heaven: The Acts of the Apostles* (Harrisburg, PA: Trinity Press International, 1997), 219–21.

7. The title now assigned to this work of Tacitus, *Annals*, was apparently not used by him or other ancient writers.

8. The translations of Josephus are those of L. H. Feldman (LCL; Cambridge, MA: Harvard University Press, 1965), vol. 9.

9. During the procuratorship of Pontius Pilate, which was from 26–36 CE, although Josephus is speaking here of the earlier phase of Pilate's time in office.

10. Berlin and New York: W. de Gruyter, 1984, with 1,055 pages!

11. Feldman has fifteen pages of *desiderata* for further study of Josephus and seventy-seven pages of addenda; the indices include references not only to all of Josephus's works, but to pagan, Jewish, and Christian writers, to Greek words, and to hundreds of modern scholars.

12. Feldman, *Josephus and Modern Scholarship*, 695.

13. The family relationship is affirmed in Mark 6:3, Matt 13:55, and by Paul in Gal 1:19. His role as apostle and leader is indicated in 1 Cor 15:7, Gal 2:9, and in Acts 12:17; 15:13, 19; 21:18.

14. 1QS VIII.

15. 1QpHab II.8–10; VII.1–5.

16. IQS iii.

17. 1QS iii.

18. 1QS ix.

19. 1QM xi. The image of a star is connected with the birth of Jesus in Matt 2:2 and Rev 22:16.

20. This feature of the Jesus tradition is discussed below, based on my analysis of the pericope offered in "Jesus: a Glutton and a Drunkard" as a main paper at the Society for New Testament Studies in Prague in 1995; see *NTS* 42 (1996): 374–93.

21. The cosmic role of Melchizedek and the perception of him as "resembling the Son of God," as set forth in Heb 7:1–10, is developed in the Letter to the Hebrews, where the priestly office of Jesus is examined (see below).

22. These roles are perceived in this document as fulfilling respectively Ps 82:2, Isa 52:7, Daniel 9:25, and Isa 61:2–3.

23. That insight is explicit in the title of his earlier work, *From Politics to Piety: The Emergence of Pharisaic Judaism* (Englewood Cliffs, NJ: Prentice-Hall, 1973).

24. Philadelphia: Trinity Press International, 1991.

25. Joseph Klausner, *Jesus of Nazareth* (trans. Herbert Danby; New York: Macmillan, 1926), 46. The implication that Jesus had five disciples is, of course, in conflict with the gospel reports of there having been twelve. Otherwise, the polemical import of this material does not call into question its correspondence in general.

26. R. Travers Herford, *Christianity in Talmud and Midrash* (New York: Ktav Publishers, 1975), 348–49.

27. Lud is Lydda, which lies inland from modern Tel Aviv.

28. Balaam was a notorious hireling prophet who caused the death of many in Israel in the time of Joshua (Josh 13:22).

29. *The Church History of the First Three Centuries* (3rd ed.; trans. Allan Menzies; London: Williams & Norgate, 1878), 1:29.

30. Ibid., 30.

31. Ibid., 49.

32. Ibid.

33. Ibid., 29.

34. Ibid., 78–81.

35. Ibid., 180.

36. Rudolf Bultmann, *Theology of the New Testament* (trans. Kendrick Grobel; New York: Scribner's, 1951), 1:3. The term *kerygma* (transliterated from Greek) means "that which is proclaimed." It has become a widely used summary term in biblical and theological circles for designating the essential Christian message.

37. Bultmann, *Primitive Christianity in Its Contemporary Setting* (trans. R. H. Fuller; Cleveland: World, 1956); see "The Eschatological Preaching of Jesus," 86–93.

38. Bultmann, *Theology of the New Testament*, 1:302–3. See also the more recent discussion of the presence of Jesus in the kerygma in Bultmann's essay, "The Primitive Christian Kerygma and the Historical Jesus," in C. E. Braaten and R. A. Harrisville, eds., *The Historical Jesus and the Kerygmatic Christ* (Nashville: Abingdon, 1964), 40–42.

39. Bultmann, *Jesus and the Word* (trans. L. P. Smith and E. H. Lantero; New York: Scribner's, 1934), gives a reconstruction of Jesus' message, but in *Theology of the New Testament*, 1: 33–34, he asserts categorically that Jesus' message is not kerygma.

40. Bultmann, "The Primitive Christian Kerygma," 40–41.

41. Bultmann, *History of the Synoptic Tradition* (trans. John Marsh; New York: Harper & Row, 1963), 338–50.

42. Ibid., 347.

43. Ibid., 350.

44. Baur, *Church History*, 50.

45. Ibid., 81.

46. A brief discussion and critique of the theory that Mark is a Pauline-oriented document appears in W. G. Kümmel, *Introduction to the New Testament* (17th ed.; trans. H. C. Kee; Nashville: Abingdon, 1975), 94–95.

47. Martin Kähler, *The So-Called Historical Jesus and the Historic, Biblical Christ* (trans. and ed. C. E. Braaten; Philadelphia: Fortress, 1964), 89–90.

48. Ibid., 72–73. The intention of historical criticism in relation to faith is a large question in itself, and one that such recent discussions as Gerhard Ebeling's ("the uncertainty created by historical criticism is the reverse side of justification by faith") have scarcely dealt with adequately; see the English edition of Ebeling's collected essays, *Word and Faith* (trans. J. W. Leitch; Philadelphia: Fortress, 1963), 17–61. But historical criticism has the necessary function of bringing into focus the issues that faith alone can decide. One must distinguish between clarity as to what the promise is and certainty that God will fulfill it. The former may be aided by the work of the historian; the latter can rest solely on faith.

49. Kähler, *The So-Called Historical Jesus*, 91.

50. Ibid., 90.

51. *Systematic Theology* (Chicago: University of Chicago Press, 1957), 2:107.

52. Ibid., 103.

53. Ibid.

54. Ibid., 114.

55. Ibid., 117–18.

56. *Theology of the New Testament*, 2:66.

57. "The Primitive Christian Kerygma," 20. For Bultmann, the essential Christian message resides in *dass* (that) = the fact that Jesus came, not in *was* (what) = facts about Jesus.

58. Schweitzer's position is sketched in *The Quest of the Historical Jesus* (trans. William Montgomery; New York: Macmillan, 1910), chap. 19. This work is a translation of *Von Reimarus zu Wrede* [From Reimarus to Wrede] (1906). But his basic study of the gospel texts is set out in *The Mystery of the Kingdom of God* (trans. Walter Lowrie; London: A. & C. Black, 1926), which is the second part of *Das Abendmahl im Zusammenhang mit dem Leben Jesu und der Geschichte des Urchristentums* [The Eucharist in relation to the life of Jesus and the history of primitive Christianity] (Tübingen: J. C. B. Mohr, 1901). A posthumously published work of Schweitzer's on the theme of Jesus' eschatology is *Reich Gottes und Christentum* [The Kingdom of God and Christianity] (Tübingen: J. C. B. Mohr, 1967). A critique of Schweitzer's position is given by W. G. Kümmel in his collected essays, *Heilsgeschen und Geschichte* [Salvation-event and history] (Marburg: Elwert, 1965), 328–29.

59. Gerhard Friedrich, evangelizesthai, "to proclaim good news," in *Theological Dictionary of the New Testament* (trans. G. W. Bromiley; Grand Rapids: Eerdmans, 1965), 2:708.

60. Ibid., 708–9.

61. In the Loeb edition of Plutarch, the treatise is found in *Moralia* (trans. F. C. Babbitt; New York: Putnam's, 1928), 2:73–89.

62. A photograph, transcription, and translation of the 9 BCE text from Priene can be found in Adolf Deissmann, *Light from the Ancient East* (rev. ed.; trans. L. R. M. Strachan; New York: Harper & Row, n.d.), 366 and fig. 70. Whether the [euangelion] is understood to be the announcement of his birth (so Deissmann) or the fulfillment of the Sibylline prophecies about Augustus (so Eduard Norden in Deissmann, 366n8), the analogy with the use of the term by Mark and the other evangelists is evident. The full Greek text is in Wilhelm Dittenberger, *Orientis Graeci Inscriptiones Selectae* [Selected Greek inscriptions from the Orient] (repr., Hildesheim: Olms, 1960), vol. 2, no. 458, lines 40–79 (the point at which the passage under study appears).

63. Friedrich, "evangelizesthai," 724.

64. For example, Bultmann, *Theology of the New Testament*, 1:87.

65. In *New Testament Apocrypha* (trans. R. McL. Wilson et al.; Philadelphia: Westminster, 1963), 72–73.

66. See the discussion by C. K. Barrett in his essay in *New Testament Essays* (ed. A. J. B. Higgins; Manchester: Manchester University Press, 1959).

67. See an important article by Robin Scroggs, "Paul: sophos kai pneumatikos, "wise and spiritual," in *NTS* 14, no. 1 (1967): 33–55. Scroggs suggests that the wisdom issue concerns the merely human wisdom of the Corinthians and "an esoteric Christian apocalyptic-wisdom teaching which [Paul] carefully guarded from immature Christians."

68. As Scroggs acknowledges, ibid., 54.

69. So Schneemelcher, *New Testament Apocrypha*, 77.

70. *The So-Called Historical Jesus*, 80n11.

71. Ibid., 81.

72. *Ecclesiastical History* (trans. K. Lake; LCL; Cambridge: Harvard University Press, 1949), 1:3.39.13.

73. Ibid., 3.39.1–17. For a critical evaluation of the significance of the Papias tradition concerning gospel origins, see Werner Kümmel, *Introduction to the New Testament* (trans. H. C. Kee; New York and Nashville: Abingdon, 1975), 42–44.

74. Ibid., 3.39.15.

75. Justin uses the phrase "memoirs of the Apostles" with great frequency in his writings; in chaps. 99–107 of the *Dialogue with Trypho*, the term appears twelve times. The "memoirs" are specifically described as documents drawn up by Jesus' apostles and those who followed them (chap. 103). In *Saint Justin Martyr* (New York: Fathers of the Church, 1949), Justin's report is based on the tradition attributed to Papias, as discussed above.

76. A summary of this discussion is provided by K. L. Schmidt in his essay "Die Stellung der Evangelien in der a *apomnemoneuma* llgemeinen Literaturgeschichte" [The place of the gospels in the general history of literature], in Hans Schmidt, ed., *Eucharisterion* [essays presented to Hermann Gunkel on his sixtieth birthday] (Gottingen: Vandenhoek & Ruprecht, 1923), 50–134.

77. See Martin Dibelius, "The First Christian Historian" and "The Speeches in Acts and Ancient Historiography," in his *Studies in the Acts of the Apostles* (trans. Mary Ling; London: SCM, 1956), 123–85. See also H. J. Cadbury, *The Making of Luke-Acts* (2nd ed.; Naperville, IL: Allenson, 1958). My analysis of "Acts as History" compares the method of the author of Luke-Acts with that of other historians of the Graeco-Roman period in *To Every Nation under Heaven*, 11–14.

78. Moses Hadas and Morton Smith, *Heroes and Gods* (New York: Harper & Row, 1965).

79. Ibid., 61.

80. Ibid., 63.

81. Ibid., 56. My detailed critique of the aretalogy hypothesis is offered in "Aretalogy and Gospel," *JBL* 93 (1973): 408–16.

82. Schmidt, "Die Stellung der Evangelien." Also Siegfried Schulz, *Die Stunde der Botschaft* [The hour of the message] (Hamburg: Furche, 1967), 36; the nature of the book's contents is described by its subtitle: *Introduction to the Theology of the Four Evangelists*. For a brilliant discussion of the uniqueness of the gospels among Hellenistic literature, see Erich Auerbach, *Mimesis* (1953; Princeton: Princeton University Press, 1974), 40–49. Analogies have been noted between certain features of the gospels and Hellenistic literary conventions (see, for example, C. H. Talbert's *Literary Patterns, Theological Themes and the Genre of Luke-Acts* [Missoula, MT: Scholars Press, 1974]), but what is demonstrated is (1) that the gospels do share certain stylistic conventions with other writings of the Hellenistic period, but (2) that the composite product, a gospel, has no real analogy in Hellenistic literature.

83. Schmidt, "Die Stellung der Evangelien," 60.

84. Ibid., 60–61, 65.

85. Ibid., 74–75.

86. Schulz, *Die Stunde der Botschaft*, 37; A. N. Wilder, *Early Christian Rhetoric* (New York: Harper & Row, 1964), 36.

87. In 1 Pet 5:13, which claims to have been written by Peter, Mark is referred to as "my son." And in Acts 12, Peter is reported as having lived in the household of Mark.

88. *Einleitung in das Neue Testament* (3 vols.; Leipzig: Weidmannische Buchhandlung, 1810–1820).

89. In *Die Predigt Jesu vom Reiche Gottes* (1892), 8.

90. Kümmel, *Introduction to the New Testament*, 68–69.

91. New York: Doubleday, 1997, 116–122.

92. See my examination of the features similar to apocalyptic to be found in Cynic-Stoic sources, Excursus 5.

93. Brown's reconstruction varies from my own in only minor details; cf. H. C. Kee, *Jesus in History* (Fort Worth: Harcourt Brace, 1996), 81–85.

94. A prime model for this theory was advanced by J. M. Robinson in his essay, "Logoi Sophon: On the Gattung of Q," in *Trajectories Through Early Christianity* (Philadelphia: Fortress, 1971), 71–113.

95. Philadelphia: Fortress, 1987.

96. In *Ancient Christian Gospels: Their History and Development* (Philadelphia: Trinity Press International, 1990), 133–34.

97. Edinburgh: T & T Clark, 1996.

98. In *Wisdom in the Q Tradition* (SNTMS 38; Cambridge: Cambridge University Press, 1979).

99. In *Jesus the Sage: The Pilgrimage of Wisdom* (Edinburgh: T & T Clark, 1994).

100. In Sir 24, a hymn in praise of wisdom culminates in the explicit statement, "All this is the book of the covenant of the Most High God, the law that Moses commanded us as an inheritance for the congregations of Jacob" (v. 23).

101. The most accessible and respected edition is *Gospel Parallels: A Synopsis of the First Three Gospels* (4th ed.; Nashville and New York: Thomas Nelson, 1979). Edited by Burton H. Throckmorton Jr., the arrangement follows that of the Huck-Lietzmann synopsis, 9th ed., 1936.

102. Luke 7:4–5, which are probably to be omitted from Q, together with the report in v. 3 that the centurion sent "elders of the Jews" with the request that Jesus come and heal his slave, since these features serve to highlight Luke's special emphasis—found in both his gospel and in Acts—on the outreach of the good news to "every nation under heaven" (Acts 2:5) and the outpouring of the Spirit of God "upon all flesh" (2:17), in fulfillment of the promise of God through the prophet Joel (3:28–32). Nevertheless, in Matthew's shorter version of the story, the initiative is taken by the centurion himself, and his trust in Jesus' ability to heal is described as unmatched "in Israel" (Matt 8:10), just as it is in Luke's version (Luke 7:9).

103. It is to Capernaum that Jesus is reported in Mark 1:21 to have taken his disciples at the outset of his public activity. From there he launched his wider work of preaching and healing "throughout all Galilee" (1:39), and to it he returned as his home base (2:1). Matthew states that Jesus left Nazareth and "dwelt in Capernaum" (4:13; 17:24). The two other canonical gospels likewise indicate that Capernaum was a major base of Jesus' operations (Luke 4:3–37 and 10:15; John 4:46–53; 6:59). The detail in Luke 7:5 that the centurion had "built us our synagogue" is almost certainly anachronistic, since in the first century this term was the designation for the gathered group, not for the architectural structure where they met, which was called a *proseuche*. Detailed analysis of the evidence for the evolution of the synagogue is offered in my introductory essay and others in *The Evolution of the Synagogue* (Harrisburg, PA: Trinity Press International, 1999).

104. Q 4:3 = Deut 8:3b; 4:10 = Ps 91:11–12; 4:12 = Deut 6:16.

105. Pg. 20.

106. Isa 29:18–19; 35:5–6; 61:1.

107. This theme is treated in detail in my essay "Jesus: a Glutton and a Drunkard," presented as a main paper at the Society for New Testament Studies in Prague in 1995. The full text is in *NTS* 42 (1996): 374–93.

108. Jesus may historically have expected a death penalty on the instigation of the religious leadership, which would have been by stoning. This may be implied by his

predicting at the Last Supper that his body will be "broken," as reported by Paul (1 Cor 11:24), but of course it was the political powers of Rome who actually executed him—on the cross, and not by stoning.

109. Mark 3:22–27; Q 11:14–23.

110. Discussion of this term in relation to magic is offered in my study *Medicine, Miracle and Magic in New Testament Times* (Cambridge: Cambridge University Press, 1986), 17–18, 73.

111. Q 13:34–35; Ps 118:26.

112. Matthew and Luke provide this parable in different forms; each seems to have adapted it to serve the specific interests and aims of the community addressed.

113. In Mark, the event is very briefly mentioned in 1:12–13, and none of the issues or specifics is mentioned, except that it lasted for forty days.

114. The allusion to God's word is implicit in Luke, but explicit in Matthew's version of this Q tradition (4:4).

115. Luke 4:10–11 quote from Ps 91:11–12, which offers assurance of God's protection of those who remain devoted to "the Most High."

116. Beelzebul is a variant spelling of the name of the god, Baalzebub, worshiped by the Philistines (2 Kgs 1:2–16). The original meaning was probably "lord of the lofty abode," but it was altered by the Israelites to Baal-zebub, "lord of the flies," and then to Beel-zebul, "lord of the dung," which is the version of the name that appears in the gospel tradition.

117. In Sir 48:5 is recalled Elijah's restoring to life the widow's son (1 Kgs 17:17–24), which led her to acclaim him as "a man of God" in whose mouth is "the word of the Lord."

118. It is significant that the quotations from Isaiah come from sections of that prophetic book now designated by scholars as apocalyptic (Isa 34–35) or postexilic (Isa 40–55) down to the fifth century BCE (Isa 56–66).

119. J. L. Kelso and D. C.Baramki, "The Excavation of New Testament Jericho (Tulul Abu el-`Aliyiq)," in *Excavations at New Testament Jericho* (ed. W. F. Albright and V. Winnett; New Haven: AASOR, 1955), 29–30.

120. The issue of divorce and remarriage is set forth in Mark 10:1–12, but in more extended form in Matt 19:1–12, where provisions are made for divorce and even for remarriage if the wife has been unfaithful, and ends with the commendation of abstinence from sex for those "who have made themselves eunuchs for the sake of the kingdom of God." Clearly, there was no single set of rules for this perennial issue among the early Christians.

121. Ibid., 74–75.

122. The most elaborate attempt to reconstruct sources behind Mark is that of W. L. Knox, *The Sources of the Synoptic Gospels* (vol. 1 of *St. Mark*; ed. Henry Chadwick; London: Cambridge University Press, 1953). P. J. Achtemeier, "Pre-Markan Miracle Catenae," *JBL* 89 (1970): 265–91, makes an excellent case for Mark's having used collections of miracle stories.

123. Bultmann, *History of the Synoptic Tradition*, 275, 279; Martin Dibelius, *From Tradition to Gospel*, (3rd ed.; trans. B. L. Woolf; New York: Scribner's, 1965), 22–23, 178–217. For evidence that Mark has created this sequential narrative, see my essay, "The Function of Scriptural Quotations and Allusions in Mk 11–16," in E. E. Ellis and E. Graesser, eds., *Jesus und Paulus* (Goettingen: Vandenhoeck & Ruprecht, 1975).

124. "The Framework of the Gospel Narrative," in his *New Testament Studies* (Manchester: Manchester University Press, 1953), 1–11.

125. These allusions to locale are possibly in contrast to references to Galilee, which R. H. Lightfoot and Ernst Lohmeyer suppose to have reflected a special interest of a hypothetical Galilean wing of the primitive church that was clearly differentiated, theologically and otherwise, from the Jerusalem church. For details, see R. H. Lightfoot, *Locality and Doctrine in the Gospels* (New York: Harper & Row, 1938).

126. See the summary below of Matthew's rearrangement of the Markan material.

127. *Der Rahmen der Geschichte Jesu* (Berlin: Trowizsch & Sohn, 1919; repr., 1964), 317.

128. Ibid., 222–24.

129. So H. Koester, *Synoptische Uberlieferungen bei den apostolischen Vaetern* [Synoptic traditions in the apostolic fathers] (Berlin: Akademie Verlag, 1957).

130. Hans Conzelmann, "Gegenwart und Zukunft in der synoptischen Tradition" [Present and future in the synoptic tradition], in *ZTK* 54 (1957): 288–96 (see esp. 294), adopts a view of Mark that is formally similar to the one proposed here; yet the substantial difference lies in the understanding of the aim of the wonder stories. These are told—not as Conzelmann suggests: to present Jesus as a divine man (*theios anēr*)—in order to show him as the bearer of the eschatological power to defeat Satan. On the imprecision of the term *theios anēr* (divine man), see D. L. Tiede, *The Charismatic Figure as Miracle Worker* (Missoula, MT: Scholars Press, 1972).

131. See Krister Stendahl, *The School of St. Matthew* (Philadelphia: Fortress, 1966), where the use of scripture in the first-discovered Qumran documents is discussed.

132. A candid and illuminating discussion of this problem has been written by Barnabas Lindars in his *New Testament Apologetic* (Philadelphia: Westminster, 1961), a book that probably owes to its misleading title its failure to receive the attention it merits.

133. This lack of exact correspondence between the prophetic promise and the Christian claim of fulfillment has been stressed by Pannenberg in his contributions to *Revelation as History* (3rd ed.; ed. Wolfhart Pannenberg; trans. David Granskou; New York: MacMillan, 1968).

134. See the excursus on Elijah in H. L. Strack and Paul Billerbeck, *Kommentar zum Neuen Testament* [Commentary on the New Testament] (Munich: Beck, 1922–61), 4:792-98. Also Joachim Jeremias, "El(e)ias, 'Elijah,'" in *Theological Dictionary of the New Testament*, 2:928–34.

135. This analysis builds on my earlier essay, "The Function of Scriptural Quotations and Allusions in Mark 11–16," in the Festschrift for W. G. Kümmel (ed. E. Graesser and E. E. Ellis; Berlin: Goettingen, 1975), 165–88; and on my further examination of this material in *Community of the New Age* (Macon, GA: Mercer University Press, 1983), 45–49, and n. 157.

136. God's gift to his people of "bread from heaven" is referred to in Psa 78:23–24, which recalls God's provision of manna to the people of Israel during their journey under Moses through the wilderness from Egypt to Sinai (Ex 16:11–36; Josh 5:12).

137. See Sigmund Mowinckel, *He That Cometh* (trans. G. W. Anderson; Nashville: Abingdon, 1956), esp. 155–86.

138. The phrase *hoi par' autou* in Mark 3:21 is wrongly translated in some editions of the RSV as "his friends." It means "his family," as 3:31–35 shows and as TEV accurately renders the phrase.

139. The fundamental essay on this subject is by K. G. Kuhn, "The Two Messiahs of Aaron and Israel," in *The Scrolls and the New Testament* (ed. Krister Stendahl; New York: Harper & Row, 1957), 54–64. Subsequent criticism of Kuhn's interpretation has

not set aside his basic position. See Matthew Black, *The Scrolls and Christian Origins* (New York: Scribner's, 1961).

140. On the theory that the *Testaments of the Twelve Patriarchs* originated at Qumran, see F. M. Cross, *The Ancient Library of Qumran* (rev. ed.; Garden City, NY: Doubleday, 1961), 198–206. On the background and intent of the Testaments, see my introduction and notes in *Old Testament Pseudepigrapha* (ed. J. H Charlesworth; Garden City, NY: Doubleday, 1983), 2:775–828.

141. It is treated along with christological titles by Ferdinand Hahn in *Christologische Hoheitstitel* [Christological titles of honor] (Goettingen: Vandenhock & Ruprecht, 1963).

142. See my discussion of aretalogy and *theios anēr* in "Aretalogy and Gospel," *JBL* 93 (1973): 408–16, and in "Aretalogies, Hellenistic 'Lives' and the Sources of Mark," *12th Colloquy of the Center for Hermeneutical Studies in Hellenistic and Modern Culture* (Berkeley, CA: Center for Hermeneutical Studies in Hellenistic and Modern Culture, 1975).

143. The three groupings of the Son of Man sayings are conveniently summarized in Bultmann's *Theology of the New Testament*, 1:30–32.

144. So Bultmann, ibid.

145. Eduard Schweizer, "Son of Man," *JBL* 79 (1960): 119–29. Also Norman Perrin, *The New Testament: An Introduction* (New York: Harcourt Brace Jovanovich, 1974), 76–77, 156–57.

146. For example, Vincent Taylor, *The Names of Jesus* (New York: St. Martin's, 1953). With many Anglo-Saxon scholars, Taylor believed that Jesus' messianic consciousness was formulated through his combining the traditional kingly messianic idea of Israel with the apocalyptic Son of Man notion and the Suffering Servant concept of Second Isaiah.

147. Philip Vielhauer, "Gottesreich und Menschensohn in der Verkundigung Jesu" [Kingdom of God and Son of Man in the preaching of Jesus], in his *Aufsatze zum Neuen Testament* [Essays on the New Testament] (Munich: Kaiserverlag, 1965), 55–91. Also, H. B. Sharman, *Son of Man and Kingdom of God* (New York: Harper & Row, 1943).

148. See the most thorough and convincing survey of the history-of-religions background of *huios tou anthropou* (Son of Man) in Carsten Colpe's article on the term in *Theological Dictionary of the New Testament*, 8:400–477.

149. H. E. Tödt, *The Son of Man in the Synoptic Tradition* (trans. D. M. Barton; Philadelphia: Westminster Press, 1965), esp. 222–83.

150. See my article on this term in *NTS* 14, no. 2 (1968): 232–46.

151. The fundamental work here is Joachim Jeremias, *Parables of Jesus* (rev. ed.; trans. S. H. Hooke; New York: Scribner's, 1963).

152. See Bultmann, *History of the Synoptic Tradition*, 120–30. G. R. Beasley-Murray has written a useful *Commentary on Mark 13* (New York: St. Martin's, 1957).

153. The relevant texts are 8:31 ("*must* suffer"), 9:11 ("Elijah *must* come first"), and 13:10 ("the gospel *must* first be preached to all nations," i.e., before the end of the age).

154. Mark 8:31; 9:12; 9:31; 10:33–34.

155. Edward Lohse, *Martyrer und Gottesknecht* [Martyr and servant of God] (Goettingen: Vandenhoek & Ruprecht, 1955).

156. Although the King James Version and a great many of the Greek and other ancient manuscripts read "new testament" (= covenant) at Mark 14:24, the Revised Standard Version follows the oldest and best Greek manuscripts in omitting the word "new." Nevertheless, the implication of this saying of Jesus is that the new basis of

man's relationship to God that Jesus is establishing will replace the basis of the Jewish covenant. Whether the claim of newness arose with Jesus or with the early church, it is clearly dependent on Jer 31:31–34: "Behold, the days are coming says the LORD, when I will make a new covenant with the house of Israel and the house of Judah, not like the covenant which I made with their fathers when I took them by the hand to bring them out of the land of Egypt, my covenant which they broke, though I was their husband, says the LORD. But this is the covenant which I will make with the house of Israel after those days, says the LORD: I will put my law within them, and I will write it upon their hearts; and I will be their God, and they shall be my people. And no longer shall each man teach his neighbor and each his brother, saying, 'Know the LORD,' for they shall all know me, from the least of them to the greatest, says the LORD; for I will forgive their iniquity, and I will remember their sin no more." Read against the background of these words of Jeremiah, the implication of this saying of Jesus (Mark 14:24) is that his death is some way seals or ratifies the (new) covenant and effects the forgiveness of sin.

157. This passage is built on the imagery of the proto-apocalyptic book of Ezekiel (esp. Ezek 34) and the apocalyptic oracle of Zech 13:7.

158. Discussion of Mark 4:11 against the background of Dan 2:30; 4:9; 7:15; 12:4 is offered in my *Community of the New Age: Studies in Mark's Gospel* (Macon, GA: Mercer University Press, 1983), 47.

159. The architectural remains of these cities still provide impressive evidence for the extent to which in the Hellenistic and Roman periods Graeco-Roman culture was a visible and powerful cultural feature of the Syro-Palestinian region—especially in Gerasa, Jerusalem, Caesarea, Herodian Jericho, Bethsaida Julius, Nablus, and Baalbek in Lebanon.

160. Lev 16:1–34; 23:26–32; Num 29:7–11.

161. Mary Magdalene is mentioned first in all the gospel listings of Jesus' disciples: Mark 15:40–41, 47, and 16:1; Matt 27:55–56, 61; Luke 8:2–3 and 24:10. These women are among those healed by Jesus.

162. Or mother of James and Joses or Joseph; or the "other Mary" (Mark 15:40; Matt 27:55–56), or the "wife of Clopas" (John 19:25).

163. Clearly, this is the phenomenon of glossalia, discussed critically by Paul in 1 Cor 12–14, since the ability to utter ecstatic speech had come to be regarded by some in the Corinthian church as evidence of divine gift. Conversely, the gift of "tongues" as depicted in Acts is the Spirit-given capacity for the apostles to address groups of listeners in foreign languages that they (the apostles) did not know. In Acts 19:6, however, the gift of "tongues" is a mode of ecstatic speech, as it seems to be in 1 Corinthians.

164. Details about Herod Agrippa I in Josephus, *Jewish Antiquities* 19.286–358.

165. Colossians is probably not by Paul; see discussion below, 258–60.

166. Raymond E. Brown draws this inference from the evidence in his *An Introduction to the New Testament* (New York: Doubleday, 1997), 158–59.

167. The link of John with Elijah remains implicit in Mark 9:13.

168. Luke 4:1–13; Mark 1:12–13.

169. The proposal to make bread from stones (Matt 4:3) is countered by quoting Deut 8:3; the proposal to test God by jumping from a pinnacle of the temple is met by Deut 6:16; the refusal of the devil's offer of all the kingdoms of the world as a reward for worshiping him is answered by quoting Deut 6:13. Appeal to the Torah is the central strategy of Jesus in rejecting Satan's offer of universal monarchy.

170. Isa 9:1–2.

171. The Hebrew text of Isa 7:14 states simply that "a young woman" will give birth to a child, and before he reaches the level of maturity for decision making, the kings of Syria and Israel will be subject to the Assyrians, which in alliance with Egypt will take over the region (7:15–17). The crucial feature of this text for Matthew, however, is in the Greek version, which designates a virgin [*parthenos*] as the mother of this child.

172. Ephratha[h] is identified with Bethlehem in Gen 35:19; 48:7; Ruth 4:11; and Ps 132:6.

173. There is a modern irony in this date, however, since it comes before what became designated as the traditional time of the birth of Christ!

174. Male nazirites had to refrain from drinking wine (Amos 2:10–12), from shaving, or from touching a corpse. Prominent in this category were Joseph (Gen 49:26), Samuel (1 Sam 1:11), and Samson (Judg 13:2–7), although his subsequent life did not fit the requirements.

175. Capernaum is identified as a town west of where the Jordan flows into the Lake of Galilee; the location "across the Jordan" is based on the text quoted from Isa 9:1–2.

176. Q 13:28–30. Luke placed this saying in the section describing Jesus' journey toward Jerusalem (13:22).

177. Matt 13:42, 50; 22:13; 24:51; 25:30.

178. Matthew's version of the commissioning of the Twelve runs from 9:37 to 10:42.

179. The charge that Jesus performed exorcisms because he was in league with Beelzebul is discussed above in the sections on Q and Mark.

180. The distinctive use of the term "our Father who is in heaven" is discussed in the analysis of the Sermon on the Mount (122–23).

181. Mark 8:28.

182. Matt 16:18. Hades, "the unseen," is a name for the Greek god of the underworld, which is the abode of the dead. It was used in the Septuagint to translate several Hebrew words for that realm: the pit, death, deep darkness, and Sheol, where oracles from the dead were thought to originate, though seeking them was forbidden in the Torah (Deut 18:11). Hades came to be perceived as the realm of the evil powers, as is evident in *1 Enoch* 18:11–16 and 108:3–7, and in 2 Esd 7:36–38; Acts 2:27, 31; Rev 1:18.

183. An insightful discussion of this matter is offered by Anthony J. Saldarini in *Matthew's Christian-Jewish Community* (Chicago: University of Chicago Press, 1994), 141–47.

184. The Hebrew text of Ps 8:2 reads, "Out of the mouths of babes and infants you have founded a bulwark because of your foes, to silence the enemy and the avenger." The significantly different version of this text as quoted in Matthew derives from the Septuagint: "You have evoked praise . . . to destroy the enemy."

185. Matt 4:16; 8:12; 25:30.

186. Similarly, in Matt 27:41 the elders are said to be plotting to kill Jesus.

187. Eusebius, *Ecclesiastical History* 5.8.3.

188. Eusebius, *Ecclesiastical History* 6.25.6.

189. The text is cited in this connection in Matthew's account of the birth of Jesus (Matt 2:1–5). Although Luke does not cite the Micah text, he has two references to Bethlehem as "the city of David" (2:4, 11), and its locus as the birthplace of the Messiah is made known to the shepherds (2:15).

190. For example, Herod of Judea (Luke 1:5), Herod Antipas (Luke 3:1, 19, 20; 8:3; 9:7; 9:9; 13:31; 23:7, 8, 11, 12, 15; Acts 4:27; 13:1); Herod Agrippa (12:1, 4, 6,

11, 19, 20, 21, 23), Emperor Tiberius (Luke 3:1), Emperor Claudius (Acts 11:28; 18:2: general references to the emperor: eight occurrences in Acts 25; 26:32; 27:1, 24; 28:18).

191. A survey of modern studies of the literary and historical methods employed in Luke-Acts is offered in the introduction to my commentary on Acts, *To Every Nation under Heaven*, 8–20.

192. This perspective on history has been labeled *Heilsgeschichte* or "salvation-history" by New Testament scholars, but the view of history in the Jewish prophetic and apocalyptic writings—which were preempted by the early Christians—is more appropriately designated as an eschatological view of history. The details vary in the adoption of this outlook among the different New Testament writers, but the basic view of history as the outworking of a divine purpose for God's new people is a central and pervasive feature in Luke-Acts. The classic formulation of the role of salvation-history in Luke-Acts is by Hans Conzelmann, *The Theology of St. Luke* (New York: Harper and Row, 1961); scholars have differed considerably with Conzelmann in details, but his overall proposal has had an enduring impact on the study of these two New Testament books.

193. Oxford: Blackwell, 1983; 103. Similar aims and strategy are noted by Reinhold Merkelbach in the romance *Chariton*, and in Apuleius's *Metamorphoses*, in *Roman und Mysterium in der Antike* (Munich and Berlin: Beck, 1962), which depicts the Isis cult.

194. This perception of human understanding and communication has been analyzed by T. S. Kuhn in his *Structure of Scientific Revolutions* (2nd ed.; Chicago: University of Chicago Press, 1970); by Peter Berger and Thomas Luckmann in *The Social Construction of Reality* (Garden City, NY: Doubleday, 1967); and by Peter Berger, *The Sacred Canopy: Elements of a Sociological Theory of Religion* (Garden City, NY: Doubleday, 1969). My own effort to show the implications of this understanding of knowledge for historical analysis of the early Christian writings is set forth in my study, *Knowing the Truth: A Sociological Approach to New Testament Interpretation* (Minneapolis: Fortress, 1989), and is employed in my study *Who Are the People of God?* (New Haven: Yale University Press, 1995), 1–16.

195. Some scholars have interpreted these texts as describing an inner experience of the kingdom by rendering the prepositions as "within," but this runs counter to the emphasis throughout Luke on the works of healing and the transformations of the sick and possessed that manifest the presence and power of the kingdom.

196. This prophetic pronouncement reflects the theme of the ultimate opportunity of the nations of the world to see God's salvation, as in Isa 49:6, that the participatory response of Gentiles to God's word made available through the renewal of his people Israel is most explicit: "I will give you as a light to the nations, that my salvation may reach to the end of the earth."

197. Two volumes in the Anchor Bible: *The Gospel according to Luke I–IX* (AB; Garden City, NY: Doubleday, 1981); and *The Gospel according to Luke X–XXIV* (AB; Garden City, NY: Doubleday, 1985).

198. Fitzmyer, *Gospel of Luke I–IX*, 153–62.

199. Josephus, *Jewish Antiquities* 18.2.1., where the date is designated as "in the thirty-seventh year after Caesar's defeat of Anthony at the Battle of Actium," which took place in 31 BCE.

200. Mic 5:2 was quoted to Herod by the chief priests and scribes, according to Matt 2:3–6. For Luke, the prophetic reference remains implicit.

201. It is significant that his name, Zechariah, means "Yahweh remembers"—as indeed God is pictured fulfilling through John and Jesus the promises to Israel conveyed through the prophets.

202. Elijah is identified in Mal 4:5–6 as God's messenger to his people denouncing their sins of sorcery, sexual promiscuity, and oppression of workers, widows, and orphans (Mal 3:1–5).

203. In Greek, the verb for anoint is *echrisen*, akin to *Christos*; in Hebrew, the verb is *mashach*, akin to *meshiach* = Messiah.

204. These stories of the miracles done by the prophets appear in 1 Kgs 17:8–9 and 2 Kgs 5:14.

205. The ancient gospel manuscripts regarded as the best include the note in Luke 4:44 that Jesus began "preaching in the synagogues of Judea," although his journey there is a central feature of the next major section of Luke, 9:51–19:27.

206. Mark 1:40–45 = Luke 5:12–16.

207. Mark 2:1–12 = Luke 17:17–26.

208. Mark 2:13–17 = Luke 5:27–32.

209. The section ends at Luke 6:48.

210. This meaning of *epitropos* may be found in Josephus, *Jewish Antiquities* 18.194.

211. For example, Aristaeus is the tutor of Dionysus, and Olympus is the tutor of Zeus (Diodorus Siculus 3.72.1). The term is used only by Luke in the New Testament, and only with reference to Jesus (5:5; 8:24, 45; 9:33, 49; 17:13).

212. Some Jewish sources indicate that the number of the nations is seventy-two, so that it is not insignificant that some ancient manuscripts of Luke give the number of those sent out by Jesus as seventy-two.

213. *Eis oikon tinos tōn archontōn [tōn] Pharisaiōn* could be understood as "a ruler who was one of the Pharisees," or "a certain ruler of the Pharisees." The latter seems to fit better in the context.

214. Cf. Matt 18:10–14.

215. While divorce is permitted for a man who "finds something objectionable about her" (Deut 24:1), rabbinic scholars of the Tannaitic period (late first century BCE to end of second century CE) debated as to whether adultery was the only ground for divorce. Luke omits the Markan tradition on this subject (Mark 10:1–12), which is expanded in Matthew (19:1–12) to include consideration of non-marriage.

216. In Matt 24:40, male workers are also present.

217. In Luke, each of the ten servants receives a pound, which was equivalent to about three months' wages, while in the Matthean version (25:15–18), three servants were given respectively five talents, two talents, and one talent, the Syrian version of which amounted to about $250.

218. Mark 12:11 includes v. 23, which asserts, "This is the Lord's doing; it is marvelous in our eyes."

219. The Markan story of the woman anointing Jesus for burial (Mark 14:3–9) was reworked by Luke and is reported early in Jesus' public career (7:36–50). See pp. 145–46.

220. The term for officer is *strategos*, which in Acts 4:1 and 5:24 refers to temple officials, as also fits this context.

221. John 19:37 directly quotes Zech 12:10 with reference to Jesus as the one "pierced."

222. *kakourgoi.*

223. *lestai.*

224. For example, Josephus, *Jewish War* 2.254 and 4.504; *Jewish Antiquities* 14.159 and 20.160.

225. This is the sole occurrence of this term in the gospel tradition. It is used elsewhere in the New Testament once by Paul (2 Cor 12:4), where he recounts his having been taken up to the "third heaven," and once in Rev 2:7, where those who are victorious against the enemy of God's people are to be permitted "to eat from the tree of life in the paradise of God"—which is an image for the renewed creation where God's people will dwell in the age to come.

226. The day of Preparation reported in John 19:42 must refer to preparation for Passover, which is said in John 13:1 to be later than the day of Jesus' final session with the disciples.

227. One of them is identified as Cleopas—who is otherwise unknown and not mentioned elsewhere in the New Testament.

228. See chap. 3 for further analyses of Acts.

229. *Das Evangelium des Johannes* (16th ed., with suppl.; Goettingen: Vandenhoeck, 1959). An English translation was published in 1971 (Philadelphia: Westminster).

230. The widespread individualism of nineteenth-century liberal Protestant Christianity is evident in hymns that were produced by it, such as "In the Garden": "I come to the garden, alone, while the dew is still on the roses. . . . And he walks with me, and he talks with me, and he tells me I am his own." A similar individualistic approach to religion is evident in the work of Martin Buber, however, and directly so in the title of his popular book published in the middle of the twentieth century, *I . . . Thou* (New York: Macmillan, 1988).

231. John Dillon, *The Middle Platonists* (Ithaca, NY: Cornell University Press, 1977), 201.

232. From my notes on "Wisdom and Poetical Writings," in *The Cambridge Annotated Study Bible* (Cambridge: Cambridge University Press, 1993), 46.

233. Major studies of Jewish mysticism that include analysis of *merkabah* mysticism are those of Gershon Scholem, *Major Trends in Jewish Mysticism*; and Ithamar Gruenwald, *Apocalyptic and Merkevah Mysticism*.

234. Edited and translated by Carol Newsom in the Harvard Semitic Museum series as *Songs of the Sabbath Sacrifice* (Atlanta, GA: Scholars Press, 1985).

235. John 2:11; "the first of his signs"; the purpose of the signs is specified in 20:30–31: to believe in Jesus as the Messiah and thereby to gain "life in his name."

236. Mark 11:15–19; Luke 19:45–48; Matt 21:12–13.

237. Shechem was the place where Abraham stayed on his arrival in Palestine (Gen 12:6) and where his bones were buried (Josh 24:32). It was in Shechem that Joshua renewed the covenant of God with Israel when they returned from slavery in Egypt (Josh 24). The city served as the capital of the kingdom formed by the northern tribes (1 Kgs 12) until it was destroyed by the Assyrian armies in 722 BCE. In 350 BCE, it was rebuilt as the religious center for the Samaritans, with their temple on nearby Mount Gerizim.

238. Unlike Matthew and Luke, which highlight Bethlehem as the place where Jesus was born in fulfillment of prophecy (Matt 2:1–12; Luke 2:4–11), John contrasts Jesus' origin in Galilee with the prophetic expectation of the Messiah "from Bethlehem" (7:41–42). Instead, John emphasizes the Galilean origin and identity of Jesus (1:46; 2:1; 7:52; 19:19).

239. Raymond E. Brown has suggested that this verse is an insert by a redactor who wanted to indicate that the faith of the Galileans was inadequate, based on the

outward deeds of Jesus rather than on their inner meaning; see *The Gospel according to John I–XII* (AB; Garden City, NY: Doubleday, 1966), 187.

240. This is referred to in John 4:54 as Jesus' "second sign," but if one understands "sign" to mean actions of Jesus that have symbolic import for God's power to heal and renew, this would be the fifth sign preceded by: (1) water into wine; (2) cleansing the temple; (3) the call of Nicodemus to new birth; (4) the interchange between Jesus and the woman at the well.

241. The major feasts for the Jews were Passover, Pentecost, and Tabernacles. Jesus was there for Passover (2:13), so this one may refer to Pentecost, which was originally a celebration of the harvest seven weeks after it began—hence fifty days = Pentecost (Deut 16:9; Lev 23:15–16). Later, it came to be a celebration of the giving of the law to Moses at Sinai, and probably has this connotation in its symbolic role in Acts 2, when the Spirit is poured out on all humanity.

242. Described by J. T. Milik in *Discoveries in the Judean Desert* (1962), 3:271; and in *CBQ* 26 (1964): 254.

243. The first of Mark's feeding stories appears in 6:30–44, and is matched in Matt 14:13–21 and Luke 9:10–17. The subsequent story of the feeding of the four thousand (Mark 8:1–10) is also in Matthew (15:32–39), but is omitted by Luke as part of the greater Lukan omission (Mark 6:52–8:26).

244. Matt 14:19; Luke 9:16.

245. Mark and Matthew use *eucharisteses* in relation to the cup (Mark 14:23; Matt 26:27), but Luke uses it for the broken bread as well (Luke 22:19). This matches Paul's account in 1 Cor 11:24.

246. Also known as Festival of Booths. With the Passover and the Festival of Weeks, it was one of the three major times for pilgrimage to Jerusalem. Cf. Exod 23:16; 34:22; Deut 16:13–15.

247. The story of Jesus refusing to accuse and condemn the woman who had been caught in adultery (7:53–8:11) was transmitted in the church independently of the four gospels. It is not found in the oldest and best manuscripts and versions of the New Testament, and its literary style does not match that of the rest of this gospel. The death penalty was prescribed in the law of Moses for adultery (Lev 20:10) and by the prophet Ezekiel (16:38–40). The mode of execution was stoning (Deut 22:21), but the witnesses essential for such a condemnation have not come forth (Deut 17:7). Jesus refuses to condemn her, her accusers leave "one by one" (John 8:9), and Jesus simply instructs her not to "sin again" (8:11). Eusebius mentions that this story appears in the apocryphal Gospel according to the Hebrews (*Ecclesiastical History* 3.9.17). The issue of dealing with an adulterous wife is discussed in the Shepherd of Hermas (*Mandate* 4.1.4–11), and was later added to the gospel tradition in Matt 19:9, as shown by comparison of this late manuscript tradition with Mark 10:11f., Matt 5:32, and Luke 16:18. Similarly, its presence in the later manuscripts of John indicates that it was added to the original.

248. Elsewhere in the New Testament, the theme is set forth that Jesus is the one who has brought God's light to the world (1 John 2:7–11) and the new people of God are depicted as those who shine as lights in the world (1 Thess 5:5; Phil 2:15; Matt 5:14). This theme of God sending light into the world is in both the earlier and later parts of the prophet Isaiah: 9:11; 42:8; 49:6; 60:1, 3.

249. Deut 17:6; 17:15.

250. Similar language is used in Isa 43:10–13, where the uniqueness of God is declared, with no divine predecessors or successors. In the LXX, 43:10 asserts that the

people are to believe and understand that I am (*ego eimi*). It is this claim of Jesus—viewed by his opponents as blasphemous—that here motivates them to execute him.

251. Stoning was a mode of capital punishment performed by the whole community to execute one who had been proved to have committed blasphemy, worship of other deities, child sacrifice, or violation of the Sabbath (Lev 24:15–16; 20:27; Num 15:32–36).

252. The *amen, amen* phrase appears in these texts in each of the three categories: (1) predictions of the future: 1:51; 12:21; 13:30; 16:20; 21:18; (2) declarations as to Jesus' role and identity: 5:19, 24; (3) promises and warnings to the new community: 3:3, 5, 11; 6:26, 47, 53; 8:34, 50; 10:1; 12:24; 13:16, 20; 14:12; 16:23.

253. Similarly, God is quoted in Exod 7:1 as saying to Moses, "I have made you like God to Pharoah."

254. One version of this anointing by an unidentified women appears in Mark 14:3–9 and Matt 26:6–13, and a more extended version—performed by "a woman of the city, who was a sinner"—occurs in Luke 7:36–50.

255. See the analyses of John 3:14 and 8:28.

256. Mark 14:17–21; Matt 26:20–25; Luke 22:14, 21–23.

257. Mark 14:26–31; Matt 26:30–35; Luke 22:31–34.

258. The parallels are in Matt 26:17–19, 26–29; and Luke 22:7–13, 15–20.

259. The term for friends here, *philoi*, is the nominal match for the verb *phileo*, which Jesus is quoted in John 5:20 as using with reference to God's love for the Son, which is manifest in his showing the Son all that he is doing and enabling him to do even greater works.

260. Other links between Judas's treachery and scripture appear in Acts 1:15–20 (cf. Ps 69:25) and Matt 27:3–10 (cf. Zech 11:12–13), but no explicit prediction is to be found.

261. Mark 14:10–11, 17–21; Matt 26:14–16, 20–25; Luke 22:3–6, 14, 21–23.

262. Mark 14:44–45; Matt 26:48–49.

263. The beloved disciple was very early identified with John and perceived to have been the author of this gospel.

264. It is only in the late additions to Mark—the so-called longer ending (16:9–20)—that the appearance of Christ to Mary Magdalene is described.

265. Raymond E. Brown, in his *The Gospel according to John XIII–XXI* (AB; Garden City, NY: Doubleday, 1970), has conveniently gathered and assessed the ancient and modern theories that offer symbolic explanations for this number, ranging from this being the number of fish "of every kind" (as in Matt 13:47; so Jerome, *Commentary on Ezekiel* 47.6–12 [PL 25:474C], to allegorical interpretations, such as that of Cyril of Alexandria in his commentary on John [*In Jo.* XII, PG 74:745]) where the number is the sum of three factors: the fullness of the Gentile nations: 100; the remnant of Israel: 50; and the Trinity.

266. The first volume of *Neutestamentliche Apokryphen in deutscher Uebersetzung* was prepared by Edgar Hennecke in 1904, and went through five editions. The 6th ed. of 1990 (Tuebingen: J. C. B. Mohr [Paul Siebeck]) was translated into English and published in 1991 under R. McL. Wilson (Cambridge: James Clarke; Louisville, KY: Westminster/John Knox) as *New Testament Apocrypha*, vol. 1, *Gospels and Related Writings*. Vol. 2, *Writings Relating to the Apostles; Apocalypses and Related Subjects*, was published in 1992.

267. Irenaeus, *Against Heresies* 3.11.8.

268. Clement, *Stromata* 3.93.1.

269. The text of this letter is translated in *New Testament Apocrypha* 1:49–50.

270. *New Testament Apocrypha* 1:66–69.

271. Schneemelcher, *New Testament Apocrypha*, 1:79.

272. This analysis of the strategy of the writers of the apocryphal gospels is set forth in detail in ibid., 1:85–91.

273. The complete list of apocryphal gospels arranged according to Schneemelcher's classification system appears in the table of contents of vol. 1 under the general title: "Gospels: Non-Biblical Material about Jesus."

274. Schneemelcher, *New Testament Apocrypha*, 1:96–99.

275. Epiphanius, *Refutation of all Heresies* 30.16.4; 30.22.4.

276. In *New Testament Apocrypha*, 1:501–36.

CHAPTER THREE

Paul and the Apostolic Traditions: Christianity Extends into the Wider Graeco-Roman World

Sources concerning Paul and the Apostles

The importance of Paul for the origins of Christianity is evident from the fact that of the twenty-seven books that comprise the New Testament, thirteen were written by him or in his name.[1] Further, the Acts of the Apostles portrays the conversion and mission of Paul and reports his message and activities in twenty-one of its twenty-eight chapters.[2] His central role in the spread of Christianity is reflected in this material, and is either described therein or may be inferred from it.

Fortunately, some autobiographical material is to be found in his letters, which also include a sufficient number of references to other apostolic leaders and to the concrete situations and actions of Christian groups across the Mediterranean world—from Jerusalem to Rome—to enable one to discern the context and content of Paul's thought and action, as well as the enduring impact of the traditions that developed in his name. This information is to some extent confirmed by the accounts of Paul in Acts, and is at a number of points supplemented considerably—although the historical reliability of the Acts material is debatable, as will be discussed below (216–20). The abundance of Pauline material in the New Testament shows clearly that his was the central role in the spread of Christianity from its geographical and cultural setting in Palestinian Judaism of the early first century CE out into the wider Graeco-Roman world.

Linked with the name of Paul in the New Testament are also sources that show the sociological development of the movement from its informal, seemingly spontaneous constituency and convictions, to a more structured organization with defined roles and beliefs and specific rules for its participants. These include writings attributed to Paul but almost certainly written by his followers: Colossians, Ephesians, 1 and 2 Timothy, and Titus.[3] Further, the description of Paul's life and thought in the Acts of the Apostles in part supplements what one may learn about him from his letters, and in part views him from a somewhat different perspective. But in any case, apart from the question of historical reliability concerning the life and thought of Paul, the diverse and dynamic Pauline traditions in the New Testament demonstrate some of the major modes and strategies by which an indigenous Jewish phenomenon spread and impacted the wider Graeco-Roman world. Basic in such an investigation is the examination of the way in which Paul's letters disclose his understanding of the role of Jesus in the purpose of God, and how this shaped his view of the new covenant community and its moral obligations to those within it and to the wider world in which its message and mission were to be proclaimed. We shall see how the later books written in Paul's name display developments in the concept of Jesus as God's agent of human renewal and in the self-understanding of the new community with regard to its structure and moral obligations.

The letters attributed to Paul may be placed in three categories: (1) those most plausibly assigned to Pauline authorship; (2) those that are likely the product of Paul's associates, showing both close relationship to and significant differences from the authentic letters; (3) those written in his name but clearly displaying that they come from a subsequent period, as evident from the social structures, leadership roles, and conceptual features they represent as operative in the Christian community. Those in category 1 are:

Galatians
1 Corinthians
2 Corinthians
Philippians
Romans
1 Thessalonians
2 Thessalonians
Philemon

In category 2 are:

Colossians
Ephesians

In category 3 are:

1 Timothy
2 Timothy
Titus

Later works attributed to Paul or purporting to describe his life or thought but not included in the New Testament canon are:

Epistle to the Laodiceans
Correspondence between Seneca and Paul
Acts of Paul

Translations and analyses of these later documents are offered in volume 2 of *New Testament Apocrypha*. It is obvious that they were produced well after the time of Paul by those who wanted to adapt his thought while also benefiting from his reputation as they set forth their subsequent theological and social schemes.[4]

Additional facets of this evolutionary process by which early Christianity developed in its diversity become evident through an analysis of other New Testament writings produced by—or in the name of—such other apostolic figures as Peter, James, and John, or anonymously, such as the Letter to the Hebrews. These works, discussed later in this chapter, document the impact on early Christianity—and, prior to that, on the Jewish community out of which it initially evolved—of concepts and insights that arose in the Graeco-Roman culture, such as Stoic ethics and Platonic ontology. Both the conceptual and the sociological developments apparent in these later writings show how the early Christian movement was able to gain stability as an institution and credibility in the various intellectual modes that it adopted—and adapted.

Our analysis of the apostolic tradition begins with a reconstruction of the career and developing thought of Paul—the central figure in this historical process that had such an enduring impact on Christianity—and then moves to the examination of his writings and those that were produced in his name[5] or provide an account of his career.[6] Before beginning the examination of the evidence concerning Paul's conversion and call to mission, however, it is essential to survey the New Testament documents that describe or report on his life and thought. As noted above, the Pauline books widely regarded as authentic are: Galatians, Romans, 1 and 2 Corinthians, 1 and 2 Thessalonians, Philippians, and Philemon. Those thought to have been written later in his name, Colossians, Ephesians, 1 and 2 Timothy, and Titus.[7]

The later Pauline tradition embodies conceptions of Christ and/or images of the church that seem to reflect theological and institutional developments after the first generation of the apostles had passed. The major feature of this tradition is, of course, the Acts of the Apostles, which, while representing a later view of Paul's life and thought, does include material that provides useful supplemental evidence about his career. Before proceeding to analyses of the letters of Paul and those attributed to him, it is essential to bring into focus the method and message of the Acts.

The Aims and Strategies
of the Acts of the Apostles

The overall aim of Acts is evident in the account of the divinely supported movement of the good news from the center of the Jewish heritage from which Jesus came—Jerusalem—to the political and cultural center of the Gentile world—Rome. But equally as important for the author as this geographical spread is the cultural outreach as evident in the concepts and modes of communication that are incorporated in the Acts account of this divinely supported move. The modes include speeches, stories, and the overall literary method of the book. Terminology and rhetorical features of Graeco-Roman culture are reportedly used by Paul in his proclamation of the gospel in the cities of the Roman world. Acts describes the journey of Paul from the center of the Jewish world—Jerusalem—to the center of the first-century CE Gentile world—Rome.

The author is not content merely to recount Paul's travels, but describes in dramatic detail his encounters with the political, cultural, intellectual, and religious features of the Roman world, with vivid accounts of his experiences in the major cities of Syria and Palestine, and then of the Greek world, in Asia Minor and in Greece itself. These narratives, which include features of the more popular types of religious communication in this culture—miracle stories and narratives of divine guidance or enablement, as in the Hellenistic romances—are important elements of Acts. Above all, the overall literary mode of Acts corresponds consistently with the histories and the romances as instruments of religious propaganda in that era.[8] In what follows we shall include examination of the narratives and speeches attributed to Paul and to other apostles, with indications of the likely degree of historical reliability of this material, as well as proposals as to the purposes served by its inclusion in the Acts account.

Features of the Acts that are of major importance for that work but are lacking in the letters of Paul or other parts of the New Testament are identified below.[9]

Following an introduction to Acts as volume 2 of Luke-Acts, there is an account of preparation for the ascension of Jesus and for the outpouring of the Holy Spirit. The replacement of the failed disciple/apostle Jude is described (1:12–26). The launching of the ethnically and geographically inclusive new covenant community begins with the coming of the Holy

Spirit, which is observed by witnesses "from every nation under heaven" (2:5). Peter explains that what is occurring is the fulfillment of God's promise through David and the prophets (2:14–36). Then the new community begins to take shape, sharing in the apostles' teaching, in fellowship, and in the breaking of bread (2:27–47). Peter's healing of a lame man at the temple gate (3:1–10) is seen as a prototype of healings to occur through the apostles across the world. Peter's speech in the Colonnade of Solomon in the temple (3:11–26) declares that what is happening is the fulfillment of God's promise to Abraham that through his descendants "all the families of the earth shall be blessed" (3:25; Gen 22:18; 26:4).

Confrontation of the apostles with the Roman authorities is the issue in 4:1–22, where the activities of the apostles are challenged by the council in Jerusalem—the *synedrion*. In spite of this official opposition, the community celebrates God's support (4:23–37) and sees divine punishment brought upon those who seek to corrupt the community (5:1–11). Conversely, crowds are attracted in Jerusalem by the signs and wonders performed by the apostles (5:12–16). Nonetheless, the trials and persecution of the apostles begin, including hostile hearings before the council (5:17–42). Although no formal charge is brought, the apostles are beaten and then discharged.

The shaping of the new community is described in 6:1–8:40. In addition to the twelve apostles, seven persons are appointed to serve in more material ways. One of them with a Greek name, Stephen, is brought to trial by the council (6:8–15), which he addresses, pointing out how God seeks to fulfill his purpose for his people in a variety of ways and in various places and cultures, choosing leaders whom the majority misunderstand and reject. In response to his claim to see Jesus "standing at God's right hand," the council stones Stephen to death as he prays for their forgiveness (7:1–8:1). The resulting dispersal of the community takes the good news of Jesus to other outsiders: the Samaritans (8:4–25) and an Ethiopian eunuch (8:26–40).

With the conversion of Saul/Paul, the new community launches a world mission (9:1–15:41). This is in fulfillment of the risen Jesus' commissioning of the disciples (Luke 4:47), and begins when Paul preaches about Jesus to a synagogue in Damascus (9:19–22). But Peter's activity also moves out of Jerusalem (10:1–48). In Caesarea, the Roman center of authority in Palestine, Peter is the messenger through whom a Roman military officer is converted— reported to and approved by the church in Jerusalem (11:1–18). The geographical outreach continues in Syria at Antioch, the city founded by the Hellenistic ruler Seleucus I and named in honor of his father, who consolidated the Seleucid empire. The city is important geographically and symbolically as evidence of the new community's reaching out to the wider Graeco-Roman world. It builds on the foundation set by Diaspora Judaism, but exceeds it in inclusiveness and mission initiative.

The theme of official hostility to the movement resumes in 12:1–17, where there is a report of the killing of the Apostle James (brother of John and son of Zebedee)[10] and the imprisonment of Peter by the civil ruler, Herod Antipas, who ruled as tetrarch of Galilee and Perea from 4 BCE until 39 CE. It was he who had John the Baptist executed, and he seized these two apostles to ingratiate himself with the Jewish leadership, who perceived the spread of the new community as a threat. Acts 12:6–17 reports that Herod wanted to bring out Peter and execute him in public (12:4) as a sign of the illegality by Roman law of schemes of political revolt, which the mission of the apostles was perceived to be. There is a double irony in this account: (1) Peter, who had been imprisoned, was set free when an iron gate opened of itself (12:10); (2) Herod, who claimed divine status and honors, was struck dead (12:20–23). In spite of official opposition, the movement continued to spread with divine support, and contact was maintained with the new community in Jerusalem (12:24–25). It is at this point that the Acts narrative begins to describe the role of Paul in the spread of the gospel in the wider Roman world.

Paul Called as Messenger to the Gentiles: The Evidence from His Letters and Acts

Examined here is the material found in what are regarded as the authentic letters of Paul (as listed above), as well as what appears to be historically reliable evidence preserved in Acts.

Paul's Life and Activity Prior to his Conversion

As noted above, some biographical information about Paul is preserved in his letters, and some can only be inferred from the later sources included in the New Testament. Of primary importance is the evidence that, in spite of the radical revision of the covenant community that Paul believed Jesus to have accomplished, he repeatedly emphasized the importance and the dynamic of the Jewish heritage in terms of which the role of Jesus was to be perceived. Especially significant is Paul's fidelity to that tradition as embodied in the Law, the Prophets, and the Wisdom writings. He affirms his having been born and reared in the traditions of Israel, with Hebrew parents and ancestry from the tribe of Benjamin (Phil 3:4–5), which fostered his remarkable commitment to Jewish legal traditions (Gal 1:13–14). His mentioning that following his conversion and subsequent conference with the apostles in Jerusalem he "returned to Damascus" suggests that he may have been in residence there at the time when he experienced the vision of the risen Christ. This city is located in what was called by the Romans the province of Syria and Cilicia, where Paul reports that he carried on his missionary activity (Gal 1:21).

Acts links Paul with Tarsus (9:11), which is also located in this province, so his origin in that vicinity is probable. This region was of major importance in the Hellenistic period, when it was designated the Seleucid realm,[11] and was subject to aggressive efforts by its rulers to impose Hellenistic culture and economics on the area. Damascus was one of the ten Hellenistic cities that were federated as the Decapolis. Built in geometric patterns, with colonnaded walks, theaters, public baths, splendid residences, these cities served as models of Graeco-Roman architectural and cultural style, mostly in the area east of Galilee and Samaria, except for Damascus to the northeast.[12] Hence, Paul's evident facility in the Greek language and literary modes are fully understandable if this was his place of origin and continuing activity

In his letters, Paul refers to remunerative work in which he was engaged, both before and after his conversion (1 Thess 2:9; 1 Cor 9:9), though he does not specify what it was. Acts 18:1–3, however, notes that he was a tentmaker (or leatherworker)—like Priscilla and Aquila, who were said to have been originally from Pontus (a province on the south shore of the Black Sea), who had moved to Rome. But they had to leave the capital city when the emperor Claudius expelled all Jews from there, so they resided in Corinth.

A personal feature of Paul indicated in his letters is that he had some sort of physical handicap that had led to his proclaiming the gospel among the Galatians, although it caused them some difficulty (Gal 4:12–14). His commendation of those who were supportive of him in spite of his "physical infirmity" declares they would have "torn out [their] eyes and given them to [him]" may reflect his having had a serious optical problem. Yet in 2 Cor 10:10, he quotes his critics as having declared that "his letters are weighty and strong, but his bodily presence is weak and his speech contemptible." Thus Paul, without specifying their nature, acknowledged his serious bodily limitations. In 2 Cor 12:1–10, he refers to the "visions and revelations" that he received from God, and repeats that he "was caught up to the third heaven" (= paradise), where he heard things that he may not repeat. He seems to have thought that, to counterbalance "the exceptional character of these revelations" he received, he was given some kind of physical disability—"a thorn in the flesh"—which he understood to be a "messenger of Satan." Although he earlier had repeatedly appealed to God to remove this handicap, he was told that the power he was receiving from God through Christ was "made perfect in weakness" (12:8–9). He no longer protested against the difficulties—including "weaknesses, insults, hardships, persecutions, and calamities"—that beset him as he sought to serve Christ. Hence, his consciousness of personal weakness confirmed his sense of God's power and strength at work through him.

The one area in which, prior to his conversion, he had achieved notable success, however, was his persecution of those who were turning to Jesus as the Messiah. He assumes that his reputation as a Jew was widely known among Christians when he "was violently persecuting the church and was trying to destroy it" (Gal.1:13). His motivation for this hostile activity toward the new movement was his being unusually "zealous for the traditions of my ancestors" (1:14), so that he "tried to destroy" this emergent community (1:13). Elsewhere he refers to himself as one who had been vigorously engaged in persecution of the church (1 Cor 15:9; Phil 3:6). This program of Paul to destroy the Jesus movement is mentioned repeatedly in Acts, as in 8:1–3, where his role in the persecution of the church is described: "Saul was ravaging the church, and entering house after house, he dragged off men and women and committed them to prison." This follows the story of the stoning of Stephen (7:54–8:1), which ends with the mention of the approval by Saul (= Paul)[13] of this execution. Acts 9:1–2 recounts his "breathing threats and murder against the disciples of the Lord," which led him to obtain from the high priest in Jerusalem letters to the synagogues at Damascus, authorizing him to bind and take to Jerusalem any whom he might find that were committed to the new movement ("the Way") or who called on the name of Jesus (9:14).

This officially authorized effort to destroy the new movement is reported again in Acts 26:4–11, where Paul is described as recounting at a hearing before the puppet king Herod Agrippa II[14] his having been reared in the Jewish tradition: ". . . a life spent from the beginning among my own people and in Jerusalem . . . that I have belonged to the strictest sect of our religion and lived as a Pharisee." These biographical details are given in more detail in Paul's reported defense before the Roman tribune after he had been arrested in the temple and was denounced by the crowd (Acts 21:27–36). Both to the tribune, speaking in Greek (21:37–39), and to the crowd, speaking in Hebrew (Aramaic) (21:40–22:5), Paul states that "Tarsus in Cilicia" was his place of birth, but that he had been "educated strictly according to our ancestral law" in Jerusalem, and that his teacher was "Gamaliel."[15]

In this Acts account, Paul also reports that he received letters from the Jewish authorities in Jerusalem to the Jews in Damascus that were intended to enable him to carry forward his program of binding and jailing men and women in the new movement, and to bring them bound to Jerusalem for punishment. There is no way to confirm or dispute the details of these reports in Acts, which offer specific claims about the strategy by which Paul may have carried forward his avowed program of persecution of the infant church. One significant detail confirmed in Paul's letters, however, is that his interpretation and appropriation of the law had been that of the Pharisees, and he does claim that, with respect to "righteousness under the law," he had regarded himself as "blameless" (Phil 3:5–6).

Paul's Initial Encounter with the Risen Christ
and His Call by God

What transformed Paul's perception of Jesus and his role in the purpose of God was, according to his own testimony, his experience of seeing the risen Christ. He understood this event as having happened as a divine disclosure and confirmation to him of the meaning of Jesus' death and as the guarantee of the resurrection from the dead that was to be experienced by all the members of the faithful community. He saw all of this as having taken place "in accordance with the scriptures" (1 Cor 15:3–4). He considered himself to be the "last of all" (15:5–9) in the series of apostles to whom the risen Christ appeared and who were commissioned by him in the apostolic role of spreading the good news. In 1 Cor 9:1, he bases his claim to be an apostle explicitly on his experience of having "seen Jesus our Lord." Paul regarded Jesus' having been raised from the dead as God's declaration that he was the Son of God, powerfully uttered through the Spirit of holiness (Rom 1:4). God's having "raised Jesus from the dead" is seen by Paul as proof that the God and Father of Jesus is "a living and true God" and that when Jesus returns to earth he will rescue his people "from the wrath that is coming" as divine judgment falls on the world dominated by evil powers (1 Thess 1:9–10). The significance of the resurrection for the formation of the new people of God and for the accomplishment of God's purpose in renewing the world is set forth in Paul's letters—especially 1 Corinthians, Romans, and 1 Thessalonians.[16]

Paul perceived this encounter with the risen Christ through divine revelation as central for his personal transformation from violent persecutor of the church to pioneer in proclaiming the good news to the Gentiles. He describes the experience as having occurred without consultation with or confirmation by the other apostles (Gal 1:13–17). He affirms it in the form of a rhetorical question in response to the challenge that had been raised about his authority as an apostle: "Have I not seen Jesus our Lord?" (1 Cor 9:1). And in his listing of those to whom the risen Christ appeared, he includes himself, while noting that he was the last and "the least of the apostles" to have this experience (1 Cor 15:8–9). The import of his having seen the resurrected Christ is indicated in more detail in his description of his having received the gospel and been commissioned to preach it among the Gentiles in Gal 1:12–17. Before examining the details of this commission, one should notice how he describes the experience: the gospel was conveyed to him not through another human being or by his being taught it, but "through a revelation [*apokalypsis*] of Jesus Christ." It was God who had chosen him for this role "before I was born," had "called me through [God's] grace," and hence "was pleased to reveal his Son to me" or "in me." This was an unprecedented encounter, since the divine purpose of this revelation was for Paul "to preach [Christ] among the Gentiles."

Paul describes this experience against the background of his own situation and activities in the Jewish tradition (Gal 1:13–14). He had been engaged in violent persecution of the church and had sought "to destroy it." He stood out in comparison with his Jewish contemporaries by reason of his zeal for "the traditions of my fathers," as evidenced by his fierce efforts to terminate this movement in the name of Jesus, which he then saw as radically subversive of the operative Jewish modes of covenantal identity and conformity.

The deeply personal context of this transforming experience is evident from Paul's note that, once the vision occurred, he did not confer with any human—not even with the Jerusalem-based apostles who had preceded him in understanding Jesus as God's agent of renewal of the covenant and in launching this message to the wider world (Gal 1:16b–17a). Instead, he went on his own into "Arabia," which was the desert-bordering Nabatean kingdom lying east of Damascus and extending south to the east of the Dead Sea and the Jordan Valley, and was ruled by Aretas IV from 9 BCE to 40 CE. Subsequently, in Damascus the governor under Aretas sought to seize Paul, but he reports how he escaped over the wall in a basket (2 Cor 11:32–33).[17]

In Acts there is a vivid depiction of Paul's transformation from violent adversary of those claiming Jesus as Messiah to a major figure in promoting that claim, but the terms used in the Acts account of this experience are different from those found in Paul's letters. Acts 1:6–8 describes Jesus as informing the apostles that the message about the establishment of God's rule on earth is not to be limited to Israel, but instead is to go out to "the ends of the earth." The power to carry out this mission will be available through "the Holy Spirit," which God is now to send down on them. The fulfillment of this promise/assignment is symbolized in the account of the outpouring of the Spirit on Jews and proselytes "from every nation under heaven" (2:1–5) and by the depiction of the ability of all these people of diverse origins to hear the message "each . . . in [their] own native language" (1:5–11). The justification for this enterprise of outreach to the wider world is provided in the Acts account by Peter's reported quotation from the prophets of Israel: "I will pour out my Spirit upon *all* flesh" (Acts 1:17).[18] Thus, in Acts, the program is set for evangelism across geographical and ethnic boundaries well before Paul is converted (Acts 9), although it is as a result of his subsequent vision (Acts 16:6–10) that the world mission is truly launched in Acts.

In Paul's letters, two potential problems related to his new conviction that Jesus was the agent of God for the renewal of his people are: (1) whether regarding Jesus' unique relationship with God involved one in polytheism, and (2) whether his having died by a pagan, bloody mode of execution meant that he should be considered accursed of God.[19] To answer these issues, in 1 Thess 1:9–10, Paul identifies the God who raised Jesus from the dead as "a living and true God." The oneness of God is affirmed, as is the insight that the seeming curse involved in Jesus' shameful death was in fact leading those who came to trust him as God's agent of human renewal to turn from idolatry, to await his return from heaven, and to be delivered from the judgment that God will send upon evildoers when the present age comes to an end. It is in light of these convictions that, for Paul, the focus for the worship of God and God's Son is not a new deity but "the true God."

The Acts account of Paul's vision of the risen Lord (9:1–19) contains features that match those mentioned by Paul in his letters, such as its occurring in the vicinity of Damascus (Gal 1:15–17). Appearing only in Acts are the exchange with Jesus, the hearing of Jesus' voice by Paul's companions, the informing of a disciple named Ananias of the central role Paul is to have in taking the name of Jesus to Gentiles and kings and "the sons of Israel," and the instruction to him to be the agent to restore Paul's sight and convey to him the Holy Spirit. Only in Acts is there a report of Saul/Paul being subsequently baptized by Ananias. Also unique to Acts is the story of his time with the disciples of Jesus there and his effective proclamation in the Damascus synagogues that Jesus is the Son of God and Messiah (9:20–22). The retaliatory plot of the Jews against him and his escape over the city wall "in a basket"[20] are described only in Acts (9:23–25).

The final account in Acts of Paul's initial associations with the Jerusalem-based disciples (9:26–30) describes his effort to join them and their disbelief that he was indeed a convert. Barnabas "brought him to the apostles" and reported on his encounter with the Lord and his bold preaching "in the name of Jesus" in Damascus. He is said to have associated with the apostles thereafter, and to have preached in Jerusalem "boldly in the name of the Lord." This led to his disputes with "the Hellenists," a term used in Acts 6:1–3 for seven men "of good repute" and with Greek names who were assigned by the apostles to handle routine daily needs of the new community there.

In Acts 9:29–30, Paul is described as engaging in debate with the Hellenists among the Christians in Jerusalem, and this evoked the response that "they were seeking to kill him." The implication is that his potential for effective appeal to Jews and Gentiles in the wider Hellenistic world was seen by them to be great, and they feared his success would seriously challenge their own identity as those reared in the Hellenistic traditions and culture who had found a new mode of participation in the covenant people different from that perceived and defined by mainstream Judaism.[21] Paul's commission to proclaim to the Gentiles the good news of what God was doing through Jesus Christ—as indicated in Gal 1:11–17 and in Acts 22:3–16 and 26:11–16—is seen in his letters and in Acts as a major challenge to the various modes of group identity operative within Judaism in the first century CE.

Paul's Subsequent Career as Evident from His Letters and as Depicted in Acts

As noted above, in chapters 1 and 2 of Galatians, Paul provides autobiographical information about his activities subsequent to his transforming vision of the risen Christ. Many other details of his apostolic career are described or referred to in his letters and in the Acts, as indicated below. Following the analysis of the biographical material, we shall examine these letters and the later letters attributed to him as offering perceptions in detail of his understanding of God's purpose through Jesus for the renewal of the covenant people, the resources available to this community to enable its members to obey and serve God, as well as how the community and its leadership subsequently came to perceive the identity and responsibilities of its members.

After Paul's vision of the risen Christ, in which God "was pleased to reveal his Son to me,"[22] he perceived that God had chosen him before he was born and was now revealing his Son to him and calling him to "preach him among the Gentiles" (Gal 1:15–16). He sought no human confirmation or authorization for this role—not even from the original followers of Jesus who now constituted the apostolic leadership in Jerusalem. As mentioned earlier, he withdrew to the barren area east of the Jordan and Dead Sea known as Arabia, and then returned to Damascus, where the vision had taken place.

His initial activity in proclaiming the good news he reports to have been carried out in "the regions of Syria and Cilicia" (Gal 1:21). Apart from his brief initial visit to the apostles in Jerusalem, he was known to the church there only by reputation: having earlier persecuted the apostolic leaders, "he is now preaching the faith he once tried to destroy" (Gal 1:23). It was fourteen years before he returned to Jerusalem, which he did for consultation with the apostles there (Gal 2:1). He mentions that he was accompanied on this visit to Jerusalem by Barnabas and Titus, who was a "Greek" and was not circumcised (Gal 2:3).

Paul's aim in visiting the apostles in Jerusalem—which he saw as having been initiated "by revelation" (2:2)—was to have the apostles review the gospel that he was preaching among the Gentiles so that he could be certain that neither his past nor his present mission activity was "in vain." The major issue was whether converts should be required to conform to the requirements of the Jewish law, specifically, whether the males who were joining the new covenant people had to be circumcised. Paul did not have to concede on this issue, even though certain zealots for the law who he says "were reputed to be something" tried to undermine what he regarded as "our freedom" and "the truth of the gospel" (2:4–5). The opinion of the apostles was that Peter had been "entrusted" by God for carrying the gospel to the circumcised, while Paul was to bring the good news to the "uncircumcised"

(2:6–8). The assignment of Paul and Barnabas to carry on their mission to the Gentiles was affirmed by the apostles and visibly confirmed by "James,[23] Cephas and John," the primary messengers "to the circumcised" (2:9), who extended to them "the right hand of fellowship."

Paul's acceptance of the obligation to "remember the poor" was his agreement to encourage the converts in the predominantly Gentile churches to contribute money for support of the new community in Jerusalem. This is directly referred to in Rom 15:22–27, where Paul reports that he is taking to Jerusalem money given by the churches in Macedonia and Achaia for "the poor among the saints at Jerusalem." It is in Gal 2:10 that Paul acknowledges the basis for this obligation to be assumed by members of the Gentile churches, and then observes that he was "eager" to accept this responsibility of collecting money, which he seems to have regarded as a tangible expression of the shared life of the scattered communities that constituted the new covenant people.

In Acts 9, there is an account of the conversion of "Saul" that differs in many details from the brief report in Galatians. His having obtained from the high priest in Jerusalem authorization to seek out any in the synagogue at Damascus who had become followers of Jesus—"who belonged to the Way" (9:2)—and to bring them bound to Jerusalem has no counterpart in Paul's letters. Nor do the details of the heavenly light and the voice that challenged this enterprise and identified itself as that of Jesus, "whom you are persecuting" (9:3–7). Led by his astounded colleagues, who could not see the one who was speaking, he was taken to Damascus, where he was sightless and speechless for three days (9:8–9). A vision is reported as leading Ananias, who had become a disciple of Jesus, to seek out Saul, but he is reluctant to do so because he has heard of Saul's authority from "the chief priests" to bind those who invoke the name of Jesus. But "the Lord" now tells him about the special role that Saul is to fulfill as the one who will carry the name of Jesus to the Gentiles, kings, and the people of Israel, and as a result will "suffer much for the sake of the name" of Jesus (9:10–16). Ananias then goes to "Saul," promising him recovery of his sight and that he will be filled by the Holy Spirit, whereupon Paul regains his sight, is baptized, and recovers his strength. After some days with the disciples of Jesus there, Paul begins to preach about Jesus in the synagogues as Son of God, confounding his Jewish hearers by the proof he offers that Jesus is the Messiah (9:20–22). None of these details has a counterpart in the letters of Paul, although there is some overlap, such as the importance of Damascus as the vicinity in which Paul reports this transformation to have taken place.

The next section of Acts (9:32–12:25) describes the mission of Peter reaching out to Gentiles and the confirmation of this by the Holy Spirit, the miraculous deliverance of Peter from prison, and the divine punishment of Herod

Agrippa I when he accepted divine honors from the people.[24] This is followed by an account of the commissioning of Paul and Barnabas by the church in Antioch to spread the gospel to the wider Gentile world (Acts 13:1–3). The journey of Paul and Barnabas to Jerusalem, accompanied by Titus, is described by Paul in Gal 2:1ff., which he says took place fourteen years after his initial contact with the apostles there. His visit was motivated by divine counsel ("by revelation"), and involved him in a private discussion with an inner circle of the apostles ("the acknowledged leaders") concerning his message to the Gentiles in order for him to be certain of the true worth of the mission in which he was engaged.

Some who falsely claimed to be members of God's new people[25] tried to discredit the freedom that Paul and his associates had shown by inviting the uncircumcised to join this new community. But Paul refused to yield on the issue, and those considered to be "of repute" did not demand that Paul add legal observance, such as circumcision, to the requirements for Gentiles to become part of the new people of God. Instead, they acknowledged a division of labor: Peter and his associates were to proclaim the good news about Jesus to the circumcised, while Paul and his coworkers would reach out to the Gentiles. This verbal agreement was confirmed by sharing "the right hand of fellowship"—thus demonstrating that membership in the new community transcended differences in perception of the legal requirements for participation (Gal 2:6–9). As a further indication of the common life that transcended the differences, the Gentile churches were urged to contribute financial support for the impoverished Christian community in Jerusalem, as indicated above.

The tradition behind Paul's second conference with the Jerusalem leadership is described in a much more elaborate and formal way in Acts 15:1–35, which follows the Acts narrative (13–14) of the mission activity of Paul and his associates among Jews and Gentiles in Cyprus and Asia Minor from their base of operations in Antioch (Acts 13:1). This material is analyzed below, but we look first at the Acts account of the Jerusalem council. The immediate occasion for it is said to have been the dispute that arose in Antioch when certain teachers from Judea declared that circumcision "according to the custom of Moses" (15:1) was essential for salvation. The resulting dispute within the Antiochene Christian community led to the assigning of Paul and Barnabas—with "some others," apparently as witnesses—to go to Jerusalem for formal consultation with the "apostles and elders" there to settle this issue (15:2). En route, they report to the Christian communities in Phoenicia and Samaria the "conversion of the Gentiles," which evokes a joyous response from "all the believers" (15:3). Their arrival in Jerusalem was welcomed by the community and its leaders ("the apostles and elders"), but their report of the success of the mission to the Gentiles evoked strong opposition from members of the community whose background in Judaism was in "the party of the Pharisees" and who therefore affirmed that circumcision and conformity to the law of Moses were still essential for membership in God's new people (15:5).

After extended debate, the first response from the "apostles and elders" is articulated by Peter (15:6–11), who recalls the dramatic outreach to Gentiles embodied in the story reported in Acts 10, when a vision seen by Cornelius, a devout officer in the Roman army (10:1–8), and one seen by Peter (10:9–16) converge to lead Peter to proclaim the forgiveness of sin that God provides through Jesus for all who believe in him, Jew or Gentile (10:34–43). This is depicted in Acts as divine confirmation through the outpouring of the Holy Spirit on the Gentile hearers, and human confirmation from the apostles and members of the church in Jerusalem when they heard Peter's report (11:1–18). Thus, Acts shows Peter as having established the precedent and receiving confirmation from the other apostles for the outreach to the Gentiles without obliging them to conform to the ritual or other require-ments of the law of Moses. Although Paul does not mention these specific developments in his letters, Acts proceeds to describe the mission to the Gentiles led by Paul and Barnabas as a consequence of this apostolic deci-sion, beginning in Acts 11:19.

The presence and activity of believers in Jesus as Messiah on the coast of North Africa (Cyrene) and the northeastern Mediterranean (the coast of Phoenicia and the island of Cyprus) is described in Acts 11:19 as a conse-quence of the persecution of the church that began in Jerusalem after Stephen's speech condemning the Jewish leaders for their continuing rejec-tion and killing of God's messengers, which had culminated in the death of Jesus (Acts 7:1–54). The scattering of the followers of Jesus is seen in Acts to have led to the Christian outreach to Samaritans (Acts 8:1–13) and to the Ethiopian eunuch (8:26–39), but also to have provoked the persecution led by Saul (9:1). The most important place to which these Christian refugees fled was Antioch in Syria. This city, located on the Orontes River in the Roman province of Cilicia and Syria, was founded in 300 BCE by Seleucus Nicanor, and became a major Hellenistic cultural and economic center for the entire region. Greek language, literature, and various modes of religion—including the mystery cults—flourished there. Travel routes by land and sea made it an ideal place for fostering the spread of Christianity. Its significance as "the starting point for the self-conscious mission to Gentiles who had not previously become Jewish proselytes" is affirmed and documented by Wayne A. Meeks and Robert L. Wilken in their excellent study, *Jews and Christians in Antioch in the First Four Centuries of the Common Era*.[26] Acts 11:26 also notes that "in Antioch the disciples were for the first time called Christians."

From this passage in Acts, one can also infer that "this mission was initi-ated by Greek-speaking Jewish Christians, 'Cypriots and Cyrenaens,' among whom Barnabas was probably the leading figure."[27] Curiously, Paul makes no further mention of Antioch after his report of the conflict there with Peter, who is said to have reneged on his program of free association with Gentiles within the Christian community (Gal 2:11–14).

In Acts 13 and 14, the itinerary of "Barnabas and Saul" is traced. Setting sail from Seleucia, a port city down the Orontes from Antioch and not far from Tarsus (which Acts 9:11 identifies as Paul's hometown), they went to Cyprus, preaching the gospel in synagogues there and engaging in an exchange with "a Jewish false prophet, named Bar-Jesus" (13:6), as well as with the chief Roman official of Cyprus (proconsul), Sergius Paulus. When their message was refuted by Bar-Jesus, described here as a "magician and a Jewish false prophet" who is also identified as Elymas,[28] Paul denounced him as a "son of the devil," and invoked the Lord to strike him blind. When this happened, the proconsul became a believer and "was astonished at their message" (13:8–12).

Setting sail from Paphos, a major port at the west end of Cyprus, Paul and Barnabas returned to the Asia Minor peninsula, landing at Perga in the district of Pamphylia and then journeying north to Antioch-in-Pisidia (13:13–14). Again engaging the Jews in the synagogue there, Paul responded to the invitation to comment on the reading of the Law and the Prophets by reviewing the history of the people of Israel from their exodus from Egypt through their coming to the land of Canaan and the establishment of David as their king. It is from his posterity that God has now raised up the promised ultimate king and savior of Israel: Jesus. The Jewish rulers did not recognize him as such or understand what the prophets had said about him, and accordingly appealed to the Roman governor to have him executed. This was done and he was buried, but "God raised him from the dead," and he appeared to his followers. Paul is quoted as claiming that Jesus is God's Son, in fulfillment of the promises uttered in the psalms of David, and as promising that those who trust in him will find forgiveness and true freedom, which the law of Moses could never provide (13:16–39). To refuse to believe this about Jesus is to invite the doom uttered by the prophet Habakkuk (1:5). The favorable response to this message on the part of many Jews and "devout converts"[29] is said to have attracted "the whole" city on the next Sabbath, but also to have evoked strong opposition from the Jewish leaders.

For the author of Acts, this reaction leads to a turning point in the mission of Paul and Barnabas that results in their taking as their major role to serve as "a light for the Gentiles" so that God's salvation may reach out "to the uttermost parts of the earth" (13:44–47). In contrast to the favorable response of the Gentiles and the resultant spread of the message "throughout all the region," the Jewish leaders try to promote the persecution of Paul and Barnabas (13:49–50), who accordingly left the city and went to Iconium, which is somewhat farther north and in Galatia—the district dominated in the last centuries before the common era by the Celtic tribe the Gauls, and hence named for them.[30]

The pattern of favorable response from Gentiles and hostility from the Jewish leaders continues in Iconium. Once more, the initial mission outreach of Paul and Barnabas is launched in the Jewish synagogue. Response to their message was from both Jews and Greeks, although some from both groups were also active in the mounting opposition the apostolic messengers encountered, including an attempt to stone them. On learning of this, the two fled southward to the cities of Lystra and Derbe (14:6–7). Curiously, Paul and Barnabas are referred to here (and in 14:4) as apostles—a term not used elsewhere in Acts with reference to Paul. The term in these texts seem to refer to their function as messengers, rather than to the formal, official role of the apostles.

Lystra is about twenty-five miles south of Iconium and had been settled by veterans of the Roman army during the reign of Augustus (37 BCE–14 CE). The impact of their living there is evident from the many Latin inscriptions that have been found and from their use of Latin titles for the city officials. The main Roman east-west trade routes on which Paul made his missionary journeys went through this city. Statues and a sculptured relief found there show how highly regarded were Zeus (the chief god of the Greeks) and Hermes (the messenger of the gods). Hence, when Paul tells the crippled man to stand and he is instantly healed, he and Barnabas are acclaimed as gods: Paul, as Hermes, since he conveyed the message, and Barnabas as Zeus. When the local priest of Zeus begins to prepare sacrifices to honor them as gods, Paul asserts the humanity of the two of them (14:8–20). But his speech seeking to honor the true creator and sustainer of the universe increases the determination of the people to offer sacrifices to them as gods. Then Jewish opponents from Antioch and Iconium arrived, and after discrediting the two messengers, stoned Paul and left him as dead outside the city. He recovered, however, and went on with Barnabas to Derbe.

In Derbe, the two preached the gospel and "made many disciples" (14:21),[31] and thereafter revisited the cities recently evangelized (Lystra, Iconium, and Antioch-in-Pisidia), edifying and exhorting the new members—while warning them of the "many tribulations" though which God's people must pass before they "enter the kingdom of God."[32] Finally, they designate those who were to be the leaders ("elders") of these communities of faith (14:21–23). Thus, the author of Acts tells these stories in the light of two issues that the churches must face: (1) the need for ongoing, responsible leadership in the individual communities; and (2) the difficulties community members will encounter in the form of opposition and suffering. Journeying south through the provinces of Pisidia and Pamphylia, Paul and Barnabas return to the port of Attalia and sail back to Antioch-in-Syria. There they report to the church the results they had achieved in opening "a door of faith to the Gentiles" (14:24–28).

It is of major importance for the interests and strategy of the author of Acts that these developments of outreach to Gentiles and their incorporation into the new community are depicted as having taken place before Paul's going to Jerusalem to attend the council of the apostles and elders there (15:1–29). In this account, the basis for the conflict is the work of Paul and Barnabas reaching out to Gentiles, rather than the precedent set by Peter in the conversion of the pious Gentile God-fearer, Cornelius (Acts 10), a move Peter defends by declaring that "God shows no partiality" but accepts "those of any nation who fear him and do what is right" (10:34–35). In the Acts account, a debate arose in Antioch when some people came there from the Judean community and insisted that circumcision was an essential requirement for membership in God's people. In the subsequent debate, it was decided to send Paul and Barnabas to raise the issue with the apostles and elders in Jerusalem. En route, they reported to the new community in Phoenicia and Samaria[33] the conversion of Gentiles, which brought "great joy to all."

In Jerusalem, they were welcomed by the church and its leaders, but the members who were from the "Pharisaic party" insisted that circumcision be required for all male members (15:5). After extended debate, it is Peter who recalls that he was the one chosen first by God to proclaim the gospel to the Gentiles, that there were those among them who believed, and that their faith commitment was confirmed by their having received the Holy Spirit. This, he claims, shows that there is to be no distinction between Jewish and Gentile converts, and that no legal burden should be placed on these new disciples. All who are granted salvation in the new community are the beneficiaries of "the grace of the Lord Jesus"—not merely those who conform to legal requirements. Indeed, he acknowledges that none of the Jewish converts had ever been able to bear "the yoke," the obligation to obey fully the law of Moses (15:6–11).

After the impressive report by Paul and Barnabas of the "signs and wonders" that God had enabled them to perform as part of their outreach to Gentiles, James,[34] the leader of the apostles, appeals to two major factors that point to support for the Gentile mission: (1) the precedent set by Peter (15:14), and (2) the words of the prophets that promise God's rebuilding of the household of faith and Gentile participation in it. His quotation of scripture (15:15–17) is composed of elements from three prophets: Jer 12:15; Amos 9:11–12; Isa 45:21. The imagery used involves God's kingdom[35] on earth, the seeking community, and the prophetic promises "from of old." But James is then reported as proposing some requirements for Gentile converts: not circumcision, but a mixture of moral and ritual obligations: "To abstain from things sacrificed to idols and from unchastity and from things strangled and from blood"[36] (15:19–20).

The formulation of these requirements in Acts differs significantly from the report in Galatians (2:10), where Paul agrees to only one obligation for Gentiles converts: that they "remember the poor"—which was carried out by offerings collected from the predominantly Gentile churches and given to "the poor among the saints in Jerusalem."[37] Gentiles have long had opportunity to know the God of Israel and to have heard his word through the congregations that gather to hear the message of Moses (15:21).

The account in Acts of the formal decision reached by the Jerusalem council and its deliverance by the two designated emissaries, Judas and Silas (15:22–33), includes features that have no counterpart in Paul's record of the agreement. The specific audience addressed in the council's letter are "the Gentiles in Antioch, Syria and Cilicia." There is acknowledgment of the troublesome words and actions of some among the Jerusalem church leaders, and a declaration that these unsettling individuals had been given no instruction by the apostles. Paul and Barnabas are commended for having "risked their lives for the sake of our Lord Jesus Christ." There is no insistence on the circumcision requirement, but there are certain ritual obligations for the members of the new community, as noted above (15:29; cf. 15:20). It is these items that have no place in Paul's account of the agreement with the apostles; they most likely represent a subsequent development in the rules in the Hellenistic churches as a consequence of two major factors: (1) the early Christian reading and appropriation of the legal traditions of the Old Testament, and (2) the growing sense of necessity for the early Christians to develop specific lines of demarcation between their community of faith and other religious movements with which they were in competition.

The community in Antioch is described in Acts 15:30–35 as receiving with joy these instructions and gaining insights and strength from the messengers sent by the apostles. After the messengers were "sent off in peace" by the Antioch community, Paul and Barnabas continued to teach and preach there (15:36–41). But disagreement arose between them when Barnabas suggested that Mark should be their colleague as they returned to visit the newly established churches of Cyprus and Asia Minor. Paul mentions that Mark had deserted them in Pamphylia (13:13), but no explanation is given in that passage or here for his departure. Yet Barnabas and Mark set out for Cyprus, while Paul chooses as his companion Silas, one of those sent to Antioch by the apostles (15:22).

Silas—who is also known by the Latin name Silvanus—is mentioned in Paul's letters as his companion or co-author (2 Cor 1:19; 1 Thess 1:1; 2 Thess 1:1). He is also identified in 1 Pet 5:12 as "a faithful brother" and as the bearer of that letter.[38] In Acts he is portrayed as a leading figure from among the Jerusalem believers in Jesus as Messiah, and as sharing with Paul in Roman citizenship (18:37) as well as in the outreach to Gentiles and the subsequent confirming of the new inclusive communities (15:40–41). Later, when Paul and Silas crossed the Aegean Sea to the mainland of Greece, they were imprisoned at Philippi (16:16–24). At Lystra they met a "disciple named Timothy," whose mother was a member of the new community but whose father was Greek—i.e., reared in and committed to the Hellenistic traditions (16:1). Timothy is designated by Paul in 1 Cor 4:17 as "my beloved and faithful child in the Lord," and is named in the earlier letters of Paul as sharing with Paul and Silas in the missions to Thessalonica and Corinth (1 Thess 1:1 and 3:2.6; 1 Cor 4:17 and 16:10; 2 Cor 1:1, 19). In these letters, the special role of Timothy is mentioned. In the deuteropauline letters, 1 and 2 Timothy, Timothy's role is perceived at a time later than Paul when the organization and worship of the church were taking on more elaborate formal structures.[39]

In Acts 16:3, Paul is described as making a major concession to those who have been insisting on circumcision as a requirement for male members of the new community when he circumcises Timothy out of deference to the Jews there. Yet in 16:4, what is communicated to the new churches is the decision "reached by the apostles and elders who were at Jerusalem," which did not include circumcision as a requirement for Gentile converts (15:28–29). Thus, in Acts there remains ambiguity on the issue of the legal obligations to be met by Gentile members of the new community, in contrast to the letters of Paul, where there are no ritual obligations for those converted. As depicted in Acts 16, there were already churches in the cities of central Asia Minor when Paul arrived, and the task for him and Timothy is to communicate the conclusions reached at the Jerusalem council. Acts reports (16:5) that the churches there grew in the faith and in numbers.

A major new development is described in Acts 16:6–10 when Paul and Silas are said to have been "forbidden by the Holy Spirit" to go into the provinces on the western and northern edges of Asia Minor (Asia,[40] Mysia, and Bithynia), and then instructed by a vision to cross the Aegean Sea into Macedonia, the northern province on the mainland of Greece. They visited the cities of Philippi (16:11–40), Thessalonica (17:1–9), Beroea (17:10–15), Athens (17:16–34), Corinth (18:1–11)—of which only Philippi, Thessalonica, and Corinth figure significantly in the letters of Paul.[41] The response Paul is reported as having received in Athens, according to Acts 17, is analyzed in our examination of Acts, as are the accounts of Paul's confrontation with the members of the synagogue in Corinth, the subsequent hearing before the Roman proconsul of Achaia, and his return to Antioch and Asia Minor (Acts 18:1–22). Also in Acts 18:24–27 is the report of a new feature in the spread of Christianity: Apollos, a Jewish convert to belief in Jesus as Messiah, was teaching in the synagogue in Ephesus, though he required additional instruction in "the way of the Lord." Paul's visit to Ephesus, after having met Apollos in Corinth, expands and deepens the understanding of the new "disciples" there, but results in a public controversy over the use of the name of Jesus to perform exorcisms that culminates in a riot and the exoneration of Paul on the charges brought against him (Acts 19). In 1 Corinthians, Paul refers to the conflicts he had experienced in Ephesus—"fought with wild animals" (15:32)—and indicates that he is writing this letter from Ephesus (16:8), where his associates, Aquila and Priscilla,[42] established a house-church (16:19). According to Rom 16:3–4, they later moved to Rome and again had a church meeting in their house. The Letter to the Ephesians, which is attributed to Paul but was written in his name subsequently, has very few personal references such as one finds in the authentic letters of Paul. The importance of Ephesus in the Graeco-Roman world and the role that it serves in Acts are considered below in our analysis of that work.

Paul's final visit to the churches of Greece, Macedonia, and Asia Minor is depicted in Acts 20, with an address to the elders of the church in Ephesus in which is set forth effectively how the author of Luke-Acts perceived Paul's strategy, message, and ministry in the churches of the Graeco-Roman world. The remaining chapters of Acts (21–28) present a dramatic account of Paul's return to Jerusalem, his visit and report to the disciples there concerning his mission to Asia Minor and Greece, a testimony to his own conversion, and an account of his hearing before the official council and the plot to kill him. The Roman authorities take him into custody and begin the process of judicial examination—which provides the occasion for his articulation and defense of his mission, culminating in his successful appeal of his case to Caesar, his dramatic journey to Rome, and his exchange there with the Jewish leaders. Analysis of this material is offered above in our examination of Acts (218–34). The only source outside of Acts that refers to Paul's journey to Rome is the concluding section of his Letter to the Romans (15:22–29), where he reports that, following his planned visit to Jerusalem, bearing the offering of the Gentile churches to "the saints in Jerusalem," he plans to travel west to Rome and to visit them there on his way to Spain.

Although there is no direct evidence from Christian or Roman sources as to the time or circumstances of the death of Paul, it is probable that it took place during the reign of Nero (54–68). In 62, Nero reinstituted the Roman law of *maiestas*, making it a capital crime to challenge or undermine imperial authority by what one said or did. It is likely that Paul was executed on this charge in 62. In Robert Jewett's detailed analysis of the data concerning the life of Paul, *A Chronology of Paul's Life*,[43] he makes a persuasive case for the proposal that Paul was executed at an early stage of Nero's persecution of the Christians as reported in the *Annals* of Tacitus (55–117).

The dubious theory that he was released from prison in Rome and returned to his mission in Asia Minor, as theoretically reflected in the deuteropauline letters, is discussed below.

We turn now to analyses of the letters of Paul, including those certainly authentic and those later written in his name. Our aim is to examine the theological and ethical substance of these letters, as well as what they convey about the changing social and cultural contexts in which they were produced.

The Letters of Paul

The thirteen letters in the New Testament attributed to Paul vary in size and strategy of communication, but for the most part they display the conventional pattern of letters that have survived from the Graeco-Roman period. By comparison with the large numbers of letters that have been found in Egypt and date from this time, the New Testament letters are mostly longer and exhibit a more literary style. Features of Paul's letters, such as liturgical passages and moral exhortations, show the influence, respectively, of Jewish liturgy (as preserved in the Dead Sea Scrolls and in the earlier strata of the rabbinic sources) and of philosophical morality, especially of the Stoic variety. Another type of communication in this period was the epistle—a more general and impersonal kind of writing, aimed at a wider range of readers or hearers.

The scholarly distinction offered by Adolf Deissmann between letter and epistle, with the former as personal and spontaneous and the latter as formal and literary in style,[44] does not suit the New Testament letters, some of which were written in careful literary manner and structure. An important factor in examining Paul's letters is that all but one of them (Philemon) were written to a community, not to an individual, although the needs and responsibilities of individuals are addressed. They reveal the concerns and convictions of Paul in relation to the needs and problems confronting the churches to which they were sent. That letters written to one church were read in other churches, however, is evident from the instruction given in Col 4:16 that the Colossians are to share their letter with the Laodiceans.

The typical features of Paul's letters are salutation, thanksgiving, concerns addressed, travel plans, and final greetings. Even in the letter as brief as Philemon these elements are present. The strategy of these letters range from an arrangement by topic of his concerns and theirs in 1 Corinthians, to the most systematic development of the role of Jesus as God's agent of renewal in Romans, and to the hasty and almost impetuous mode of addressing controversial issues with the Galatians. Our analytical procedure is to offer an examination of each of the letters—first those very likely written by Paul, and then of those written in his name. We shall look at the issues and concerns in each of the churches, and at Paul's way of dealing with these problems.

1 Thessalonians

This letter was written by Paul jointly with two of his associates, Silvanus and Timothy (1:1), and is addressed to the church in Thessalonica, the capitol of Macedonia and the eastern terminus of the Via Egnatia, one of the main Roman routes for travel and commerce. Located on the western side of the Aegean Sea, this city was named for the wife of Cassander, a general in the army of Alexander the Great. In 146 BCE, it became a Roman province, and was of major importance in the Roman period, both administratively and economically. There was a strong Jewish community there, but it had long been a center for the Graeco-Roman religious cults of Serapis and Kabeiroi. The latter mysteries were considered by the Greeks to be age-old; the principal site where the rites were performed was on the island of Samothrace, but there developed a center for them at Thebes, which attracted men who were perceived as in need of transformation so that they might experience the true sources of life and gain the basic forms of humanity.[45]

An inscription from the first century CE found at Thessalonica offers legitimation for the mystery cult of Isis and Serapis, which had been established there by the second century BCE.[46] Isis came to be regarded as the divine agent of justice and of healing, through whom the ailing or the pious seekers could find not only healing, but also meaning and renewal in life. This is her role in the *Metamorphoses* of Apuleius (123–180 CE). It was to those hearing claims of divine agents for human renewal that Paul and his companions proclaimed the message and meaning of Jesus among the Thessalonians.

Paul's initial expression of thanks to God for those addressed highlights the three features that were to characterize the new community: faith, love, and hope.[47] He praises them for the love that characterizes their life together, including all the people of faith throughout Macedonia (4:9–10). But above all, Paul here emphasizes the hope of the coming of Christ: they are "to wait for God's Son from heaven, whom he raised from the dead, Jesus who delivers us from wrath to come" (1:10). The term for his coming, *parousia*, occurs more frequently in this than in any other of Paul's letters (2:19; 3:13; 4:15; 5:13). He gives a detailed description of the Parousia in 4:13–17. The Thessalonians have been grieving—and perhaps despairing—because some of their members have not survived until Christ's promised return in triumph. They are to regard their deceased members as having "fallen asleep"; they will be awakened as Christ descends from heaven, heralded by the cry of the archangel and the trumpet of God, and they will be the first to be called forth before being taken up to meet him, along with the living faithful. All of them will then remain "always with the Lord." It is this promised triumph of the living Christ that is to provide comfort and assurance for the bereaved in the present.

Similarly, the suffering they are experiencing as members of the community of faith is not to be considered a punishment or a sign of divine abandonment, but is part of the process by which God's chosen people and agents undergo suffering and death in order that God's purpose may triumph. This was true of the prophets and especially of Jesus, and has been experienced by Paul and his associates at the hands of Jewish leaders who violently opposed the apostles' reaching out to include Gentiles in the people of God. Already God's punishment of them has begun to take place (2:14–16). Paul may well be referring here to actions taken by the Romans against Jewish revolutionaries, whose program was to come to a climax in the revolt of 66–70 CE, and which ended in disaster for the Jews at the hands of the Romans, including the destruction of the Jerusalem temple.

Paul speaks about suffering also on the basis of his own experience of being "shamefully treated at Philippi" (2:2). His strategy and that of his associates was not to engage in flattery as a tactic for gaining human approval nor make demands on the community by reason of their apostolic status. Instead, they were gentle and affectionate, sharing "not only the gospel but also our own selves" (2:4–8). The Jewish opposition in Thessalonica had hindered them from preaching the gospel and apparently caused them to leave. Their efforts to return were frustrated by "Satan" (2:18), but Paul was able to get a report of their progress from Timothy, whom he sent to them from Athens[48] and who told him of their growing faith and love (3:1–6). He offers prayers and thanks to God in their behalf and hopes to return so that he may "supply what is lacking in [their] faith" (3:7–10).

He then proceeds to offer instruction concerning their way of life and their expectations concerning the future (4:1–5:11). Their lives are to be characterized by holiness ("sanctification," 4:2), which will manifest itself in their adopting pure sexual and marital practices, in their avoidance of vengeance in dealing with fellow members, and in moral purity of life. Above all, it is to be evident within the community through mutual love, respect for others, and self-maintenance of the members by working for their own financial support.

Following his description of the coming of Christ indicated above (4:13–17), Paul alerts the members to the necessity of their being ready for the coming of Christ and their avoidance of complacency or false reliance. As "children of light and of the day," they are to be always on the alert for this event, wearing the armor of God: "the breastplate of faith and love, and for a helmet, the hope of salvation" (5:8). There is to be constant assurance of God's ultimate deliverance of his people, and ongoing mutual support to "build one another up" (5:11). The moral exhortations and prayers that bring the letter to a close (5:12–24) culminate in the petition to "the God of peace" to sanctify them completely: in "spirit, soul and body." A final note calls for them to read this letter to the whole community of faith (5:27). Clearly, the letters are not intended for individuals or for the leaders alone, but for the instruction and illumination of the entire body of the faithful.

The strong emphasis in this letter on being prepared for the coming of Christ and the consequent end of the present age has its conceptual antecedents in the apocalyptic tradition among the prophets of Israel and in the extra-canonical writings now designated as the Old Testament Pseudepigrapha.[49] The conceptual kinship of this material with aspects of Stoic philosophy is traced below in Excursus 5, Facing the Future: Common Themes in Jewish Apocalyptic and Graeco-Roman Philosophy and Literature. Thus, for Paul to have placed so strong an emphasis in a letter to a Greek community on this aspect of Christian faith and its implications for moral behavior is wholly appropriate. Also noteworthy is the fact that the *Sibylline Oracles* were originally produced to express the fears and hopes of peoples subjected to what they regarded as alien rule in the Graeco-Roman world. J. J. Collins has observed, "The most characteristic feature of Sibylline oracles is the prediction of woes and disasters to come upon mankind." Written in Greek hexameter, the Sibyl "is always depicted as an aged woman uttering ecstatic prophecies." The words of doom are often followed by "a ray of hope . . . indicating restoration after destruction."[50] Remarkable is "the attribution of inspired Jewish and Christian oracles to the pagan Sibyl." These documents show that Jews and subsequently Christians took up and adapted this literary mode to convey to their constituents their anxieties and aspirations, and especially their confidence in the divine ordering of history and of the life of God's people.

2 Thessalonians

This letter has the same cowriters as 1 Thessalonians, highlights the same theme of being prepared for the coming of the kingdom of God,[51] and commends the community for its fidelity in spite of the persecutions and other difficulties that it is undergoing. Indeed, both the community members' faith and love are growing. Once again, the suffering they are undergoing is part of God's process of testing and purifying them. And they can be assured that God will punish those who have been causing them harm, but above all that they are about to have revealed to them "the Lord Jesus" and the army of angels that will accomplish his purpose. This will include severe punishment for those who "do not know God" as well as for those who have heard the good news about Jesus but have failed to obey it (1:3–8).

The determinative event will be his coming: the wicked will be punished and excluded from the presence of the Lord and from the mighty disclosure of his glory. At the same time, his people, who will be astounded by his presence and power, will glorify him. The reason they will be able to respond to him in this way is that they heard and believed the testimony that was given by Paul and his associates concerning God's purpose that is being achieved through Jesus. They continue to pray for the Thessalonian believers: that their lives may be characterized by qualities and actions that befit the role as God's people to which they have been called, and that by the power God provides for his people they will carry through on their decisions and subsequent actions. The result of their fulfilling this kind of life will be to bring glory and honor to the name of Jesus—and to themselves, as the ones who have been the trusting beneficiaries of the kindness bestowed on them by the grace of God and the agent through whom that grace has been revealed: "the Lord Jesus Christ" (1:9–12).

The letter then turns to some of the major problems that beset the community in Thessalonica (2:1–11). The first concerns the claim that some have made to them that the coming (*parousia*) of Christ has already taken place. Paul warns them not to be misled, troubled, disheartened, or excited by that claim, and certainly not to be taken in by those who base this assertion on what is purported to be a letter from him (2:2). Before Christ's coming occurs, there will be a major rebellious movement[52] on the part of the powers of evil and a public disclosure of Satan, who is here designated as "the man of lawlessness" and "the son of perdition." In Jewish apocalyptic thinking, an upheaval was expected at the end of the present age, which would disrupt the political and religious life of the Jewish covenant people. In the Septuagint, the "lawless one" is used to translate the Hebrew word "Belial," which means "wickedness" or "worthlessness" and is used for Satan in the Dead Sea Scrolls as well as in other Jewish apocalyptic literature (*Testaments of the Twelve Patriarchs, Jubilees*, the *Sibylline Oracles*), and the rabbinic literature. As in 2 Cor 6:15—where the name is transliterated as Beliar—it is a designation for the cosmic leader of the opposition to God, his purpose, and his people. He and those who follow him are doomed for destruction (2:3). Satan—or his agent—will claim priority and superiority to all other deities, and will enthrone himself in the temple of God, claiming to be God. The Roman emperor Gaius Caligula, who reigned from 37 to 41, promoted his own deification. As the Jewish philosopher Philo of Alexandria wrote in his *Embassy to Gaius*[53], Gaius gave orders "for a colossal statue [of himself] to be set up right inside the shrine [of the Jerusalem temple] and named after Zeus himself." Gaius is said by Philo to have denounced the Jews as "the only people in the whole world who do not acknowledge Gaius as a god."[54] There was fear among Jews and Christians in the subsequent decades that the Roman emperors would make similar claims for themselves and force their subjects throughout the empire to offer them divine honors. This anxiety is reflected in these words about "the man of lawlessness," who is here pictured as the agent of Satan who will claim to work wonders through him and thereby deceive those who have "refused to love the truth" (2:10) and who take "pleasure in unrighteousness" (2:12).

Some scholars have concluded that this picture of an extended program by Satan to persuade the masses to acknowledge the divinity of an earthly ruler is incompatible with Paul's statements in 1 Thessalonians about the imminence of the triumphant return of Christ. But in fact, apocalyptic literature—Jewish and early Christian—affirms the coming of the Messiah in the near future, yet also expects a program of satanic acts that are aimed to coerce the populace to offer divine honors for a human ruler or agent. Thus, 2 Thessalonians gives a picture of the evil aspects of the future, while 1 Thessalonians emphasizes the divine triumph. The faithful are "the first fruits" produced by God's work through the Holy Spirit, which will result in their moral renewal ("sanctification") and their grasp of "the truth" about God's purpose through Jesus for the renewal of the creation and of the covenant people (2:13).

The promise to them that they "may obtain the glory of our Lord Jesus Christ" is an aspect of a theme that runs throughout Paul's letters. It builds on the concept in ancient Israel that the radiant cloud that hovered above the altar in the inmost sanctuary of the tabernacle and temple was the visible evidence of God's presence among his people, as it did when the law was given at Mount Sinai.[55] Those who come to know God through faith in Jesus as Messiah thereby experience the divine radiance, sharing God's glory (Rom 5:3; 8:17, 21; 9:23), and are transformed into the likeness of Christ as its visible evidence (2 Cor 3:18), shining in their hearts "to give the light of the knowledge of the glory of God in the face of Jesus Christ" (2 Cor 4:5).

Their continuing in this relationship with God is sustained by their remaining firm in "the traditions that you were taught by us"—insights communicated both by "word of mouth" when Paul was present among them, and by letters he sent to them subsequently (2:15). Through Christ and "God our father," they will experience hope, reassurance, insight, and strength to carry forward their role in the community by word and deed (2:17). He asks for their prayers, that the good news may continue to spread rapidly and meet with a glorious response "everywhere," and that he and they may be protected from the evil schemes of hostile people and particularly from those of "the evil one." He prays that their lives may be characterized by "the love of God" and by fidelity in spite of adversity, as was exemplified by Christ (3:1–5).

Before ending the letter, he gives a word of warning to the members who—apparently on the basis of hope for impending divine deliverance and in reliance on the generosity of the new community—have ceased gainful employment. Paul points to his own diligent work when he was among them, by which he provided for his own basic needs: this is to be a model for the members' quietly attending to their own support, rather than living off the resources of others. These dependent members are to be separated from the others and warned that they are irresponsible, not rejected as enemies (3:14–15).

The final prayer for peace perceives it as comprehensive in its effects: "at all times and in all ways" (3:16). As the entire letter shows, it is not only peace with God, but peace even when confronted by Satan and his agents, and peace that reaches across divisions and conflicts within the community. The final note seems to have been some sort of distinctive "mark" that was to be found in each of his letters, which may have been dictated but included a final personal sign (1 Cor 16:21; Gal 6:1; Phlm 19).

Galatians

Galatia was the name given by the Romans to a province located on a wide strip of land in central Asia Minor that extended from the Black Sea to the Mediterranean. It was so designated because it included the south-central region, which was the place of origin of the Gauls, a Celtic tribe famed for its military skills. The reference to Galatia in Gal 1:2, and three others references to it (in Acts 16:6; 18:23; 1 Cor 16:1), are linked with Paul's ministry and hence probably refer to this traditional territory. But 1 Pet 1:1 and 2 Tim 4:10 may refer to northern parts of the province, for which there is no evidence of a Pauline visit. He writes this letter to report his astonishment at the claims that others have made in this region that those who are followers of Christ must conform to the requirements of the Jewish law—especially to the circumcision of the males.

The letter begins with a salutation similar to those in Paul's other surviving letters (1:1–5). But the emphasis is on the purely divine source for the message and mission in which he has been engaged among them: God the Father and the risen Christ. Sharing with him in this message are "all the members of God's family"; hence, he is presenting a widely held point of view, not one held by merely a minority. He begins by making three assertions that are central for his aims throughout the letter. The first is that Christ gave himself as a sacrifice to deal with the sins of his people. The second is that this action of Christ has the potential to liberate his people from the claims and evil forces that powerfully influence the present age. The third is that what he perceives to have been accomplished and planned for God's people is in accord with God's will (1:3–5). Thus, the resolution of the controversy with these purveyors of falsehood and the fulfillment of God's purpose for the new community are to be carried out by God's grace alone and not by human achievement, as the advocates of conformity to the law maintain.

There is no other gospel to replace the one that Paul proclaimed to them: to make such a claim is to open oneself to a divine curse. Those offering this "different gospel" are hoping for gratification from human support for their program: salvation would be seen as the result of human accomplishment. Instead, as a servant of Christ, Paul is proclaiming the message based on what God has done and continues to do through Christ for the renewal of his people (1:6–10). His is a perception of human salvation that honors God and his agent, Jesus Christ; it is not a source of human gratification based on what is viewed by these misguided people as personal achievement.

Paul's call to be an apostle and the message he was commissioned to proclaim are not the product of human accomplishment or instruction. Instead, they originated with God alone, and were disclosed to Paul through his revealing vision of the risen Christ (1:11–12). The outcome of Paul's encounter is particularly amazing, given his pre-conversion orientation and activity, which he here describes (1:13–14). He was violently active in seeking to persecute and destroy the church. He exceeded the majority of his Jewish contemporaries in his devotion to the Jewish traditions, with their strong emphasis on ritual purity and legal conformity. In retrospect, he perceives that this preparatory stage of his life was divinely planned and carried out in order to make him a dramatic, effective messenger of the good news to those who had no such religious heritage: the Gentiles. When God chose "to reveal his Son" to Paul in order for him to carry out this mission as an apostle of Christ, he did not seek confirmation from any human source, including the apostles in Jerusalem. Instead, he went out into the barren land east of Syria—the Nabatean kingdom, known then as Arabia. Apparently, he had some kind of mystical encounter there, and then returned to Damascus, where earlier he had been carrying out his hostile program toward the emerging church.

Paul's initial contact with the other apostles consisted of a visit for two weeks with Peter (Cephas, 1:18) and a visit of some sort with "James the Lord's brother" (1:19), who is mentioned in Mark 6:3 and Matt 13:55. In 1 Cor 15:7, he is named as one of those to whom the risen Jesus appeared, and in Acts 1:14, 15:13–21, and 21:18, he appears as a leader of the new community in Jerusalem. Josephus reports that he was put to death by the priestly authorities in Jerusalem a few years before the Romans destroyed the temple there in 70 CE (*Jewish Antiquities* 20.17). Paul returned to the region of Syria and Cilicia, where both Damascus and his native home, Tarsus, are located. The churches of Judea did not see him, but they rejoiced that the former leading persecutor of the church was now preaching the faith he had earlier sought to destroy (1:23–24).

During Paul's subsequent visit to Jerusalem, accompanied by Titus and Barnabas, there was controversy about his role and his message, but he was given official approval—"the right hand of fellowship"—by James, Peter (Cephas), and John to continue his mission of proclaiming the gospel to the Gentiles (2:9). The other apostles would maintain their program of preaching the message to the Jews. When Peter subsequently visited Antioch, the main city of the province of Syria and Cilcia, he was intimidated by some who were associated with James, and ceased having fellowship with uncircumcised Gentiles in the community. Paul denounced him for the inconsistency of his behavior in wanting Gentiles to conform to Jewish legal requirements (2:11–14).

Galatians continues with a compact statement of Paul's perception of justification by faith (2:15–21). He and other Jews have come to realize that to gain acceptance and right relationship with God is not a human achievement through conformity to the requirements of the law of Moses. The law leads to death for disobedient humanity. But Christ, who was obedient unto death, was raised from the dead by God. Those who discern this sacrificial role and divine confirmation of Jesus by God may now—through trusting in Christ—enter new life in him and experience a new relationship with God as members of his new people. This takes place solely based on God's grace, not through human ritual or moral achievement. The Spirit of God, which is now at work within his new people, is likewise the gift of God and not a reward for human accomplishment through conformity to the law (3:1–5).

The precedent and model for the community of faith were set by Abraham, who, in spite of his childlessness, believed what God promised him concerning his posterity—"I will make of you a great nation"—and hence was set in right relationship with God. This divine blessing was to benefit not only his offspring, but "all the families of the earth" (Gen 12:2–3). All this occurred because Abraham believed the promise of God (Gal 3:6–9). Paul offers a sharp contrast between (1) those who rely on their own achievements to gain acceptance with God and hence are under a curse for their failure to meet the total requirements; and (2) those who trust in God's remedy for human sin: the death of Christ on the cross, by which he took the curse[56] upon himself (Gal 3:13). By the cross, the blessing of the Gentiles promised to Abraham is now taking place, as is confirmed by God's Spirit at work within the life of the new community (3:14). Jesus is the "offspring" of Abraham through whom this promise of an inclusive covenant has been carried out by God, and it was not superseded by the giving of the law through Moses centuries after the time of Abraham (3:15–18). The law was given as an interim provision, and it has served as a binding, restricting, separatist,[57] disciplinary factor for those involved in the law-based covenant.

Christ has freed his people from these obligations and separatist restrictions through faith and the public rite of baptism, by which their commitment to the new covenant is given expression. Thereby, they share in the new life that his death and resurrection have made possible. No humanly imposed distinctions are any longer valid: not ethnic-religious differences between Jews and Gentiles; not social status as slaves or free; not gender distinctions between male and female. The new unity that has come into being through Christ dissolves all of these ritual, social, and traditional barriers, and has brought into being the new inclusive covenant people promised to Abraham: it is now actualized through Christ (3:19–4:5). As children of God, through the Spirit that Christ has made available, they enjoy a close, loving relationship with God, who is here addressed by the affectionate term "Abba," and who has promised them a heritage of blessing in the future (4:6–7).

For the Galatians to turn to the law as the ground of their relationship with God, as evident through their observance of holy days and times, is as deplorable as their original devotion to false gods—"the weak and beggarly elemental spirits" (4:8–10). Paul exhorts them to follow his example: in spite of his ailment or physical handicap, they welcomed him as God's messenger. He now is experiencing pain, as if bearing a child, and will continue to do so until he learns that they have experienced renewal of their lives through Christ (4:12–20). They have the choice to make between adopting as their model one or the other of Abraham's two sons: (1) Ishmael, born of a slave woman taken as wife by Abraham to provide the offspring he seemed unable to produce by Sarah (Gen 16); or (2) Isaac, who was promised to Abraham and Sarah in spite of their scornful skepticism (Gen 18), and who was born in spite of Abraham's advanced age (Gen 21). Paul allegorizes these stories, identifying (1) Hagar, the slave woman, with Mount Sinai and the law of Moses and earthly Jerusalem, where the ritual and moral requirements are observed and fostered; and (2) the free woman, Sarah, is identified with the heavenly Jerusalem, from which God has sent Jesus to die on the cross and to which he has been taken up as a guarantee of the ultimate liberation of God's new people (4:21–5:1).

Paul appeals to the Galatians to rely on the Spirit that Christ has sent among them for moral renewal, not on such legal requirements as circumcision, as urged by the instructions from the misinformed. Their proper goal is to gain true freedom, which will manifest itself through the power of love for one's neighbor, not through self-indulgence or conflict within the community (5:2–15). If they rely upon their own inner resources, the results will be moral disaster—the "works of the flesh," which he describes as social, sexual, and personal moral failure, and which are wholly incompatible with the hope to share in the kingdom of God (5:16–21).

But if the Spirit of God is allowed to become the dominant force in the life of God's new people, the results will be moral renewal that conforms to ethical norms of the Bible as well as to those espoused by Stoic philosophers. With the exception of love and joy, what the Spirit produces in the lives of the faithful are the virtues that Stoic philosophers were promoting: peace, patience, gentleness, kindness, goodness—and especially, self-control.[58] For Paul, it is the work of the Spirit within that enables one not only to perceive what is ethically proper, but also to perform it. Specific results of this inner moral renewal are indicated in 6:1–10 with respect to restoring an erring member to the community and sharing the burdens being experienced by others. Also essential is self-examination in order to determine what one's own motivations are and to take on obligations that result from one's actions. The insights gained from these experiences are to be shared with others in the community. Social and moral responsibility will one day bring the reward of sharing in life eternal, which is granted through the Spirit of God. The aims and motivations for one's moral life are to take fully into account their impact on "the family of faith" (6:1–10).

Romans

Christians in Rome

From Paul's Letter to the Romans, one can infer information as to the origins and constituency of the church in that city. That those who came to comprise this church in Rome were part of the Jewish community that had been there from before the turn of the eras is attested by Latin historians, who note that Jews there were eager to develop proselytes.[59] This is confirmed by Josephus, who describes a Jewish resident there in the reign of Tiberius (14–37 CE) who made off with a contribution for the Jerusalem temple that he had received from a "woman of high rank who had become a Jewish proselyte."[60] As a consequence, Tiberius "ordered the whole Jewish community to leave Rome," and four thousand Jewish males were drafted for military service. Others were penalized for refusing to serve because they believed it would result in violation of their law.

On the other hand, Philo extols Augustus for his approval of the Jews in Rome, most of whom were Roman citizens. Their community gatherings[61] and observance of the Sabbath were respected by the authorities, and they were permitted to send contributions to Jerusalem.[62] That Greek was the common language of the Jewish community in Rome, as it was in the city as a whole, is attested by the Jewish funerary inscriptions that have been found there from the first century CE.[63]

The continuing links of Jews in Rome with Jerusalem is attested (1) by Philo, who reports the journey to Jerusalem made by some of the Roman Jews;[64] and (2) in Acts where "visitors [*epidemountes*] from Rome" are reported as "dwelling [*katoikountes*] in Jerusalem" (2:5–10). It is likely that some of these Jewish sojourners in Jerusalem who were converted by the apostles' preaching returned to Rome, and hence would have represented the strongly Jewish orientation of Peter and James within the new covenant community there. In any case, Paul's letter to the Roman community deals explicitly and at length with the relation of the church as the new covenant community with that of traditional covenant people, Israel.

As indicated in chapter 2, in his *Lives of the Twelve Caesars*, Suetonius describes a disturbance that took place among the Jews in Rome during the reign of Claudius (41–54 CE). Although the provocation is attributed to "Chrestos," it more likely was the result of successful efforts to evangelize the Jews there in the name of *Christos*, which probably led to the conversion of some Jews there to Christianity as early as 49–50 CE. This would have been well before Paul's projected visit there. In his *Annals* (15.44), Tacitus points out that the fire that destroyed much of Rome during the reign of Nero (54–68 CE) and that was widely thought to have been set by him was blamed by him on the Christians. Accordingly, they were mocked and tortured and crucified in Nero's gardens for the crowds to see. Thus, the Christians by the time of Paul had become an identifiable group in Rome and were differentiated from the Jews, and so it is wholly credible—even from non-Christian sources—that there was a visible Christian community there with which Paul was in correspondence.

There has been an ongoing debate among scholars as to the original extent of Paul's Letter to the Romans and whether it is of composite origin.[65] The most plausible conclusion, however, is that it comprises a unified whole, and embodies an encompassing presentation of many of the topics that Paul had written about in earlier letters. As Joseph Fitzmyer concludes, Romans is not a dogmatic treatise but "a didactic and hortatory letter, intended for discussion by the Jewish and Gentile Christians of Rome, for their understanding and their conduct."[66] Further, this letter is unique among Paul's letters in that he wrote to a church that he had not founded or visited, although he had had as coworkers in Ephesus and Corinth two members of the Roman community, Priscilla and Aquila, who may well have been among its earliest members. The fact that such an extended section of the letter (Rom 9–11) is devoted to the place of historic Israel in the future purpose of God is a likely indication that most of the original members were Jewish or proselytes, and hence for them this would be a major issue.

As Fitzmyer has observed, in his Letter to the Romans, Paul uses conventional features of letter writing of that time, but his style "is more that of an orator than a writer," and he probably intended for it to be read aloud to those addressed.[67] The occasion for his writing is explicit: he plans to visit Rome on his way to Spain and to spend some time with the church there (15:24). His carrying out the divine commission "to win obedience from the Gentiles" had taken him across the Mediterranean world from Jerusalem to Illyricum on the east of the Adriatic Sea. Since Rome had already received the gospel, he now planned to go beyond Italy to Spain, because his call has been "to preach the gospel not where Christ has already been named" (15:20), and there is no such territory left in the northern Mediterranean area east of Rome. His plan to bypass southern Gaul may indicate that that area had already been evangelized, but it is clear that his primary goal is Spain (15:24, 28). That there was a Christian community in Rome long before Paul wrote to them is made explicit in this letter, since he declares, "I have longed for many years to come to you." His visit will be brief, and his journey to un-evangelized Spain will be continued "once I have enjoyed your company for a little" (15:23–24). He sends greetings and recommendations concerning several whom he knows in the Roman community, including Phoebe, a dea-coness from the church at Cenchreae, the port on the east side of the Corinthian peninsula, and his former associates, Prisca and Aquila. The mobility of people in the Roman world is attested by the many individuals now in Rome whom Paul mentions by name as former associates, converts, acquaintances, and coworkers (16:3–16)—including his first convert in the eastern province of Asia!

First, however, he must go back to Jerusalem with the offerings to the "poor among the saints" there. These funds came from the Gentiles, who had shared the "spiritual blessings" and were now going to serve the original community with "material blessings" (15:27). This collection has been gath-ered from the churches of Asia Minor and Greece. He asks for the prayers of the community in Rome that he might be delivered from hostile acts on the part of nonbelievers in Jerusalem, and that his act of service (*diakonia*) may be acceptable to the Jerusalem believers—some of whom might be unwilling to accept anything from ritually impure Gentiles.

The Strategy of the Letter to the Romans

Paul is seeking in this letter to confirm his role as an apostle, which is based on his encounter with the risen Christ, and to show that the message he is preaching concerning Jesus as Son of God is grounded in both (1) scripture, and (2) historic experience. Jesus' human descent from David is affirmed, as is his being the Son of God, which has beendemonstrated for human wit-nesses by his having been raised from the dead. What is distinctive about Paul's role as apostle is that he has been called and empowered to bear wit-ness to Jesus "among all the nations," including this community in Rome

(1:1–6). Following the introduction (1:1–15), which includes his address to the Romans (1:1–7), his thanksgiving for the depth and worldwide repute of their faith, his attestation of prayers on their behalf (1:8–9), and his declaration of his continuing desire to visit them (1:10–15), he turns to the main body of the letter. This consists of two major parts: (1) the doctrinal section (1:16–11:36); and (2) the hortatory section (12:1–15:13). These are followed by a statement of his plans and a request for their prayers (15:14–33), concluding greetings, advice, and warnings (16:1–23), and a doxology (16:25–27). The result is the most comprehensive statement of Pauline theology and ethics that has been preserved.

His role as an apostle is to proclaim the good news from God, which was promised through the prophets and fulfilled through the crucifixion and resurrection of Jesus, God's Son, and is now being made known through the apostles, including Paul. The response that is called for is "the obedience of faith among all the nations" (1:5)—which is a phrase unique to this letter of Paul,[68] and which implies that the good news of what God has done for the renewal of the covenant people through Christ calls for trust and commitment on the part of the professed believer. Although the gospel had its origins among the Jewish people, it is now to be offered to "all the Gentiles" as well. The power of this message and the benefits from the divine actions through the life, death, and resurrection of Jesus are now extended to all humanity (1:16–17).

The common translations here—"the righteousness of God" and "the one who is righteous"—are misleading, since these English words imply the moral character of God and humans. Implicit in these terms is not simply divine quality or ethical behavior, but divine action and appropriate human responses that overcome human disobedience and alienation and bring humans into the relationship with God that was intended from creation: "Let us make humankind in our image, according to our likeness" (Gen 1:26–27). Righteousness (*dikaiosune*) is a verbal noun, pointing to God's work through Jesus to accomplish human renewal. The only appropriate human response is "faith" understood as "trust" and "reliance," not as merely belief. One may paraphrase Paul's quotation from Hab 2:4, "The one who gains right relationship with God by trusting in what God has done will truly live" (1:17).

The refusal of humans to acknowledge and honor God as creator and sovereign, and their turning instead to the worship of created things or objects they had made, led to their complete estrangement from God and the corruption of human relations and mode of life. Paul lists the "debased" and hostile modes of human relations that on the whole characterize the human race, whom he describes as "foolish, faithless, heartless, ruthless" (1:26–31). Their doom is the result of willful moral perversion, not of moral ignorance (1:32). God has not overlooked this moral corruption, but has acted and will continue to hold humans accountable, whether they know the divine law through their conscience (the Gentiles, 2:12–16) or through the law given to Moses (the Jews, 2:17–24). True obedience to the law of God is not achieved by "external and physical" means, such as the rite of circumcision, but by inner renewal of the heart and will (2:25–29). God's just dealing with humans involves his judgment on the disobedient, which includes both Jews and Gentiles, as attested in the psalms.[69] The conclusion—that no humans will be set right with God through their conformity to the demands of the law—is based on Ps 143:2, since law brings "knowledge of sin," not motivation or empowerment for humans to obey the will of God.

The new remedy for human moral corruption is perceived by Paul as foreseen in the Torah and the Prophets, but the true renewal of human relationship to God has already been accomplished. This is essential, because the original creation of humans in the divine image, sharing the "glory of God" (3:23; cf. Ps 8:5), has been lost as a result of their failure to seek to reflect that image in their way of life. Now, instead of the altar of sacrifice in the temple as the locus where human sin is dealt with by God, God has put forward the perfect sacrifice, which demonstrates the divine purpose in setting things right and achieves that aim for those who trust in the crucified Jesus. Now both Jews and non-Jews may share the new relationship with God and his people—which does not "overthrow the law" but exhibits how God has dealt with the sin of disobedient humanity (3:21–33).

The roots of this divine transaction are to be traced back to the time of ancient Israel, with Abraham and David as major examples. It was Abraham's trust in God's provision of the covenant that put him into an enduring right relationship with God (4:1–5; Gen 15:6). David foresaw that God would provide a base for the forgiveness of human sin (4:6–8; Ps 32:1–2). Abraham was the prototype and ancestor of those who would trust God's promise and share in the life of the covenant people without having been circumcised. Further, he did not rely on human capability to beget or to conceive a son or on any human strength, but solely on the promise of God. Just so, those who trust in Jesus depend solely on his atoning death and his resurrection as the basis of their relationship with God (4:9–25). In this way, humans are reconciled to God, in spite of their inherent sinfulness, and receive new character and hope through the Spirit of God that has been poured into their hearts (5:1–11).

A vivid contrast is offered between the disastrous effects of Adam's disobedience to God, with its corrupting effects on the whole human race, and the free gift through Jesus of righteousness—in the sense of moral renewal as well as of being placed in right relationship with God. The law simply multiplied human disobedience and alienation, but God's grace is disclosed and experienced through the death and resurrection of Jesus (5:12–21). To accept baptism is to identify oneself publicly with the crucified and risen Jesus, and should lead to transformation of one's life so that one may serve as God's instrument for the renewal of others as well. One will then be enslaved, not to sin as formerly, but to the work of God in renewing his people—which will culminate in one's sharing in eternal life (6:1–23). Like a woman freed from a marriage by the death of her husband and able to enter a new relationship, so those who commit themselves to Christ are discharged of their obligation to the law, which leads to death, and are called to enter a new life, one empowered by the Spirit of God. This new life is confirmed by the close, loving relationship to God as father ("Abba"), and enables one to endure suffering, weakness, and even martyrdom through assurance that one's physical body will ultimately be transformed and renewed in conformity to the image of God's son (7:1–8:30). In spite of all present difficulties, God's people can be certain that none of the powers of evil that plague human existence will ultimately separate them from the love of God (8:31–39).

In chapters 9 to 11, Paul turns to the questions concerning the place of historic Israel in the purpose of God now being revealed through Jesus. This question was obviously of great importance to the new community in Rome, with its predominantly Jewish membership, and for Paul himself, who attests his previous devotion to conformity to the demands of Torah. He conveys his sorrow that many who are part of the historic people of Israel and their descendants—blessed by God with the law, the covenants, the worship of God, and the prophetic promises—do not share in God's fulfillment of those promises. In his sovereign way, God has been disclosing his purpose not only to Jews but also to Gentiles, thereby fulfilling the prophetic promise given through Hosea that "those who were not my people . . . shall be called children of the living God" (9:25–26; Hos 2:23). Because most Jews sought right relationship with God ("righteousness") on the basis of their conformity to the law, they were offended ("stumbled") at the new means that God provided through Jesus for the renewal of the covenant people (9:30–10:4). The invitation is now open to all—Jews and Gentiles—to experience salvation given by God through trusting in Christ as the divine remedy for human sin: "Everyone who calls on the name of the Lord shall be saved" (10:13; Joel 2:32).

In Torah itself there is a warning that the people of Israel will become jealous of another "nation" with which God will establish a special relationship (10:19; Deut 32:21), and thus God will be found by those who did not seek him (10:20; Isa 65:1). This new, inclusive view of the covenant people does not imply that the historic people of Israel have no role in this community of faith (11:1–10). Even in times of serious disobedience on the part of Israel, as in the days of Elijah, there has always been a remnant that has remained faithful. Then, as now, the faithful have been chosen by divine grace, not because of their religious accomplishments. Others have experienced hardened hearts, sluggish spirits, and darkened eyes, as foretold in the scriptures (Isa 29:10; Deut 29:4; Ps 69:22–23). Their present stumbling (*paraptoma*) in rejecting Jesus will lead ultimately to Israel's full participation (*pleroma*) in God's purpose for his people. In his images of the leavening effect of dough and the grafted branches that receive life from the root of the tree, Paul points to the renewal and revivification that God will accomplish for his covenant people in spite of the present alienation of some of them (11:11–24). The ultimate outcome will be the transformation of Israel and the fulfillment of God's purpose for and through his people. This is now being accomplished through "the Deliverer" who has come "out of Zion" (11:25–27).[70] In a rhetorical question, Paul extols the rich wisdom and knowledge of God that surpass human ability to evaluate or penetrate fully—a position he confirms by quoting Isa 40:13 and concluding with a doxology (Rom 11:34–36).

Paul introduces the concluding section of the letter—in which he addresses practical issues—with images drawn from worship, with the dedication of oneself to God as the essence of sacrifice and purity (12:1). Linked with this is the need to free oneself from the demands and values of the present age and from the human tendency to self-promotion. Instead, one must recognize and respect the diversity of capacities and roles that are essential for the life of the community—as members of the body of Christ (12:2–8). All of these features are charismatic gifts (*charismata*) from God: prophecy, ministering (*diakonia*) to the needs of others, teaching, exhorting, giving, exhortation, administration, showing compassion. Clearly, the churches have developed into complex organizations, requiring a range of capabilities and functions to meet the needs of their members and for the leaders to fulfill their roles responsibly. The implications in this letter are of a structure and a common life considerably more complex than the one addressed in the Corinthian letters. But as in 1 Corinthians, love is to prevail as the basis of their mutual relationships, as well as in their relationships with outsiders. This love is to manifest itself in caring for the needs of others, in associating "with the lowly," in refusing to respond to evil with evil but to care for the needs of one's enemies—thereby "overcoming evil with good" (12:9–21), and in fulfilling the law of love (13:8–10).

In this commitment of the community to love and compassion, even toward enemies, the members are to subject themselves to the civil authorities, who are depicted here as having been placed in power by God. They are to pay their taxes and show respect toward the secular powers (13:1–7). The purity of their lives is to model "the Lord Jesus Christ," especially in view of the soon coming of the end of the age and the triumph of God's purpose in the world (13:11–14). They are to accept one another within the community in spite of differences of opinion on matters of diet, holy days, and lifestyle, and are not to pass judgment on the behavior of other members, since it is

God alone who will bring them into judgment (14:1–23). They are to seek to live in harmony in spite of differences among them, joining in one voice to "glorify the God and Father of our Lord Jesus Christ" (15:1–6).

Returning to the theme with which the letter began—God's purpose in bringing Jews and Gentiles into the new covenant community—they are to live in hope, as promised through the prophet (15:12; Isa 11:10) and experienced by the power of the Holy Spirit (15:13). It is by the Spirit that Paul has been enabled to carry out his pioneering ministry to the Gentiles in the eastern Mediterranean world (15:14–21). As indicated previously, he plans to take the symbolic offering from the Gentile churches to the community in Jerusalem, and then to extend his mission westward beyond Rome, which he will visit en route (15:22–33). The letter closes with many greetings to those he has come to know elsewhere but who are now in the community in Rome (16:1–16), and a final plea to overcome the differences that have developed among them. They are to await the soon and final defeat of Satan, and to rejoice in the revelation that God has granted to the Gentiles, based on the Jewish prophets, which will lead to the new era characterized by "the obedience of faith . . . through Jesus Christ" (16:17–27).

Thus, Paul's Letter to the Romans sets forth in a comprehensive way his understanding of the purpose and program of God to renew his covenant people. And at the same time, it discloses the person of Paul and the mission in which he was engaged across the Roman world.

Philippians

According to Acts 16:11–12, Philippi was the first center for Paul's missionary activity on the mainland of Europe. The city was founded and named for himself by Philip II of Macedonia, who ruled from 359 to 336 BCE and who was the father of Alexander the Great. The location for the city was chosen because of its proximity to gold and silver mines along the northwestern Aegean seacoast. In Roman times, it became of major commercial and military importance, since it was near the eastern end of the Via Egnatia, which served as the main route from Rome and the Adriatic across northern Greece to the Aegean Sea. The deities worshiped there were Greek gods and goddesses, as well as those imported from Rome, Egypt, and Asia Minor—including Jupiter, Mars, and Cybele. Philippi became the capital of the Roman colony that this northern Greek region comprised.

The narrative in Acts describes Paul going outside the city of Philippi to where, as he supposed, there was a Jewish "place of prayer" (*proseuche*) (16:13). That it was on a Jewish base that the new community in this thoroughly Graeco-Roman city emerged and grew is evident from Paul's allusions to features of the Jewish scriptures, but especially to his articulating personal claims to authentic Jewish ancestry and tradition (Phil 3:4–6). Paul has obviously had long association with the church there, and is deeply grateful for the relationships that have developed over the years: "your partnership in the gospel from the first day until now" (1:5). They have continued to share concern for him during his time of imprisonment and in his need to defend and confirm the gospel (1:7), and he commends them for their "love . . . knowledge and discernment" (1:9). The community of "the saints" there has assigned leaders for its shared life: bishops and deacons (1:1). The first of these terms, *episkopos*, is not found elsewhere in the letters of Paul, and the second, *diakonos*, is used by Paul as a descriptive term for his own role as an agent of Christ and the gospel, but only once. As discussed below, the offices of deacon and bishop are described and defined in the later letters attributed to Paul. Even *apostolos*, a term that in Acts is a designation for the Twelve chosen by God as the official witnesses and messengers for Christ, is used by Paul in this letter with reference to Epaphroditus, his coworker and personal supporter, whom he has commissioned to carry out a special task among the Philippians (1:25). Clearly, Paul saw no need to develop organizational roles in the churches, since he expected the end of the age to occur very soon. In this late letter—and especially in those subsequently written in his name—the formal assignment of responsibility becomes important and the designation of offices begins to emerge.

The autobiographical and confessional notes of Paul in 3:5–16 are unique and informative. He was a birthright Jew, as is evident from his having been "circumcised on the eighth day"—the proper time as indicated in the report of God's covenant with Abraham (Gen 17:9–12) and in the Levitical code (Lev 12:3). He claims descent from Israel, and specifically from the tribe of Benjamin. His self-designation as a "Hebrew of Hebrews" may mean that he was born and reared in the Hebrew-speaking Jewish tradition, although obviously he was fluent in Greek as well. His approach to understanding and conforming to the law of Moses was that of the Pharisees. Anthony J. Saldarini, in his study *Pharisees, Scribes, Sadducees in Palestinian Society: A Sociological Approach*,[71] effectively summarizes the features of Paul's pre-conversion life that derive from his Pharisaism:

(1) His adherence to the Pharisaic mode of interpreting the law led him to attack a group which mounted a major challenge to the Pharisaic way of life. As some of the Pharisees had challenged and plotted against Jesus (according to the gospels), so Paul the Pharisee attacked the followers of Jesus who threatened Pharisaic influence on Jews and who more and more taught a significantly different understanding of Torah and the Jewish way of life. The Pharisees and the followers of Jesus especially clashed on the importance of purity laws, tithes and other "boundary mechanisms" for maintaining the integrity of God's people. (2) Paul kept the law as one was supposed to and achieved the righteousness from the law that was proper to it, Paul is not

referring to a highly complex doctrine of works-righteousness vs. grace-right-eousness, but simply saying that he lived a good life according to the rules. Paul's point is that he was humanly acceptable according to the ordinary Jewish norms for proper behavior toward God and fellow Jews; he had lived up to the expectations of [that] society's code of behavior and could not be rejected as a disgruntled failure.[72]

Although Paul's perception of the criteria for participation in the covenant people has changed radically as a consequence of his encounter with the risen Christ, his central concern continues to be the foundation God has provided for sharing in the life of his people, as well as how they are to become God's truly obedient children. His perception of "righteousness" is no longer what humans may achieve by strict conformity to the law of Moses, but an act of God through Jesus Christ. Jesus' faithfulness to God, his conse-quent suffering and death at the hands of the civil authorities, and God's vindication of him by raising him from the dead are the basis of this new relationship and the divine action to which humans are called to respond with trust, rather than in their own presumed moral capabilities. It is this right standing with God that is attained by trusting in what God has pro-vided: "the righteousness from God that depends on faith" (3:9). This con-trasts radically with the Pharisees' formula for gaining acceptance with God by full conformity to the demands of the law of Moses as perceived by their scholarly analysis. Paul's ultimate hope is that he and other members of the community of faith will share in the resurrection of the dead (4:11), which he hopes will occur within his own lifetime.[73] He sees his present sufferings and those of the faithful, obedient members of the community as sharing in the sufferings of Christ, which may well lead to martyrdom (3:10).

The renewal and transformation of the lives of God's new people are signs of their growth toward maturity in the faith community (3:12–16). Paul sets himself forth as an example of someone who is eagerly seeking to grow, for-getting his past errors and "straining forward to what lies ahead," which will culminate in God's upward call of him and his people. Paul laments those whose enmity toward the cross is evident in their gross desires, in their shame-ful delight in their own achievements, and in personal gratification. God's people share in the life of a new people—a new commonwealth—for which the model is in heaven, from which they await the return of Christ to accom-plish (1) their bodily transformation into his image, and (2) the complete sub-mission of the creation to God. With this hope in mind, Paul appeals to the Philippians for firm commitment to God's glorious purpose (3:17–4:1).

The letter concludes with personal greetings, with hope for settlement of disagreements, and assisting those in need, and for joy in what the Lord has done and is soon to do, which will lead to freedom from anxiety and peace of heart and mind (4:2–9). Gratitude is expressed for the Philippians' concern for Paul, as evident in the material support they have provided for him through the contributions they have sent to him. He assures them that God will likewise supply their needs, in keeping with the divine riches disclosed through Jesus, for which he offers thanks to God.

His closing greeting is from members of the new covenant community in Rome, whose membership includes "those of Caesar's household," which could refer to servants or agents in the royal establishment (4:22). This passing note shows in a dramatic way how the message concerning the one crucified by a minor Roman official in Jerusalem has now had a transforming effect among men and women across the empire—penetrating the imperial household itself!

Philemon

This is the shortest of the surviving letters of Paul, and the only one written to an individual, Philemon, who is identified in Col 4:9 as a member of the church in Colossae, a small city about one hundred miles east of Ephesus in the Asia Minor region of Phrygia. Several of those mentioned in the letter also appear in other New Testament writings: Timothy, the co-sender of the letter (v. 1);[74] Onesimus (Col 4:7–9); Archippus (Col 4:17); Luke and Mark (Col 4:10, 14). Paul is writing from prison, as he mentions was often the case (2 Cor 6:5; 11:23), but the location of it in this instance is not clear. Proposals have included Caesarea in Palestine, where Acts reports him in extended Roman custody (Acts 23:23–17). Others have suggested Rome, since in Phil 1:13 he mentions the imperial guard, but units of the Praetorian Guard were stationed in major cities across the empire. His expectation of returning to visit Philemon (v. 22) suggests that his imprisonment may have been in Asia Minor or Greece, probably in Ephesus.

The letter is addressed not only to Philemon, who is described as a "fellow worker," but also to "Apphia our sister and Archippus our fellow soldier." Inscriptions from Phrygia show that Apphia was a common name there. Apphia was probably a leader in the Christian community there, as was Archippus, who is here called "our fellow soldier." In Col 4:17 he was given the instruction to "fulfill the ministry [diakonia] which you have received in the Lord."[75]

Archippus's designation as a soldier suggests that he may have shared in the conflicts Paul experienced in the service of the gospel. The style and strategy of the letter match very well the deliberative rhetoric mode of the classical Greek tradition. As Scott Bartchy has shown,[76] the letter—in addition to the traditional greetings at the beginning and at the end (1–3, 23–35), in which the addressees and the co-senders are identified—follows the tripartite pattern that goes back to Aristotle, Cicero, and Quintilian: (1) exordium, vv. 1–3; (2) the body of proof, vv. 8–16; (3) peroration, vv. 17–22. The aim of the exordium was to set up the mood and win the favor of the hearer/reader in dealing with the subject at hand. The main body presents the subject of the letter in such a way as to appeal to the honor and to point out the advantage to the recipient of the letter if the proposed line of action is followed. The peroration restates the argument and the appeal and seeks to place the reader in a positive, sympathetic frame of mind.

Seen from this perspective, the letter to Philemon may be analyzed as follows. The salutation (vv. 1–3) is typical of Paul's letters, with an indication of his present situation and associates and identification by name of the individuals and the church that he is addressing, followed by a stylized liturgical greeting.

The exordium (vv. 4–7) offers praise and thanksgiving to Philemon as an individual.[77] He is praised by Paul for his love and faith—that is, trust—which he has not only toward "the Lord Jesus," but also "in all the saints." These attitudes have resulted in his sharing the faith and in fostering "knowledge" of all the benefits that are accessible for those who are "in Christ Jesus." This love has brought "joy and encouragement" to Paul, but it has also been a source of renewal and refreshment for "the saints"—those who responded to God's call through Jesus and are now set apart as the new covenant people. It is with this expression of gratitude and the specifying of the benefits that have come to the community through Philemon with which the letter proper begins.

The occasion for the letter and Paul's main concerns regarding Philemon and the church that meets in his house (v. 2) are set out in vv. 8–16. Paul is sending back to Philemon a former slave of his, Onesimus, whom he wants Philemon to receive as "a beloved brother" (v. 16).[78] Paul could have used his authority as an apostle of Christ to "command" Philemon to follow his order, but instead he "appeals" to him on two bases: as an "older" member of the covenant people, and as someone "in bondage to Jesus Christ" (v. 9). Another love-based appeal to Philemon to accept a new relationship with Onesimus is Paul's description of him as his child whom he sired while imprisoned (v. 10). With a wordplay on the name of Onesimus, which means "useful," Paul notes that formerly this man had been "useless" to both of them, but now he can be "useful" to "both you and me" (v. 11). As a faithful member of the new community, he can carry forward the mission launched across the Mediterranean world by Paul and whatever new work will be fostered by Philemon in Phrygia. The role of Paul implicit in this letter matches that known from Roman law, according to which a third party was sought to effect restoration of a slave to the owner under improved conditions. It is possible that Onesimus had chanced to find Paul, whom he would have known during the earlier period of Paul's association with his master, Philemon, and had sought to have him fulfill this mediatory role. But now he was going back to his master, not merely as a slave seeking restoration of a relationship, but as a brother in the community of faith. If Paul still held to the view set forth in 1 Cor 6:20–22, he would have assumed that the actual slave-master relationship would continue, but the implication in v. 16 is that the relationship is to be transformed: "no longer as a slave, but as more than a slave: as a beloved brother."

Paul's sending Onesimus back to his former owner is an act of love, concern, and self-sacrifice. He could have performed important work for the imprisoned Paul, but Paul did not want to presume on his use of Onesimus as an aide in his work without approval from his owner, Philemon. Further, Paul had a loving relationship with Onesimus at both the personal level and in relation to the mission of the gospel (vv. 15–16). Paul is sending him as a partner, a coworker, to be received as a member of God's new people, not as a runaway slave who has been captured and is now ready for punishment (v. 17). If during his life as a slave he had done anything wrong or in any way took what belonged to his owner, Paul is ready to repay anything he owes. Yet he reminds Philemon that he owes to Paul his very self—which indicates that it was through Paul that he became persuaded to have faith in Jesus Christ and to find his place in the covenant people (v. 19). The "benefit" he wants to receive from Philemon is not financial, but spiritual, and will derive from the transformed relationship between the former master and slave— who are now "beloved brothers" in the new people of God (v. 20).

The issues arising from relationships within families as a result of the conversion of members or heads of the family were examined and solutions offered in the literature subsequently written in Paul's name and building on the social foundations that had been established in the communities of faith that arose under his leadership. It is to these documents, their theological insights, and the social formation they represent that we now turn.

Paul as Portrayed in Letters Attributed to Him

The letters attributed to Paul but presumably written by others in subsequent generations of the church who were influenced by Paul and who sought to demonstrate the relevance of the Pauline tradition for the altered circumstances of the church's life may be grouped in three categories: (1) those close to Paul in style and concerns, but representing a significant shift in the conception and the structure of the church; (2) those that concentrate on defining structure and leadership roles; (3) those indulging in pious tradition or fantasy concerning Paul, which have been grouped by scholars within the New Testament Apocrypha. Accordingly, the specific works involved may be grouped as follows:

1. Colossians and Ephesians
2. The so-called Pastorals: 1 and 2 Timothy; Titus
3. Paul in the New Testament Apocrypha
   a. The Correspondence between Seneca and Paul
   b. The Pseudo-Titus Epistle
   c. Acts of Paul
   d. Apocalypse of Paul

Colossians

Colossae was located in the district of Asia Minor known as Phrygia, just over one hundred miles east of Ephesus. Its status as a large and prosperous city in the Hellenistic era rested chiefly on the location there of textile and cloth-dying industries, but other cities surpassed it in productivity in the first century BCE, and disaster struck around 60 CE through a severe earthquake. Cicero[79] reports that there was a large Jewish community there, and by the middle of the first century CE, there was also a Christian community. Epaphras, who is identified by Paul as a coworker of his in Phlm 23, is referred to twice in this letter (1:7; 4:12–13). His designation in 1:7 as the "fellow servant" from whom the Colossians "learned" the gospel and "understood the grace of God in truth" (1:6) may point to his role as the founder or the major teacher of the church in that city—and perhaps as the author of this letter written in the name of Paul. The reference to the prayers of Epaphras that the Colossians "may stand mature and fully assured in all the will of God" (4:13) fits well with the evidence from this letter that the perception by the new community of the purpose of God revealed through Jesus is significantly different from what appears in this regard in the authentic letters of Paul.

The overall structure of this letter matches that of the authentic letters of Paul, however: (1) in 1:1–14, the sender and recipients are identified, with prayers and thanksgivings for the church in Colossae; (2) vv. 1:15–2:15 are a declaration of the role of Christ in the purpose of God and an expression of concerns for the community addressed; (3) vv. 2:16–4:6 include advice and exhortations; (4) in 4:7–18 are additional advice and final greetings. The significant differences between this letter and those certainly written by Paul appear (1) in the descriptions of the role of Jesus in the purpose of God, (2) in the perception of the nature of the evil opposing that purpose, and (3) in the details of the structure and members' roles in the new community. Especially important in this letter is the emphasis on knowledge—including the emphatic differentiation between true and false knowledge.

The Pauline elements of faith, hope, and love are present in this letter (1:3–5), but there is a different perception of the gospel, with an emphasis on the "word of truth" (1:5b), which should lead to full comprehension of that truth (1:6). In these deuteropauline writings, the term for knowledge, *epignosis*, appears with twice the frequency that it does in the authentic Pauline letters. In Romans, for example, the term has negative connotations: proud humans chose not to have God in their knowledge (1:28); through the law comes the knowledge of sin (3:20); Israel's zeal for God is "not according to knowledge" (10:2). It does have positive connotations in Phil 1:9, however, where it is linked with true discernment.

Far more frequent in Paul's letters is *gnosis*,[80] although it too is often negative in import: the law is not to be viewed as the embodiment of knowledge (Rom 2:20); knowledge inflates the ego and is never complete or wholly accurate (1 Cor 8:1–2); those who claim to possess knowledge often pervert others (1 Cor 8:10–11); without love, knowledge is nothing (1 Cor 13:2–3) and will pass away (13:8); the ability to speak in tongues is of value only if it conveys revelation and true knowledge (1 Cor 14:6). So deep and rich are true knowledge and wisdom that they are beyond human capacity to penetrate (Rom 11:33); yet those who possess knowledge and goodness are able to instruct others in the community (Rom 15:14).

Paul prays that the Corinthians may through Christ be enriched in all speech and knowledge (1 Cor 1:5), which are gifts of the Spirit (12:8). God has given to his people the "fragrance" and the "light of the knowledge of God in the face of Jesus Christ" (2 Cor 2:14; 4:6). Paul encourages the Corinthians to excel in generosity as they now do in "faith, utterance, knowledge and love" (2 Cor 8:7). The primary focus of knowledge for Paul is not wisdom or information that has been gained from God or from others, but personally "knowing Christ Jesus my Lord" (Phil 3:8).

An emphasis on conceptual knowledge is evident in Colossians, on the other hand. Thus, in Col 1:9–10, the author prays that they may be filled with knowledge of God's will, with wisdom and spiritual understanding, and for an increase in their good work and their knowledge of God. They have heard this message in "the word of the truth of the gospel," which has been taught to them and is now growing throughout "the whole world." When the author details what this knowledge implies, however, he portrays Jesus in modes that are more abstract than those used by Paul and involve an ontological contrast between the eternal and the temporal (ontological) rather than between the present age and the age to come (eschatological).

Knowledge of God's will is here perceived as conveyed through "spiritual wisdom and understanding" and will result in the community's growth "in the full knowledge [*epignosis*] of God" (1:9–10). The author prays that they will be endued "with all the strength that comes from his glorious power in order to endure the difficulties they will experience" (1:11). In what follows, the emphasis is not on what God is going to do in the future when the Parousia (coming) of Christ takes place and the powers of evil are overcome with the establishment of the kingdom of God (as in 1 Cor 15:24), but on the transformations and new resources that have already been made available through him. His new people already "share in the inheritance of the saints in light": they "have been delivered from the dominion of darkness and have been transferred into "the kingdom of [God's] beloved Son" (Col 1:13).

In the hymn-like passage that follows (Col 1:15–20), there is praise for what God has already done for his new people and for the cosmic renewal that has come through Jesus. Instead of the mystery concerning the future return of Christ and the change that will take place in the covenant people (1 Cor 15:51–57), this mystery (Col 1:25–28) is now fully made known to the new community and affirms the presence of Christ within "his saints," which will result in even the Gentiles' sharing in this mysterious wisdom that God has revealed.

It will make possible maturity among the members, and is the objective for which "Paul" is devoting all the energy God has provided for him (1:29–2:5). In addition to the encouragement and unity that is sought for them, there is the hope that the saints will be enriched by "assured understanding" and "knowledge [*epignosis*] of God's mystery—which is Christ, in whom are hid all the treasures of wisdom and knowledge." These insights are conveyed to the Colossians in order to stave off the efforts of those who purvey false teachings and thereby undermine the "good [moral] order and the firmness of your faith in Christ" (2:5).

Clearly, this letter is written at a time and under circumstances in which correct behavior and well-grounded faith are central concerns for the church leadership. Members' "faith" and the moral order that is to characterize their lives were the result of what they have been "taught," and they are here called to conform to both standards (2:6–7). This is contrasted with the false teaching that some are seeking to promote among them—"philosophy and empty deceit" (2:8)—which derive from *stoicheia*,[81] and not from Christ. The direct mention of philosophy here shows that the encounter between Christians and pagans is taking place at an intellectual level, and that *stoicheion* is not simply a designation for basic features of personal piety such as ritual requirements or personal relations, as in the letters of Paul (Gal 4:3–11), although that issue and terminology do appear in Colossians (2:16–18). Instead, here there is a radical contrast between (1) the law-observers' time-bound religious regulations and human doctrines, which claim to be wisdom and foster "self-abasement and severity to the body"; and (2) the heavenly realities that have been disclosed through Jesus, which transform life now for his people and which will culminate in their being united with him at his glorious, triumphal appearance (3:1–4). Those who trust in him are called to moral renewal, which is here designated as putting off "the old nature" and putting on "the new nature, which is being renewed in knowledge [*epignosis*] according to the image of its creator" (3:9–10). The moral renewal that will result within the community (3:12–16)—"compassion, humility, meekness, lowliness, patience . . . forgiveness, perfect harmony"—is to be fostered by instruction and admonition "in all wisdom" and by the community's joining in song and worship.

All this is to be lived out "in the name of the Lord Jesus" and in gratitude "to God the Father" (3:17). The moral renewal described here is grounded on a dualistic point of view that contrasts earthly and heavenly, temporal and eternal, physical and spiritual. Influenced by Platonism, the perspective in the Pauline letters has here been significantly modified by those writing in his name, who shift the contrast from (1) the eschatological distinction between this age and the age to come, as in Paul's writings, to (2) the ontological difference between temporal and eternal. This intellectual shift is evident in such Jewish writers from around the turn of the eras as Philo of Alexandria[82] and became a major feature in the interpretation of the New Testament by such Christian scholars as Origen of Alexandria.[83]

Ephesians

Unlike the authentic letters of Paul, the oldest copies of this letter do not indicate the church to which it was sent. Only later copies mention the "Ephesians" as the recipients. The specific needs and concerns of a particular church are not addressed here as they are in the Pauline letters. The vocabulary, style, and structure of this letter likewise differ from those of Paul, but there are some parallels with the Letter to the Colossians, which we have noted is probably by someone in the subsequent Pauline tradition and not by Paul himself. The letter consists of a long formal introduction that culminates in a prayer (1:3–3:21), followed by a string of recommendations as to how the members of the community should live (4:1–6:24). Missing are the main features of Paul's letters: presentation of theological insights relevant for the needs of the church addressed, and direct discussion of local issues within that church. Further, the vocabulary of the letter includes terms not used in the other letters attributed to Paul. But above all, the emphasis throughout is on the unity of the church as an established structure, the ranks within the community, and the specific responsibilities of the members: husbands and wives, children and parents, masters and slaves. In short, the church here appears as an ongoing institution, with this letter as a kind of book of order.

The anxiety about the end of the age and the conflict with civil and religious authorities in Paul's letters have given way to joy and gratitude for what God has already accomplished through Christ. The "age to come" is still expected (1:21), but the emphasis here is on what God has already achieved through Christ for the renewal of his people and of the world. Not only forgiveness of sins has been granted, but also wisdom, which has made known "the mystery of [God's] will" and his plan for bringing the universe under divine control (1:10–12). The gift of the Spirit to the new community is the guarantee of their sharing in these cosmic triumphs (1:14). God's control of the universe and its hostile forces is already achieved through the resurrection and heavenly enthronement of Christ, who has been made by God to be "head over all things for the church" (1:20–23). The eschatological promises in the Jesus tradition and in the Pauline letters are not dismissed, but they are eclipsed by the emphasis on the victory God has already attained through Christ.

This triumphant motif also appears in this letter in relation to the lives of the members of the community (chap. 2). The faithful, who were once "dead through trespasses and sin" when they followed the course of the present age, having submitted to the "prince of the power of the air" and hence doomed for destruction, have been raised with Christ and are already "seated with him in the heavenly places." Although they were once Gentiles—and hence ignorant of the covenant and excluded from sharing in the promises of God to his people—they are now reconciled to God by the cross. They have access to God through the Spirit, and share with the saints in "the household of God," which is built on the "foundation of the apostles and prophets," with "Christ Jesus himself as the cornerstone." This new structure—earlier pictured as a body, and then as a household—is now the "holy temple" where God dwells and which continues to grow. The community of faith is perceived as having been "saved" (2:8), in contrast to Paul's description of the cross of Jesus as "the power of God" by which the believers in Christ "*are being saved*" (1 Cor 1:18).

Chapter 3 describes the process through which Gentiles came to share in this new people. Paul is said to have been uniquely commissioned by God to disclose to Gentiles this wisdom: the mystery of divine renewal of the covenant people and the divine program to carry out their participation in it. His prayer is that, by the power of the Spirit and the indwelling of Christ in their hearts, they may come to comprehend this divine truth, to experience the love of Christ, and to be "filled with all the fullness of God." Clearly, the emphasis here is on the now available, divinely provided resources for the renewal of the community rather than on the expectation of the future return of Christ and the end of the present age, as in the authentic letters of Paul.

In 4:1–16, the major theme is the unity of this new community: the body of Christ. The members of this body share a common calling, a common hope, a common faith in Christ as Lord, a common rite of admission (baptism), and a common commitment to God the Father and universal Lord. Yet to these people of God has also been given a variety of gifts[84] to enable them to fulfill their roles within the community. The gifts are here said to have been given by Christ following his descent to earth and his exaltation to heaven, and they include a range of roles to be carried out within the new community: apostles, prophets, evangelists, pastors, teachers. The task of these leaders is to enable the members ("saints") to carry out their particular ministry (*diakonia*), which will result in the "building up of the body of Christ." Their goal is to be the achievement of a uniform doctrine ("the unity of the faith"), of "knowledge of the Son of God," of spiritual maturity, and of growing to match "the full stature of Christ." Instruction and spiritual growth are the primary goals of the community as depicted here, and "speaking the truth" is to foster love within the new "body," for which Christ serves as "head" and model.

The rules for the life of the new community as set forth here contrast the dominant lifestyle of the wider world and the way God's people are to live (4:17–5:2). The plight of the Gentiles is the futility of their intellectual endeavors, their lack of understanding, their alienation from God, their ignorance and hardness of heart, licentiousness, and impurity, which they are in fact "greedy to practice" (4:17–19). Hence, there is a call to separate oneself from pagan ways (5:3–20) and specific advice is given for the roles of the members within the community as well as within their families and wider households (5:21–6:9). As in Col 3:18–41, there are specific instructions for wives and husbands, slaves and masters (5:21–33; 6:5–9), but here there are also brief suggestions for relations between children and parents (6:1–4). This is further evidence of the sense of need within the ongoing life of the Christian community for rules by which personal relations are to be handled within the household, as well as the reactions of the members toward the wider secular world.

The closing advice concerns the struggle confronted by God's people and the resources God has provided for them (6:10–20). This conflict is not with local or imperial political powers but with diabolical forces of evil: "the spiritual forces of evil in the heavenly places." Preparation for it involves utilizing spiritual resources, "the whole armor of God": the belt of truth, the breastplate of righteousness, the shoes as one enters the role of mission, the shield to protect one's faith, the helmet of salvation to guard one's existence and life and to enable one to function in the new role, and "the sword of the Spirit, which is the word of God." Here, then, is the equipment for effectiveness and for safeguarding oneself as the soldier of Christ, waging the battle of proclaiming the good news of Christ in a hostile world. The possibilities for the messengers of the gospel, as well as the danger from imperial opposition, have increased in what seems to be a generation after the initial apostolic period. What is articulated here was appropriate and relevant for this new stage in the spread of Christianity across the Roman world around the turn of the second century CE.

In Pauline fashion, a personal aide is mentioned in the concluding lines (6:21–22), followed by a benediction (6:23–24). Yet the letter as a whole represents an adaptation of the Pauline tradition in a period when the imminence of the Parousia is no longer a major question. Now the community must be instructed how to live and behave as an ongoing institution in the wider Roman world.

The Pastoral Letters:
Structure and Order in the Churches

As noted above, there are three letters included in the New Testament that are frequently designated as the Pastorals, since they are concerned with advice and warnings to churches and their leaders. Though attributed to Paul, they give clear evidence of having been written in a later generation in that they reflect circumstances in the church that have altered significantly from those of the time of Paul. These writings are 1 Timothy, 2 Timothy, and Titus.

1 Timothy

Timothy is described by Paul in 1 Cor 4:17 as "my beloved and faithful child in the Lord," and in Acts 16:1 as "a disciple . . . the son of a Jewish woman who was a believer, but whose father was Greek." He was a resident of Lystra, and Paul had him circumcised in order to avoid offending Jewish converts who learned that his father was a Gentile (16:3). According to 1 Tim 1:3, he took up residence in Ephesus when Paul was there, and carried on instruction there for correction of teachers who were promoting "different doctrine," promulgating "myths" and "speculation" rather than "the order [which derives] from God" that is in accord with "the faith" (1:4). The goal that Paul is said to seek to achieve is "love from a pure heart, a good conscience, and genuine faith" (1:5). These concepts and terminology show the substantial influence on the author of Stoic thought, with its emphasis on natural law and the conscience as the human capacity to perceive and conform to that law. "The faith" is not so much trust in God—as it is in Paul's letters—but correct doctrine as contrasted with mythic speculation.

"Certain persons" have deviated from these perceptions, however, and hence, though it is their aim to be "teachers of the law"—a term antithetical to Paul's estimate of the law and its place in the purpose of God[85]—they understand neither the subject of their teaching nor the terms by which they seek to communicate (1:7). The author then states that "the law is good," though it serves as a rebuke to those who violate it and whose way of life is "contrary to sound doctrine as perceived through the glorious gospel with which [Paul] has been entrusted" (1:9–11). Here there is no longer an antithesis between law and gospel, as in the authentic letters of Paul. The author describes the pre-conversion Paul (1:12–16) as characterized by blasphemy, persecution, and insult of Christ, as having received mercy though he "acted ignorantly in unbelief" until the faith and love that are in Christ—who "came into the world to save sinners"—overflowed for him. "Paul" is now the prime example of a sinner who has been transformed by the grace and mercy of God in Christ, who is described here as "the king of the ages, immortal, invisible, the only God," worthy of eternal honor and glory (1:17). The author here directly identifies Jesus as "God," in contrast to Paul, who speaks rather of what God is doing *through* his unique agent, Jesus, such as "reconciling the world to himself" (2 Cor 5:19), and the one who was "designated Son of God in power according to the Spirit of holiness by his resurrection from the dead" (Rom 1:4). The defining of the relationship of Jesus to God became a subject of major debate in the church, the early stages of which are reflected in this later Pauline tradition, as well as in the Johannine tradition.[86] Here the activity of Paul is designated as a mode of service, *diakonia*, in which he was judged faithful and for which he was empowered by Christ (1:12).

Divine support for the role of Timothy as a leader of the new community was indicated "by prophetic utterances" that pointed to his initiative in the sacred "warfare." The resources for this are "faith and good conscience," which here connote sound doctrine, departure from which led "Paul" to turn over "to Satan" two who had uttered blasphemies in the name of truth, and thereby "made shipwreck of their faith" (1:18–20).

The community is to have as a major objective "a quiet and peaceable life . . . godly and respectful in every way" (2:1–3), which is expected to foster a positive image from the viewpoint of outsiders. To achieve and maintain this, prayers are to be offered for all civil rulers, but it is also essential that there be no conflict within the community (2:8). The divine aim is for the salvation of "all humans" and that they will "come to the knowledge of the truth" (2:4). Once more, this letter perceives faith in terms of correct knowledge, as reflected in the description of the role of Paul as "a teacher of the Gentiles in faith and truth" (2:7). That truth is declared to affirm (1) the being of "one God," and (2) the role of Jesus as the "one mediator between God and humans," whose self-sacrifice was for the benefit of all (2:5). It was to proclaim this truth and to serve as an authorized leader ("apostle") of the new community that Paul was divinely appointed (2:7).

A description of the new community follows, with a differentiation of the roles of men and women (2:8–15). Men lead the group in prayer, while women—modestly attired—bear testimony to their "piety"[87] through the good deeds they perform. They are to "learn in silence," to be completely submissive, and to abstain from teaching or exercising authority over men. The reason for this submissive role is that it was a woman who was first deceived and then led Adam into trouble as well. It is the pangs of childbirth that will make possible her salvation, though she must also continue modestly in "faith, love and holiness." The thoroughly secondary and subservient status of women greatly reduces their role as reflected in the letters of Paul. They are to be evaluated and respected solely on the basis of personal piety.

The personal qualifications for those who aspire to leadership roles within the new community are indicated as well (3:1–12). The bishops[88] must be "above reproach" in their marital status, parental role, and way of life—exemplifying the virtues also fostered in the Stoic tradition: temperate, sensible, dignified, hospitable, and free of violence, contentiousness, and greed. A bishop's effectiveness in managing his own household and maintaining control of his children will have its counterpart in his leadership of the new community and will result in high esteem for him among outsiders. The detail that "he must not be a recent convert" is an additional indication that these Pastoral Letters attributed to Paul were written in a later generation of the church's existence, since in Paul's time of pioneering mission there would have been no members who were not "recent converts."

The designation of deacons (1 Tim 3:8–12)—which means "servant, helper"—as those who are servants of the gospel or of Christ or of the new covenant—is found in Paul's letters (1 Cor 3:5; 2 Cor 3:6; 1 Thess 3:2), but in Phil 1:1 it appears in combination with "bishops" and seems to be used as a title with reference to the church leadership, as is clearly the case in the deuteropauline letters (1 Tim 3:8–13; Titus 1:9). The deacons are to be serious, straightforward, and abstemious with regard to wine or wealth, but the major qualification is their adherence to "the mystery of faith" with no inner qualifications, and hence "a clear conscience." The verse implies a theological debate within the church engaged in by its leaders, who may have had basic disagreements on certain features of "the faith." Instead, they are to affirm the true faith "with great boldness."

These instructions and the norms for leadership (3:14–16) pertain to proper behavior and correct beliefs within the church, which is here designated as "the household of God." Its role is to affirm and defend the true faith: "the pillar and bulwark of the truth." To the church, God has committed "the mystery of our religion." The latter term, *eusebeia*, which occurs nine times in the Pastoral Epistles, is never used in the letters of Paul, and is found only once in Acts (3:12), where it is given a negative force. Here it connotes reverence toward God and a way of life characterized by personal piety and devotion, as is made explicit in 4:7, where the readers are urged to train themselves in *eusebeia*.

It is significant that in this hymn-like summary of "the mystery" (3:16)—which includes the revelation of God "in the flesh" of Jesus, his vindication in the Spirit,[89] his having been seen by angels, and the subsequent preaching and the response of faith among the nations—there is no mention of the cross or explicitly of the resurrection, which are, of course, of central importance in the letters of Paul.

Additional indication that this writing comes from a time later than Paul is provided in the reference to "the later times" when apostasy is to be expected, which is here designated as involving renunciation of *the faith* (4:1). Those fostering the false teachings—"the liars whose consciences are seared"—are setting up ascetic rules, forbidding marriage, and insisting on dietary restrictions. These regulations conflict with the goodness of the creation, which is affirmed in gratitude by those who have the correct doctrine: that is, "who believe and know the truth" (4:3-4). These features give evidence of development in the direction of Gnosticism—a radically dualistic movement that began in the early second century CE; its major precepts and assumptions were based on what Bentley Layton has described as "an elaborate symbolic poem" that "unfolds a mythic drama in four acts":

I. The expansion of a solitary first principle (god) into a full non-physical (spiritual) universe.
II. Creation of the material universe, including stars, planets, earth and hell.
III. Creation of Adam, Eve and their children.
IV. Subsequent history of the human race.[90]

The latter stage of this drama was perceived as offering the liberation of the knowledgeable community (the gnostics) from the physical world and enabling them to enter the timeless realm of the spirit.[91] In contrast to this developing perception of reality, which is here denounced in the later New Testament writings, there are two aspects of truth that have been set forth and that are to be followed: "the words of the faith" and "the good instruction."[92] The radical distinction made by these predecessors of the gnostics between the spiritual and the material world led to the second century CE proposal for humans to understand the nature of the world and to seek the conceptual and ritual means by which one might escape from it through the divinely provided knowledge: Gnosis (see Excursus 3 on Wisdom and Gnosticism, 443–50).

Here in 1 Tim 4:7-8, these proto-gnostic ideas are denounced as "worldly old wives tales." In contrast to these false teachings, there is an appeal in 4:8-10 for the members to train themselves in true piety (*eusebeia*). This is seen as a form of self-discipline analogous to bodily development through physical exercise—which is said to be of some value. But true piety is of value in every way, providing benefits for life in the present and assurance about a blessed future destiny: hope for "the life to come."

The leadership of the new community is called to command and, through both speech and conduct, to teach the proper life for the members (4:12). This is to be carried out through public reading of the scriptures, as well as by exhortation and instruction, which may take the form of teaching or of prophetic utterances confirmed by the ceremonial laying on of hands (4:13–14). Carrying out this role will have salvific benefits for both the divinely empowered agent and for the hearers (4:16).

A set of detailed instructions follows about enrolling members in the community (5:1–6:13)—including overcoming the gaps between the older and the younger, and between men and women. Although the words *presbyteros* (regularly translated "elder" or transliterated as "presbyter") and the feminine counterpart *presbytera* are used here, it seems in this context to refer to age differences among members, not to the issue of male and female officers.

The "enrolling" of widows involves a process by which the economically deprived female members of the community are given material assistance. The recipients must be those whose husbands are dead or gone, and who therefore have no means of support: "real widows" (5:3). Those whose primary obligation is to these destitute widows are their own family and offspring. The bereaved widow is filled with hope in God, and devotes herself continually to prayer, while other widows who live voluptuously may be regarded as "dead" (5:4–5). People of faith must support such genuinely needy widows: to fail to do so is to adopt the way of life of unbelievers (5:8–9). Benefits are to be extended by the community to widows who are over sixty, who have been married only once, and who are known to have been responsible toward their children and toward the needy within the community—"devoting herself to doing good in every way" (5:10). Support is not to be offered to younger widows, however, since their aims involve getting married again and spending time in gossip (5:11–13). They should marry, however, and fulfill responsibilities toward children and household, and thereby avoid reproach from outsiders (5:14–16). If relatives can provide support, they should do so, rather than burdening the church (5:15).

Returning to the matter of the role of official "elders" (5:17–22), there are now explicit rules for identifying them, supporting them, and dealing with charges brought against them. Their task is to teach and preach; their support comes from the community; charges brought against them are to be dealt with responsibly. The first of the two quotations here—not muzzling an ox as it treads out the grain—is from Deut 25:4, and appears in Paul's First Letter to the Corinthians (9:9). The second quote is perhaps derived from a saying of Jesus in Matt 10:10, "The laborer deserves his food." Accusations against elders may be brought before the community only when supported by "two or three witnesses"—a principle laid down in Torah (Deut 19:15). Unlike Paul's view in Romans and Galatians of Christ having brought to an end the law as the basis for humans to gain acceptance with God (Rom 10:4), the author here charges his readers to "keep the rules without favor" and to execute judgment on those who violate them (1 Tim 5:21). Decisions about appointing them to the role of elders are not to be made hastily. To choose unworthy leaders contaminates the membership: "Keep yourself pure!" (5:22).

Attention must be paid as well to the moral behavior of members of the community (5:23–25), including avoidance of overindulgence in wine. There are also guidelines for the relations between slaves and their masters within the community (6:1–2). Slaves are to take care to honor and obey their masters—else they will bring dishonor to "the name of God" and to the "teaching" that is promoted by the community. There is no hint here of Christianity as a movement fostering social revolution.

Of primary value are piety or reverence and contentment with a modest level of material support, as contrasted with the love of money, which entices people "away from the faith" (6:3–10). The goal of life is to achieve the virtues—which correspond to those of Stoic piety. As for leadership within the community, there is to be caution regarding teachers who are proud and whose teachings are counter to those of Christ (6:3–10). They are craving attention and fostering controversy for foolish, selfish reasons. Though they are bereft of the truth, they promote their own kind of piety as a means of financial gain. Instead, they should accept the status of having limited personal possessions, and be content so long as their basic needs are supplied. A statement here has become a widespread proverb: "Love of money is the root of all evil." Recalling ancient Jewish wisdom,[93] they should realize that humans "brought nothing into this world and can take nothing out of it."

Instead of succumbing to the urge for material gains, they are to aim to achieve the moral qualities—which, as listed, include those of Stoic origin as well as those from the biblical tradition. Thus, "righteousness" is here a moral quality rather than the outcome of the divine program by which things were set right between God and humans, as set forth in Paul's letters to the Romans and Galatians. This commitment to correct doctrine and morality will result in a battle for the cause of "the faith" (6:12). But if the members conform to the commandments (6:14), they will gain confirmation and reward when the epiphany of Christ occurs and he is acclaimed as "King of kings and Lord of lords" (6:15). Paul refers to the triumphant coming of Christ at the end of the age as the Parousia, but it is here and elsewhere in the Pastoral Letters designated by the common Greek term for divine disclosure: *epiphany*. Similarly, the resurrection of the body—which was a Christian concept taken over from Judaism—is replaced by the Hellenistic concept of *immortality*. And the kingdom is perceived here as an "eternal dominion" rather than as a new age that will be established by God through Christ when he returns in triumph.[94]

The final group addressed in this letter is comprised of the rich (6:17-19), which shows clearly that by the time this letter was written there were wealthy members of the churches. They are here called to use their wealth to perform "good deeds, liberal and generous," and to do so with confidence that their generosity will store up as a treasure —a term found only here in the New Testament.[95] Their true treasures are the good things that God provides for his people, and their wealth consists of the good deeds they perform and that provide for them "a good foundation for the future": the true life that God provides for his people. The good deeds of those who seek to share in the people of God are not what qualifies them for admission. Yet such misdeeds as those here enumerated do result in the exclusion of the one who does them (Gal 5:21).

The last word of counsel to Timothy (6:20-21) involves his carefully guarding the message and understanding that have been entrusted to him, and avoiding the "godless chatter and contradictions of what is falsely called knowledge [*gnosis*]." This seems to be an indication that Gnosticism has evolved into a religious mode and conceptual framework that is in direct competition with more traditional Christianity—presumably in the mid-second century CE. We have, however, noted how its antecedents had already begun to influence Christian thinking as set forth in the letters to the Colossians and the Ephesians. The result of this deviation from the true faith is that some have "erred concerning the faith." This term for heretical departure from the truth is found only in the Pastorals.[96] Thus, these letters display the beginnings of an effort by those who consider themselves to be orthodox to combat what they regard as heresy.

2 Timothy

Timothy is identified here as Paul's "child," as he is in 1 Tim 1:2. Paul is here said to affirm that his service of God rests on "a clear conscience" (as in 1 Tim 3:9) like that of his "fathers," recalling his ancestry, as in Phil 3:5. His continuing support of his readers through prayer matches Rom 1:9. His commendation of Timothy's "sincere faith" echoes 1 Tim 1:5, and is described here as having been transmitted through three successive generations: son, mother, and grandmother (2 Tim 1:5). Clearly, this passage implies that the church is an ongoing community, extending over time, not a newly founded movement. The indwelling spirit that God has given to his people—including Timothy, who reportedly received it by imposition of Paul's hands—is to be rekindled.[97] It conveyed to him, and to others who receive it, not only freedom from timidity induced by the prospect of persecution by the civil authorities, but "power and love and self-control"[98] (1:7). There is to be no anxiety or shame in bearing witness to the Lord Jesus, or of acknowledging affiliation with a now-imprisoned leader of the movement in his name.

Highlighted here are the achievements and the display of God's purpose that have already taken place. Salvation in the authentic letters of Paul is depicted as an ongoing process: "to us who are *being* saved" (1 Cor 1:18); God is now "*justifying* the one who has faith in Jesus" (Rom 3:24). But here, in a hymn-like passage, the process is described as having already taken place: "he saved us and called us with a holy calling; . . . God's purpose and grace . . . he gave us in Christ Jesus ages ago . . . He abolished death and brought life and immortality to light through the gospel." The faithful are called to "follow the pattern of sound words" and to "guard the truth which has been entrusted . . . by the Holy Spirit" (2 Tim 1:9–12). The timeless quality of the gospel and what has been achieved by God through Christ are basic, rather than an appeal as in Paul's letters to share in this ongoing salvific process.

This message is to be entrusted to faithful men who will be able to instruct others (2:1). The images used to depict these leaders imply hard work and discipline: soldiers, athletes, and farmers (2:3–6). They are to endure the difficulties and to remain faithful to the enterprise. Central to the leadership role is the ability "to handle properly the word of truth" (2:15) and to be forewarned about those who engage in "godless chatter" and are leading others into "ungodliness" because they are deviating from "the truth," hence upsetting "the faith of some" (2:17–18). Faith is primarily correct doctrine here, rather than the emphasis on ongoing trust in the message and actions of God in Christ that characterizes the authentic letters of Paul.

Similarly, the moral renewal of the community is perceived here as based on personal consecration and self-discipline rather than by the renewal of the faithful through the Holy Spirit, as set forth by Paul (Rom 8:1–17). Moral purification is seen as the outcome of personal effort aimed at consecration, righteousness, love, and peace, developing out of "a pure heart" (2:21–22). One must be gentle with one's doctrinal opponents, "correcting [them] with gentleness" in the hope that they will change their minds and "come to know the truth" (2:24–26). In the time of stress that lies ahead, the worst features of humanity will be abundantly evident: self-love, disobedience, inhumanity, treachery, conceit, loving pleasure rather than loving God. Only the external form of religion will be maintained—not its essential power—by those who are exploitive and burdened with sin. They will never listen to proper instruction, and hence will never arrive at "knowledge[99] of the truth," which they oppose because they have a "corrupt mind and a counterfeit faith" (3:7–8). Thus, "the faith" consists of a fixed set of correct beliefs rather than Paul's idea of faith: primarily, trust in God, in the divine promises in scripture, and in the remedy for the human condition that God has provided through the life, death, and resurrection of Jesus Christ.

The readers are called to continue in fidelity to the instruction that Paul is said to have conveyed to them, as well as imitating his perseverance in spite of persecution—which is to be expected and prepared for by all the people of faith (3:10–12) in spite of "evil men and impostors" who will plague the community. The true members have had instruction in the truth since childhood, and are to continue in it—firmly believing it and recognizing its correspondence with the "sacred writings" (3:14–15). Confirmation of this faith will be gained through their reading and study of "the sacred writings," which here surely refers to the Jewish scriptures as adopted and interpreted by the early Christians, but which may also include the earliest of the Christian writings—possibly parts of the gospel tradition and the authentic letters of Paul. Instruction in these scriptures was begun when the readers were children, and is to be continued, since these writings are "divinely inspired" and serve essential functions in "teaching, reproof, correction and training in righteousness." Proper use of scripture will produce proficient and efficient workers in the church (3:16–17).

As noted above, the term in 4:1 for the awaited coming of Jesus is *epiphaneia*, rather than Paul's customary term, *parousia*.[100] Epiphany is linked here with "the kingdom," which Paul refers to seven times in his letters.[101] Before that takes place, however, the leaders of the community are to continue with diligence and patience to preach the word, to rebuke and exhort the members—forewarning them that their hearers will include those who will "not endure sound teaching" but will turn away from "the truth," seeking out false teachers and "wandering into myths" (2 Tim 4:1–5). In contrast to these who want the instruction to match their own prejudices, the author here announces that he awaits martyrdom. Having "kept the faith"—here clearly a body of orthodox doctrine—he is confident of his being rewarded "on that day," as will all who love Christ's "appearing" (*epiphany*; 4:6–8).

In contrast to the punishments that await those who have wronged the author and his colleagues and his regret that members of the community did not rise to support him when he was making his defense (*apologia*), God has been faithful to him and continues to strengthen him to carry out his mission to the Gentiles. He is confident that God will rescue him from every evil and "save [him] for the heavenly kingdom" (4:16–18). The confrontation of the Christians with the secular authorities is clear and produces anxiety, but the appeal here is to remain faithful in spite of threat and persecution, confident in the triumph of God's purpose through and for his people.

Titus

Titus is mentioned in Gal 2:3 as a Gentile Christian whose not having been required to become circumcised led to the crucial decision by the leaders of the church not to prescribe circumcision for the male non-Jews who joined the new community. Highlighted in the opening lines of this letter (1:1–13) are "the faith of God's elect," their "knowledge of the truth," and the accord of the latter with true piety (*eusebeia*). Clearly, here a balance is perceived between the central factor of correct doctrine ("the faith we share") and proper behavior at both the moral and ritual levels. Titus's task in Crete was to assign leadership roles ("elders" and "bishops") to those who were morally qualified ("blameless") and who had a firm and reliable "grasp" on the "word" that is to be proclaimed and taught. The result will be preaching in accord with "sound doctrine" and the capability to refute those whose teaching is false (1:5–9). An interesting detail in this description of the leadership is the mention that elders are to be monogamous and that their children are to be believers. For them there is clearly no celibacy requirement.

The primary focus of the church leaders is to "give instruction in sound doctrine" as well as to confute those who contradict it, including those who give heed to "Jewish myths" and reject the truth—thereby showing that their minds and consciences are corrupted (1:14–15). Instead, the leaders are to communicate "what is fitting for wholesome [moral] instruction"[102] (2:1) within the community, which consists of proper teaching about the behavior and relationships shared by its members, including special advice given to distinct groups within the community: older men, older women, young women, younger men, and slaves (2:2–10). Many of the moral characteristics used here to instruct the members of the community about their way of life are found in the New Testament only in the Pastorals,[103] but some also appear in Paul's letters and in the gospels. The older males are told to be "temperate, serious, sound in faith, in love, and in steadfastness" (2:2). The older women are to be reverent in their behavior, avoiding slandering others and alcoholism (2:3), and they are to train younger women to foster love, chastity, and kindness, to manage their households well, and to be submissive to their husbands (2:4–5). The young men are told to exercise self-control[104]—which is a major factor in Stoic ethics—and they are to live in such a way as to serve as models of good deeds and to contribute to the instruction of the members of the community.[105] The lives of the members are to be characterized by freedom from corruption, dignity (or holiness), healthy speech that is beyond reproof—all terms found only here in the New Testament.[106]

Another group given special instruction in this letter consists of slaves (2:9–10). They are to maintain their enslaved status as members of the community, and are to be fully obedient to their masters: they are to please them wholly, avoiding any kind of disobedient obstinacy or misappropriation of the master's possessions, showing instead complete fidelity to their owners. By doing so, they will in every way display publicly the worth of the moral instruction that has come from "God our savior."

This is the purpose disclosed by the grace of God with its potential for the moral renewal[107] of all humans (2:11–14). This human transformation takes place through proper instruction that leads to the renunciation of "irreligion" and of "worldly passions," and instead brings one to live in this present age under self-control, righteously and piously, as one awaits fulfillment of the "blessed hope: the disclosure [*epiphaneia*] of our great God and savior, Jesus Christ." It is he who gave himself for his people, in order to free them from every kind of lawlessness and to purify for himself his own chosen, special people, who now are earnestly seeking to perform good deeds. The instruction, exhortation, and reproof that are linked with this mode of ministry are to be carried out "with all authority" (2:15).

The detailed moral teaching also calls for submission to civil authorities, for obedience—apparently to the political powers—for engaging in honest work, for avoiding demeaning others or engaging in quarrels, and for demonstrating gentle and courteous attitudes toward everyone (3:1–7). This contrasts sharply with the author's characterization of the former way of life of those who have now joined the new community: previously they were "foolish, disobedient, wandering, slaves to various passions and pleasures, spending their lives in malignity and jealousy, hated and hating one another." The new hope for renewal of the members is set forth here in hymn-like fashion: "But when the goodness and love for humanity of God our savior were disclosed, he saved us—not by deeds which we performed in the arena of righteousness, but by reason of his mercy, which is based, not on acts of righteousness which we have performed, but on the ground of his own mercy." We have access to this transformation through a ritual act—"the washing of regeneration" (= baptism)—and through divine action: "rebirth by the Holy Spirit," which has been made "richly" available to the new people of God "through Jesus Christ our Savior." The result of these divine acts of human renewal is that this new community has been set in right relationship with God "by his grace" and the members now are certain of sharing in "the hope of eternal life."

These truths and insights are to be affirmed and emulated, with the result that the lives of members of the community will be good and morally productive (3:9–11). To be avoided are controversies and disputes over such foolish matters as genealogies and interpretations of the law, since they will produce no constructive outcome. Those who foster such debates are to be advised about their harmful consequences (3:9), but are to be given only a few opportunities to desist. If they continue in this perverse kind of relationship, they are to be dismissed as "perverted and sinful," since their attitudes and actions are having harmful effects on the community as a whole. They are themselves responsible for the condemnation[108] that is being assigned to them by that community.

The closing personal messages mention Artemas, Tychicus, Zenas (the lawyer), and Apollos (3:12–13). The name of the first of these does not appear elsewhere in the New Testament, but is probably a shortened form of Artemidoros, meaning "gift of Artemis," the center of whose worship was at Ephesus (Acts 23:39–41). Zenas the lawyer is not named elsewhere in the New Testament either, but mention of such a figure suggests that by the early second century, the church was including in its membership men and women of significant social status. Apollos may possibly be a reference to Paul's coworker mentioned in 1 Cor 3:1–9; Acts 18:24 and 19:1. The final appeal is for the members of the community "not [to] be unproductive," but to perform "good works" intended in part to "meet urgent needs" of the underprivileged members. This echoes Paul's appeal to the Thessalonians to emulate him by being diligent in their work, just as he was able to achieve self-support, based on his own remunerative employment (2 Thess 3:6–12). It would appear that both the social and economic situation of the churches were undergoing significant change by the time these letters were written in Paul's name.

The factors that bind together the leaders and the members of the diverse churches (3:15) are three: one is "love"—which rests on the love of God evident in his having sent Jesus Christ to redeem his people and in the work of the Spirit in the hearts of the new community. The second is "faith," which rests on proper beliefs about God and Jesus and manifests itself in the morality and uprightness of the community. The third is God's "grace," which lies behind and energizes the whole process of human transformation to which the author is pointing in these letters written in the name of Paul.

Apocryphal Pauline Writings

The Epistle to the Laodiceans

This writing, which purports to be the Letter to the Laodiceans referred to in Col 4:16, is mostly a patchwork of phrases and passages from the authentic letters of Paul, and especially from Philippians. It is possibly a product of the Marcionites, who followed Marcion (ca. 100–160 CE) in differentiating between (1) the demiurge described in the Old Testament that created the physical universe and led to the development of the law, the synagogue, and the sacrificial cult; and (2) the exalted, loving God who sent Jesus in human form for the transformation of the people of true faith.[109] Yet it shows no clear evidence of Marcionite views, and has been characterized as "a clumsy forgery" and a "carelessly compiled concoction," the aim of which was to supply the epistle mentioned in Col 4:16.[110]

Correspondence between Seneca and Paul

There are fourteen surviving letters that purport to have been exchanged between Paul and Seneca, the Roman philosopher. Born into a wealthy family in Spain ca. 4 BCE, Seneca was brought up in Rome, where he studied law, preparing for an official career, as well as Pythagorean, Stoic, and Cynic philosophy. Although he was banished to Corsica, through Agrippina, who had married the emperor Claudius and who persuaded him to make her son, Nero, his heir, Seneca was recalled and invited to be Nero's tutor. Seneca possessed enormous wealth, which he used to aid Nero in his struggle to maintain control of the empire. In despair, however, he committed suicide, but his many writings survived. Reflecting chiefly Stoic principles, they included essays on such themes as peace of mind, anger, clemency (addressed to Nero), and natural questions, which deals with physics as well as ethics. In his letters, he discusses the importance of finding friends and maintaining mutually supportive relationships with them. In Letter V, for example, he declares, "[T]he first thing philosophy promises us is the feeling of fellowship, of belonging to the human race and being members of a community." The peace and stability of such a life are attained when one learns "to live in conformity with nature."[111]

The central importance of making and establishing friendship, as well as building new friendships, is asserted in Letter IX. This is to be sought in order to achieve mutual benefits, and not simply for personal, individual support. One should seek a human model of goodness to emulate (Letter XI), but the community with which one identifies should be characterized by wide and encompassing interests that are shared by the group as a whole (XLVIII). One should not allow one's spiritual enthusiasm to wane (XVI), even though one must expect a time of judgment and testing to be experienced in the near future (XVI; XXVI), which is to be followed by entering into a final blessed abode (LXIII). The Spirit of God dwells presently within the members of this community, who are to be ruled by the Spirit and not by the body, but who are to prepare themselves for confronting difficulties while living in accord with reason (CXXIII). Meanwhile, they are to live in hope, accepting without complaint the difficulties they experience (CV), ever aware of the presence of God within them: "God is near you, is with you, is inside you. There dwells within us a divine spirit which guards and watches us in all the evil and good we do. . . . No one is good without God." Seneca goes on to quote the poet Virgil: "In each and every good man a god . . . dwells," though he acknowledges that who the God is, is uncertain. "Humans are to be seen as rational animals, for whom the ideal state is realized when they fulfill the divine purpose for which they were born" (XLI).

Major features of Seneca's view of humanity and the possible relationships with God that show kinship with the thought of Paul include the following:[112]

1. Emphasis on community, which enables one to experience "the true full force of friendship" (III). "The first thing philosophy promises us is the feeling of fellowship, of belonging to humankind and being members of a community" (V). The wise will continue to make friends (IX), maintaining established friendships and building new ones. Thereby one will experience mutual benefits, not merely personal support (X). Friendship will create a community of interest with the others, so that "You should live for the other person if you wish to live for yourself" (XLVIII). The kinship of this concept of community with that of early Christians is clear.

2. Central to achieving a life of freedom is the pursuit of wisdom, the primary aim of which is to learn virtue, and which will enable one to perceive what purity is, how much value there is in it, and whether it lies in the body or the mind (LXXXVIII). One must learn never to give in to adversity or to trust prosperity, taking always into account "fortune's habit of behaving just as she pleases" (LXXVIII). The major qualities to be sought are bravery, self-control, humanity, and mercy. Wisdom will disclose the origins of the universe, and the nature of the soul: its origins, history, transformation, and its ultimate departure from the body (LXXXVIII). Those schooled in these qualities are brought to perfection (XC).

3. The soul is in captivity to the body, unless philosophy comes to its rescue. One should seek freedom of the spirit from the body, since it is in the human spirit that God is present (LXV), just as the soul of Scipio Africanus returned to heaven, from which it came (LXXVI). All human works are subject to mortality, and death is a blessing to some, since it frees them from suffering (XCI). The worst thing about death is fear of it. One should refuse to be bothered about what the future will bring and should instead stand confident, ready to take "without flinching whatever the future hurls at us" (CIV). By cultivating continuous reflection, one can "ensure that no form of adversity [will] find you a complete beginner," and thus achieve "a noble spirit . . . so that we may bear up bravely under all that fortune sends us" and thereby "refrain from railing at nature" (CVII). The human spirit must prepare itself to show endurance when confronting difficulties, and live according to reason, avoiding association with or emulation of the self-indulgent and snobs. One must put "good living before a good reputation," recognizing that "virtue has to be learnt" (CXXIII). These are also the major themes in the authentic letters of Seneca.

Although the fourteen brief letters attributed to Paul and Seneca[113] were considered authentic by Jerome and Augustine, they do not deal with issues that Seneca discussed and probably date from the fourth century. In content, they are little more than exchanges of mutual admiration between the two:

Seneca praises Paul for his "wonderful exhortations to the moral life" (I); hopes Paul can join him in offering insights and instruction to the emperor Nero (III); reports the sorrow of the empress that Paul has departed from the rites and beliefs of Judaism (V); is glad to have seen some of Paul's letters and is persuaded that the Holy Spirit is what empowers his thoughts and gives him the ability to express them, since the gods speak "through the mouth of the innocent" rather than of the educated (VII).

Paul expresses gratitude for Seneca's favorable response to his letters (II), but apologizes for aspects of his thought that were offensive to the emperor (VIII) and for having chastised Seneca, instead of being "all things to all men" (X; 1 Cor 9:27; 10:33). Seneca deplores the hostility of the Roman judges to Paul and his people in having blamed the Christians for the burning of Rome (XI), and affirms his sense of kinship with Paul, whom he sees as not only a Roman citizen but also as a "second self" (XII). He notes the great power evident in Paul's writings, as well as in the role that he carries out (XIII). Paul declares that Seneca has received revelations from the Deity and has become a "new herald of Christ," using his rhetorical power and his wisdom, by which he may now convey these insights to the imperial couple, so that the Word of God may be "instilled in them as a vital blessing" (XIV). Clearly, apart from the reference to the Holy Spirit, there are no specifics as to the revelation that has avowedly been conveyed through Paul to Seneca. The apologetic theme of these brief letters is that such divine disclosure has taken place—but any indication of its content is lacking.

The letters do deal with issues central in Stoic philosophy in the Roman period, however, and focus on matters that were of primary concern for Paul: (1) the criteria for sharing in a community of those attuned to the divine purpose; (2) the circumstances and divine strategy by which that purpose will be accomplished in the future—a theme that is treated below in Excurses 4, The Multiple Impact of Stoicism on the Origins of Christianity, and 5, Facing the Future: Common Themes in Jewish Apocalyptic and Graeco-Roman Philosophy and Literature. It was the convergence of these early Christian concerns and perceptions with those formulated by Stoic philosophers in the Roman period that led to the creation of these pseudonymous letters purportedly exchanged between Seneca and Paul.

The Pseudo-Titus Epistle

This letter attributed to a colleague of Paul was found in 1896 in a Latin manuscript dating from the eighth century CE. Its language has been characterized as "barbarous," and it calls for a life of asceticism that has no counterpart in the authentic Pauline or in any other New Testament writings. Its appeal is based on selective quotes from the gospel tradition, from the Old

Testament—chiefly the Prophets—and from various apocryphal writings. The major thesis is that "Salvation is to be preserved in solitary celibacy."[114] The Law and the Prophets are interpreted in symbolic mode, as, for example, Neh 8:15, "Come ye from all cities to Jerusalem to the mount and bring with you cypress and palm leaves and build you detached booths." This is explained as follows:

> Thou seest then, O holy man, that the hope described by the authors named holds good for us that, pure in body, we may live in solitude in our booths, and that no one of us suffer himself to be fettered by carnal love. For according to the question and answer of Christ, our lord, "the cypress is a mystery of chastity."[115] Its spike on a single stalk aims rightly at the sky. By the palm leaves he signifies the victory, the glory of martyrdom. Out of these two kinds of trees are booths built, which are the bodies of the saints. And since he added "out of the mount", i.e., from the body of Christ, he meant doubtless the *substancia conexa*.[116] Blessed then are those who preserve this *substancia*! These the Lord praises through Isaiah: "Every one that does not profane the sabbath but keeps it and takes hold of my covenant, them will I bring to my holy mountain and make them joyful in my house of prayer, and their offering and burnt offering will be acceptable on my altar." So saith the Lord. The keeping of the Sabbath clearly means not to defile the pure flesh. And thus it was ordered in the books of the patriarchs[117] that no unprofitable work should be done on the Sabbath. Clearly then it is a positive fact that God forbids the doing of the works of this world in the flesh that is dedicated to him.

The interpretation of these scriptures—canonical and apocryphal—treats them as symbolic appeals to abstain wholly from sexual activity. The standard of true purity is "holy celibacy," when "the lusts of the flesh are to be deplored." This is summarized in a beatitude near the end of this writing that described those who abstain from all sexual acts urges: "Blessed then are those who have remained holy in body and united in spirit, for they will often speak to God! Blessed are those who have kept themselves from the unchastity of the world . . . They will enjoy eternal delight . . . To the victor will I give to eat of the tree of life which stands in the paradise of my God." Instead of challenging the conviction that it is obedience to the law that brings one into right relationship with God, as Paul does, the writer of this document intensifies the demands of the law and makes its primary focus to be the divine call to total abstinence from sexual activity. This moral position is set forth in the name of Titus, one of Paul's associates: "Blessed then are those who have remained holy in body and united in spirit, for they will often speak to God!"

Clearly, this attitude toward sex and marriage is incompatible with the biblical tradition as a whole and with the attitude evident in the authentic Pauline letters. In the Old Testament, marriage and sexual relations are essential features of God's creation of humans and include the responsibility placed upon them to beget and bear children (Gen 2:21–24). Fidelity in marriage was an important item in both the wisdom and the legal traditions (Prov 5:18–29), as is explicit in the Ten Commandments (Exod 20:14; Deut 5:18). In the prophetic and poetic traditions of Israel, marriage is a metaphor for the relationship of God to his people (Hos 3; Song of Solomon). In the New Testament, it serves as a figure for the people of God awaiting the coming of the Messiah, as in the parable of the Maidens in Matt 25:1–13, and in the apocalyptic vision of Rev 19:7–10. Thus, this renunciation of sex and marriage, as attributed to an associate of Paul,[118] is totally out of keeping with Paul's letters as well as with the biblical tradition as a whole.

Paul as Portrayed in the Apocryphal Acts of the Apostles

Paul is not the only apostle to be portrayed and celebrated by new versions of Acts of the Apostles in the second and third centuries and subsequently, portions of which have survived. In addition to the *Acts of Paul* are "Acts" of Andrew, of John, of Peter, of Thomas, of Peter and the Twelve Apostles, and, still later, *Acts of the Apostles*.[119] These writings are not unified in literary mode or in theological point of view. Their main focus is not on theological or ecclesiastical issues or on historical information, but they tend toward hagiographical matters: fostering veneration of the saints.

The influences of the Hellenistic romance on these works are evident in their attention to travel and to aretalogical and teratological wonders,[120] but there is not total conformity to these models. There are also erotic features, but they present motifs of love mostly in positive terms, rather than adopting the ascetic and encratitic perspectives of the developing gnostic outlook. There are legends about the apostles, but these appear to be merely passed on, rather than invented. The apostles are portrayed as divinely endowed humans (*theioi Andres*) whose words and acts point the hearers/readers to the divine way of salvation.[121] Popular from the third to the ninth century, these "Acts" tend to be dualistic and ascetic. Though officially condemned, they were widely read and influential on the popular perception of the apostolic traditions.[122]

The *Acts of Paul*,[123] which probably dates from about 200 CE, uses the we-style employed in the canonical Acts of the Apostles, and appears to have been written by a native or resident of Asia Minor. Paul's journeys often take him where churches already exist. The stories aim to edify the community addressed, as well as to entertain it. There is no debate with Judaism, which, of course, is a major feature in the authentic letters of Paul and Acts. The emphasis falls rather on continuance of the apostolic traditions, but in the process, the readers or hearers are to be entertained by the vivid stories. Nothing of historical significance about Paul is added by this document to the information from his authentic letters and the canonical Acts.

The Apostles as Portrayed
in the Apocryphal Acts

There is no uniform literary mode or structure in these writings, and no discussion of either theological or ecclesiastical issues. Instead, the aim is to foster veneration of the apostles as saints. A plausible theory is that these were
brought together by Photius, patriarch of Constantinople in the later ninth
century, as part of his project to preserve and to foster study of ancient writings—including Greek classics and early Christian works, as well as medical
and scientific works. They were attributed by Photius to a disciple of the
Apostle John named Leucius Charinus, and are said to have been adopted as
authoritative by the Manichees.[124] Although they implicitly base their claim
to authority on the alleged links with the apostles, they provide no reliable
historical evidence from the first or second centuries CE, but instead manifest the radically ascetic features of certain later claimants to the Christian
tradition. The writings employed the style of ancient popular narratives of
the adventures, exploits, and love affairs of great men, now adapted in literary form and religious mode to further their religious cause. The Christians
adopted and adapted these literary types to serve their own distinctive ends.
The works of this type included in the Manichaean collection are: *Acts of
Andrew, Acts of John, Acts of Paul, Acts of Peter,* and *Acts of Thomas.*[125]
   These apocryphal Acts of the apostles combine entertainment and edifi-
cation, but they also are hagiographical literature—showing the grounds for
divine honors to be given to these apostolic saints. The typical style of these
writings is twofold: to highlight the deeds of the apostles and to depict them
as prime examples of the faithful who have suffered martyrdom. Examples of
these Acts have been preserved in Greek, Latin, Syriac, Slavic, Arabic,
Ethiopic, Croatian, and Armenian—clearly indicating the widespread role
that they served. Their historical value concerns the piety of the church in
the post-Constantinian period, rather than furnishing historical information
about thought or action in the apostolic period.
   A document that manifests these functions while purporting to recount
the commissioning of Peter and the other apostles for their mission to the
world is *Acts of Peter and the Twelve Apostles.* This short work exists only in a
Coptic translation, which was among the Nag Hammadi gnostic writings discovered in Egypt in 1954.[126] The text shows that it is based on an original
Greek document. It probably dates from the second or early third century
CE, and represents an early state in the development of Gnosticism, purporting to convey a message received in heaven by those who are now sent
by God to "preach in all the world." It builds on material from the canonical
gospels—especially the passages in the gospels that speak of casting pearls
before swine, and of the merchant who was seeking a pearl of great price

(Matt 78:6; 13:36). Schenke has proposed that this writing is a combination of three original texts: (1) an account of the voyage of Peter out of space and time to an imaginary small island; (2) the story of Peter's vision of the pearl merchant, Lithargoel (= Jesus), who is preaching the good news; (3) a post-Easter account of an appearance by Jesus to the eleven. The result is an elaborate mingled metaphor of Jesus as the pearl merchant who provides for the poor, and as the physician who brings health and wholeness. But like the other apocryphal Acts, this work shows the radical ways in which the perception of Jesus and his divine role, as well as that of the apostles, evolved during the second and third centuries, but—like them—it offers no additional historical information about the apostles or their activities.

Other Canonical Apostolic Traditions

The Apostles as Portrayed in Acts

In contrast to the gospels, where the core of followers of Jesus are referred to mostly as the disciples, in Acts they are called "apostles" from the opening lines (1:2) onward. In Mark 3:13–19, however, Jesus simply designates twelve men to accompany him, to go out to preach, and to "cast out demons."[127] After their return from this mission, however, they are referred to as "apostles" (6:30), just as they are from the outset in the Matthean and Lukan versions of Jesus' commissioning the Twelve (Matt 10:12; Luke 6:13). Luke further develops the use of this term for Jesus' followers in 17:5, and "the Twelve" of Mark 14:17 are identified as apostles at the Last Supper in Luke 22:14. Similarly, the women who found the tomb of Jesus empty—and report it to no one in Mark 16:8—inform the apostles of their discovery in Luke's account (24:10). Clearly, for Luke, in both volumes the apostles' authoritative role as agents and spokesmen for the risen Christ is of major importance. The term appears twenty-three times in the book of Acts!

Apostolos is identified from the outset in Acts as a formal, authoritative office, as is indicated by its association with the term *episkopos*—a term quoted in 1:20 from Ps 69:26, and which means "guardian" or "overseer." A specific qualification for the role of apostle according to Acts was that one had been an associate and witness of Jesus from the time of his baptism by John until his resurrection (1:21–22). The functions they fulfilled included service, or ministry (*diakonia*, 1:25). In addition to choosing the Twelve (1:2), the risen Christ is said to have demonstrated to them his resurrection "by many proofs," to have informed them over a period of forty days concerning the coming of "the kingdom of God" (1:3), and to have promised the outpouring upon them of the Holy Spirit (1:4–5). By the Spirit, they will be empowered to carry the message of the gospel from Jerusalem "to the end of the earth."[128] After Jesus' ascension takes place, they are informed that he will return "in the same way" (1:11). Just as Jesus' ministry, which was launched by the coming of the Spirit, is seen in Luke 4:17–21 as fulfillment of the prophetic promise of "good news to the poor . . . release to the captives and recovering of sight to the blind," so the beginning of the worldwide mission of the apostles is inaugurated by the outpouring of the Spirit upon them in Jerusalem on "the day of Pentecost" (Acts 2:1–4).

Those who witness this event have come from a worldwide range of ethnic, geographic, and religious backgrounds (2:8–12), and are astounded that each of them hears the message in his or her own native language. This phenomenon is perceived to be the fulfillment of the prophecy of Joel (3:1–5) as a sign of the potentially universal access to the power and purpose of God (Acts 2:17–21). It is the resurrected Jesus who has poured out the Spirit in this manner, and the apostles are now witnesses to this momentous divine action (2:29–36). Three thousand respond to the apostles' invitation to repent and to be baptized, and they then become devoted to the apostles' teaching and the fellowship of the new community (2:37–42). The divine approval of this development is provided by the "wonders and signs" done through the apostles (2:43). These developments lead to the formation of a fully shared life of the new people of God: sharing in convictions and commitments, possessions, instruction, and ritual (2:42, 44–46).

When the lame man is healed by Peter at the gate of the temple, the astounded witnesses are assured that this gift of human renewal is not the result of the apostles' innate power or piety, but comes through faith in the name of Jesus, God's servant (3:12–13). Through him God is fulfilling his promise of a new covenant people in which "all the families of the earth shall be blessed," as was promised to Abraham (3:25; Gen 22:18; 26:4). The question by the Jewish elders and scribes as to the source of power by which the apostles were able to effect this healing receives the answer: "By the name of Jesus Christ of Nazareth" (4:5–10). The apostles Peter and John have no human credentials: they are "uneducated, common" individuals, but they have "been with Jesus" and say they cannot remain silent about "what we have seen and heard" (4:13, 20). Their prayer is that God will empower them to "speak the word with boldness" and will use them as agents for healing, and for performing "signs and wonders through the name of [God's] holy servant, Jesus" (4:29–30).

Their prayer is fulfilled, and the apostles unite in the sharing of possessions, empowerment by the Spirit, and effective speaking of "the word of God" (4:31). Violators of this sharing are divinely punished (5:1–11), but the faithful continue to be the instruments through whom signs and wonders are performed and to whom the sick are brought to be healed (5:12–16).

Their effectiveness in actions and message evokes hostility from the high priest and other religious leaders, however, and hence the apostles are imprisoned (5:17). But divine action results in their liberation, though the prison doors remain locked. Called before the high priest and the council, they articulate their conviction that God, the risen exalted Jesus, and the Holy Spirit must be obeyed. The hostile rage that this claim evokes is countered by the warning from Gamaliel the Pharisee that God punishes those who act contrary to the divine purpose, and that if God is behind this movement, the council will not be able to "overthrow" these leaders (5:33–39). The apostles are released, and their preaching and instruction in the temple and in homes continue (5:42).

Only in Acts is there evidence of a division of responsibility on the part of the new community between the twelve apostles and seven others, who are assigned the task of "serving tables"—which apparently means that they are to see that the material needs of the members of the community are met. A problem arose when "widows were neglected in the daily distribution" (6:1), which is probably a reference to a practice of distributing food and basic necessities to the members. The issue and an arrangement to deal with it are described in 6:1–6, although no term is indicated as having been assigned to this group of seven. As is discussed in chapter 5, in this passage, "disciples" is the broad term used with reference to the converts and members of the new community. The seven chosen in this account are clearly differentiated in function and qualifications from the apostles. What seems likely is that the original meaning of the term *apostolos*—which derives from *apostello*, "to send forth"—was "emissary," indicating that someone was commissioned and sent out with a message or an assignment to be carried out under the authority of the sender. It came to be used by the community behind Luke-Acts, however, as the designation for an authority figure whose actions and judgments provided the norms for the movement. It is this perception of "apostle" that led to the assignment of subsequent writings to apostolic authorship, as is evident in the New Testament Apocrypha,[129] and to the identification of subsequent leaders and thinkers in the early Christian movement as "The Apostolic Fathers," whose writings are discussed below (343–54).

The dispute described in Acts 6:1–6, however, arose within the Jerusalem Christian community. It involved the charge that the members from more a traditional Jewish background ("Hebrews" as contrasted with the "Hellenists," who were Jews whose language and cultural orientation were directly influenced by the Graeco-Roman ethos) were being given preferential treatment in the daily distribution—presumably of food and tangible resources—to the membership as a whole. The Hellenistic orientation of these newly chosen Jewish leaders is evident from their Greek names (Stephen, Philip, Prochorus, Nicanor, Timon, Parmenas, and Nicolaus) and from the fact that the last named was a "proselyte," hence not born into a Jewish family. The imposition of hands on this seven is a clear sign of the distinctive authority seen to be possessed by the apostles. The message grew in effectiveness, apparent when the membership of the new community increased "greatly," and included a large number of priests (6:7). The diversity and inclusiveness of this new covenant people —in spite of differences in cultural orientation—is dramatically evident in this account.

Ironically, in Acts 6:8–12, those who take the initiative to silence the most effective messenger of the good news to those in the wider Graeco-Roman world—Stephen—are Jews who are resident in Jerusalem, but whose origins are in the wider Mediterranean world: from Cyrene, Alexandria, Cilicia, and Asia (6:9). Their struggle to maintain Jewish identity in these pagan regions seems to have made them especially sensitive and hostile on this issue of inclusiveness. After fostering opposition to Stephen among the Jewish leaders, these severe critics took him before the regional council, the *synedrion*, to bring charges against him of subversion of temple and Torah (6:12–14). In his defense before the council—which is the longest speech in Acts and thus the most important statement on the inclusiveness of the new community[130]—the following themes are set forth:

1. God is at work for the achievement of his purpose for the apostles and through them—not in a single location but across the wider world. The leaders must be prepared to move about, and to do so in confidence as to God's continuing presence and power through them.

2. The leaders of God's people have historically experienced trials and difficulties at the hands of hostile authorities as the divine purpose has been conveyed and become operative through them.

3. Stephen's account of God's work on behalf of his people refers repeatedly to "our" ancestors (7:2, 11, 12, 18, 38, 39, 44, 45)—thus making clear that the God of Israel is the God who is now at work on behalf of the new covenant people in process of formation.

4. Unlike the self-appointed leaders of the people, those whom God has chosen and empowered for this role have been granted special wisdom and insight into the divine purpose. This has enabled them to understand, to convey, and to carry out God's purpose for his people (7:10, 22).

5. Yet the chosen leader of God's covenant people has frequently been misunderstood, or even rejected by his people (7:35).

The thrust of this message is to claim that neither Stephen nor the Jesus whom he proclaims as God's agent of renewal is a threat to the covenant tradition. Rather, they are the divine agents and messengers through whom the transformation of the covenant community is taking place. That process of renewal was begun by Jesus and will continue to occur through the divinely chosen "son"—as has been the case from Isaac (7:8) to Jesus. Obedience to God is called for no matter where his people may live, as was the case with Israel's call by God in "the land of the Chaldeans" (7:4) and their extended time in Egypt, followed by the subsequent journey to the promised land during which the divine disclosure of the law took place on Mount Sinai (7:30–35). The "wonders and signs" that occurred in Egypt and at the Red Sea manifested God's power and presence among his people (7:36), and the coming of a prophet was promised (7:37). The "tent of witness" (the tabernacle) was a continuing sign of God's presence among his people, which reached its climax when the portable tent was replaced by the splendid temple of Solomon (7:44–47). But "the Most High does not dwell in houses made with hands," as the prophet Isaiah affirmed (7:48–49). Down through history, the leaders of the covenant people have resisted the messages conveyed to them by the Holy Spirit, however, and have persecuted the messengers God sent to them, with the result that they have killed those who foretold the coming of the Messiah. Now he has come, but he has been rejected and executed by these leaders, just as they have failed to obey the Torah "delivered by angels" (7:51–53). The climax of their failure to respond to God's message came when they participated in the trial and death of "the Righteous One" (7:52). Now they denounce Stephen's message as blasphemous, and stop their ears to hear no more of it. Yet Stephen is able to see that the one whom they rejected is now exalted by God: "The Son of Man [is] standing at the right hand of God" (7:55–56). The leaders call for and carry out the execution of Stephen by stoning him to death, which they see as called for in Torah (Lev 24:13–14; Num 15:32–36; Deut 17:2–7).

With supreme irony, there then appears on the scene one who has taken initiative in the persecution of the church: Saul (7:59; 8:1, 3), who subsequently becomes the leading apostle for the outreach of the church to the wider Gentile world—Paul, as recounted in Acts and as evident in his letters. The resulting persecution of the church leads to the scattering of its members throughout Judea and Samaria, although the apostles remain in Jerusalem. Appropriately, the outreach of the gospel to non-Jews begins with one of the Hellenistic leaders of the movement: Philip (8:5; cf. 6:5). His proclamation of Christ to the Samaritans evokes a positive response on the part of "multitudes," which is confirmed by the signs, exorcisms, and healings (8:5–8), and is publicly demonstrated by their accepting baptism (8:12). The apostolic observers, Peter and John, confirm these conversions by transmitting the Holy Spirit to the new believers (8:14–17) and by extending the gospel outreach to "many villages of the Samaritans" (8:25).

Philip is instructed by an angel to go down the desert road toward Gaza (8:26–40). On the way, he meets someone ethnically, culturally, physically, and religiously disqualified from participation in the covenant people: an Ethiopian eunuch[131] who is an official in the service of the Ethiopian queen. He is coming to Jerusalem to worship the God of Israel, and en route is reading the Jewish scriptures—specifically, the prophet Isaiah (53:7–8). When Philip joins him in his chariot, the eunuch asks the meaning of the passage that compares the cruel fate of someone to the slaughter of a lamb and the removal of his life from the earth (Acts 8:32–33). Philip explains it as a prediction of the suffering, death, and resurrection of Jesus Christ, which evokes faith in the Ethiopian. His request to be baptized is promptly performed by Philip, who is then transported elsewhere by the Spirit (8:34–39). He continues to preach the good news in the other towns along the coastal area—all of them Hellenistic, from Azotus (Ashdod) to Caesarea, the center of Roman rule for the region (8:40). The program of outreach to non-Jews is set by this divine action, although the policy has not yet been approved by the apostles.

The major agent in the persecution of the church in Jerusalem (8:1–3) becomes converted and soon serves as the leader of the mission to the wider world of the Gentiles: Saul/Paul. The transformation is vividly and repeatedly described in Acts.

The apostles are divinely commissioned and set out for the wider outreach—to Cyprus, Syria, and such cities as Antioch, Iconium, and Lystra (13:1–14:28). The confirmation of the divine purpose at work in this outreach is provided by the conversion of the Gentiles, the healings that occur, and the outpouring of the Holy Spirit. The soundness of this missionary enterprise is formally confirmed by the apostolic council in Jerusalem, which makes a decision in support of the inclusion of Gentiles in the new covenant community (15:1–29). The subsequent mission and inclusiveness are based on this apostolic decision (16:4), and divinely confirmed by the strong faith and increasing numbers of these communities (16:5).

Paul's vision of a call to come to Macedonia on the mainland of Europe represents a major advance in the outreach of the apostles, and is confirmed by the conversions that occur in Greece. But it also involves major contravening factors that the church was to face in the first and subsequent centuries: conflict and official opposition from Jewish and Roman authorities as well as from representatives of historic religious and philosophical traditions, such as in Athens (17:16–32). The conflict of the new movement with Jewish tradition and leadership and its divinely intended replacement of the older covenant community are pictured in vivid detail in Paul's actions and statements in Corinth (18:1–17), in Antioch (18:18–21), and in Ephesus (18:24–19:40). In his final address to the elders of the new community in Ephesus (20:17–38), Paul describes his ministry since he first "set foot in Asia

[Minor]," and the opposition it had evoked from Jewish leaders eager to preserve their unique, traditional identity as the covenant people. He had proclaimed the message of grace to Jews and Gentiles, calling for "repentance toward God and faith in our Lord Jesus" (20:21). He states that the Spirit has led him to expect "imprisonment and afflictions" as he goes to Jerusalem, and possibly even loss of life (20:22–24). His sole aim is to carry out the program and the ministry that has been given to him by "the Lord Jesus," and hence he does not expect that his hearers will "see [his] face" again.

He urges those who have been made leaders ("overseers" = *episkopoi*) to care for "the church of God which he obtained with the blood of his own Son" (20:28). The community will be attacked after Paul has gone: the opponents will seek to draw off some of the "disciples," but his prayer is for God to build them up and to grant them "the inheritance" that belongs to all who have chosen the sacred role and way of life of "the sanctified" (20:32). He reminds them that he had never sought economic benefit from his work among them, but saw to his own "necessities" (20:34). He then quotes a saying of Jesus that is not otherwise preserved in the New Testament tradition: "It is more blessed to give than to receive." Clearly, the author of Acts wants to portray Paul as one whose sole purpose was to bring to the wider world the message of God's grace made known through the life and death and resurrection of Jesus Christ, and one who had no interest in personal gain. After he bade the Ephesian elders farewell, they accompanied him to the ship in which he was to sail off toward Jerusalem (20:33–38).

Paul's encounter there with the Jewish and the Roman authorities leads to a plot, first to kill and then to arrest him. Seized by the authorities, including those appointed by the Romans as regional civil leaders,[132] he denies any violation of either Jewish or Roman law (25:8), and on the basis of his Roman citizenship (22:25–29), appeals his case to Caesar—where he is sent following the hearing of his case by the puppet Jewish king, Agrippa (25:23–26:32).

What is evident in the Acts account of these developments is that this new movement is to be perceived as not in violation of Jewish tradition, as properly understood by its adherents, nor is it a challenge to imperial authority. Also clearly pictured in Acts is the divine support of the leaders and faithful members of the new community who are risking their lives in carrying out the mission to which they believe they have been called and for which the Holy Spirit provides direction and enablement. The apostles are depicted as the divinely chosen and enabled leaders of this movement as it spreads across the known world. The divine support for this outreach is indicated by the miraculous deliverance of the apostle from the shipwreck en route. The ultimate goal is to be foreseen in the symbolic climax when the message of Jesus as Lord is proclaimed in Rome, the capital of the Gentile world (27–28), "quite openly and unhindered" (28:31).

The Acts account, therefore, is not merely a fascinating narrative of the shift from the proclamation of the good news at the center of Judaism to the center of the Gentile world—Rome. Together with the Gospel of Luke, Acts offers ongoing evidence of divine leadership and enablement for the spread of this message to the wider Gentile world about God's renewal of human beings through Jesus' life, death, and resurrection, and for the development of an enduring and inclusive structure for the new covenant community. This enterprise is perceived in Acts as the role assigned to the divinely called and enabled apostles, which leads to the outreach of the good news to "every nation under heaven" (Acts 2:5). As this process gets under way, the evolution of the leadership roles in early Christianity moves forward, as is discussed below in chapter 5.

The Johannine Traditions

The Letters of John

The writings traditionally linked with the name of John include not only the Gospel of John[133] and the letters of John, but also the Revelation of (or to) John. This name (the original is Johanan, or Jehohanan) was common among Jews from the second century BCE on. For example, it was the name of the grandfather and the brother of Judas Maccabeus, who led the successful Jewish revolt against the Syrian Seleucids that began in 167 BCE. John is also the name of (1) the one who baptized Jesus, of (2) the father of Peter (John 1:42), of (3) a member of the high priestly family (Acts 4:6), of (4) a disciple of Jesus who was a son of Zebedee (Mark 10:35), and of (5) the author of the book of Revelation (Rev 1:1, 4, 9), as well as (6) the surname of Mark (Acts 12:12). The two kinds of New Testament writings linked with this name—(1) the Gospel of John and the letters of John, and (2) the Revelation of John —are radically different in style and perspective. The first are mystical, picturing participation in the community of faith in terms of divine illumination and spiritual group imagery and experience,[134] while the latter is the single thoroughly apocalyptic document in the New Testament. We turn first to the letters of John.

In 1 John, eternal life is seen to have been disclosed by Christ and launched through the contact on the part of his earthly followers with Jesus, through whom they now have access to and fellowship with Christ and with God (1:1-3). The imagery by which this mystical association is pictured is joy (1:4), but preeminently as light. God is light (1:5), and the faithful are called to walk in that light, which offers a shared fellowship with those who have been cleansed from sin by the blood of Christ. Having confessed their sins, they have received forgiveness and are wholly cleansed (1:6). God has made provision for those who do commit sin, however, through Christ who is advocate for the sinners and whose death served as an expiation for the sins of his people (2:1–6). If they now live in obedience and confess their sins, they may be confident of continuing in this divinely established relationship, and are cleansed "from all unrighteousness" (1:9). And now they may walk as he walked through life: in full obedience to God.

Instead of the law of Moses, they now live by the "new commandment," which is demonstrated by love for one's brothers and sisters within the new community. They are to live in this light, and to avoid hatred, which leads to darkness (2:7–11). Advice is offered to various subgroups within the community: to little children, to fathers, and to young men. The call is to remain faithful and obedient; by doing so, one gains strength, God's word has a continuing influence, and "the evil one" is overcome (2:12–14). All this is in sharp contrast to life according to the values and motivations of "the world"—the society and norms of the dominant culture. That way of life results in estrangement from God, and a life according to the lusts, self-seeking, and pride of ordinary human life. It demonstrates that those who live in that way have no significant relationship to God "the Father," which leads to doom and the destruction of their world. This is in radical contrast to those who do God's will and are enabled to live forever (2:15–17).

The letter proceeds with contrasts between these two outlooks and ways of life (2:18–25). The model for the path to disaster is the anti-Christ, who has fostered defection from the faith and denial of Jesus as the Christ and of God as the Father. The model for the community of faith, however, is evident in those "anointed by the Holy One," who know the truth, are confident in the enduring value of what they have heard, and therefore continue to live on the basis of the promise of the Father—which results in their sharing in eternal life. Through the divine provision—"anointing"—of information and insight, they understand what is true, and thus remain firmly in the framework of knowledge provided through their union with Christ (2:26–27). If they remain faithful and obedient, they will be confident until he comes for them, following the example and instruction of their righteous savior (2:28–29).

The present status and responsibilities of the people of God (3:1–18) are sketched. They must be aware that the world around them will not understand them any more than it understood Jesus. But they should be confident that when he appears, they will be transformed into his image of purity, toward which they have already been striving. They must continue to choose between lives of righteousness or of sin. Their model is, of course, Christ, who came "to destroy the works of the devil." They have within them the seed of the divine nature: if they allow their lives to be shaped by this model, they can overcome sin and will stand as examples of "the children of God"— in radical, visible contrast to those who are "children of the devil." The prime evidence of this divine transformation will be that they love one another—unlike Cain, who emulated "the evil one" and murdered his brother out of resentment for his righteous life.

The members of the new community must be aware that they will be hated by the people of this world, who do not affirm or conform to the law of love of one's brothers and sisters (3:19–24). The law of life is the law of love of neighbor, as exemplified most powerfully by Christ's having "laid down his life for us." They must be willing to sacrifice their lives for the benefit of others and to share their possessions with others who are in need. By doing so, they are concrete examples of the love of God, which is not an abstract principle or merely a motto, but is a transforming inner power that is to be manifest through them "in deed and truth." The experience of this power of love provides assurance that one is in right relationship with God's "truth" and overcomes feelings of guilt. The basis of this relationship is trust in what God has done through Jesus Christ, matched with concrete obedience to the love commandment.

There is a warning that evil spirits and false prophets may promote false ideas and deny that Jesus came from God (4:1–12). The new community stands in sharp contrast to those who submit to "the spirit of anti-Christ," which is at work in the world and has its staunch adherents. The true community may be confident in the ultimate defeat of these false ideas, and instead may be certain that God hears their prayers and is conveying to them divine truth. Central in that truth is that "God is love," and thus love should characterize the relationships within the community. That love has been preeminently revealed to humans by God's having "sent his only Son into the world" to provide a way of life and to remove "our sins" as a barrier to our becoming members of God's people. This act of divine love has provided access to God, although no mere human ever sees God (5:12a). Yet it makes possible the experience of God's loving presence and transforming power in the lives of his people.

They live in confidence that they already share in eternal life (5:13), that whatever they ask in prayer will be heard by God (5:14–15), and that participation in the life of God's people will be preserved even for those who commit sins, so long as their misdeeds are not "mortal"—that is, are not so gross as to be beyond forgiveness. According to the gospel tradition (Mark 3:28–29), such an unforgivable sin would be attributing an action mistakenly to the Spirit of God. Those who are members of God's people—born of God—characteristically do not sin, because God keeps them safe from the influence of the Evil One, whose power pollutes the whole of the present world order. God gives his people understanding of the truth embodied in Christ and a share in eternal life. Hence, they are to beware of "idols," which are merely images of divine beings, but which embody false concepts or claims for loyalty or devotion on the part of humans. As in the Gospel of John, the community shares in the new life that God has provided in Christ for his people, and they are now members of God's family. They live by one rule: the commandment of love, and God protects them from the Evil One. They understand and affirm the truth as it is disclosed and embodied in Jesus Christ (5:18–21).

2 JOHN

This letter emphasizes the importance of knowing "the truth," which is here sharply contrasted with the teaching by some that Jesus was wholly divine and not really human, and who deny "the coming of Jesus Christ in the flesh" (v. 7). This doctrine, which seems to have developed by the early second century, claimed to present a more exalted image of Christ: he was one who did not really share human limitations, but merely appeared to do so. The critics of this viewpoint referred to it as "Docetism"—a term from the Greek word *dokeo*, which means "seem." It was a radically dualistic notion that built on Graeco-Roman stories of the deities masquerading as humans, and thereby enabling their devotees to escape the physical and temporal limits of human existence. The author of 2 John insists instead on the full, bodily humanity of Jesus—"the coming of Jesus Christ in the flesh" (7), and advises the community that those who challenge this basic belief in Jesus as both divine and fully human are to be expelled and not given even a greeting by the members of the faithful community (10–11). As though to match the belief in the incarnation of Christ, the author declares that he is eager to visit his readers in person—not merely by letter—in order to convey to them more fully his message and to make "our joy more complete" (12).

3 John

This letter is addressed to an individual, Gaius, and deals more with issues relating to individuals than with the community as a whole, but its major concern is with the dispute over authority within the church (9–10), as represented by the hostile and authoritarian actions of one Diotrephes. This kind of struggle evolved as the churches shifted from the original charismatic leadership to community structures and formal leadership roles. It is similar to what is evident in the changes from the authentic letters of Paul to those written in his name that define the increasingly authoritarian ecclesiastical offices: the Pastoral Letters. It is also apparent in the gospel tradition, as one moves from Mark, with its eschatological urgency, to Matthew, where rules, structure, and authority are central concerns.

In this letter, Gaius is commended for the hospitality he has shown—apparently to itinerant Christian messengers—and for the material support with which he has sent them forth. They are dependent solely on community support, and refuse to accept any from non-Christians (5–7). Presumably, Gaius is a wealthy member who has the space and the resources to enable the community to meet at his place and to benefit from the messages brought by such visitors. Such generous individuals serve as "fellow-workers in the truth" (8).

In complete contrast, however, is Diotrephes (9), who rejects the authority of "the elder" who is writing this letter. When the elder visits the community here addressed, he will bring up this issue. He will recall the evil words of Diotrephes, pointing out his ruthlessness in refusing hospitality or support for the itinerant messengers with whom he disagrees, and in seeking to exclude them from contact with the community. The author appeals to the community to match the generous, open model provided by Gaius, and to deplore and reject the tactics of Diotrephes. The good done by Gaius is the work of God, while the evil done by Diotrephes shows that he has never so much as "seen God."

A third individual named in the letter is Demetrius (12). He is probably one of the itinerants excluded by Diotrephes, but here he is given a strong recommendation by the author. His reputation has broad support and is in harmony "with truth itself"—and the author now adds his own witness to the integrity of Demetrius. The references to the friends who send greetings and to those who are greeted here fit with the implications that there were major divisions within this community in which Diotrephes was exercising unwarranted and wholly misguided authority. Thus, the letter shows the depth and breadth of issues related to doctrinal, social, and leadership authority in the churches by the early second century.

The Revelation to John[135]

THE CONTENT AND INTENT OF THE MESSAGE

The claims concerning the source, content, and intent of this "revelation" (1:1) are made explicit: it is given by God; it consists of a "revelation of Jesus Christ," and the intended recipients are God's "servants," to whom it shows what "must soon take place" in the fulfillment of God's purpose. A messenger from God has communicated this to "his servant John" (1:2). This revelation is based on "the word of God" and "the testimony of Jesus," in that he is perceived to be the divine instrument through whom God's message for his people is being conveyed. But Christ and his role in the purpose of God in the world and for his people are also the content of the revelation—which has been foretold in the Jewish scriptures.[136] The message is to be read aloud, to be listened to, and, above all, to be heeded. Thereby will come the fullness of God's blessing on his people in the near future. These intentions for the role of this writing are reaffirmed in 22:6–7, following the climactic disclosure of "the holy city Jerusalem coming down out of heaven from God" (21:10, the central features of which are "the throne of God and of the

Lamb," 22:1). The source and substance of this prophetic revelation (1:3) are what God has announced in scripture and through Jesus and has already accomplished through him. John is to communicate what has been disclosed to him, based on the "word of God and the testimony of Jesus" (1:2), addressed especially to "the seven churches that are in Asia." The specific addressees are located in seven of the major cities in the Roman province of Asia, as noted below. The continuity between this message and what has been disclosed and promised in the scriptures—"the word of God"—is evident from an analysis of the huge number of references to and quotes from scripture in Revelation. Of the 404 verses in this book, 278 contain at least one reference to the Old Testament—with the dominant links to Daniel, Ezekiel, Isaiah, Zechariah, as well as Psalms and Exodus.[137]

In addition to taking into account the parallels in content and mode of communication between the Revelation to John and other Jewish and early Christian writings, it is important to note how basic features of these apocalyptic writings have parallels in the literature of the Graeco-Roman world. These similarities are documented in Excursus 5 of this volume, "Facing the Future: Jewish Apocalyptic and Graeco-Roman Philosophy and Literature." Especially relevant as a parallel phenomenon to Revelation are the *Sibylline Oracles*, which were produced in the Hellenistic and Roman periods, advancing claims of prophetic insight with promises of divine support as well as of conflict in response to the powers of evil.[138] The Revelation to John was not a document embodying a view of history and a strategy of cosmic understanding that was strange or without parallel in the Roman world in the early centuries of the common era; it had counterparts in these oracles. It is not at all surprising that Jews and Christians would develop their own versions of these oracles, details of which are also indicated in Excursus 5.

The message of Revelation serves as a solemn warning to the new community that there is going to be severe and deadly confrontation between the Roman Empire and the new people of God, who are here seen as benefiting from forgiveness of their sins through the blood of Jesus, and as thereby gaining the right to fulfill royal and priestly roles: "a kingdom, priests to God and his Father." Their priestly role consists in their providing both access to God and spiritual purity through the message they proclaim about Jesus' redemptive death and through the new community of God's people. Their royal role involves their shared life in that community where the power and purpose of God are already manifest and dominant. Christ's future coming in triumph is affirmed, and is to be visible to all humanity, but especially to the Roman authorities, who "pierced him" when they put him to death. All these peoples will "wail" out of contrition for having rejected and executed him (1:6–7).[139] In response to the prayer of John in which these past, present, and future events are described, there comes a pronouncement by God affirming his eternal being and all-encompassing authority: the beginning and ending of all communication, symbolized by the first and last letters of the Greek alphabet (Alpha and Omega); the One whose purpose and power cover the whole of time; and the direct declaration of God's omnipotence (1:8).

In sharp contrast to these symbols of divine universal dominance are the identification of the writer of this apocalypse by name, an indication of his specific location (the island of Patmos), a description of his personal experience as he heard the message, and the naming of the seven locations of those who are to receive it (1:9–11). John's banishment to Patmos—one of a group of islands known as Sporades, off the southwest coast of Asia Minor—is reported by him in 1:9 to have been the result of "the word of God and the testimony of Jesus." Pliny and Tacitus note that some of these islands were used by Roman authorities for retaining dissidents. Hence, the radical critique of Roman authority conveyed in the message of John may well have been the cause for his being sent to Patmos.

Under the power of the Spirit and on "the Lord's day," which commemorates his resurrection from the dead, John was instructed by a voice "like a trumpet"—a repeated figure in this work for the communication of God's purpose[140]— to write "in a book" what he has seen in this divine disclosure and to send it "to the seven churches" (1:10–11). The book is by no means a routine account of observed past events, but claims to be a divinely intended and enduring record of the cosmic purpose of God—a theme developed throughout this writing. In 5:1, 8–9, John is told that what is being revealed to him corresponds to what is written in a scroll that is in the presence of God—hence, a divinely determined program for the renewal of the creation and for the redemption of his covenant people.[141] Its message is not to be accessible to people in general, just as the content of the vision granted to Isaiah was regarded as "a sealed document" (Isa 29:11–12). Similarly, the message and vision that Daniel received were to be "kept secret . . . until the time of the end" (Dan 12:4, 9). There is only one who is qualified to open the scroll in which this plan is described: he is "the Lion of the tribe of Judah, the Root of David"—that is, Jesus, who has triumphed over sin and death, and through whom the divine program is being carried out. He is authorized not only to "open the scroll" but also to unfasten its "seven seals"—thereby launching the successive stages of cosmic renewal. His designation as "the Lion of the tribe of Judah" recalls the promise to Judah made by Jacob in his final words, comparing his heir to a "lion's whelp" and assuring him of an enduring rule over an obedient people (Gen 49:8–10).[142] The "root of David" is an image used in Isa 11:1–8 to depict the transforming power of God that will be at work in the renewed Davidic dynasty, overcoming injustice and inequality and transforming the whole of creation. Above all, this "root of Jesse" is to serve as the instrument to spread God's message of renewal to "the nations" (Isa 11:10).

Ironically, the one authorized to "open the scroll" (5:5)—that is, to bring about what has been promised through the prophets—is not a Lion, but "a Lamb"—once "slain," but now alive. The completeness of his capacity to carry out this transforming role is described in terms of his total—sevenfold—capacities: horns, the symbols of power; eyes, the signs of discernment; spirits of God, combining divine wisdom and capability (5:6). The number seven—deriving obviously from the tradition of seven days for completion of the creation—is pervasive throughout this book. Seven is the number of:

The spirits before the throne of God (1:4).

The churches addressed here (1:11).

The golden lampstands in the vision (1:12).

The stars in the hand of the "one like a son of man" (1:16).

The identification of the stars and lampstands as the seven churches (1:20); subsequent references in 2:1; 3:1.

The torches at the throne of God (4:5).

The seals on the scrolls (5:1).

The horns and eyes of the Lamb (5:6).

The seals opened by the Lamb (6:1).

The angels and the trumpets given to them (8:2, 6).

The thunders evoked by the outcry of the angel (10:3-4).

The mystery declared by the seventh angel's trumpet (10:7).

The dragon with seven heads (12:3).

The heads of the beast from the sea (13:1).

The angels with the seven plagues (15:1, 6-7).

The bowls of divine wrath (16:1; 17:1; 21:9).

The heads of the scarlet beast (17:9).

The mountains on which the woman is seated (17:9).

The seven kings (17:10).

It is one of the seven angels with the bowls who announces the consummation of God's purpose for his people—a group identified as "the bride, the wife of the Lamb." These people take up residence in the new city of God, which is built on the foundation of the twelve apostles (21:9-14). The implication of this last detail, as well as of the reference to the apostles in 18:20, is that the author of this work is not an apostle, but one who deeply honors and is grateful for the apostles' original, basic role in preparing for the renewal of God's people and of the creation.

The pervasive importance of "the book" in this writing is evident in the account of the Lamb's opening the seals that have marked off the stages of the divine scheme of renewal—the seventh of which (7:1) opens the way for the seven trumpets that announce the divine purpose (8:1–9:19). The seventh in that series (10:1–7) leads into the seven thunders, which are the discernible evidence of the carrying out of that plan: "the mystery of God, as he announced to his servants the prophets." A variant of the book image appears when John is instructed by a voice from heaven to "take and eat the scroll which is open in the hand of the angel standing on the sea and on the land" (10:8). It is this "little scroll," taken and eaten by the apocalyptic seer, which enables him to discern the further details of the purpose of God—some of it pleasant ("sweet as honey") and some of it distasteful ("bitter"). The purpose of his absorption of these insights from the "little book" is to enable him to "prophesy about many peoples and nations and tongues and kings" (10:11). The eternal destiny of members of the human race who yield to the pressure to worship "the beast," who is the God-opposing power ruling the world, is linked with the note that their names "were not written before the foundation of the world in the book of life" that lists those who trust in "the Lamb that was slain" (13:8).[143] At the final judgment (20:11–15), the dead are judged by what was "written in the books" about what they had done: those whose names are not written in "the book of life" were "thrown into the lake of fire." By contrast, blessing is pronounced on anyone "who keeps the words of the prophecy of this book" (22:9). There is a final warning of judgment on anyone who adds to or takes way from "the book of this prophecy": those who do so will lose a share "in the tree of life and in the holy city which are described in this book" (22:18). The documents of past behavior and of future fulfillment of the divine purpose—these "books"—are central for its definition and consummation.

The initial image in this message of the fulfillment of God's purpose for his people and for the creation is the vision of "one like a son of man"[144] (1:12–16), clothed in a long robe and a golden girdle, with white hair and flaming eyes. The long robe indicates his role as ruler and priest; the girdle is a sign of his authority. Symbolic indications of his central role in disclosure of the divine presence and power are the images of seven golden lampstands and his possession of seven stars, as well as the sword from his mouth and his shining face. If the tradition that is being drawn on here is from such Torah texts as Exod 26:35 and 40:4 and Num 8:2–3, what is pictured is probably not seven different lampstands, but a single lampstand with a central shaft and three branches on each side, on each of which was placed a lamp.

Later the lampstand was perceived as a stylized tree of life, but in Zech 4:1–6 and 11–14, the seven lamps are said to be "the eyes of the Lord, which range throughout the whole earth." Located as they were in the inner sanctuary of the temple, they represented the visible presence of God among his people.[145] This role is seen by John as now being carried out by "the one like a son of man" (1:13), who in place of seven lamps has in his hands "seven stars" (1:16). The stars are then identified as "the angels of the seven churches," and the lampstands are "the seven churches." These serve the author of Revelation as the visible presence of God among his people and in the world. And in the diversity of the churches as they are depicted in the ensuing letters, the reader can see the range of challenges and responses that are engaged in by the new people of God. Before examining the seven letters, however, it may be useful to look at the qualities that are to be displayed by this new community and the divine blessings that attend them, as indicated in the seven beatitudes reported in this book. "Blessed are those . . ."

1. Those who read aloud the words of this prophecy and . . . hear and keep what is written therein (1:3).

2. The dead who die in the Lord . . . they rest from their labors, and their deeds follow them (14:13).

3. Those who are awake and properly clothed—that is, prepared for the sudden coming of Christ—are warned to be ready even as the fearful outpouring of the powers of evil is taking place (16:15).

4. Those who are invited to the marriage supper of the Lamb, the members of the elect community, are to be ready to share in the joyous celebration of the consummation of God's purpose in the world (19:9).

5. Those who share in the first resurrection because they had died as martyrs—continue their testimony to Jesus and the word of God, and refuse to participate in divine honors to the emperor: "the beast or its image" (20:4).

6. "The one who keeps the words of the prophecy of this book," that is, those who not only read this apocalypse, but who have the wisdom and courage to obey its counsel concerning their personal lives and sociopolitical relationships (22:7).

7. "Those who wash their robes," that is, those are careful to gain and maintain purity of life and thought in spite of threats and suffering that they undergo at the hands of the demonic political rule and its cruel challenges to the new community (22:14).

The supreme irony is that the impending time of struggle and suffering will be for the faithful and obedient ultimately a time of divine blessing.

THE LETTERS TO THE SEVEN CHURCHES (2:1–3:22)

The seven letters are addressed by Christ to the seven churches, whose experience and needs are symbolic and representative of what is faced by all the churches. Each of the letters consists of three parts: (1) commendation and encouragement; (2) criticism and warning ("I have this against you"); and (3) promise of divine support ("I will come . . . I will give"). The letters are addressed in each case to "the angel" of the particular church—who is perceived to be the divine messenger communicating Christ's assessment, critique, and advice to each of these communities.

The Letter to the Church in Ephesus (2:1–7)

Ephesus, located on the western coast of Asia Minor (the Roman province of Asia) at the mouth of the Cayster River, was famed as the location of a temple of the fertility goddess, who was identified by the Greeks as Artemis.[146] An earlier temple for the fertility goddess of unknown name was rebuilt by Alexander the Great, and then under his Seleucid successors was elaborately redesigned. The resulting columned structure was considered to be one of the wonders of the Hellenistic world. In addition to Ephesus's function as a port, which gave access to the whole of the province of Asia for travel and commerce by an elaborate system of highways, the shrine of Artemis was a major attraction, bringing the pious and the curious from across the world. Numerous other deities were worshiped in Ephesus as well,[147] but the veneration of Artemis was a major factor in the life of the city.

According to the account in Acts 19:21–41, Paul's stay in Asia was when he was en route from Greece ultimately to Jerusalem (21:1–15). There was fierce resentment of the widespread abandonment of worship of these traditional deities as a consequence of his preaching (19:26). This had an economic impact as well, in that (1) sales of silver miniature shrines of Artemis dropped off sharply, and hence the income of the silversmiths that made them declined radically; and (2) fears arose that the numbers of those coming to visit the city and temple would decline greatly as well (19:27). After the hostile group's charge that Paul and his associates would discredit the temple and even the goddess, the crowd engaged in extended shouting, "Great is Artemis of the Ephesians" (19:28). Some of Paul's coworkers were reported to have been dragged into the great theater (which seated 25,000), but he was advised by some sympathetic civic leaders called Asiarchs[148] not to join the throng there (19:31). The author is clearly indicating that the message proclaimed by Paul had already begun to penetrate the upper levels of society in the Roman world. The attempt by an unidentified Jew named Alexander to present a statement in defense of Paul was thwarted by the crowd, which shouted the praise of Artemis for two hours (19:34).

The official response to the charges and the hostile reaction against Paul were offered by the town clerk. He noted that the authorized "temple-keeper" for the shrine of Artemis was the city of Ephesus, which also was guardian of a meteorite that was believed to have come from her.[149] This enduring sign of divine approval for the worship of Artemis, in addition to the fact that no charges of sacrilege had been brought against Paul, were said to preclude any hostile action on the part of the people. Any accusations the Ephesians might wish to make must be presented in the courts or before the proconsuls, the resident Roman authorities. The author of Acts is here making the point that the apostles were not engaged in anti-Roman propaganda or activity. Instead of their being accused of such by the regional authorities in Ephesus, their innocence of such charges is declared publicly and officially in this Acts account. In Paul's first letter to the Corinthians, there is mention of his having "fought with beasts at Ephesus" (1 Cor 15:32), which is probably a vivid metaphor for the fierce opposition he encountered there. The continuity of the Pauline tradition in Ephesus historically is evident from the messages in the deuteropauline letters of Timothy addressed to Pauline associates located there: Timothy (1 Tim 1:3); Onesiphorus (2 Tim 1:16); Tychicus (2 Tim 4:12).

The message to the church in Ephesus (Rev 2:2–7) includes commendations and warnings. The members are commended for their "patient endurance" of the hostility and consequent suffering that they have experienced as members of the new community, and for their perceptiveness in recognizing those among them whose teachings and claim to apostolic authority are false. Yet they are challenged for having lost the love and obedience that they earlier had, and are called to repent, lest they lose their place on the "lampstand" of communities called and illumined by Christ. Their continuing wisdom is evident in their rejection and opposition—"hatred"— of "the works of the Nicolaitans," which is said here to be the attitude of Christ toward this deviant group.

The specifics of the teaching of the Nicolaitans cannot be determined with certainty, but in 2:14–15, this erring group is linked with "the teaching of Balaam." That non-Israelite hireling prophet (Deut 23:4–5; Josh 13:22), although he refused to curse Israel when ordered to do so (Num 22–24), was killed when his advice to Israel resulted in their fall into infidelity and their receiving divine punishment (Num 31:1–16), as noted in 2 Pet 2:15 and Jude 11. The evils promoted by Balaam that have reappeared in this false teaching of the Nicolaitans include immorality and eating food sacrificed to idols. Some scholars have conjectured that there is a parallel between the Semitic name of this false prophet—Balaam, which derives from Baal-`am, meaning "lord of the people"—and the Greek name, Nicolaus, which means "conqueror of the people." Irenaeus saw a link between this heretical group and Nicolaus,[150] who is mentioned in Acts 6:5 as one of those chosen to handle the ongoing needs of the community in Jerusalem, but there is no hint there or elsewhere of his involvement in false teaching or practices. Modern scholars have perceived the Nicolaitans as Judaizers, but a much more plausible description is that of Elizabeth Schüssler-Fiorenza, who sees them to have been "enthusiasts": those who claimed "to have received ultimate perfection and salvation through baptism and 'gnosis,' to belong already to the heavenly, spiritual world, and to be able to express this spiritual freedom by eating meat sacrificed to idols and in committing immoral acts."[151] Those who heed the Spirit will be enabled to discern and to fulfill the life of obedience in the face of suffering, and thus to share in the new life that God will provide in the new age: "the paradise of God" (2:7).

The Letter to the Church in Smyrna (Rev 2:8–11)

Smyrna (modern Izmir) on the west coast of Asia Minor had a fine harbor and fertile farmland around it. A major highway across central Asia Minor terminated there. Settled by the Greeks in the tenth century BCE, and geometrically laid out, the acropolis of the city was located on a hill five hundred feet high, and was referred to as the "crown." The city was rebuilt by the successors of Alexander the Great, and then early on entered into an alliance with the Romans. In 195 BCE, there was a temple erected there for the goddess Roma. After a brief period of control by the Parthians (41–39 BCE), Smyrna regained independence and was acclaimed by the geographer Strabo as "the most beautiful city of all." The civic structure was that of Greek cities taken over by the Romans, with a council (*boule*) composed of the richest citizens, an assembly of the people (*demos*), a council of elders (*gerousia*), and magistrates (*strategoi*), who served as administrators.

From the early second century CE, there are documents that indicate the presence there of a substantial Christian community. These include two writings by Ignatius, the third bishop of Antioch in Syria: one to the community in Smyrna, and one to its bishop, Polycarp (both preserved in the Apostolic Fathers). Eusebius reports that Polycarp was a companion of the apostles, and that he was condemned to be eaten by beasts in Rome. En route there, he visited churches in Asia Minor and wrote to others,[152] and died under Trajan in Rome in 103 CE. Ignatius's letter to Smyrna calls for submission to the bishops, the presbyters, and the deacons, and encourages cordial contacts to be made and sustained with churches in other cities. He warns against denial of the bodily nature of Jesus and of his resurrection (Docetism), and asserts the importance of participation in the Eucharist and of belief in the passion and resurrection of Jesus. He explains that he was willing to submit to martyrdom as an expression of his bodily, physical commitment to Christ—"near the sword is near to God"—and his expectation of the bodily resurrection.

The letter to Smyrna in Rev 2:8–11 begins with the words of Christ, who is not named here, but who is identified in terms echoing 1:17–18, which are spoken by "one like a son of man" (1:13). He affirms that he is the one who has a role in the purpose of God that sweeps from "first" to "last," as evident by his life, his death, and his resurrection (2:8). He declares that, in spite of the "rich" resources that God has provided for his people, they are now experiencing "tribulation"[153] and poverty." What has provoked this severe difficulty is that the Jews there have differentiated between themselves (a religious movement accepted by the Romans) and this new movement, whose members claim to be the true heirs of the tradition and covenant promises of ancient Israel. This hostility toward the new covenant people on the part of the Jews is perceived by John as evidence that they are not a gathering of God's people but are a "synagogue of Satan" (2:9).

The members of the church in Smyrna are to see a parallel between the ultimate outcome of what they are about to experience and the death and resurrection of Christ (2:8). For a brief period of time they will have to endure "tribulation"—suffering, trials, imprisonment, and even death—as they maintain their stand against the present Roman political and cultural order. Here and throughout the New Testament, tribulation[154] is seen as a necessary feature of the divinely effected transition from the present evil age to the age to come, when God's purpose will triumph and the Messiah and the new covenant people will be vindicated. The relevant metaphor for this painful but productive process is employed in John 16:21–22: the pain and travail experienced by a pregnant mother, which leads to the joyous result of the delivery of her child. The tribulation of the faithful will not last long—"ten days"—and their fidelity will be rewarded by a "crown of life." Their triumphant delivery from "the second death" is later contrasted in Rev 20:6–15 with the ultimate destiny in "a lake of fire" for the powers of evil and all wicked and faithless human beings. The ability of the faithful to "conquer" derives from their trust in the divine provisions for the people of God.

The Letter to the Church in Pergamum (Rev 2:12–17)

The message is sent to the church in Pergamum by one whose mouth is like a "two-edged sword"—echoing the description of the servant of Yahweh in Isa 49:2 and the role of God's word in accomplishing the divine purpose for deliverance of Israel from slavery in Egypt according to Wis 18:1–19. The church is located in the city "where Satan's throne is" (2:13)—that is, the altar in a vast temple of Zeus, built in Pergamum by the Hellenistic ruler Eumenes II (197–159). Domitian (who reigned 81–96) was identified with Zeus, and the friezes in this temple depict his victory over his cosmic enemies, which became a central locus for divine honors to the Roman emperor and the major center for the imperial cult in the whole of the eastern Mediterranean world.[155] This began when Augustus agreed to be called "Son of the Deified," but insisted that the worship be linked with Roma, the goddess of Rome. It was on this basis that the great temple was erected in Pergamum, and it was pictured on the reverse side of a coin of Augustus in 19 BCE. The divine designation of the emperor was continued under his successors. When Gaius was serving as deputy for Augustus in the East, he settled some disputes concerning Roman control and was accorded divine honors as the emperor's heir.[156] They were also offered to Nerva (96–98 CE), who was designated in Pergamum as Common Benefactor and Savior of the province and city, and to Trajan (98–117), who was called Lord of Land and Sea and Savior of the World, and honored throughout the region. The chief locus for these rites was this temple located near the summit of the great acropolis of Pergamum, where a recurrent festival of divine honors to the emperor was established. Clearly, this is "where Satan's throne is" (Rev 2:13).

The prime example of the threat to Christians in this context of conflict concerning the imperial cult is Antipas (2:13), the "faithful one" whose role as a "witness" for Christ (*martus*) resulted in his martyrdom. There is a solemn warning (2:14–15) recalling the dangerous teaching of the Nicolaitans mentioned in 2:6, which fostered moral and ritual irresponsibility.

Two kinds of divine support are promised for those who resist the demands to conform to the pagan cult: (1) "hidden manna" and (2) "a white stone" (2:17). The first recalls God's provision for his people as they escaped from slavery in Egypt (Exod 16; Num 11), feeding them with "the grain of heaven . . . the bread of angels" (Ps 78:24–25). The second results in the inscription on a white stone of a "new name," which matches the promise in Isa 62:1–12, where the vindication of God's people leads to a new name for them and a new network of relationships with God: "the Holy People, the Redeemed of the Lord." Only those who receive this "new name" from God will understand the depths and riches of this new relationship.

The Letter to the Church in Thyatira (Rev 2:18–29)

Located between Sardis and Pergamum, Thyatira was the residence and place of business for Lydia, Paul's first convert in Macedonia, across the Aegean Sea from Asia Minor. She is identified in Acts 16:14a as a seller of purple goods—a luxury item for royalty and the wealthy (Rev 18:12, 16)—and "a worshiper of God." Paul reportedly met her outside the city gate of Philippi, where he "supposed that there was a place of prayer" (*proseuche*) and where he encountered her among a group of women worshipers. She was persuaded by Paul's message and was baptized—hence she was his first convert on the mainland of Europe, according to Acts 16:14b–26. She then provided her house as a residence for him and as the meeting place for the congregation that was beginning to form in Philippi.

The church in Thyatira is commended for its "works," which are identified as (1) "love and faith"—faith here means fidelity rather than simply belief—as well as (2) "service and patient endurance" in response to the difficulties, demands, and needs that are being met by the members. Yet they are sharply criticized for their tolerance of a woman here given the symbolic name of Jezebel: wife of Israel's king Ahab, who perverted his people's worship of God by establishing an altar and fostering worship of the Canaanite god, Baal. This was an erotic deity thought by his devotees to be the source of human, plant, and animal fertility, and identified with storm clouds that brought rain (1 Kgs 16:29–33). In sharp contrast to Lydia is this woman identified as Jezebel, who claimed to be a "prophetess," but who fostered idolatry and immorality (Rev 2:20). Since she refused to repent of her false beliefs and sinful practices, warning is here given that she and those who join with her will be stricken with illness, will undergo "great tribulation," and will suffer the loss of her children (2:21). These could be her actual offspring or her converts. Those who remain faithful—if they reject this false teaching, including that of those who claim to have special information and insights about Satan—are not to be placed under additional obligations,[157] but are encouraged to stand fast in their beliefs and way of life until Christ returns (2:24–25).

The last lines of this letter describe the role of the faithful, brave, obedient new people of God in the period until Christ's coming again: it is to be one of power that they will come to exercise over the nations. Their rule is to be firm, and strong initiative is to be taken against the hostile, evil people/nations, which will be shattered like "earthen pots," just as Jesus struck out against the demons and the powers of evil that he encountered. A notable expression of this claim is in Luke 11:20, where Jesus declares that his casting out demons is "by the finger of God" and has resulted in this: "the kingdom of God has come upon you." As instruments of God's power and purpose, the faithful will share in the establishment of God's rule on the earth. What is foreseen here is the fulfillment of the promise articulated in the oracle of Balaam (Num 24:17), where hearing, knowing, and seeing God and his purpose in the world are to take place when "a star shall come out of Jacob, and a scepter shall rise out of Israel," and the enemies of God and his people will be destroyed. Similarly, in Ps 2:7–9, the son of God will take possession of the nations as far as "the ends of the earth," will "break them with a rod of iron, and dash them to pieces like a potter's vessel." As in the days of David depicted in this psalm, the letter to Thyatira announces the overcoming of the earthly powers of evil.

The Letter to the Church at Sardis (Rev 3:1–6)

Located about one hundred kilometers east of Ephesus and Smyrna, this former capital of the empire of Lydia in the sixth century BCE was the seat of power of Croesus, who ruled as king from 560 to 546, when his alliance with Egypt and Babylonia against Persia failed and the Lydian kingdom was brought to an end. When Alexander conquered the region, Sardis surrendered to him and was permitted to operate by its own laws. Lydia was the richest of all the provinces in Asia Minor, with wealth generated by its forests and mines but even more by its fertile valleys, which produced fruits and grains, especially wine. In the reign of Croesus, Sardis benefited from these products and became a renowned center for arts and letters. Under the Seleucid successors of Alexander, the city became the administrative center for Asia Minor, and when the Romans took over in the first century BCE, it had become an independent city-state, famed for its textiles, including wool, linen fishnets, and luxury linen interwoven with gold thread. Later in that century, Sardis and other cities in the region fostered the worship of Roma and Augustus. In the second century, Sardis was among those Greek cities that acclaimed the emperor Hadrian (117–138) as the "new Dionysus," the god of wine and of mystical communion.

The Christian community there is sharply criticized in this letter, and warned that its "works" are "not perfect in the sight of God" and that Christ will come to them at a time they do not expect (3:4–6). Only a "few" of the members have not become stained by participation in local pagan practices: it is they who will be fit to "walk with [Christ] in white," whose names will be retained in "the book of life," and who will be acknowledged by him in the presence of "my Father." Meanwhile they are to be attentive to "what the Spirit says to the churches."

The Letter to the Church at Philadelphia (Rev 3:7–13)

This city was founded in the mid-second century BCE by a king of Pergamum named Attalus II Philadelphos, and at the death of his successor in 173, it was bequeathed to Rome. Located in a fertile valley east of Smyrna and Sardis, the area was subject to severe earthquakes, the most violent of which was in 17 CE, and resulted in the populace having to move outside the city to avoid falling structures. The emperor Tiberius (14–37 CE) removed the city's obligation to pay tribute to Rome so that rebuilding could be carried out. These developments may lie behind the letter's commendation of the church there for its fidelity in spite of difficulties, but also as a warning of the difficulties that will beset the whole world: the cosmic conflict that will bring an end to the present age, as well as the promised soon return of Christ to establish his people like "a pillar in the temple of God." What is predicted is the coming of a new city—Jerusalem—which will "come down from God out of heaven," in association with the "new name" of Christ as God's agent to rule the world (3:11–12). Calling this city Philadelphia is appropriate, since it is a new city of interfamilial love that receives this cosmic assurance.

Letter to the Church at Laodicea (Rev 3:14–22)

Laodicea was founded by the Seleucid ruler, Antiochus II, and named in honor of his wife. Located in the Lycus River valley on a major highway, its commercial activity and especially textile manufacture made it a prosperous city. It adopted a pro-Roman policy as the Romans were taking over Asia Minor, and became thoroughly Romanized. Accordingly, the efforts of the emperor Vespasian (69–79) to gain allegiance of the cities of Asia was particularly effective in Laodicea. An inscription there attests that he was acclaimed as Benefactor of the World and Savior of all Humankind. Festivals honoring the emperor as divine took place there from the time of Claudius (41–54) and continued under Vespasian (69–79).

The city became a major center for medical practice. A significant feature of the city was its water supply, which came from a spring and was brought into the city by an aqueduct, where it was accessible in fountains and basins. Excavations of the ruins of the city have disclosed several theaters, a council chamber, a gymnasium, and a large stadium, but all these were destroyed by an earthquake to which the area was often subject. Before the turn of the eras, there was a large settlement of Jews who had come from Babylonia to the districts of Lydia and Phrygia, many of whom chose to live in Laodicea. Josephus[158] reports a statement by the local magistrates that Jewish residents were permitted to observe the Sabbath and other features required by their law. The fact that this kind of issue was handled in such a formal, official manner indicates that there was a sizeable Jewish population in the vicinity.

The church in Laodicea is mentioned in the Letter to the Colossians (4:16), and is directly addressed in an apocryphal *Epistle to the Laodiceans*, which claims to have been written by Paul but which consists mostly of phrases borrowed from his authentic letters.[159] The challenge to the church there in Rev 2:15–22 is based on the charge that its members have taken pride in its material wealth and prosperity (3:17a) while ignoring the fact that spiritually they are "wretched, pitiable, poor, blind and naked" (3:17). Hence, the members are summoned to be purified and refined like gold or white cloth. Acknowledging their moral and spiritual "nakedness," they are to have their spiritual vision salved in order to give them true insights. What they are going to suffer is to be understood as divine purification, since those whom God loves are the ones here seen as being reproved and chastened—"refined by fire" (3:18–19). If they accept this cleansing and renewal, they will have conquered the powers of evil, will experience fellowship with Christ (3:20), and will sit with him on his throne—sharing in the divine rule of the kingdom of God (3:21). They must be ready to hear and obey what God is conveying through the Spirit to "the churches" (3:22).

THE HEAVENLY DISCLOSURE OF THE FUTURE
PLAN OF GOD (REV 4:1–20:15)

The substance of the revelation that follows involves access for the faithful to heaven itself and a vision granted of the throne of God (4:1–11). A detailed picture of heaven and the throne of God there leads to an account of Christ's role as the Lamb who alone is worthy to open the sealed scrolls in which are described the fulfillment of God's purpose for his people and for the renewal of the creation. All creatures in heaven and earth join in offering praise to him and to God: "Blessing and honor and glory and might forever" (4:1–5:14). Christ is seen to be both the one through whom this plan of cosmic renewal is being disclosed and the one through whom it is to be achieved. The churches addressed in the preceding letters represent the various facets of the new people of God—their strengths, their needs, and the divine provisions to enable them to fulfill God's purpose for them. But here their serious weaknesses are also indicated.

John is called up to heaven to be shown what is to take place in the outworking of God's cosmic plan for his people, for the creation, and for the defeat of the powers of evil: "What must take place after this" (4:1–11), which involves the consummation of that divine plan. The details here are variants on the prophet's vision in Ezek 1, when before the throne of God he sees four living creatures, each of which has four faces—that of a human, a lion, an ox, and an eagle. John is not transported bodily into the divine presence but "in the spirit" or "by the Spirit" (4:2). There is no description of "the one seated" on the throne—that is, of God (4:3)—except for some comparisons with glistening jewels and an indication of the divine radiance surrounding it. Present there are twenty-four elders, each on a throne, granted power ("golden crowns"), and serving as models of purity ("in white robes," 4:4). The number of the elders represents a combination of the twelve tribes of Israel and the twelve apostles commissioned by the risen Christ and empowered by the Holy Spirit. Radiating from the throne are signs of cosmic power ("lightning and thunder") and of divine outreach and purpose ("seven flaming torches" = the "seven spirits of God," 4:5). Surrounding the throne are "four living creatures," each with "six wings" and "full of eyes," which resemble respectively a lion, an ox, a human, and an eagle (4:6–8a). The "seven spirits," which are before the throne of God (1:4b), are linked in 3:1 with Christ, who is pictured as standing among the "seven golden lampstands" and holding the "seven stars" (1:12–16) as he addresses the seven churches. Here these seven spirits are pictured as "flaming torches" before the throne of God (4:5). But in 5:6, they are linked with the eyes and horns of "the

Lamb," and are foreseen as being sent out by God "into all the earth." Thus, they symbolize insight into the divine purpose through Christ and the instruments of power by which that purpose will be achieved and made known throughout "all the earth." The sevenfold work of the Spirit of God recalls the promise in Isa 11:1–3, which will bring to the one so empowered seven capabilities: wisdom, understanding, counsel, might, knowledge, fear of the Lord, and "delight in the fear of God."

The "sea of glass" before the throne (4:6) recalls the divine control of the waters at the creation of the earth (Gen 1:1–10; Ps 104:1–13). Although the description of the four "living creatures" (4:6–9) matches Ezekiel's vision in Ezek 1—"like a lion . . . an ox . . . a human . . . an eagle"—there is no clear indication of their symbolic significance here. But their role is of major importance: they are those who offer unceasing praise to God. This is articulated here and throughout Revelation in phrases echoing praise to God in the prophets. The trishagion here builds on Isa 6:3, expanding the praise to include the eternity of God and the divine purpose: "who was, and is, and is to come." The four living creatures in Ezekiel symbolize the range of powers and activities by which God's rule is operative in the world, but in Revelation, they are the communicators of the message concerning the nature and purpose of God in the world. The lion symbolizes strong initiative; the ox has the strength and endurance to carry out the divine purpose; the human represents both the values and the concerns operative for God's people; and the eagle embodies the lofty, effective fulfillment of this hope for cosmic renewal. Yet it is God alone who is worthy and able to accomplish all this, and who is here praised for creating and sustaining the universe (4:11).

The specifics of that purpose of renewal are indicated in the "scroll" (5:1–5). A question is raised concerning the identity of the one who is qualified to disclose and to achieve that goal—that is, "Who is worthy to open the scroll and break its seals?" (5:2). The answer is ironic: it is one who is identified as "Lion of the tribe of Judah" (5:5), but who is also "a Lamb" (5:6). In Gen 49:9–10, the lion is promised an enduring rule, just as in Isa 11:1–9, the "root of David" is promised enablement by God's Spirit that will lead to justice, equity, defeat of the powers of evil, cessation of hostility between animals and of their role endangering human life—and, above all, the Lamb will provide universal "knowledge of the Lord." The Lamb (5:6) conveys a complex of images, recalling the prospect of death for the gentle prophet (Jer 11:19) and for the faithful servant of Yahweh (Isa 53:7), but also of one who has triumphed over death ("as though it had been slain"), and who has been given the complete number ("seven") of (1) instruments to achieve God's purpose ("horns," Zech 1:18–21), of (2) perspectives on that purpose ("eyes," Zech 4:10), and of (3) the divinely granted capabilities to carry it out ("spirits," Zech 4:6). These divine resources are now operative throughout "all the earth" (5:6).

The multiple eyes recall the prophetic image of the wheels rimmed with eyes that were seen beside the four living creatures in the vision of Ezekiel (1:15–21). They seem to represent both the perception of the divine purpose that is in process and the divine movement by which it will be accomplished. The access of these creatures to God is pictured in the succession of structures above them: a dome (1:22–25), a throne (1:26a), a human form (1:26b), and the radiant divine glory (1:27–28). In John's vision, the agent of fulfillment is not a figure of power, however, but the Lamb: these promises of renewal are foreseen as now being fulfilled through Christ in Rev 5:6–14. They include his carrying out both the royal and priestly roles in the establishment of God's kingdom on earth and in the offering by his people of unending praise to the enthroned Lamb. He alone is qualified to "open the scroll" and thereby to launch the divine process of renewal of the creation and of God's people that is depicted therein. This movement toward fulfillment of God's rule is described through complex and intertwined imagery, which opens with these "seven seals" (Rev 6–7) but then moves to seven trumpets and seven bowls of divine wrath, culminating in the destruction of "Babylon" (Rev 8–18), and finally in the vision of the renewal of heaven and earth (Rev 19–22). The succession of visions of this process of accomplishment of God's renewal of his people and of the world order resembles the eight visions of Zechariah, which culminate in the coronation of the king ("branch") and of the priest who are to guide God's people.[160] Just as in that prophecy "many nations and strong nations" are foreseen as "seeking the Lord of Hosts" and "entreating his favor" (Zech 8:22), so the opening of the scroll that contains the divine cosmic purpose and the sacrifice of the Lamb leads to the assurance that by his blood are to be "ransomed for God saints from every tribe and language and people and nation" (5:9). It is they who will share with the triumphant Christ in his "reign on earth" (Rev 5:10). The four living creatures and the elders join with "every creature" throughout the universe in offering everlasting praise to the one "who sits upon the throne" and to the enthroned Lamb (5:14).

The Seven Seals and the Seven Trumpets (Rev 6:1–12:17)

Now begins the process of opening the scroll's seven seals, which makes possible the depiction of the events that will lead to the time of divine punishment of the powers of evil in the world and ultimately to the triumph of the divine purpose. The first four of these seals bring about the disclosure of four riders, each mounted on a horse of a different color. This imagery once again recalls the prophecy in Zech 1:7–17, where the horsemen explain that their role is to patrol the whole of the earth and to maintain peace.[161] Here, however, the roles of the horsemen are diverse and judgmental. The "voice of thunder," which comes from one of the "living creatures" and is the instrument foretelling and effecting the purpose of God, calls forth a rider on a white horse (6:1–2). He is the agent of power and rule, equipped with a bow and a crown. The next creature calls out the rider on the red horse, who is the instrument of warfare, symbolized by his "great sword" (6:3–4). The third horse is black, and is a sign of famine, indicated by the cost of a quart of wheat: a day's wages (6:5–6). The fourth horse is pale green: the symbol of death, as shown by his name and by Hades,[162] who is his companion here and the instrument of famine, pestilence, and warfare (6:7–8). The fifth seal results in a vision of the souls of martyrs and an inquiry as to when they will be avenged, followed by assurance that it will indeed take place (6:9–11). The sixth seal leads to seismic disturbances, which are recognized by the earthly rulers and leaders as portents of divine judgment to be administered by the one "seated on the throne" and by the Lamb. This doom will fall on all evil humans, ranging from kings and generals to ordinary individuals, slave and free. From this triumph over evil, none of the wicked can escape (6:12–17).

Before the seventh seal is opened (8:1), with the consequent cosmic disaster that is to befall the world (7:1–3), there is a description in two stages of the enduring constitution of the people of God before the divine judgment is poured out on the world. This process is launched by the seven trumpets (8:6). The first image of God's people (7:1–8) is presented in a strictly formal mode, comprised of exactly the same number of members (twelve thousand) from each of the twelve tribes of Israel. Implicit in this image is that what God is doing through Jesus Christ for the renewal of his people is in continuity with and represents a mode of fulfillment of the covenant promises that were made to the people of historic Israel, here referred to in a stylized mode. But then we see "a great multitude which no one could number"— including people "from every nation, from all tribes and peoples and language groups [*tongues*]" (7:9–12). The covenant promises of God are not for the heirs of traditional Israel alone, but are extended to potentially the whole of humanity. Standing before the throne of God and before the Lamb, and joining with the angels and the white-robed elders in the praise of God (7:10–12; cf. 4:2–4), those from the whole range of ethnic and political traditions also are clad in white robes, symbolizing the purity they have gained through "the blood of the Lamb" (7:14). They remain forever in the divine presence, free from hunger and thirst and from oppressive heat (7:16). Since the Lamb is their shepherd, he will "guide them to springs of living water,"[163] and God will remove from them all causes of sorrow: "The Lord God will wipe away the tears from all faces" (Isa 22:8; Rev 7:13–17).

When opened, the seventh seal leads to a brief period of heavenly silence, followed by the appearance of seven angels before the throne of God. To each of them is given a trumpet, the blowing of which will lead to a series of divine judgments on a hostile, evil world (8:1–6). This series of eschatological announcements is seen as taking place at an altar before the throne: there the souls of the martyrs are gathered (6:9), and from it arise prayers of the saints (8:3), which another angel causes to mingle with the smoke arising from the incense on the altar. This angel filled his golden censer with fire from the altar, which is then thrown down upon the earth, resulting in cosmic and seismic disturbances (8:5). These dramatic developments prepare for the sounding of the seven trumpets by the seven angels, thereby foretelling the divine judgment that is to take place on the earth (8:6).

The first three trumpets bring down on the earth (1) a mixture of fire, hail, and blood, which destroys a third of the forests and all the green grass; (2) a flaming mountain that converts a third of the sea into wormwood, destroying a third of its living creatures and a third of its ships (8:8–9); and (3) a great star, named Wormwood, which dries up rivers and fountains and poisons humans who drink of this water. Thus, both natural life and interregional commerce are severely harmed. The fourth trumpet (8:12–13) leads to a cosmic crisis: loss of part of the light of the sun, moon, and stars, thus producing more darkness during day and night. This serves as a warning of greater difficulties that are to follow the sounding of the next three trumpets.

The fifth trumpet (9:1–11) opens the "bottomless pit," from which emerge polluting and destructive forces that leave the world of nature unharmed, but a plague of scorpion-like locusts[164] brings torture for five months to those who lack "the seal of God." Their ruler is an angel from the bottomless pit named "destroyer"—in Hebrew, Abaddon, and in Greek, Apollyon. What results from this and from the next two trumpets is identified in 9:12 as "woes."

The sixth trumpet is sounded (9:13–19), and its consequences are a series of cosmic catastrophes designated as the "second woe" (9:20–11:14). At the divinely predetermined "hour, day, month and year" (9:15), the four angels assigned to the military role dispatch cavalry troops numbering 20 million, with the riders wearing multicolored breastplates and the horses with lion heads, smoke coming from their mouths and tails like deadly serpents (9:19). Most of humanity does not repent of its evil deeds and idolatries (9:20–21), however. The angel that appears, radiant with celestial features, announces with a voice of thunder the message from heaven that is not to be disclosed but is now to be fulfilled when the seventh angel conveys with a trumpet call "the mystery of God" (10:1–7). This is inscribed on a scroll in the hand of an angel, which the writer is instructed to take and eat: it will taste sweet, but will be bitter in the stomach—pleasant to hear initially, but sad to experience its doleful consequences. An order is given to measure the central part of God's temple, but not the Court of the Nations, since the Romans have polluted both the temple and the city of Jerusalem. "Two witnesses" will continue to convey God's message for three and one-half years,[165] during which the temple will have become a pagan shrine. But God's agents will bring drought and plagues, and will destroy their opponents by fire, with the result that "the beast"—Satan—will come and make war on them, and accordingly these faithful witnesses will die in Jerusalem as their Lord did. They will lie unburied and their enemies will rejoice at the seeming end of these two radically critical prophets. But after a short period ("three and a half days"), God will raise them back to life and they will be taken up to heaven, while the city and seven thousand of its inhabitants will be killed in a great earthquake (11:11–13). This is "the second woe" (11:14).

The seventh trumpet heralds the triumph of God's purpose in the world: "the kingdom of our Lord and of his Christ," which is to endure forever (11:15). Although the nations rage (11:18), it is the time for the dead to be judged, for the faithful to be rewarded—saints, prophets, and all who fear the name of God—and for the "destroyers of the earth" to be destroyed (11:18). God's temple in heaven is open, with the ark of the covenant visible as well as cosmic signs evident (11:19). A dual vision highlights the triumph of God over the powers of evil (12:1–6): (1) the woman—arrayed with heavenly symbols and symbolizing the people of God—gave birth to a child, who was to be ruler of the nations and was taken up to God, while she escaped under divine protection for the three and one-half years; (2) the deceitful dragon—who is "the Devil and Satan"—the opponent of God and the accuser of the faithful, is ironically defeated by "the blood of the Lamb" and the testimony of the faithful martyrs. His efforts to destroy the "woman"—the new community— became ferocious, pictured here with intricate symbolism (12:13–13:18) that points to the power of the Roman Empire and its program requiring divine honors to the emperor, making war on the faithful community, and taking total control over all the subject peoples. The only nonconformists are those whose names have been in the Lamb's book of life since before the creation of the world (13:8), and they must remain faithful (13:10).

Symbols of Cosmic Evil and of Divine Triumph (13:11–20:15)

In depicting this diabolical program, a second "beast" is described (13:11–18) that mimics the qualities of a lamb but speaks like a dragon. Its role is to promote a wicked imitation of Christ. "The first beast," who is said to have recovered from a mortal wound and therefore appears as a pseudo-Christ, is probably Nero.[166] The prophet-like second beast promulgates and enforces divine honors to the emperor, and claims that there are communications from this divinity who is said to have come back from the dead. In public acknowledgment of this divinity, his devotees are to receive some sort of mark on the forehead or right hand. Such public sign of the deity of the emperor is requisite for any economic transaction—which some scholars have proposed may refer to the use of Roman coins on which the emperor was depicted as a divinity, and which many Jews and Christians accordingly refused to use.[167] The enigmatic identification of the beast by the number 666 may well have developed from the use of Hebrew letters as numbers: specifically, the numerical equivalent of Nero Caesar would be this number. The only explicit reference to Nero's persecution of Christians is linked with the burning of Rome, for which he wanted to make them the culprits.[168] This is the first indication in Roman sources of an imperial attack on the Christians.

The vision that follows depicts the symbolically complete new community (14:1–5). It is located in the central place where God is among his people—Mount Zion—and the major figure is "the Lamb," but the details of the sights and sounds of the divine presence match those of the throne of God in heaven in the earlier visions of this book. The redeemed community numbers 144,000—which is the number of the tribes of Israel, times the number of the apostles, times the number of years of the triumph of God's plan for his people. Their chastity—implying here moral and religious purity and not merely sexual abstinence[169]—and their commitment to truth make them exemplars and prototypes of God's new people. The potential membership includes "every nation and tribe and tongue and people" (14:6), and all are warned of the impending day of divine judgment to be carried out by the creator of the universe (14:7).

In complete contrast to this assurance of divine renewal is the message of the second angel announcing the destruction of "Babylon" (= Rome; 14:8–11), and the ensuing judgment that will fall on the evil world for its participation in divine honors to the "beast" (= the emperor). This is pictured in multiple images: a divine harvest, "the wine of God's wrath," and the fire of unending torment to be experienced by those who join in worship of the emperor (14:14–20). The blood is said to flow from the winepress for about two hundred miles at a depth of five or six feet.

The next and final series of symbols of the outpouring of God's wrath consists of seven angels with seven plagues represented by seven golden bowls (15:1–16:21): "With them the wrath of God is ended." The faithful community that resisted the imperial worship is seen as assembled in the presence of God, playing harps and joined in the praise of God with the songs of Moses and of the Lamb, the words of which build on the psalms and the Prophets,[170] celebrating God's outreach to all the nations (15:4). The wicked suffer sores, darkness, pain, and transformation of their rivers into blood (16:1–6). From the heavenly altar comes assurance of the omnipotence of God (16:7), but from the successive bowls come the punishment of the evil worshipers, culminating in a combined assembling of the worldly kings to battle "God the almighty" at Armageddon (16:12–16). This is not an otherwise known place, but is probably a reference to the coastal mountain range at Mount Carmel near Megiddo, where battles were fought in ancient Israel (Judg 5:19; 2 Kgs 9:27; 23:29). Only the faithful will be alert and ready for this battle (16:15), which is here symbolic for the ultimate confrontation between the people of God and the powers of the idolatrous empire. Horrendously heavy hail symbolizes the cosmic destruction that falls on the evil world and destroys "Babylon" (= Rome; 16:19–21), which will be made to "drain the cup of fury of God's wrath." This is further depicted through various images in Rev 17–18.

The first of these is that of a harlot who commits fornication with the "beast": the empire whose successive rulers are pictured as multiple "heads" and "horns" enticed into fostering this imperial idolatry. She becomes drunk on the blood of the saints and martyrs who refuse to conform to the imperial decree (17:1–6). The heads and horns are then explained to be the emperors, who will "make war on the Lamb," but who will be conquered by him who is "King of kings and Lord of lords" (17:14). The woman is directly identified as Rome, which "has dominion over the kings of the earth" (17:18). The fall of "Babylon" is then pictured in vivid detail. It becomes a "dwelling place of demons" and foul spirits, since kings have gained power and merchants have gained wealth through a vast spectrum of economic activities and cooperation with "her," proud and foolishly self-reliant as she is (18:1–19). God's people are urged to leave this city, whose wealth and splendor are to be destroyed—an event that will bring joy to the leaders of God's people (18:20). Her destruction is symbolized by the casting of a great millstone into the sea, which will mark the end of the light, life, music, and merchant activity there (18:21–23)—developments that are described in terms echoing the prophets of Israel.[171]

Following the heavenly hymn of praise to God for the manifestation of "salvation and glory and power," as well as for the carrying out of judgment against the wicked city that has "corrupted the earth" (19:1–4), the apocalypse turns to portray "the marriage supper of the Lamb" (19:5–10), by which God and his people—"the Bride"—are ultimately joined together. This leads into the second of a series of unnumbered visions (19:11–21:8).[172] The first in this series is of a bridegroom, Christ, who appears as a rider on a white horse and is acclaimed as "faithful and true," as one who settles issues and triumphs in conflict with evil (19:11). He also is designated as "The Word [*logos*] of God," and as "King of kings and Lord of lords," in which capacity he leads "the armies of heaven" (19:13–16). His qualification for these roles is evident from his robe dipped in blood—symbolizing his sacramental death—and from the sharp sword issuing from his mouth, indicating that he is the one who declares and accomplishes the purpose of God in overcoming evil and fulfilling his plan for his people.

The second vision (19:17–18) is an invitation to what will be a ghastly scene of "the great supper of God," in which God's enemies, their leaders and all their subjects, are to be devoured. This leads into the third vision of cosmic battle (19:19–21). Enticed by the false prophet and his signs, many have shared in the worship of the "image" of "the beast." The leaders and the participants in this idolatrous worship are thrown into fire and their bodies are devoured by ravenous birds (19:21).

The fourth vision is of the binding of Satan, who is also identified as the dragon and the devil and the serpent (20:1–3). He is to be thrown into a pit to stop his deceiving the nations, although after the one thousand years he will be released for a time, in accord with the divine plan as indicated by the prophets (Isa 24:21–22; *1 Enoch* 10:4–6). Satan is resilient, in spite of divine opposition, but will ultimately be destroyed. The establishment of the kingdom of God through the Messiah and the final defeat of Satan are foreseen in the fifth vision (20:4–10). Those martyred for their testimony and loyalty to Christ and for their refusal to honor the "beast" are raised to life and share in his thousand-year reign. Their roles are dual, combining royal and priestly functions. The resurrection of other dead humans comes only at the end of the millennium, but the death they will experience—"the second death"—has no power over the raised martyrs, who have already shared in the reign of God.

There will be a period of resumed evil activity on the part of Satan at the end of the millennium with the aim "to deceive the nations," which are spread out to "the four corners of the earth" (20:8). The evil agents are here identified as "Gog and Magog," whom Satan will gather for battle in numbers as great as the "sand of the sea." The name Gog, which probably derives from Gyges, king of Lydia in the seventh century BCE, appears in the biblical prophets with reference to enemies that are to invade Israel from the north, but are to be destroyed by God (Ezek 38–39).[173] Magog is the land from which he comes, but in *Sibylline Oracles* 3.315, Gog is linked with Ethiopia. The prophecy in Ezekiel mentions Persia and Ethiopia (38:5), which indicates that this text originated late in the history of ancient Israel.[174] Here the two names are symbols for the pagan nations that will seek to take over Jerusalem and the new community that is to be gathered there, but they are to be consumed by fire, as are the devil, the "beast," and the false prophet, and all those whose names are "not written in the book of life" (20:9–10, 14–15). All the dead are raised and are brought to judgment before the throne of God on the basis of how they have lived, as it is recorded in the book of human deeds (20:12a). The evildoers, as well as Death itself and Hades, the abode of the dead, are thrown into the lake of fire (20:13–15). The final sorting out of humans and superhuman forces in the universe is seen here as being carried out.

NEW HEAVEN, NEW EARTH (REV 21:1–22:5)

What follows is the transformation of the creation into "a new heaven and a new earth." The dramatic, symbolic event by which this is begun is the coming from heaven to earth of the "holy city, new Jerusalem" (21:2). This vision recalls the prophetic expectation in Isa 65:17–25 of the renewal of the creation, including the removal of hostility between animals ("the wolf and the lamb shall feed together").[175] It results in the enduring presence of God among his people, with the consequent removal of all pain and sorrow, as promised in Isa 25:6–8; 35:10; 65:19. A series of images point to the source of this cosmic renewal: God's self-designation as the beginning and the end of the alphabet and of all reality, the free-flowing fountain of life, the conqueror of the forces of evil through Christ, the Son, and the one who assigns all these evildoers to the "second death" in the lake of fire (21:6–8).

A detailed description of the Holy City follows, with its multiple features of twelve: gates, angels, tribes of Israel, and apostolic foundations (21:10–14); its dimensions of twelve thousand stadia (about fifteen hundred miles); its walls 12 x 12 cubits high, the twelve jewels[176] adorning the city wall; and the city gates of enormous pearls (21:15–21). The streets are paved with transparent gold, just as the city as a whole is made of "pure gold" (21:18, 21).

Unlike the historical Jerusalem, there is in this new city no temple—because God is present there and accessible to all. The division of time into day and night ends, since the ever-present God provides everlasting light, conveyed through the Lamb. In that light all the nations will walk, and their rulers will bring to the city the esteem and authority—the "glory and honor"—that they have received from their people (21:24–26). This access to divine light echoes the prophetic promise in Isa 60:19–20, where darkness and sorrow shall be no more, and in Tob 13:11, where the bright light that honors God's "holy name" summons nations from the ends of the earth. With this eternal light shining, the city gates will always be open, and "there shall be no night there." Unclean people and unclean objects are to be excluded, since those guilty of lying or defilement—ritual or moral—are excluded (21:27).

The imagery shifts from light to the river that is "the water of life"—bringing life in the kingdom of God to all who come in faith and obedience (22:1–5). The source of this life-giving water is "the throne of God." On each side of the river is "the tree of life," the fruit of which is produced every month, and the leaves of which bring healing to the nations. The prophetic model for this scene is Ezek 47, where the life-giving and creation-renewing water flows from the new temple. The tree of life with its twelve kinds of fruits is of course an echo of the garden of Eden story, where eating this fruit would have enabled one to "live forever" (Gen 3:22–24). Now humans are purified through Christ, and the option to share in eternal life is offered here before "the throne of God and of the Lamb" and has been chosen by the "servants" who "worship him" and who share with God and the Lamb in the eternal reign (22:5).

AWAITING THE COMING OF CHRIST (22:6–21)

The Identity and Role of God's Messenger to His People (22:6–9)

The trustworthiness and truth of the messages that are being communicated to John are affirmed: it is God whose spirits have been communicating through the prophets who has now sent his messenger to inform those who serve him concerning what is about to occur: Christ is to return soon to his people (22:6–7). The messenger conveying what he has heard and seen is John, who recalls how he initially bowed at the feet of the angel who was bringing God's message to him, and was reminded that the angels and the prophets—and now John himself and those who preserve and promote its message—are but servants of God.

The Warning concerning Response to the Message (22:10–11)

What is essential is to "keep the words of this book" (22:8–9) by concurring with its promises and conforming to its demands. The message is to be proclaimed, but one must be prepared for a range of responses—from filthy thoughts and behavior to righteous obedience: only the latter will lead to holiness.

The Identity and Role of God's Agent of Renewal (22:12–13)

Christ here promises his imminent return to earth, when he will respond appropriately to what all humans have done—whether they have been obedient or disobedient to the will of God as he has declared and demonstrated it. Here he affirms his comprehensive role in the purpose of God—from its design and inauguration (*Alpha*) to its consummation (*Omega*), "the first and the last, the beginning and the end."

Assurances and Warnings (22:14–15)

First is a reiteration of the promise to those whose right to share in the life of God's new people is based on their having gained forgiveness and purity through their trust in the sacrifice of Christ: "They washed their robes and made them white in the blood of the Lamb" (7:14). They now share in both the royal and the priestly roles of God: in God's sheltering, ruling presence, and through worship of God in his temple. All their needs are met, and protection is provided by the Lamb even from discomforts symbolized by the burning sun (7:15–17). Excluded from the city are the evildoers and the agents who foster both cultic and moral misdeeds (22:15).

God's Agent of Cosmic Renewal: Christ (22:16–21)

The identity of the agent of God who has made possible the renewal of God's people as it is now embodied in the churches is Jesus, who is here seen as the true heir of God's promises to David, the agent for establishing God's rule in the world (22:16).[177] Jesus identifies himself here as "the bright morning star"—an image that corresponds to the oracle in Num 24:16–17, where the "star out of Jacob" is foreseen as ruler of God's people and the one who will overcome their enemies. Those who utter the invitation to share in this new community are "the Spirit" and "the Bride"—the latter is an image of those who are already participating in its common life. In this way, the respondents can freely enjoy the divine provision for ultimate and ongoing human needs: "the water of life" (22:17).

The apocalypse ends with a solemn warning to those who hear it that, since this document originates with God, no human is to add to it or reduce it. Those who do so will not be able to share in the renewed "life" of this new community of God's people: "the holy city" (22:19). The final words of the writing repeat the assurance that Christ will soon return to carry out this cosmic plan of God for the renewal of his people and of the whole creation, and close with a prayer for the ongoing presence and experience of God's grace as revealed through Jesus (22:20–21).

The Peter and Jude Tradition

Two of the apostles in whose name writings were produced that came to be included in the New Testament canon are Peter and Jude. We have already discussed the role of Peter as portrayed in Acts. But mentioned in Luke 6:16 as one of Jesus' disciples and in Acts 1:13 as one of the twelve apostles is one Judas, who in some manuscripts is identified as "son of James" and in others as a brother of Jesus.[178] It is as the former that the author of this letter is identified in Jude 1:1.[179] Thus, there is an implicit triple claim for the authority of this book: the writer was a disciple, an apostle, and a brother of Jesus the Lord.

The two canonical letters attributed to Peter are different from each other in style and conceptual orientation, but both are written in learned literary modes and employ rather sophisticated vocabularies that would not likely be used by a Galilean fisherman. First Peter is strongly influenced by Graeco-Roman culture as well as by apocalyptic tradition, while 2 Peter shows a major impact of apocalyptic perspective, and incorporates material from the book of Jude (as noted below) as well as from Greek mythology about the fate of the dead, as in the description of the fate of the fallen angels consigned to "pits of nether gloom" (2:4). The term used there, *tartarosas*, refers to Tartarus, the subterranean place where Greeks believed divine punishment was brought upon the wicked.[180]

1 Peter

Although Acts 9–11 describes the pioneering outreach of Peter to Gentiles in Lydda, Joppa, and Caesarea—cities strongly influenced by Graeco-Roman culture—and the confirmation of this mission by the apostles as a whole (11:18), it is Paul who is seen in Acts 13–14 as having launched the gospel mission in Asia Minor. It is to members of the new community in northern Roman provinces on the shore of the Black Sea that this letter is addressed.[181] The letter not only refers to the members in Jewish terms—"exiles of the Dispersion" (1:1), "holy priesthood" (2:5), "chosen race, holy nation, God's own people" (2:9)—but it also foresees their destiny in "Zion" (2:6), and refers to Jews as "your ancestors" (1:18) and to nonmembers as "Gentiles" (2:12). Thus it is clear that the new community is perceived here as the replacement for historic Israel. Hence, it is designated in a quotation from Hos 2:23 as "God's own people" (2:10).

The basis for the life of the community is the sacrifice of Christ, which was foretold in the scriptures, conveyed by the Holy Spirit, enacted in the death of "the lamb without defect or blemish," and confirmed by God's having raised him from the dead (1:18–21). Symbolic participation in this transforming sacrifice is possible through the rite of baptism, which leads to moral renewal and prefigures the ultimate triumph of God over the powers of evil.

One of the few Roman historical texts that refer to the Christians originated in Bithynia, the correspondence between Pliny the Younger (62–113 CE) while he was governor of Bithynia and the emperor Trajan (98–117). Pliny reports the rapid spread of the Christians in the region and the resultant decline in attendance at the imperial shrines.[182] This was not the first instance of Roman historians reporting imperial persecution of Christians: Suetonius tells how Nero (reigned 54–68 CE) sought to place the blame on Christians for the burning of Rome, resulting in their slaughter by wild animals and by crucifixion.[183] Domitian (reigned 81–96) insisted that he be addressed as "lord" (*dominus*) and "god" (*dues*).[184] Thus, the "testing by fire" of the faith of Christians in Asia Minor (1 Pet 1:7) had antecedents that went back to the time of Nero, but was acute there in the late first century. This is, of course, the major issue confronted by Christians in that region according to the book of Revelation.

For the author of 1 Peter, faith is not simply trust in the promises of God—as it is primarily in the Pauline and canonical gospel traditions—but a coherent and defensible set of correct beliefs. The faith is to be confirmed through conceptual testing (1:7), and those who affirm it are to be prepared to offer a rational defense (*apologia*) of it (3:15). The scriptures quoted in this letter for recalling the divine promises and perceiving the outworking of the divine purpose through Christ for the new community are, of course, from the Septuagint—which would scarcely have been a source utilized by a Galilean fisherman!

Yet there is in 1 Peter as in Revelation a continuing effort to assert the continuity between the new community and the divine actions and promises bestowed on historic Israel. The members are addressed as "the exiles of the Dispersion" (1:1). They are being formed by God into "a spiritual house" and are to serve as "a holy priesthood." Their service in this setting constitutes "spiritual sacrifices acceptable to God through Jesus Christ" (2:5). What is happening is perceived to be in fulfillment of the scriptural promises to Israel. In supreme irony, but in keeping with the scriptures, this new structure is being erected on "a cornerstone . . . in Zion"—a stone that the traditional builders rejected (2:6–7; Isa 28:16; Ps 118:22). Drawing on a range of texts from Torah and the Prophets, the community is described as "a chosen race, a royal priesthood, a holy nation, God's own people."[185]

The imagery of household and family is developed as well. This new people of God (1:3, 14; 2:10) lives as a "spiritual household" (2:5; 4:17), as a brotherhood (2:17; 5:9) characterized by filial love (1:22; 3:8; 4:8), and as God's children (1:14–17; 4:19; 5:6–7, 10). The social attitudes of those who are members of families are specified, including submissiveness and consideration (3:1–7), as are the leadership roles within the community (5:1–5). The members are to take care to maintain a good reputation among their pagan contemporaries (2:11–12), and to conform to the order imposed by the imperial establishment. Thereby they can maintain a good reputation in the wider social context, including their patient acceptance of cruel treatment by the secular authorities—just as Christ experienced suffering as the sacrifice for sinners (2:16–24; 5:1). Yet the ultimately evil nature of the Roman Empire is indicated symbolically in the final greeting from the church: "She who is at Babylon" (5:13), Rome, which is here compared with the city and imperial power that brought about the exile of Israel.

As noted above, the community is called a "priesthood" (2:5) and a "brotherhood" (2:17; 5:9), but the only reference to *episkopos* is to Christ's role as "shepherd and overseer" of God's people, rather than to an ecclesiastical office. There is mention of "elders" who have the responsibility to "tend the flock of God" (5:1–2), but specific roles are not indicated. There is an indication in 3:21–22 that the sacrament of baptism was regarded as an instrument of salvation, in that participation in it was to be seen as a sign of sharing in Christ's triumph over sin by his resurrection and ascension—a victory that is now evident in his victory over the God-opposing powers.

Jude

The author of this letter identifies himself as a "brother of James"—which recalls that in Mark 6:32 and Matt 13:55 these two are listed as brothers of Jesus. Clearly, the aim is to link the message of this letter with the historical Jesus. But both the style and the contents of it show that it was produced at a much later stage of the life of the church than in the first generation of the disciples.

Faith is perceived as trust in what God has declared and accomplished through Jesus, but as a fixed and unchanging body of truth that was "once for all delivered to the saints" (3). The community of the faithful has been corrupted by infiltration of ungodly individuals who are doomed to divine condemnation. That process of purgation of the unworthy has precedent in the biblical tradition: the unfaithful among the people of Israel were destroyed after leaving Egypt; the wicked who lived in Sodom and Gomorrah had fire from God fall on them (Gen 19); the wicked angels are imprisoned as they await divine judgment; those who rebelled against God perished (Gen 4:3–8; Num 22–24); Cain committed the first murder; Korah led a rebellion against God. Those who have lived and acted in such ways are doomed for destruction.

It was Enoch, in whose name apocalyptic writings were produced in the centuries before and after the turn of the eras, who is said to have predicted the coming of myriads of angels to judge and punish the wicked (14–16). These predictions are said to have been reaffirmed by the apostles, and already the corrupters and perverters of the truth are at work among God's people—who are here called to maintain a firm stand on their "most holy faith" as they await eternal life (20–21). The wavering are to be snatched from the fire, and all are to rely upon God through Christ to keep them true to the faith and "without blemish" in their way of life (24).

2 Peter

Although the letter purports to have been written by Peter the apostle (1:1), its clear dependence upon the Letter of Jude and its use of Stoic and neoplatonic philosophical concepts and terminology show that it is pseudonymous. The special knowledge and insights claimed by the author are based on his claim to have shared in the vision of the transfiguration of Christ described in the gospels (1:16–18; Matt 17:1–8; Mark 9:2–8). The goal of the faithful as here perceived is to become a "partaker of the divine nature" (1:4). The moral qualities that are thereby to be manifest are the Stoic virtues of knowledge, self-control, steadfastness, piety, brotherly affection (*philadelphia*), and love (1:5–7). By maintaining these moral qualities, one can be confident of gaining access to "the eternal kingdom of our Lord and Savior Jesus Christ" (1:10–11).

The members of the community are to be confident that God's purpose of cosmic renewal will triumph through Christ (1:16–19), but they should deplore the fact that corruption of the faithful will occur through false teachers and prophets (2:1–22). The corrupt will deny the triumphant coming of Christ, ignoring the fact that God's computation of time is utterly different from that of humans, so that "a thousand years is as one day" (3:8). The faithful must persevere in confidence that the divine punishment will come on the earth and then the vindication of the righteous will occur (3:11–13). The author's wrestling with the problem of the delay of Christ's return—as well as the designation of the letters of Paul as "scripture" (3:16)—point to the probability that this work was produced at a late date, well into the second century CE.

James

The identity of the author of the Letter of James cannot be determined with certainty. The Greek version of the name, *Iakobos*, is obviously a transliteration from the Hebrew, Jacob, and is used in the New Testament with reference to at least five different men: (1) James, a disciple of Jesus, the son of Zebedee and brother of the disciple John (Mark 1:19–20; 3:17); (2) James, the son of Alphaeus and a disciple of Jesus (Mark 3:18; Acts 1:13); (3) James, the father of Jesus' disciple, Judas (Luke 6:18); (4) James, the brother of Jesus,[186] who was initially hostile to him and his message (Mark 3:21, 31–35), but who became a follower of Jesus, a witness to his resurrection (1 Cor 15:7), and a leader in the Jerusalem church (Gal 2:1–12); (5) the author of the Letter of James (James 1:1).[187]

A perceptive and useful indicator of the subject matter of this writing is provided by the topical headings included in the New Revised Standard Version:

Faith and Wisdom (1:2–8)

Poverty and Riches (1:9–11)

Trial and Temptation (1:12–18)

Hearing and Doing the Word (1:19–26)

Warning against Partiality (2:1–13)

Faith without Works is Dead (2:14–26)

Taming the Tongue (3:1–12)

Two Kinds of Wisdom (3:13–18)

Friendship with the World (4:1–10)

Warning against Judging Another (4:11)

Boasting about Tomorrow (4:13–17)

Warning to Rich Oppressors (5:1–6)

Patience in Suffering (5:7–12)

The Prayer of Faith (5:13–20)

A common assumption has been that it was the brother of Jesus who wrote this book, but the rather sophisticated Greek literary style, the evidence of impact from Stoic thought, and the learned vocabulary of this writing—as well as substantive differences in content from the Jesus tradition—point to its having been written by someone steeped in Graeco-Roman culture, including exposure to Greek philosophical traditions.[188] Although there are references to specifics of Jewish law (such as adultery and murder),[189] the perception of law as universal and obligatory for all humanity is offered in a perspective akin to Stoicism. This wisdom "from above" is identified as *logos*—word of truth (1:18)—and is detailed in terms close to the Stoic notion of universal reason. Thus, the prototype for the Letter of James is Jewish wisdom tradition of the type strongly influenced by Hellenistic philosophy, such as is evident in the Wisdom of Solomon.

The writer addresses his readers on the ground that members of the new community are wealthy, unscrupulous, and self-serving—which scarcely fits the emphasis in the gospels on proclaiming "good news to the poor." There is a solemn warning about the punishment that will come to unscrupulous members who have cheated others, including their employees, and have wallowed in luxurious living (5:1–6). Instead of attention to the basic details of the death and resurrection of Christ, the religious orientation is defined in the more abstract terms of "pure and genuine religion" (*threshkeia*).

There are no specifics of doctrine in James. Indeed, there are no allusions in this writing to the suffering, death, or resurrection of Christ. The emphasis here is instead on human obligation to conform to divine law, which fits the viewpoint of such Cynic-Stoic philosophers of the early centuries CE as Seneca and Epictetus. There is no evidence of an impact from the New Testament commandment to love God and neighbor, or any other of the details of either the ethics of Jesus or the concept of the moral renewal effected by the Holy Spirit that one finds in Paul and in the Gospel of John. Indeed, the book seems to embody a reaction against the Pauline perception of salvation by grace. As already noted, this writing has no reference to the crucifixion or resurrection of Christ, which are so central for Paul and for the passion narratives included in the canonical gospels. Instead, there is a plea to those who "wander from the truth" that they will conform to correct doctrine. This will result in the salvation of the soul from death and "cover a multitude of sins" (5:19). There is evidence for formal procedures to be carried out by church leaders for care of the ill—praying for them and anointing them with oil (5:14–15)—and for confession of sins (5:16). Institutional structures and rules for the community seem to have developed here in ways analogous to those evident in the deuteropauline letters.

The suitability of James for inclusion within the New Testament canon has been a matter of dispute from early times in the life of the church, and the relationship of its perception of the law to the viewpoints of Paul and the gospels has been debated for centuries. Martin Luther wanted to dismiss James from the New Testament, but—as noted below[190]—it was included in the canon, and serves as clear evidence of the diversity that was operative in early Christianity, and of the range and depth of influence effective there literarily and conceptually from the wider Graeco-Roman world.

Anonymous Apostolic Tradition: The Letter to the Hebrews

Although designated in the Authorized and Revised Versions as "The Epistle of the Apostle Paul to the Hebrews," the authorship of this "letter" has been debated from the early centuries of the common era. Pantaenus—who about 180 CE left his post as head of the school of Christian studies in Alexandria to serve as a missionary in India—asserted that this letter was written by Paul. But his successor, Clement of Alexandria, said that Paul had written it originally in Hebrew, which was then translated into Greek by Luke. He added that the stylistic difference of this letter from the others by Paul was the result of Luke's translation, and that the omission of Paul's name as author was out of deference to the "Hebrews," since he was "a preacher and apostle of the Gentiles."[191]

Origen of Alexandria, however, noted the radical difference between the "apostle's rudeness . . . in style" and the superior Greek of this writing. He concluded that, while "the thoughts are the apostle's . . . the style and composition belong to one who called to mind the apostle's teachings, and as it were, made short notes of what the apostle said." But as for "who wrote the epistle, in truth God knows"![192]

Origen's conclusion about the identity of the author is surely correct, but the conceptual framework in which the role of Jesus and the nature of the new covenant people are portrayed in this writing is significantly different from that in the genuine letters of Paul.[193] Further, the form of this writing is markedly different from that of Paul's letters. Missing are the epistolary introductions and conclusions, although there are a few personal notes and greetings at the end (13:22–25). Mention of "those who come from Italy" may indicate that the author was writing to the church in Rome, and was sending greetings from Italian expatriates who were then in the region from which this writing was sent. But the genus of this "letter" is that of a treatise rather than an epistle. Its style and concepts are closer to that of sophisticated Jewish wisdom tradition—especially of the Wisdom of Solomon—including Greek philosophical and rhetorical modes. Anthony Saldarini has noted how that Jewish work describes wisdom in Greek categories and builds on the Platonic philosophy of emanations, including the contrast between timeless archetype and time-bound types or copies of the ideal realities.[194] This philosophical contrast is an essential feature of the Letter to the Hebrews, in explicit statements and in the imagery that is used to portray the role of Jesus and the new community that has come into being through him.

From the opening lines of this work and throughout it, there is evidence of the impact of Platonic-type perceptions of the divine, of the universe, and of human destiny—synthesized with Jewish wisdom concepts. The contrast between the many messages from God conveyed through the prophets and the ultimate word communicated through the "Son" (1:1–2a) recall the Platonic distinction between the eternal ideas and the ephemeral copies. Christ is the one through whom the world was created; the one in whom the radiant glory of God as well as the nature and purpose of God are disclosed; and the one through whom sin and evil are overcome. All the features of the created world are subject to change, but Jesus is God's Son—the eternal model of the divine—and the agent of divine rule of the universe, seated "at the right hand of the Majesty on high" (1:3–12).

In keeping with the Jewish tradition, a major role of Christ is to overcome the powers of evil and to transform the people of God from their sinful state into a holy community. Christ is depicted in 2:10 as the agent and prototype of this program of divine renewal. The term used here with reference to Jesus, *archegos*, is found in Plato as (1) a depiction of ultimate being—the greatest and first leader of all the elements[195]—by which their role is shaped, and (2) as the ruling power of all that is.[196] Throughout this writing there are contrasts between temporal and eternal—the former represented by historical individuals and practices, and the latter by Christ and his divinely determined role of human renewal. It is God, the creator and sustainer of the universe, who is accomplishing this salvific purpose for his people through Jesus, who is seen as God's agent—both eternal and historically disclosed.

Before continuing the description of the process through Christ of the transformation of God's people, one should note the range of images by which both Christ and the people are depicted in Hebrews. As noted above, Jesus is designated as Son of God and primary agent (*archegos*) of human renewal. The identification of Jesus as son in 1:5–14 builds on scriptural pronouncements. Hebrews 1:5a is from Ps 2:7 and 2 Sam 7:14/1 Chron 17:13: these are based on the concept of God's covenant with David as king, and what is affirmed is the father/son ground of the royal relationship. Hebrews 1:6 quotes from Deut 32:43 and Ps 96:7, in which the king is described as God's "firstborn," and all the angels are instructed to worship him. Hebrews 1:7–9 contrasts the role of the angels and servants of God ("winds" and "flames"; Ps 45:6–7) with that of the Son, who is addressed as divine and told that God has "anointed [him] with the oil of gladness" and bestowed on him a "righteous scepter" with which he shall rule his "kingdom." Further, he will live and rule forever (1:10–11), unlike the time-bound heavens and earth that were created through him (Ps 45:6–7; 102:26–28). Thus, the Messiah is seen as an eternal rather than as a time-based person. Yet change will come in the course of his reign: the angels will be God's agents to overcome the powers of evil and to minister to the needs of those who share in the life of God's people and thus "obtain salvation" (1:12–14; Ps 110:1). The eschatological contrast in the Jewish traditions between the present age and the age to come (when God's purpose triumphs) has been adapted in Hebrews to the ontological contrast between temporal and eternal reality, in the Greek philosophical tradition.

The roles of Christ as perceived in this writing are likewise described as moving beyond the time-bound experiences of historic Israel and embodying eternity. The people of Israel who had left Egypt for the promised land under the leadership of Moses and Joshua were not permitted to enter that place of "rest" because of their disobedience and lack of trust in God (3:16–4:8). David is said to have continued to warn against disobedience that would prevent the people from entering the place of rest (3:7; Ps 95:7).

What will prepare people "to enter that rest" is for them to be open to the penetrating, morally critical power of "the living, active word of God" that has come through Jesus, and that—in implied contrast to the law of Moses, which did not produce this moral renewal—penetrates and transforms "the thoughts and intentions of the heart" (4:12). Unlike the temporally, morally, and functionally limited roles of the high priests of historic Israel, Jesus is the "high priest forever"[197]—the eternal and "perfect" model (5:8–10). Melchizedek is the appropriate prototype of Christ as high priest for the author of Hebrews, since the lack of mention of ancestry or lifespan of Melchizedek in the scriptures where one might expect it (Gen 14:17–20) is here perceived as an indication that he was a timeless divine being, and thus "resembles the Son of God" in his eternal priesthood (7:3). Christ is the eternal, "holy, blameless, unstained, separated from sinners, exalted above the heavens" priest—a status depicted in conformity to the Platonic concept of the ideal.

That perception is described more fully in 8:1–7, where the "true"—that is, ideal and eternal—priest serves in the true sanctuary, of which the earthly temple is only "a copy and shadow" (8:5). Indeed, Moses was enabled by God to see the eternal model, "the heavenly sanctuary," but the earthly copy and the cultic activity carried out there did not fulfill the function that God intended as the basis for his relationship with his covenant people. That has now been accomplished through Christ's "more excellent ministry," which has come to fruition in "the true tent"—the heavenly, eternal ideal (8:5–7). Similar contrasts are set forth in this writing concerning the true covenant of God with his people (8:8–12; 9:15–22), the true sanctuary (9:15–22), and the perfect sacrifice of Christ (9:23–28). The cultic system enjoined in the Law is no more than a "shadow" of the substance: the realities are those that have been accomplished through Christ and that are now eternally effective in the renewal of the covenant people (10:1–4).

Christ's offering of himself is the ultimate sacrifice, and has confirmed the words of scripture that contrasted the emptiness of the sacrificial system enjoined in the Law with true dedication and full obedience to God's will, as set forth in the Psalms (Heb 10:5–8 = Ps 40:7–9). Again are contrasted the repeated, ineffective sacrifices under the legal code with the single, perfect sacrifice of Christ, which results in the inner moral renewal ("hearts, minds") of God's people (10:9–18). Consonant with Platonic theory, there is a sharp distinction here between the eternal ideal and the imperfect copies, and between the changing external evidence and the inwardly perceived, changeless truth. Those who discern that truth "with full assurance of faith" will have their minds renewed ("[their] hearts sprinkled from an evil conscience") and their outward lives purified ("washed with pure water," 10:2).

Further, the images of the new people of God set forth in Hebrews are communal rather than individualistic. Four may be noted: (1) house, (2) covenant people, (3) heavenly sanctuary, (4) city of the living God.

House

In 3:1–6 are contrasted the roles of Moses and Jesus within God's house— that is, where God dwells among his people. Moses is depicted as a faithful servant who conveyed to the people God's promises and intentions for them, preparing them for what God would declare to them in the future. But Jesus' role is that of the son of the builder of the house—God. That dwelling place of God is the new community, in which the members participate based on confidence and pride in the hope as to what God is doing and has promised for his people.

In 10:21, the "house of God" is pictured by the imagery of the sanctuary, access to which has been provided through "the blood of Jesus." He is the one who presides over this house as "great priest," and through him the members of this people come to God with hearts that have "full assurance of faith," "hearts sprinkled clean from an evil conscience," and "bodies washed with pure water." God's people within this new "house" may now participate in the functions and transforming effects of the historic temple and its cultus.

New Covenant People

Interwoven with the theme of the new covenant that God has established with his people through Jesus is the image of the heavenly sanctuary where they now have access to the presence of God. Before turning to the details of that model, we may consider details of the new covenant. Jesus is declared to have been given "a more excellent ministry than that of Moses"—who initially shaped the covenant people by conveying to them the law of God and by establishing the portable sanctuary where God was present among them. But now Jesus is said to be "the mediator of a better covenant" than the one based on conformity to the law of Moses—the ineffectiveness of which is evident in the necessity for God to have announced through the prophet Jeremiah his intention to "establish a *new* covenant" (8:6–7). Hebrews then offers an extensive quotation from Jer 31:31–34 in which the promise of the new covenant is contrasted with the one that was "made with the ancestors" as they were being led out of Egypt (8:8–9). Now God's purpose for and expectations from his people will not be set down on tablets of stone, as the Torah was, but inscribed "in their minds" and "on their hearts" (8:10). The basis of this new relationship will be direct, personal knowledge of God on the part of all the people, "from the least of them to the greatest" (8:11). The divine response will be mercy and forgiveness toward their sins (8:12). Once more, the emphasis on internal moral renewal rather than external laws is consonant with Platonic ethical concepts.

There follows in 9:1–10 a sketch of access to God's presence and the repeated mode of redemption of human sin as set forth in the old covenant, which is then contrasted with the basis of the new covenant, by which Christ's sacrifice has taken place "once for all at the end of the age" (9:26). His total devotion to the will of God has made his "single sacrifice" effective for all who trust in him (10:12–18). Part of the quotation from Jeremiah is repeated (10:16–17 = Jer 31:33–34), which leads to the declaration of the new way that Christ has opened the way into the presence of God for participants in the new covenant people.

The Heavenly Sanctuary

Hebrews 9 presents a somewhat detailed picture of the "earthly sanctuary," including the lampstand, the Bread of the Presence, the altar of incense and ark of the covenant (which contained the manna), Aaron's rod that budded,[198] and the tablets of the covenant that Moses is said to have received from God on the mountain and then to have taken down to the people[199] (9:1–5). Above the ark were the winged angels, the cherubim, symbolizing the presence of God among his people at the mercy seat in this most holy place.[200] It is into the presence of God—the heavenly sanctuary—that Jesus has gone, taking his blood as purification of the "conscience" of his people, having offered himself as a sacrifice "through the eternal Spirit" (9:11–14), thereby "securing an eternal redemption." This is in contrast to the oft-repeated sacrifices offered in the earthly temple. The ontological contrast is made explicit in 9:23–24, which describes the earthly sanctuary as a transitory copy of the heavenly archetype of the divine presence—a concept closely resembling the Platonic distinction between an ideal or archetype and its earthly copy. Christ's sacrifice was presented once-for-all in the heavenly abode of God. From there he will one day return to earth to gather his forgiven and purified new covenant people (9:26–28).

The law of Moses, with its call for repeated sacrifices, cannot effect true human renewal. But Christ has achieved that through his complete commitment and conformity to the will of God, as foreseen in Ps 40:7–9. His "single sacrifice" has brought about the moral perfection of all those who are "sanctified" through trusting in his self-offering—accomplished on earth and accepted in heaven. The new relationship to God that this effects results in the inner acceptance of and moral conformity to the intent of the divine law. It is on the basis of "the blood of Jesus" that the new community has "confidence to enter the sanctuary" (10:19).

City of the Living God

That community is also pictured in Hebrews as the city of God. Abraham had been willing to move about as an itinerant and a sojourner—living in tents, as did his descendants, Isaac and Jacob—although all of them shared in the covenant of promise. This tradition is now to culminate in a new structure for God's people: "the city which has foundations, whose builder and maker is God" (11:8–10). Jacob and his innumerable descendants in the covenant community, recognizing that their common life was alien to the ways of this world in which they were "strangers and exiles," looked forward to the homeland and the heavenly city that God was preparing for them (11:11–16). Hence, Jacob expected the exodus of the Israelites; Moses prepared to lead his people out of Egypt to the promised land. They subsequently experienced success in conquering the new land, but also conflict and persecution, "wandering over deserts and mountains, and in dens and caves of the earth" (11:38). Yet they did not "receive what was promised" (11:39), because God had foreseen for his people "something better," which has now been fully revealed to the new community (11:40). They have now "come to Mt. Zion and to the city of the living God, the heavenly Jerusalem . . . and to the assembly of the first-born who are enrolled in heaven, and to a judge who is God of all, and to Jesus, the mediator of a new covenant" (12:22–24). The shared life of the people of God for whom God's purpose of renewal has been achieved is here pictured as the true city of God. In the present, earthly situation, God's people have no enduring city: instead, they seek "the city which is to come"—the community through and for whom the divine purpose in the creation of the world and of the human race is to achieve its ideal goal (13:14). They are now being prepared for this new mode and context of life as the covenant people through the Christ who dwells among them and through whom the will of God is being accomplished (13:20–21).

The perspective in which the destiny of these people is viewed is thus a combination of the Judaeo-Christian eschatological view and the ontological assumptions about reality that had developed in those traditions, based on Platonic philosophy. The way was being prepared for the emergence of Platonic interpretation of the Christian tradition evident in the so-called Alexandrine school represented by Clement and Origen, which built on the intellectual strategy of Jews in Alexandria before the common era, as represented most extensively by Philo. It was this kind of synthesis of biblical tradition and Platonic ontology that was to have such profound and enduring impact on the intellectual life and thought of the Christian community.

Notes

1. The probably authentic letters of Paul included in the New Testament are Galatians, Romans, 1 and 2 Thessalonians, Philippians, and Philemon. The evidence concerning the authentic and the pseudonymous letters of Paul is considered below.

2. As noted above (136), Acts was written as vol. 2 following the Gospel of Luke. It was probably written a generation after Paul's lifetime, but in spite of its stylized accounts of Paul's activities and preaching, it very likely includes some historically valuable information as well as some adaptation and additions. The historical method of Acts is discussed in Excursus 1, Changing Historical Models in the Biblical Tradition, where Acts is perceived as a useful though tendentious historical source, especially in relation to the Graeco-Roman literary mode, the romance. Acts certainly embodies a reconstruction of the aims and significance of Paul's work, and is here used cautiously as a historical source.

3. These writings are analyzed and evaluated later this chapter, in "Paul as Portrayed in Letters Attributed to Him," "The Apocryphal Pauline Writings," and "The Apostles as Portrayed in the Apocryphal Acts." Information that is likely compatible with or supplemental to the letters of Paul is included in the reconstruction of the life and thought of Paul offered here.

4. The translations, with useful introductions to these writings, appear in *New Testament Apocrypha* (2 vols.; rev. ed.; ed. W. Schneemelcher; trans. R. McL. Wilson; Louisville, KY: Westminster/John Knox, 1992), 2:42–53, 213–70.

5. The so-called deuteropauline writings, especially the Pastorals: 1 and 2 Timothy and Titus.

6. Clearly, the chief example is the Acts of the Apostles. Its importance and significance as a source for knowledge of Paul's apostolic career are noted in its correlations with and differences from Paul's own letters.

7. Some scholars would add 2 Thessalonians to this deuteropauline list, but the reasons for its probable authenticity are offered below, 239.

8. The romance and its historical mode are discussed in Excursus 1, Changing Historical Models in the Biblical Tradition.

9. The details and descriptions of these features of the Acts account are based on my commentary on Acts, *To Every Nation under Heaven* (Harrisburg, PA: Trinity Press International, 1997).

10. Mark 3:17; 5:37.

11. This was distinct from the Egyptian area, which became dominated by the Ptolemies as successors to Alexander the Great.

12. These cities are listed by the Roman historian Pliny the Elder (23–79 CE) as Damascus, Philadelphia (Amman), Raphana, Scythopolis (Beth Shan, Beisan), Gadara, Hippos, Dion, Pella, Gerasa, and Canatha.

13. In the letters of Paul, there is no reference to himself by the name of Saul, but it may have been used by him in an Aramaic-speaking environment. Since his mission was to reach out to the Gentile world, it is understandable that in this role he would have been identified solely by his Greek name, *Paulos*.

14. Herod Agrippa II was the son of Agrippa I and the great-grandson of Herod. Brought up in Rome at the court of the emperor Claudius (ruled from 41–54 CE), he was only 17 when his father died. The emperor Gaius Caligula (37–41 CE) had made him king of the region north and east of the Sea of Galilee, but Claudius had considerably enlarged his realm to include Judea and Samaria, and Nero (54–68 CE) added the district of Tiberias. It was this Herod who urged the Romans to send troops when his initial efforts failed to halt the Jewish revolt in 66 CE. As reported by Josephus (*Jewish Wars* 2.344–407), he tried in vain to persuade the Jewish leaders that their effort to gain independence would result in the destruction of Jerusalem and its temple—as it did.

15. In rabbinic literature, Gamaliel is identified as "Gamaliel the Elder." In the Pirke Abot section of the Mishnah, he is listed as one of the patriarchs of Judaism, but Jacob Neusner has noted the absence from the Gamaliel material of any discussion of the issues of table fellowship and purity rules that were of paramount importance for the Pharisees. Neusner has conjectured that Gamaliel was a public official rather than a leader of the sect of the Pharisees (in his *The Pharisees: Rabbinic Perspectives* [Hoboken, NJ: KTAV, 1985], 23–58).

16. 1 Cor 15:42–50; Rom 1:3–6; 1 Thess 4:13–18.

17. According to Acts 9:23–25, Saul (Paul) was similarly rescued from hostile Jews in Damascus.

18. The quotation combines elements from Joel 2:28–32 and Zech 12:10.

19. Gal 3:13; Deut 21:23. Since Jesus spoke of his impending death in terms of a broken body (Mark 14:22), it is possible that he expected to be executed by stoning, the standard Jewish mode of execution for those who were considered guilty of blasphemy (Lev 24:15–16; 1 Kgs 21:9–14) or who encouraged the worship of other gods (Deut 13:6–10). Instead, he was put to death by the standard Roman mode: crucifixion.

20. A report of an ancient escape over a city wall in a basket is found in Josh 2:15.

21. The nature of the dispute with the Hellenists is discussed in my study of Acts, *To Every Nation Under Heaven*, 88–89, 122–23.

22. The Greek text reads, literally, "in me," which may be understood as the vision occurring as inward experience, but he perceives this seeing Christ as of the same order as his appearances to the other apostles.

23. This James is identified by Paul (1:19) as "the Lord's brother"—a relationship also asserted in Mark 6:3, where the brothers and sisters of Jesus are mentioned (cf. Matt 13:55).

24. Agrippa I reigned in Palestine from 41–44 CE.

25. *Pseudadelphous*; literally, "false brothers."

26. SBLSBS 13; Missoula, MT: Scholars Press, 1978, 15.

27. Ibid.

28. Elymas sounds Semitic, but has no parallel use and does not mean "magician." See my *To Every Nation under Heaven*.

29. *Tōn sebomenōn proselutēn*.

30. The region dominated by the Gauls until the Roman takeover of the whole of Asia Minor in the first century BCE was a part of the larger area that was designated as the province of Galatia by the Romans. There is no mention of Paul's having visited cities in the northern part of the province, which was the older Galatian territory. The reference to Galatia in 2 Tim 4:10 and 1 Pet 1:1 seem clearly to refer to the province rather than to the northern territory.

31. The term, "make disciples" (*mathēteuein*) appears in the New Testament only here (14:21) and three times in Matthew (13:52; 27:57; 28:19). In all these occurrences, it implies a more formal instructional program for those who have joined the covenant community rather than merely conversion.

32. See Excursus 7, The Kingdom of God in the Pauline Letters.

33. Stephen's evangelism in Phoenicia is described as having been limited to Jewish hearers. But the conversion of Samaritans is reported in Acts 8:4–13—approval of which by the apostles receives divine confirmation in the outpouring of the Holy Spirit on these Samaritan converts (8:14–17).

34. See n. 23 above. This is James, the brother of Jesus, as indicated by Paul in Gal 1:19.

35. See Excursus 7, The Kingdom of God in the Pauline Letters.

36. Some ancient manuscripts of Acts omit the phrase "and from what is strangled." This is apparently a reference to the rule laid down in Lev 17:15 against eating meat from animals that were not properly slaughtered. From this omission, some interpreters of Acts have concluded that the decision of the apostles did not include any ritual issues, but concerned only moral and basically religious issues: idolatry, lack of chastity, and murder (shedding of blood). Other scholars have assumed a link between these rules and those set forth in the rabbinic tractate, *Sanhedrin*, in which the seven commandments are given to Noah and his sons are said to be binding on all humanity. But this rabbinic text dates from later than Acts (as late as the sixth century CE). A more plausible link is with Lev 17–18, where rules are set forth on the same issues raised here in Acts: eating meat offered to idols, partaking of blood, eating meat not properly slaughtered, and having sexual intercourse with someone of close kin. A fuller analysis of this passage from Acts in relation to Jewish law is set forth in my commentary on Acts, *To Every Nation Under Heaven*, 181–82.

37. Another designation for this assistance to "the poor" is "the contribution for the saints" (1 Cor 16:1–3). The Gentile churches of Corinth and Galatia were directed by Paul to take up weekly collections and retain them until he came and dispatched their authorized representative to take the gifts to Jerusalem. An extended section of 2 Corinthians (8–9) includes commendation for the generosity of the churches in Macedonia and Corinth in collecting these contributions for "the saints"—the members of the Jerusalem community. Further praise is for the Gentiles, who have shared in "spiritual blessings" with the saints in Jerusalem and have now also been of service to them by sharing "their material blessings" (Rom 15:26).

38. First Peter is one of those writings that represent the subsequent development of the church, its organization and doctrine, from a generation later than that of the historic apostles.

39. Discussed below in "Letters Attributed to Paul."

40. The letters at the beginning of the Revelation to John (1–3) are addressed to "the seven churches of Asia," which were located in the area where Paul was forbidden to go in Acts16:7.

41. Athens is merely mentioned in 1 Thess 3:1 as a place where Paul, Silvanus, and Timothy were present. Beroea is not referred to at all in Paul's letters.

42. Called Priscilla in Acts 18:2, 18, 26, she is identified as Prisca by Paul (1 Cor 16:19; Rom 16:3).

43. Robert Jewett, *A Chronology of Paul's Life* (Philadelphia: Fortress Press, 1979), 96–104.

44. A. Deissmann, *Light from the Ancient East* (trans. L. R. M. Strachan; New York and London: Harper, 1927), 227–29.

45. See Excursus on "Bridal Imagery in the Mysteries of the Kabeiroi and of Serapis."

46. A survey of the documents attesting the spread of these ancient mysteries is offered by Douglas Edwards in *Religion and Power: Pagans, Jews and Christians in the Greek East* (Oxford: Oxford University Press, 1996), 32–33. An inscription from Thessalonica may be found in *New Documents Illustrating Early Christianity* (ed. G. H. R. Horsley; North Ryle, Australia: Macquarrie University Press, 1981), 1:31, which describes a man being instructed by the god Serapis to worship him and Isis. Coins of the Graeco-Roman period from various parts of Asia Minor attest the widespread worship of these deities perceived as agents for enabling devotees to share in the divine life and to benefit from their healing powers.

47. These are declared to be the three chief qualities of the community at the end of perhaps the most famous passage in Paul's letters, the hymn of love in 1 Cor 13, where love is said to be "the greatest" (13:12).

48. This is the single reference to Athens in the letters of Paul. Unlike Acts (17:16–34), he gives no report of his activities there.

49. The apocalyptic writings and testaments in the Old Testament Pseudepigrapha include the following:

Apocalypse of Abraham	*Questions of Ezra*
Apocalypse of Adam	*Revelation of Ezra*
Testament of Adam	*Vision of Ezra*
3 Baruch	*Fragments of Pseudo-Greek Poets*
Apocalypse of Daniel	*Testament of Job*
Apocalypse of Elijah	*Testament of Moses*
1 Enoch	*Apocalypse of Sedrach*
2 Enoch	*Treatise of Shem*
3 Enoch	*Sibylline Oracles*
Apocryphon of Ezekiel	*Testament of Solomon*
Fourth Book of Ezra	*Testaments of the 3 Patriarchs*
Greek Apocalypse of Ezra	*Testaments of the 12 Patriarchs*
	Apocalypse of Zephaniah

These documents are found in this sequence in translation, with introductions and notes, in *The Old Testament Pseudepigrapha* (vol. 1; ed. James H. Charlesworth; Garden City, NY: Doubleday, 1983).

50. *The Sybilline Oracles* are translated and annotated by J. J. Collins in *The Old Testament Pseudopigrapha* (ed. James H. Charlesworth; Garden City, NY: Doubleday, 1985).

51. See Excursus 7, The Kingdom of God in the Pauline Letters.

52. The term used here for "the rebellious movement," *apostasia*, is used in *Jubilees* 23:14–23 with reference to an expected revolt of Israel against God's law, and by Josephus for the Jewish revolt against Rome in 66–70 CE (*Vita* 43).

53. Philo, *On the Embassy to Gaius* (Loeb Classical Library; Cambridge, MA: Harvard University Press, 1929),186–89.

54. Philo, *On the Embassy to Gaius,* 263–68. Further analysis of these passages is offered in my *The New Testament in Context: Sources and Documents* (Englewood Cliffs, NJ: Prentice-Hall, 1984), 37–42.

55. Exod 16:10; 24:16–17; 40:34; Num 20:6; Pss 24:7–10; 78:60–61.

56. The curse on one who "hangs on a tree" (Deut 21:22–23) is here perceived as having been fulfilled by the suspension of Jesus by crucifixion on a wooden cross. The legal prohibition against allowing the corpse to remain exposed over night is conformed to by the authorities in the Johannine account of the passion (19:31).

57. The image Paul uses here is of being imprisoned (Gal 3:22–23): the law divided the people of Israel from everyone else.

58. Self-control, *egkrateia*, is a common term in later Stoicism, but appears infrequently in the Septuagint (Sir 18:29; 4 Macc 5:34; *Letter of Aristeas* 278) and only three times in the New Testament: Acts 24:25; 2 Pet 3:7; and here in Gal 5:23. In the Stoic tradition, it was used with reference to the human capacity to exercise moral influence based on what one knew inherently through the inner power of reason (*logos*).

59. Horace, *Satires* 1.4, 142ff.; Tacitus, *History*, vol. 5.

60. Josephus, *Jewish Antiquities* 18.81–83.

61. Paul mentions in 16:5 the *ekklesia* that meets in the house of Prisca and Aquila, but makes no reference to a *proseuche* as a place of meeting, which was the term in use in the late first-century Jewish tradition, as evident from its occurrence in Acts 16:13. My essay, "Defining the First Century C.E. Synagogue," which deals with the relation of *proseuche* to *synagoge*, is in *The Evolution of the Synagogue* (Harrisburg, PA: Trinity Press International, 1999), 17–26.

62. Philo, *On the Embassy to Gaius* 155–58. Initially, this favorable policy toward Jews in Rome was continued by Tiberius.

63. A study of funerary inscriptions recovered from this period in Rome shows that of the 534 Jewish inscriptions found in catacombs in Rome, 405 were in Greek, 123 were in Latin, only five use Hebrew or Aramaic, and one of the latter is in Greek and Latin (J. B. Frey, *Corpus inscriptionum iudicarum* (Vatican City: Institute of Christian Archaeology, 1936–1952), I:lxv–lxvi. Cited by Joseph Fitzmyer, *Romans: A New Translation with Introduction and Commentary* (AB; New York: Doubleday, 1993), 33:89–90.

64. Philo, *On the Embassy to Gaius* 23, (156).

65. A superbly perceptive analysis of the evidence for the original form and content of Romans is offered by Joseph Fitzmyer in his masterful commentary on this letter. He concludes that, in spite of scholarly conjectures about the composite origins of the letter, it was written as a unit, with the exception of 16:25–27, which he considers to have been a later addition. In one manuscript, it appears after chap. 14, and in another, after chap. 15. It is, in any case, wholly compatible with the thought of Paul in Romans and in his other letters.

66. Fitzmyer, *Romans*, 73, 79.

67. Ibid., 92.

68. It is found also in Rom 6:17 and 16:26, and resembles a similar phrase in 2 Cor 9:13.

69. The composite quotation in 2:10–18 derives from Ps 14:1, 3; 14:2; 53:3; 5:9; 140:3; 36:1. Rom 2:15–17 is based on Isa 59:7–8, with influence from Prov 1:16.

70. The quotation derives from Isa 59:20–21; 27:9; cf. Ps 14:7; 53:6; 110:2.

71. Wilmington, DE: Michael Glazier, 1988; 134–37.

72. Ibid.

73. 1 Thess 4:15; 1 Cor 15:51.

74. Timothy is also indicated as joint sender of 1 and 2 Thessalonians, 2 Corinthians, Philippians, and Colossians. The two letters addressed to him, 1 and 2 Timothy, are from after the time of Paul, as discussed below.

75. The theory that Archippus was the head of the household addressed by Paul in Philemon and the owner of the slave Onesimus is not persuasive (John Gillman, "Archippus," *Anchor Bible Dictionary* (vol. 1; ed. D. N. Freedman; New York: Doubleday, 1992).

76. S. Scott Bartchy provides a detailed, perceptive analysis of this letter in his article on Philemon in the *ABD*, 5:305–10. His equally insightful study, "Slavery in the Greco-Roman World," in which he analyzes features of slavery as they bear on the events that form the narrative background for Philemon, is in *ABD* 6:65–73.

77. In the Greek text, every occurrence of "you" from v. 4 through 22a is in the singular. This is clearly a primarily personal communication, though at the end greetings are also extended to the community as a whole (vv. 22b–25).

78. The attempt by Allen D. Callahan in *Embassy of Onesimus: The Letter of Paul to Philemon* (Valley Forge, PA: Trinity Press International, 1997) to show that Onesimus was not a slave but the brother of Philemon is totally unconvincing. Clearly, "brother" in v. 16 means a fellow member of the covenant community, not a literal sibling.

79. In *Pro Flacco* 68.

80. *Gnosis* occurs in Paul's letters eighteen times; more than half of the instances have negative connotations. Excursus 3 is an analysis of the background of Gnosticism and its impact on early Christianity.

81. The term, *stoicheion*, obviously is linked with Stoics, whose view is that the world consists of matter (*hyle*) that is formed and moves by reason (*logos*). Of the four basic elements—earth, air, fire, water—fire is the most important and produces the other three. The reasonable power that formed and operates the universe is *logos*, and it is the manifestation of the ultimate creative power that the Stoics called Zeus. In the Hellenistic period of Judaism, those who worshiped the elements were denounced (Wis 12:2–3), as they are by Paul in Gal 4:8–10, where *stoicheia* is used with reference to the cultic requirements based on the calendar and set forth in the Jewish law. In Colossians, however, the term is used in the more abstract sense of the cosmic elements.

82. Evident pervasively in Philo's allegorical method of interpreting scripture.

83. Most notably, in Origen's *Commentary on the Gospel of John*.

84. Eph. 4:8 is a paraphrase of Ps 68:18, which describes someone—probably God—ascending Mount Sinai and receiving gifts from the people, including non-Israelites. In the interpretation of this verse in Ephesians, God is the donor, not the recipient of the gifts: instead, they are divine enablements, not material grants.

85. The attack on those who promote the law of Moses among members of the new community is the major theme in the first half of Paul's letter to the Romans, as well as in Galatians.

86. Analysis of Christology is offered in the studies of the Gospel of John and the letters of John.

87. The term *theosebeia*, widely used in the Graeco-Roman literature for "fear of God" or religiousness, is found only here in the New Testament.

88. The term translated "bishop" is *episkopos*, which means "overseer," but in Titus 1:5–9 it seems to be equated with elder (*presbyteros*).

89. "In the Spirit" could connote by the Holy Spirit, or in the new body fashioned and empowered by the Spirit for the people of faith.

90. Bentley Layton, *The Gnostic Scriptures* (New York: Doubleday, 1987).

91. An analysis of Gnosticism and its origins in response to the later Platonic tradition is offered in Excursus 3, 443–50. In *The Gnostic Scriptures*, Bentley Layton offers a translation of the gnostic texts and a perceptive introduction and analysis of these documents.

92. The Greek term here, *didaskalia*, is often translated "doctrine," but the connotation of the term here and throughout the deuteropauline letters is closer to that of moral instruction.

93. Eccl 5:15–16; Job 1:21.

94. The future kingdom of God is a major feature in the synoptic gospel tradition, but also has a significant role in the thought of Paul. He indicates what qualities characterize those who will share in the new circumstances of God's rule over his people—a context of righteousness, peace, and joy in the Holy Spirit, rather than by strict adherence to such laws as the dietary rules (Rom 14:17). Yet moral failure will result in disqualification for sharing in the kingdom: excluded are the "fornicators, idolaters, adulterers, male prostitutes, sodomites, thieves, the greedy, drunkards, revilers, robbers" (1 Cor 6:9–10). In Gal 5:19–21, a similar list of modes of sinful behavior—"the works of the flesh"—repeats that such an immoral way of life precludes sharing in the kingdom of God. 1 Thess 3:12 declares that through Christ, God calls his people to share in the kingdom of God and his glory. In 2 Thess 1:5, the persecutions and afflictions endured by the faithful come from God, but their faithfulness to God shows them to be "worthy of the kingdom of God." Similar to the texts quoted above from Paul, Eph 5:3–5 announces that those guilty of obscenity, fornication, greed, or other modes of immorality are to have no share in the kingdom of God. In 1 Tim 4:1–5, there is a warning that the time is coming when some from within the community of faith will "depart from the faith" and espouse "the doctrines of demons," insisting on radical asceticism and giving credence to "silly myths." Instead, they are to be instructed in "the words of faith and sound doctrine" (4:6) and to "train [themselves] in piety" (*eusebeia*, 4:7).

95. The term is *apothesaurizontas*, which matches the concept of good works as stored treasures—a repeated feature in the synoptic tradition: Mark 10:21; Matt 19:21; Luke 18:22; Matt 6:20–21; Luke 12:33. Yet there is no comparable image in the letters of Paul of storing up good deeds, although he does refer to the divinely granted "light of the knowledge of the glory of God in the face of Jesus Christ" as "this treasure" that is contained in the "clay jars" that are the earthly bodies of God's new people (2 Cor 4:3–7).

96. In addition to this occurrence, it appears in 1 Tim 1:6 and 2 Tim 2:18.

97. This term, *anazopurein*, appears only here in the New Testament.

98. This term is also found only here in the New Testament; it echoes the Stoic perception of morality as fostered by inner awareness of the good (conscience) and the capability to conform to that moral standard (self-control).

99. The term here is *epignosis*, a term seldom used by Paul, but frequently appearing in the deuteropauline writings, as noted above.

100. Epiphany means illumination, but in Greek usage, it connoted public disclosure or formal appearance of deities or of royalty. In Paul's letters, the more frequent term is *parousia*, which emphasizes the public presence of the person or authority involved. Paul refers to the coming of Christ in triumph eight times in his letters as *parousia*, but he also uses the word with reference to the presence of ordinary humans

(as in 1 Cor 16:17; 2 Cor 7:6–7; 10:10; Phil 1:26; 2:12). The expectations of Christ's return are in 1 Cor 15:23; 1 Thess 2:19; 3:13; 4:15; 5:23; 2 Thess 2:1, 8, 9. It appears that this expectation of Christ's coming was no longer perceived as imminent, so the term for that event shifted to the widely used designation of divine, illuminated disclosure: *epiphany*, as in 1 Tim 6:14; 2 Tim 1:10; 4:1, 8; Titus 2:13. In 2 Thess 2:8, the two terms are combined, implying that the divine disclosure of Christ (*epiphaneia*) will take place when he is visibly present on the earth among his people (*parousia*).

101. See Excursus 7, The Kingdom of God in the Pauline Letters.

102. The term used here for instruction, *didaskalia*, is found only twice in Paul and twice in the gospels, but seventeen times in the deuteropauline letters.

103. Unique to the Pastorals are the following terms; *nephalious* [temperate], *sophron* [prudent], *hieroprepes* [worthy of reverence], *katastema* [behavior].

104. The term is *sophronein*, "to be in one's right mind."

105. Statistics for this term, *didaskalia*, are offered above in n. 102. Its repeated use here shows clearly the post-Pauline emphasis on moral instruction within the church.

106. Incorruption (*aphthoria*); dignity or holiness (*semnotes*), which also is used in 1 Tim 3:4; healthy speech that cannot be censured (*akatagnostos*).

107. This is the implication of *soterios*, a term that does not appear in the letters of Paul, which connotes simply moral renewal rather than the transfer of humans from their alienated status as children of Adam, the innovator of human sin and alienation, to becoming children of God in Christ, the wholly obedient one, through his reconciling death and triumphant resurrection, as declared in 2 Cor 5:17–19.

108. *Autokatakritos*, "self-condemned," appears only here in the New Testament.

109. The form of the New Testament canon promoted by Marcion is discussed below.

110. So W. Schneemelcher in his introduction to the epistle in *New Testament Apocrypha*, 2:44.

111. Seneca, *Letters from a Stoic* (ed. and trans. Robin Campbell; New York: Penguin Books, 1969, 1982), 37.

112. The references are to the letters of Seneca, with assigned Roman numerals, in ibid.

113. An introduction, bibliography, sketch, and translation of the correspondence between Seneca and Paul is in *New Testament Apocrypha*, 2:46–53.

114. An insightful introduction and translation (with notes) of this writing are in "The Pseudo-Titus Epistle," in *New Testament Apocrypha*, 2:35–74. The quotations here are from this translation, by Aurelio di Santos Otero.

115. This is quoted from an unknown source.

116. Literally, "a unifying substance," but its intended meaning here is unclear.

117. There is no indication which "books of the patriarchs" are being referred to here.

118. In Paul's authentic letters, Titus has an important role as an associate and coworker with Paul: he accompanied Paul to Jerusalem (Gal 2:1–10) to report the success of his mission to Gentiles and was the bearer of a letter of Paul to the Corinthians (2 Cor 7:5–16), who is commended for not having taken advantage of them (12:14–18). There is no hint of his serving as a model of complete chastity, as the pseudepigraphic *Letter of Titus* implies.

119. Introductions, translations, and analyses of these texts are in *New Testament Apocrypha*, 2:75–482.

120. "Aretalogical" concerns the powers of the wonder worker; teratological features describe cosmic miracles.

121. *New Testament Apocrypha*, 2:85.

122. Ibid., 2:104.

123. Introduction, translation, and notes by Wilhem Schneemelcher in *New Testament Apocrypha*, 2:213–70.

124. Mani founded this religion in Persia in the third century CE after a mysterious voice enjoined him to abstain from wine, meat, and sex in order to prepare for sharing in the divine nature. He formed a purist sect, saw himself as a successor of the heavenly messengers—Adam, Zoroaster, Buddha, Jesus—and launched a mission to spread this universal message, which reached from India to the Atlantic and continued until the fifteenth century. Detailed analysis of the evidence for Manichean use of the apocryphal Acts is offered by Knut Schaeferdiek in *New Testament Apocrypha*, 2:87–100.

125. Introduction to these writings and translations of them are available in *New Testament Apocrypha*, 2:75–411.

126. An introduction to this document is provided by Hans-martin Schenke in *New Testament Apocrypha*, 2:412–25. The gnostic documents from Nag Hammadi were edited in translation by James M. Robinson in *The Nag Hammadi Library* (3rd ed.; San Francisco: Harper & Row, 1988). Other ancient writings linked with Gnosticism are available in translation by Bentley Layton in *The Gnostic Scriptures* (Garden City, NY: Doubleday, 1987).

127. The further designation of them as apostles does not appear in the oldest and best manuscripts of Mark. However, in Matt 10:2 and Luke 6:13; 9:10; 17:5; 22:14; and 24:10, as well as in Mark 3:13–19, they are identified as "apostles."

128. More detailed studies of this theme are in my *Good News to the Ends of the Earth: The Theology of Acts* (Philadelphia: Trinity Press International, 1990); and in *To Every Nation Under Heaven*.

129. For example, among the New Testament Apocrypha are gospels, acts, and apocalypses attributed to such apostolic figures as Peter, Philip, James, and Thomas. The texts and introductions to these writings are in *New Testament Apocrypha*, vols. 1 and 2. See n. 126 above.

130. A fuller analysis of Stephen's speech is offered in my commentary on Acts, *To Every Nation under Heaven*, 95–102.

131. Cf. Deut 23:1.

132. This includes the Roman tribune (21:30–40), the crowd before the temple (21:40–22:21), the chief priests and the council (22:30–23:10), and Felix the governor (23:23–24:27).

133. The Gospel of John is analyzed in chapter 2, "The Community of Mystical Participation" (163–92).

134. An important antecedent example of the mystical perception of Jesus as the revealer of God is in the *Odes of Solomon*, which purport to have been written by Solomon, but which seem to have been written from the outset in Greek. These Odes highlight the incarnation and the role of the Logos as the agent of complete revelation: "Blessed are they who by means [of the Logos] have understood everything, and have known the Lord in his truth" (Ode 12). Perceptive analysis of this document is provided by Johannes Quasten in *Patrology* (vol. 1; Westminster, MD: Christian Classics, 1986), 160–68.

135. Excellent analyses of Revelation to John, its origins, its literary antecedents, its aims and structure are offered (1) by W. G. Kümmel, in his study of "Apocalyptic and Apocalypses" and of "The Apocalypse of John," in his *Introduction to the New Testament* (trans. H. C. Kee; Nashville and New York: Abingdon, 1975), sec. 33 and

sec. 34, 452–74; and (2) by Adela Yarbro Collins, in "Book of Revelation" (*ABD*; New York: Doubleday, 1992), 5:694–708. Her perceptive study builds on her earlier, creative analysis in her dissertation, *The Combat Myth in the Book of Revelation* (Missoula, MT: Scholars Press, 1976). A fine commentary on Revelation is that of Frederick J. Murphy, *Fallen Is Babylon: The Revelation to John* (Harrisburg, PA: Trinity Press International, 1998).

136. The factor of foretelling through scripture is implicit in the term used here, *semaino*, which is often translated as "report" or "communicate," but which implies something that is being foretold, as when Agabus predicts a famine in Acts 11:28. The term appears in Josephus: (1) in *Jewish Antiquities* 6.50, where the story is retold of Saul and Samuel, when God reveals that it is Saul who is to rule; (2) in 8.409, where there is a report of a false prophet predicting that Ahab will conquer all of Syria (1 Kgs 22:6).

137. These figures are provided by Jean-Louis D'Aragon in his analysis of Revelation in *The Jerome Bible Commentary* (Englewood Cliffs, NJ: Prentice-Hall, 1968), 468.

138. An analysis of the *Sibylline Oracles* is offered in chapter 1.

139. The piercing of Jesus is a term based on Zech 12:10, which is a source for the prophetic note in Rev 1:7.

140. 4:1; 8:2, 6, 8, 10, 12, 13; 9:1, 13, 14; 10:7; 11:15.

141. This function of the scroll corresponds to the one depicted in Ezek 2:1–3:11: its significance is as the medium by which is to be communicated to the people the message from "the Lord God."

142. In the oracle of Balaam (Num 24:9), the promise of Israel's ability to establish a kingdom in the land of Canaan is expressed in imagery that includes a powerful lion and lioness.

143. In 17:8, there is a prediction of the destruction of the powers of evil, as well as of the earth-dwellers whose names are not written in the book of life.

144. A. Y. Collins has advanced an innovative theory about the son of man in Jewish and early Christian literature in *Cosmology and Eschatology in Jewish and Christian Apocalyptic* (JSJSup 50; ed. J. J. Collins; Leiden/New York: Brill, 1996). She proposes that Jesus spoke of the son of man, but did not identify himself by that designation. She perceives it to have been for him an alternative to other symbols of authority (emperor, messianic claimant, King Herod), and that it appears here in Revelation in a form older than in the synoptic or Q tradition as an expression of what she calls "angelic christology" (159). She concludes that in Revelation it refers to the risen Jesus, but is not a title, as it became in the gospel tradition (159–97). Yet one must take into account the fact that the use of this term in the Q and Markan traditions appear to predate the book of Revelation.

145. Perceptive analysis of the Torah texts and a plausible reconstruction of some of the different lampstands that may have been used in the tabernacle and temple are offered by Carol Meyers in her article on "Lampstand" in the *ABD*, 4:141–43.

146. An enduringly useful study of Artemis of Ephesus is that of Lily Ross Taylor in *The Beginnings of Christianity* (ed. F. J. Foakes Jackson and Kirsopp Lake; repr., Grand Rapids: Baker, 1966), 5:251–56.

147. The names of deities worshiped there, as found in literary sources and inscriptions, include: Aphrodite, Apollo, Asclepius, Athena, Cabiri, Demeter, God Most High, Hecate, Hephaestus, Hercules, Pluto, Poseidon, and Zeus. In addition, there was veneration of heroes, from Alexander the Great to the Roman proconsul, Publius Servitus Isauricos.

148. Asiarch was a title assigned to leading citizens of the province of Asia who formed a league that gave a degree of local autonomy to the region while fostering loyalty to the empire. Earlier analyses of the limited evidence led to the conclusion that it was used to promote divine honors to the emperor, so that Asiarch was an alternative for *archierus Asias* = high priest of the imperial cult (so Lily R. Taylor, in *The Beginnings of Christianity*, 5:258). More recent examination of the evidence from relevant inscriptions, however, shows that "the duties of an asiarch fell within the sphere of civic administration" (so R. A. Kearsley in the Appendix on the Asiarchs, in *The Book of Acts in Its Graeco-Roman Setting* (ed. D. W. J. Gill and C. Gempf; Grand Rapids: Eerdmans, 1994), 2:364–76.

149. The Greek term is *diopetes*, which means, "that which fell from Zeus." It may have been merely a meteorite, but it may have resembled the goddess. In either case, it was believed to be a tangible sign of her divine presence among the Ephesians. In Pausanias's *Description of Greece*, there is a story that images of the Greek goddess Athena fell from the sky. Such images were thought to be of divine origin and authority.

150. Irenaeus, *Against Heresies* 1.26.3.

151. E. Schüssler-Fiorenza, *The Book of Revelation: Justice and Judgment* (Philadelphia: Fortress Press, 1985), 120.

152. Eusebius, *Ecclesiastical History* 3.36.

153. "Tribulation" (*thlipsis*), perceived as suffering experienced by the faithful covenant community, is an important feature in the apocalyptic worldview, as is made explicit in the gospels and the Pauline literature, but especially in Rev 7:14 (see n. 154 below).

154. Tribulation (*thlipsis*) is a significant theme throughout the writings of the New Testament. The Synoptic Gospels include predictions of tribulations and persecution (*diogmos*) that will arise for God's people as a result of the message of Jesus (Mark 4:17; Matt 13:21). These tribulations will be unprecedentedly severe, and will be followed by a time of darkness and cosmic disturbances prior to the coming of the Son of Man (Mark 13:19, 24; Matt 24:9, 21, 29). Quoted in this connection are Isa 13:10; 34:4, and alluded to are themes found in Joel 2:2 and Dan 12:1. "Tribulation" is also a significant feature in Acts: allusions to the afflictions of Joseph in Egypt (7:10–11) and to those of Stephen (11:19) and Paul (20:23). In his Letter to the Romans, Paul rejoices in the sufferings he has experienced, since they produce endurance and hope (Rom 5:3). He finds comfort from God in all his afflictions (2 Cor 1:4–9), which he sees as a share in Christ's sufferings and as having increased his reliance upon God. He exhorts the Thessalonians (1 Thess 3:3, 7) not to have their faith threatened by the afflictions he has experienced, but to see these trials as having been foretold by him and as providing a basis for comforting him when he hears of their abiding faith. In 2 Thess 1:4, 6, Paul reports that he boasts to other churches that the Thessalonians have remained steadfast in spite of the persecution and afflictions that they have undergone. Clearly, for Paul, tribulation has constructive and enduring results.

155. Abundant evidence for the rise and development of the Roman imperial cult is provided by David Magie in his *Roman Rule in Asia Minor to the End of the Third Century after Christ* (2 vols.; Princeton University Press, 1950; repr., New York: Arno Press, 1975).

156. Gaius, known as Caligula, was emperor from 37 to 41.

157. The term translated "burden" (*baros*) here is found in the Acts report (15:28–29) of the decision made by the apostolic council in Jerusalem as to what legal obligations are to be placed on Gentile converts: "To abstain from what has been sacrificed to

idols and from blood and from what is strangled, and from unchastity." The requirements in both texts are basically the same.

158. Josephus, *Jewish Antiquities* 14.241–243.

159. The *Epistle to the Laodiceans* is examined on p. 305.

160. Zech 6:9–15. Many features of the prediction of the divine triumph in Revelation resemble those of the prophecies in Zechariah: nations other than Israel will also be drawn to honor Yahweh (Zech 8:20–23); judgment will fall on pagan cities and people, in contrast to the triumph of the king in Jerusalem (9:9ff); Judah and Israel will be restored to their traditional lands (9–11); Jerusalem will triumph over its enemies (12); there will be mourning by the house of David and Jerusalem for the one "whom they have pierced" (12:10–13:1); the shepherd and his sheep will be scattered [the Diaspora] (13:7–9). The ultimate conflict will involve attack on Jerusalem by all the nations and seismic disturbances, but will lead to the victory of God and his people, renewal of the land, the temple, the city, and the outflow from Jerusalem of wealth and blessing to all nations as they observe the festivals of Israel (14:1–21).

161. Other prophetic passages in which horsemen are seen as agents or images of divine punishment or renewal include: Isa 21:7, where they bring word of the fall of Babylon; Isa 22:6–7, where they are agents for the destruction of Jerusalem; Isa 31:1, where they symbolize the folly of Israel's reliance on Egypt; Jer 4:29, where they symbolize the impending desolation of Judah; in Jer 46:4, they represent the defeat of Egypt; in Ezek 26:10; 38:4; Dan 11:40, they show the defeat of Israel's enemies; in Hab 1:8, they are those who attack Israel.

162. Like *sheol* in the Hebrew tradition, Hades (Greek for "the unseen") was the abode of the dead (Acts 2:27, 31). In Rev 1:18 and in Matt 16:18, the risen Christ has power over life and death, as symbolized by his having "the keys of death and Hades."

163. Isa 49:10; Ps 23:2.

164. The complex imagery by which these locusts are depicted includes battle horses, human faces, women's hair, teeth like lions, scales like iron breastplates, noisy wings, and tails like scorpions.

165. This brief period is otherwise designated as forty-two months and 1,260 days (11:3).

166. Identification of the first beast by modern scholars has included proposals of Gaius Caligula, who reigned from 37 to 41 CE, and who claimed to be divine. But a more likely choice is Nero (54–68 CE), who built on the tradition by which the Senate, following the death of Augustus in 14 CE, had identified him as one of the gods of the state. Nero vetoed a proposal that a temple be erected in Rome for the Divus Nero, however, but permitted coins honoring him as divine to be used in Asia Minor and permitted inscriptions identifying him with various gods.

167. Insights on the factor of the divine image of "the beast" are offered by A. Yarbro Collins in *The Apocalypse* (Wilmington, DE: M. Glazier, 1979).

168. In Tacitus, *Annals* 15.44.

169. There is a scholarly debate as to whether John is here calling for literal virginity or using it as a symbol for moral purity in a broader sense. The former interpretation is offered by A. Yarbro Collins in "Women's History and the Book of Revelation," *SBLSP* 26:80–91, and the latter by Frederick J. Murphy in *Fallen Is Babylon*, 314–19.

170. Quoted or alluded to in this song are Ps 86:9; 111:2; 139:14; 145:17; Amos 3:13; Jer 10:7.

171. Allusions or quotes appear in 18:18–23 from Ezek 26–27; Jer 7, 25, 27; and Isa 23–24.

172. The two series of unnumbered visions in Revelation have been identified by A. Yarbro Collins in *The Apocalypse*, xiii.The first is in Rev 12:1–15:4; the second is here in 19:11–21:8.

173. The defeat of the invaders from the north is also prophesied in Jer 1:14–19.

174. Some scholars propose that the present text of Ezekiel may date from as late as the time of Alexander the Great or his successors in the fourth century BCE.

175. Similar visions of cosmic renewal appear in *1 Enoch* 45:4–5; 4 Ezra 7:75; 2 Bar 32:6.

176. The twelve jewels in the city wall recall both the adornment of the priestly breastplate in Exod 28:15–21 and the twelve signs of the zodiac.

177. The promised heritage of David as shepherd and ruler of God's people is recounted in 2 Sam 5:1–3 and celebrated in Pss 2 and 110.

178. Mark 6:3; Matt 13:55. The other brothers of Jesus named are James, Joseph, and Simon. From ancient times, it has been theorized that these were Joseph's sons by a former wife.

179. In referring to the other apostles in 1 Cor 9:5, Paul includes among them "the brothers of the Lord," though without mention of their names.

180. It is also used in Jewish apocalyptic texts: Job 41:24; *1 Enoch* 20:2; *Sibylline Oracles* 2.302; 4.186.

181. Paul's mention of his having avoided extending his mission to portions of Asia Minor that had already been evangelized (Rom 15:20), when combined with the report in Acts 16:6–7 of the Spirit's having prohibited him from going into Bithynia, might reflect the fact—or the tradition—that Peter had preached the gospel there before Paul went to the area. Certainly, Acts portrays Peter as the pioneer in the outreach to Gentiles and God-fearers in parts of Palestine dominated by Graeco-Roman culture: Lydda, Joppa, Caesarea. Yet it is Paul who launches the mission in Asia Minor (Acts 13–14). Silvanus and Mark, who are mentioned in this letter (1 Pet 5:12–13), are also linked with Paul (Silvanus in Acts 15; 1 Thess 2:6; 2 Cor 1:19; Mark in Acts 12:25; 13:5; Phlm 24). The historical basis of these traditions is difficult to determine.

182. Pliny, *Letters* 10.94, in *Fifty Letters of Pliny* (ed. A. N. Sherwin-White; New York: Oxford University Press, 1967).

183. Suetonius, *Life of Nero* 16.

184. Suetonius, *Life of Domitian* 13.

185. These designations come from Isa 42:12; 43:21, 30; Exod 19:6; 23:22; Mal 3:17; Hos 1:6, 9; 2:25.

186. To avoid questioning the virginity of Mary on the ground of her having given birth to other children, it has been conjectured that James was the son of Joseph by a previous marriage, as is implied in the *Protoevangelium of James* 9.2.

187. There is a possible reference to yet another James, who is called simply "the younger" or "the less" (Mark 15:40).

188. The substantive use of concepts and terminology from the Graeco-Roman world, and the features that correspond to those of the Shepherd of Hermas (written in Rome around the middle of the second century CE), confirm the deduction that the Letter of James was written by a quite sophisticated author steeped in Stoic philosophy and Cynic modes of communication. This is shown effectively by Sophie Laws in her article on James in *ABD* 3:621–28, and by Raymond E. Brown in his analysis of James in *An Introduction to the New Testament* (ABRL; New York: Doubleday, 1997), 725–47.

189. James 2:11; Exod 20:13–14; Deut 5:17–18.

190. On the formation of the New Testament canon, see below.

191. In Eusebius, *Ecclesiastical History* 6.14.

192. In Eusebius, *Ecclesiastical History* 6.25.

193. Detailed and perceptive analyses of the Letter to the Hebrews, including conceptual content and literary structure, are offered by Raymond E. Brown in *An Introduction to the New Testament*; and by Harold W. Attridge in *The Epistle to the Hebrews* (Hermeneia; Philadelphia: Fortress, 1989), 683–704.

194. A. J. Saldarini, "Jewish Responses to Roman Culture," in *The Cambridge Companion to the Bible* (ed. H. C.Kee, John Rogerson, Eric M. Meyers, and Anthony J. Saldarini; Cambridge: Cambridge University Press, 1997), 406–7.

195. Plato, *Sophist* 243D.

196. Plato, *Cratylus* 401D.

197. Quoting Ps 2:7—a passage especially appropriate with reference to the role of Jesus, in that it combines kingly and priestly offices.

198. Num 17:1-11.

199. Deut 9:10-15.

200. Exod 25:17-22.

CHAPTER FOUR

The Noncanonical
Apostolic Traditions

"Apostolic" became the designation for later Christian sources regarded as authoritative because they were perceived to embody God-given insights and information transmitted through the apostles. Three groups of writings received this label: (1) the Apostolic Fathers; (2) the *Apostolic Constitutions*; and—using modern terminology—(3) the Apostolic Pseudepigrapha. In spite of major differences in perspective, mode of communication, and contextual origin, all these writings claim to be divinely granted communications transmitted through the special core of divinely informed and empowered followers of Jesus: the apostles.

Created following the period of the apostolic leadership of the church, these writings claimed to have been written by the apostles or asserted that they fostered and developed the insights and traditions founded by them. These include the somewhat later documents known as *The Apostolic Tradition* (produced by Hippolytus in the second century), the *Didascalia*, and the *Apostolic Constitutions*. The content, context, and aims of these groups of writings are analyzed below.

The Apostolic Fathers

The Corpus of Apostolic Fathers

This title for a collection of early Christian writings is based on the assumption that they were produced by persons directly associated with the apostles—a link that was perceived to lend authority to them. The first group to be published under this title appeared in 1602; edited by J. B. Cotelier. It included the writings attributed to Barnabas, Clement, Hermas, Ignatius, and Polycarp—all of whom were identified as contemporaries of the apostles.[1]

The designation of this material as "Apostolical Fathers" was made by William Wake, who in 1693 published a translation of a group of these writings. The subtitle he used claimed that, together with the New Testament scriptures, these writings were "a complete collection of the most primitive from antiquity for about CL years after Christ," that these were authentic writings produced by those whose names they bear, and that they represent the doctrine, government, and discipline of the church as received from the apostles.[2] The instructions these documents contain were said to have come from Christ and from the Holy Spirit, who directed the Fathers in what they taught. The designation "Apostolic Fathers" was adopted by Lutheran, Reformed, and Anglican scholars—all of whom perceived these writers to have been the immediate successors of the apostles, and hence to be those who represent the direct development of the authentic apostolic teaching.

Additional items were included among the Apostolic Fathers by later scholars on the basis of writings found in the nineteenth century among ancient manuscripts of the New Testament. Included were *1–2 Clement* and the Shepherd of Hermas. Some of these writings were also quoted as authoritative by Christian scholars of the second to the fourth centuries—including Irenaeus, Clement of Alexandria, Origen, and Eusebius—who clearly assumed that this material had originated in association with abiding apostolic authority. For example, Clement of Alexandria considered the following to be canonical: *1 Clement*, Shepherd of Hermas, *Barnabas*, and the *Didache*. There is also evidence that these writings, and especially the letters of Clement, were appealed to in christological debates down into the fifth and sixth centuries. Works included by modern scholarship among the Apostolic Fathers[3] are:

1. *1 Clement* to the Corinthians
2. *2 Clement* to the Corinthians
3. Letters of Ignatius: *To the Ephesians, To the Magnesians, To the Trallians, To the Romans, To the Philadelphians, To the Smyrnaeans, To Polycarp*
4. Polycarp, *To the Philippians*
5. *Martyrdom of Polycarp*
6. The *Didache*
7. Letter of *Barnabas*
8. The Shepherd of Hermas
9. *Diognetus*

Some of these documents show the strong influence of Graeco-Roman culture—especially *1 Clement*, the letters of Ignatius, and *Barnabas*, which has utilized the Letter to the Hebrews.[4] Others are directly dependent on earlier Jewish and Christian traditions. For the Jesus tradition, the *Didache* builds chiefly on the Gospel of Matthew, while *2 Clement* shows links with the wider synoptic traditions. As a whole, the writers seem to have had access to a harmony of the gospels, but in several of them of major importance is the Gospel of Matthew, which is perceived as detailing the Christian reappropriation of the law. The aims in most of these writings include:

1. To show that what has resulted from the teachings, death, and resurrection of the Christ in the founding of the new community is in accord with the Jewish scriptures.

2. The moral life of the members is to be guided by the teachings of Jesus, with additional insights and concepts borrowed from Graeco-Roman philosophical traditions.

3. It is essential that the members respect and obey their leadership—from the bishops to the elders and deacons. The authority of these leaders has been defined by the apostles, but now that it has been established, it is to be maintained by the power of God at work among them.

4. A major goal of the community is to achieve unity, in spite of the diversity that is apparent in the various traditions.

Analysis of the Apostolic Fathers

1 Clement

In this letter addressed to the Corinthian church, the beliefs in such matters as the resurrection and the omniscience of God are defended by appeal to the Jewish scriptures. For example, in chapter 26, the resurrection is supported by references to Ps 3:5; 28:7; and Job 19:26. God's comprehensive knowledge is defended by quoting Ps 139:7-8. But there are also supporting claims based on Graeco-Roman texts and concepts, such as the myth of the phoenix as a sign of the resurrection, and allusions to Herodotus (2.73) and Pliny's *Natural History* (10.2).

Christians are said to be made righteous by true faith, and not by good deeds or wisdom (32.8.4), although they are to continue in good works, for which they will be rewarded (33-34). The community is urged to seek to achieve "concord in our conscience" (34.7) and "continence" (35.2)—which is the major virtue in the Stoic tradition.[5] Jesus is perceived as the high priest in terms akin to those in the Letter to the Hebrews (36), serving as the model of moral perfection, of fullness of immortal knowledge, and of triumph over

evil and God's enemies in the present world. There is need for faithful, obedient assumption of a range of roles within the community, which is here
compared to the diversity of officers in the imperial army (37). The leaders'
aims are to be for the promotion of mutual help among the members: failure
to do so will result in divine punishment (38–39).

As in the organization of a sociopolitical structure, it is essential for members to respect the range of rank and position "which grace bestowed on
each." The goal is to be mutually helpful. Members must accept correction
and chastisement when the leaders point out to them their boastful and
erring ways. One must keep in mind the catastrophic judgment that Wisdom
foretold would befall the wicked (57). The members must adopt an attitude
of self-control, patience, obedience: thereby they may live in peace and harmony (62–63). Thus, they may achieve well-pleasing qualities of life through
Christ, "our high priest and defender" (64).

Divine knowledge has been granted to God's new people so that the
cycles of worship and ministration can be carried out properly (40). Order is
to be observed in the religious services, following the models of the apostles,
who are the foundation of the church and were appointed by Christ to foster
correct faith and to employ the proper strategies in spreading the gospel,
developing the churches, and appointing bishops and deacons. These roles
are said to have been perceived by the prophets and outlined by Moses
(40–43).[6] Thus, the organization of the church and the appointment of its
leaders are in accord with an ancient divine plan—which includes decisions
to release bishops and elders from their roles at the appropriate times (44).
The reference to the apostles in a retrospective mode (44:1) is a clear indication that this writing dates from a postapocalyptic time—probably well into
the second century.

2 Clement

Also addressed to the Corinthian church, this writing is more of a sermon
than a letter. Its aim is to promote a high Christology and to encourage belief
in the resurrection of the flesh. In both style and content, it appears to have
been written by a different author than the writer of *1 Clement*, and probably
dates from the middle of the second century.[7]

A major goal of the church is perceived in this letter to be to call sinners
to repentance, leading them to true knowledge and obedience to the will of
God (1–4). This will require the members' performing the works of love and
turning away from the evil and hostile way of life that characterizes this
world. Instead, one should live in expectation of the coming of the kingdom
of God (5). The purity that was obtained through baptism is to be preserved:
one is to persevere in penitence and in the works of piety and righteousness
(6–8). Since the resurrection of the flesh is expected, one must maintain

purity, be zealous for virtue, avoid doubt, and be single-minded in obedience (9–11). One is not to seek to please other humans, except by acts and attitudes of righteousness (13).

The church is said to have been in existence since before the creation of the sun and the moon. The biblical account of the creation of male and female is said to signify Christ and his church, which has existed from the beginning (14:2). Though it is spiritual, it was made manifest "in the flesh of Christ." Those who guard the church in the flesh without corruption "shall receive her back again in the Holy Spirit" (14:3). Hence, there is a call to holiness and to prayer, by which God will be with his people. The faithful are to be aware of the danger of coming judgment, and are hence to live in penitence, to give alms, and to perform good works (16). They are to obey the leaders fully in their daily lives, not merely when they are in church (17). Aware of the impending divine judgment, they are to overcome temptation and to follow righteousness—giving heed to the scriptures and obeying the God of Truth. Aware that the benefits to the righteous will come in the future, they are now to pursue piety: *theosebeia*; *eusebeia*.[8] Similarly abstract, the final doxology identifies God as "the father of truth" and Christ as the "prince of immortality" (20). Unlike the earlier New Testament writings, which highlight the divine works through the life and teachings, death and resurrection of Christ, and the personal relationship of the people to God, these later writings employ abstract terminology to describe the nature and timeless acts of God.

Letters of Ignatius of Antioch

Eusebius reports that Ignatius was the second to succeed Peter as bishop of Antioch, and that he was taken by Roman authorities to Rome, to be eaten by wild beasts there. En route, he wrote letters, of which seven have been preserved—six to churches, and one to Polycarp, the bishop of Smyrna. It seems that he was allowed to visit with churches and their leaders as he was on his way to martyrdom in Rome.[9] The features emphasized in these letters are (1) the authority of the bishops and other church officials, and (2) conformity to correct doctrine and liturgical practices.

TO THE EPHESIANS (I)

Here the call is to become one with the bishop, just as the church is one with Christ. There is praise for the orderly life of the members, which is in accord with the truth (I.5–6). Through Christ, they have already achieved the heights in piety and obedience (I.9), but the last days are at hand and they must continue to live in reverence and fear if they are to avoid the judgment of God (I.11). They are urged to meet frequently, since by this mutual support, the powers of Satan can be overcome (I.13). They must not corrupt the faith, but should avoid bad doctrine (I.61). Ignatius asks for their prayers that he may be a worthy sacrifice to God in Christ's name as he experiences martyrdom in Rome.

TO THE MAGNESIANS (II)

Comparisons are offered between the authoritative role of God and that of the bishops, and between those of Christ and of the apostles, to whom his ministry was committed (II.6). The members must do nothing without consulting the bishops and the council of the priests, just as Christ, in union with God, worked only through the apostles (II.7). One must obey the bishop (II.13). The faith of the church rests upon Christ's birth, passion, and resurrection, and the hope of renewal through him (II.11).

TO THE TRALLIANS (III)

The emphasis in this letter is on the authority of the bishops, leaders, and deacons, and heresy is to be avoided (III.2, 4). "No one who acts apart from the bishops and the priests and the deacons has a clear conscience" (III.7). Attacked is the belief that Christ did not have a true physical body, and merely seemed to suffer (III.10). "Faith is the body of the Lord; love is the blood of Christ" (III.8).

TO THE ROMANS (IV)

The martyrdom of Ignatius is to take place in Rome, where the church is without blemish and has primacy as the community of love. Ignatius hopes to be devoured there by wild beasts, and through suffering martyrdom there, to reach God. Hence, he does not want them to pray or scheme for him to avoid his suffering and death.

TO THE PHILADELPHIANS (V)

The emphasis in this letter is on the authority of churchly leadership and the unity of the church. There is one bishop, one mode of sacrifice, and one church. Strange doctrine is to be avoided: those who follow heretical teachings will not inherit the kingdom of God. Christ is the High Priest: He is "the door . . . through which Abraham, Isaac, Joseph and his prophets, and the apostles of the church all enter into the unity of God" (V.9).

TO THE SMYRNAEANS (VI)

Here is offered a summary of true doctrine of Christ, with an emphasis on his bodily resurrection (VI.1–3). There is a warning against heretical teachers, especially those who deny Christ's bodily resurrection. There is a call for submission to the bishops and elders (VI.8–9): "Anyone who acts without the knowledge of the bishop is serving the devil." The church is urged to send a messenger to the church in Syria to congratulate them for having regained peace and unity.

IGNATIUS, *TO POLYCARP* (VII)

The appeal here is for Polycarp in his role as bishop of Smyrna to carry out the following responsibilities:

1. To fulfill the office of bishop with all diligence, caring for unity of the people, helping and loving all, seeking wisdom, and speaking to the needs of individuals.

2. Special care is to be given by him to the weaker members. He is to seek wisdom and spiritual gifts from God in order to carry out his tasks as bishop.

3. He is to stand firm against heretics, enduring all things for the sake of God.

4. The needy in the church are to be cared for, and all members are to be treated equally, including the slaves—who are to be set free by the community.

5. Love between husbands and wives is to be fostered.

6. Submission to those in authority is to be encouraged: to bishops, leaders, and deacons.

7. The bishop is to lead the church council in choosing a messenger to convey the love of the community to the church in Syria.

8. Polycarp should write to other churches in order to encourage them to perceive and obey the mind of God. The letter ends with personal greetings.

Polycarp, *To the Philippians*

Polycarp is sending the Philippians a cover letter for the collection of letters of Ignatius that is being prepared for them. It includes credal features and a call to obey the commandments of Jesus as preserved in the gospel tradition, as well as the injunctions found in the letters of Paul and the other New Testament epistles.[10] These are to be studied in order that the members may "be able to build yourselves up into the faith given you" (III.2). There are special instructions for wives and widows (IV), a call to deacons for lives of purity (V), and the duties of presbyters are set forth (VI). There are warnings against heresy (VII) and a call for perseverance in true faith and obedience (VIII), with the martyrs set forth as examples of true fidelity (IX), and a plea for philanthropy and good works (IX). The erring are called to repent, which should lead to forgiveness by the community (XI). Prayers are to be uttered for the saints, but also for the secular leaders—even for those who persecute the faithful (XII).

Martyrdom of Polycarp

An account of the martyrdom of Polycarp—very likely genuine—was preserved in a manuscript by Irenaeus (lived 130–202?), which was reported to have been found in the fourth century.[11] A nearly complete version of this text was included by Eusebius in his *Ecclesiastical History* (5.15), where Polycarp's death is described as taking place probably in 156 CE. The report is a letter sent by the church in Smyrna to the church in Philomelium, which was about two hundred Roman miles to the east, but it is addressed as well "to all the sojourners of the holy catholic church in every place." It tells how Polycarp—whose death is said to have brought to an end the Roman program of persecuting the Christians (1.1)—was put to death after he had first sought escape by fleeing to farms. But he was betrayed to the authorities, who came to seize him. He refused their demand that he "swear by the genius of Caesar" and deny that he was a Christian. After being threatened with death by wild beasts, he was set afire and—after affirming his confidence in the resurrection—died as had been foretold to him in a dream. His bones were claimed by the Christians, and served as a continuing reminder of his courageous faith, as well as of the ongoing threat of martyrdom for Christians.

The *Didache*, or Teaching of the Apostles

This manual of instruction for the church has three main themes:

1. Ethical norms and injunctions: the Way of Life and the Way of Death (1:1–6:2).[12]
2. Guidelines for sacramental procedures (7:1–10:7; 14:1–3).
3. Rules for church leaders (15:1–3).

The concluding section (16:1–8) offers signs and warnings about the coming of the end of the age.

The injunctions concerning the Way of Life (1:1–4:14) build primarily on synoptic tradition, especially from Matthew with its legal orientation and the Jewish tradition that underlies it.[13] There is a call to love one's enemies, to abstain from carnal lusts, to give alms, but not to accept them if one is not in need (1). Practices to be avoided include sexual misdeeds, magic, theft, abortion or infanticide, covetousness, astrology, deceit, and hatred (2). Instead, one is to be merciful, guileless, and humble, honor the Lord, overcome divisions, and be generous and responsible in handling one's children and slaves (3–4). The depiction of the Way of Death (5:1–6:3) includes a list of deeds of greed, falsehood, and cruelty, with warnings against deviation from the Way of Life or partaking of food offered to idols (5:1–6:3).

There are also instructions concerning baptism (7), for fasting and prayer (8), for preparing and participating in the Eucharist (9–10), and for supporting itinerant teachers,[14] prophets, and others (11–12). Christians in need are to be given "firstfruits" (13) of one's resources. Advice is offered about preparing for worship on the Lord's Day (14), the appointment of bishops and deacons (15:1–2), and for the resolution of conflict between members (15). The final exhortation is for all to be prepared for the coming of the end of the age, to beware of false teachers, and to await the heavenly signs that will precede the Lord's return (16).

Letter of *Barnabas*

Although it is known as the letter of *Barnabas*, this document is in fact anonymous, but has been ascribed since ancient times to the companion and coworker of Paul mentioned twice in his letters (1 Cor 9:6; Gal 2:1, 9), and frequently in Acts. According to Acts, he had an important role in introducing Paul to the apostles (9:27), and in appraising for them the results in Antioch of preaching the good news to Greeks/Hellenists. This led to the two sharing a ministry for a year in the large, ethnically mixed community there. Their joint ministry was extended to Cyprus, Antioch-in-Pisidia, Lystra, and Derbe in Asia Minor (Acts 14), and the outreach to Gentiles is reported to and confirmed by the apostles in Jerusalem (Acts 15). Subsequently, they split in carrying out their missions—Barnabas joined by Mark, and Paul by Silas (15:36–41). Ironically, the probably pseudopauline letter to the Colossians includes a greeting to Paul from Mark, who is identified as "the cousin of Barnabas" (Col 4:10).

Barnabas combines features that build (1) on the Jewish wisdom traditions, as well as (2) on ethical features from Hellenistic philosophy (II.2–3), and from (3) apocalyptic eschatology, with its expectation of the imminent coming of the new age—quoting the book of *Enoch* and alluding to Daniel.[15] The apocalyptic hope builds on the new wisdom that God has provided for his people, as well as on the conviction that the promises recorded in the scriptures are now being fulfilled. Joy is evoked by this wisdom,[16] and it leads to removal of the traditional Jewish covenantal features of Sabbath, festal observances, and fasting. What is called for is moral renewal (II–III): the new covenant has supplanted the old (IV:6–14; XIV), and the temple has been replaced by the new community, which is spiritual and dedicated to God (IV.11), while the true temple is heavenly (XVI). The prophets foretold the suffering and death of Jesus (VI–VII), which are also foreshadowed by the sacrificial system of the law of Moses (VIII). The importance of water in the ritual symbolizes cleansing and renewal, just as the death of Jesus on the cross is anticipated by Moses stretching out his hands to aid Israel's victory (XII; Exod 17:8–18) and by the graven serpent on the pole (Num 21:6; Deut 17:16). It is also foretold in *4 Ezra* 4–5, which speaks of blood flowing from a tree. The name of Jesus is anticipated by Joshua[17] (XII; Num 13:17), and

Christ's exaltation to God's right hand is foretold in Ps 110:1, as is the submission of the pagan nations to Christ (Isa 45:1). The completion of the creation in six days will be matched by the renewal of creation—and the end of the present age—in six thousand years (XV).[18] The true temple will come when God dwells among his people: "a spiritual temple for the Lord" (XVI).[19] Humans must choose between the Way of Light—which leads to humility, love, obedience, fidelity, sharing, and peace—and the Way of Darkness— which leads to idolatry, arrogance, adultery, murder, malice, fraud, covetousness, lying, evil speaking, and oppression (XVII–XX).The faithful who obey the just requirements of the Lord (*dikaiōmata*) will enter the kingdom of God, and are to receive wisdom, understanding, prudence, knowledge of the divine ordinances, and patience. Seeking out what the Lord requires, they will be found faithful in the Day of Judgment (XXI).

Robert A. Kraft has correctly observed that the letter of *Barnabas* is not a collection of rules or proof-texts, but represents a school of thought in early Christianity that was "closely related to Hellenistic Judaisim."[20]

The Shepherd of Hermas

This is the longest of the works that comprise the Apostolic Fathers, and is divided into (1) five Visions (I.1–V.7); (2) twelve Mandates (I.1–XII.6); and (3) ten Parables (I.1–X.4). All of these employ allegorical methods in conveying to the reader the purpose of God for his people as disclosed to Hermas by angels and by the venerable lady—the church. Although one of those greeted by Paul in his Letter to the Romans is named Hermas (Rom 16:14), this was also the name of a brother of Pope Pius (140–154 CE). The fact that issues discussed in the Shepherd of Hermas are those debated with the Montanists[21] further points to a date during the Antonine period of the Roman Empire (138–238 CE).

In Vision 1, Hermas is called to convert his family and correct his children, and to call the people to "keep the ordinances of God." In Vision 2, there is a call to the church leaders to reform their ways, to endure persecution, and to live in simplicity and temperance.[22] The lady through whom these truths are revealed is not the Sibyl, as in Graeco-Roman tradition, but the church. It is the church that is depicted symbolically in Vision 3: a tower built on the water with square, shiny stones and founded on the Almighty Name. Out of the sea are brought the stones, who suffered for the Name and obeyed the commandments of God, in contrast to the broken, cast-aside stones (hypocrites and the wicked) and the round stones (the rich, who are useless in the kingdom of God). Defectors from the faith are the stones cast aside. The tower is still being built, as mutual support develops among the members. Vision 4 offers symbolic insight for facing the Beast (the anti-

Christ) in the cosmic struggles before God's purpose triumphs through Christ. The fifth vision is of the coming shepherd, who calls for obedience to the commandments and offers insight into the meaning of the visions and parables that follow.

The Mandates call for (1) faith; (2) simplicity; (3) truth; (4) purity in thought, action, and human relations, including marriage; (5) longsuffering, or persistent courage and joy in spite of difficulties; reaffirmed (6) are the need to trust the righteous and to seek to achieve moral transformation through the angel of righteousness; (7) who brings godly fear and conformity to the commandments. Life is to be characterized by self-control in moral behavior and by ministry to those in need (8). Double-mindedness is to be overcome, and trust is to be solely in God and his great power (9). Grief is to be put away (10), and overcome by reliance on the Holy Spirit, replaced by joyfulness (*hilarotēta*). Careful distinctions must be made between false and true prophets (11): the latter are meek and gentle, empowered by the Holy Spirit; they take no fees and are the agents of divine power; (12) they desire what is good and holy (*semnē* = pious), avoiding indulgence and luxury, fostering faith, meekness, and obedience to the commandments. Humans were commissioned by God to be lord of all creatures, and should master and exemplify the divine commandments in spite of the devil's efforts to hinder obedience by God's people.

The parables of similitudes here are largely ethical allegories, calling for servants of God to live as aliens in this world, pursuing only the spiritual wealth that God provides (1). The rich and poor need each other (2): the former provide for the latter in obedience to the law of God. Trees look alike (3), but must be differentiated: the righteous are the budding trees; the withering trees are the wicked (4). Fasting means avoiding evil and serving the Lord with a pure heart, not literal abstinence from food (5) but repression of evil desires. The servant is the Son of God; the weeds are the iniquities of God's servants; the master's absence is the delay of the Parousia. The son is not the servant of the father, but his agent of renewal, transforming the lives of the faithful. The parable of the shepherd (6) presents a call to faith and righteousness as well as a warning to those doomed to punishment because they have been lured away from God by the lusts of this world. The penitents receive instruction and are made strong in the Lord, serving the Lord for the rest of their days. Parable 7 warns against the afflictions to be suffered until one is truly penitent and purified: God will be compassionate toward such persons, will heal them, and affliction will depart. The parable of the willow tree (8) depicts the variety of moral fruitfulness represented by the members of the community, with special attention and concern for those like dry stalks, who produce little virtue.

The parable of the twelve mountains (9) represents the apostles sent to twelve nations, and the variety of responses that were evoked, but results in the sharing of the faithful in the one tower. The mountains again represent apostates, hypocrites, those faced with difficulties as they seek to enter the kingdom, double-minded believers, those troubled by false understanding and by adoption of senseless folly, leaders who err and exploit the people and are valueless to the Lord. Yet they continue to have a chance to repent and be saved. On the other hand, the trees sheltering the sheep are the responsible bishops and faithful members, who, to the glory of God, care for the destitute and the suffering. The twelfth mountain is white, and represents those who remain in innocence or reduce their wealth, and so are qualified to find their place in the tower: the kingdom of God. The final parable (10) teaches that to be certain of success in every good work, one must keep the commandments, undertake perfection and moderation through submission to the Lord's power and rule, and rescue others from distress by doing good deeds. Otherwise, one will be excluded from a place in the tower that is God's people.

Diognetus

Found in a single manuscript from the thirteenth or fourteenth century, this work is in two parts: (1) a letter (1–10), and (2) a homily (11–12). The author says that he is "a disciple of the apostles," and that the letter is an apology for the divine piety (*theosebeia*) of the Christians, which engages in a challenge to the beliefs in and worship of the traditional Graeco-Roman gods (2). It also differentiates Christians from Jews (3), making the case that Christians sojourn in an alien world, loving those who hate them (4–6) and trusting in the One whom God sent as a human, calling and loving humanity. But this One will return as judge, savior, teacher, and counselor (7–9). Disparaged is the notion of God as an element of the physical universe (8). Instead, the claim is that the mystery of God's purpose has been disclosed through his Son, and that through him the sins of humanity are forgiven. This involves complete knowledge of God, of the divine ordering of the world, and of the promise of sharing in the heavenly kingdom (9–10). Identifying himself as a disciple of Christ, the author rejoices in the ongoing divine disclosure through God's grace, which has taken place through the prophets, the gospels, and the apostles, and which continues to "give understanding, make mysteries clear, announce the acceptable times." Therefore, one "rejoices over the faithful." There is an appeal to "let your heart be knowledge and your life be true reason, properly understood." Thus, *Diognetus* constructively combines faith and reason. In this respect, it is a prime example of the perceptions that dominated the church in the early centuries, as evident from the Apostolic Fathers.

The Apostolic Tradition

This was written by Hippolytus, a Roman priest in the early third century, whose knowledge of Greek philosophy and mystery traditions suggests that he was of Greek origin. He was critical of the pope, Callistus (217–222), and was elected an anti-pope, but then was exiled to Sardinia, where he died. Then his body was returned to Rome for burial. His writings include *Philosophumenē* (The Refutation of All Heresies), *Syntagma* (Against All Heresies), commentaries on Old Testament books, retelling of Old Testament stories, and chronological treatises (including the date of Easter)—and the *Apostolic Tradition*. This document includes rules for the ordination and function of church officials, and for celebrating the Eucharist and performing baptism. Only fragments of the Greek original have survived, but several translations were made, including a Latin version that is so pedantic that from it one can reconstruct the Greek original. The translations show that the work was especially well received in the Near East and North Africa. In the prologue, Hippolytus claims to be using older traditions, and emphasizes apostolic succession in leadership and in practices. The prayers and liturgy included set the rules for both clergy and laity—especially for dealing with new converts, for specifying which professions are forbidden to Christians, and in indicating procedures for confirmation of church leaders.

The Didascalia

A document with major impact in setting norms for leadership and membership in the church is the *Didascalia*, which was produced by the church in northern Syria and was initially aimed for instruction of converts from paganism. It claims to have been produced by the apostles soon after their council in Jerusalem (Acts 15), but was most likely written in Greek early in the third century. The Greek original has survived in only a few fragments, but a complete Syriac translation was soon made, and it served as the main source for the *Apostolic Constitutions* in the fourth century (see below).

The book offers instruction regarding Christian behavior in a pagan world, procedures for the election of bishops, the ordination of priests and deacons, and the instruction of catechumens. There is advice about how to care for the poor and to deal with lawsuits, but especially about the conduct of worship and the seating for it, as well as the roles of bishops, elders, and deacons. Also presented are guidance for observing feast and fast days, the education of children, and dealing with heresy, heretics, and schismatics. There is special concern for penance and the forgiveness of sins, including what sins can and cannot be forgiven.

Apostolic Constitutions

The *Apostolic Constitutions*, which were apparently compiled in Syria in the later fourth century, include eight books:

Book 1: To the laity, male and female, concerning moral and social behavior.

Book 2: Bishops, Presbyters, and Deacons—qualifications for the offices, as well as responsibilities in dealing with the innocent, the guilty, and the penitent, building on the Old Testament as well as on the forgiveness available through Christ. The roles of bishops and deacons are defined. Disputes are to be settled within the church, and there is a call to the faithful to attend worship and to abstain from all modes of impiety.

Book 3: Rules are set forth for widows and other women in the church. Neither they nor faithful laymen are permitted to teach or to hold offices in the church. There is also a discussion of rules regarding baptism.

Book 4: Advice on helping the poor, avoiding love of money, and instruction concerning domestic and social life of members: parents, children, and virgins.

Book 5: Instruction about martyrs and the resurrection of the faithful; the holy days and the resurrection of Christ.

Book 6: A response to heresies and wrongful practices.

Book 7: The Christian life, the Eucharist, initiation into Christ, and sacred mysteries.

Book 8: Spiritual gifts, ordaining bishops, preparing catechumens for membership, ordination of presbyters; rules for the clergy, prayers,[23] and liturgy.

This work is the largest collection of liturgical and socio-structural material that has survived from Christian antiquity. It is a crucial source for analysis of the emergent leadership and social structures within Christianity of the early centuries. The texts were published in 1848: *The Apostolic Constitutions* (New York: D. Appleton & Co).

Apostolic Apocrypha[24]

The twelve disciples are pictured in the New Testament as companions of and coworkers with Jesus—preaching the good news and performing exorcisms in his name. But in Luke 6:13, as well as in some of the most reliable manuscripts of Mark, they are also designated as "the apostles." Matthew equates the disciples and the apostles (10:1; 11:1). Paul identifies Cephas and the Twelve as "the apostles" (1 Cor 15:3–7), but then claims that he is the final apostle (15:8–9). The role of the Twelve is defined in Mark 3:14–15 as being sent out (*apostellē*) in Jesus' name "to preach and to cast out demons." In Acts 1:21–22, Peter is reported as offering a definition of apostle as "one of the men who have accompanied us during all the time that the Lord Jesus went in and out among us, beginning from the baptism of John until the day when he was taken up from us—one of these men must become with us a witness to his resurrection." Matthias is chosen and "enrolled with the eleven apostles" (1:26). Of the twenty-eight occurrences of *apostolos* in Acts, all refer to the Jerusalem-based apostles, except for 14:4 and 14:14, where Paul and Barnabas are called apostles. Somewhat ironically, in Acts 15:2, it is these two who are appointed by the church in Antioch "to go up to Jerusalem to the apostles and the elders" to get their opinion as to whether circumcision is a prerequisite for male membership in the new community. In Acts 9:30, "the brethren" in Jerusalem sought to save Paul from his attackers, took him to Caesarea, and sent him off (*exapesteilan*) to Tarsus. The root *apostellō* here implies dispatching him, not formally authorizing him in an apostolic role. But the term *apostolos* clearly came to connote those who from the beginning of the Jesus movement were witnesses and authorized messengers of the good news, which was now to go out "to the end of the earth" (Acts 1:8).

It is thoroughly understandable why documents produced in genera-tions after the time of the apostles would seek authority and primacy by claiming apostolic origin. It was with this aim in mind that a range of allegedly apostolic documents was produced: the Apostolic Apocrypha, which may be grouped as (1) Apostolic Psedepigrapha (a variety of writings in the name of the apostles); (2) Apocryphal Acts (claiming to depict the activities of various apostles); and (3) a diverse group labeled here as Other Apocryphal Documents.

Apostolic Pseudepigrapha and Apocryphal Documents

Kerygma Petri (*Preaching of Peter*)

Based on quotes and allusions to this writing by such figures as Clement of Alexandria, Origen, and Heracles the Gnostic, it can be dated to the second century—possibly earlier—and probably originated in Egypt. The name refers to the message allegedly preached by Peter, which implies that it is the basic apostolic proclamation. There is no evidence, however, of a link in content with the Gospel of Mark, which has traditionally been perceived as associ-ated with Peter.[25] What is affirmed is the following: the oneness of God, regarded as incomprehensible, inconceivable, everlasting, imperishable, and uncreated. Rejected are polytheism and worship as carried out by the Jews. The Old Testament is claimed for the church, Christ is seen as the Law and the Word (with no developed Christology), and Christians are seen as the "third race"—as distinct from Jews and Gentiles—with whom God has established a new covenant through Christ. The apostles are the Twelve who were chosen as disciples of Jesus and then as proclaimers of the message and revealers of the future of God's purpose.

Epistle to the Laodiceans

Apparently intended to supply the otherwise unknown correspondence between Paul and the church in Laodicea referred to in Col 4:16, this letter consists largely of some twenty-five quotations from or allusions to the known letters of Paul. Its style is also derived from the letters of Paul, but it has been characterized as "a clumsy forgery" and "a paltry and carelessly compiled concoction."[26] There are no christological or other theological assertions, and the dominantly ethical intent of the work is epitomized in v. 15: "What is pure, true, proper, just and lovely, do."

Other Apocryphal Documents

Pseudo-Clementines

A considerable body of literature has been preserved in the name of Clement of Rome: two letters to James (one from Peter and one from Clement); two letters addressed to virgins; twenty Homilies; ten books of Recognitions;[27] the Clement Romance; and the *Kerygmmata Petrou*. The most likely place of origin of these writings is Syria, and the time of their writing is probably mid-third century. Significant in them are the aims to show divine support for the authority of the successors of the apostles while demonstrating the compatibility of Christian doctrine with features of Graeco-Roman philosophy. Insightful analyses of these writings are offered by Johannes Quasten and by Johannes Irmscher and Georg Strecker.[28]

The biographical information reports Clement's birth in an aristocratic family in Rome, his inquiries about religious matters, his journey to Judea to learn about the claim that the Son of God had appeared there, and his encounter there with Peter. Persuaded by Peter's message about Jesus as the Word of God, and impressed by the manifestations of divine power in the contest with Simon Magus, Clement traveled with Peter on his missionary journeys and is reported to have been ultimately designated by Peter as bishop of Rome. The writings attributed to or describing the career of Clement—

including the Recognitions, the Homilies, and the Letters—continued to evolve into the fourth century.

The most comprehensive work in the Clementine material is the *Kerygmata Petrou*, which purports to be the messages preached by Peter. The central figure in this work is "the true prophet," Christ, who is contrasted with Adam. Christ is depicted as coming "from the hands of the Creator of all things," and as possessing "the great and holy Spirit of divine knowledge." Throughout universal time, he changed his form and names until he was anointed by God in his own time, and will have rest forever.[29] His role as the divinely endowed agent is that he "loves pious, pure and holy men . . . preaches peace, commends temperance, does away with sin . . . leads all humans to charity . . . commends justice, seals the perfect, and publishes the word of peace."[30] As the prophet of truth, he knows that the world has fallen into error, and by fostering knowledge, he slays ignorance—thereby separating the living from the dead. A female being, created as his companion, is far inferior to him, promotes earthly riches and self-deification, and leads astray those who turn to her for truth.[31] The true law of God was given to Moses, who delivered it orally to seventy wise men to prepare the people to receive it, but it was not written down until after his death, and was found in the temple five hundred years later.[32] The promise was made that a leader would come from Judah who would be awaited by the Gentiles (Gen 49:10) and who would show which parts of the scriptures were true and which were false, while affirming the eternal power of the law.[33]

Also in this document is a polemic against Paul, whose vision of Christ differs from that of Peter and the other apostles. It is asserted that what must be affirmed is ritual as well as internal cleansing. Baptism is essential (John 3:5), as is the avoidance of lust—not merely of overt adultery. The faithful Gentiles must exceed in purity those who conform to the Jewish ritual laws.[34] One must not only believe what is taught by Jesus and Moses, but must live in accord with their instructions.

The Clement Romance contains a report of Peter's having healed the crippled hands of a woman, who turned out to be the mother of Clement. In Epitome II is an account of Peter's designation of Clement as bishop of Rome—a role which he was reluctant to accept, but was encouraged by Peter to assume. Thus is affirmed in these Clementine writings continuity of divine power and purpose, of religious insight, and of ecclesiastical authority.[35]

Apocalypses and Related Documents

Building on the Jewish apocalyptic tradition and with the major emphasis on apocalyptic expectations and roles in the Jesus, Pauline, and Johannine features included in the New Testament—as well as on the analogous elements in the Stoic tradition—the post-canonical writers of early Christianity dealt with the expectation of divine defeat of the powers of evil and the transformation of the cosmos through Christ in a variety of apocalyptic modes. They perceived evil to be operative through the Roman imperial power, as well as in more personal ways through the demonic forces evident in the lives of individuals and through the sociopolitical powers. Examples of these apocalyptic features are examined below.

In the Jewish tradition, the typical elements of apocalyptic are as follows:

1. Pseudonymity, in that the vision and messages reported are conveyed mostly through famous figures of the past: Elijah, Daniel, Isaiah, Moses, Ezra, Enoch. Thereby, the divine origin of these insights is perceived to be confirmed, as is their transcending of time and the limitations of human insight.

2. Visionary mode of communication, so that the message is transmitted through dreams or ecstasy, or heavenly rapture, and is conveyed by symbols and allegories—which require interpretation. They often involve surveys of history, which extend into the future from creation or from some point in the past.

3. The verbal communication of the divinely determined course of history is conveyed through speeches, dreams, and *parainesis* (exhortation), and is articulated in ways that include prophecies and farewell discourses.

4. The concepts include divine secrets, a pattern of two ages (pessimism for the present and hope for the future) culminating in the hope for cosmic renewal, which is to have universal impact but which now calls for individual response. The apocalypses purport to be secret wisdom that is being disclosed to the faithful, obedient community.[36] Representative examples of this apocalyptic mode follow.

Martyrdom and Ascension of Isaiah

Dating from the first century CE, its references to the community leaving Bethlehem and taking up life in the desert may be an indication that it was produced at Qumran. There is a sharp sense of conflict with the powers of evil, in that following the death of King Hezekiah, power passes to Manasseh, here seen as the agent of Beliar, the satanic power. In this account, Isaiah withdraws to the desert with other prophets, and predicts the coming of the Beloved from the seventh heaven in human likeness, and his suffering persecution, dying, and being raised on the third day. Thereafter he sends out twelve disciples to take his message to all the nations. Although false teaching will arise, the Christ will return, the pious will be raised, the hosts of evil will be destroyed, and heaven and earth will be transformed. This writing may have had a Jewish antecedent, but it is clearly Christian in its extant form and shows the enduring power of the apocalyptic hope. Noncanonical features include the river of fire that brings destruction and the details of the agony suffered by the wicked.

Early Christian Apocalypses

Other early Christian apocalypses—in some cases based on prior Jewish texts—include the fourth and fifth books of Esra, the *Book Elchasai*, the *Apocalypse of Paul*, the *Apocalypse of Thomas*, and Coptic gnostic apocalypses of Paul and Peter.[37] Thus, the power and substance of the apocalyptic world-view—including the identification of the covenant community as comprised of those to whom God has granted special insights and hopes of deliverance—continued to have a significant impact on Christians from the patristic period down to the Middle Ages. One feature of apocalyptic that has often been overlooked, however, is the kinship that existed between this Jewish-Christian worldview and analogous hopes and fears that were being expressed in the Graeco-Roman world in relation to the divinely empowered agents known as the Sibyllines. It is to the Christian version of this mode of divine disclosure concerning the future triumph over the powers of evil that we now turn.

Christian *Sibylline Oracles*

The role of the Sibyl as the instrument through whom the future is disclosed was affirmed by such major intellectuals of the Graeco-Roman world as Plato and Heraclitus. Around 500 BCE, Heraclitus declared, "By uttering things not to be laughed at, unashamed, unscathed, the Sibyl penetrates with her voice through millennia with the aid of the godhead."[38] Plato, speaking in the name of Socrates in the *Phaedrus* (244), notes the "Sibyl and all others who by prophetic inspiration have foretold many things to many persons and thereby have made them fortunate afterwards." It was based on this tradition that the Jewish Sibyllines were produced—and adapted by Christians. The kinship with apocalyptic is pervasive and constitutive in these writings.

The Christian Sibyllines are adaptations of Jewish oracles, and in their tracing of the course of history through successive world powers match Daniel. A fine introduction to these oracles and an annotated translation of them has been prepared by John J. Collins.[39] The oracles build on Old Testament tradition, but have been adapted to employ the aims and methods of the Graeco-Roman Sibylline traditions, just as the Hebrew mythological features are linked with those of the Graeco-Roman world. Thus, Book 1 contains a combination of the creation accounts in Genesis with aspects of creation theory in the Jewish wisdom tradition[40] and in later Jewish apocalyptic. The story of Noah's ark ends with its landing in Phrygia—Ararat is located in Armenia—and his three sons receive the Greek names of Chronos, Titan, and Iapetus. History is perceived to have moved through successive stages of good and evil, with the divine solution provided by the coming of Christ (1.324–400), who will transform and illumine those who heed him—though the Jews will reject him. The temple will be replaced by the house of heaven (1.38f.), and a new community will emerge: "a new shoot will sprout from the nations, while the temple will be destroyed" (387–400).

In Book 2, there is a prediction of disaster that will befall the human race in the tenth generation, but God will act to save the pious and to restore fertility in the earth. Elijah will reappear, and following the divine destruction (187–200), the dead will be raised, the wicked punished and the righteous rewarded, and the earth will be renewed (313–38). Book 3 pictures the successive world kingdoms that culminate in Rome's universal rule, followed by cosmic destruction and the accession to power by Beliar. Oracle 4 is an older Hellenistic document, picturing the four world kingdoms (Assyria, Media, Persia, and Macedonia), but it has been adapted to describe the destruction of the Jerusalem temple, Nero's flight to the Parthians, the eruption of Mount Vesuvius, and the devastation of Jerusalem. Baptism is seen to be necessary to avoid judgment, and what is called for is moral purity. Ultimate conflagration will burn the earth, destroying its cities and most of its population (171–92), except those who have participated in the Christian factors of conversion and baptism (171–78). The pious will escape the doom of Gehenna, and will live on a renewed earth (179–92).

Oracle 8 sketches the history of the Roman Empire from Julius Caesar to Marcus Aurelius (161–180 CE), and predicts the destruction of Egypt and its cities, as well as of Nero, who is expected to return but will be destroyed by "a certain king . . . sent from God against him," as will "all the great kings and noble men" (5.93–110). The eastern territories are also to be destroyed: Babylon and "all Asia." Britain and the Gauls, as well as the Ethiopians, are warned of the doom that is to befall them. On the other hand, there is praise and divine honor for the Jews, with blessing and honor for Jerusalem and the Holy Land, and especially for the righteous. Although the temple will be destroyed by the Romans, a savior figure will appear, and the city and temple will be renewed in great splendor. The earthly struggles will be accompanied by cosmic conflict, which will result in destruction of stars.

Oracles 11 to 14 outline history from the flood to the Arab conquest of the Middle East—building on what were originally Jewish traditions, but expanding and adapting them to the Roman and Byzantine periods. The hope is that the evil nations will be overcome, and the holy nation of God's people will be granted control over all the earth. Fragments of other oracles likewise affirm monotheism and universal divine sovereignty. God is ruler of all, and those who honor him will inherit life and dwell in paradise. Thus, the hope and expectation of universal divine sovereignty and the vindication of the faithful expressed in the earliest Christian traditions continue to be affirmed.

Notes

1. The title begins *Patrum qui temporibus apostolicis floruerent* [Fathers who flourished in the times of the apostles] (2 vols.; Paris).

2. This description is part of an excellent analytical summary of these works by William Schoedel in his article "Apostolic Fathers" in the *Anchor Bible Dictionary* (ed. D. N. Freedman; New York: Doubleday, 1992), 1:313–15.

3. The most useful edition of these works is the Greek-English version translated and edited by Kirsopp Lake, *The Apostolic Fathers* (LCL; Cambridge, MA: Harvard University Press; and London: Wm. Heinemann, 1950–1952). Another accessible English translation with useful notes is *The Apostolic Fathers* (Fathers of the Church; trans. Francis X. Glimm, Joseph M.-F. Marique, and Gerald G. Walsh; New York: CIMA Publishing Co., 1947).

4. Analysis of the Hellenistic features of the Letter to the Hebrews is offered on pp. 323–29 of this book.

5. There are other appeals to features from Stoic ethics in chaps. 62 and 64. Fuller consideration is offered in Excursus 4, "The Multiple Impact of Stoicism on the Origins of Christianity," 451–62.

6. The prophetic quote is from Isa 60:17, and general terms for leadership are equated with church offices. The appeal to Moses builds on Num 12:7.

7. Francis X. Glimm, in the volume on the Apostolic Fathers in which he participated, identifies this writing as "The So-Called Second Letter of St. Clement." He proposes that it should be considered pseudonymous, and that it may well have originated in Corinth (61–63). A similar conclusion is drawn by Johannes Quasten in *The Beginnings of Patristic Literature* (vol. 1 of *Patrology*; Westminster, MD: Christian Classics, 1986), 53–58.

8. These abstract terms in chap. 20 appear in only the later New Testament writings and would not likely have been in the vocabulary of the original apostles.

9. The sending of the letters as Ignatius journeyed to Rome is explicitly indicated in his letter *To the Romans* (4.9–10). All the other cities to which letters were sent for the Christian communities are located in western Asia Minor.

10. Quotes include some from Acts, 1 Peter, Ephesians, and the Pastorals.

11. A critical edition of the text of this document is in K. Lake, ed., *The Apostolic Fathers*, 2:312–45.

12. The Two Ways are featured also in another of the Apostolic Fathers: the letter of *Barnabas*, discussed below.

13. In addition to the examination of the Gospel of Matthew as part of the synoptic tradition (121–36), see the analysis in chap. 5, pp. 367–424, Community Structures in the Early Church.

14. Curiously, these traveling teachers are referred to as "apostles."

15. Quoted or alluded to in IV:3–5 are *Enoch* 89, 61–64; 19:17, as well as Dan 7:7–8, 24.

16. The Hellenistic terms for wisdom here include *sophia, epistēmē, gnōsis,* but there is no hint of the radical dualism—ethical or ontological—which was essential for the gnostics.

17. The Semitic equivalent of Jesus is *Yeshua,* which is akin to *Yehoshua* (= Joshua).

18. This argument builds on Ps 90:4, which compares 1,000 years and a day.

19. Dan 9:24–27.

20. Robert A. Kraft, *Didache and Barnabas* (vol. 3 of *The Apostolic Fathers*; New York: Thomas Nelson, 1965), 20.

21. Montanism began in Phrygia in the middle of the second century CE. Montanus, its founder, claimed to speak the words of the Holy Spirit, which were transmitted through the mouths of men and women who thus conveyed new perceptions of the coming millennium, but also interpreted in new ways the teachings of Jesus and Paul, with emphasis on the importance of ecstasy, which the Spirit brought, and insights about life in the age to come. A perceptive summary of Montanism is provided by Robin Lane Fox in his *Pagans and Christians* (New York: Alfred Knopf, 1986), 404–16.

22. The crucial term here is the Stoic virtue, *egkrateia* (= self-control), which is listed by Paul as one of the fruits of the Spirit (Gal 5:22–23).

23. David A. Fiensy, in his *Prayers Alleged to Be Jewish: An Examination of the Constitutiones Apostolorum* (BJS 65; Chico, CA: Scholars Press, 1985), has made a persuasive case for the Jewish origin of the prayers included in this Christian document.

24. Translations of these pseudepigraphic writings attributed to the apostles, with scholarly introductions, are available in *New Testament Apocrypha* (Cambridge: Jas. Clarke; Louisville: Westminster John Knox, 1992).

25. The traditional link between Peter and the Gospel of Mark is discussed above in the analysis of that gospel (119–20).

26. So W. Schneemelcher, in the introduction to the *Epistle of Laodiceans,* in *New Testament Apocrypha,* 2:44.

27. The Recognitions purport to be autobiographical.

28. By Quasten, in *Patrology,* 1:53–62; and by Johannes Irmscher and Georg Strecker, in *New Testament Apocrypha* (Louisville: John Knox, 1992), chap. 18, "The Pseudo-Clementines, 2:483–541." Extensive bibliographies are offered in both volumes, which are referred to below as NTA.

29. This section is designated in the NTA edition as H.III.17–20.

30. H.III.26.

31. H.III.22–25.

32. H.III.38.

33. H.III.48–52; XVII.13–14; XL.22–33.

34. II.16–17; 43–44; XVII.13–14; XL.25–33.

35. A superb series of studies of the patristic literature—with careful translations, analyses and references to relevant literature—has been published by Johannes Quasten in *The Beginnings of Patristic Literature,* vol. 1 of *Patrology,* which covers the material from the Apostles' Creed to Irenaeus. Vol. 2 provides translations and analyses of the ante-Nicene literature after Irenaeus.

36. This summary of Jewish and early Christian apocalyptic features builds on the insights set forth by Phillip Vielhauer and Georg Strecker in *New Testament Apocrypha*, 2:544–54.

37. Translations, introductions, and bibliography are provided in *New Testament Apocrypha*, 2:691–752.

38. Quoted in a fragment (92) published in Hermaun Diels, *Sibyllinische Blätter* (Berlin: Verlag, 1890).

39. In *The Old Testament Pseudepigrapha* (ed. J. H. Charlesworth; Garden City, NY: Doubleday, 1983), 1:317–472.

40. Wis 2:23; 9:1; Sir 25:24; *1 Enoch* 6–16; 60:4–18.

CHAPTER FIVE

The Emerging Structures of Early Christianity: Modes of Achieving Theological and Social Unity

Methodological Orientation

Crucial sociological insights directly relevant to the origins of Christianity were articulated by Max Weber (1862–1920) in the early decades of the twentieth century, and very quickly affected the historical study of Christianity in the English-speaking world.[1] In the introduction to a volume of selected essays by Weber, *Max Weber: On Charisma and Institution Building*, S. N. Eisenstadt shows the major historical impact of Weber's sociological insights—especially on the sociology of religion—in his perceptive analyses of the social processes explicit in the title, as evident in a wide range of societies and cultural contexts. Weber's concerns were "the problems and predicaments of human freedom, creativity, and personal responsibility in social life in general, as well as in modern society." These human experiential features were perceived as functioning within the arena of "interpersonal relations, organizations, institutional structures, and the macrosocietal setting in which freedom, creativity, and responsibility could become manifest."[2] Institution building and social transformation were conceived by Weber as manifest in creativity and freedom, but as often effecting in the process "destruction of institutions."[3] Pure charisma "is rooted in the attempt to come into contact with the very essence of being, to go to the very roots of existence, of cosmic, social and cultural order, to what is seen as sacred and fundamental."

And it may involve challenge or dismissal of traditional and "formalized forms" of what has previously been assumed as sacred order, and hence may be regarded as "antinomian and anti-institutional."[4]

Often a similarly antiestablishment factor in charismatic movements is the negative view adopted toward wealth and possessions. As Weber stated it, "Frequently *charisma* quite deliberately shuns the possession of money, and of pecuniary income *per se*. . . . In general, charisma rejects all rational economic conduct. . . . In its pure form charisma is never a source of private gain for its holders."[5] Directly relevant to this subject are the teachings of Jesus as reported in the gospel tradition, where Luke quotes Jesus as declaring in his inaugural sermon in the Nazareth synagogue that he has been anointed by "the Spirit of the Lord . . . to preach good news *to the poor*" (4:18). The first of Jesus' beatitudes announces that it is the poor who will be granted a share in the kingdom of God (Luke 6:20). The folly of reliance on personal possessions is further pointed out in Jesus' instructions: (1) to the rich young man— "It is easier for a camel to go through the eye of a needle than for a rich man to enter the kingdom of God" (Mark 10:25); (2) in the parable of the Rich Fool (Luke 12:16–20); and (3) in the story of the Rich Man and Lazarus (Luke 16:19–31). Indeed, Weber observed, "The existence of charismatic authority is specifically unstable. . . . The charismatic leader gains and maintains authority solely by proving his strength in life," and by his "devotion to the unheard of, to what is strange to all rule and tradition—and which is therefore viewed as divine."[6] Jesus' reversal of common perceptions of wealth and poverty is made explicit by Paul in his commendation of the generosity of the impoverished Macedonian churches: "Though he was rich, yet for your sake he became poor, so that by his poverty you might become rich" (2 Cor 8:9).

Yet, as Gerth and Mills note in their introduction to Weber's essays, "Weber sees the genuine charismatic situation quickly give way to incipient institutions, which emerge from the cooling off of extraordinary states of devotion and fervor." The result is that charisma becomes "routinized into traditionalism or into bureaucratization as the institutional framework of the movement evolves."[7] It is precisely these modes of origin and development from charismatic to institutional forms that we may see as having taken place in early Christianity, and thus as evident in the later New Testament writings and those of the second century. These evolutionary features involve both leadership roles and community structures. Our procedure will be to look first at the convictions shared by the emergent early Christian communities, with the aim to discern how the shared beliefs and practices—including the evolving forms that these took—influenced the structures and leadership roles that emerged in the early church. The evolution of these roles will be traced from their charismatic origins to the development of assigned official roles. Paralleling these changes are the various modes of community structure that developed in early Christianity, with their diverse models and terminology. Finally, we shall examine the process by which the decisions were made as to which of the early Christian writings were to be regarded as authoritative: the emergence of the Christian canon.

It is essential in such an analysis of historical development to bear in mind how Weber emphasizes "not so much the charismatic leader, but the charismatic group or band" for which "the charismatic qualities are transferred from the unique personality or the unstructured group to orderly institutional reality."[8] Eisenstadt also points out that "the test of any great charismatic leader lies not only in his ability to create a single event or a great movement, but also in his ability to leave a continuous impact on an institutional structure . . . by infusing into it some of his charismatic vision, by investing the regular, orderly offices, or aspect of social organization, with some of his charismatic qualities and aura."[9] Thus, in the development of early Christian offices and structures, we may expect the transformation of traditional features rather than mere innovations. As a result, we shall see developing in the beginnings of Christianity not only features sharply critical of both Judaism and the Roman social and imperial systems, but also correlative features of community structures and organizational leadership. As the movement continued to develop over the years, institutional features and authoritarian roles gained in importance.

Structures of Faith and Practice: Kerygma, Creed, Liturgy, and Ethical Rules

The Nature and Ground of Faith: Changing Perceptions

In the traditions of ancient Israel, faith consists of trust in the Lord—in what God has done for his people, and continues to do. For example, this is celebrated in the harvest festival of the firstfruits (Deut 26:5–11) and in the Passover—which may have originated as an agricultural or sheep-herding ritual, but which came to be linked with God's care for his people, freeing them from bondage in Egypt and leading them into their own land. Central events that manifested the trustworthiness of the God of Israel were God's call of Abraham, the liberation of Israelites from slavery, their settlement in the promised land, and the enduring presence of Yahweh among his people in the temple. By identifying with these historic divine actions, and by affirming their continuing, constitutive import for the covenant people, the faith of those who shared in the covenant community was confirmed and renewed.

Analogously, in the new covenant community, faith involves affirmation of and gratitude for what God has done through Jesus Christ to defeat the powers of evil, to grant forgiveness of sins, and to constitute a new people of God that is inclusive across traditional ethnic and cultic boundaries. It is trust in this new work of God in the world among human beings—accomplished through the message, life, ministry, death, and resurrection of Jesus Christ—that is the basis of faith for the new community. The specifics of this divine action are affirmed in the good news proclaimed by Jesus and the apostles. When the focus is on the proclaiming of this message, the New Testament writers employ the verb *kerysso* or the cognate noun *kerygma*: proclamation or announcement. When the emphasis is on describing and communicating as good news God's historic actions through Jesus, the terms used are the verb *evangelize* or the noun *euangelion* (gospel). In the gospels are accounts of how it is that what Jesus said, did, and experienced were divine acts of transforming power, resulting in the forgiveness of sins, the defeat of the powers of evil, and the consequent inclusiveness of the covenant community that turned to him with faith. There are summary statements in Acts and in the letters of the New Testament that point to these divine salvific events that occurred through Jesus of Nazareth.

Artur Weiser correctly notes that the Greek term for faith, *pistis*, is linked with the Hebrew term *amen*, in that the latter is "an expression of the particular being and life of the people of God which stands both individually and collectively in the dimension of a vital divine relationship [which] embraces the whole span of this form of life, even to the final depths which are disclosed only when, under the threat to human existence, certainty in God releases new energies of faith and life."[10] R. Bultmann noted that in the New Testament, faith as trust is closely linked with hope, since through Christ the hope of the reconstitution of the community and for the renewal of the creation is reaffirmed but also redefined.[11] For the New Testament writers, hope is based on what God has newly done for renewal of his people and of the creation, as evident in Christ's triumph over human evil and death, as well as over the cosmic forces of evil. The invitation to share in this new reality is extended to all who respond in faith, regardless of their ritual condition, their ethnic background, or their social or moral status. By the impact of the later prophetic tradition and especially the apocalyptic hope of vindication of the faithful and defeat of the powers of evil, the hope set forth in the New Testament shows a transformation from older ethnic separatist views to an ethnically and culturally inclusive hope for human renewal. These hopes rest on what it is perceived that God has now done through the life, message, death, and resurrection of Christ, and they are being confirmed by the outpouring of the Holy Spirit. A vivid example of this conviction is the word of Jesus in the Q tradition: "If it is by the finger of God that I cast out demons, then has the kingdom of God come upon you" (Luke 11:20). Such confidence in the inbreaking of God's rule into the present situation is affirmed from the outset of Jesus' public mission according to Mark, the oldest of the gospels: "After John [the Baptist] was arrested, Jesus came into Galilee, preaching the gospel of God and saying, 'The time is fulfilled, and the kingdom of God is at hand: Repent and put trust in the gospel'" (Mark 1:14–15).

The aim and substance of the ministry of Jesus are summarized in the Gospel of Matthew (4:23): "Jesus went about all Galilee, teaching in their synagogues and preaching the gospel of the kingdom and healing every disease and infirmity among the people." The program for the worldwide spread of the good news is announced in Matt 24:24, "The gospel of the kingdom shall be preached throughout the whole world as a testimony to all nations, and then the end will come." The cost of discipleship and its subsequent reward are stated in Mark 10:24, "Truly . . . there is no one who has left house or brothers or sisters or mother or father or lands for my sake and for the gospel, who will not receive a hundred-fold now in this time, houses and sisters and mothers and children and lands, with persecution, and in the age to come, eternal life" (Mark 10:29).[12] The gospel tradition anticipates that this message will reach out to the whole world, as is evident in the claim that the pious act of the woman who anointed Jesus' head was a perceptive anticipation of his death on the cross, and thus it is to become known as the gospel is proclaimed throughout the whole world (Mark 14:9; Matt 26:13). Indeed, Matthew and Mark report an explicit instruction of Jesus to his disciples that the gospel is to be preached to all nations (Mark 13:10; Matt 24:14).

Jesus' outreach with his message and acts of liberation and renewal is depicted in all the gospel tradition, but especially in Luke and Acts, as noted above and in the analysis of Luke.[13] In all these versions, Jesus reaches out in violation of traditions of ethnic and ritual limitations in order to meet the needs of the suffering and oppressed. The sole requirement to share in the personal and group renewal enacted and promised by Jesus is to trust in him as the agent of God's power and purpose for achieving this cosmic goal.

The significance of the message, the career, the death, and the resurrection of Jesus and the cosmic consequences are spelled out in a variety of forms in the other New Testament writings—all of which call for trust in the God who is working through Jesus for renewal of the world, and especially of his covenant people.

Kerygmatic Summaries

The letters of Paul include concise versions of the *kerygma* that he proclaimed, as well as indications of the distinctive ways in which he was convinced God had called him to convey this message. The challenge to spread the good news to the wider Gentile world came through Paul's vision of the risen Christ: "[God] was pleased to reveal his son to me, in order that I might preach him among the Gentiles" (Gal 1:16). The nearest to a summary of the gospel in Paul's letters appears in 1 Cor 15:1–8, where he reviews "the gospel which I preached to you . . . Christ died for our sins in accordance with the scriptures; he was buried, and he was raised on the third day in accordance with the scriptures; he appeared to Cephas, the twelve [disciples], more than five hundred brethren[14] . . . to James and to all the apostles. Last of all, as to one untimely born, he appeared also to me."

The appearance to Paul of the risen Christ was more than a personal confirmation of the redemptive role and significance of Jesus in the purpose of God for his people and for the renewal of the creation. It put into focus the place of Christ in the eternal purpose of God, as well as Paul's role in proclaiming it, which he set forth in the opening lines of his Letter to the Romans:

> Paul, a servant of Jesus Christ, called to be an apostle, set apart for the gospel of God which he promised beforehand through his prophets in the holy scriptures, the gospel concerning his Son, who was descended from David according to the flesh and designated Son of God in power according to the Spirit of Holiness by his resurrection from the dead, Jesus Christ our Lord, through whom we have received grace and apostleship to bring about the obedience of faith for the sake of his name among all the nations, including yourselves who are called to belong to Christ. (1:1–6)

It is for the spreading of this message throughout the world that Paul sees himself to have been called (1:9), and he has no shame or disappointment about his role in this enterprise, since this gospel "is the power of God for salvation to everyone who has faith—to the Jew first, and also to the Greek" (1:16). The significance of the crucifixion and resurrection of Christ is that they are to be seen as the divine factors that evoke trust on the part of those who hear this message. Any other message or interpretation of the death of Christ is subject to a divine curse (Gal 1:8–9). The true meaning of the gospel is to be proclaimed by Paul not only among Jews, but also among the Gentiles (Gal 1:16). It is a supreme irony that Paul, who once sought to destroy this faith, is now proclaiming it across the Gentile world (Gal 1:23).

The sermons attributed to Peter in Acts make claims similar to those of Paul. The basic affirmation is that through Jesus the age of fulfillment of God's promise in the scriptures for the renewal of his people and of the whole creation has dawned (2:16; 3:18, 24). This has been launched through the ministry, death, and resurrection of Jesus, who is depicted as descended from David (2:30–34), and as one whose ministry was characterized by power, prodigies, and signs (2:22). He is a prophet—one who speaks for God—like Moses (3:22), but his role in the purpose of God culminated in his death (2:23; 3:63–74), his resurrection (2:24–31; 3:15; 4:10), and his exaltation to God's right hand (3:15; Ps 110:1). Hence, he is the cornerstone of the new covenant people (Ps 128:22).

Further divine confirmation of what Jesus has launched has come through the outpouring of the Holy Spirit (2:17–21, 33; Joel 2:28–32). The messianic age is about to be inaugurated (3:21). In response to what God has done and continues to do through Christ, humans are called to repentance and promised forgiveness, a share in the Holy Spirit, and in the life of the age to come (2:38–39; Joel 2:32; Isa 57:19). There is no other source for salvation of human beings (4:12; 5:31). Omitted from the kerygmatic summaries in Acts are the designation of Jesus as Son of God, his death for human sins, and his intercession for his new people. But shared by Paul and the sermons in Acts are affirmations of Jesus' descent from David as Messiah, his death according to the scriptures, his resurrection and exaltation at God's right hand, the assurance of human deliverance from sin through him, and of his return to bring in the new age. In both sources, importance is also declared for the role of the Spirit in the life of the new community, and for the designation of the church as the new Israel of God. Thus, the claims made concerning the role of Jesus in his career, death, and resurrection differ in detail in the various New Testament writings, but in all of them the emphasis is on trust in what God has done and continues to do through Christ—all of which is seen as fulfillment of the promises made of old to Israel.

Confession of Faith

An essential complement to this personal trust in what God has done and continues to do through Christ for the renewal of the covenant people is the importance that those who share this faith give public testimony to their convictions. To engage in such public declaration is designated as "confession" (in Greek, *homologeo*), by which one identifies with the community that shares these convictions.[15]

Paul sets forth this public act as an essential feature of becoming a member of the new community: "If you confess with your lips and believe in your heart that God raised Jesus from the dead, you will be saved. For a person believes with his heart and so is set right with God, and he confesses with his lips and so is saved" (Rom 10:9). The term "confess" is also used for statements of personal identity, as when John the Baptist "confessed and did not deny" that he was neither the Messiah, nor Elijah, nor the eschatological prophet whose coming was predicted (Deut 18:15), but that he was the herald who announced the coming of God's ultimate agent of human redemption. Details of Paul's affirmation of faith are given in Acts 24:14, indicating what features of his pre-conversion beliefs are perceived to have been carried over into his new convictions concerning Christ as God's agent of covenantal renewal: ". . . According to the Way, which [the opponents] call a sect, I worship the God of our fathers, believing everything laid down by the law or written in the prophets, having a hope in God which these themselves accept, that there will be a resurrection of both the just and the unjust." Subsequently in Acts, Paul explains to King Agrippa that his beliefs rest on "nothing but what the prophets and Moses said would come to pass: that the Messiah must suffer, and that, by being the first to rise from the dead, he would proclaim light both to the [Jewish] people and the Gentiles" (Acts 26:22–23). The puppet king Agrippa is quoted as saying that if he were to believe these claims, he would "become a Christian." What is occurring when one moves from the earlier traditions in the gospels and the Pauline letters to the later New Testament writings is that faith is not only trust in what God has done, but also correct belief. This shift is even more apparent in the deuteropauline letter 1 Tim 6:12: "Take hold of eternal life to which you were called when you made good confession in the presence of many witnesses."

In 1 John 4:2–3 and 2 John 7, there are warnings against those who do not "confess that Jesus Christ has come in the flesh." Thus, this affirmation reflects the emergence among some adherents of the new movement of what was regarded by those who identified with the apostolic tradition as a heretical teaching known as Docetism: that Jesus was a divine being who had only the outward appearance of a human: a physical body. This issue is reflected in the later New Testament and other early Christian writings. Thus, in the second century CE, as is clearly evident in the Apostolic Fathers, there developed erroneous teachings that affirmed the divinity of Christ but denied his physical, human existence. Designated as Docetism (derived from the Greek word for "seem"), this doctrine sought to portray Jesus as an exalted divine being, but discredited his incarnation: he only *seemed* to be human. Clearly, the Gospel of John, with its assertion that in Jesus "the Word was made flesh," is seeking to combat this false teaching. Countering this heresy were also statements in the early second century such as those by Ignatius of Antioch about the true birth, suffering, and death of Jesus.[16] It is in this period that formal, credal statements began to emerge, and faith came to be perceived as not merely personal convictions, but as based on public affirmation of sound doctrines.

Before turning to the question of the origin of the Christian creeds, it is important to note that in the Letter to the Hebrews yet another perception of faith is evident—one which was also to have enduring import in the subsequent centuries of the life of the church. In this document, there is a shift from the temporal, apocalyptic base in the teachings of Jesus and Paul concerning the new age inaugurated by Jesus to perceiving faith on an ontological basis. This perception derives from the Platonic contrast between the eternal realm of the ideal and the ephemeral, worldly realm of the transitory, physical universe, as noted above in the analysis of Hebrews (324). The author of Hebrews portrays Jesus and his activity as constituting a disclosure of the eternal realm of the divine, rather than merely the temporal earthly sphere. The contrast is between time and eternity, and the way was thereby open for an interpretation of Christ and of God's purpose through him that was not primarily eschatological in perspective, but was shaped by this Platonic distinction between the temporal and the eternal.

The major Alexandrine Christian thinkers, Clement and especially Origen, reinterpreted the Christian tradition in accord with this ontological mode. Not surprisingly, therefore, one of Origen's most significant works was his study of the Gospel of John, where the *logos* and the symbolic imagery of both the narratives and the teachings of Jesus lent themselves readily to this mode of interpretation. For Origen and those of similar persuasion, the contrast was no longer between this age and the age to come, but between the temporal and the eternal.

Jaroslav Pelikan has effectively traced these developments in his study of "The Faith of the Catholic Church," specifically in terms of the section of that analysis designated "The Apocalyptic Vision and its Transformation" and "The Supernatural Order."[17] The delay in the Parousia of Christ, which was clearly a problem in the later New Testament period, is specifically addressed in 2 Pet 3:1–10. There the seeming delay is explained based on the difference between divine and human calculations of time: "With the Lord one day is like a thousand years, and a thousand years like one day." The non-fulfillment of the earlier expectation of the soon coming of the end of the present age is no longer to be regarded as a problem for the faith. An analogous shift is evident in the change from (1) kerygma as a call to trust in what God has done through Jesus for renewal of his people and for transformation of the world to (2) a set of beliefs that are to be affirmed: a creed. It is to this process of change that we now turn.

The Transition from Kerygma to Creed

In the kerygmatic summaries that appear in the New Testament and in the epitomized sermons of the apostles reported in Acts, the mode of communication is basically narrative: reporting what Jesus did and said and how he was mistreated by the civil and religious authorities, which resulted in his death and then his divine vindication by resurrection. In the second century CE, however, this mode of affirmation of the significance of Christ was replaced by what came to be known as rules of faith, or creeds. This development is described at the end of that century by the church fathers, Irenaeus and Tertullian, and is embodied in the creeds that began to appear about this time. A central factor in this development, however, is the claim of continuity between the testimony of the apostles and the affirmations embodied in the creeds.

Jaroslav Pelikan, in *The Christian Tradition: A History of the Development of Doctrine*,[18] points out that with the passing of the generation of the apostles, there was a shift in the thinking of the Christian leaders from the categories of an awaited cosmic drama—in anticipation of the new age promised in futuristic terms by the defeat of the powers of evil and the triumph of God's purpose for his people—to analyses based on modes of being, contrasting the present world bound in time and space with the supernatural realm of eternity and divine order.[19] Continuing to use the Old Testament as a base—especially the prophetic tradition—together with the apostles' perceptions and appropriation of their traditions, true faith for Christians was perceived by major thinkers of the second and third centuries to be based on the doctrine taught by the apostles. Thus, apostolic dogma came to be a standard term for what was believed, taught, and confessed by the orthodox Catholic Church, and was affirmed to be based on the Word of God.[20] The two major elements that constituted this faith in the early creeds were (1) the Trinity, and (2) the life, death, and resurrection of Christ.[21] These beliefs were affirmed by such major early Christian thinkers as Origen, Tertullian, and Irenaeus.

The collection of writings that comprise the New Testament was too long, diverse, and complicated to serve as a rule of faith. It was essential to have a condensed version of that rule, therefore, and this was accomplished in the later second century when such a rule of faith was formulated. Antecedents of the formation of a creed are evident in the early second century letter *To the Trallians* from Ignatius of Antioch, in which he warns those addressed to avoid the notion promoted by the Docetists[22] that the historical life of Jesus was unreal:

> Be deaf, therefore, whenever anyone speaks to you apart from Jesus Christ, who is of the family of David, and of Mary, who was truly born, both ate and drank, was truly persecuted under Pontius Pilate, was truly crucified and died in the sight of those in heaven, on earth, and under the earth; who also was truly raised from the dead, when his Father raised him up, as in the same manner shall raise up in Christ Jesus us who believe in him, without whom we have no true life.[23]

Similar credal statements appear in the *Epistula Apostolorum*, which was produced in Asia Minor or in Egypt in the mid-second century, where one is called to believe:

> In the Father, the Ruler of the Universe,
> And in Jesus Christ, our Redeemer,
> In the Holy Spirit, the Paraclete,
> In the Holy Church,
> And in the Forgiveness of Sins.[24]

By the early third century CE, a creed had developed in Rome that was to be the ancestor of the Apostles' Creed. The early version of this is preserved in a document known as Interrogatory Creed of Hippolytus, dating from about 215 CE:

> Do you believe in God the Father All Governing [*pantokratora*]?
> Do you believe in Christ Jesus, the Son of God, who was begotten by the Holy Spirit from the Virgin Mary, who was crucified under Pontius Pilate, and died (and was buried) and rose the third day living from the dead, and ascended into the heavens, and sat down on the right hand of the Father, and will come to judge the living and the dead?
> Do you believe in the Holy Spirit, and in the resurrection of the body [*sarkos*: flesh]?[25]

The final, enduring version of this creed seems to have been prepared about 700 CE, probably in southern France:

> I believe in God the Father almighty, creator of the heaven and the earth;
> And in Jesus Christ, His only Son, our Lord, Who was conceived by the Holy Spirit, born of the virgin Mary, suffered under Pontius Pilate, was crucified, dead and buried. He descended into hell, on the third day rose again from the dead, ascended to heaven, and sits at the right hand of God the Father almighty; thence he will come to judge the living and the dead;
> I believe in the Holy Spirit, the holy catholic church, the communion of the saints, the forgiveness of sins, the resurrection of the body [*carnis*], and the life everlasting. Amen.

A legend arose that claimed that this creed in what became its official form was composed by the apostles through inspiration of the Holy Spirit on the tenth day after Jesus' ascension. Clearly, the major motivation in the fashioning of this legend was the sense of importance for establishing continuity between the developing faith and practice of the church and those of the apostles as reported in the New Testament and other ancient traditions.

What seems to have happened in response to claims made by Marcion[26] and by the Montanists[27] is a pair of developments: "The decline in the eschatological hope and the rise of the monarchic episcopate are closely interrelated phenomena . . . in the second century church, and perhaps earlier, by which many Christians were beginning to adjust themselves to the possibility that the church might have to live in the world for a considerable time to come." There was a decline in both intensity and frequency "of the charismata that had been so prominent in the earlier stages of the Christian movement."[28] Thus, the church in its ethnic, cultural, and conceptual diversity began to seek out modes of organizational and structural formation, confirmed by defined leadership and by confessional unity. These developments involved not only conceptual matters, as reflected in kerygma and creed, but also the shaping of the patterns of worship and, above all, the specifying of the leadership roles in the church.

Ritual Formulations

Another mode of structuring that is evident in the New Testament involves the emergence of ritual and liturgical formulas by which the members celebrated their identity as God's people and the divinely initiated events that brought into being the new community. The basic ritual acts by which participation in the new community was affirmed were (1) the initiatory rite of baptism, and (2) the ongoing celebration of the founding events in the rite of the Eucharist.

Baptism

The prototype for the baptism of Jesus and subsequently of his followers was, of course, the baptism practiced by John, as reported in the Markan, Lukan, and Q traditions.[29] As noted in our analysis of the gospels, baptism signified one's public commitment to the new life, to the new community, and to God's agent of renewal—Jesus. Those who shared in this rite were to be the true and faithful "children of Abraham" (Luke 3:8). Their public testimony to this change was their participation in baptism. In Matthew's gospel, Jesus instructs his followers to go forth and "make disciples from all nations." The confirmation of this new relationship was to be given by the disciples through "baptizing them in the name of the Father and of the Son and of the Holy Spirit," followed by instructing them to observe the new commandments taught by Jesus (Matt 28:19–20). Acts 2:37–42 is an account of the response of thousands to Peter's address to the throng following the outpouring of the Holy Spirit on the Day of Pentecost. They were called to be "baptized every one of you in the name of Jesus Christ" so that they might "receive the gift of the Holy Spirit." Those who "welcomed the message were baptized" and "devoted themselves to the apostles' teaching and fellowship, to the breaking of bread and the prayers."

Eucharist

"Breaking of bread" is, of course, another way of referring to the Lord's Supper or Eucharist. The two earlier accounts of Jesus' instituting this rite appear in Mark 14:22–25 and 1 Cor 11:23–26. Just before the crucifixion, the shared loaf and cup at the celebration of the Passover by Jesus and the disciples are said to symbolize his body broken for them and his blood, which confirms the new covenant. It also looks forward to his being reunited with them when the kingdom of God has fully come (Mark 14:25). Their continuing sharing of the loaf and cup are an essential mode for "proclaiming the Lord's death until he comes" (1 Cor 11:26). The gospels declare that

Jesus will not share these elements with them again until the kingdom of God has come (Mark 14:25), when they will join him on his "glorious throne" and have a role in the judging of the people of God (Luke 22:15, 28–29; Matt 26:29; 19:28). Thus, the words of Jesus became the liturgical basis for the ongoing performance of this ritual.

Liturgical Structures

Other modes of structuring evident in the early stages of Christianity also have to do with ritual and liturgical features. The patterns adopted in the early Christian hymns and prayers derived in large measure from the psalms and prophetic oracles.

As indicated above, the eucharistic ritual is evident from both the gospel and the Pauline traditions. Paul's version is very likely an earlier literary document than what appears in Mark's gospel, but they are remarkably consonant. Paul claims to have received the eucharistic liturgical tradition "from the Lord"! It reads: ". . . the Lord Jesus on the night that he was betrayed took a loaf of bread, and when he had given thanks [*eucharistesous*], he broke it, and said, 'This is my body which is for you. Do this in remembrance of me.' In the same way also the cup, after supper, saying, 'This cup is the new covenant in my blood. Do this as often as you drink it, in remembrance of me.' For as often as you eat this bread and drink this cup, you proclaim the Lord's death until he comes." In the account of Jesus' final Passover meal with his disciples,[30] Mark reports, "While they were eating, he took a loaf of bread, gave it to them, and said, 'Take; this is my body.' Then he took a cup, and after giving thanks he gave it to them, and all of them drank from it. He said to them, 'This is my blood of the [new][31] covenant which is poured out for many. Truly I tell you, I will never again drink of the fruit of the vine until that day when I drink it new in the kingdom of God.'" The Lukan version of the establishment of the Eucharist, however, includes the reference to "the new covenant" (Luke 22:20). Thus, the fluidity of this ritual formula in the early centuries of the church is evident.

The liturgical features of the practice of baptism are fewer and less clear. The most familiar indication of a baptismal liturgy is in Matt 28:19–20, where the risen Christ instructs his disciples, "Go therefore and make disciples of all nations, baptizing them in the name of the Father and of the Son and of the Holy Spirit." This baptismal formula is followed by Jesus' call to "teach [these newly-baptized converts] to observe all that I commanded you." In Acts 2:38, the converts are told by Peter that they should "repent and be baptized in the name of Jesus Christ," which will result in their receiving forgiveness of sins and the gift of the Holy Spirit. In the letters of Paul, it is clear that baptism was "into Christ" (Gal 3:27), or into the body of Christ

(1 Cor 12:13), and resulted in one's being "clothed with Christ" (Gal 3:27). As one descended into the baptismal water and then emerged, one was perceived as having been buried with Christ and then raised to new life (Rom 6:3). This transforming rite was seen as the outcome of being "baptized in the name of Jesus" (Acts 19:5).

The community's celebration of what God has done and continues to do for the new covenant people is expressed in liturgical fashion. This embodies terms and modes adapted from the liturgical features in the psalms and the prophetic oracles, as noted above. These are evident in both the gospels and the letters of the New Testament. In Rom 11:33–36, following citations from Psalms and Prophets,[32] Paul offers a hymn-like conclusion to his examination of the fate of Israel (Rom 9–11) that combines allusions to scripture (Isa 40:13; Job 41:11) with his own poetic utterances of praise to God for the deep and rich knowledge divinely provided, joined with the affirmation of God's universal sovereignty.

In his appeal to the Philippians for humility, unity, and mutual concerns, Paul cites a hymn that celebrates the incarnation of Christ (2:6–11). He urges them to gain the same mindset or aspiration that was embodied by Jesus, who did not exploit his divine status, but took on the role of a slave—human in form, and obedient to God to the extent of accepting death on a cross, which was an agonizing and utterly humiliating kind of death. Yet God has rewarded him by exalting him above all others, and decreed that at his name every human being should ultimately bow and publicly acknowledge his lordship, thereby glorifying the Father whose plan this was for the renewal of his people. The poetic style and the rhythmic mode of this hymn is Jewish, as is the centrality of Jesus' role as God's servant (Isa 52:13–53:12). Other later hymnic features in the Pauline and deuteropauline letters include Paul's hymn concerning God's love in 1 Cor 13, Eph 1:3–14, Col 1:15–20, and hymn-like utterances in 1 Tim 1:17 and 3:16.

The two major examples of formal prayers in the New Testament are both in the gospel tradition: the Lord's Prayer (Matt 6:9–15) and Jesus' final prayer for the disciples in John 17:10–26, which in both style and substance serves as a model for the community. As noted above, the formal development of the Lord's Prayer is apparent when one compares the older, shorter, and simpler Q version, as it appears in Luke 11:2–4, with the fuller version in Matt 6:9–13. This formalizing development is also evident in what might be called the liturgical mode of ethical and social instruction as it appears in the third-person, generalized Matthean version of the Beatitudes (Matt 5:3–12). In contrast with this is the Lukan form of the Beatitudes, where they are set forth in a prophetic mode as personal, direct address to the disciples in the second person. The worship life of the new community, though diverse in details, shares the foundational feature of building on the hymnic traditions of Israel, especially as found in Psalms and the Prophets.

The New Testament writing with the highest degree of hymnic material is the Revelation to John. Written in a time and circumstance of oppression and grave threat for the church at the hands of the Roman imperial authorities, the book opens with the pronouncement of divine provision of peace from God through Christ, and an expression of gratitude for the relationship God has established with his people through him, whose triumphant return is now awaited (1:5–7).

Other liturgical features in Revelation include the trishagion (thrice-holy) uttered by the four living creatures who surround the throne of God (4:8), and the song of the twenty-four elders praising the glory and power of God (4:11). In 5:9–13 is a series of hymns in adoration of Christ the Lamb, through whom God's purpose for the creation is to be achieved. In 7:9–12, an innumerable multitude gathers to honor God and the Lamb. As the last of seven trumpets sounds (11:15), the heavenly voices proclaim the universal and everlasting rule of God through Christ, to which the leaders respond with gratitude and praise (11:16–18).

Revelation 12:10–12 is a hymn of gratitude for the coming defeat of Satan and for the vindication of the faithful. Pronouncements of doom for the powers of evil and of praise for the blessing awaiting the faithful are in 14:8, 13. A song of Moses and the Lamb praising God the Father for his wonderful deeds is offered in 15:3–4, and in 16:5–7 there is a song of gratitude for God's punishment of the enemies of his people. Revelation 18:2–3 is a hymn rejoicing in the fall of Babylon—which symbolizes the imperial power of Rome—that is followed by a hymnic appeal to the faithful to flee the city before God's judgment falls on it. Mourning for the wicked city and joy for the deliverance of God's people and their leaders are offered in hymnic form in 18:19–20 and 21–24.

The heavenly hosts join in praise to God for his triumph over the powers of evil, and there follows an utterance of joy at the vindication of God's people (19:5–8). As the divine overcoming sin and death comes to completion, there are songs of praise and promise from the heavenly throne (21:3–4). Thus, formal expressions of praise for the divine triumph over the powers of evil and for the accomplishment of God's renewal of his people and of the creation pervade Revelation.

The outstanding feature of the New Testament that contributed to the shaping of the church's enduring liturgical tradition, however, appears in the stories of the birth of Jesus in Luke 1 and 2. There are six liturgical sections in these chapters of Luke, three of which came to be used widely in the church and are identified on the basis of the titles assigned to them in the

Latin-speaking church: Magnificat (1:46–55), Benedictus (1:68–79), and Gloria in Excelsis (2:14). They draw on the Old Testament, especially Psalms and the Prophets, but are incorporated into the narrative of Luke as he describes the preparations for the birth of Jesus the Messiah.[33]

The first of these canticles comes as the angelic message to Zechariah the priest that his wife is to bear a son. He will come to be known as John the Baptist and will prepare the way for God's Messiah (1:13–17). The son will be an ascetic who will resemble Elijah as an agent of the power of the Spirit, will call parents to greater responsibility toward their children, and will prepare a true people of God, bringing the disobedient to wisdom.[34]

The second canticle is uttered by the angel Gabriel to the virgin Mary (1:30–33). The message is that she, as a virgin, will give birth to a son, whose name will be Jesus,[35] and whose role as "son of the Most High" will be to serve as king forever. His birth will be the work of the Holy Spirit, and he will be acclaimed as the Son of God. The third canticle in Luke is Mary's song of praise, which came to be known as the Magnificat (1:46–55), echoing the theme in Ps 69:30, where the name of God is praised and magnified. Other elements in this song that recall the Law, the Prophets, and the Writings of the Old Testament include the acclaim of God as "my salvation" (Ps 25:5; Isa 12:2: Mic 7:7); the declaration of the blessedness of women (Gen 30:13); the affirmation of the great things God has done (Deut 10:21); the holiness of God's name (Ps 119:9; Isa 57:15); God's mercy (Ps 103:17); mighty arm (Ps 89:11); and aid to Israel (Isa 41:8–9). These developments will result in the ultimate fulfillment of God's covenant promises to Abraham and Jacob (Mic 7:20).

The fourth canticle is the Benedictus, uttered by Spirit-filled Zechariah, the father of John the Baptist (1:67–79). Here, too, the imagery and affirmations echo the history and prophetic traditions of Israel: the blessedness of God (Ps 41:14; 72:18; 106:48; 1 Kgs 1:48); the identification of God's agent for renewal of his people as "a horn of salvation" (1 Sam 2:10; Ps 18:3; 132:17); the recalling of God's promise to Abraham (Gen 26:3; Mic 7:20) and to the ancestors of the people of Israel (Jer 11:5); the light that will come to God's people in darkness (Isa 59:8); and the way of peace that God will show them (Isa 59:8).

The "multitude of the heavenly host" that joins the angel to address the fearful shepherds at the birth of Jesus in "the city of David" (2:4, 11) identifies the one to be born there as Savior, Messiah, and Lord, calling for praise to God in the heavenly realms (*Gloria in excelsis*), and proclaiming peace on earth for those with whom God is pleased (2:14).

The last of this series of canticles, which came to be known as *Nunc Dimittis* (2:29–32), is uttered by Simeon, a devout man to whom it had been revealed that he would live to see "the Lord's Messiah." When Jesus is brought to the temple to be circumcised, Simeon recognizes him to be God's agent for the salvation that God has prepared "in the presence of all peoples: a light for revelation to the Gentiles, and for glory to [God's] people Israel." God's invitation to share in the life of his new people goes out to all humanity. Simeon has seen God's agent for this—the child Jesus—and so he is now ready to depart from this life, but he adds a note to Mary that the son to be born to her will be a cause for divergence in Israel, and that she will suffer deeply as he fulfills his divinely ordained role. He will be the one through whom the inner thoughts of humans will be disclosed (2:33–35).

Thus not only the general structural format but also specific features of worship in the early church are provided in the Gospel of Luke. These hymnic materials build on liturgical elements in the Jewish scriptures, and have continued to be used by the church down to the present day.

Leadership Roles

Antecedent Leadership Roles in Judaism, and Christian Adaptation of Them

Although the early Christians had distinctive features in their claims as to what God had launched and was carrying out through Christ—factors that are evident from the constant claims in the New Testament that scripture is being fulfilled through him and the community he launched—one sees that both the models for the new community and the defining of the leadership roles build on biblical and subsequent Jewish precedents, while modifying them in significant ways in response to the concurrent sociocultural developments in the Graeco-Roman world. The role analyses that follow seek to show both the antecedents in Judaism and the presence of innovative features in the early Christian writings.

Prophets

Although the roles of the prophets are depicted in a variety of ways in the Old Testament and other ancient Jewish sources, the one common feature in these documents is that the prophet serves as a medium of communication between God and his people. The aims and modes of communication differ, however, as do the specifics of the prophetic role and the major emphases operative in their messages. In the Jewish biblical tradition, those identified as prophets or prophetesses include not only the writers of the prophetic books of the Bible, but such figures from the early history of Israel as Abraham, Aaron, Miriam, and Deborah.[36] Moses is said to have had no match as a prophet (Deut 34:10), but it is predicted that he will be followed in later times by one whose message will include all God's commandments, and that all God's people are to heed his message (Deut 18:15–18). In Peter's sermon in Acts (3:17–24), this prediction is said to have been fulfilled through Jesus, and the result of it will be blessing for "all the families of the earth," in accord with the promise of God to Abraham (Gen 22:18).

When the writings were assembled by Jewish leaders to form the Hebrew Bible, a distinction was made between the Former Prophets (Joshua, Judges, the books of Samuel and Kings) and the Latter Prophets: Isaiah, Jeremiah, Ezekiel, and the Twelve Prophets (which were treated as one book). Daniel was included in the section called simply the Writings. Modern scholarship, however, differentiates between the roles of the prophets before and after the exile in Babylon as well as noting the features characteristic of their respective writings—as described below. But it should be recognized that there are also a number of persons identified as prophets in the biblical tradition who predate the writing prophets—and even the monarchy. Thus Samuel, who is called a prophet (1 Sam 3:20), uses the prophetic formula, "Thus says the Lord" (10:18; 15:2). By him the word of the Lord "came to all Israel" (1 Sam 4:1), and he was the one commissioned by God to anoint Saul as Israel's first king (1 Sam 9:15–17; 10:1).

Other non-writing prophets include Elijah and Elisha. In 1 Kgs 16 to 2 Kgs 2, there is a series of stories reporting the critical message and the impact of the prophet Elijah on the policies and acts of the successive kings of Israel. The most dramatic of these accounts describes Elijah's challenge to the kings, which produces a remarkable result: Elijah's triumph over the priests of Baal, the god whose worship was brought to Israel by King Ahab's Tyrian wife, Jezebel. The prophet Malachi predicts Elijah's future return and his effective call of the people to repentance in preparation for "the great and terrible day of the Lord"—God's final and cosmic defeat of the powers of evil (Mal 4:5–6). His successor in the northern kingdom of Israel, Elisha (2 Kgs 2–9), was primarily seen as God's agent who called Israel back to obedience to Yahweh. Similarly, Nathan the prophet served as the crucial advisor to King David in the carrying out of the covenant relationship between God and his people (2 Sam 7:1–16).

The earliest prophets whose oracles were preserved in writing date from the eighth century BCE: Amos, Hosea, Micah, and Isaiah;[37] these were followed in the seventh century by Zechariah, Jeremiah, Nehemiah, Habakkuk, and Ezekiel. In the sixth century, the prophecies that scholars have come to call Second Isaiah (40–66) were written, addressed to the people of Israel in exile in Babylon, before and subsequent to the triumph of the Persian ruler, Cyrus,[38] over the Babylonians. This was followed by his decision and program for the return of the Israelites to their own land and for the restoration of the ruined temple in Jerusalem (44:28)—all of which were seen as the outworking of God's plan for the renewal of his people (45:11–19).[39] The composite book of Isaiah conveys the twofold message of the prophets concerning: (1) God's sovereign rule in history, which brings judgment on the disobedient people and the powers of evil; and (2) the divine plan and capacity to triumph over these powers, to renew his covenant people, and to establish a universal rule.

The theme of this divine triumph came to be perceived in ways that built on the Jewish prophetic tradition, but were also akin to a comparable hope for moral and cosmic renewal in the Graeco-Roman world: divine sovereignty over the natural world and the realm of history was expected to lead through a succession of periods to a climactic new age in which peace and justice would prevail. This view of history found expression in apocalyptic literature, features of which are evident in Isa 24–27, but which is fully developed in the basic perspective and mode of communication embodied in the book of Daniel. It is found later in such writings as the books of *Enoch*, the *Apocalypse of Abraham*, and other documents among the Dead Sea Scrolls. Analogous features of this material appear also in Graeco-Roman philosophy, as discussed in Excursus 5.

As noted above,[40] the *Sibylline Oracles*—found initially in Graeco-Roman writings and subsequently in Jewish and Christian literature, with dates ranging from the second century BCE to the seventh century CE—highlight the advent of a glorious kingdom and the transformation of the earth under a ruler who affirms and seeks to put into effect the cosmic purpose of the one God who rules the universe. There are solemn warnings of destruction that will come on evildoers, and an appeal to the people for obedience and gratitude toward the deity whose purpose is being worked out in human history.

One of the most vivid and powerful expressions of this worldview in Roman literature appears in the Fourth Eclogue of the Latin poet, Virgil. He reports a message from the Sibyl based in Cumae in Sicily, in which is proclaimed that a new cycle of the ages is soon to begin. This will lead to the emergence of "a golden race throughout the world" in which human heroes will mingle with the gods. The resulting virtues will bring peace: hostility between animals will cease, the powers of evil will be overcome, and every land shall produce all the fruits with unprecedented fertility. Accordingly, those who hear and heed this message will unite in praise: "All things exult in the age that is at hand."

As John J. Collins has noted, "All the Sibyllline Oracles were essentially religious. Prodigies, portents, and political crises were all related to the will of the gods and then to matters of right worship. . . . The pagan Sibyl spoke for Apollo, as surely as her Jewish counterpart spoke for Yahweh."[41] The periodization of history in these oracles probably developed under Persian influence after the fourth century BCE, and is reflected in Virgil's reference to the "final age." The high esteem in which the oracles were held in the Roman world seems to have led Jewish and Christian writers to adopt this mode.

Antecedents were already present in the later Jewish prophetic tradition, which sought to convey the message of cosmic renewal to the prophets' contemporaries. Evidence of their use of this medium of instruction and propaganda extends from the second century BCE to the seventh century CE, building on the oracles from the Hellenistic world that depicted the coming of a glorious kingdom and the transformation of the earth and its people—together with solemn warnings of the destruction that awaits evildoers. The appeal is for recognition and honoring of the God who rules the universe and human history,[42] who through Christ will bring judgment on all of disobedient humanity, including the wicked church leaders who are more concerned to gain wealth than to deal justly with those in need (*Sib. Or.* 2:252–282). The wicked are to be thrown into hell, but the faithful will be taken into the presence of God and granted eternal life (2:315ff.).

Thus, both the major thrust of early Christian apocalyptic—the expectation of God's action through his chosen and empowered agent, Jesus Christ, to renew his people and establish the divine rule on earth—and the literary mode through which this hope was conveyed had antecedent models in the wider Graeco-Roman world. These features and historical antecedents of apocalyptic are discussed more fully in Excursus 5, "Facing the Future: Common Themes in Jewish Apocalyptic and Graeco-Roman Philosophy and Literature." This conceptual kinship helps to account in a significant way for the rapid spread of the Christian message and convictions throughout the Roman world.

Priests

The Old Testament references to priests link them and at times contrast them with the Levites. The roles of both these groups undergo change in the biblical tradition, reflecting a range of circumstances under which these agents functioned. In the tribal period of Israel—following the exodus, when the Levites cared for the ark of the covenant—they also served as priests. They continued to do so when the tribes settled in the land of Canaan and established a central shrine in which the ark was the major feature. They claimed to be descendants of Moses or of Ithamar, Aaron's youngest son, through whom the father's priestly role was continued (Exod 6:23). When the central sanctuary was located in Jerusalem in the reign of David—with other sanctuaries operative with their own priests in many places in the land—the claim was made that only descendants of Levi could perform the sacred rites in "the house of God" in Jerusalem. They also transmitted and administered the divine law (Deut 17:18; 33:10). But in other biblical traditions, the Levites' role was to convey the purpose of God for his people

(Judg 18:3–6) and to give instruction to them in the divine law (Deut 33:10; 2 Chron 17:7–9; 35:3). In Ezek 44:10–14, however, they are denounced for erring from the true worship of God, and their role is reduced to that of caretakers in the temple rather than priests. In addition, two of the collections of Psalms are attributed to Levitical groups: the Korahites (Ps 42, 44) and Asaph (Ps 73–83).

In the postexilic period, however, the Levites are depicted as having a special role in relation to the ark of the covenant (1 Chron 15): they alone can carry the ark (15:15). They take it to a tent in Jerusalem, and they alone can serve "as ministers before the ark of the Lord" (1 Chron 16:4). The ark was the embodiment of two major factors: (1) the joint commitment of the Israelite tribes to God and to his covenant with them; (2) the visible symbol of God's continuing presence among his people. Hence, priests and Levites were perceived as the intermediaries between God and his people: conveying messages from God to them, serving as the agents to offer sacrifices as signs of gratitude and commitment, as well as the means whereby the sins and failures of the people could be atoned for and forgiveness granted. The priests announced God's blessing of the people (Num 6:22–26), and blew the trumpets on the occasion of the holy days (Num 29:1), especially on the Day of Atonement to mark the fiftieth year.[43] This action served as an expression of gratitude, penitence, and covenant renewal (Num 29:7–11).

When the Jews under their Maccabean rulers gained independence from the Hellenistic powers (from 65 BCE), the priests were the dominant group, with the royal and priestly roles mingled. The Dead Sea sect became critical of the official priests in Jerusalem, however, and so established its own priestly group. They expected a priestly messiah who would be co-ruler with the royal messiah. Because of the major economic and sociological role of the high priest in this period under the Roman rule, he was appointed by the Romans. His function was not only religious, but also financial, since the largest source of income in that region came from contributions to the temple made by pious visitors and by those who wanted to give concrete evidence of their commitment to the God who was believed to dwell there. Thus, in the time of Jesus, the priests were of major importance religiously, socially, economically, and politically.

The priestly roles involved the diagnosis of diseases that individuals had, which led to the performance of appropriate rites of purification. The priests were forbidden to have physical contact with the dead, including their own parents and offspring. The priesthood defined, embodied, and sought to enforce sanctity as it was perceived in the Torah. Jesus' social and physical contact with the diseased and the ritually impure was thus seen by his law-abiding Jewish contemporaries as a major violation of covenant obligations—and therefore as disqualifying him from fulfilling a priestly role.

Elders

The elders—who were heads of families or clans—were the representatives of the people of Israel as a whole.[44] It is they who came to Moses to offer sacrifices to God, and to receive "the words of the Lord and all the ordinances" (Exod 24:2). These functions provided the basis for the ongoing covenant relationship and for the responsibilities of the people. In Num 11:16–37, Moses has been instructed to gather seventy elders of the people, to whom God will talk and who will receive some of the Spirit that has come upon Moses. But they shall also "bear the burden of the people along with Moses" for the level of their obedience. As a sign of the divine presence and power, the Spirit comes upon them and they prophesy. Subsequently, the elders conveyed to Samuel the judge the people's request to have a king (1 Sam 8:1–9). In the time of the judges and kings, the elders were leaders of the municipalities, and made important judicial, military, and political decisions. Even though their power declined with the rise of the monarchy, the kings continued to turn to the elders for counsel in critical situations (1 Kgs 20:7–8; 21:8, 11).

Joshua 23–24 is the account of Joshua's summoning "all Israel, their elders and heads, their judges and their officers" in order to inform them of his departure and to call them to obey "all that is written in the law of Moses," including warnings of dire consequences if they fail to obey the covenant. Analogously, the prophets later tell of the judgment of God that is to fall on Jerusalem and Judah because the elders and princes have exploited the rest of the people (Isa 3:14). The significance of Jeremiah's symbolic act in shattering an earthenware jug as a sign of the judgment that is to fall on the city and nation is conveyed to the leaders and some of the senior priests (Jer 19:1). When Jeremiah utters to the officials and to all the people a warning of the city's destruction, it is the elders who explain that this will be divine judgment (16:17). Ezekiel predicts that, in spite of the people's search for peace and for a vision from the prophet, instruction from the priests and counsel from the elders will soon come to an end (Ezek 7:25–26).

During the exile, the elders appear to have been the chief leaders in self-government among the exiles—apparently deriving their authority from their position as head of aristocratic families. During the Hellenistic and Roman periods—probably with antecedents during the time of Persian dominance of Palestine—the elders were major figures, constituting, with the priests, the council (*synedrion*), which gave a degree of local autonomy to the native groups. It was this mode of leadership that constituted the council that convened at Jamnia after the fall of Jerusalem in 70, providing structures and guidelines for the continuing life of the Jewish community. It is against this historical background that one must (1) assess the dominant role of the Jewish elders in the gospel narratives, and (2) discern the role of elders in early Christianity.

The elders were the representatives of the people of the land (1 Kgs 20:7; 21:8, 11). When David escaped from the plot of Absalom to assassinate him (2 Sam 16–18), he mourned for Absalom and then sought the support of elders in Jerusalem to restore him to authority there (2 Sam 19:11–15). They urged him to return to the city with his royal retinue, which he did, and he was met with a promise of support and obedience from the people (19:16–18). The elders were the representatives of all the people of Israel as Solomon prepared for the dedication of the temple, and they are linked in 1 Kgs 8:1 with the "heads of the tribes and the leaders of the ancestral houses of the Israelites" (1 Kgs 8:1). They joined the Levites to carry the "ark of the Lord" into the tent of the covenant (8:4). In Deuteronomy, they are the agents to accomplish just punishment of evildoers (19:11–13) and to aid in just settlement of legal disputes (22:15; 25:7–8). The elders meet to carry out their judicial functions in the city gates (Prov 31:23).

A more formal role for the elders developed in the Hellenistic period. When Antiochus III and his troops entered the city of Jerusalem, they drove out the Egyptian troops that had occupied the citadel and provided the Jews with the food and supplies they needed—not only to survive, but also to resume the worship of God in the temple, which was to be rebuilt—"making the restoration of the temple more splendid"—and establishing the indigenous form of government. This was to be "in accordance with the laws of their country" and to involve not only the priests and scribes of the temple, but primarily "the senate."[45] This body is here designated as the *gerousia,* but references in the books of Maccabees to the members of this official body call them *presbyteroi*. Thus, this group was a Council of the Elders, serving in both legislative and judicial capacities.

Scribes[46]

It is estimated that in the ancient Near East, as well as in Graeco-Roman society, 90 percent of the populace were illiterate—most of them farmers. But the literate minority included those who served as administrative and financial officials, educators, and religious functionaries: for them, an overarching term was "scribes" (Hebrew, *sopherim*). The courts of Egypt and Mesopotamia had elaborate systems of scribal training and administration—which was probably imitated in Israel from the time of Solomon on—including financial, administrative, and policy-making functions. Second Kings 22 describes the major role of Shaphan in the seventh century BCE as secretary or scribe to the youthful King Josiah of Judah. In this capacity, he distributed funds to the workers repairing the temple and reported to the king the recovery in the temple of a copy of the "book of the law" (22:1–13). On hearing the law as Shaphan, the scribe, read it to King Josiah, the monarch was overcome with contrition, and launched his historic reform (22:14–23:25). Other scribes kept records of the prophets, as Baruch did in the time of Jeremiah (Jer 36:32). At the time of the return of the Israelites from Persia, King Artaxerxes sent instructions for the life of this people through "the priest Ezra, the scribe, a scholar of the text of the commandments of the Lord and his statutes for Israel," identifying him as "scribe of the law of the God of heaven" (Ezra 7:11–12). Study of the Law was fostered by the scribes, whose associates gave instruction in the law, and who were given considerable authority by the king over the Jewish community (Ezra 7:21–26).

In the Graeco-Roman period, Eleazar, a scribe in a high position, defied the Syrian powers' decree that he must eat pork, and was accordingly tortured and put to death (2 Macc 6:18–31). In the works of Josephus, the roles of scribes range from village copyists to members of the Jerusalem-based regional council.[47] The term *sopherim* (= people of the book) came to be used chiefly for teachers devoted to study and interpretation of the law of Moses—a role that was subsequently taken over by those who called themselves "rabbis."[48]

At the time of the return of the people of Israel from exile in Babylon, Ezra is pictured as fostering the study of the law of Moses and keeping the records of what was required for settling in the traditional land (Ezra 7:11–23). As a scribe, it was his responsibility to appoint the judges who enforced the law. Others who earlier served as record-keeping scribes included Shemaiah, a Levite in the reign of David according to 1 Chr 24:1–6. Ezra and his associates continued to give instruction in the Law (Neh 8), and were granted limited authority over the Jewish community by the Persians (Ezra 7:21–26).

In the Graeco-Roman period, however, the term *sopherim* (= people of the book) was used for scholars and teachers devoted to the study and interpretation of the law of Moses—a role that was later formalized and designated as "rabbi." But in the Hellenistic era, it was the scribes who carried out this mode of ministry. When a leading scribe died for the law, the scribes sought reconciliation with Alcimus, the high priest. He had been appointed by the Seleucid ruler, Demetrius (1 Macc 7:1–19), and killed many of the Hasideans[49] in one day.

Some Jews in this scribal role are referred to in the gospel tradition, including those of Pharisaic persuasion who are pictured as opposing Jesus. In Mark, the scribes associated with the chief priests as part of the government of Judea are a politically unified group, and function as the authoritative teachers of Jewish law and custom (1:22; 9–11). In Matthew, they comprise learned groups, in villages as well as in Jerusalem, and this gospel is severely critical of the scribal opposition to Jesus. In Luke-Acts, they are linked with the chief priests and are the learned leaders of Jews in Jerusalem. Luke at times replaces "scribe" with "lawyer" (Luke 10:25/Mark 12:28/Matt

22:35), but the role implicit in the texts is that of the scribes (Luke 7:30; 11:45; 14:8). They are experts on Jewish life and piety, and learned leaders, based chiefly in Jerusalem, seeking to protect the covenant people from pagan pollution. Within the Jewish community, however, they have a kind of bureaucratic role in the interface between Jews and the Romans. And that role as low-level officials and judges in Jerusalem, as well as in other Jewish towns and villages, may have gained for them an authority recognized by the Romans.

In 1 Cor 1:20, Paul groups three types of Jewish leaders whose roles are interrelated—"wise man . . . scribe . . . debater"—and whose claims to wisdom and authority he denigrates, in contrast to "Christ the power of God and the wisdom of God" (1:24). The scribe in the first century CE is not merely a copyist of documents, but a teacher and interpreter of the sacred texts, showing their relevance for their contemporaries. It was this scribal function that was continued in Judaism by those calling themselves rabbis in the period after the fall of Jerusalem to direct Roman control.

A central feature of Judaism and of emergent Christianity in this period developed when the roles of the scribes and the rabbis became formalized: the need arose for instruction and for orientation of the members of these communities, given the transition of the Jewish movements from their spontaneous and charismatic origins to their requisite structuring. Such developments involved the defining of leadership roles and patterns of instruction. As we shall see, a similar pattern of sociological and conceptual change is evident within early Christianity as one moves from the earlier to the later New Testament writings. The specifics of these latter changes were understandably influenced and shaped in part by conscious similarities and contrast with analogous developments in both Jewish and Graeco-Roman culture of the time.

Rabbis

Originally a general title of honor, meaning "my lord" or "my master," *rabbi* came to be used for one who was regarded as a master of Torah.[50] Earlier, the role of interpreting and putting into operation the law was carried out by a judge or administrator, but "rabbi" came to be used for those who lived and functioned in the rabbinical academy. This was not only a school for the study of Jewish law, but was also a holy community that sought to foster convictions of its members as to the relevance of Torah for the lives of individuals and communities committed to the will of God. Participants in such academies wanted to live in conformity to ethical and ritual requirements that would lead them to obedience and purity. The deliberations carried out by such groups and the decisions reached by them produced the vast body of material that came to be known in the fourth and fifth centuries and subsequently as

rabbinic literature: the Mishnah and the Talmud.[51] The role of rabbis as ana-
lysts and formulators of the ongoing meaning and relevance of Torah, however, is directly anticipated at an earlier stage within Christianity: in the New
Testament, and especially in the Gospel of Matthew, which is analyzed above
as the product of the Law-Abiding Community.

The term *rabbi* appears in the New Testament only in the gospel tradition—in Mark, Matthew and John. In the account of the transfiguration of
Jesus (Mark 9:2–8)—seen by Peter, James, and John—Peter addresses Jesus as
"rabbi," and suggests that three booths be made: for Jesus, Moses, and Elijah,
who are perceived to be major agents of divine disclosure. The return of the
latter two is anticipated in scripture: the appearance of a prophet like Moses
in Deut 18:15; the return of Elijah in Mal 3:1; 4:5, who will turn the hearts
of parents and children to obedience to God before the land is to be struck
with a curse. In Mark 11:21, as Jesus and the disciples pass the fig tree that
Jesus had cursed, Peter calls him "Rabbi" and notes that the tree has withered. In Mark 14:45, Judas identifies Jesus to the crowd assembled from the
chief priests, scribes, and elders by addressing him as "Rabbi" and then kissing him. A kindred term, *Rabbouni*, is used by the blind man who asks Jesus
to restore his sight (Mark 10:51). In Matthew, the term *rabbi* appears in only
two passages: (1) in 23:1–8, the scribes and Pharisees are denounced for
claiming to be the ultimate interpreters of the law of Moses, while placing
moral and ritual burdens on others, engaging in public display of their
allegedly pious status, seeking places of honor in the synagogues, and insisting that they be addressed in public as rabbi. Instead, they are told that God
is to be their sole father, through whom they are to experience commonality
as God's people, acknowledging Christ alone as their authoritative teacher
(*kathegetes*; 23:10). And (2) ironically, Judas, as he engages in betraying Jesus
to the civil and religious authorities, addresses him as Rabbi (= "master")
(Matt 26:25, 49).

In the Gospel of John, *rabbi* first appears when Jesus is addressed with
that term by two of the disciples of John the Baptist, who ask where he is
staying and are invited there by him. Rabbi is said to mean "teacher" (John
1:38). When Nathanael is being called by Jesus as a follower, he declares to
Jesus, "Rabbi, you are the Son of God" (1:49). Similarly, Nicodemus, "a ruler
of the Jews," addresses Jesus as "Rabbi . . . a teacher come from God" (3:2).
When Jewish critics report to John the Baptist that Jesus is also engaging in
baptism and rallying followers, they call him "Rabbi" (3:26). Clearly, it is
seen here as a term for the leader of a reforming religious movement in the
Jewish tradition.

In the Johannine account of Jesus' extended engagement with the woman
at the well in Samaria (4:1–42), the disciples are concerned that Jesus should
take some food, addressing him as "Rabbi" (v. 31). After Jesus had walked on

the water (6:16–21), his disciples reach him in Capernaum and ask, "Rabbi, when did you come here?" (6:25). When they see a man blind from birth, they ask Jesus, "Rabbi, who sinned, this man or his parents that he was born blind?" (9:2). When Jesus plans to go to Judea, his disciples say, "Rabbi, the Jews were but now seeking to destroy you" (11:8). Thus, the then current Jewish term for the one who provides leadership, insight, and authority for a community seeking to define itself as God's people and to conform to the divine purpose is *rabbi*. It is significant and wholly appropriate that this term is not used in Luke or Acts, since that two-volume work was addressed particularly to Gentile readers, living in and shaped by the Graeco-Roman culture, rather than in the Jewish teacher/learner tradition that is a central feature in the other gospels.

Receivers/Conveyors of Wisdom: Schools, Teachers, and Disciples/Learners

The first evidence for a formal process of instruction in Israel is linked (1) with the account of building the temple in Jerusalem and establishing worship there, for which it was necessary to have personnel trained to lead the worship; and (2) with the development of national leadership. Both kinds of leaders needed to be informed concerning the historical traditions of the people. Hence, the basis for the learning was primarily biblical (2 Chron 17:7–9). Literacy seems to have permeated the society (Deut 6:9; 11:20), and to have manifested itself in the appointment of royal scribes who dispensed and kept records of royal funds (2 Sam 8:17; 20:24–25; 1 Kgs 4:3; 2 Kgs 12:9–16).

In later times, individuals were given training in order to qualify for official positions (Ezra 1:8–11; 2:2ff; 7:12–16). In the Hellenistic period, there is a story that the Babylonians, on taking over Jerusalem, gave orders for establishing learned young Jews in the royal court: ". . . Some of the Israelites of the royal family and of the nobility, young men without physical defect and handsome, versed in every branch of wisdom, endowed with knowledge and insight and competent to serve in the king's palace; they were to be taught the literature and language of the Chaldeans . . . [and] were to be educated for three years, so that at the end of that time they could be stationed in the king's court" (Dan 1:3–5).

At the end of Ecclesiastes—the Hebrew title for which is Qoheleth, which means "Teacher"—it is reported that, "Beside being wise, the Teacher also taught the people knowledge, weighing and studying and arranging many proverbs. The Teacher sought to find pleasing words, and wrote words of truth plainly" (Eccl 12:9–10). In Prov 23:12, there is an appeal to "apply your mind to instruction, and your ear to words of knowledge," which is followed by advice to discipline one's children. In the prophetic tradition, it is implied that the young or the simple are to be taught: "Whom shall we teach knowledge, and to whom will he explain the message? Those who are weaned from milk, those taken from the breast? For it is precept upon precept, precept upon precept, line upon line, line upon line, here a little, there a little" (Isa 28:9–10). Similarly, the prologue to Sirach offers advice about fostering and gaining "instruction and wisdom," with praise to those who read and understand "the Law and the Prophets and the other books of our ancestors . . . and acquire considerable proficiency in them." But the translator of this text[52] then notes that he has "applied [his] skill day and night to complete and publish the book for those living abroad who wished to gain learning and are disposed to live according to the law." Of central importance for the ongoing life of the community is instruction in the Law and the Prophets: "Fear of the Lord is wisdom and upbringing, fidelity and humility are his delight" (Sir 1:27).

Thus, in those features of Judaism that developed as intentional outgrowths of the biblical traditions, as well as in those that evolved under the influence of Graeco-Roman culture, there was a growing emphasis on the need for institutions and modes of instruction that could—in the changing situation in which the communities found themselves, including the loss of the temple, the priesthood, and the Jewish royal political entity[53]—ensure the preservation of values, insights, and the roles of agents that had derived from the tradition. For example, in 2 Chron 17:8–10 is a report that as early as the reign of Jehoshaphat, king of Judah (874–850 BCE), there was a royal decree that "Levites, priests, and heads of families" were to settle cases of dispute, but also to give instruction in "the law or commandment, statutes or ordinances," so that the divine wrath might not fall on the disobedient people.

A most significant and enduring conceptual and leadership development in Judaism in the postexilic period—though with antecedents in the earlier period—was linked with the concept of wisdom. In Ecclesiasticus, or the Wisdom of Jesus Son of Sirach, written in Egypt early in the second century BCE, there is consideration of the qualifications for teaching (24:30–34), including the ability to "make instruction shine forth like the dawn," and the importance of the teacher's extended experience and travel (34:9–13). The effective teacher is compared with a grape picker: "Consider that I have not labored for myself alone, but for all who seek instruction." The teacher is to search out and then to share divinely granted insights.

It was probably in the mid-second century BCE, when there was a radical conflict as to who should be the high priest,[54] that a group of Jews led by some of the dissenting priests withdrew to the wilderness of Judea area, overlooking the Dead Sea—there living together what they perceived to be the true life of moral and cultic purity under what they regarded as the proper leadership. There they were awaiting divine intervention on their behalf, which was to be followed by their establishment in power in the Jerusalem temple. During this time of waiting, they believed that they were being instructed in the truth about God's purpose for his people, based on the insights of a leader—or perhaps the founder of the movement—whom they designated The Teacher of Righteousness. This may have had the intended meaning of "the one who teaches righteousness," but it could also have implied "the one who teaches how things are to be set right." A document found among the scrolls at this site, Qumran, was a commentary on the prophet Habakkuk,[55] in which the author identifies the chief opponents of God's people as the Man of Lies and the Wicked Priest. The group is persuaded that God has granted to this community true perception of the divine purpose. Righteousness as they perceived it involved the right living of the members, as well as how they were convinced God was going to set things right in the world.

The Dead Sea Scrolls, which this group produced,[56] attest the deep discontent within Judaism of the Graeco-Roman period toward the Jewish political and sacral leadership, who were perceived as collaborators with the pagan powers. These dissident Jews were persuaded that only those who believed and behaved as they did were faithful to the Jewish tradition. Their writings attest that the members were confident that they were being informed by God through his chosen agents concerning the renewal of the covenant people that was soon to occur. Hence, they were awaiting the impending divine changes. Central to such dissent from the roles and policies of the official leadership sanctioned by the Hellenistic and then the Roman powers was the expectation of divine intervention. This was to take place through the agents who would bring insights and foster the development of a community to which the purpose of God was being disclosed and through whom it would be accomplished.

In the Dead Sea community, two divinely empowered agents were expected: a royal messiah and a priestly messiah. It was through disclosures concerning the divine purpose for the covenant people—as conceived by the founders and leaders of this movement—that the dynamic of these hopes was being revealed and conveyed. The members were to fulfill the ethical and cultic obligations set forth in the Dead Sea Scrolls—especially in the *Manual of Discipline* and the *Damascus Document*—if they were to share in this eschatological community. It was this divine purpose and the rules for those by and through whom it would be carried out that were reported in these documents.

The strict cultic and social requirements that separated this community from the rest of the human race—including other Jews—stand in sharpest contrast to those of Jesus and the early Christians as reflected in the New Testament—although both groups believed that through their founder, God had launched renewal of the covenant people. In sharp contrast to the fierce exclusivism of the Dead Sea Scrolls, the gospels and letters sound the pervasive theme that participation in the new community being convened by Jesus and in his name is ethnically, culturally, and even morally inclusive. The wisdom that Jesus brings into the world is seen to be potentially "the true light that enlightens every human" (John 1:9).

A more purely conceptual and intellectually oriented approach to communicating divine wisdom to the people of God is found in what is now known as the Wisdom literature of Judaism. The Wisdom of Solomon, which probably comes from the first half of the first century CE,[57] includes a list of subjects that are taught by wisdom, "the fashioner of all things." They consist of what we would now call ontology (the nature of true being), cosmology (establishing the cosmic order), physics, history, astronomy, biology, botany, and ethics—thus encompassing the fields of science, philosophy, and history—all examined within a theistic context. These subjects appear to have been on the curriculum of the Jewish-founded *gymnasia* (a major feature of the Graeco-Roman school systems) and are here said to be important concerns of those Jews engaged in instruction. How widely this range of subject matter was promoted by Jewish teachers cannot be determined, but this highly respected book—the Wisdom of Solomon—shows what was considered by some leading Jews to be the ideal range of intellectual inquiry and perception.

Also in the Hellenistic traditions, a keenly personal relationship between the teacher and his pupil/learner (= *mathetes*) developed. The term was used for those engaged in learning, from apprentices to masters of certain skills such as weaving or medical practice, but especially for the pupil of a philosopher or a religious leader. Socrates and Plato fostered cordial personal relations with those studying with them: in the Academy of Plato, members were designated as *hetairoi* (= companions, or comrades of the master teacher). Students of earlier philosophers such as Pythagoras and later ones such as Epicurus formed communities with their followers and came to regard their teachers as divine agents of wisdom. Schools developed that preserved and handed down the traditions of their founders, or even claimed divine origin for what they perceived to be ultimate truths.[58] The divine insights and resources provided through these teachers were handed down to later generations through their *mathētai* (disciples or students).

The impact of these understandings of divinely bestowed wisdom on early Christianity is evident in both negative and positive ways. The most direct evidences of this impact from Graeco-Roman wisdom are (1) in the Stoic-influenced ethics of Paul; (2) in the perception of Jesus as the divine Logos in the Gospel of John; and (3) especially in the Letter to the Hebrews, where the Platonic ontological distinction between the eternal ideal and the ephemeral copy is adapted for interpreting the nature and role of Christ. In sharp contrast to this ontological philosophical distinction are such declarations in the New Testament as that of the Prologue to the Gospel of John that in Jesus the eternal Word/Logos of God took on human form: "became flesh and dwelt among us" (John 1:14). The divine wisdom is disclosed to humans, not in abstract, timeless intellectual concepts, but in the life and activity, death and resurrection of a historical individual: Jesus.

It is essential to recognize, however, that in addition to such explicit import of Hellenistic concepts of wisdom and its conveyors, there was in the Jesus tradition of the Synoptic Gospels a major feature directly related to Jewish wisdom: Jesus as teacher. He conveyed to his hearers the purpose of God and the criteria for participation in the achievement of that purpose for human renewal. As we shall discuss below, Jesus' function as teacher is given considerably more attention in the gospel tradition than his identification as Messiah. These roles are by no means antithetical, however: essential to the messianic community taking shape was its perception of its place in the divine purpose as the fulfillment of the divine promises uttered through the prophets of Israel and now through Jesus. The detailed import of this claim and the consequent expectation of the new community are pointed out above in our analysis of the gospel tradition.

The biblical terminology concerning instruction that developed among the Greek-speaking Jews and Christians built on three logistical/conceptual modes of teaching, which are represented by three Greek verbs related to learning: *manthano*, *didasko*, and *paideuo*. These terms reflect the three instructional functions that were operative in these movements: learning, instructing, and childrearing or attainment of status as son and heir.[59] The corresponding English noun for the first is "disciple"; for the second, "teaching"; for the third, "child" or "son." Examples of each of these terms within the gospel tradition are (1) Jesus' followers, who are identified as "disciples" (Matt 5:1; John 2:11); (2) Jesus' hearers, who were "astonished" at his "new teaching" (Mark 1:27); (3) in the Beatitudes, those who serve as peacemakers are called "the children of God." Further, Paul declares that through Christ, God's people are no longer under a child-tutor, but have achieved status as mature "sons of God" (Gal 3:25–26; 4:5). Thus, they are no longer servants but those who share in the resources and responsibilities as mature offspring and heirs of God (Gal 4:7).

The essential role of the leaders of the Christian movement was to persuade and enable members to serve as disciples/learners of the good news and its implications for the renewal of human life. This required instruction—"teaching"—to provide knowledge and understanding of the tradition, the resources, and the responsibilities in which members of the new community now participated. The aim of these instructional endeavors was to foster growth toward the maturity of these members, so that they might more fully share in the new life that God made available to them through Christ. These are the tasks to which the "teachers" have been called, and for which they have been divinely enabled by the Spirit of God.

Subsequently, the instructional role came to be perceived and carried out in more nearly catechetical terms. But Paul denounces those who, in what he perceived to be the predominant Jewish tradition, "rely upon the law and boast of your relation to God and know his will and approve what is excellent, because you are instructed in the law," and hence regard themselves as "a guide to the blind . . . a corrector of the foolish, a teacher of children, having in the law the embodiment of knowledge and truth" (Rom 2:17–20). Teaching in the new community, as Paul perceives it, is not to be carried out in such a catechetical fashion. He asserts, "Whatever the law says it speaks to those who are under the law" (Rom 3:19). Humans are set right with God on the basis of their trust in what God has done through Christ, and this is "apart from works of law" (Rom 3:28). The moral renewal will come when they yield themselves to God and their bodily capabilities to God as instruments of righteousness (Rom 6:13). "It is the Spirit who bears witness with our spirit that we are children of God" (Rom 8:16), and who produces within the lives of God's people the moral and spiritual qualities that Paul lists—drawing on both the biblical traditions and on the ethical insights of the Stoics: "love, joy, peace, patience, kindness, goodness, faithfulness, gentleness, self-control." Moral instruction is clearly a matter of central importance, but for Paul this takes place through the working of the Spirit within the life of the community and its members.

The ability to carry out the various roles essential for the founding and functioning of the churches is understood by Paul to be the consequence of God's assigning and enabling members to fulfill such actions. The functions of these various divinely granted gifts, *charismata*, are compared with those of parts of the body. A list of the resulting roles—including the order of their importance—is offered by Paul in 1 Cor 12:28: apostles, prophets, teachers, workers of miracles, healers, administrators, speakers in various kinds of "tongues" (languages).

Equally important as fostering the development of instructors and curriculum in Judaism of the Graeco-Roman period was the defining of the role of the student—regularly referred to as disciple (*mathetes*)—and carrying out the process of instruction. The central focus for study was the law of Moses. To study the law is enjoined in Exod 13:9, and in Deut 5:1 there is an order to "learn and observe the statutes and ordinances" addressed to the covenant people by Moses. It is to be studied "day and night" (John 1:8; Ps 1:2) and is to be taught to children (Ps 78:5). Ezra "set his heart to study the law of the Lord" (Ezra 7:10), and the Levites went to him to study the teachings of the Law (Neh 8:13). In the wisdom tradition there is a call to engage in extended study (Job 5:27), and the truth is to be taught by the fathers to the children (Job 15:18). Intelligent people who are eager and ready to learn do themselves a favor by engaging in continuing study (Prov 18:15; 19:8). One should buy into truth and understanding (Prov 23:23). The prophet Daniel calls for the people to keep God's commandments and to give heed to the prophets (Dan 9:4–6), which requires careful study of the scriptures. That call is similarly articulated in the gospels (John 5:39; 7:52) and Acts (17:11). Thus, throughout the biblical tradition, study and learning are central and essential responsibilities for the covenant people.

It is in conformity with this perception that one of the dominant designations of the followers of Jesus is *mathetes*, which is used in the New Testament 250 times. It means "one who learns," and is usually translated "disciple," although not all those so mentioned are among the core of twelve disciples of Jesus. Rather, the word assumes a pattern of instruction by which the teacher, Jesus, has passed on insights and knowledge to the "learners." As noted above, this connotation is clear and central in the Greek tradition and became a major feature of early Christianity. In addition to the designation of a pupil or learner, "disciple" came to connote membership in the new community. This is a dominant factor in the gospel tradition, where the twelve disciples constitute the core of the new community, but are also the agents and messengers by whom those who hear their message and see the power of God at work through them are persuaded by it. They thus become "disciples" of Jesus in their convictions and by the transformation of their lives. This role is highlighted in both the Q and the Markan traditions. In Luke 14:25-27,[60] heeding Jesus' call to discipleship requires a break with one's family obligations, and will likely result in martyrdom—taking up one's cross—as a follower of Jesus. The same basic point is made in Mark 8:34, where there is emphasis on self-denial as a prerequisite for discipleship. Luke 14:28-32 expands on this feature, comparing it with the cost of building a tower, and with the need for a king to be certain he has the forces to succeed before he goes to war. He ends by warning that the disciple must "renounce all that he has." What must be learned is the nature of the dynamic enterprise that Jesus has launched in announcing the coming of the rule of God and preparing for this cosmic event by his message, by his transforming his hearers through works of healing and exorcism, and by his calling them to participate in a new community of God's people.

Charismatic Roles in Early Christianity

There is a wide range of roles for which responsibility and enablement are provided in the new community by the power of the Spirit of God at work. The form and function of these modes of leadership built on the Jewish traditions, but developed as well their own distinctive features. In 1 Corinthians, these roles are designated by Paul in two modes: as divine appointments (12:28), and as spiritual (12:1) or charismatic gifts (12:4). But in any case, they are not seen as manifestations of native human capabilities, but as purposive, divine enablement of committed individuals. The gifts range from authoritative roles (apostles, elders, bishops, deacons, and administrators) through agents of communication (prophets, teachers, speakers, and interpreters of tongues), to instruments of divine empowerment (healers, workers of miracles), and to those who come to the aid of members of the community who are confronting difficulties (helpers).

A vivid metaphor for one kind of divinely provided guidance of the covenant people is that of the helmsman (*kybernetes*, 12:28).[61] That role is most important in time of storm, which here points to the need for the leadership required in the face of conflict or major difficulties. The church fathers took up the image of the church as a ship, but pictured Christ as the helmsman. As Hippolytus wrote, "The sea is the world in which the church is surrounded by storms like a ship on the sea, but it does not founder because it has on board the experienced pilot: Christ."[62] For Paul, however, the pilot is Christ's chosen and empowered agent within the community of faith, who is to give guidance to the ship, which is the people of God as they pass through the storms of life in a hostile world. But also from the beginning of the church, roles developed that were perceived to possess and exercise several levels of authority: apostles, bishops, elders, and deacons.

Apostles

As noted above in our analysis of Paul and the Apostolic Traditions, the role of apostle was perceived to be based on the commissioning by the risen Christ of certain persons who had seen him after he was raised from the dead and who were now commissioned by him to bear the good news of the gospel to all people. We also noted that the office of apostle took on authoritative features, since those to whom this role had been assigned were seen as the prime messengers and agents for the founding and spread of the new covenant community. Hence, the apostolic claim provided the motivation for assigning later writings to one or another of the apostles, in order to bestow authority on the message and to assert continuity between later developments and the origins of the movement.

Prophets

Shaped by both the traditions of the prophets of Israel and by thinkers in the Graeco-Roman world who were predicting cosmic renewal as taking place in a coming age,[63] a useful and insightful definition of early Christian prophecy is: "The early Christian prophet was an immediately inspired spokesperson for God, the risen Jesus, or the Spirit, who received intelligible oracles that he or she felt impelled to deliver to the Christian community or, representing the community, to the general public."[64] A crucial factor in the ongoing decision-making process of the church was the wisdom and insights provided by the Spirit of God at work through those chosen and empowered to be the bearers of the divine purpose for his people: the Christian prophets.

Teachers

As noted above, there was a continuing need for the community to provide instruction in the scriptures and the Christian traditions. The role was perceived as conveying perceptions of God's purpose for his people, which was to be carried forward in the changing circumstances of the life of the church and the consequent social and political challenges that its leaders and members faced. The insights and capacities to carry forward this diverse program for the members of the community are perceived to have been provided by God through the Holy Spirit at work among his people.

Capabilities through the Work of the Spirit

In 1 Cor 12:28, following the list of the three more formal roles—apostles, prophets, and teachers—Paul shifts to the results of the charismatic gifts of the Spirit (1 Cor 12:29b–30) that members are empowered to perform by the Spirit (1 Cor 12:9–10): healings, helpful deeds, prophecy, distinguishing the spirits that produce good or evil results, speaking in tongues, interpreting tongues.

Before examining the roles of healing and working miracles, of "helpers" and "administrators," we must consider the import of the strange term "tongues" among the charismatic gifts. The references here to "tongues" recalls that in the Greek religions—from the Thracian cult of Dionysus to the divinatory manticism of the Delphic Phrygia and the Sibyls—there was the phenomenon of ecstatic utterances that were perceived as conveying divine truths to humans.[65] The gift of tongues and of interpreting them are the early Christian counterpart to this feature of the pagan world. The ability to understand and communicate the divine message is as important as the capacity to speak in tongues. In the New Testament, the divine communication through "tongues" appears in two different senses: (1) the charismatic gift described by Paul; and (2) the miraculous event on the Day of Pentecost, when the apostles were divinely enabled "to speak in other tongues, as the Spirit gave them utterance," reported in Acts 2:1–4. The result is that the assembled throng is able to hear and understand the message, "each of us in his/her own language" (2:8). The range of lands and languages represented by the hearers is enumerated in 2:9–11. Peter is reported to have explained that this miracle of Spirit-empowered speech and comprehension is the fulfillment of the prophecy of Joel that God will "pour out my Spirit upon all flesh" with the result that "whoever calls upon the name of the Lord shall be saved" (Acts 2:16–21; Joel 3:1–5). Both these phenomena are here attributed to the power of the Spirit of God. While the members of the new community will not reenact this symbolic event that took place at Pentecost, they are expected to be the agents of the Spirit for conveying the message of God through Christ to receptive listeners. This is to occur through ecstatic utterances, the meaning of which is then to be offered to the hearers by those gifted for interpretation of the "tongues."

The divinely granted capabilities for leading members of the church are ranked in 1 Cor 12:28, but, as noted above, to them is added the role of administrator, which is the standard Greek term for helmsman or pilot of a ship. As noted above, the use of this word with reference to God's guidance of the world is to be found in both classical Greek and Jewish sources.[66] Thus, for Paul, the Holy Spirit is the divine resource at work through the members of the new community to accomplish the renewal of God's people and of the creation. Equally important are the services that the leaders are to provide for those who are in need, including healing, wonder-working, and helping.

These last three roles, which are to be carried out with aid of the Holy Spirit (12:29), match well the tasks that Jesus performed in his earthly ministry as reported in the gospel tradition. The nature and significance of this kind of activity by Jesus is powerfully pointed out in Luke's account of Jesus' reading and claiming fulfillment of the scripture (Isa 61:1–2) in the synagogue at Nazareth.[67] In all the gospel tradition, it is the healing activity and the wonder-working by him—casting out demons, restoring the crippled and the dead, enabling the blind to see—which serve as both symbol and substance of Jesus' role in overcoming the powers of evil[68] and renewing the life of those who trust in him as the agent of divine renewal.

This carrying forward of Jesus' works of love and renewal by which the powers of evil and the consequences of human sin are overcome is epitomized by Paul in 2 Cor 5:17–20 as "the ministry of reconciliation" (*ten diakonian tes katalages*). This was launched by God, who in Christ is "reconciling the world to himself." It is as part of this divine enterprise that the powers of evil are being overcome and the people of God renewed. As noted above, the message from God in language that all in the diverse Roman world may potentially understand, regardless of cultural or ethnic origins, is conveyed and enhanced by the work of the Spirit through the members of the new community. At the same time, the guidance and leadership of this community are empowered by the Spirit of God through the charismatic gifts. The overall aims of this divine activity are to foster the unity of the church in spite of the diversity of origins of its members, to develop leadership empowered to carry forward effectively the ministry of the church, and to build the community in terms of unity and effectiveness of its mission.

Assigned Official Roles in the Church

Apostles

As discussed above, the designation of leaders of the church as apostles served to affirm continuity between Jesus and his original circle of followers. With the aging and passing of the first generation of these apostles, it was seen as essential to demonstrate continuity between the apostles and the appropriation of their tradition in the church's theological, ethical, leadership, and organizational structures. This accounts for the attribution to apostles of letters and other writings produced in the late first and early second century—including the canonical letters of Peter and John, the Pastorals, and Acts of the Apostles, as well as the many writings now designated as the New Testament Apocrypha.[69]

We have observed that the four canonical gospels were given status and authority by the early traditions that linked them with apostles. As reported by Eusebius,[70] quoting Papias of Hierapolis, the Gospel of Mark was assigned by him to Mark, who "became Peter's interpreter and wrote accurately all that he remembered," taking care "to leave out nothing of what he had heard and to make no false statements." Papias is also quoted as saying that "Matthew collected the oracles [of Jesus] in the Hebrew language, and each interpreted them as best he could." This tradition, linked with the special importance attached to the role of Peter as presented in the Gospel of Matthew, emphasizes the continuing significance of links with the apostles and probably accounts for its being placed at the head of the Christian canon.

Similarly, the authority of the Gospel of Luke and of Acts of the Apostles rests in large measure on the links between Luke and the Apostle Paul, as noted earlier. The anonymous Gospel of John was also perceived as of apostolic origin, as were the many writings now classified as New Testament Apocrypha.[71] Thus, the authority perceived to reside with the apostles of Jesus continues to be a significant factor in the Christian traditions of the subsequent centuries.

The effectiveness and substance of the historic apostles' role in spreading the good news was perceived to be based on their having been direct witnesses of the message and ministry of Jesus, of his sacrificial death, and of the divine confirmation of him through God's having raised him from the dead, as well as the continuity of divine enablement provided to them by the presence and power of the Holy Spirit.

Elders

We have surveyed the important role of elders in Judaism, from ancient times to the Graeco-Roman period as consultants, leaders, and both formulators and enforcers of policy. They are directly and frequently referred to in the gospels and Acts (1), but there are also references to Christian elders in the later New Testament letters (2), as well as visions in Revelation of elders around the throne of God (3).

In the gospel tradition, Jesus foretells that a coalition of chief priests, scribes, and elders will collaborate with the Roman authorities to have him put to death.[72] It is a similar group, including elders, who challenge Jesus as he is walking in the temple courts.[73] Other reports of plots by the Jewish officials—including elders—to have Jesus put to death appear in Mark 14:43 and Matt 26:3, 47. The elders share in the council of collaborators with the Romans: the *synedrion*, and in Luke 22:52 they are among those addressed by Jesus with the question, "Have you come out with swords and clubs as if I were a bandit?" On the other hand, in Luke 7:1-10, a story from the Q source,[74] the request of a Roman army officer, a centurion, for Jesus to heal his ailing slave, is conveyed by some "elders of the Jews," who note that the centurion "loves our nation and built for us our synagogue."[75]

In Acts 4:5, hostile reaction to the preaching by Peter and John resulted in a hearing for them before the Jews' "rulers, elders and scribes assembled in Jerusalem" and the high priests, which led to their being threatened and released (4:21). Similarly, negative reaction to the signs, wonders, and message of Stephen leads to his being brought before the council in Jerusalem, including the leaders and the scribes (Acts 6:8-15). The charge of insurrection is also made against Paul before the Roman governor by the high priest and "some elders" (24:1). Thus, the elders are clearly pictured as major elements in the leadership of the Jewish community in the first century.

Christian elders appear—not in the gospels or in the letters of Paul—but frequently in Acts and the deuteropauline writings. Following the mission of Barnabas from the church in Jerusalem to the rapidly growing group in Antioch and the prediction there of a famine (Acts 11:19-30), the members—here called "disciples"—decided to send a "relief" contribution to "the elders by the hand of Barnabas and Saul." In every church these two founded by their preaching the gospel, "they appointed elders" (Acts 14:23). Clearly, the latter are to provide leadership for these newly founded communities.

When the issue was raised by some Judeans about requiring circumcision of converts, Paul and Barnabas decided to go to Jerusalem in order to confer there with "the apostles and elders" (15:2). They were welcomed there by "the church and the apostles and the elders"; the latter two groups soon "gathered to consider this matter" (15:6). After reaching the decision that conformity to Torah should not be required of Gentile converts—though they are "to abstain from the pollution of idols and from unchastity and from what is strangled and from blood"—Paul and Barnabas are authorized to convey this message to the Gentiles in Syria, accompanied by two of their leaders, Judas Barsabbas and Silas (15:19–29). The authoritative role of these leaders in the Jerusalem church is indicated by their self-designation as "apostles and elders," and it is in these terms that the message is conveyed (16:4). When Paul and his companion reach Jerusalem at the conclusion of his missionary activity (according to Acts), the assembled leadership consists of "James and all the elders" (21:18).

Though absent from the authentic letters of Paul, in 1 Timothy—where instructions are given about community relationships with various kinds of members, such as the elderly and widows (5:1–16)—there is advice about dealing with elders. Those who rule effectively are to be honored—especially those engaged in preaching and teaching. Here is explained how they are to be compensated and how charges against them are to be handled. Communities in every town are to have elders appointed in order to provide leadership and authority (Titus 1:5). In Jas 5:14, it is elders who are to pray for the sick and "to anoint them with oil in the name of the Lord" so that they might be restored to health. If the ailing have sinned, they will be forgiven (5:15). The pastoral role of the elders is described in 1 Peter, where Peter is depicted as "a fellow elder, a witness of the sufferings of Christ as well as a partaker in the glory that is to be revealed" through Christ for his people.[76] The elders are "to tend the flock of God that is in your charge, exercising the oversight, not under compulsion but willingly, as God would have you do it—not for sordid gain but eagerly."[77] The leadership role of the elder is implicit in the identification of the sender of 2 John and 3 John as "the elder." The letters warn against turning from the teaching of Christ (2 John 10) and call for adopting the model of "what is good" (3 John 11). Thus, the elders are depicted in the later New Testament writings as divine agents for exhorting and rebuking the new community.

In the Revelation to John, an elaborate picture of the throne of God (Rev 4–5) is followed by an account of the succession of events that depict the triumph of God over the powers of evil, the vindication of his people, and the establishment of his rule over the creation (Rev 6–22). Throughout this series of apocalyptic visions are references to the elders, who have a leading role in bringing honor to God and to Christ, God's agent in the achievement of this cosmic triumph. God is never described, but there are vivid and detailed features of what and who surrounds the throne of God: these depict or symbolize the nature, the power, and the purpose of God. They join in praise to God, celebrating his lordship over human history as the holy one who was, and is, and is to come (Rev 4:8).

Surrounding the divine throne are (1) four living creatures, who resemble a lion, an ox, a human, and an eagle,[78] and (2) twenty-four thrones, on which are seated that number of elders—thus doubling the model of the twelve tribes who comprised the Jewish people of God. It is one of these elders who declares that the scroll that contains the divine plan can be opened only by one who perceives the purpose of God and is morally qualified to work for its fulfillment: Jesus Christ, the Lamb of God, the Lion of Judah, the Root of David (5:1–6). As he takes from God's right hand the scroll —to disclose and to launch the divine purpose of cosmic renewal—the four creatures and the twenty-four elders prostrate themselves in honor of the Lamb, offering prayers and praise for the people of God: the saints from every tribe and language and people and nation whom the Lamb has ransomed by his death and has made to be a kingdom and priests serving God (5:7–10). All creatures—numbering in the "thousands of thousands," and including the elders—join in praise to God and the Lamb (5:11–14). Similarly, in 7:9–12, there is a vision of an innumerable multitude from every nation who join in worship of God and the Lamb surrounded by angels. There are seven trumpets blown (8:6–11:19), heralding the establishment of God's rule through the Messiah, who is honored by the twenty-four elders.

In the midst of a series of visions of evil powers at work in the world—dragons and beasts (12:1–18:24)—144,000 appear, symbolizing the multiple renewal of God's new Israel,[79] who sing praise to God before the throne, with its four living creatures and the elders (14:2–3). The triumph of God over the powers of evil is celebrated by "the great multitude in heaven," who are joined in worshiping God by the elders and the four living creatures (19:4). Thus, the elders symbolize the faithful people who honor God and are enabled to share in the fulfillment of the ultimate triumph of the divine renewal of the creation. Yet in the post-apostolic tradition, they are portrayed as the authoritative leaders of the new community of God's people.

Bishops

The Greek term *episkopos* is the designation of one who watches over or oversees, a guardian, supervisor, or inspector, or a tutor in an educational capacity, including a guardian of the mind. It is found in the Septuagint with reference both to God and to human roles. In Job 20:29, the heritage of the wicked is decreed by the Overseer (= God). In Wisdom of Solomon 1:6, God is the true observer of the hearts and the speech of humans. Human overseers include those who provide oil and incense for the sanctuary (Num 4:16), officers in the army (Num 31:14), those who supervise the Levites (Neh 11:9, 14, 22), those who oversee the repair of the house of the Lord (2 Chron 34:12, 17), and those who are appointed by Antiochus IV as inspectors or overseers of all the people (1 Macc 1:51).

Episkopos occurs only once in the letters of Paul—in Phil 1:1, where it is linked with *diakonoi*,[80] and refers to those members in supervisory and subservient roles, respectively. Similarly, in Acts when Paul is reported as addressing the elders of the church in Ephesus, he describes them as "overseers" (*episkopous*), whose role is "to shepherd the church of God" (20:17, 28). Similar imagery, though with different personal reference, appears in 1 Pet 2:25, where Christ is declared to be "the shepherd and guardian [*episkopos*] of your souls."

Episkopos as an official category of church leadership first appears in the Pastoral Letters, attributed to Paul but deriving from a later generation. A detailed description of the requirements for bishop is offered in 1 Tim 3:1–7. It is a "noble task," requiring that one be "irreproachable," married only once, "temperate, sensible, dignified, hospitable,[81] and an apt teacher." Drunkenness, violence, contentiousness, and greed are to be avoided by the bishop, and he is to maintain submission and respect on the part of his children. His effectiveness as the head of a family bodes well for his leadership role in the church. The relatively late date of this document is indicated by the specification that he is not to be "a recent convert," but of course, in the first generation of Christianity, all leaders and members would be recent converts! He must avoid conceit and should enjoy respect among nonmembers if he is to be safe from subversion by the devil. Similar virtues are expected of the bishop according to Titus 1:7–9: he is the "steward of God" (*oikonomos*), and is to be "a lover of goodness, master of himself, upright, holy and self-controlled." His instructional role requires him to "hold firm to the sure word as [he was] taught, so that he may be able to give instruction in sound doctrine and also to confute those who contradict it." Thus, the bishop is now seen to be conveyor of truth and an effective discreditor of false teaching.

It is in the Apostolic Fathers that the role of bishop is more fully described. In *1 Clem.* 42–44 is depicted the process of appointing bishops to carry forward the preaching of the kingdom of God. These replacements for those who have died are to be eminent men who have a fine record in their ministry to the flock of Christ. Justification for this process is provided by a quotation from Isa 60:17[82]—although the Septuagint version of this text lacks the term "deacons." Other occurrences of *episkopos* in the LXX show that the supervisory role was by no means limited to religious leadership, as bishop came to be understood.[83] In the letters of Ignatius of Antioch are such themes as (1) subjection to the bishop and living in harmony with his will;[84] (2) regarding the bishop as the Lord himself, and following him in discerning truth and avoiding heresy;[85] (3) respecting the bishop in spite of his youth, and perceiving God the Father as the "bishop of us all."[86] The exalted rank and role of the bishop are indicated by the call to live in harmony with God, with the bishop who presides in God's place, and with the elders who took the place of the council of the apostles.[87]

Similar emphasis on the authority of the bishop and the obligation to obey him appears in the Shepherd of Hermas. There is a call for members of the new community to be subject to the bishop as to Christ[88] and to follow the bishop as Jesus Christ follows the Father and as the presbytery follows the apostles. Those who honor the bishop will be honored by God, and whoever does anything without the bishop's knowledge and approval is serving the devil.[89] The bishop is the divinely empowered leader who is to guide the church in all that it does.

Deacons

The Greek verb, *diakoneo*—with the cognate noun, *diakonos*, from which "deacon" is transliterated—means to render a service to oneself, to others, or to a deity. In ordinary Greek usage, it often connotes menial work, however, such as waiting at tables. Yet it differs from other modes of service: as a slave (*douleuo*), or for wages (*latreuo*), or for the state (*leitourgeo*), or mere subservience (*hypereteo*). Instead, *diakoneo* implies personal service rendered to another, providing and caring for others in need. It is not found in the LXX, where service to God is expressed in more formal terms (*latreuo* and (*leitourgeo*). In Josephus, *diakoneo* is linked with serving at tables, but also with obedience to God and rendering priestly service. Serving others in this Jewish tradition is limited in scope because of the narrow definitions (1) of the "neighbor" (Lev 19:18) who is to be served; and (2) of what constitutes pious service to God, which is perceived primarily as taking place at the altar in the temple.[90]

In the gospel tradition, serving—*diakoneo* and cognate terms—moves far beyond waiting tables or offering gifts on the altar: it involves providing for the needy and the ritually excluded (Luke 10:40; Matt 25:42–44). The model for sacrifice is suffering for the benefit of others, as enacted by Jesus Christ (Luke 22:26; Mark 10:45; Matt 20:28). Serving the community is made possible by the charismatic gift of God to his people (1 Pet 4:10–11). The model for serving is the Pauline collection for the saints (2 Cor 8:19; Rom 15:15), but *diakonia* is a term also used for Paul's broader ministry, and involves his troubles and difficult responsibilities (2 Cor 6:3; 11:23). This follows the model set forth by Jesus in the gospel tradition (Mark 10:45): "For the Son of Man came not to be served [*diakonthenai*] but to serve [*diakonesai*], and to give his life as a ransom for many." It is in this perspective that the office of service—*diakonia*—developed in the early church.[91]

The role of "deacon" is perceived in three different ways in the New Testament: (1) the role of servants of God, carried out by the disciples and the apostles; (2) Christ as servant of God; (3) the earthly rulers who unwittingly serve as agents to fulfill God's purpose in the world.[92] In Jesus' response to the request of James and John for special places of honor in the kingdom of God, he tells the disciples that "whoever would be great among you must be your servant [*diakonos*], and whoever would be first among you must be slave [*doulos*] of all."[93] A similar designation of the obedient follower of Jesus is offered in John 12:26. In Paul's First Letter to the Corinthians, he and Apollos are identified as "servants [*diakonoi*] through whom you believed" (1 Cor 3:5). In 2 Cor 3:6, he identifies himself and the apostles as "ministers" (*diakonous*) of a new covenant, and in 6:4 as "servants [*diakonoi*] of God." Some versions of the text of 1 Thess 3:2 identify Timothy as the *diakonos* of God. The same term is also used by Paul with reference to the human agents of Satan, however (2 Cor 11:15).

In the deuteropauline literature, the term is used as well: in Col 1:7, Epaphras is also identified as "a faithful minister [*diakonos*] of Christ"; the author refers to himself as a *diakonos* of the gospel (1:23) and of the church. This role is described as "a divine office" (*oikonomian tou theou*) in which he was to make known fully God's word: "the mystery hidden for ages and generations but now made manifest to his saints" (1:25). The concept of *diakonia* as an office for conveying divine mystery is further developed in Eph 3:7, where the operation of divine power is described. Specific qualifications for deacons—male and female!—are laid down in 1 Tim 3:8–13, including moderation in mode of life, integrity of faith, and domestic responsibility. Those who warn the members of coming apostasy in the form of rigid asceticism will be serving as good ministers (*diakonos*) and will be promoting true piety (*eusebeia*) as well as sound doctrine (4:6–8). Thus, the role of deacon has become a formal office, with the assignment of specific modes of leadership responsibility within the new community.[94]

The Christian Role of Priest

A recurrent metaphor in Paul and the later New Testament for the meaning of Christ's sacrificial death and its appropriation within the new community of faith is that of the priest. Paul explicitly uses the image of priestly role and sacrifice once: in his letter to the Romans (15:16), he describes his ministry "of Jesus Christ to the Gentiles" as "priestly service of the gospel of God." The term for "minister" here is *leitourgos*—akin to our word "liturgy," and implying sacramental service. That implication is confirmed by two other terms found here: "priestly service of the gospel of God" (*hierourgonta*) and the depiction of the Gentiles as the sacrificial offering (*prosphora*) that is presented to God.

The most elaborate occurrence of the priestly imagery is in the Letter to the Hebrews, as indicated above in our analysis of that writing in chapter 3, Paul and the Apostolic Traditions. But the priestly features of the new community are pointed out in two of the later New Testament writings: 1 Peter and Revelation. In 1 Pet 2:5, the community is called to be "built into a spiritual house, to be a holy priesthood, and to offer spiritual sacrifices acceptable to God through Jesus Christ. In 2:9, the members are depicted in mixed metaphors that build on the Jewish tradition of the covenant community as "a chosen race, a royal priesthood, a holy nation, God's own people." Similarly, in Rev 1:5–6, the community is depicted as having been "freed from our sins by [Christ's] blood and made . . . a kingdom, priests to his God and Father." In the hymn of praise to the Lamb in Rev 5:9–10, Christ is acclaimed because "you were slaughtered and by your blood you ransomed for God saints from every tribe and language and people and nation," and "you have made them to be a kingdom and priests [in service] to God, and they will reign on earth." Sung by "the twenty-four elders" (5:8), this hymn celebrates the joining of the two covenant peoples symbolized by twelve: the twelve tribes of Israel and the twelve disciples/apostles of Christ. Those who share in Christ's triumphant reign have been restored to life because they refused to take part in the worship of "the beast"—the emperor worship demanded by Roman law. "They will be priests of God and of Christ, and they will reign with him a thousand years" (20:4–6). Thus, in these later New Testament writings, the linked eschatological roles of king and priest are epitomized by Christ, but are also shared by his faithful people. It is important to note, however, that priest is not used in the New Testament as a designation or title for an official leader in the church.

Roles Chosen by Individuals: To Love One Another

In addition to the formal leadership roles that were assigned in early Christianity, the individual members had the opportunity, and—in terms of the teaching tradition attributed to Jesus and the apostles—the responsibility to live lives of service and to foster loving relationships with the members of the community, but also with their fellow humans who were in need. This opportunity and obligation were perceived in several ways, one of which was to manifest love, which surpasses in significance both faith and hope, as well as such charismatic gifts as prophecy and wisdom (1 Cor 13:13). Love involves the complete fulfillment of the law (Gal 5:14). It should manifest itself in loving one's neighbor as oneself (Rom 13:8–9). In the later Pauline tradition, love is seen as a way of life in imitation of Christ: "Walk in love, as Christ loved us and gave himself for us" (Eph 5:2). Even in the Letter of James, which is opposed to the Pauline doctrine of justification by faith, loving one's neighbor as oneself is called "the royal law according to scripture." Like the Gospel of John, 1 John places the emphasis on loving other members of the community of faith: love one another, or one's brother,[95] although in the Gospel of John the cosmic model for love is God's gift of his only Son (3:16). Emphasis on love within the community is also evident in 1 Pet 1:22. And in every case, the prime factor in the transformation of human relations from conflict into harmony is love. The supreme expression of love—as exemplified by Christ—is that "someone lay down his life for his friends" (John 15:13).

This theme is a major feature of the gospels, as well, in both the Markan and the Q traditions. In Mark 12:28–34, Jesus' response to the disciples' question as to which is the chief commandment is to quote from Deut 6:4–5—"Hear, o Israel . . . you shall love the Lord your God with all your heart . . ."—and then to add from Lev 19:18, "You shall love your neighbor as yourself." But unlike the injunctions in the law of Moses, which assert the divine aim to keep God's people "separated from the other peoples" (Lev 20:24, 26), Jesus enjoins his followers to include in love and service those who are morally, ritually, or ethnically outsiders in terms of this law. The call to love is extended even farther in the Q tradition, where Jesus commands his disciples to love their enemies, to do good to those that hate them, to bless those who curse them, to pray for those who abuse them, and to respond to misdeeds of others by acts of generosity (Luke 6:27–31).

In the Gospel of John, a central feature in the representation of God is his love as evident in his having given his Son (3:16). The import of the command to love in this gospel, however, focuses on loving "one another"—that is, within the membership of the community of faith (13:34; 15:12, 17). The essential manifestation of love is that Jesus has "laid down his life for his friends" (15:13).[96]

Love is far more than a matter of attitude or feeling. Especially in 1 Corinthians, Paul makes the point that the exercising of the charismatic gifts is to be for the benefit of the community as whole (1 Cor 14). In the same way, suffering is to be for the benefit of others. And the overall aim of all the service and leadership roles in the church is the good of all (1 Cor 14:26ff).

Community Structures in the Early Church

We have noted that throughout the New Testament writings there is a central theme: that Jesus is the agent of God through whom the new covenant community is called into being and commissioned to carry out its role in the purpose of God. We have seen in the analyses of the various types of New Testament material that the Christian communities were defined in a variety of ways given the input from the traditions that they adopted and the expectations of divine development that they shared. The major modes evident in the early Christian literature are the following:

1. The eschatological community, which builds on the acts and promises of divine deliverance and renewal based on the death and resurrection of Jesus and conveyed by Jesus to the apostles. These features are dominant in Q, in Mark, and in the letters of Paul.

2. The community that sees itself as the new Israel, to whom God has disclosed his purpose and the rules and agents by which that will accomplished. The prime example of this is the Gospel of Matthew.

3. The emphasis falls in Luke and Acts on the potential and divinely intended inclusiveness of the community, which is to reach out geographically, ethnically, and culturally "to the ends of the earth."

4. Evident in the letters of Paul and in Luke-Acts, but dominant in the strategy of the Letter to the Hebrews—as it was in the writings of Philo of Alexandria, of the Christian *Sibylline Oracles*, and such studies as those of Clement and Origen of Alexandria—is the synthesis of biblical features with conceptual insights in the Graeco-Roman tradition, especially those of Plato and the Stoics. The community sees itself as called to understand and communicate its message and build its common life based on divine action and revelation, which are conveyed through concepts and insights present in the wider culture.

5. Akin to this strategy, but with major emphasis on mystical participation in the divine life by individuals and the sacred community, is the Gospel of John.[97] The images of Christ and the community of faith, as well as the depiction of the work of the Spirit in their common life, are seen as leading to transformation of life for both individuals and the community. These developments are analogous to the reclaiming in the Graeco-Roman culture of older religious traditions in the centuries just before and after the turn of the common era—especially the mysteries of Isis and Osiris, and the Iranian mysteries of Mithras.[98]

6. The new community's developing of defined leadership roles and hierarchical structures is most clearly evident in the deuteropauline writings, although antecedents of this process appear in Paul's authentic letters.

Further evolution of these institutional roles and forms appear in the Apostolic Fathers and other post-apostolic writings.[99]

Thus, throughout this literature, the defining of the new community, its leadership, the rules by which its members are to live, and the images of the new life in which its members will share are in process of formation and specification. The sociological features of growth of religious movements from charismatic origins to institutional forms are clearly evident. The details of the community structure vary significantly within the New Testament and the early Christian literature, and the preference of a facet of early Christianity for one of those models led to the diversity that is evident in early and subsequent Christian history.[100]

It is through analysis of the range of contexts in which the Christian traditions emerged and in which they subsequently evolved that one can discern the diversity of social and conceptual features that characterized Christianity in its early history.

Other Early Christian Models and Terminology for the New Community

Antecedent features of the structured images of the church that developed in the second century are already present in the letters of Paul, and especially in letters attributed to him: the so-called Pastorals.

Images in Paul's Letters

In Gal 6:10, Paul refers to the people of God as *oikeios tes pisteos*. The term, *oikeios*, is used for members of a household, for blood relatives. Hence, this community is defined by the faith that is shared by its members and provides the basis for their common identity. This is the common locus in which and for which they all live. The family relationship is a repeated theme in Paul's letters, as in Rom 8:12–17, where he uses a variety of terms to describe the links with God's people: sons (*huioi*), children (*tekna*), co-heirs (*sugkleronomoi*), brothers [and sisters] (*adelphoi*). This relationship is confirmed by the Holy Spirit: "The Spirit bears witness with our spirit that we are children of God" (8:16).

Images in Deuteropauline Letters

The images of the relationship between God and his people of the new covenant appear in more structured form in the deuteropauline writings. The crucial text is in Eph 2:19, where the writer declares that the members of the new community "are no longer strangers and sojourners"—which they would be as non-Israelites, or those who were only inquirers or on the periphery of the traditional covenant people. Instead, they are now declared "fellow citizens with the saints and members of the household of God" (*sympolitai ton hagion kai oikeioi tou theou*). The structure of the community and the identity of its members are now well-defined. The strength and stability of this new people, as well as its growth potential and destiny as the divine dwelling place, are affirmed (2:20–21). The foundation on which this structure is erected is the testimony of "the apostles and prophets": the apostles have born witness to their convictions that the promises made through the prophets concerning God's renewal of his people and ultimately of the whole creation are now being fulfilled. The base on which this new reality is manifesting itself is "Christ Jesus . . . the cornerstone." Unlike human edifices, which are constructed from lifeless materials such as wood, stone, and metal, this building is alive—its components are growing together as it becomes the divine replacement for what is seen as the now-destroyed traditional temple of Israel. This new structure will be the place of God's presence, the center of his purpose and power, where God will be present and active through the Spirit. There, God's true people will share with God their new life together.

Social Structures in the Pastoral Epistles

As discussed in chapter 3, in the Pastoral Epistles, the focus shifts to the leadership roles and the community norms—doctrinal and ethical—that are to characterize God's covenant people. In these letters, major attention is given to defining the roles that the leaders of the churches are to fulfill: bishops, elders, and deacons. There are strict requirements for those who aspire to leadership in the church. Faith is perceived not merely as trust in God and the divine provisions for renewal of his people, but as correct doctrine (2 Tim 3:8; Titus 2:1).

Members of the church are to affirm true doctrine and to exhibit true piety, which is to be fostered through wholesome moral instruction and is to correspond to apostolic traditions. At the same time, the leaders are to be aware of and to expel those who become apostate by opposing the truth, adopting instead a "corrupt mind and counterfeit faith" (2 Tim 3:8). Social differentiation is to be maintained among the members, with slaves continuing in servitude to their masters (Titus 2:9–10). There is to be no civil disobedience: instead, members are to be "submissive to rulers and authorities" (Titus 3:1). The leaders must test the integrity of the faith and the practice of the members while avoiding the adoption of rigid ascetic rules on such matters as food and marriage (1 Tim 4:3). Thus, the new community is to have a

clear authority structure, to encourage civil obedience, to beware of the ascetic beliefs and practices that were to characterize Gnosticism as it developed
in the second century.[101] The more public role of Christians in the empire of
the second century CE is apparent and is being responded to in these Pastoral
Letters—socially, conceptually, and organizationally.

These features of Christian encounter with Roman culture and political
power are also dealt with in the *Didache* and the Apostolic Fathers. As noted
above,[102] the major themes in those documents are submission by members
to the church leadership, affirmation and enforcement of unity in spite of
the diversity of background and origins of members, and affirmation of the
true faith. The appeal to authority is especially strong in the letters of Ignatius
of Antioch, where conformity to correct doctrine and liturgy are enjoined.

From Scriptures to Christian Canon

An issue that became important for the early church was which scriptures
were to be considered as authoritative. This was an implicit factor, for example, in the declaration by Paul that the death and resurrection of Jesus were
"in accordance with the scriptures" (1 Cor 15:34). The gospels have many
references to what is "written" or has been "fulfilled" through Jesus: these
refer, of course, to the Jewish scriptures.[103] But the question for both Jews
and Christians was which of these writings comprise the basic documents for
the covenant people? That is, for the people of Israel, what constitutes their
authoritative texts? It was, of course, these writings that Christians came later
to designate as the Old Testament. In addition, for Christians, the important
question was: Which of their writings linked with Jesus and the apostles were
to be included in the New Testament?

To select the list of those writings to be designated as authoritative, or
canonical,[104] involved not only identifying the prior Jewish documents but
also assumptions as to the nature and source of the authority that they car-
ried. For Christians in the first century CE, in accord with contemporary
Jewish traditions, these writings included not only the Law of Moses and
the collection of the Prophets; there are also references in the New
Testament to another set of documents, known as simply *kethuvim*, "the
Writings." The content of this third group was not clearly defined within
Judaism until after the end of the first century CE, when it was attested in 2
Esdras 14:44–46 as comprising eleven books: Psalms, Proverbs, Job, Song of
Solomon, Ruth, Lamentations, Ecclesiastes, Esther, Daniel, Ezra-Nehemiah,
and Chronicles. (This writing is included in the Roman Catholic Vulgate
Bible where it is called 4 Esdras.) A different sequence of the sacred books
was offered in the Septuagint, however, ancient copies of which reveal a

wide range of differences in the grouping and order of the writings. Further, it was this extended group of Jewish writings that indeed constituted the Septuagint, which became the scripture to which the Christians frequently appealed. But how were these documents selected?

A writing known as the *Letter of Aristeas* purports to describe the process by which the translation of the Hebrew writings into Greek that came to be known as the Septuagint was carried out.[105] This letter reports that, in order to provide the text and translation of the Jewish laws for inclusion among the collection of all the books in the world being assembled in the library of Alexandria by order of Ptolemy II (285–247 BCE), there were seventy-two translators—six from each of the twelve tribes of Israel—sent from Jerusalem by the Jewish high priest. Their translation was designed to be the official Greek text, and indeed functioned in this way, not only for the Jews, but subsequently for the early Christian community as well. Modern editions of the Septuagint, as well as some of the ancient copies, however, include books that are not found in the Hebrew scriptures,[106] and the Greek translations frequently evidence a Hebrew original slightly different from the dominant Old Testament textual traditions. These non-Hebrew writings came to be included in the Christian editions of the Old Testament—although some were later designated as Old Testament Apocrypha—and are quoted often in early Christian writings.

Ancient evidence thus shows the actual diversity within first-century Judaism as to which books were to be regarded as the scriptures. Primary evidence on this issue is to be derived from the Dead Sea Scrolls, among which were found copies of all the books of the Hebrew canon except Esther, although the Psalter was not fixed in terms of content or order. On the other hand, the rabbinic story that a group of rabbis met at Jabneh (Jamnia) in the late first century CE after the fall of Jerusalem and drew up an official canonical list is almost certainly legendary. What is more likely is that the Jewish canon was formed by the rabbis in the late first century CE to differentiate what they regarded as authoritative documents from the early Christian writings and the Jewish literature that they regarded as aberrant because it was apocalyptic or involved synthesizing features of Hellenistic culture. Thus, the canon of scripture adopted in postbiblical Judaism was significantly different from what Christians from the outset perceived to be the antecedent scriptural sources, which comprise what they called the Old Testament.

As the Christians produced their own texts, authority was soon extended to the writings that comprise the Christian canon of scripture. The authority for which the apostles were the agents was perceived to be embodied in their writings, as expressed, for example, in 1 John 2:7–14: to heed this message will lead to life in the name of Jesus, to confirmation of forgiveness, to knowledge of God, and to triumph over "the evil one." The aim of these new writings is epitomized in John 20:30–31: "That you may come to believe that Jesus is the Messiah, the Son of God, and that through believing you may have life in his name." These aims were shared by the other early Christian writings as they came to be brought together as a group, which included the gospels, the letters, Acts, and Revelation.

The reconstruction of the development of this New Testament canon has been effectively and perceptively traced by Bruce M. Metzger in *The Canon of the New Testament: Its Origin, Development, and Significance.*[107] He notes that, among the Apostolic Fathers,[108] the words of Jesus had supreme authority, and they evaluated traditions based on their degree of conformity to the four gospels. In the East, there was a consensus on the authority of these gospels, of the Pauline and other letters considered to be of apostolic origin, in addition to Acts and Revelation. A prime witness is Eusebius's summary of the writings that should be included in the New Testament:[109] the "recognized books" are the four gospels, Acts, the epistles of Paul, 1 John, the Epistle of Peter (= 1 Peter), and the Revelation of John. The "disputed books" according to Eusebius are James, Jude, 2 Peter, 2 John, and 3 John. He then lists books that were taken to be not genuine: *Acts of Paul*, the Shepherd of Hermas, the *Apocalypse of Peter*, and the *Didache*. This is followed by the names of other books that are mostly rejected. Writings ultimately included in the New Testament but considered doubtful or noncanonical by many were Hebrews, James, and the letters of Peter, John, and Jude. In Origen's *Homilies on Joshua* as edited by Rufinus, however, all twenty-seven books of the New Testament are included as authoritative.[110] But Origen also quotes, or refers to as "divinely inspired," Clement of Rome, the epistle of *Barnabas*, and the Shepherd of Hermas.

Clearly, in the early centuries of Christianity, neither the definition nor the dimensions of the New Testament canon were set. The Christians' defining of the canonical scriptures was an ongoing process that produced diverse results. The list of the early Christian books not included in the canon of the New Testament is available in the introduction to *New Testament Apocrypha*, as are translations of (1) writings purporting to be gospels, and (2) accounts of the acts and writings of the apostles.

Concluding Observations: Diversity and the Search for Unity

The social, conceptual, and cultural diversity of early Christianity is obvious in the New Testament and the patristic writings. In the gospel tradition, Jesus is challenged for including among his followers those who by ethnic or religious traditions, by occupation, or by cultural identity were outside the limits of Jewish covenantal definition and conformity. In a challenge to that tradition, however, Jesus is reported to have prayed that those who trust in him through the word of his followers "may all be one" (John 17:20–21). Paul develops the image of the body as diverse in functions yet one in essence: "For as in one body we have many members, and all the members do not have the same function, so we, though many, are one body in Christ, and individually members one of another" (Rom 12:4–5). This diversity of the new covenant community as evident in the gospels and the early apostolic tradition continues to be both a challenge and a central feature in the Christian movement of the second and subsequent centuries. The ongoing effect of the church's fresh and faithful appropriation of the New Testament and the insights offered by the leaders of the church in the early centuries has been to call its members to recognition and affirmation of the unity in the midst of diversity that characterized the Jesus movement from the outset. These differences are reflections of the diverse contexts in which the first followers of Jesus lived, thought, acted, and perceived their identity in the new movement.

Thus, the diversity is evident in roles, in theological and ethical standards, and in models for the community of faith. Yet careful attention to the New Testament evokes consciousness of the central events and messages conveyed through Jesus to his followers that constitute the basic unity. Thus, one must examine and analyze the various social, cultural, literary, and conceptual features of the changing context of Jesus and the movement he launched if one is to recognize the transforming consequences of the diverse settings in which the movement in his name took root and flourished.

Notes

1. Weber's works began to be translated into English as early as 1927. A complete list of his works and their translations is offered in the introduction to his *On Charisma and Institution Building* (Chicago: University of Chicago Press, 1968), ix–lvi. Analyses of the major impact of Weber on sociology in the English-speaking world are offered by Eisenstadt in the introduction to that volume, x–xvi.

2. Eisenstadt, introduction to *Max Weber: On Charisma and Institution Building*, xvi–xvii.

3. Eisenstadt, in Weber, *On Charisma*, xvi–xvii.

4. Ibid., xix.

5. "The Sociology of Charismatic Authority," in *From Max Weber* (ed. and trans. H. H. Gerth and C. Wright Mills; New York: Oxford University Press, 1946), 247.

6. Ibid., 247–48.

7. From *Max Weber*, 54.

8. Eisenstadt, *Weber: On Charisma*, xxi.

9. Ibid., xxi–xxii.

10. Artur Weiser, in the article on *pisteuo*, in *Theological Dictionary of the New Testament* (ed. G. Friedrich; trans. G. W. Bromiley; Grand Rapids: Eerdmans, 1976), 6:196.

11. R. Bultman, *Theological Dictionary of the New Testament*, 6:207–8. Regrettably, however, Bultmann's analysis of faith in Judaism includes a distorted view of faith as abstract and as based on human merit. Further, his view of faith in the New Testament is based on existentialist philosophy, which results in a radically individualistic perspective—ignoring the powerful and pervasive effort in the New Testament to redefine covenant participation and consequent group identity.

12. This mixture of promise and warning is given in abbreviated form in Matt 19:29 and Luke 18:20.

13. The outreach of the gospel to all nations is a major theme in Luke and is demonstrated in Acts.

14. "Brethren" here refers not merely to male witnesses, but to all the "siblings"— male and female—who comprised the earliest Christian community. Luke-Acts gives special attention to the place of women among the faithful from the outset of Jesus' career.

15. That *homologeo* connotes statements of belief, or credal affirmations shared by a community, is evident from Acts 23:8, where we read that the Sadducees did not "confess" the resurrection, angels, or spirits, but the Pharisees confessed/affirmed them all.

16. Ignatius, *To the Trallians*.

17. J. Pelikan, *The Emergence of the Catholic Tradition: 100–600* (vol. 1 of *The Christian Tradition: A History of the Development of Doctrine*; Chicago and London: University of Chicago Press, 1971), 123–41.

18. Ibid., 1:117–21.

19. The philosophical influence in this conceptual shift was Platonic, as has been noted above in relation to the change in the perception of faith that is evident in the Letter to the Hebrews (323–29).

20. Pelikan, *Emergence of the Catholic Tradition*, 120–21.

21. Ibid., 117.

22. As noted above, this term derives from the Greek word, *dokeo*, which means "to seem," as distinct from what actually exists.

23. The translation is from the Loeb Classical Library edition of *The Apostolic Fathers, To the Trallians* 1:9.

24. This creed is quoted from J. N .D. Kelly, *Early Christian Creeds*, (New York: D. Mackay Co, 1972), 82.

25 Variant versions of this creed appeared in the Creed of Marcellus submitted to Julius I in 340, and the Creed of Rufinus of Aquileia, dating from ca. 404.

26. A Roman Christian thinker who came to be regarded as a heretic, Marcion is reported by Tertullian to have insisted on a radical distinction between two Gods: (1) the Creator of the world, who was "judicial, harsh, mighty in war," and (2) a God who was mild and placid, simply good and excellent. The former was the God of the Old Testament; the latter was the Father of Jesus Christ, who had come to earth during the reign of the emperor Tiberius Caesar (in *Against Marcion* 1.6.1).

27. Montanus in the mid-second century sought to "shape the entire life of the church in keeping with the expectation of the return of Christ, immediately at hand; to define the essence of true Christianity from this point of view; and to oppose everything by which conditions in the church were to acquire a permanent form for the purpose of entering upon a longer historical development." This analysis of

Montanism is paraphrased by J. Pelikan in *Emergence of the Catholic Tradition*, 98–99, from G. Nathaniel Bonwetsch, *Geschichte des Montanismus* (Erlangen, 1881), 139.

28. Pelikan, *Emergence of the Catholic Tradition*, 98–99.

29. Mark 1:2–11; Luke 3:7–14.

30. Mark 14:22–25.

31. The Greek manuscripts regarded as most reliable (Codex Sinaiticus, Vaticanus) but also others down to the fifth century, as well as some early papyri, omit "new," which has broad attestation only in later manuscripts and versions. What is implicit in the reference here to "covenant" as to its newness, therefore, was made explicit in later textual traditions.

32. Rom 11:8–9 derives from Deut 29:4; Isa 29:10; Ps 69:22–23 in the LXX. Rom 11:26–27 consists of quotes from Isa 59:20–21 and Isa 27:9.

33. These Lukan canticles have been superbly analyzed by Raymond E. Brown in pt. 2 of his *The Birth of the Messiah: A Commentary on the Infancy Narratives of Matthew and Luke* (Garden City, NY: Doubleday, 1977); and by Joseph A. Fitzmyer in pt. 1, "The Infancy Narrative," in *The Gospel according to Luke (I–IX)* (Garden City, NY: Doubleday, 1981), 303–448.

34. Cf. 2 Sam 7:24; Exod 19:10–11; Mal 3:24; Sir 48:10.

35. The Semitic original of this name, *Yehoshua* (= Joshua), is that of the one chosen by God to lead his people Israel into the promised land (Josh 1).

36. Gen 20:7; Exod 7:1; 15:20; Judg 4:4.

37. The older part of Isaiah (1–35) is followed by a narrative account (36–39), and then by so-called "Second Isaiah" (40–66), which is postexilic.

38. Isa 44:24–45:8.

39. Scholars have made a plausible case that Isa 55–66 should be considered Third Isaiah, and dated to the fifth century BCE.

40. The *Sibylline Oracles*—Graeco-Roman and Christian—are analyzed in chap. 4.

41. John J. Collins, "Introduction to the Sibylline Oracles," in *The Old Testament Pseudepigrapha* (ed. J. H. Charlesworth; Garden City, NY: Doubleday, 1983), 1:317–24. Collins sees no real link between these oracles and Babylonia or Berossus, a Chaldean priest of the seventh century BCE who described the history of Babylon from creation to final destruction. There is no certain evidence regarding the origin of the Sibyl; instead, there are legends concerning her from the fourth century BCE on, linking her to many places, but especially to Erythrea and Marpessus in Asia Minor, and to Cumae in Sicily. The Prologue to the Oracles, which is probably from the sixth century CE or later, identifies her as a daughter of Noah (30).

42. Ibid., 320–23.

43. Fifty had symbolic significance as the joining of the multiple of the sacred number seven, plus one: 49 + 1 = 50.

44. Exod 18:13–17; 24:1–11. In both Hebrew and Greek, the term for elder is used with reference (1) to those who are literally older, and (2) to those who are designated as members of the leadership council of the community.

45. Josephus, *Jewish Antiquities* 12.138–42.

46. Fine analyses of the role of scribes in Judaism are offered in the articles on "Scribes" (1) in the *Dictionary of Judaism in the Biblical Period* (ed. Jacob Neusner and William Scott Green; Peabody, MA: Hendrickson, 1999), 554–55; and (2) by Anthony J. Saldarini, in his article on "Scribes" in *Anchor Bible Dictionary* (ed. D. N. Freedman; New York: Doubleday, 1992), 5:1012–16).

47. This was the Jerusalem-based council known as the *synedrion*.

48. Analysis of "rabbi" is offered below.

49. The Hasideans are described in 2:42–47 as a pious group who joined in the Hasmonean counterattack on the Syrian efforts to impose Hellenistic culture and lifestyle on the Jews in order to make certain that Jews could live in accord with the law of Moses.

50. This analysis is based in part on the article "Rabbi," in *Dictionary of Judaism in the Biblical Period: 450 B.C.E. to 600 C.E.* (ed. Jacob Neusner and William Scott Green; Peabody, MA: Hendrickson, 1999), 516–18. The earlier uses of the term are inferred from the New Testament texts themselves. Neusner has produced an enormous body of writings in which these developments of Rabbinic Judaism are traced and demonstrated.

51. The Mishnah dates from the fifth century CE; the Talmud from the early seventh century CE.

52. Only Latin and Greek versions of the complete Sirach have survived, but fragments of the Hebrew original have been found in Egypt and Palestine. The translator dates his version from the reign of the Egyptian ruler in the Hellenistic period, Ptolemy VIII Euergetes Physcon, who ruled from 170 to 116 BCE. The influence of Stoic philosophy is evident at several points in this text.

53. The Jewish kingdom, which was established under Hellenistic rule and then was revived by the Romans, had become a puppet mode of government with the Herodians designated by the Romans as the royal family, but it went out of existence by the later first century CE.

54. A detailed analysis of the evidence of the controversy over who was qualified to serve as high priest in the mid-second century BCE is offered by J. Murphy-O'Connor in his article, "Teacher of Righteousness," *ABD*, 6:340–41.

55. The scholarly designation for this writing is 1QpHab. A reliable translation by Florentino Garcia Martinez is available in *The Dead Sea Scrolls Translated: The Qumran Texts in English* (2nd ed.; trans. Wilfred G. E. Watson; Leiden: E. J. Brill; Grand Rapids: Eerdmans, 1996).

56. These documents were found in the middle of the twentieth century, although some of them were previously known. An excellent survey of the discoveries and the documents, as well as of the movement within Judaism that launched this group, is provided by John J. Collins in the *ABD*, 2:85–101.

57. A plausible case has been made by David Winston (in his article on the Wisdom of Solomon [*ABD*, 6:122–123]) that the apocalyptic vision in 5:16–23 grew out of the experience of the Jewish community in Alexandria during the reign of the emperor Gaius Caligula (3–41 CE), when Jews were denounced as "aliens and foreigners" (Philo, *In Flaccum* 54).

58. A notable example of the claim to divine connections is that of Chrysippus, the third-century BCE Greek philosopher who taught that the Stoic sage alone could achieve immortality.

59. The Greek term, *huiothesia*, is often translated as "adoption as son," but it connotes attainment of status as son, moving from rank as child to full participant.

60. The Matthean parallel is in 10:37–38.

61. The literal references to this role include Acts 27:11; Rev 18:17; the term is used metaphorically in Prov 1:5; 11:14; 24:6.

62. Hippolytus, *De antichristo* 59.

63. Discussion of prophecy in the Jewish tradition is offered above, 35–40, including references to comparable phenomena in the Graeco-Roman world. Perceptive

analyses of early Christian prophets and prophecy are offered by David E. Aune in *Prophecy in Early Christianity and the Ancient Mediterranean World* (Grand Rapids: Eerdmans, 1983); by M. Eugene Boring in the article "Prophecy (Early Christian)," *ABD*, 5:595–2; and by David L. Tiede in *Prophecy and History in Acts* (Philadelphia: Fortress, 1980).

64. This quote is adapted from one offered by the 1973 SBL Seminar on Early Christian Prophecy.

65. A perceptive analysis of the phenomenon of *glossalalia* in the Graeco-Roman world and in Judaism of that period is offered by Johannes Behm in his article on *glossa* in G. Kittel, *Theological Dictionary of the New Testament* (trans. G. W. Bromiley; Grand Rapids: Eerdmans, 1964), 1:722–26. Plato describes the divine gift of "true and inspired [*mantikes*] divination," which is conveyed through "dream or waking vision by the divining and inspired nature," which are to be analyzed "by means of reasoning to discern about them all wherein are significant and for whom they portend evil or good in the future, the past, or the present" (*Timaeus* 71E–72A).

66. Prime examples are Plato (*Statesman* 272E; *Euthydemus* 291C), and Philo of Alexandria (*On the Migration of Abraham* 67).

67. Luke 4:16–21.

68. A notable text in this regard is Luke 11:20—"If it is by the finger of God that I cast out demons, then the kingdom of God has come upon you."

69. *Gospels and Related Writings* and *Writings Relating to the Apostles, Apocalypses and Related Subjects* (vols. 1 and 2 of *New Testament Apocrypha*; rev. ed.; ed. E. Hennecke and W. Schneemelcher; trans. R. McL. Wilson; Cambridge: James Clarke; Louisville, KY: Westminster/John Knox, 1991–1992).

70 In *Ecclesiastical History* 3:29.15–16.

71. Titles of some of these apocryphal writings are provided above (30–34).

72. Mark 8:31; Luke 9:22; Matt 16:21.

73. Mark 11:27; Matt 21:23; Luke adds that Jesus was teaching in the temple and preaching the gospel (20:1).

74. Cf. Matt 8:5–13.

75. Since the term synagogue in the first century CE is used for gathered groups, rather than for the buildings where they assemble, these details are anachronistic. Cf. the essays in *Evolution of the Synagogue: Problems and Progress* (ed. H. C. Kee and L. H. Cohick; Harrisburg, PA: Trinity Press International, 1999).

76. 1 Pet 5:1.

77. 1 Pet 5:1–2. There is a play on the chronological implications of "elder" in 5:4, where it is stated that the "younger must accept the authority of the elders."

78. These visions of kingdoms as animals recall those in Dan 7, where the successive kingdoms of the Middle East are depicted as weird animals whose rule is replaced by the kingdom of God.

79. The number of the tribes of Israel and of the apostles—twelve—is multiplied by itself and by the symbolic number of divine triumph: one thousand.

80. The terms linked here, *episkopoi* and *diakonoi*, are probably not instances of the use of these words that developed subsequently as designations of formal roles in the church leadership, as described below (406–9). Cf. Joseph A. Fitzmyer, *The Jerome Biblical Commentary* (Englewood Cliffs, NJ: Prentice-Hall, 1968), 2:246.

81. As in the Pauline description of the gifts of the Spirit, these moral qualities match those of the Stoic virtues esteemed in the Graeco-Roman world.

82. In the Hebrew version, the closing part of the text reads, "I will appoint peace as your overseer and righteousness as your taskmaster."

83. The LXX reads literally, "I will give your rulers in peace and your overseers in righteousness." The Hebrew text translates, "I will appoint Peace as your overseer and righteousness as your taskmaster." The LXX uses *episkopos* with reference to a variety of supervisory roles: military officers (Num 31:14; Judg 9:28; 2 Kgs 11:15; overseeing the Levites (Neh 11:9, 14, 22) and the repairs of the sanctuary (2 Chron 34:12, 17); dispensing oil and incense for the sanctuary (Num 4:16).

84. Ignatius, *To the Ephesians* II; IV.

85. Ibid., VI.

86. Ignatius, *To the Magnesians* IV; *To Polycarp*, preface.

87. Ignatius, *To the Magnesians* VI.

88. Ignatius, *To the Trallians* II.

89. Ignatius, *To the Smyrnaeans* VIII.

90. Josephus, *Jewish Antiquities* 3.155.

91. The verb, *diakoneo*, akin to *diakonos*, is one of several in Greek that refer to modes of service: *douleuo* = serve as a slave; *therapeuo* = serve with concern and respect; *latreuo* = serve for wages; *leitourgeo* = perform public service to people or to the state; *hypereteo* = steer or follow the commands of the master. *Diakoneo* means to perform service for another in a close relationship, and hence it covers a range of functions from waiting on tables (Luke 10:40; 17:18; Acts 6:2) to service for others in need (Mark 10:43–45; Luke 22:26; 1 Pet 4:10–11). The acts of help and support for others enjoined by Jesus (Mark 10:44–45) are akin to loving one's neighbor (Lev 19:18). *Diakoneo* becomes, however, a designation for a service function within the new community.

92. The term is also used with reference to an ordinary domestic servant, as in John 2:5.

93. Mark 10:43; Matt 22:11. The same point is made in Mark 9:35.

94. Evidence of the more formal nature of the function of the deacon appears in *1 Clem.* 42:1ff. and *Didache* 15:1.

95. 1 John 2:8–11; John 13:34; 15:12, 17.

96. The mystical union of the community of faith in the Gospel of John is traced below in the analyses of the various models of community structures in the early church.

97. Mystical participation as depicted in the Gospel of John is analyzed in chap. 2.

98. A fine survey of the mystery religions and of their relationship to early Christianity is offered by Marvin W. Meyer in his article in *ABD*, 4:941–45.

99. Analysis of the deuteropauline literature is offered in chap. 3.

100. I have offered a more detailed analysis of the range of communities that developed within the early Christian movement in my book *Who Are the People of God? Early Christian Models of Community* (New Haven and London: Yale University Press, 1995).

101. The development of Gnosticism is discussed in Excursus 3, "Wisdom and Gnosticism."

102. Analysis of the *Didache* is included in the review of the Apostolic Fathers in chap. 4.

103. Examples of these explicit appeals to the Jewish scriptures include Matt 2:6; 4:4; 4:6; 4:10; 11:10; 21:13; 26:24, 31; Mark 1:2; 7:8; 9:12, 13; 11:17; 14:21, 27; Luke 3:4; 7:27; 21:22; 24:44; John 6:31, 35; 12:16.

104. Canon is derived from a Semitic root, *kaneh*, which meant "reed." In Greek, *kanon* was used for "straight rod" or "plumb line," and hence for a standard or rule, as in the rule regarding circumcision (Gal 6:16). A superb analysis of the evolution of the threefold Jewish canon of scripture is provided by James A. Sanders in his article in the *ABD*, 1:837–53.

105. An insightful introduction and translation of this letter by R. J. H. Shutt are in *Old Testament Pseudepigrapha* (ed. J. H. Charlesworth; Garden City, NY: Doubleday, 1985), 2:8–34.

106. Writings not found in the Hebrew texts but included in ancient copies of the Septuagint are: Additions to the historical books (*Paraleipomena A and B*), other books of Ezra, Judith, Tobit, Wisdom of Solomon, Psalms of Solomon, Sirach, Additions to Daniel, and four books of Maccabees.

107. Oxford: Clarendon Press, 1987. This study includes a survey of literature on the canon and analyses of the formation of the canon and of the historical and theological problems concerning the canon.

108. Analyses of features of the Apostolic Fathers are offered above in the examination of the post-gospel traditions concerning Jesus.

109. In *Ecclesiastical History* 3.25.

110. Metzger, *The Canon of the New Testament*, 139.

Changing Historical Models
in the Biblical Tradition

Historical Models in Judaism

Models in the Biblical Period

The historical dimensions of the Jewish scriptures are central—not only in such unmistakably historical writings as the books of Samuel, Kings, and Chronicles, but also in those sections often identified as Law, Wisdom, or worship. The overall thesis of these works is that it is through history that God has established his covenant people and conveyed to them his purpose and destiny for them. The details and the emphases differ in these books, but this basic assumption is consistent in all of them.

The Canonical Histories of Israel/Judaism

The fundamental document for Judaism in all its forms is Torah, also known as the Pentateuch, or the law of Moses. Scholarly analysis has long recognized that this body of literature developed in four major streams of tradition, conveniently designated as J, E, P, and D.[1] The first strand designates the God of Israel as Yahweh,[2] and represents the interests of the southern tribes of Israel, based in Jerusalem, dating from the mid-tenth century BCE. The E tradition prefers to call God El (or Elohim), and reflects the perspective of the northern tribes, based in Shechem and Samaria and produced in the mid-eighth century. D was probably produced in the time of

King Josiah (late seventh century), when there was a reform of the laws and a reworking of the historical narrative of Israel's history, which highlighted the role of Joshua and the phenomenon of the Holy War by which Israel was able to take over the land of Canaan. P reflects the reworking of the tradition from the priestly point of view, and constitutes the major segment of the Pentateuch.

The Deuteronomic history describes in stylized fashion the multi-tribal settlement in the land of Canaan, and how the twelve tribes' way of life under charismatic leaders was organized in a stable form by David, who succeeded Saul as king, taking authority first over the tribes of Judah and then over the northern tribes as well. Yahweh is depicted as choosing Jerusalem for the place of his own special presence, and as the chief city of his people. David and his descendants will rule in an unending dynasty, and the temple (built under Solomon) will be the central shrine, where God would "cause his name to dwell." Jerusalem will be preserved so long as a descendant of David rules and the people are obedient to Yahweh. This promise continued as the basis for Israel's hope of restoration beyond the exile in Babylon.[3] The northern kingdom broke away in 931 under Jeroboam, and came to end when attacked by the Assyrians in 722. Subsequently, the Babylonians took over the southern kingdom in 587, and Jerusalem was destroyed. The historical account in Kings ends here, but hope for the future in spite of disaster is expressed in 1 Kgs 8:12–53, and is included in Solomon's prayer at the dedication of the temple.[4] In the face of Israel's defeat, there remains expectation of divine vindication. These historical books were probably written in two stages: (1) during the reign of Josiah in the seventh century BCE; and (2) after the return of the people of Israel from the exile in the fifth century BCE.

Also probably written after the return of Israel from exile in Babylon were 1 and 2 Chronicles, which call all Israel to obey the law while awaiting divine vindication. Historical accounts of the subsequent history of Israel were written in the fourth century BCE, and offer two slightly different versions of (1) the project of restoration of the city and the temple of Jerusalem with the encouragement of the Persian rulers, and (2) of the leadership that developed there with the aim of calling the people to obedience to the law and to the proper worship of the God of Israel. These books convey the hope that God will reward the fidelity of his people. As historical narratives, they report not only what God has done in behalf of his people over the centuries, but what the divine expectations are for obedience on their part in the future and for punishment in the event of their infidelity to the covenant relationship. In all of these diverse historical modes in the biblical tradition, therefore, history points not merely to the past, but also to the present and the future.

The books of Ezra and Nehemiah provide a major source of evidence for the history and social conditions that obtained at the time of the writing of the books of Chronicles. Their reports do not always match in detail, but the major theme is consistent: the necessity of rebuilding the city of Jerusalem and the temple as the place where God dwells among his people. Ezra begins with the decree of Cyrus the Great, who ruled Persia from 559 to 529 BCE, granting permission for the Jews to return to their land and reestablish the city and its temple. This matches the message of the prophets Haggai and Zechariah, who announced that rebuilding the temple would usher in a new era, in which the hostile nations would be overthrown and the people of Judah would be established as a people of power.[5] It is perceived to be essential that Jews refrain from marrying pagan wives, and that they divorce them if already married to non-Israelites.[6]

Ezra returned to Jerusalem in order to promote the rebuilding of the temple, and Nehemiah is to encourage the rebuilding of the city. These enterprises are confirmed by decrees of the Persian rulers, Cyrus, Darius (522–486 BCE), and Artaxerxes (464–424 BCE).[7] The primary role of Ezra is described as "a scribe skilled in the law." He went to Jerusalem accompanied by priests and Levites, singers and temple servants,[8] but his major role is to call for and foster obedience to the law of Moses. He offered a prayer of confession on behalf of the people, and they responded to his word and work by renewing their commitment to the covenant with God.[9] The sequence of events and the names of central figures are not always consistent between these two books, but the main historical themes they share are: (1) the divine initiative to restore the people of Judah to their land where God dwells among them in the temple; (2) in their land they are to respond by obedience to the law and carrying out the proper cultus in the temple; (3) they are to maintain separate ethnic identity; and (4) they are to study and obey the law of God.

Other Modes of the Perception of History in the Biblical Tradition

History in the Prophetic Tradition

The chief function of the prophet in the traditions of Israel was not foresight, but insight. There are predictive features in the pronouncements of the prophets, but the crucial factor is their perception of the purpose of God for his people as it has been revealed in the past and as that is now relevant for the present.[10] A prime instance of this appears in Hos 11–12, where the predictions of the exile and the suffering that the people will undergo are set in the context of how God has sought to deal with his people in the past, and especially when he led them from slavery in the land of Egypt to the promised land. In earlier times, prophets served as advisors to kings—as Nathan offered warning to David,[11] and Elijah confronted Ahab.[12] Elijah is depicted as having a direct encounter with Yahweh, who gives him explicit instructions about changing the leadership of God's people in order to overcome the defection of the people to Baal.[13]

The prophets Amos and Hosea foresee divine judgment on disobedient Israel, and Jeremiah foretells the impending destruction of Jerusalem. The prophetic term, Day of the Lord, initially referred to the coming day of divine vindication of God's people, but in Amos, Isaiah, and Zephaniah it is seen as a day when God will appear in order to punish his disobedient people. In the subsequent apocalyptic tradition, as represented by Zech 9–14 and Joel, the Day of the Lord is the final battle in which God will triumph over evil in behalf of his people. The theme of restoration of God's people is dominant in Isa 40–55, which was written in Babylon at the time of transition from indigenous rule to dominance by Persia under Cyrus, who is acclaimed as God's "anointed"—in Hebrew, *meshiach*; "messiah" (Isa 45:1). What is proclaimed here is God's superiority and ultimate triumph over the evil earthly rulers.

In Isa 24–27—known as the "Little Apocalypse"—the theme of triumph is extended to include victory over the cosmic agents of evil and the slaying of the major agent of the evil powers (the dragon), the resurrection of the dead, and the vindication of the faithful. In the final section of Isaiah (56–66), the climax is the depiction of the new heaven and the new earth.[14] In the midst of Jeremiah's warnings of coming judgment and oracles of the doom of nations[15] appear promises of restoration, and especially the renewal of the covenant with God's people.[16] The book ends with a report of the destruction of Jerusalem and the release from captivity of the king of Judah, Jehoiachin. Thus, these prophetic books mingle history with the features of analysis of the present and predictions of the future.

Similarly, Ezekiel highlights the restoration of Jerusalem and the renewal of the temple. Habakkuk's denunciation of the disobedient people is followed by expressions of hope for their ultimate renewal.[17] It is significant that this prophetic book appeared among the Dead Sea Scrolls with a commentary to show its relevance for the future of that community. Zechariah comprises two books: (1) 1–8, which portrays two anointed figures: the royal Zerubbabel and the priestly Joshua; and (2) 9–14, in which the restoration of Judah is foretold, as well as the battles of nations against Jerusalem, and the divine condemnation of that city's unworthy shepherds/leaders. The prophet offers perceptions about past, present, and future as the successive arenas in which the purpose of God for his people will be accomplished, as well as the defeat of the powers of evil. History—especially its ultimate goal—is the common theme that runs through these diverse prophetic traditions.

History as Perceived in the Liturgical Tradition

In Deut 26:1–11, the people of Israel are instructed that when they enter the land of promise, they are to dedicate to God a token of the produce that comes as a bounty of that land. This pious act is "a response to the Lord your God," and is to include a celebration of God's historical deliverance of the people from slavery in Egypt and his having led them into their new dwelling place. Central to this act of gratitude and offering reassurance of God's continuing care of them in the future is the historic experience of the "mighty hand and outstretched arm" by which they were "brought out of the land of Egypt." Similarly, in the prophetic tradition, there are recitals of God's historic deliverance of his people, as in Hos 11:1–4, where God's care for them is compared with a parent's nurturing a child.[18]

In Psalms, the historic acts of God to nurture and care for his people are expressed in liturgical terms in relation to David's triumph over his enemies (Ps 18) and his enthronement (Ps 72). Praise is offered to God for having established and maintained the king's rule of peace and justice for the needy, as well as the defeat of their enemies. God's historic actions celebrated in Psalms include the exile (Ps 137) and the subsequent return to the land, where rebuilding of the people has occurred (Ps 51, esp. 18–19).

History in the Wisdom Tradition

Wisdom of Solomon 10:1–19:22 contains an extended series of depictions of the role of wisdom in the unfolding historic experiences of God's people—from Adam, the first-created human (10:1), through Moses, the crossing of the Red Sea, the settlement of Israel in the promised land, the defeat of the human agents and demonic powers of evil, and the promised renewal of the covenant people and of the whole creation (19:18–22). A similar section of Sirach (44–50) "sings the praises of famous men" (44:1), describing the crucial roles of the divinely provided leaders of God's people. These major historical figures are distinguished for their wealth, intelligence, musical and poetical skills, and their "righteous deeds" (49:10). This list of those depicted and praised for their historic deeds begins with Enoch and Noah and concludes with Simon, son of Onias the high priest (ca. 220–195 BCE), under whom the temple and its precincts were restored and the daily pattern of sacrifices resumed (50:1–21).

The Impact of Graeco-Roman Historiography on Judaism

Graeco-Roman Historiography: Representative Historians

Hecataeus of Miletus, in Ionia on the east side of the Aegean Sea, has been characterized as "the first assured historian and . . . the founder of geography."[19] Although his writings at the turn of the sixth/fifth century BCE were titled *Map of the World* and *Genealogies*, he did not simply report traditions about the past, but asserted, "What I write here is the account which I considered to be true. For the stories of the Greeks are numerous, and in my opinion ridiculous."[20] He directly criticizes the mythography that claimed to report the origins of humans and society. But it was Herodotus (484?–425? BCE) who launched disciplined history and did so on a universal scope. Herodotus undertook to write a universal history, contrasting Hellenic and other cultures, collecting, evaluating, and conveying older historical sources. He perceived human life to be controlled by superhuman powers, acting on principles of justice and retribution and punishing evildoers, as in the disaster that befell the Persian invaders of Greek territory. His historical accounts drew upon records of geography and ethnography, as well as ancient myths of earlier peoples.

Thucydides (471–400 BCE) was the founder of political history, in which he described the defeat of the Persians and the rise of the Athenian empire. His historical method sought to achieve both accuracy and relevance, based on information he obtained from persons involved, if possible. For him, the speeches offered in a history must show why things happened, and what forces were at work to achieve these results—including the character and motives of the actors involved. He eliminated such factors as divine providence and oracles, insisting rather on human responsibility and the operation of chance. His major aim in writing history was to show what best served the interests of the Athenians. Actions were evaluated in accord with reason, based on success or failure. Similarly, Polybius (198–117 BCE)—taken as a hostage from Greece to Rome after the Battle of Pydna—gained firsthand knowledge of the Romans and their traditions, and planned to write a comprehensive history of the Roman ascendancy as a world power. He insisted on accurate presentation of the facts, and in the knowledge of causes—among which he included natural and human causes, as well as *Tyche* ("fortune, fate"). He later came to accept the Stoic view of history as a succession of forms of government and the transitory nature of noble institutions. For Polybius, the aim of history is to instruct the mind, and to do so in terms of historical truth and impartiality—even though he was strongly influenced by the philosophical and ethical tendencies of his age.

Among the Roman historians, two outstanding figures are Livy (59 BCE–17 CE) and Tacitus (55–117 CE). Livy's chief aim was to give Romans a picture of the growth of their nation. He wrote during the tranquil period of Augustus's reign, and did not bother to seek precise knowledge by visiting historical scenes or consulting primary sources. As an optimistic court historian, he sought to foster the political ideals of the emperor. Tactitus's aims were more ethical, in that he strove to exhibit the motives and personalities of the historical actors through the speeches he attributed to them. His *Annals* advanced the ideals of virtue and nobility, while disclosing to his readers the crimes of the Julio-Claudian dynasty.

Designed as a universal history of forty volumes—from the Trojan War to the death of Alexander the Great—Diodorus Siculus in the middle of the first century CE set forth in detail his aims in this undertaking, which is known as *The Library of History*. He praises those who have written "universal histories,"[21] since their aim is to help human society as a whole. Instruction about historical failures and successes is essential for the human race. He observes that there are two views of human origins: (1) that the universe and humans have always existed; (2) that the universe had a beginning and will decay and humans came into being at a definite time, developing control of animals and food as well as speech and symbols to understand the changing and difficult world in which they lived. He sketches the progressive history of humankind and reports the myths of the origins of the universe and of the deities.[22] A notable feature of this history is the author's reporting of a story about Semiramis, who is depicted as having built the city of Babylon.[23] The story is attributed to Ctesias, whose *Persica* describes the founding of the Persian empire, and is a prime example of the historical romance—a literary mode popular in the Hellenistic world, and adapted by Jewish writers in the Graeco-Roman period, as noted above. Josephus, of course, best represents a similar comprehensive, didactic view of Jewish history, with respect to both content and historical method.

Didorus Siculus's perception of the role of history—to foster justice and piety, to denounce evil, to develop a comprehensive view of the world and its destiny—was clearly shared by the early Christian writers, from the author of Acts down to Eusebius and subsequently.

Notes

1. Details of analysis and chronology of the Pentateuch and the historical writings are based on material offered by Eric M. Meyers and John Rogerson in *The Cambridge Companion to the Bible* (ed. H. C. Kee; Cambridge: Cambridge University Press, 1997), 114–60.

2. Earlier transliterated as Jahveh, or Jehovah.

3. Isa 2:2–3.

4. 1 Kgs 8:12–53, esp. 47–50.

5. Hag 2:23; Zech 3:6–10.

6. Ezra 9:1–4; 10:1–44; Neh 13:1–3, 27–43.

7. It is possible that the Artaxerxes mentioned in Ezra 7:11 is the second ruler by that name, whose reign was from 404 to 358 BCE.

8. Ezra 7:1–10.

9. Ezra 9:5–10:15.

10. Details of this sketch of the prophetic tradition derive from the analysis offered by Meyers and Rogerson in *Cambridge Companion to the Bible*, 161–228.

11. 2 Sam 12.

12. 1 Kgs 17–18.

13. 1 Kgs 19:11–18.

14. Isa 65:17–25.

15. Jer 1–25; 46–51.

16. Jer 30–33; the renewed covenant in 31:31–34.

17. Hab 3:17–18.

18. This theme recurs in Hos 12:9 and 13:4–5.

19. By Herbert Butterfield, in *The Origins of History* (New York: Basic Books, 1981), 134.

20. Quoted from J. B. Bury, *The Ancient Greek Historians* (New York: Macmillan, 1909), 13. The sketches offered below of Greek and Roman historians are indebted to his analyses in this volume, which have been modified by Truesdell S. Brown in *The Greek Historians* (Lexington, MA: D. C. Heath, 1973).

21. *Tas koinas historias* 1.1.

22. Diodorus, *Library* 1.7–29.

23. Ibid., 2.4–20.

Changing Historical Methods in the Study of Christian Origins

The Range of Historical Resources in the New Testament

The gospels, which are the opening documents in the New Testament, are by no means reports produced by detached, objective observers analyzing the career of Jesus. They all constitute portrayals of Jesus and reports of his words and works by those who are convinced that he was God's agent for the establishment and nurturing of a new covenant people. Yet, as is indicated in the analyses of the gospels in chapter 2 of this volume, each of the gospel traditions represents a different perspective on the role of Jesus and a different definition of the divinely assigned role of the new community that he was calling into being. The historical sources that portray these features include sayings sources, a distinctive narrative mode—which came to be known as a gospel—as well as both the canonical gospels, which portray Jesus in a range of roles and modes, and the noncanonical gospels. Further, there are references to other Jesus traditions in the letters and treatises that came to be included in the New Testament. Analysis of these documents are offered in chapters 2, 3, and 4 of this volume.

The writings in the New Testament that most closely match the style and communication modes of Graeco-Roman historiography are the twofold books of Luke and Acts. The explicit historiographic features are pointed out in our analyses of them. These writings are propaganda for the origins, spread, and aims of the program perceived to have been launched by Jesus and being carried out by agents appointed by him and empowered by the Holy Spirit. This program represents the author's perception of the process leading to culmination of God's purpose for the renewal of his people and, through them, of the creation. Although the details differ in significant ways, this basic hope shaped the other New Testament writings as well.

Details of the historical setting for this movement are also provided by Roman and Jewish sources from the first centuries of the common era, including Jewish and Roman historical sources, as well as religious documents produced by mainstream Jews and by such dissident groups as those who produced the Dead Sea Scrolls.

Efforts by the early Christians to supplement their literary base are apparent in the great body of literature now known as the New Testament Apocrypha and in the writings of the so-called church fathers. The objective to impose harmony on the diverse gospel accounts of Jesus in the canonical gospels is manifest in the document known as the *Diatessaron* ("through the four") produced by Tatian. This Christian scholar left his native land east of the Euphrates and moved to Rome.[1] His major scholarly contribution was a harmony of the career of Jesus, which he produced by weaving together the elements of the four gospels. By so doing, he sought to overcome the historical problems raised by the differences in sequence and content between these sacred writings. More recently discovered gospels and Acts of the Apostles have, on the contrary, complicated the historical picture of Jesus and the spread of the movement in his name.

Early Christian Perspectives
on History as a Whole

The first comprehensive history of Christianity was that of Eusebius, who around 315 became bishop of Caesarea in Palestine. He wrote his great *Ecclesiastical History* during the reign of the emperor Constantine, to whom he served as advisor on religious issues. His aim in this history was to show that the purpose of God was being worked out by the divine Logos, and that all history involved the struggle of the Evil One against God. Central for history is accurate chronology—the time in which the unified, divinely ordered and accomplished growth of the church was taking place. He denied, however, that its institutional development and change of doctrines were part of the divine program. Instead, the church was to be one in teaching and order. The sources he used for his history included the Jewish writers Josephus and Philo, as well as both orthodox and heretical Christian writers, such as Clement of Alexandria, Clement of Rome, Papias of Hierapolis, Tatian, Justin

Martyr, Irenaeus, and gnostic writings. Using these writings enabled him to document the issues in doctrinal controversies.

Another Christian scholar whose writings later provided perspective and content for the history of Christianity was Augustine of Hippo (354–430). He perceived that in history there had been two concurrent societies:

> [1] Worldly society has flowered from a selfish love which dared to despise even God, whereas [2] the communion of the saints is rooted in a love of God that is ready to trample on self. . . . This latter relies on the Lord, whereas the other boasts that it can get along by itself. . . . In the city of the world both the rulers themselves and the people they rule are dominated by the lust for domination, whereas in the City of God all citizens serve one another in charity, whether they serve by the responsibilities of office or by the duties of obedience.[2]

Augustine's analysis of historical events and documents is based on this distinction. He regarded history as moving through six ages, which corresponded to the six days of creation but which would culminate in the final divine judgment.

Enlightenment and Post-Enlightenment Historical Reconstructions

The development of history as a science, as Donald R. Kelley has pointed out,[3] began under the joint impact of the Renaissance—with its recovery of ancient culture—and the Reformation—with its reexamination of the biblical and historical traditions of Christianity and Judaism. This involved investigation and authentication of ancient data. Scholars over the centuries have proposed different epochs of history and different modes of analysis of the historical evidence. For example, in his *Discourses on Universal History*, Jacques Benigne Bousset (1627–1704) divided history into a succession of epochs, in each of which the central focus was on religion and political government, with the changes occurring as a result of divine action. His theory was that the long concatenation of particular causes that made and remade empires depends on the secret decrees of Divine Providence: "From the highest heaven God holds the reigns of every kingdom and holds every heart in his hand. . . . What is coincidence to our uncertain foresight is concerted design to a higher foresight; that is, to the eternal foresight which encompasses all causes and effects in a single plan."[4] A similar view of history was articulated by Foustel de Coulanges: "History is not an accumulation of events of all kinds which happened in the past: it is the science of human communities."[5] This methodological feature with its emphasis on community formation has come to be recognized in the twenty-first century in the form of insights in sociology of knowledge, a method that perceives that both the framework and details of what is "known" are shaped by the assumptions and values of a community that makes the claim to possess knowledge of reality.

After the Renaissance, a treatise that had an enormous and enduring impact on scholarly perceptions of history as reflected in the gospels and epistles was John Locke's *The Reasonableness of Christianity, as Delivered in the Scriptures*.[6] In this study, Locke (1632–1704)—who was involved in political conflict, but spent years as a scholar at Christ Church, Oxford—makes a sharp distinction between (1) the gospels and Acts, which he takes to be documents demanding faith in Jesus' messiahship and resurrection; and (2) the epistles, in which he thinks the true gospel has been diluted and mingled with alien ideas that pervert the simple gospel.[7] As a result of this thesis, scholars began critical analysis of the New Testament, and felt free to discredit certain features of it as marginal or contrary to true faith.

Locke's view of knowledge has been summarized as follows:

> [1] It is evident that all relations [to Christian faith] terminate in, and are ultimately founded on, those simple ideas we have received from sensation and reflection. [2] . . . In relations we have for the most part, if not always, as clear a notion of the relation as we have of the simple ideas whereon it is founded. [3] That in the so-called moral relations we have a true notion of the relation by comparing the action with the rule, whether the rule be true or false.[8]

Thus, the pattern was set for differentiation within the New Testament writings as to original context and intent—a critical method advanced by a scholar within the major university! Locke's basic point of view was what has been called deism: the belief that God, or the gods, exist and function in a sphere removed from humanity, so that understanding of divine being and activity is in the realm of the theoretical or abstract. This worldview is in contrast to theistic perspectives, which claim to discern divine presence and action in the earthly, human sphere.

The deistic view became dominant among biblical scholars in Europe, as is shown in the survey by W. G. Kümmel under the theme, "English Deism and its Early Consequences."[9] But a philosophical mode that also powerfully influenced critical analysis of the New Testament subsequently was that of Georg W. F. Hegel (1770–1831), whose career culminated as professor in Heidelberg and Berlin. He perceived the course of the world process to be dialectical, by which seemingly antagonistic features—thesis and antithesis—are reconciled or combined to form a synthesis in which such differences are overcome. The force that effects this cosmic renewal and unification he called the Absolute Spirit. This is a process of becoming, and leads ultimately to the perception of true Being. Hegel discerned these features in the physical, moral, political, historical, and religious spheres. Christ appeared as a finite individual who is also a particular manifestation of the infinite, the universal, and the self-existent. In him are fused the universal and the particular, the divine and the human. Although Hegel believed that the combined church and state for centuries countered the possibility of true freedom, he thought that the Reformation freed individual humans to obey God directly, without political or ecclesiastical control. He was convinced that this access to freedom for the individual was confirmed intellectually by the Enlightenment, in which each scholar highlighted his or her value and subjective experience. Hegel's dialectical approach to understanding had direct effects on scholarly exegesis of the New Testament.

Two New Testament scholars methodologically influenced by Hegel were David Friedrich Strauss (1808–1874) and Ferdinand Christian Bauer (1792–1860). Their theories had major influence on the studies of early Christianity in Europe in the mid-nineteenth century. Strauss made a sharp distinction between myth and history, but assumed that myth was not untrue but an important symbolic mode of conveying timeless truth. This notion matches well Hegel's theory that human thought is to occupy itself with the universal by contemplation of the truth and by participation in the absolute Spirit that is at work to carry forward the unending process of change and spiritual renewal. The Hegelian mode of truth advancing in the universe through the process by which thesis and antithesis give rise to a new synthesis is perceived by Strauss to be operative in the shift in viewpoint concerning Jesus from the Synoptics to the Gospel of John. Hegel makes a sharp distinction between the natural and the mythical perceptions of truth in the gospels: "The natural system of interpretation, while it seeks to preserve the historical certainty of the narratives, loses their ideal truth—sacrifices the essence to the form; whereas the mythical interpretation by renouncing the historical body of such narratives, rescues and preserves the idea which resides in them, and which alone constitutes their spirit and vitality."[10]

Similarly impacted by the theories of Hegel in his analysis of the New Testament was F. C. Baur. In his detailed examination of the Pauline letters, he came to the conclusion that from the beginning Christianity was shaped by the tension that arose between law-abiding Jewish Christians and law-free Gentile Christians. The results of this synthesis he saw in the later New Testament writings, where there was emphasis on obedience to the law—as in James and 1 Peter, but especially in 2 Peter. This last writing Strauss regarded as inauthentic, but as reflecting the emergence of a Christian combination of freedom and moral structure. Here is a prime example of a Hegelian process by which conflicting concepts are overcome and transformed in new syntheses that are seen as disclosing and confirming concepts of ultimate reality.

An analogous and equally powerful methodological synthesis of philosophical theory and historical interpretation of early Christianity is evident in the extensive historical writings of Adolf von Harnack—who was likewise influenced by the radical individualism of Hegel. In his book on the essence of Christianity,[11] he defined the core of the Christian faith as consisting of three basic items: the fatherhood of God, the brotherhood of humankind, and the infinite worth of the human soul. He closed this widely influential work with the declaration that by tracing the history of the human race we may perceive "upward development and . . . the communion of minds" and so "become certain of the God whom Jesus Christ called his Father, who is also our Father." The subsequent diversity of the early Christian writings was acknowledged by von Harnack, but the underlying unity was seen by him as central and basic.

· In the twentieth century, an analogous development in the historical analysis of Christian origins was offered in the extensive and highly influential New Testament studies of Rudolf Bultmann. Bultmann made a major contribution to New Testament studies by developing a method of analysis of the component elements—narrative and sayings material—which were brought together to constitute the gospels.[12] This method came to be designated form criticism. In addition to the formal distinctions (such as "tales" and "myths," which imply negative judgments about historical reliability), these scholars differentiated functional distinctions: preaching or instruction. The form critics also sought to determine the *Sitz-im-Leben*—life situation—of the formal units. But these scholars did not take into account sufficiently the diverse modes of community definition that we have seen to be so central a feature in the shaping of the various gospel traditions.[13] Instead, Bultmann adopted[14] the radically individualistic perspective of existentialist philosophy, with its primary concern for the decisions one makes as determining one's destiny.[15] Accordingly, Jesus' role was perceived by Bultmann as primarily a call of the individual to the decision to obey God. Left out of consideration by him was the community that shares this call. Nevertheless, form criticism has proved to be of enduring value in the process of detailed analysis of the gospels. Though its significance for historical reconstruction of the original settings has not followed the individualistic approach of Bultmann, this analytical method instead has pointed to the adaptation of the traditions by the various gospel writers, reflecting the distinctive mode of community in and for which they were writing.

Martin Hengel's monumental study, *Judaism and Hellenism: Studies in their Encounter in Palestine during the Early Hellenistic Period*,[16] demonstrated by detailed analyses of the relevant evidence that the radical distinction scholars have found between Judaism and Hellenism as backgrounds of early Christianity were contrary to the abundant evidence of the extent of shared literary and conceptual modes between these cultures. Subsequent analyses of the literature and other relevant material have confirmed the high level of impact of Hellenistic philosophy, literature, and social structures on Judaism, and subsequently on early Christianity.

The sociological dimensions of such studies in cultural history have been highlighted by both sociological and biblical scholarship. Of central importance are T. S. Kuhn's *The Structure of Scientific Revolutions*[17] and the study by Peter Berger and Thomas Luckmann, *The Social Construction of Reality: A Treatise in the Sociology of Knowledge.*[18] Kuhn offers detailed analysis of the process by which scientists through the centuries chose different paradigms by which they interpreted the evidence that they perceived, with the result that "the whole conceptual web has to be shifted and relaid; a whole new way of regarding the problems and factors in their solution emerges." He raises questions that in my view are also important for examination of the complex process of Christian origins: "How does one elect or is one elected to membership in a particular community, scientific or not? What does the group see collectively as its goals; what deviations, individual or collective, will it tolerate?"[19] It is this mode of investigation that must be engaged in if one is to discern more accurately the specifics of claims and affirmations that are evident in the diverse communities and modes of understanding that developed in the beginnings of Christianity. The rationale for this historical method based on sociology of knowledge is set forth in my study, *Knowing the Truth: A Sociological Approach to New Testament Interpretation,*[20] and is operative in my monograph, *Who Are the People of God? Early Christian Models of Community.*[21]

The Reversion to Reductionist Methods

In spite of what seems to be a clearly apparent scholarly strategy among responsible biblical scholars in these days, which takes into account conceptual and cultural diversity from the beginnings of Christianity, there continue to be proposals of reductionist strategies in the reconstruction of early Christianity. These are evident in the so-called new search for the historical Jesus—for which the Jesus Seminar has gained the most publicity. Prime examples of the results of this approach have been set forth in a brief analysis by John Dominic Crossan, *The Essential Jesus: Original Sayings and Earliest Images,*[22] and in his comprehensive study, *The Historical Jesus: The Life of a Mediterranean Jewish Peasant.*[23] A composite record of the results of the Seminar has been prepared by Robert Funk: *The Gospel of Jesus according to the Jesus Seminar.*[24] In the latter volume are presented the sayings of Jesus and the accounts of his activities that the Seminar considers to be authentic, with brief comments on the component features of this gospel. The work draws on all four of the canonical gospels, but also on others—especially the *Gospel of Thomas*—in order to distill what are regarded by the group as the essential teachings and events in the life of Jesus.

In the *Gospel of Thomas*, the kingdom of God is perceived as a life of obedient serenity, rather than as an age to come. True followers of Jesus are to prepare for breaks with their families and for the experience of bad elements: "weeds among the wheat." They are to rely on divine support, which God will provide like a loving parent. The kingdom of God is not an age to come, but an already present reality for the obedient. Severe discipline is called for from the members, whose lives are to be characterized by love and compassion and by generosity to the needy. Only brief mention is made of the arrest, trial, and crucifixion of Jesus, but an epilogue recounts his appearances to his disciples. This gospel builds on not only the Synoptics, but also on the Gospel of John, the Acts of the Apostles, and the letters of Paul.

It is significant that the leaders of the Jesus Seminar have come from backgrounds based on traditional beliefs—evangelical and Roman Catholic. What seems evident in the Seminar's proposal, which claims to be *The Gospel of Jesus*, is that the members have sought to construct an alternative Jesus with whose words and works they feel more comfortable than with the older traditions. The pervasive apocalyptic features of the gospel tradition have been removed—apparently because these scholars felt uncomfortable with the nonfulfillment of that expectation. With regard to scholarly method, the decisions as to authenticity of Jesus tradition rest on preference for traditions for which the modern mind has less intellectual discomfort. Significantly absent from these publications are any substantive efforts to deal with the diversity of sociocultural contexts in which the Jesus traditions were preserved and by which they were adapted. The result is what its proponents seem to view as a more broadly comfortable alternative picture of Jesus. The motivation for such undertakings might be seen as a modern variant of the divine utterance in the Genesis creation story (Gen 1:26): "Let us create Jesus in our own image!" But truly responsible historical study of Christian origins calls instead for analysis of the variety of sources and historiographic modes that are apparent in the early Christian writings.

Notes

1. The only certain date for the career of Tatian is the report that he returned from Rome to the Middle East in 172 CE.
2. Augustine, *City of God* (ed. Vernon J. Bourke; Garden City, NY: Doubleday, 1958), 14.28.

3. Kelley's perceptive study, *Version of History from Antiquity to the Enlightenment* (New Haven: Yale University Press, 1991), demonstrates the shift from history as an art to a science (370ff.).

4. Quoted in ibid., 433.

5. Quoted in Geoffrey Barraclough, *Main Trends in History* (New York and London: Holmes & Meier, 1978), 91.

6. A useful edition of this work, with an insightful introduction by Benjamin Rand, is *An Essay Concerning the Understanding, Knowledge, Opinion and Assent* (Cambridge: Harvard University Press, 1931). A perceptive analysis of Locke's theses is offered in *Locke and the Compass of Human Understanding* (Cambridge: Cambridge University Press, 1970).

7. W. G. Kümmel, *The New Testament: The History of the Investigation of Its Problems* (trans. S. M. Gilmour and H. C. Kee; Nashville: Abingdon, 1972), 51.

8. Introduction to Locke's *Essay*, liii.

9. *The New Testament: The History*, pt. 2, sec. 2, 51–61.

10. Kümmel, *The New Testament: The History*, 124.

11. In German, the title was *Das Wesen des Christentums*; in English, it was *What is Christianity?* The work went through fourteen editions and as many translations. Its basic perspective was documented in a greatly expanded form in von Harnack's seven-volume *History of Dogma*, produced between 1886 and 1890.

12. As did his contemporary New Testament scholar, Martin Dibelius. They developed a method of analysis of the gospel tradition that they designated as *Formgeschichte*, translated as form criticism. This analytical mode identified a variety of forms in which both the narrative and the sayings features of the gospel tradition were preserved in the canonical gospels. Dibelius's analysis of the gospels sought to show the similarities between the originally oral units of tradition preserved in the gospels and forms preserved in folk literature. His work (*Formgeschichte*) built on studies by Karl Ludwig Schmidt, who in 1919 proposed that the gospels had been compiled from units of tradition preserved by the church to serve its needs for conversion and instruction of inquirers (in *Der Rahmen der Geschichte Jesu* [The framework of the history of Jesus]). Dibelius in that same year pointed this out in his *Die Formgeschichte der Evangelien*, translated as *From Tradition to Gospel*. In 1921, Bultmann published his monumental analysis of the material brought together from its original oral form to shape the written gospels: that these forms of communication were used to serve the two basic needs of the church: preaching and moral teaching: *Die Geschichte der synoptischen Tradition*. This was published in 1963 in an English translation by John Marsh as *The History of the Synoptic Tradition*.

13. Analyses of these various community settings for the gospel tradition are offered above in chap. 2.

14. In Bultmann's studies of the gospels, but also in his *Theology of the New Testament*, where he seeks to trace what he regarded as the regrettable evolution of Christianity from the basic call of the individual to decision for the will of God to the institutional modes taken on by the Christian communities.

15. A leading German existentialist philosopher was Martin Heidegger, who shared the existentialist view that "to think of man as being really meant to think of him as *potencia*, or becoming. To exist meant literally to stand out, to emerge, to choose, to transcend the forces operating upon one, not to be bound entirely by the past, but to point toward the future." From Franklin L. Baumer, *Modern European Thought: Continuity and Change in Ideas, 1600–1950* (New York and London: Macmillan, 1977), 436.

16. 2 vols.; trans. John Bowden; London: SCM; Philadelphia: Fortress, 1974.
17. 2nd ed.; Chicago: University of Chicago Press, 1970.
18. Garden City, NY: Doubleday, 1967.
19. K. G. Kuhn, *The Structure of Scientific Revolutions*, 206–9.
20. Minneapolis: Fortress, 1989.
21. New Haven: Yale University Press, 1995.
22. San Francisco: HarperSanFrancisco, 1994.
23. San Francisco: HarperSanFrancisco, 1991.
24. Santa Rosa, CA: Polebridge Press, 1999.

Wisdom and Gnosticism: Origins and Impact on Christianity

In the Graeco-Roman world, there were three alternative perspectives concerning wisdom and knowledge that had pervasive influences on perceptions of human destiny in the wider culture, including those that arose within Judaism and early Christianity. The antecedents of these various modes of wisdom are evident in the Jewish biblical tradition, but also in literature of the wider world of the ancient Near East. The first of these perspectives sought to discern and define timeless truths, which claimed to transcend social and cultural features of any specific epoch or historical setting and found expression in both proverbial and philosophical modes.[1] The second mode of wisdom did concern history—past, present, and future—in its social, political, and cultural aspects, as well as the destiny of the individual. This was embodied in the Judaeo-Christian traditions in the form of prophetic pronouncements, and subsequently in what has come to be designated as apocalyptic.[2] The third perspective on wisdom and knowledge viewed them as esoteric information and insights, reserved for a favored elite—a point of view that came to full expression in the writings of the gnostics in the second century CE.

Since wisdom in its various modes has an important role in the New Testament and early Christian writings, it is essential to examine these parallel features from the wider culture. In his superb survey, "Wisdom in the Old Testament," Roland E. Murphy observes:

> there seems to be a general consensus that biblical wisdom connotes a search for "order" . . . that is to say, the sages held that there was a fundamental order in the world, and their teachings were designed to bring about conformity [by the wise, or gnostics] with this order that had been determined

by God . . . [But] at most the sages perhaps impose an order on experience; they present conclusions drawn from observation. [Yet] despite the dogmatic form of their statements, they were also aware of mystery and uncertainty.

They allowed for a margin of error in their analyses, as well as the possibility of self-deception, and raised questions, articulated by Job, whether one can fully understand the mystery of God: "Can you penetrate the designs of God? Dare you vie with the perfection of the Almighty? It is higher than the heavens; what can you do? It is deeper than the nether world; what can you know?"[3]

In spite of the acknowledged limits of humans to grasp divine wisdom, there are in the Jewish scriptures express and vivid pronouncements about the role of wisdom in disclosing and achieving the purpose of God for his people. Psalm 136:5 declares God's wisdom or understanding to have been the instrument through which God created the heavens, just as Job 26:12 links God's power with his divine understanding in order to achieve the events that made possible Israel's exodus from Egypt. The role of God as maker of the universe is linked by the prophets with the personal relationship of God to his people, as in Isa 54:5, where the "maker" is also "the husband" of Israel, and in Job 10:2–12, where the God from whom forgiveness and renewal are sought is addressed as "the one who fashioned me like clay," and also "granted me life and steadfast love."

Wisdom is not an abstract entity or tool for creation, but a deeply personal feature, as evident in the repeated references to Lady Wisdom (Job 28; Prov 1, 8, 9), whose role in the purpose of human renewal is detailed in Sir 24:1–22. In Prov 8:22–36, the role of Wisdom in creation is linked with her capacity as teacher and giver of life to those who heed her instruction. The divine bestowal of wisdom is also to be found in the Prophets (Isa 11:2; 33:6). Her prophet-like role is indicated in Prov 1:20–33, where she threatens her audience with doom if they disobey God, but promises peace and security to those who obey her. The priority of being in right relationship with God is set forth in Prov 1:7 and 9:10, where "the fear of the Lord" is declared to be "the beginning of wisdom."

But wisdom in the third sense indicated above is depicted in both the prophetic and the apocalyptic tradition. For example, the ruler chosen by God for his people will be enabled to carry out his role by the divinely bestowed spirit: "The spirit of the Lord shall rest on him, the spirit of wisdom and understanding, and spirit of counsel and might, the spirit of knowledge and fear of the Lord" (Isa 11:2). Divine wisdom disclosing the future of the world and of God's people is made explicit in the grateful prayer of Daniel reported in Dan 2:20–23:

Blessed be the name of God from age to age, for wisdom and power are his. He changes times and seasons, deposes kings and sets up kings; he gives wisdom to the wise and knowledge to those who have understanding. He reveals deep and hidden things; he knows what is in darkness, and light dwells with him. To you, O God of my ancestors, I give thanks and praise, for you have given me wisdom and power, and have now revealed to me what we asked of you.

Wisdom is here perceived not as personal insight, but as disclosure of the cosmic divine purpose, with direct relevance for the people of God as they face the future and are granted a vision beyond the current threat and persecution they are experiencing, and thus can perceive the ultimate triumph—for them and through them—of the purpose of God for his people and for the renewed creation.

Under the impact of the Platonic tradition as it was being reconceived and appropriated in the final centuries BCE, both Jewish and early Christian thinkers—influenced by philosophers in the wider Graeco-Roman world—developed new perspectives on what divinely granted esoteric wisdom communicated to the insiders who saw themselves as comprising the community of the truly wise. It was this intellectual movement, with clear antecedents in the Middle Platonic tradition,[4] which by the early second century CE came to be designated Gnosticism, and is examined here in both its theoretical and mystical dimensions. Evidence of its impact on early Christianity is to be noted, beginning with the antecedents evident in the letters of Paul, and turning to the clear development of this conceptual view in the later letters attributed to Paul and other later writings included in the New Testament.[5] Bentley Layton has correctly observed, however, that the earliest surviving explicit reference to the sect of the gnostics is by Irenaeus about AD 180 concerning Valentinus of Alexandria, on whom "the gnostics were a major influence."[6] Layton thinks it is likely that Valentinus had encountered in Egypt the esoteric Hermetic literature, which included *Poimandres*, offering a description of the creation of the world and the origins of humanity, engaging in an allegorical interpretation of ancient cosmological myth, drawing on both the *Timaeus* of Plato and the biblical account in Genesis as Philo of Alexandria had done earlier in his treatise, *On the Creation of the World*. From Irenaeus's *Against Heresies* can be reconstructed the basic features of the gnostic myth of creation as offered by Valentinus, which presents four acts: the emission of the spiritual universe; the creation of the spiritual universe; the creation of Adam and Eve; the subsequent history of the human race, which includes the emission of the Holy Spirit and the emanation of Jesus.[7] Thus, although there are antecedents of Gnosticism in Judaism as early as Philo (30 BCE–45 CE), there is no firm evidence for it as a theological system until the time of Irenaeus.

Layton perceives Gnosticism as "the literary creation of theological poets—an elaborate symbolic poem," which unfolds a mythic drama in four acts:

I. The expansion of a solitary first principle (god) into a full non-physical (spiritual) universe.
II. Creation of the material universe, including stars, planets, earth and hell.
III. Creation of Adam, Eve and their children.
IV. Subsequent history of the human race.

This is interwoven with a subplot of theft and loss, but of ultimate recovery of a part of the divine "as mystic souls are summoned by a savior and a return to God."[8]

The dates for this literature cannot be determined with certainty, but Layton notes that some of these gnostic works (*Zostrianus* and *The Foreigner*) were brought to the attention of Plotinus about 250 CE, and some very probably pre-date Valentinus. Even those gnostic writings that do not include explicitly Christian features are so closely akin to the other gnostic writings that they cannot with any probability be assigned to pre- or non-Christian origins.[9]

Careful analysis of the Neoplatonic sources has shown that gnostic thought was decisively influenced by the Platonic tradition as it was perceived and expounded in the second and third centuries CE.[10] John D. Turner has shown the Platonizing influence evident in the Sethian texts found among the Nag Hammadi documents, such as *The Treatise of the Allogenes*: the derivation of "the ontological structure of their transcendent world and the structures of the visionary ascent through it, as well as the Sethian negative theology applied to the invisible spirit from sources that are ultimately at home in Platonism." These concepts stem from Middle Platonism, based on exegesis of the *Timaeus*, *Sophist*, *Parmenides*, *Symposium*, *Republic*, as well as the reminiscences of Plato's teaching in Aristotle's *Metaphysics*.

Knowledge of this gnostic type shared a widespread philosophical view in this period that focused on wisdom as providing access to personal meaning and destiny, claiming that access to divinely communicated knowledge enabled one to escape the limitations, tragedies, and routines of ordinary human life and to gain not only knowledge of the realm of the divine but participation in it in a personal way. The crucial term for such divinely communicated knowledge that came to be used for this claim was obviously one of the Greek words for knowledge: *gnosis*. The adherents of this concept of knowledge were called "gnostics"—implying that in a special way they were "in the know."

Scholarly interest in this subject, which the writings of the Fathers show to have been a major area of controversy in the early centuries of the church's existence, was greatly increased in the twentieth century as the result of the discovery in 1945 of thirteen gnostic books. Found at Nag Hammadi in upper Egypt and written in Coptic—the native Egyptian language in the Graeco-Roman period—they were recorded in a script very different from that of the older Egyptian records. These writings supplement in a significant way other documents quoted and contested by the church fathers, as well as those found and/or published since the late nineteenth century that had also been produced by Egyptian gnostics. The earlier finds included *Pistis Sophia*,[11] the *Apocryphon of John*,[12] and the *Sophia Jesu Christi*.[13] Others long known, which some scholars have claimed to be gnostic, are the *Odes of Solomon*,[14] and the *Hymn of the Pearl* (which is included in the apocryphal *Acts of Thomas*).[15] But as H. J. W. Drijvers has noted in his analysis of the latter document,

> Philosophical and religious knowledge plays a central role, not as the instrument of redemption but in order to lead to the true action which effects salvation. Yet all the characteristic marks of the classic gnostic systems are completely lacking in the *Odes* and the *Hymn of the Pearl*. There is no mention of a fall in the Pleroma;[16] the creation is not the work of a wicked Demiurge, and matter is therefore not in itself evil. Man's freedom is the primal cause of good and evil, death and life, and this stands in sharp contrast to gnostic determinism.[17]

Especially in the twentieth century, scholars have sought to discern and describe the rise of gnosticism and the specifics of the gnostic claims to possess knowledge of the divine, comparing these writings with religious documents from Greece and various parts of the Near East, and with the canonical texts of early Christianity. Theories about the origins of Gnosticism were propounded in the nineteenth century, and continued down to the twenty-first century. An influential hypothesis was that of Rudolph Bultmann, who declared that Gnosticism was "a religious movement of pre-Christian origin" that invaded "the West from the Orient as a competitor of Christianity," and "assumed the form of mystery cults" so that "the Gnostic motifs took on concrete form in one of the mysteries." It is said by him to have "penetrated to the philosophical literature of Hellenism," and thus to have influenced both Philo and Neoplatonism. The so-called gnostic myth is said to have concerned the fate of the soul, which had its origin in the realm of light, but became imprisoned in the body, from which it now awaits its final deliverance and its ascent to the world of light. The supreme deity took pity on humans, sent down his Son as "the heavenly figure of light," who arouses his own from sleep, inviting them to join him. He teaches them how to find their way to their true heavenly home, for which he grants them the sacred passwords and insights by which they can achieve this goal.[18]

Bultmann constructed this mythical pattern based on material preserved by the Mandaeans, a small religious sect existing in Iraq and Iran down to the twentieth century. Their beliefs and practices are recorded in texts, some of which probably date from as early as the third century CE, but which also include ritual books, theological tractates, and magical texts, mostly from the fourth or fifth century CE. The writings depict a world of light and one of darkness, with a struggle going on between the king of light and the powers of darkness. There is an emphasis on ritual—especially baptism—as the divinely granted means by which the faithful can gain deliverance from the powers of evil: baptism leads to the ascent of the soul to the heavenly realm of light. There are, however, no historical redeemer figures who perform redemptive roles comparable to that of Jesus—although one of the Mandaean messengers is reported to have confronted Jesus, denouncing him as a liar. The soundest conclusion to be drawn from this evidence, therefore, is that Mandaeism developed in the form in which it has survived in reaction to Christianity—not as an antecedent.

Another scholarly theory about the origins of Gnosticism propounded in the middle of the twentieth century was that this perception of human origin and destiny developed as Jews and Christians abandoned their apocalyptic hopes of divine social or political vindication in the face of the Roman takeover of the land of the Jews and the destruction of the temple, the priesthood, and any agency of social or cultural autonomy. All the aspirations were crushed by Hadrian with the failure of the Second Jewish Revolt and the radical restructuring of life for what had been the land of the Jews. Both the Jews and the Christians came to doubt the traditional concepts of the omnipotence, omniscience, and providential care of God, and sought new ways in which to interpret the prophecies and expectations of their traditions by turning in upon themselves as the locus of divine renewal. The interpretation of the prophecies supposedly shifted the focus from the corporate renewal of the people of God to spiritual, personal, and internal transformation.

A far more likely accounting for the rise of Gnosticism than the theories sketched above, however, is the perception that it resulted from significant changes that took place in the early centuries of the common era in a broad intellectual context: scholars dealing with such basic philosophical issues in the Platonic tradition as the ground of human knowledge. The process of recasting the Platonic concept of being—and hence, of knowledge—began in the period of philosophical evolution now known as Middle Platonism and reached its climax in the philosophical development known as Neoplatonism.[19] The conceptual and intellectual interchange between this philosophical tradition and the gnostic features in early Christianity is evident from the explicit engagement with the latter that was undertaken by such leading later Platonic thinkers as Plotinus. It is highly significant that Plotinus directly engaged the gnostics in the Ninth Tractate of his Second Ennead, "Against the Gnostics." In his *Life of Plotinus*, Porphyry gives another title to this essay, "Against those who say that the maker of the universe is evil and the universe is evil" (24.56–57). A. H. Armstrong observed that this treatise:

is a most powerful protest on behalf of hellenic philosophy against the un-Hellenic heresy (as it was seen from the Platonist as well as the orthodox Christian point of view) of Gnosticism. . . . Plotinus disliked [the Gnostics] so intensely and thought their influence harmful [because] "they despise and revile the ancient Platonic teaching and claim to have a new and superior wisdom of their own; but in fact anything that is true in their teaching comes from Plato, and all they have done themselves is to add senseless complications and pervert the true traditional doctrine into a melodramatic, superstitious fantasy designed to feed their own delusions of grandeur. They reject the only true way of salvation through wisdom and virtue, the slow patient study of truth and pursuit of perfection by men who respect the wisdom of the ancients and know their place in the universe . . . Worst of all, they despise and hate the material universe and deny its goodness and the goodness of its maker."

Yet Plotinus's view of the creation is opposed to orthodox Christianity as well as to Gnosticism, since, as Armstrong notes, "the idea that the universe could have a beginning and end is inseparably connected in [Plotinus's] mind with the idea that the divine action in making it is arbitrary and irrational. And to deny the divinity . . . of the world soul, and of those noblest of embodied living beings—the heavenly bodies—seems to him both blasphemous and unreasonable."[20] Thus, it is evident that the gnostics, in dealing with the major themes of their theological construct, were wrestling with and debating precisely those issues central to Middle Platonism. It must be recognized, however, that related issues had already emerged in the development of Jewish and early Christian wisdom traditions. As noted in the analyses of Paul's letters and those subsequently written in his name,[21] the role of wisdom is important, as it came to be in the gnostic tradition. The initial stages of the evolution of the concept of knowledge in that direction are already evident in these documents written in the name of Paul, as well as in the Letter to the Hebrews. The changing conception of wisdom (*sophia*) in the deuteropauline letters shows the influence of gnostic-type perceptions.

Notes

1. Translations of proverbial wisdom from cultures other than that of Israel in the ancient Near East are in *Ancient Near Eastern Texts Relating to the Old Testament* (ed. James B. Pritchard; Princeton: Princeton University Press, 1955; 3rd ed. with suppl., 1969).

2. The apocalyptic mode of wisdom is analyzed in Excursus 5, "Facing the Future: Common Themes in Jewish Apocalyptic and Graeco-Roman Philosophy and Literature."

3. R. Murphy, "Wisdom," *Anchor Bible Dictionary* (ed. D. N. Freedman; 6 vols.; New York: Doubleday, 1992), 6:922–23.

4. A superb analytical survey of Middle Platonism is offered by John Dillon in his *Middle Platonism: 80 B.C. to 220 A.D.* (Ithaca, NY: Cornell University Press, 1996).

5. Analysis of the features of the letters of Paul that show the influence of what became Gnosticism—and of the deuteropauline letters that show this even more clearly, are offered in chapter 3.

6. The reference to the gnostics is in Irenaeus's treatise *On the Gnostics* (1.29); Layton mentions it in his *The Gnostic Scriptures* (Garden City, NY: Doubleday, 1987), 5. Irenaeus lived from ca.100 to ca.175 CE.

7. Layton, *Gnostic Scriptures*, 223–27.

8. Ibid., 12–21.

9. Ibid., 21.

10. Richard T. Wallis, *Neoplatonism and Gnosticism* (Albany, NY: SUNY Press, 1992), 125.

11. *New Testament Apocrypha* (Louisville, KY: Westminster/ John Knox, 1991), 1:361–69.

12. An English translation is included in *The Nag Hammadi Library in English* (ed. W. Schneemelcher; English translation by R. McL. Wilson; rev. ed.; Leiden: Brill, 1988), 104–23.

13. Ibid., 220–43.

14. Translation in *Old Testament Pseudepigrapha* (ed. James. H. Charlesworth; Garden City, NY: Doubleday, 1985), 2:735–71.

15. *Apsotle of Thomas*, 108–13.

16. Kurt Rudolph has described the *pleroma* in the gnostic system of Valentinus as a feature of the basic belief in the idea of emanation from the primordial beginning, consisting of "at least thirty aeons arranged in fifteen pairs," of which the most important are "primal-depth" (*bythos*) and "thought" (*ennoia*); "grace" (*charis*) and "silence" (*sige*); then "mind" (*nous*) or the "only-begotten" (*monogenes*) and "truth" (*aletheia*); "word" (*logos*) and "life" (*zoe*); "man" (*anthropos*) and church (*ekklesia*); and finally "wisdom" (*sophia*), which out of ignorance creates the world. To overcome the difficulty this fosters, there are created two aeons, Christ and the Holy Spirit. Christ brings Sophia back to harmony with the pleroma, but her passionate desires are separated from her and become features of the later created cosmos, which is dominated by the demiurge. Man is part of this material world, from which he is in need of liberation, and which is made possible through Christ.

17. *New Testament Apocrypha*, 2:337.

18. R. Bultmann, *Primitive Christianity in Its Contemporary Setting* (Cleveland and New York: Meridian, 1956), 162–65.

19. A superb study by John Dillon is *The Middle Platonists: 80 B.C. to 220 A.D.* (rev. ed.; Ithaca, NY: Cornell University Press, 1996). R. T. Wallis has made a fine study of *Neoplatonism* (New York: Scribners, 1972), and co-edited a collection of essays on *Neoplatonism and Gnosticism* with Jay Bregman (Albany: State University of New York Press, 1992). Another group of relevant essays on the import of Neoplatonism for the evolution of Christian thinking is *Neoplatonism and Early Christian Thought* (ed. H. J. Blumenthal and R. A. Markus; London: Variorum Publications, 1981).

20. In the introductory note, *Against the Gnostics* (LCL; Cambridge: Harvard University Press, 1966), 2:220–22.

21. Colossians, Ephesians, and the Pastorals.

The Multiple Impact of Stoicism on the Origins of Christianity

Traditional Links of Paul with Stoicism

An encounter between Paul and representatives of two of the major Greek philosophical traditions—Epicureans and Stoics—is described in the vivid scene in Acts 17:16–34, where Paul engages in a public encounter with those depicted as intellectual inquirers at the Areopagus in Athens, who "spent their time in nothing except telling or hearing something new" (17:21). The group addressed by Paul may be simply a crowd of city-dwellers gathered in the public space on the Areopagus, but on the other hand, they could represent the official Areopagite body of public officials charged with overseeing the intellectual and cultural life of the city. In either case, those assembled are identified by Paul as "Men of Athens" (17:22). It should be noted that this account in Acts is from a book that almost certainly was written no earlier than the later first century, long after the fall of Jerusalem and the death of Paul.[1] While Acts includes some reliable historical material, it cannot be assumed that all the evidence in this book constitutes an accurate historical report.[2]

In Paul's address at the Areopagus, as reported in Acts, he affirms the transcendence of God, the divine role in the creation of the world, and the common origin and destiny of the human race. He further asserts the divine immanence for all humans by quoting an apparently well-known Greek poet:[3]

The God who made the world and everything in it, he who is Lord of heaven and earth, does not live in shrines made by human hands, nor is he served by human hands, as though he needed anything, since he himself gives to all mortals life and breath and all things. From one ancestor[4] he made all nations to inhabit the whole earth, and he allotted the times of their existence and the boundaries of the places where they would live, so that they would search for God and perhaps grope for and find him—though indeed he is not far from each of us. For in him we live and move and have our being, as even some of your poets have said, "For we are his offspring."

Since we are God's offspring, we ought not to think that the deity is like gold, or silver, or stone, an image formed by the art and imagination of mortals. While God has overlooked the times of human ignorance, now he commands all people everywhere to repent, because he has fixed a day on which he will have the inhabited world judged in righteousness by a man whom he has appointed, and of this he has given assurance by raising him from the dead. (Acts 17:22–31)

Scholars have long advanced the theory that the declaration in v. 28, "in him we live and move and have our being," is a quotation from the Cretan poet, Epimenides, who is included by Diogenes Laertius as one of the seven sages in his *Lives of the Philosophers* (1:109–15).[5] He is a semi-mythical figure from the sixth century BCE who is said to have lived for a century and a half, and who is mentioned by Plato and Aristotle. Another quotation from him appears in Titus 1:12, where he is reported to have denounced Cretans as "gluttons, lazy beasts, and liars." Although the source of this first quotation or allusion is debatable, the explicit reference to a poet in the latter part of Acts 17:28 has long—and accurately—been recognized as coming from Aratus, a poet of the early fourth century BCE. It was also quoted by Aristobolus, a Jewish theologian who wrote in Egypt, probably during the reign of Ptolemy Philometor (155–145 BCE).[6] Yet his work survives only in fragments preserved by Eusebius in his *Ecclesiastical History*[7] and his *Praeparatio Evangelica*.[8] Quoted by Aristobolus from Aratus's *Phaenomena* are the following lines:

From Zeus[9] begin the song, nor ever leave
his name unsung, whose godhead fills all streets,
all thronging marketplaces of humans,
the boundless sea and all its ports.
All mortals need God everywhere,
for we are his offspring. And he kindly
reveals to humans good omens of success,
stirs them to labor by the hope of food,
tells when the land best suits the grazing ox.
or when they should plough; when the seasons are favorable
for planting the young tree, and sowing the various seeds.

Aristobolus then declares that these factors show that the power of God is operative through all things.[10] We shall note below that he perceives the correspondence in point of view between the Stoic philosophers and the Jewish scriptures to be the result—not of the Jewish thinkers having read and been influenced by the Stoics, but of the Stoics having read and been persuaded by Moses! He declares, "It seems to me that Pythagoras, Socrates, and Plato with great care follow [Moses] in all respects. They copy him when they say that they hear the voice of God, when they contemplate the arrangement of the universe, so carefully made and so unceasingly held together by God."[11] This apologetic tactic demonstrates the concern of Jewish scholars to show the correlation between the biblical tradition and the philosophical insights of Greek and Roman thinkers—a goal that found its most extended expression in the writings of Philo of Alexandria, with his elaborate allegorical exposition of the Jewish scriptures.[12]

Another encounter between Paul and the civil authorities depicted in Acts 18:12-17 may involve—at least, implicitly—a contact between Paul and an outstanding figure in the Stoic tradition: Seneca. Gallio, the Roman proconsul of Achaia, before whom Paul is reported in Acts to have been summoned after accusations were brought against him by the Jewish leadership in Corinth, found him guilty of no "crime or serious villainy." Instead, Sosthenes, the leader of the local synagogue, is said to have been beaten by the local Roman authorities.[13] The only reliable historical report of this account comes through analysis of fragments of an inscription that were found at Delphi: they indicate that Gallio's term in office in the region was during the reign of the emperor Claudius (41–54 CE), which may be compatible with the chronology that can be inferred from the Pauline letters. But the notion of a direct link between Paul's views and those of the Stoics probably developed (1) from the fact that Gallio was known to have been the brother of the Stoic philosopher, Seneca (ca. 4 BCE to 65 CE), and (2) from the consequent assumption in the early church that Gallio's refusal to punish Paul was accompanied by a favorable reaction to Paul's teaching, and that his positive estimate of Paul's teachings was subsequently conveyed by Gallio to his brother, Seneca, whose philosophical concepts are considered below.

But also linked with the name of Seneca is another body of early Christian literature that purports to document the close connection that Paul had with the Stoic tradition, and the mutual respect that obtained between Seneca and Paul. It exists only in the fragments of alleged correspondence between these two, which were edited for the American Academy in Rome by C. W. Barlow in 1938, with a perceptive introduction,[14] and more recently by Cornelia Romer, in "The Correspondence between Seneca and Paul," in vol. 2 of *New Testament Apocrypha*.[15] This material consists of fourteen brief letters, eight from Seneca and six from Paul. Their content is largely reciprocal praise between these two for the wisdom and skills in communication that each declared the other to possess. For example, in Letter XIV, Paul commends Seneca for his "irrefutable wisdom." In Letter XI, Seneca mentions Paul's

Letters to the Galatians, the Corinthians, and the Achaeans—probably meaning 2 Corinthians, which is addressed to "all the saints throughout Achaia"
(1:1). In this letter of Seneca, Paul is identified as a Roman citizen, but the
Jews and Christians are blamed for the burning of Rome.

When and how did these letters originate? In 392, Jerome, in *De viris
illustribus* 12, refers to the correspondence between Paul and Seneca, and to
the execution of Seneca by Nero two years before "the glorious martydom of
Peter and Paul." This tradition is also transmitted by Augustine, Alcuin, and
Peter Abelard. But earlier (in 324), Lactantius, referring to Seneca with respect
for his philosophy, observed that *if he had been a Christian*, he would have
been a true worshiper of God.[16] This implies that the traditions of mutual
admiration and shared beliefs between Paul and Seneca were unknown in
325 CE. Thus, it seems clear that the correspondence between these two was
produced in the mid-fourth century, and that only in the fifth century and
subsequently[17] was this claim taken as historical fact. Doubts concerning the
authenticity of these letters began to emerge in the fifteenth century, and
modern scholarly study has confirmed their apocryphal origins. But even if
they were to be adjudged authentic, it would be inexplicable that in these letters there is no documentation for features of either Stoic philosophy or of
the theology of Paul. An analysis of the philosophy of Cicero and Seneca
and other Roman Stoic philosophers, however, and a comparison of major
features of this tradition with the letters of Paul and other early Christian
writers, shows that the Stoics and the early Christians did in fact share a significant range of concepts and perspectives.

Stoic Views on the Divine Order of the Universe and on Human Destiny

The Stoic school, which was established ca. 300 BCE by Zeno of Citium (in
Cyprus), developed in three successive periods: (1) the first, led by Cleanthes
and Chrysippus from 300 to 200 BCE; (2) the second headed by a chain of
instructors that began with Zeno of Tarsus, and whose leadership continued
with Diogenes of Babylon and Antipater of Tarsus; (3) the third launched by
Paenetius of Rhodes (200–250 CE) when he introduced Stoicism in Rome
and his pupil, Posidonius of Apamea, taught M. Tullius Cicero there. It is
worth noting that two of these philosophers came from Tarsus—the city Paul
is reported in Acts to have named as his native place![18] Yet neither in Acts
nor in his letters does he suggest that Stoicism in Tarsus had any influence
on his intellectual development or concepts.

Stoicism had begun in Athens about 380 BCE, when Zeno (350–260
BCE) founded a school there, following an extended period of study of vari-

ous philosophies, including those of Socrates, Plato, and Heraclitus. We look first at some of the typical features of the earlier Stoicism before turning to an examination of aspects of Roman Stoicism, especially as evident from the writings of Cicero and Seneca. Central was the conviction that the Logos, or divine reason, shaped and rules the universe, and should serve as a guide to right reasoning and to perception of the divine natural law. For individuals, the goal of human life was to live "according to nature"—a phrase that may have originated with Zeno or with his successor as head of the school, Cleanthes (331–232).

Chrysippus, who followed Cleanthes as head of the school from 232 to 206, sought to strengthen and systematize the Stoic doctrines. He propounded a concept of the human soul as *pneuma* (spirit), which is "inborn in us, continuous, extended throughout the body . . . The command center of the soul is the part where all things come together and is located in the heart."[19] Chrysippus propounded a theory of cosmic spirit (*pneuma*), which he saw as equivalent to God and to divine reason (for which he used both *nous* and *logos*), and which he described as pervading the entire universe as the soul does the body, and as corporeal (*sōma*). In some parts of the universe, it merely stabilizes, but in others it functions as mind, imparting coherence to the whole. Because of this spatial and corporeal coherence of the universe, there is also temporal extension of the *pneuma*, so that just as all the cosmic parts are interconnected, so all events are linked to one another by spiritual power (*dynamis pneumatikē*). From this cosmological concept arises the Stoics' notion of the chain of fate, on which their deterministic view of human existence is based, and which may "number among its descendants the Holy Ghost."[20]

Cicero, born in Italy in 106 CE, studied law, oratory, literature, and philosophy in Rome under the Stoic Posidonius. After a brief career in the military and then as a lawyer, he continued his studies of philosophy in Greece and Rome, to which he returned in 77 BCE. He aligned himself with Pompey in the struggle for power, and entered the Senate in 74. Exiled for a time, and after serving as consul in Cilicia, he returned to Rome in 50 and allied himself first with Pompey and then with Julius Caesar. He supported Octavian after Caesar's death in 44 CE, became involved in the ensuing power struggle with Mark Anthony, and in 43 BCE was himself murdered. Among his treatises that have survived, most relevant for our purposes are his *De Haruspicium Responsis*, *De divinatione*, and *De natura deorum*. In the first of these, Cicero urges his readers to heed the messages of the gods, whether through augurs or portents such as earthquakes (xi; xxviii), and recalls that it was through instructions by the Sibylline oracles that significant developments had taken place in the life of Rome (xi).[21] In the treatise *On Divination*, Cicero describes the significance of oracles "uttered under divine inspiration," and of those humans enabled by the gods to interpret these messages from the gods (I.xvii.34). The gods are the friends and benefactors of humans, and they grant to them both signs and the ability to interpret them (I.xxxviii). He asserted further that the existence and work of the gods is to be inferred from the following: the beauty and order of the heavens; the evidence of divine providence (II.xxix–lxii), as well as from epiphanies experienced by humans at crucial moments in history; and from divination, portents, omens, prophecies, including the Sibyllline oracles (II.iii–iv). The world is pervaded by reason, which is divine, animate, and the governing principle of the universe.

It is in Cicero's *De natura deorum*, however, that features showing kinship with early Christianity are most clearly evident. He rejects the belief of other Stoics in the notion of recurring cycles in the world, and infers instead the existence and action of the gods from the beauty and order of the heavens and from the epiphanies of the gods at crucial moments in history, which have been discernible through divinations, prophecies, and signs—including the Sibylline Oracles.[22] He cites Chrysippus's affirmation that the order of the universe proves that it is "maintained in union by a single divine and all-pervading spirit," which is reason, and which has granted wisdom to the world, all of the forces of which are held together by the divine nature. Nature is "the sustaining and governing principle of the world."[23] As a result of the interaction of the elements of the universe—particularly, fire and water—there will come a cosmic conflagration, from which only the fire will remain, but then a new world will be created and the ordered universe restored.[24] The divine purpose embodied in this plan is seen to be that "the world itself was created for the sake of gods and men, and the things that it contains were provided and contrived for the enjoyment of men. For the world is as it were the common dwelling place of gods and humans, or the city that belongs to both; for they alone have the use of reason and live by justice and law."[25]

Cicero describes the greedy schemes of Dionysius the Cynic by which he robbed temples and sold the sacred objects for his own gain in the marketplace, so that thereby "to impiety toward the gods he added injustice towards men," who were under obligation to restore the holy things to the shrines from which they came. But Cicero declares that he is not promoting sin, since "an innocent or guilty conscience" is "so powerful a force in itself," and operates to effect "divine governance of the world," as part of a rational system which brings rewards for right conduct and punishments for transgression.[26] Conscience, therefore, is seen by this Stoic as the divinely granted human capacity to be aware of and to move one to obedience regarding the moral standards of the law of nature that pervades and orders the universe. To ignore its urgings is to leave oneself vulnerable to the divinely instituted punishment of the wicked. Cicero's prime interest was ethics, but he appealed to logic and the natural sciences to make his case for moral responsibility. Thus, the animating principle of reality is the *logos*, which he considered to be divine reason, consisting of a fine material: fire.[27] The chief manifestation of the *logos* is the human soul, which is summoned to live in accord with the divine order by conformity to natural law. This will foster human brotherhood and the practice of the four chief virtues: wisdom, courage, justice, and temperance. As we shall observe, these appear as prime features of the ethics of Paul.

It is with a Stoic contemporary of Paul—Seneca—that the nearest conceptual kinship between Stoicism and nascent Christianity is evident. Born in Spain about 4 BCE and educated in Rome in rhetoric and philosophy, he was made a praetor[28] in 49 and became a tutor of Nero—very likely contributing to what was initially the latter's decent and reasonable rule, which began in 54. By 62, however, Seneca was estranged from Nero and took part in a conspiracy to kill him, which resulted in his being forced to commit suicide in 65. Central in Seneca's philosophy was the principle of living according to nature: this was the highest good that humans could achieve.[29] The essential factor for conformity to the true good is a good conscience,[30] which links the individual to honorable purpose and right action. Dwelling within the individual is the divine presence: "God is near you, he is with you, he is within you"—which Seneca designated as the holy spirit and which he defined as soul and reason (*ratio*) brought to perfection in the soul.[31] The norm for proper behavior is temperance, which is achieved through self-control of the body—a feature that we shall see was also significant in the moral perspective of Paul.[32] Thereby, a good conscience leads to an even and calm way of life.[33]

Although Seneca observes that in this world persons are diverse in social status and power, he sees also the possibility of achieving unity of life: this is created by reason, which is nothing else than a portion of the divine spirit set in a human body.[34] This makes possible the experience of union with the divine:

> When a soul rises superior to other souls, when it is under control, when it passes through many experiences as if it were of small account, when it smiles at our fears and at our prayers, it is stirred by a force from heaven. A thing like this cannot stand upright unless it is supported by the divine. Therefore, a greater part of it abides in that place from which it came down to earth. Just as the rays of the sun do indeed touch the earth, but still abide at the source from which they are sent; even so the great and hallowed soul, which has come down in order that we may have a nearer knowledge of divinity, does indeed associate with us, but still cleaves to its origins; on that source it depends, thither it turns its gaze and strives to go.[35]

Seneca did not share with Cicero any skepticism about the possibility of divine disclosure of the future of the cosmos. In his treatise *On Providence*, he affirms the universality of the divine order,[36] and in *To Marcia on the Death of Her Son*, he describes how the world is renewed over and over within the bounds of time, with cyclic conflagrations and cosmic renewal.[37] Death is not the end of existence but results in a journey to the gods, who look down with detachment on human affairs and take the souls of the blest to a realm of eternal peace,[38] from which one can enjoy "the noblest spectacle of things divine."[39] The present cosmic order will perish in the conflagration, but it will come into existence again, and the righteous will share in it. Like Cicero, Seneca perceives a cosmic purpose that shapes both cosmic history and the destiny of the individual.

The Impact of These Aspects of Stoicism on Judaism in the Graeco-Roman Period

Jewish writers of this period who give evidence of basic influence from Stoicism—in addition to Aristobolus, mentioned above—include the author of the *Testaments of the Twelve Patriarchs*, the author of 4 Maccabees, and Josephus. In the *Testaments of the Twelve Patriarchs*, moral requirements for the Jewish people are identified with the Stoic concept of living "according to nature" (*T. Naph.* 3). From the opening lines of 4 Maccabees (which dates from the late first or early second century CE), the story of the struggle of the Maccabees is retold as a philosophical lesson, the aim of which is to foster the Stoic virtues: self-control, courage, justice, and temperance. Obedience to the law of Moses enables one to perceive and embody these cardinal moral qualities. In his *Against Apion* (*Contra Apionem*), Josephus points out parallels between the law of Moses and Greek philosophy: Moses' primary concern is for piety and virtue, and his view of God emphasizes these qualities, which are described by the Pythagoreans, the Platonists, and the Stoics, and which are unbegotten, eternal, immutable, superior to all mortal conceptions. The chief virtues are justice, fortitude, temperance, and the universal moral laws. Like Plato, Moses insisted on seeking to achieve the true commonwealth in which all people would obey the laws. Josephus declares that the reason the philosophers parallel the insights of the law of Moses is that they all derived their insights from that source which sets forth "the truest piety in the world" (2.4–42).

It is clear from these Jewish writers as well as from their Gentile contemporaries around the turn of the eras that the distinction often made by scholars in the present era between wisdom and apocalyptic would be meaningless in the first century CE. Instead, writings from this period and culture assume a divine design to be operative universally—both in the lives of individuals and in the course of world affairs. Influenced substantively by the Stoic tradition, the task of the philosophical and religious leadership—Jewish and

Gentile—is seen to be discerning and conveying this wisdom in order to achieve individual and corporate renewal. It is in this perspective that the early Christian literature should be understood as well.

Features of the Early Christian Tradition Akin or Analogous to Those in Roman Stoicism

It is significant—and perhaps symbolic—that in the so-called Q material included in the gospels of Matthew and Luke,[40] where Jesus is depicted as one whose wisdom is greater than that of Solomon or Jonah, the essence of his insights concerns his call to repentance in the light of impending divine judgment on the current evil generation. Jesus' wisdom does not consist of pious, timeless aphorisms on an allegedly Cynic model, as a contingent of New Testament scholars have tried to show.[41] The true analogue between Jesus and the Stoic-Cynic tradition is rather what might be called an eschatological-ethical theme: the gods will reward and sustain the king who honors virtue, who is humane, and who is characterized by prudence (*phronesis*), temperance (*sophrosune*), justice (*dikaiosune*), and courage (*andreia*).[42]

It is in the letters of Paul that these features of ethics and social renewal evident in the Stoic tradition are explicitly present and powerfully operative, especially in his exposition of (1) divine justice, (2) natural law, (3) conscience, (4) moral renewal, and (5) the ultimate establishment of divine rule in the world. Later New Testament writers incorporated similar features in their worldviews, as well.

The import for Paul of the word *dikaiosune* is clouded by the traditional translations, "righteousness" and "justification." The function of this term in the letters of Paul is not a moral quality as such, or a judicial process leading to legal vindication. Rather, God is the agent at work in *dikaiosune* to bring his people into right relationship with him and with each other as members of the covenant community. Through the cross and resurrection of Jesus, the obstacles to achieving that relationship—sin and consequent death—have been overcome. The model for setting humans right with God is, of course, Abraham, who—in spite of his advanced age and his wife's barren condition—trusted God's promise and thus received a son to carry forward the covenant people in right relationship with God.[43] Now the new people of God enter that right relationship through the benefits deriving from the sacrificial death and the resurrection of Jesus.[44]

Paul asserts that both Jews and Gentiles are called to this relationship, but that they are unable to attain it by their own efforts. All humans who turn from worship of and obedience to God the Creator are abandoned to lives in violation of the order of nature.[45] Yet there remains the possibility that some Gentiles do hear and obey the law of nature, the requirements of which are written on their hearts, as they are made aware through their conscience.[46] For Paul, conscience is awareness of and sensitivity regarding the moral order of the creation, as in the Stoic tradition. Subjection to the civil authorities is to be carried out, not merely out of fear of divine judgment, but in response to the stimulus from the conscience.[47] Those limited in their awareness of the divine order assume that they are still prohibited from eating food that had been offered to idols, whose sham and impotent nature they ignore.[48] Sensitivity to the divine purpose and order and living in response to it are the basic role of conscience in the life of the new people of God.[49] Those who will share in the new life in "the kingdom of God" will be enabled to do so by the Spirit,[50] which recalls Cicero's citation of Chrysippus concerning the single divine and all-pervading spirit that has brought wisdom to the world and enables humans to live by justice and the law, as well as Seneca's description of the role of the "holy spirit." What the Spirit produces in the life of this new people is the configuration of virtues that include those asserted by Dio Chrysostom and other Stoics as characterizing the life of the wise and just: "love, joy, peace, patience, kindness, goodness, faithfulness, gentleness, self-control."

In the later New Testament material, including letters attributed to Paul, the perception of conscience shifts to moral standards for the life of the community, which is characterized as "good,"[51] "clean,"[52] or "defiled."[53] In the Letter to the Hebrews, the work of the Holy Spirit purifies the conscience.[54] In 1 Pet 3:21, baptism is a symbolic reenactment of the resurrection of Jesus and it should lead to one's yearning for a good conscience.

Moral renewal is linked in 2 Pet 1:4 with participation in the divine nature, which brings "life and piety through the knowledge of the one who has called us to his own glory and virtue," and enables the faithful to "escape the corruption that is in the world in the form of lust." The consequence of this process of moral renewal is that "faith is enhanced with virtue [*arête*], virtue with knowledge [*gnosis*], knowledge with self-control [*engkrateia*], self control with perseverance [*hypomone*], perseverance with piety [*eusebeia*], and piety with mutual affection [*Philadelphia*], and mutual affection with love [*agape*]." Here, then, is an extended list of the Stoic virtues that are attainable through "knowledge of our Lord Jesus Christ," and which provide access into his "eternal kingdom."[55] It is this last theme of the ultimate divine order of the universe that, in a highly elaborated form, brings to a close the Revelation of John. There—following the millennial prelude of the defeat of Satan and the vindication of the righteous[56]—the ultimate renewal of heaven and earth occurs and the City of God comes down out of heaven for the righteous to enter.[57]

Notes

1. A discussion of the origin and date of Acts is offered in my commentary on Acts, *To Every Nation under Heaven: The Acts of the Apostles* (New Testament in Context; Harrisburg, PA: Trinity Press International, 1997), 13–14.

2. On the historical strategy and value of Acts, see the discussion in ibid., 11–20.

3. Identified by ancient and modern scholars as Aratus (so Clement of Alexandria, in *Stromata* 1.19.91.4f.) or as Epimenides (*Stromata* 1.14.59).

4. Literally, "from one blood."

5. Discussed by Kirsopp Lake in *Additional Notes to the Commentary*, vol. 5 of *The Beginnings of Christianity* pt. 1, The Acts of the Apostles (ed. F. J. Foakes-Jackson and K. Lake; New York: Macmillan, 1920–1923; repr., Grand Rapids: Baker, 1966), 240–50.

6. Insightful analysis and translation of the surviving texts are in the section on Aristobolus by A. Yarbro Collins in *The Old Testament Pseuepigrapha* (vol. 2; ed. J. H. Charlesworth; Garden City, NY: Doubleday, 1985), 831–42.

7. LCL; vol. 1; trans. Kirsopp Lake; Cambridge, MA: Harvard University Press, 1949; and vol. 2; trans. J. E. L. Oulton; Cambridge, MA: Harvard University Press, 1953.

8. *Eusebius: Preparation for the Gospel* (Oxford: Oxford University Press, 1903).

9. Aristobolus makes the point that he replaces the name of Zeus, as used by Aratus, with the direct designation of "God" (666d).

10. These lines are recorded in Eusebius's *Praeparatio Evangelica* 13.13.6.

11. Aristobolus, Fragment 4 (= Eusebius, *Praep. ev.* 13:3–4).

12. A fairly recent and highly perceptive study of Philo's mode of interpretation of scripture is that of Peder Borgen, *Philo of Alexandria: An Exegete for His Time* (NovTSup 86; Leiden and New York: Brill, 1997).

13. Detailed analysis of the hearing of Paul before Gallio and a defense of its general historical reliability are offered by Klaus Haacker in his article on Gallio (*ABD*; New York: Doubleday, 1992), 2:901–3.

14. Claude W. Barlow, *Epistolae Senecae ad Paulum et Pauli ad Senecam [Quae Vocantur]* (vol. 10; Papers and Monographs of the American Academy in Rome, 1938).

15. Ed. E. Hennecke and W. Schneemelcher; trans. R. McL. Wilson; Louisville, KY: Westminster/John Knox, 1992.

16. 6.24.13–14.

17. The tradition is reported in the early fifth century by Augustine (Ep. CLIII.14), and later by Alcuin, Peter Abelard, and Peter of Cluny.

18. Acts 9:11; 21:30; and 22:8–although Paul never mentions Tarsus in his letters.

19. Quoted by Galen; SVF 2.911.

20. This analysis of Chrysippus is based on the essay of Michael Lambidge, "Stoic Cosmology," included in *The Stoics* (ed. John M. Rist; Berkeley: University of California Press, 1978), 164–79.

21. The importance of the role of the Sibylline oracles is confirmed by the fact that they were frequently consulted by the Roman Senate (*De divinatione* I.xliii).

22. *De natura deorum* II.ii.4–6; iii.7; iv.12.

23. Ibid., II.ix.29–32; xxxii.

24. Ibid., II.118.

25. Ibid., II.lxii.154.

26. Ibid., III.85.

27. Here Cicero's view of fire as the central element seems to have been influenced by Heraclitus.

28. *Praetor* is the Latin term for the chief magistrates, who aided the consuls by administering justice or commanding armies. During the Roman Republic, there were two consuls, chosen from the patricians, who were the chief magistrates for the entire state.

29. Seneca, *Epistulae morales* xvi.7; lxvi.40.

30. Ibid., XXIII.7.

31. Ibid., XLI.1, 7.

32 The Greek term used by Paul, *egkratieia*, has several synonyms in Latin: *moderatio*, *continentia*, and *temperantia*.

33. Seneca, *Ep.* XXIII.7.

34. Ibid., LXVI.12, 35.

35. Ibid., xli.

36. I.1.

37. XXI.1–3.

38. XXIV.5.

39. In *Helvia on Consolation* XX.1–2.

40. Luke 11:29–32; Matt 12:38–42.

41. Insightful studies of Cynicism have shown that the Cynic Epistles, to which some have turned as models for interpreting the teachings of Jesus, developed only in the second century CE (e.g., Donald R. Dudley, *The History of Cynicism* [London: Methuen, 1937]), and that the earlier Cynics depicted the ideal ruler, who resolved to follow the divine model of *paideia* and sought to produce among humans "the divine and royal nature" (Dio Chrysostom, *Kingship 1* 1.65). The New Testament scholars who have misused the Cynic evidence to create a Jesus who spouted timeless aphorisms are represented by the so-called Q Seminar.

42 Expounded by Dio Chrysostom, *Kingship 3* 45–47. A perceptive study of kingship in the Cynic tradition is that of Ragnar Hoistad, *Cynic Hero and Cynic King: Studies in the Cynic Conception of Man* (Uppsala: Gleerup, 1948).

43. Rom 4:13–22.

44. Rom 4:23–24; 5:6–11.

45. Rom 1:24–26.

46. Rom 2:14–15.

47. Rom 13:5.

48. 1 Cor 8:7–12; 10:25–29.

49. 2 Cor 1:12; 4:2; 5:11.

50. Gal 5:21–23.

51. 1 Tim 1:5, 18–20.

52. 2 Tim 1:3.

53. 1 Tim 4:2; Titus 1:15.

54. Heb 9:8–9, 14; 10:2, 21–22.

55. 2 Pet 1:8, 11.

56. Rev 20:1–6.

57. Rev 21:1–22:15.

Facing the Future: Common Themes in Jewish Apocalyptic and Graeco-Roman Philosophy and Literature

Many scholars in the field of biblical studies seem to suffer from a chronic case of what might be called "abortive Hegelianism." The symptoms of this ailment are that its victims feel compelled to establish a pair of conceptual dichotomies, but instead of working toward a new synthesis, they try to make a case for one option over against the other. Nowhere is this more evident than in the analyses of wisdom and apocalyptic, earlier in studies of the Jewish scriptures, but more recently in New Testament studies as well. Fortunately, the protracted debate as to whether apocalyptic developed out of prophecy (as asserted by H. H. Rowley,[1] among others) or out of the wisdom tradition (as maintained by Gerhard von Rad[2]) has been answered by mediating voices seeking to show how both factors contributed to the rise of apocalypticism.[3] More recently, however, the rich complexity of the situation has been more fully demonstrated in brilliant essays that have shown that Jewish apocalyptic had counterparts in non-Jewish literature of the Hellenistic and Roman periods and that it was powerfully influenced by mantic wisdom that can be documented in later material from the Near East.

A pioneer in this approach was Jonathan Z. Smith, whose essay "Wisdom and Apocalyptic" first appeared in 1975.[4] He begins by affirming a declaration of H. D. Betz that "Jewish and subsequently Christian apocalyptic cannot be understood from themselves or from the Old Testament alone, but must be seen and presented as peculiar expressions from the entire development of Hellenistic syncretism."[5] We shall see that features analogous to those of apocalyptic are evident in a wide range of both Hellenistic and Roman documents. In his illuminating article, Smith concentrates on apocalyptic-type elements as evident in the following sources: (1) Berossus, the Babylonian historian who was writing in Greek at the time of Alexander. He drew on astronomical and astrological material, and as a mythographer and historian writing in relation to the Babylonian Sibyl, he compiled "a history of the cosmos and a people from creation to final catastrophe which is dominated by astrological determinism."[6] (2) From Egypt come three apocalyptic writings: the *Demotic Chronicle*, *The Curse of the Lamb*, and the *Potter's Oracle* (which we shall examine later in some detail).

J. Gwyn Griffiths and Walter Burkert, in essays contributed to the Congress on Apocalyptic in Upsala,[7] point to the documents mentioned by Smith but also to philosophers—especially Hesiod and Plato—where the course of history is seen as divinely determined and moving toward cosmic renewal. It is in David Aune's excellent monograph, *Prophecy in Early Christianity and the Ancient Mediterranean World*,[8] however, that the fullest account is provided of the similar features of prophetic speech in the Graeco-Roman world and that of postbiblical Judaism and early Christianity. Aune analyzes in detail the various forms of prophetic utterance in the Greek world and the roles performed by diviners, especially by the sibyls and the collections of their oracles so highly prized over the centuries down into the Roman era. Included is a description of what he terms "eschatological prophets," such as Virgil in his Fourth Eclogue, and other utopian visions of the future from the seventh century BCE to the third century CE,[9] with oracle collections known from Herodotus (fifth century BCE) to Plutarch and Pausanias in the first and second centuries CE. The Sibylline oracles disclosed the purpose of the gods in the present but looked back to divine activity in the past and forward to the accomplishment of a divine purpose in the future: in both cases, these cosmic changes were perceived to be linked with the role of rulers. Plato affirmed the validity of these inspired oracular instruments to deal with questions and responses.[10]

Two very different studies of the *Sibylline Oracles* show how documents that in their present form were preserved by Jews are basically products of Hellenistic culture as adopted and adapted by the Romans. John J. Collins's study, *The Apocalyptic Imagination*,[11] includes at the outset a useful definition of apocalyptic developed by the SBL Genres Project[12]—"A genre of revelatory literature with a narrative framework in which a revelation is mediated by an otherworldly being to a human recipient, disclosing a transcendent reality which is both temporal, insofar as it envisages eschatological salvation, and spatial, insofar as it involves another, supernatural world." An apocalypse is intended to interpret present, earthly circumstances in light of the supernatural world and of the future, and to influence both the understanding and the behavior of the audience by means of divine authority.

In *The Old Testament Pseudepigrapha*,[13] Collins's translation of the *Sibylline Oracles* and notes therein demonstrate in detail the author's (or authors') use of imagery from the Bible but also from older Near Eastern and Graeco-Roman sources, with the result that motifs are transferred from one context to another.[14] In apocalyptic writings, Collins writes, wisdom is not inductive, as in Proverbs or Ben Sira, but *mantic*, as in the Babylonian tradition. Its language is expressive rather than referential, symbolic rather than factual.[15] The course of history is viewed in light of transcendent reality, which enables the beneficiary of this disclosure to see the hidden world that is shaping the present as well as the ultimate destiny of the favored group. The Roman originals of the *Sibylline Oracles* were formally consulted by the Senate and served as confirmation for takeover of territory or resistance to hostile programs by ethnic or political groups throughout the empire. The documents include the periodization of history, reaching back to the ancient world and involving Assyrians, Persians, Macedonians, but looking forward to the new age of peace. They were adapted by Jews and then by Christians to interpret such developments as the Roman attack on Jerusalem and the destruction of the temple. They foresee the appearance of a divine savior figure who will vindicate God's holy people,[16] and offer scathing denunciations of the emperors, such as Nero, while reporting the tradition of his expected future return.[17] Descriptions of the Roman emperors are offered from Augustus to Alexander Severus (reigned 232–235). The Oracles were adapted by the Jews, but manifest numerous added Christian features, as well. A pervasive feature, however, and one that reflects the Roman origins of these documents, is their eschatological vision of divine judgment of the wicked and vindication of the just. The cultural climate was there in the early centuries CE for documents like the Revelation to John, with its message of divine purpose and punishment, and of vindication of the righteous.

Collins infers from these documents that they originated as apologetic literature of Hellenistic Judaism, affirming a common human basis for the origins and destiny of Jews and Gentiles. They were produced during the period from the second century BCE to the seventh century CE. Of the fourteen books of Oracles that have been preserved, only three (11–13) lack eschatological passages. The majority are political in perspective, expecting the advent of a glorious kingdom and the transformation of the earth, as well as the destruction of the earth by fire, to be followed by the great year of cosmic renewal. History is perceived as divided into ten generations, or four successive kingdoms (as in *Sib. Or.* 4). Only the Christian editions of these Oracles show concern for the destiny of individuals, however.

A notable testimony to this kind of expectation of cosmic change is the Fourth Eclogue of Virgil, in which the Cumean Sibyl foretells the coming of the *ultima aetas*—"the final age." The Roman Oracles were entrusted to special keepers and consulted in times of crisis. Though the collection was destroyed when the temple of Jupiter burned in 83 BCE, it was rebuilt in 76 and gathered there were copies of the oracles from other Sibylline centers. These were preoccupied with portents and prodigies, and highlighted the birth of an *androgyne* (bisexual). Used for political propaganda purposes, the oracles foretold the coming of the Golden Age and the Ideal Monarch. Warnings about falsification and manipulation of them were included in the writings of Cicero and Plutarch. Jews and Christians adapted this literary and conceptual form to promote their own messages and hopes of political and cosmic renewal. The historical value of the Oracles lies not in historical information that they contain, but in their display of popular attitudes toward history and power, as well as the legend-laden views of kings and empires, the hopes and fears of Eastern peoples, and the widespread resistance to the Romans in the eastern Mediterranean world. It is not surprising that both Jews and Christians would have adapted this literary and conceptual mode to convey their hopes and fears concerning their destiny as those who claimed to be the people of God.

Another extremely useful analysis of the Sibyllines is that of D. S. Potter in *Prophecy and History in the Crisis of the Roman Empire: A Historical Commentary on the Thirteenth Sibylline Oracle*.[18] He shows how the single Sibyl of the late fifth century BCE is transmuted into a series of sibyls from Babylonia across the Mediterranean world following Alexander's conquests, and how other cultures appropriate the Sibyl as a prophetess among their own people "in their efforts to claim intellectual respectability in a Greek context."[19] By the first century BCE, she was linked with official collections of oracles in Rome and "elevated to the position of the greatest prophetess of antiquity." An official committee was assigned to preserve and interpret her oracles, which bore directly on the conduct of wars and public policy. Victors were identified with Ares, and thus received divine sanction for their exploits.[20] The *Thirteenth Sibylline Oracle* concerns the struggle for political and cultural power in the Eastern empire at the great city of Palmyra in the third century CE, when Persia was threatening to resume control over this region. The reigns of the various emperors are evaluated based on their military and economic impact on the region. Far from being an esoteric treatise for intellectually and culturally fringe people, this oracle is dealing with the most basic issues that confronted the Roman Empire and its leaders in the crisis of the third century. Clearly, Jew and Christians in the Roman period shared the anxieties about Roman rule and the hopes for divine deliverance, which found expression in their adaptation of this view of the triumph of divine purpose in history and the oracular mode for conveying such hopes.

James C. Vanderkam's fine study, *Enoch and the Growth of an Apocalyptic Tradition*,[21] while carefully differentiating Mesopotamian mantic material from Israel's prophetic tradition, notes that the former "provided a considerable part of the context from which Jewish Enochic literature arose and grew,"[22] with possibly additional contribution from Persian eschatology. The length of Enoch's life—365 years—and the contents of the Astronomical Book (*Enoch* 72–82), as well as details in the Book of Watchers (*Enoch* 1–36), show how central for apocalyptic was the cosmic order of the universe as evident in the movement of the heavenly bodies.[23] Although Vanderkam points out the absence of several typical features of apocalyptic, it is in this Astronomical Book that Enoch "assumes the role of antediluvian sage who still experiences intimate contact with the divine realm and who bridges the gap between human and divine by conveying his special knowledge to humanity,"[24] like the role of the Mesopotamian *apkallus*.

George Nickelsburg, in addition to his useful analyses of the Jewish literature of the Hellenistic period,[25] has made an important methodological contribution to the area of our investigation by calling attention to "The Social Aspects of Palestinian Jewish Apocalypticism."[26] Noting the generalizations about apocalypticism that have been made on the basis of inadequate evidence or by imposition of modern sectarian models, Nickelsburg raises a long series of substantive questions to be addressed to the texts by those analyzing them. These questions concern the political, economic, cultural, and religious circumstances of the writer and his potential readers; the response of the writer to the crisis that he and his community confront; the self-definition of the community expecting divine action on its behalf; and the distinctive features of each apocalypse as compared with others. As a test case, he raises these questions with regard to *1 Enoch* 92–105, the so-called *Epistle of Enoch*, which sketches the history of Israel in the Apocalypse of Weeks. His proposal for a date is the early second century BCE. Possibly this work was produced at Qumran, since it shares with the Dead Sea Scrolls the critique of the Jerusalem priesthood. His questions require the interpreter to take into account the diversity of details represented in apocalyptic literature in order to see how they shed light on the origins of each document.

David Winston's superb commentary on the Wisdom of Solomon[27] has been supplemented by an essay, "The Sage as Mystic in the Wisdom of Solomon."[28] He shows that wisdom is concerned with the entire scope of human and cosmic history, and the search for wisdom is described in mystical, even erotic, language (7:25–26, 29–30; 8:2–3, 9), for which he notes analogies in Philo, especially in his "On Mating with Preliminary Studies."

Wisdom is seen as essential not only for the immortality of the soul but also for effective rule by monarchs (6:17–21). The goal, therefore, is not the attainment of timeless proverbial truths but achieving personal union with wisdom (6:12–16), for which the analogy is union with Isis, as in Apuleius's *Metamorphoses* 11.23, 25, 29.

In spite of these important insights and the availability of newly recovered sources that document the shared concerns of apocalyptic literature and wisdom of the Graeco-Roman period, there has developed in New Testament studies in the past decade a counterpart to the false wisdom/apocalyptic dichotomy that once pervaded studies of Jewish sources. Some scholars are now seeking to show that the apocalyptic features of the gospel tradition are later accretions, behind which can be discerned Jesus' authentic words of wisdom.[29] The latter are said to be purely aphoristic in style and timeless in intent. They allegedly mirror the style of Cynic-Stoic philosophers of the Graeco-Roman era. The theory runs that it was later dull-witted early Christian editors who amended these texts and supplemented them with apocalyptic and miracle-working features, in accord with popular but intellectually inferior religious impulses of the era, and thus produced the gospels as we have them in their canonical form. The new model for the historical Jesus fits this wisdom-purveying construct on the hypothetical Cynic-Stoic model.

It was over a century ago (in 1891) that Albert Schweitzer posed the problem of apocalyptic in early Christianity when he published his analytical survey, *Das Messianitats und Leidensgeheimnis: Eine Skizze des Lebens Jesu,*[30] with its portrait of the thoroughly apocalyptic Jesus. Schweitzer's conclusions were more systematically formulated a few years later in his critical survey of scholarly analyses of the life of Jesus, *From Reimarus to Wrede: A History of Research on the Life of Jesus,* which is of course better known in its English translation as *The Quest of the Historical Jesus.*[31] In both works, Schweitzer developed the evidence for a thoroughly apocalyptic framework for Jesus' self-understanding and career, and asserted that Jesus' eschatological view of himself and his work "can only be interpreted by the aid of the curiously intermittent Jewish apocalyptic literature of the period between Daniel and the Bar-Cochba uprising."[32] Having arrived at these results of his investigation—which he regarded as incompatible with the intellectual values gained from his own post-Enlightenment training and orientation and which the subsequent history of early Christianity proved to have been wrong—Schweitzer adopted two tactics: (1) He affirmed a Jesus who was "absolutely independent of historical knowledge" (including his apocalyptic outlook) and who "can only be known by contact with his Spirit which is still at work in the world."[33] (2) Schweitzer turned from theological and biblical studies to medicine, and devoted the rest of his life to noble humanitarian service among indigenous Africans.

Among the other escape routes from apocalyptic taken by scholars in the earlier decades of the past century were the reductionist modes of (1) Adolf von Harnack, for whom the essence of Jesus' message was (in pre-feminist days) the fatherhood of God, the brotherhood of man, and the infinite worth of the human soul;[34] and (2) Rudolf Bultmann, for whom the essence of Jesus was his individualistic, existentialist call to radical decision—to which he thought that the Jesus tradition could be conveniently reduced by demythologization.

As we have seen, however, more recent analyses of documents from the Graeco-Roman world puts the eschatological mode of the gospel tradition in a very different historical light from that assumed by those engaged in the flight from apocalyptic throughout most of the past century of scholarly inquiry. Instead of Graeco-Roman wisdom providing a refuge from apocalyptic, it is now evident that precisely among the intellectual and political leaders of the emergent Roman imperial world were to be found the very issues that—differently formulated and drawing on different mythological traditions—are represented in the apocalyptic documents of Judaism and early Christianity. Politicians, poets, and philosophers of the late Roman Republic and early Roman Empire were dealing with just these issues. The assumptions of some recent scholars about an exclusively aphoristic mode of Cynic-Stoic wisdom in this period may be shown to be in fact a mixture of inaccuracy and anachronism. The questions about human destiny that in spite of cultural differences are evident in both the Jewish/Christian apocalyptic and the Roman literature (especially the Stoic sources and the *Sibylline Oracles*) may be formulated as follows:

1. Concern for the maintenance of cosmic order.

2. Conviction about human moral accountability before the gods.

3. Confidence in oracular disclosure of the divine purpose.

4. Belief in divine choice of human agents to fulfill the divine purpose.

5. Use of traditional mythic imagery to depict the course of human destiny and the consummation of the divine purpose.

What is called for in responsible historical analysis of Christian origins is to highlight the various facets of the religious and philosophical literature of the centuries before and after the turn of the eras with the aim of discerning how certain aspirations and claims about human destiny were shared by Graeco-Roman philosophers and leaders *and* Jewish and early Christian writers. As noted above, the answers will differ in imagery and in detail, but the basic human questions are common features. Our analysis of the evidence involves an examination of the divinatory and oracular sources preserved from the wider Graeco-Roman world in the period from the second century BCE to the second century CE, and then—more briefly—from Jewish and early Christian sources. Next, we move to an examination of some of the most important philosophical and literary sources of this period. Based on these lines of investigation, we may demonstrate the presence of common issues in Jewish and Graeco-Roman sources, in spite of the obvious differences in cultural and mythological tradition drawn upon by each.

The Potter's Oracle *as an Apocalyptic Document*

The subtitle of Ludwig Koenen's analysis of the *Potter's Oracle* is of fundamental significance: "A Prophecy of World Renewal Becomes an Apocalypse."[35] The document shows the "intellectual resistance on the part of Egyptian national groups to Greek hegemony and of the aspiration enkindled among these groups by the bloody strife in the royal house [Ptolemaic] about 130 B.C." Eschatological prophecy projects the myth and rite of enthronement into the future during a period of desperation.[36] The collapse of the order of nature will be followed by political, social, and economic chaos, from which deliverance will come through a savior-king, who is described in imagery drawn from Egyptian mythology (Horus/Isis). Koenen notes a similar mode of expectation of a king-deliverer on the mythological model in the *Demotic Chronicle*,[37] who appears as "a long-awaited savior-king after a period of domination by godless foreigners."[38] (251). Later interpretations of the *Potter's Oracle*, after differences were settled between the Egyptians and the Ptolemies, recast the prophecies in a cyclical mode, projecting the hope of fulfillment into the future in true apocalyptic style.[39]

The Imperial Roman Adoption of Astrology *as an Official Mode of Divine Confirmation*

Too often overlooked by biblical scholars is the pervasive and widely valued role of astrology in the thought and literature of the Graeco-Roman period. Frederic H. Cranmer, in *Astrology in Roman Law and Politics*,[40] points out the discussion of astrology by Plato's student Eudoxus[41] and by Aristotle, whose view of the structure of the stars and planets was used by early astrologers. Alexander's successful invasion of Persia was accounted for by Chaldean astrologers (Diodorus Siculus 17.112.2ff). Stoicism fostered the surge of Hellenistic belief in "the science of fatalistic astrology."[42] According to Josephus, it was Berossus who introduced priestly astrology among the Greeks, and Pliny tells how he was honored at Athens "on account of his divine prophecies" (*Natural History* 7.37, 123). Refinement of astrology by the Greeks took place in 300–150 BCE, with two goals: mystical participation in the divine purpose, and scientific, mathematical calculation of the course of the universe.[43] Dozens of existential questions—about family, love, prosperity, journeys—were answered by an appeal to astrology.[44] Through the concept of cosmic cycles, in which various planets were successively dominant, there was foreseen an eternal sequence of fiery consummation (*ekpyrosis*) and rebirth (*palingenesis*), with the interval between these events known as the "great year."[45]

An initial period of skepticism about astrology on the part of philosophers gave way at the end of the Roman Republic to the affirmative point of view articulated by Posidonius of Apamea, so that with the establishment of the empire, the rulers sought and gained support of astrologers in the belief that the stars controlled human destiny—a view that was dominant from Augustus to Domitian. Varro and Virgil, in his Fourth Eclogue (as we shall note below), affirmed the controlling effects of the astrological powers.[46] Julius Caesar promoted astrology to gain popular support, and based on it revised the calendar. Octavius (or Octavianus) exploited the appearance of a comet to prove the heavenly assumption of Julius Caesar and his own placement in power by the gods.[47] Astrology provided a link between mundane causality and the cosmic laws that regulated the movement of the stars and of human history. This reliance on astrology reached its zenith in the Julio-Claudian and Flavian houses. The divine powers were perceived to be directly and effectively at work shaping human destiny and the history of the state in a larger cycle of cosmic renewal—features that are shared formally with the apocalyptic worldview.

James H. Charlesworth has assembled the evidence for credence in astrology on the part of Jewish writers from the first century BCE down to the Talmudic period.[48] In one section of *1 Enoch*, astrology is denounced as demonic (8:3), but in the portion known as the Astronomical Book (72:1–37; 75:3), the features of the zodiac are prominent, as they are in *2 Enoch*. The first century BCE *Treatise of Shem* is an astrological tract that seeks to show how human fortune, the fertility of the land, and the movement of the stars are all dependent on the powers resident in the houses of the zodiac.[49] Fragment 4Q186 from Qumran is a horoscope based on astrological beliefs in the powers that shape human life and character.[50] Surveys of the iconography of Palestinian synagogues more recent than that of Charlesworth show that those of the third and fourth centuries CE regularly had the signs of the zodiac at the center of the hall, with Yahweh pictured as Helios, driving the chariot of the sun. One must acknowledge that the astrological symbolism was not merely decorative, but was an expression of the conviction that the God of Israel was responsible for the ordering of the universe and the course of human events. That conviction also found expression in the early Roman imperial period through the writings of Stoic philosophers, to which we now turn.

Historical Determinism and Stoic Philosophy in the Roman Period

Largely neglected by scholars dealing with the factors of wisdom and apocalyptic in the Graeco-Roman period is the discussion of this dimension of historical expectation by Stoic philosophers of the period. We select for examination here the writings of two philosophers who were directly involved at the political center of the Roman Empire: Cicero at the time of its establishment and Seneca when the crisis arose at the end of the Julio-Claudian succession of emperors. Both were central wisdom figures at the political heart of their world.

The importance of the issue concerning a divine purpose at work in human history is highlighted in Cicero's treatise *On the Nature of the Gods* and is then more directly addressed in his work *On Divination*. Although he makes an assertion that he does not share the conviction that the divine purpose for the world is communicated through oracles, dreams, and other modes of divination, Cicero documents fully how deeply engrained these beliefs were in the minds of Stoics of the first century BCE. Balbus, who presents the Stoic position in *De natura deorum*, first makes a case for the rational ordering of the universe by the gods. In the course of describing the spherical form of the divine nature, he pictures the movement of the world as also spherical, and corresponding to it is the "great year" when the heavenly bodies complete their prescribed courses and return to their original relative positions. Only humans have been granted prophecy and divination: through auguries, oracles, dreams, and portents, "the power or art or instinct has clearly been bestowed by the immortal gods on man, and on no other creature, for the ascertainment of future events" (II.65). Oracles, including the Sibyllines, show that the gods disclose the future as a warning and a counsel to humanity (II.3-4). That the stars are divine, and that they possess consciousness and intelligence, is evident in their orderly motion. Divine nature is spherical and its motion is rotary. Hence, the "great year" is the span of time when the heavenly bodies will return to their same relative positions as at the beginning (II.15-20). Only human beings have been granted "this power or art or instinct" to discern the future and avoid its dangers (II.65).

In *De divinatione*, Cicero, writing in the middle of the first century BCE, notes the universality of the belief among Assyrians, Babylonians, and Greeks that the gods communicate concerning the future through divinatory signs.

He describes the importance of augurs in Rome since its founding by Romulus, the practice of consulting the *auspices* on all important state issues, and the appointment of the ten supervisors of the Sibylline Oracles to shed light on major decisions. He recalls the accuracy of dreams and oracles that foresaw the future of Greece and Rome, and the support for this understanding of divine communication on the part of Socrates, Plato, and Aristotle. The reputation for reliability is well deserved by the oracles at Delphi and Cumae. Throughout history, divination has flourished in the best-regulated states, as evident in the Senate's regular, official consultation of the Sibyl. Central to this are God, Fate, and Nature, but especially *heimarmene*, which is the orderly succession of causes. The gods know what will happen; humans presage the future by certain signs, which include the movement of the stars and the entrails of sacrifices. Effect follows cause; sign precedes event. The study of these signs is divination. Cicero recounts a scathing critique of this Stoic point of view by Cotta, who denounced the whole enterprise as superstition, but then Cicero commends the Stoics for the skill of their arguments and leaves to the thoughtful inquirer the judgment concerning the truth.

Writing in the middle of the first century CE, Seneca shows no trace of the skepticism—or more accurately, ambivalence—of Cicero on the subject of divine disclosure of the future of the cosmos. In his *On Providence*, Seneca affirms the universality of the divine order, so that the stars and their revolutions are ruled by eternal law (I.1). Humans differ from the gods only in relation to time: they are pupils of the gods, imitators and true offspring. The highest god holds them to account for their moral behavior (1.5). Difficulties humans experience are part of the process of divine discipline, and adversities are for the good of those who endure them: "God hardens, reviews and disciplines those whom he approves, whom he loves."[51] He quotes with approval Ovid's *Metamorphoses* (2:79ff.) on the hero's following the divinely prescribed track of testing and struggle through the signs of the zodiac (V.11).

In his letter *To Marcia on the Death of her Son*, Seneca describes how the world renews itself over and over within the bounds of time, with cyclic conflagrations and renewal of the creation (21.1–3). Death is not the end of existence, but the journey to the gods, who far aloft throughout the universe look down with detachment on human affairs (23.1). The soul struggles for release from the body in order to ascend to the place from which it came (24.5), a place of eternal peace, where all is bright and pure. The stars and all the fiery matter of the world will be "caught up in a common conflagration. Then also the souls of the blest, who have partaken of immortality, when it shall seem best to God to create the universe anew—we, too, amid the falling universe, shall be added as a tiny fraction to this mighty destruction and shall be changed again into our former elements" (26.6). In *On the Shortness of Life* (19.1), Seneca asks about the fate that awaits the soul, "where nature lays us to rest when we are free from the body"—a hope that recalls that of Paul in 2 Cor 5:8: "Absent from the body, present with the Lord." Writing to his mother from exile, in *Helvia on Consolation* (20.1–2), Cicero says that his philosophical thoughts transport him "to the heights above," where he can enjoy "the noblest spectacle of things divine," and his soul, "mindful of its own immortality, proceeds to all that has been and will ever be throughout all ages to come."

The divine determination of the course of history was affirmed in Roman culture at the outset of the empire by Virgil as well. In his *Aenid*, he traced the origins of Rome back to Troy, thereby demonstrating the continuity of the purpose of the gods in human history. More enigmatic but also more complex is his Fourth Eclogue, in which he describes the birth of Caesar Augustus as a divinely ordained child ("offspring of the gods, mighty seed of Jupiter") who in maturity will bring in a new and joyous era of human existence, recalling the reign of the Olympian deities. All this has been heralded through the Sibyl at Cumae: the new age of peace, prosperity, and plenty is about to begin. Studies of Stoic cosmology[52] have shown that the Stoics depicted the cosmos as a living animal, ensouled and possessing a mind and reasoning powers. The world soul is identified with *pneuma*, which is an air/fire mixture permeating the universe.[53] The present cosmic order will perish in the *ekpyrosis*, but it will come into existence again and individuals will reappear. The themes of cosmic fire and cyclical periods derive from Heraclitus by way of Aristotle. The continuity of the human species is affirmed. The rational seeds (*spermatikoi logoi*) of this process were described by Zeno,[54] but it was Chrysippus (late fourth century) who described the *pneuma* as the principal cosmic agent that controls the movements of the cosmos, as is evident in the astrological forces that shape human destiny. Seneca articulates a Roman intellectual's version of this view of cosmic purpose shaping history and individual destiny.

Three Jewish writers who give evidence of basic influence from Stoicism are Ben Sira, Josephus, and the author of the *Testaments of the Twelve Patriarchs*. David Winston, in his article "Theodicy in Ben Sira and Stoic Philosophy," points out that in dealing with the difficult problem of theodicy, Ben Sira "seems to have consciously followed in the footsteps of the Stoics," especially "their self-satisfied and supremely optimistic faith in a perfect, all-embracing Nature."[55]

In his *Contra Apionem*, Josephus points out parallels between the law of Moses and Greek philosophy. Moses is concerned primarily with piety and virtue. His view of God emphasizes just those divine qualities (unbegotten, eternal, immutable, superior to all mortal conceptions) that are described by the Pythagoreans, the Platonists, and the Stoics. Similarly, the chief religious virtues—justice, fortitude, temperance, universal laws—match those of Greek philosophy. Like Plato, Moses insisted on achieving the true commonwealth in which all people obey the laws. According to Josephus, the reason that the philosophers parallel the insights and requirements of the Jewish law is that they all derived their insights from Moses, who taught the "truest piety in the world" (2.40–42). From this perspective, there is no basic difference between the law revealed to Moses and the insights of the philosophers, including the Stoics. From the Jewish side there are some criticisms of reliance on dreams and divination (as in Sir 34:1–7), but the basic convictions are shared about universal law, divine disclosure through historical events, moral accountability to the divine—conveyed through the prophets—and an ultimate consummation of the divine purpose.

In the *Testaments of the Twelve Patriarchs*, moral requirements of the Jewish people are identified with the Stoic concept of living "according to nature" (*T. Napht.* 3). From the opening lines of 4 Maccabees (dating from the first or second century CE), the story of the struggle of the Maccabees is retold as a philosophical lesson, with emphasis on the Stoic virtues: self-control, courage, justice, and temperance. Obedience to the law of Moses enables one to perceive and embody these cardinal moral qualities. The correspondences between this point of view and Paul's appeal to universal natural law in Romans and to the Stoic virtues as manifestations of the fruit of the Spirit in Galatians are obvious.

Thus, in both Jewish and early Christian writings—as in Stoic writings of the first century—what modern scholars often have differentiated as "wisdom" in contrast to "apocalyptic" (understanding the latter to be divinely revealed insight as to the moral and cosmic ordering of the universe) are in both bodies of literature different facets of analogous comprehensive worldviews. Thus, Paul, in the very letter where he describes Christ as the "first fruits" of the dead and the one who will destroy "every ruler and authority and power" (1 Cor 15:20–28), also refers to him as "the power of God and the wisdom of God" (1 Cor 1:18–30). Similarly, in the Q source, where Jesus is depicted as one whose wisdom is greater than that of Solomon, that wisdom is conveyed in a context of universal eschatological judgment and implies the clear superiority of Jesus to both Solomon as bearer of wisdom and Jonah as prophet of divine judgment (Luke 11:29–32). Neither in Paul nor in Q is the truth about God and his activity in the world in behalf of his people conveyed in timeless aphorisms, any more than it is in Stoic wisdom contemporary with these early Christian writers.

The communication of wisdom through aphorisms does take place in one body of literature that some New Testament scholars have pointed to as their proposed historical prototype for the teaching of Jesus: Cynicism. The assumption is that there was a philosophical school of the Cynics, reaching back to the time of Diogenes (fifth/fourth century BCE) and extending down into the Byzantine period, that sought to expose the falsity of accepted patterns of life and norms of human behavior and did so by the use of clever witticisms and aphorisms. Its devotees adopted a mendicant style of life in protest to the social and economic values of their epoch. Donald R. Dudley, in his *History of Cynicism*[56]—which remains a landmark in this field of historical inquiry—declares that "it would be an exaggeration to speak of any Cynic 'school' in the regular sense of organized teaching and a common body of doctrine."[57] He describes the shift away from the philosophical systems of Plato and Aristotle as follows: "From the noble quest to satisfy the curiosity of the intellect it descended to become Daily Strength for Daily Needs." The earlier Cynics described the ideal ruler, which they saw embodied in Cyrus, who was not only efficient as a ruler but also manifested courage, helpfulness, and self-control, and whom they characterized as shepherd of the flock. Dio Chrysostom recounts that Heracles was made ruler of the world because he resolved to follow the divine model of *paideia* (instruction), which is the gift of the gods, and serves as a guard against human folly, producing divine and royal nature (*he theia kai basilike physis*).[58] As a result, Heracles is characterized by the royal values of peace, law, and right reason; he is made king and savior of all humanity but chastises savage and wicked humans and crushes the power of tyrants. The gods will reward and sustain the king who honors virtue, is humane, and is characterized by prudence (*phronesis*), temperance (*sophrosune*), justice (*dikaiosune*), and courage (*andreia*).[59]

Although the Cynics may initially have been in conversation with the Stoics, by the time of Cleanthes (330–240) and Chrysippus (291–205), Stoicism distanced itself from the more popular Cynic features, turning instead to physics and logic in the tradition of *egkyklia mathemata*. As Dudley puts it, "The new Stoicism was determined to have no truck with Cynicism in its own day."[60] By the second and first centuries BCE, Cynicism did little more than gain a footing in Rome, was unknown elsewhere in the West, and survived in obscurity in the eastern half of the Mediterranean world.[61] The issues of royal authority and social responsibility that had been addressed by the earlier Cynics were taken up by the Stoics in the early Roman period. A surge of Cynicism came only well into the common era, in the period from Vespasian to Marcus Aurelius (69–180). It was then that the Cynic Epistles were produced—all of them pseudepigraphic, and all seeking to lend authority to their ideas by purporting to come from the classical period of Greek philosophy.

It is evident, therefore, that Cynicism did not provide Jesus or his earliest followers or any other pre-70 Christians with a specific model for attracting a wide popular following or for communicating wisdom in the form of Cynic-Stoic–style aphorisms. Instead, the oldest layers of the early Christian tradition disclose thinkers and writers engaged in their own version of answers to the pervasive human questions that were indeed being addressed from a different cultural point of view by the popular Stoic philosophers of this epoch. It is to some of the points of correspondence between the Stoic and Jewish-Christian sets of responses to the central human issues that we turn in conclusion.

Conclusion

Reviewing the agenda of Graeco-Roman philosophers and oracles, as well as that of Jewish and Christian writers in the period before and after the turn of the eras, we may repeat our summary of the paramount issues for them as follows:

- Concern for the maintenance of cosmic order.
- Conviction about human moral accountability before the gods.
- Confidence in oracular disclosure of the divine purpose for the future.
- Belief in divine choice of human agents to fulfill that divine purpose for the universe.
- Use of traditional mythic imagery to depict the course of human destiny and the consummation of the divine purpose.

We have seen that by the time of the establishment of the Roman Empire in the first century BCE these were major issues among philosophically inclined Romans as well as among Jewish thinkers concerned about the prophetic promises and the current state of political impotence and moral ambiguity of the Jewish people. How would the cosmic order be renewed? How would the traditional deities/deity accomplish this? How would human beings be called to account for their moral behavior? Who were the agents through whom this renewal would come?

The answers to these questions were believed to be in process of disclosure through certain chosen instruments for the benefit of the people, and especially for the guidance of their leaders. Dreams, portents, cosmic signs, and especially oracles—with proper interpretations—were the instruments through which the divine purpose was being revealed. The actual renewal was to be achieved through divinely empowered agents, who were identified with the ancestral figures of mythological and historical tradition: for example, Horus and Osiris; the Cumean Sibyl and the reign of Jupiter or Saturn; in the Jewish tradition, the new Israel and the royal heir of David or the archetypal Son of Man. These ancient hopes were now expected to be achieved through contemporary historical figures.

These promises of social and political renewal, with their corollaries of hope for personal meaning and moral vindication, were represented across the Graeco-Roman world. Far from dismissing these Stoic visions as meaningless or idolatrous, the Jewish and early Christian visionaries presented their own alternative responses to these longings for renewal and order. Pagans, Jews, and Christians in this period would have subscribed to the declaration in the Letter of James that true wisdom is "from above" (Jas 3:17). While they would have also agreed with Paul that the wisdom of God was "mysterious, hidden, and predetermined before the ages," they would likely have dissented from his claim that "none of the rulers of this age" perceived that wisdom (1 Cor 2:7–8). Formally speaking, both the intent and the mode of communication of divine wisdom were shared by Jews and Christians with the contemporary Graeco-Roman culture. The crucial divergence came in the specific content of each of the cultural systems, which derived from their respective historical and cultural heritages, and which produced significantly different parameters by which the enlightened community and its destiny were defined.

Notes

1. In *The Relevance of Apocalyptic* (2nd ed.; London: Lutterworth, 1947).
2. In *Wisdom in Israel* (Nashville: Abingdon, 1972).
3. E.g., Paul D. Hanson, *The Dawn of Apocalyptic* (Philadelphia: Fortress, 1975); William McKane, *Prophets and Wise Men* (SBT 40; London: SCM, 1965).
4. In Birger Pearson, ed., *Religious Syncretism in Antiquity*, 131–56, repr. in *Scriptures, Sects and Visions* (ed. J. Neusner; Philadelphia: Fortress, 1980), 101–20.
5. In *ZTK* 63 (1969): 155.
6. J. Z. Smith, "Wisdom and Apocalyptic," 108.
7. J. G. Griffiths, "Apocalyptic in the Hellenistic Era," in *Apocalyptic in the Mediterranean World and the Near East* (ed. David Hellholm; Tübingen: Mohr, 1983), 273–93; Walter Burkert, "Apokalyptik in früher Griechentum: Impulse und Transformation," 235–53.
8. Grand Rapids: Eerdmans, 1983.
9. Ibid., 43.
10. Plato, *Timaeus* 71c–72b.
11. Subtitle: *An Introduction to the Jewish Matrix of Christianity* (New York: Crossroads, 1989).
12. Published in *Semeia* 14 (1979).
13. "The Sibylline Oracles," in *Old Testament Pseudepigrapha* (ed. J. H. Charlesworth; Garden City, NY: Doubleday, 1983), 1:317–472.
14. Collins, *Apocalyptic Imagination*, 16.
15. Ibid., 14.
16. *Sib. Or.* 5, 108, 151–61, 256–59, 414–25.
17. Ibid., 5.94–110, 361–85.
18. Oxford: Clarendon Press, 1990.
19. Ibid., 109.
20. Ibid., 138–39.
21. CBQMS 16; Washington, D.C.: Catholic Biblical Association, 1984.
22. Vanderkam, *Enoch*, 70.

23. Ibid., chap. 4.

24. Ibid., 106.

25. *Jewish Literature between the Bible and the Mishnah* (Philadelphia: Fortress, 1981).

26. In *Apocalyptic in the Mediterranean World and the Near East*, 641–54.

27. *Wisdom of Solomon* (AB; Garden City, NY: Doubleday, 1979).

28. In *The Sage in Israel and the Ancient Near East* (ed. J. G. Gammie and L. G. Perdue; Winona Lake, IN: Eisenbrauns, 1990), 383–97.

29. This assumption is basic to the analyses of Q (1) by the group calling itself The International Q Project; (2) by Helmut Koester (in *Ancient Christian Gospels: Their History and Development* [Philadelphia: Trinity Press International, 1990]); (3) by James M. Robinson in an essay, "The Q Trajectory: Between John and Matthew via Jesus," for the Koester Festschrift (*The Future of Early Christianity: Essays in Honor of Helmut Koester* [ed. Birger A. Pearson et al.; Minneapolis: Fortress, 1991], 173–94), who pictures the original Q as devoid of apocalyptic or christological features; and (4) by Burton L. Mack (in *The Lost Gospel: The Book of Q and Christian Origins* [San Francisco: Harper, 1994]). All simply posit a radical disjunction between wisdom and apocalyptic in the developing Jesus tradition. Although Robinson appeals to Ronald A. Piper's study, *Wisdom in the Q Tradition* (SNTSM 61; Cambridge University Press, 1989) for support of his position, Piper notes the links in Q between aphorisms and eschatological pronouncements, and observes the continuity implied between past, present, and "the nature of the eschaton which confronts [the author of this source]" (154–55), and between aphoristic wisdom and revealed knowledge (178–79).

30. Subsequently published in Tübingen by J. C. B. Mohr in 1901.

31. A. Schweitzer, *The Quest of the Historical Jesus* (New York: Macmillan, 1910).

32. Ibid., 367.

33. Ibid., 401.

34. A. von Harnack, *What Is Christianity?* (trans. T. B. Saunders; New York: Putnam, 1900; repr., New York: Harper and Row, 1957). The title is an inaccurate rendering of the German original, *Das Wesen des Christentums* [The Essence of Christianity].

35. "The Prophecies of a Potter" is the main title in *Proceedings of the Twelfth International Congress of Papyrology* (ed. D. H. Samuels; Toronto: American Studies in Papryology, 1970), 248–54.

36. Koenen, "A Prophecy," 248.

37. From Papyrus #215 in the Bibliotheque Nationale, Paris; published by W. Spiegelberg, "Die sogennante demotische Chronik . . . ," in *Demotische Studien* (Leipzig: J. C. Hinrichs, 1914).

38. Koenen, "Prophecy," 251.

39. Ibid., 252–53.

40. American Philosophical Society 37; Philadelphia, 1954.

41. Quoted by Cicero, *De divinatione* 2.87.

42. Cranmer, *Astrology in Roman Law and Politics*, 13.

43. Ibid., 15.

44. Ibid., 19–24.

45. Ibid., 25.

46. Ibid., 61–65.

47. Ibid., 78.

48. "Jewish Astrology in the Talmud, Pseudepigrapha, the Dead Sea Scrolls and Early Palestinian Synagogues," *HTR* 70 (1977): 183–200.

49. J. H. Charlesworth in *The Old Testament Pseudepigrapha*, 1:473–86.

50. Geza Vermes, *The Dead Sea Scrolls in English* (London: Penguin, 1987), 305–7.

51. The theme here recalls Heb 12:6, which quotes Prov 3:11.

52. David E. Hahm, *The Origins of Stoic Cosmology* (Columbus, OH: Ohio State University Press, 1977). Michael Lapidge, "Stoic Cosmology and Roman Literature," in *ANRW* II, 36.3 (1379–1429).

53. Hahm, *Origins of Stoic Cosmology*, 137.

54. *Stoicorum veterum fragmenta* (ed. J. von Arnim; Leipzig, 1903–1924; repr. Stuttgart, 1966; New York, 1986), 1.98.171.

55. In *Of Scholars, Saints and their Texts: Studies in Philosophy and Religious Thought* (ed. Ruth Link-Salinger; New York: Lang, 1981), 239–46.

56. London: Methuen, 1937.

57. Dudley, *History of Cyncism*, 36–37.

58. Dio Chrysostom, *Kingship 1* 1.65.

59. Dio Chrysostom, *Kingship 3* 45–47. An insightful study of the kingship theme in Cynicism is that of Ragnar Hoistad, *Cynic Hero and Cynic King: Studies in the Cynic Conception of Man* (Uppsala: Gleerup, 1948).

60. Dudley, *History of Cyncism*, 102.

61. Ibid., 124.

Bridal Imagery in the Mysteries of the Kabeiroi and of Serapis

A most useful analysis of "The Mysteries of the Kabeiroi" is offered by C. Kerenyi in his paper bearing that title included in *The Mysteries: Papers from the Eranos Yearbooks* (Bollingen Series 30, no. 2; New York: Pantheon, 1955), 32–63. He shows that the *mysteria* referred to in Greek literature of the Graeco-Roman period "took the initiate back to the very beginning of life, its natural genesis, and not to any philosophical 'principle,' though this too is called the *arche*." These rites were initiatory actions, including closing the eyes and falling into darkness. They were perceived and enacted in festive marital contexts, mythologically represented and experienced as related to the primeval marriage of a divine bride and a divine bridegroom. The preliminary act was veiling, which then led to the unveiling: "the fulfillment and culmination of an initiation." The basic theme of this rite was that ancient man was primarily procreator of his family and race, but participation in it enabled humans to transcend this status through deeper understanding and exalted experience (43–44).

The symbolism of the center for this mystery at Thebes is significant: it was approached from the north by way of an open plain filled with light and culminating at a dark mountain. The mystery celebrated the experience of the morning light. No details of the mythological base for the rites have survived, and the identity of the deities involved are secret as well. They appear to have consisted of the Great Mother, with the mysteries initiated by Demeter. The divine women were represented by images of storks and swans, whose maternal role was devoted to renewing life, symbolized as the sun rising in the human body. Masculinity was perceived as displaying on

481

its surface destructive aggression; only beneath the surface can man's true fruitfulness be discerned. The mission of the divine woman is to open for males the path to the depths, to the source of life, to the most metaphysical roots of human being.

The Kabeiroi were perceived as primeval men in need of initiation. In their original state, they were characterized as "bull-roarers," the simplest forms of humanity, in need of transformation into manifesting the true sources and aim of life.

The cult of Serapis developed from mythology and mystery practice in Egypt, but spread throughout the Graeco-Roman world. Serapis (at times spelled Sarapis) was named for an Egyptian deity, Apis, and was earlier identified with Osiris, the consort of Isis. Osiris had been perceived as presiding with Isis over the world below, and as judge of the departed spirits. Isis, sister and spouse of Osiris, taught humans the cultivation of grain and served as the goddess of fecundity. Subsequently, she came to be viewed as embodying the power to conceive and bring forth life in the earthly sphere. When Osiris died, she buried him and then restored him to life, thereby symbolizing the renewal of the annual agricultural cycle, but also the transformation of the life of her devotees. The later cult of Serapis promised the sustaining of the earthly cycle of fertility, but also participation in a new and enriched kind of life.

Some of these cultic features from both types of mystery have a counterpart in Judaism and early Christianity. The promises of being "born again" or "from above" (anothen) in John 3 resemble this mystical imagery. And the way in which the Song of Songs came to be perceived as a poetic symbolic portrayal of the divine purpose for uniting God and his people matches the Hellenistic myths of the love shared by Venus and Adonis, and by Isis and Osiris. In the Hebrew Bible, the date of the Song of Songs from the Hellenistic period is indicated by its use of Persian and Greek words (4:8; 8:5).

The bridal imagery for the relation of Christ to the church is present in the symbolic language of Mark 2:19 and in the parable of the Ten Bridesmaids in Matt 25:1–13, as well as in the report in John 3:25–30 of John the Baptist contrasting himself with the bridegroom: Jesus. In Rev 19 and 21, the image is made even more explicit: the marriage of the Lamb has come, and the bride (the church) has made herself ready. In Rev 21:2, 9, the new Jerusalem coming down from God out of heaven is likewise compared to a bride. The bridal imagery is thus explicit for portraying the ultimate relationship of the new community to the one through whom it was called into being. It is through awareness of the presence and power of this kind of imagery in the Graeco-Roman culture of the early centuries of the common era that one can perceive how the bearers of the Christian message were able to direct it effectively to its hearers, Jewish and Gentile.

EXCURSUS 7

The Kingdom of God in the Pauline Letters

The future kingdom of God is a major feature in the synoptic gospel tradition, but it also has a significant role in the thought of Paul. He asserts the qualities that characterize those who will share in the new circumstances when God's rule takes on its encompassing role over God's people and the world as a whole. That context will be characterized by righteousness, peace, and joy in the Holy Spirit, rather than by strict adherence to such laws as the dietary requirements (Rom 14:17). Yet moral failures will result in disqualification for sharing in the kingdom. Excluded are "fornicators, idolaters, adulterers, male prostitutes, sodomites, thieves, the greedy, drunkards, revilers, robbers" (1 Cor 6:9–10). In Gal 5:19–21, a similar list of modes of sinful behavior—labeled "the works of the flesh"—is linked with the assertion that such an immoral way of life precludes sharing in the kingdom of God. On the positive side, 1 Thess 3:12 declares that through Christ, God calls his people to share in the kingdom of God and his glory. In 2 Thess 1:5, the persecutions and afflictions endured by the faithful are part of God's plan, so that by enduring them, their faithfulness will show that God deems them to be "worthy of the kingdom of God."

The dietary and other ritual laws in the tradition of Torah are not binding for Christians, Paul declares (Rom 14:13–22). Indeed, "The kingdom of God is not food and drink, but righteousness and peace and joy in the Holy Spirit." Yet if for one member of the community to eat nonkosher food offends another member, each one should be careful not to indulge one's freedom from these regulations.

In the deuteropauline letters, there are similar warnings of the dire consequences of violation of the moral norms. Yet the radical renewal that will take place with the coming of the kingdom is also affirmed. Colossians 1:12–13 expresses thanks "to the Father, who has qualified [his new people] to share in the inheritance of the saints in light," and who "has delivered us from the dominion of darkness and transferred us to the kingdom of his beloved Son, in whom we have redemption, the forgiveness of sins."

Ephesians 5:3–5 announces that those guilty of obscenity, fornication, greed, or other immorality are to have no share in the kingdom, which is here linked with both Christ and God. In 1 Tim 4:1–5, there is a warning that the time is coming when some from within the Christian community will "depart from the faith" and espouse "the doctrines of demons," insisting on radical asceticism and giving credence to "silly myths." To counter this trend, the members are to be instructed in "the words of faith and sound doctrine" (4:6) in order to "train [themselves] in piety" (*eusebeia*; 4:7).

In 2 Tim 4:1, the kingdom of Christ is linked with his "appearing" (*epiphaneia*), which probably refers to his future return, since it is linked with his judgment of "the living and the dead." There is a final expression of confidence by the author that "the Lord will rescue me from every evil and save me for his heavenly [*epouranion*] kingdom" (4:18). This implies that the kingdom will bring to earth the power and purpose of God for the creation and for his people, rather than that it will involve the transport of the saints to heaven, as has often been a popular perception based on Matthew's version of the Beatitudes. There the "poor in spirit" and "those who are persecuted for righteousness' sake" (5:3, 10) are promised a share in the "kingdom of heaven." This has been widely perceived as finding fulfillment in heaven, even though Matthew's version of the Lord's Prayer asks that God's will might be done "on earth as it is in heaven" (6:10).

Index